Global Environmental Politics

Dilemmas in World Politics

Series Editor: Jennifer Sterling-Folker, University of Connecticut

Why is it difficult to achieve the universal protection of human rights? How can democratization be achieved so that it is equitable and lasting? Why does agreement on global environmental protection seem so elusive? How does the concept of gender play a role in the shocking inequalities of women throughout the globe? Why do horrific events such as genocide or ethnic conflicts recur or persist? These are the sorts of questions that confront policymakers and students of contemporary international politics alike. They are dilemmas because they are enduring problems in world affairs that are difficult to resolve.

These are the types of dilemmas at the heart of the Dilemmas in World Politics series. Each book in the Dilemmas in World Politics series addresses a challenge or problem in world politics that is topical, recurrent, and not easily solved. Each is structured to cover the historical and theoretical aspects of the dilemma, as well as the policy alternatives for and future direction of the problem. The books are designed as supplements to introductory and intermediate courses in international relations. The books in the Dilemmas in World Politics series encourage students to engage in informed discussion of current policy issues.

BOOKS IN THIS SERIES

Global Environmental Politics, Seventh Edition
Pamela S. Chasek, David L. Downie, and Janet Welsh Brown

The United Nations in the 21st Century, Fifth Edition
Karen A. Mingst, Margaret P. Karns, and Alynna J. Lyon

Global Gender Issues in the New Millennium, Fourth Edition
V. Spike Peterson and Anne Sisson Runyan

United States Foreign Policy in the 21st Century: Gulliver's Travails
J. Martin Rochester

Democracy and Democratization in a Changing World, Third Edition
Georg Sørensen

International Human Rights, Fourth Edition
Jack Donnelly

Southern Africa in World Politics
Janice Love

Ethnic Conflict in World Politics, Second Edition
Barbara Harff and Ted Robert Gurr

Dilemmas of International Trade, Second Edition
Bruce E. Moon

Humanitarian Challenges and Intervention, Second Edition
Thomas G. Weiss and Cindy Collins

The European Union: Dilemmas of Regional Integration
James A. Caporaso

International Futures, Third Edition
Barry B. Hughes

Revolution and Transition in East-Central Europe, Second Edition
David S. Mason

One Land, Two Peoples, Second Edition
Deborah Gerner

Dilemmas of Development Assistance
Sarah J. Tisch and Michael B. Wallace

East Asian Dynamism, Second Edition
Steven Chan

SEVENTH EDITION

Global Environmental Politics

PAMELA S. CHASEK

DAVID L. DOWNIE

JANET WELSH BROWN

Westview Press was founded in 1975 in Boulder, Colorado, by notable publisher and intellectual Fred Praeger. Westview Press continues to publish scholarly titles and high-quality undergraduate- and graduate-level textbooks in core social science disciplines. With books developed, written, and edited with the needs of serious nonfiction readers, professors, and students in mind, Westview Press honors its long history of publishing books that matter.

Published by Westview Press, an imprint of Perseus Books,
a Hachette Book Group company
2465 Central Avenue
Boulder, CO 80301
www.westviewpress.com

Library of Congress Cataloging-in-Publication Data

Names: Chasek, Pamela S., 1961– author. | Downie, David Leonard, author. | Brown, Janet Welsh, author.
Title: Global environmental politics / Pamela S. Chasek, David L. Downie, Janet Welsh Brown.
Description: Seventh edition. | Boulder, CO : Westview Press, [2017] | Series: Dilemmas in world politics | Includes bibliographical references and index.
Identifiers: LCCN 2016011543 (print) | LCCN 2016016932 (ebook) | ISBN 9780813349794 (paperback) | ISBN 9780813350356 (e-book)
Subjects: LCSH: Environmental policy. | BISAC: POLITICAL SCIENCE / Public Policy / Environmental Policy. | NATURE / Environmental Conservation & Protection. | LAW / Environmental.
Classification: LCC GE170 .C46 2017 (print) | LCC GE170 (ebook) | DDC 363.7/056—dc23
LC record available at https://lccn.loc.gov/2016011543

10 9 8 7 6 5 4 3 2 1

Contents

Illustrations

Tables

Figures

Photos

Text Boxes

Preface and Acknowledgments

Environmental issues affect the welfare of all humankind, both directly and through their interaction with other aspects of international politics, including economic development, trade, humanitarian actions, social development, and even security. For twenty-five years, *Global Environmental Politics* has sought to provide an up-to-date, accurate, and unbiased introduction to the key issues in the study and practice of international environmental politics and policy.

Like global environmental politics itself, this book has gone through significant transformations. Although its purpose remains the same, the contents of *Global Environmental Politics* have evolved significantly since 1991, and each new edition contains a significant amount of new material. This new edition builds directly on the sixth edition with updated discussions of key historical developments and trends in global environmental politics; the major national, institutional, and subnational actors; the factors that enhance or diminish prospects for effective policy; insights provided by the scholarly study of global environmental politics; and the development, content, remaining challenges, and potential future paths of global policies that address climate change, biodiversity, chemicals and wastes, desertification, forests, endangered species, fisheries, the stratospheric ozone layer, sustainable development, and many other issues.

The seventh edition also contains entirely new sections that examine critical developments that have occurred in global environmental politics since the sixth edition, including the adoption of the Sustainable Development Goals and the 2030 Agenda for Sustainable Development, the December 2015 Paris Climate Change Conference, the historic 2013 and 2015 joint meetings of the major chemi cals conventions, efforts to increase financing for environmental protection and sustainable development, and important developments in the regimes covered by the case studies in Chapter 3 and 4. We have also added new timelines and other boxes that break out key issues and significantly restructured the discussions of the intersection of environmental, economic, and social development issues. In addition to entirely new sections, we have updated each part of the book to reflect important developments in the practice and study of global environmental politics.

This book has been made possible by the inspiration, encouragement, and assistance of our colleagues at Manhattan College, Fairfield University, Columbia University, the *Earth Negotiations Bulletin*, and the United Nations. We also want to thank our editors, Kelli Fillingim and Katie Moore, and everyone at Westview Press for their support and positive attitude throughout this process. In addition to all of our colleagues who were thanked in earlier editions of this book, we thank Nicole Cappiello and Maria Leal Giraldo for their research assistance. We are grateful to the peer reviewers and users of previous editions who provided feedback and suggestions.

Most important, David Downie thanks his family—Laura, William, and Lindsey; Bonnie and Carl Sims; Janice and Leonard Downie; Marina and Robert Whitman; and Scott, Joshua, Sarah, Malcolm, and Tracy—for their fun, patience, good humor, support, and making the good things in his life possible. Pamela Chasek thanks her family—Kimo, Sam, and Kai Goree; and Arlene and Marvin Chasek—for all of their patience, support, and love.

Pamela Chasek
David Downie

Acronyms

AAAA	Addis Ababa Action Agenda
ADP	Ad Hoc Working Group on the Durban Platform for Enhanced Action
AILAC	Association of Independent Latin American and Caribbean States
ALBA	Bolivarian Alliance for the Peoples of Our America
AOSIS	Alliance of Small Island States
APEC	Asia-Pacific Economic Cooperation
BRICS	Brazil, Russia, India, China, South Africa
CBD	Convention on Biological Diversity
CBDR	common but differentiated responsibilities
CFCs	chlorofluorocarbons
CITES	Convention on International Trade in Endangered Species of Wild Fauna and Flora
CO_2	carbon dioxide
COFI	Committee on Fisheries (FAO)
COP	Conference of the Parties
CSD	Commission on Sustainable Development
CTE	Committee on Trade and Environment (WTO)
DDT	dichlorodiphenyltrichloroethane
EC	European Community
ECOSOC	United Nations Economic and Social Council
EEZs	exclusive economic zones
EU	European Union
FAO	Food and Agriculture Organization of the United Nations
FfD3	Third International Conference on Financing for Development
FSC	Forest Stewardship Council
FTA	financial and technical assistance
G-77	Group of 77
GATT	General Agreement on Tariffs and Trade
GDP	gross domestic product
GEF	Global Environment Facility
GHGs	greenhouse gases
GNP	gross national product
HCFCs	hydrochlorofluorocarbons
HLPF	High-Level Political Forum on Sustainable Development
HFCs	hydrofluorocarbons

HIPC	heavily indebted poor country
IAF	International Arrangement on Forests
ICJ	International Court of Justice
IFF	Intergovernmental Forum on Forests
IGOs	intergovernmental organizations
IISD	International Institute for Sustainable Development
IMF	International Monetary Fund
INC	International Negotiating Committee
INDC	intended nationally determined contribution
IPBES	Intergovernmental Science-Policy Platform on Biodiversity and Ecosystem Services
IPCC	Intergovernmental Panel on Climate Change
IPEN	International POPs Elimination Network
IPF	International Panel on Forests
ITTA	International Tropical Timber Agreement
IUCN	International Union for the Conservation of Nature and Natural Resources
IWC	International Whaling Commission
LDC	least-developed country
LMDC	like-minded developing country
LMMC	Group of Like-Minded Megadiverse Countries
LMO	living modified organism
LMO-FFP	living modified organism intended for food, feed, and processing
MARPOL	International Convention for the Prevention of Pollution from Ships
MDGs	Millennium Development Goals
MEAs	multilateral environmental agreements
MOP	Meeting of the Parties
MSC	Marine Stewardship Council
NAFO	Northwest Atlantic Fisheries Organization
NASA	National Aeronautics and Space Administration
NDB	New Development Bank
NDC	nationally determined contribution
NEPAD	New Partnership for Africa's Development
NGOs	nongovernmental organizations
OAS	Organization of American States
ODA	official development assistance
ODS	ozone-depleting substance
OECD	Organization for Economic Cooperation and Development
OPEC	Organization of Petroleum Exporting Countries
PACE	Partnership for Action on Computer Equipment
PCBs	polychlorinated biphenyls
PFOS	perfluorooctane sulfonate
PIC	prior informed consent

POPRC	Persistent Organic Pollutants Review Committee
POPs	persistent organic pollutants
PPP	public-private partnership
SDGs	Sustainable Development Goals
SPREP	Pacific Regional Environment Programme
SSC	South–South Cooperation
TED	turtle-excluder device
TEEB	The Economics of Ecosystems and Biodiversity
TFAP	Tropical Forestry Action Plan
TRAFFIC	Trade Records Analysis of Flora and Fauna in Commerce
UN	United Nations
UNCCD	United Nations Convention to Combat Desertification
UNCED	United Nations Conference on Environment and Development
UNCSD	United Nations Conference on Sustainable Development
UNDP	United Nations Development Programme
UNEA	United Nations Environment Assembly
UNEP	United Nations Environment Programme
UNFCCC	United Nations Framework Convention on Climate Change
UNFF	United Nations Forum on Forests
UNGA	United Nations General Assembly
WHO	World Health Organization
WMO	World Meteorological Organization
WSSD	World Summit on Sustainable Development
WTO	World Trade Organization
WWF	World Wildlife Fund/Worldwide Fund for Nature

Chronology

1800 Atmospheric carbon dioxide (CO_2) and methane concentrations in the atmosphere hover around 280 parts per million (ppm) and 700 parts per billion (ppb), respectively. Most scientists today use these numbers as a pre–Industrial Revolution baseline for comparison.

1827 Jean-Baptiste Joseph Fourier, a French mathematician and physicist, publishes perhaps the first paper speculating on the existence of what we now call the *natural greenhouse effect*.

1859 John Tyndall, an Irish physicist, publishes results of laboratory experiments detailing the relative radiative forcing (greenhouse effect) of different gases in the atmosphere, including CO_2.

1872 Yellowstone National Park, the first national park in the United States, is created.

1892 Sierra Club is established by John Muir and others to defend Yosemite National Park.

1896 Svante Arrhenius, a Swedish scientist, publishes an article that concludes that doubling the amount of CO_2 in the atmosphere would raise temperatures by 5°C to 6°C.

1900 CO_2 concentration in the atmosphere reaches 295 ppm.

1902 The Convention for the Protection of Birds Useful to Agriculture is adopted.

1903 The first international conservation nongovernmental organization is formed: the Society for the Preservation of the Wild Fauna of the Empire.

1909 US president Theodore Roosevelt convenes the North American Conservation Conference in Washington, DC.

1911 The Treaty for the Preservation and Protection of Fur Seals is adopted.

1933 The London Convention on the Preservation of Fauna and Flora in Their Natural State is adopted.

1938 G. S. Callendar revisits Arrhenius's 1896 publication and argues that increases in CO_2 concentration could explain recent warming trends.

1945 The United Nations is established.

1946 The International Convention for the Regulation of Whaling is adopted; the International Whaling Commission (IWC) is established.

1947 The International Union for the Conservation of Nature and Natural Resources is established, becoming the first international nongovernmental organization with a global outlook on environmental problems.

1949 The International Convention for the Northwest Atlantic Fisheries is adopted.

1950 The World Meteorological Organization is established.

— The International Convention for the Protection of Birds is adopted.

1952 A toxic mix of dense fog and sooty, black coal smoke kills at least four thousand people, and perhaps as many as twelve thousand, in the worst of London's "killer fogs."

1954 The International Convention for the Prevention of Pollution of the Sea by Oil is adopted.

1956 Roger Revelle and Charles David Keeling publish a paper showing the increasing atmospheric concentrations of CO_2 over the past century.

1962 Rachel Carson publishes *Silent Spring.*

1963 The Agreement for the Protection of the Rhine Against Pollution is adopted.

1967 The supertanker *Torrey Canyon* runs aground in the English Channel, causing a massive oil spill and raising public awareness of environmental issues.

1970 US Environmental Protection Agency is established.

1971 The Ramsar Convention on Wetlands of International Importance is adopted.

1972 The United Nations Conference on the Human Environment convenes in Stockholm.

— The United Nations Environment Programme (UNEP) is established.

— *The Limits to Growth* report is published.

— The Convention on the Prevention of Marine Pollution by Dumping of Wastes and Other Matter (London Convention) is adopted.

— The Convention for the Conservation of Antarctic Seals is adopted.

1973 The Convention on International Trade in Endangered Species of Wild Fauna and Flora (CITES) is adopted.

— The International Convention for the Prevention of Pollution from Ships (MARPOL) is adopted.

— The US Endangered Species Act becomes law.

1974 M. J. Molina and F. S. Rowland publish their theory that chlorofluorocarbons (CFCs) threaten the ozone layer.

— The World Population Conference is held in Bucharest, Romania.

1975 The UNEP Regional Seas Programme is created.

1976 The Convention for the Protection of the Mediterranean Sea Against Pollution is adopted.

— The UNEP International Register of Potentially Toxic Chemicals is established.

1977 The United Nations Conference on Desertification adopts the Plan of Action to Combat Desertification.

1979 The Convention on the Conservation of Migratory Species is adopted.

— The First World Climate Conference warns of the danger of global warming.

— The Convention on Long-Range Transboundary Air Pollution, the first international legally binding instrument to deal with problems of air pollution on a broad regional basis, is adopted.

1980 The Convention on the Conservation of Antarctic Marine Living Resources is adopted.

1982 The IWC approves a five-year moratorium on commercial whaling.

1984 The International Tropical Timber Agreement (ITTA) is adopted.

— The Union Carbide disaster occurs in Bhopal, India.

1985 The Vienna Convention for Protection of the Ozone Layer is adopted.

— The Antarctic ozone-hole discovery is published in *Nature*.

— Canadian scientists discover abnormally high levels of persistent organic pollutants in some Inuit communities in northern Canada, revealing the global transport of toxic chemicals.

— Parties to the London Convention vote to ban dumping of low-level radioactive wastes in oceans until it is proven safe.

1987 The Montreal Protocol on Substances That Deplete the Ozone Layer is adopted.

— The Report of the World Commission on Environment and Development (the Brundtland Report) is published as *Our Common Future*, introducing the concept of sustainable development to the general public.

1988 The Intergovernmental Panel on Climate Change (IPCC) is established.

1989 The Basel Convention on the Control of Transboundary Movements of Hazardous Wastes and Their Disposal is adopted.

— The European Community agrees to ban hazardous waste exports to African, Caribbean, and Pacific countries that do not possess the capacity to dispose of them safely.

— Sixty-seven governments attending the Ministerial Conference on Atmospheric Pollution and Climate Change call for stabilizing CO_2 emissions by 2000.

— CITES bans trade in African elephant ivory products.

1990 Parties to the Montreal Protocol significantly strengthen the Montreal Protocol by agreeing to eliminate CFCs and establish the Multilateral Fund.

— The IWC extends the ban on commercial whaling.

— The IPCC releases its First Assessment Report, concluding that the average global surface temperature has increased by 0.3°C to 0.6°C since 1980.

1991 The Global Environment Facility is established.

— The Bamako Convention on the Ban of the Import into Africa and the Control of Transboundary Movement and Management of Hazardous Wastes within Africa is adopted.

— The Protocol on Environmental Protection to the Antarctic Treaty is adopted.

1992 The United Nations Conference on Environment and Development convenes in Rio de Janeiro and adopts Agenda 21, the Rio Declaration, and the Forest Principles.

— The United Nations Framework Convention on Climate Change is adopted.

— The Convention on Biological Diversity is adopted.

1994 The United Nations Convention to Combat Desertification is adopted.

— The International Conference on Population and Development convenes in Cairo.

1995 The World Summit for Social Development convenes in Copenhagen.

— The Agreement on the Conservation and Management of Straddling Fish Stocks and Highly Migratory Fish Stocks is adopted.

— The World Trade Organization is established.

1996 The IPCC releases its Second Assessment Report, which concludes that there is a discernible human influence on the global climate.

1997 The Kyoto Protocol to the Framework Convention on Climate Change is adopted.

1998 The Rotterdam Convention on the Prior Informed Consent Procedure for Certain Hazardous Chemicals and Pesticides in International Trade is adopted.

1999 The Protocol on Liability and Compensation to the Basel Convention on the Control of Transboundary Movements of Hazardous Wastes and Their Disposal is adopted.

2000 The Cartagena Protocol on Biosafety is adopted by the Conference of the Parties to the Convention on Biological Diversity.

— The United Nations Forum on Forests is established.

— The Millennium Summit is held at the United Nations in New York; the Millennium Development Goals are adopted.

2001 The Stockholm Convention on Persistent Organic Pollutants is adopted.

— The IPCC's Third Assessment Report concludes that the evidence of humanity's influence on the global climate is stronger than ever.

— The International Treaty on Plant Genetic Resources for Food and Agriculture is adopted.

2002 The World Summit on Sustainable Development convenes in Johannesburg.

2003 The African Ministerial Conference on the Environment adopts the New Partnership for Africa's Development's Environment Action Plan.

2004 CO_2 concentration in the atmosphere reaches 379 ppm.

2005 The Kyoto Protocol enters into force.

— The Millennium Ecosystem Assessment is released; thirteen hundred experts from ninety-five countries provide scientific information concerning the consequences of ecosystem change for human well-being.

— The European Union's Greenhouse Gas Emission Trading Scheme begins operation as the world's first multicountry, multisector greenhouse-gas (GHG) emission trading scheme.

2006 The ITTA successor agreement is adopted in Geneva.

— UNEP initiates the Strategic Approach to International Chemicals Management.

— The Stern Review on the Economics of Climate Change makes a convincing case that the economic costs of inaction on climate change will be far larger than the costs of reducing GHG emissions.

— The National Aeronautics and Space Administration (NASA) reports that recovery of the ozone layer has begun as a result of reduced emissions of CFCs under the Montreal Protocol.

2007 The IPCC Fourth Assessment Report confirms that climate change is occurring, that the human contribution to this change is unequivocal, and that impacts are already apparent and will increase as temperatures rise.

— The Nobel Committee awards the 2007 Nobel Peace Prize to the IPCC and former US vice president Albert Gore for their efforts to disseminate knowledge about climate change.

— The European Union (EU) announces that it will cut its GHG emissions by 20 percent from 1990 levels by 2020 and require that 20 percent of total energy consumption come from renewable energies.

2009 The parties to the Stockholm Convention significantly expand the regime, limiting the production and use of nine additional toxic substances. Additional chemicals are added in future years.

2010 The Conferences of the Parties to the Basel, Rotterdam, and Stockholm conventions meet together for the first time, a milestone in attempts to coordinate action among global environmental treaties in related issue areas.

— The Nagoya–Kuala Lumpur Supplementary Protocol on Liability and Redress to the Cartagena Protocol on Biosafety is adopted.

— The Nagoya Protocol on Access to Genetic Resources and the Fair and Equitable Sharing of Benefits Arising from Their Utilization is adopted.

2011 The International Renewable Energy Agency Assembly convenes for the first time.

2012 The United Nations Conference on Sustainable Development convenes in Rio de Janeiro.

— Governments agree to create a second commitment period for the Kyoto Protocol that will address GHG emissions during the period 2013–2020 and work toward a universal climate-change agreement covering all countries from 2020, to be adopted by 2015.

2013 The Minamata Convention on Mercury, a global treaty to limit mercury emissions, is adopted.

2014 The IPCC Fifth Assessment Report reconfirms that climate change is occurring, that human contributions are unequivocally the dominant cause, and that negative impacts are already apparent and will increase significantly as temperatures rise.

— The EU announces that it will reduce its GHG emissions by 40 percent from 1990 levels by 2030 and reaffirms its objective to reduce emissions by at least 80 percent by 2050.

2015 CO_2 levels in the atmosphere exceed 400 ppm on a regular basis, the highest level in eight hundred thousand years. NASA and other organizations conclude 2015 was the hottest year since temperature records began in the 1880s.

— Parties to the Montreal Protocol agree to negotiate policies to control hydrofluorocarbons.

— The Third International Conference on Financing for Development adopts the Addis Ababa Action Agenda.

— The UN adopts the 2030 Agenda for Sustainable Development, including the seventeen Sustainable Development Goals.

— The UNFCCC adopts the Paris Agreement, the first-ever universal, legally binding climate agreement.

1

The Emergence of Global Environmental Politics

Until the 1980s, most governments regarded global environmental problems as minor issues, marginal both to their core national interests and to international politics in general. Then the rise of environmental movements in industrialized countries and the appearance of well-publicized global environmental threats that affect the welfare of all humankind—such as ozone layer depletion, climate change, and dangerous declines in the world's fisheries—awarded global environmental issues a much higher status in world politics. Today, environmental issues are globally important both in their own right and because they affect other aspects of world politics, including economic development, trade, humanitarian action, social policy, and even security.

Global concern about the environment evolved in response to expanded scientific understanding of humanity's increasing impact on the biosphere, including the atmosphere, oceans, forests, soil cover, and a large number of animal and plant species. Many by-products of economic growth—such as the burning of fossil fuels, air and water pollution, hazardous waste, release of substances that destroy stratospheric ozone, production of toxic chemicals, increased use of natural resources, and decreasing forest cover—put cumulative stresses on the physical environment that now threaten human health and economic well-being. The realization that environmental threats have serious socioeconomic and human costs and that unilateral actions by individual countries cannot solve these problems produced increased international cooperation aimed at halting or reversing environmental degradation.

This chapter provides an introduction to global environmental politics. It highlights key economic and environmental trends, introduces and defines important concepts, and traces some of the major intellectual currents and political developments that have contributed to the evolution of global environmental politics.

GLOBAL MACROTRENDS

Global demographic, economic, and environmental macrotrends describe key factors that drive global environmental politics.[1] Humanity's potential stress on the environment is to some extent a function of three key factors: population, resource consumption, and waste production. One way to measure this impact is through an ecological footprint, which measures humanity's demands on the biosphere by comparing humanity's consumption against the earth's regenerative capacity, or biocapacity.[2] The ecological footprint measures the sum of all cropland, grazing land, forest, and fishing grounds required to produce the food, fiber, and timber we need and to absorb the wastes emitted. Since the 1970s, humanity's annual demand on the natural world has exceeded what the earth can renew in a year. This ecological overshoot was at a 50 percent deficit in 2010.[3] This means that it now takes natural systems about 1.5 years to regenerate the renewable resources that we use and absorb the waste we produce in a year, and it could reach three years by 2050 in a business-as-usual scenario.[4]

Population Growth and Resource Consumption

Population growth affects the environment by increasing the demand for resources (including energy, water, food, and wood), the production of waste, and the emission of pollution. These relationships are not fixed, however, and most of the negative impacts result from how we carry out certain activities. Nevertheless, given the dominant economic and social patterns that have existed since the Industrial Revolution, the rapid growth of human population over the last one hundred years has significantly influenced the environment and will continue to do so throughout this century.

In 1900, global population stood at approximately 1.6 billion. Today it is more than 7.3 billion. It took fifty years for global population to go from 1.6 billion in 1900 to 2.5 billion in 1950. It then took only thirty-seven years for it to double, reaching 5 billion in 1987. It passed the 6-billion mark only twelve years later, reached 7 billion in late 2011, and is on pace to reach 8.5 billion by 2030, 9.7 billion by 2050, and 11.2 billion by 2100[5] (see Figure 1.1).

Projections of future population growth depend on fertility trends, which can be affected by economic development, education, widespread disease, and certain population-related policies. The world's human population is currently growing at a rate of 1.18 percent annually.[6] Although significantly less than the peak growth rate of 2.04 percent from 1965 to 1970, this still means a net addition of eighty-three million people per year.[7] Most of this growth, as much as 92 percent,[8] will occur in Africa and Asia. China and India alone already account for 37 percent of

FIGURE 1.1 **World Population Growth 1950–2050 (Projected)**

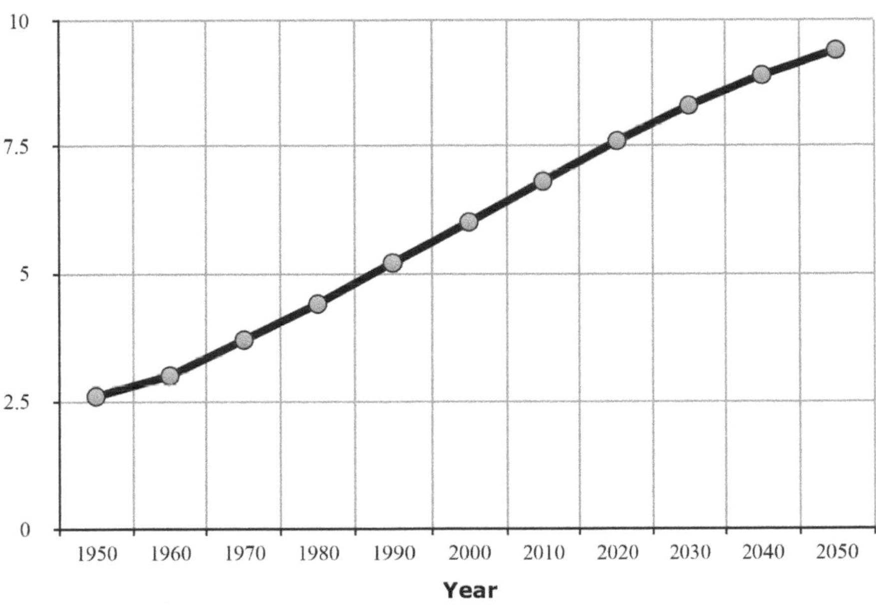

Source: "World Population," United States Census Bureau, www.census.gov/population/international/data/worldpop/table_population.php.

the world's population. Moreover, the population in the forty-eight least-developed countries is projected to grow dramatically, from 954 million in 2015 to 1.9 billion in 2050 and 3.2 billion in 2100.[9] Population increases have been accompanied by large increases in the consumption of natural resources, including fresh water, forests, topsoil, fish stocks, and fossil fuels. In addition, per capita consumption of natural resources has been rising much faster than population growth. For example, private consumption expenditures (the amount households spend on goods and services) increased more than fourfold from 1960 to 2000, even though the global population only doubled during this period.[10] This increase is positive in that it reflects growth in the standard of living for billions of people. At the same time, the aggregate human consumption of natural resources has largely passed sustainable rates.[11]

As more developing countries pursue the lifestyles of North America, Japan, and Europe, the future will likely bring higher per capita rates of consumption unless resources are both consumed more efficiently and recycled more effectively. For example, the population of middle-income countries (including many of the world's emerging economies, such as Brazil, China, India, Indonesia, Russia, and South Africa) has more than doubled since 1961, while the ecological footprint per person has increased by 65 percent.[12] The United Nations (UN) estimates that the global middle class will grow from 2 billion today to 4.9 billion by 2030, with consequently large increases in demands for energy, food, water, and material goods.[13]

Despite large increases in the consumer class in a number of developing countries, the gulf in consumption levels within and among countries continues to draw attention. High-income countries, such as the United States, have an ecological footprint per capita that is roughly four times that of middle-income countries and five times that of low-income countries.[14] The 12 percent of the world's population that lives in North America and Western Europe accounts for nearly 60 percent of private consumption spending, whereas the 33 percent of the population that lives in South Asia and sub-Saharan Africa accounts for only about 3.2 percent.[15] The United States has had more private cars than licensed drivers since the 1970s, and the average size of new, single-family houses in the United States has grown by more than 60 percent since 1973[16] despite a decrease in the average number of people per household.[17] If everyone consumed resources at the level Americans do, it would take the planet 3.9 years to regenerate the renewable resources used and absorb the wastes produced.[18]

At the other end of the spectrum, nearly 1.2 billion people—one out of five—live on less than $1.25 a day, and 2.5 billion people live without basic sanitation, the overwhelming majority of whom live in Southern Asia and sub-Saharan Africa.[19] A 2014 study estimated that 1.8 billion people drink water contaminated by human or animal waste and even more drink water delivered through systems that lack adequate protections against sanitary hazards.[20]

Today, the world's richest countries use on average eleven times more energy than the poorest ones; the richest comprise only 18 percent of the world's population but use nearly 40 percent of the world's energy (see Figure 1.2). The United States, with less than 5 percent of the global population, uses about 25 percent of the world's fossil-fuel resources—coal, oil, and natural gas.[21] Sub-Saharan Africa accounts for about 13 percent of global population but only 4 percent of global energy demand.[22] The average American consumes 3.5 times more energy than the average global citizen, 3.3 times more than the average Chinese, and 11 times more than the average Indian (and the vast majority of this energy still comes from burning fossil fuels).[23] Approximately 590 million people in sub-Saharan Africa and 300 million people in India live almost entirely without access to electricity.[24]

However, energy consumption in developing countries is increasing, driven by industrial expansion, infrastructure improvement, population growth, urbanization, and rising incomes (see Table 1.1). In 1980, China and India together accounted for less than 8 percent of the world's total energy consumption; by 2014 their combined share had grown to 28 percent.[25] In contrast, the US share of total

FIGURE 1.2 **Global Energy Use, 2013**

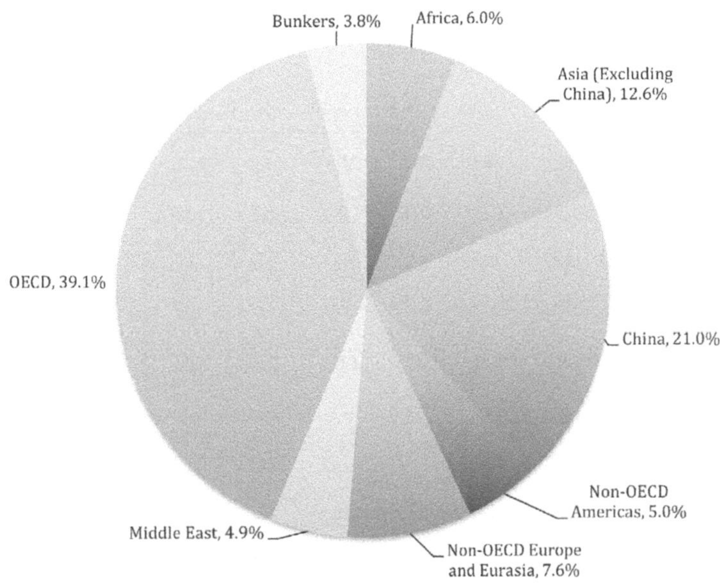

Note: The term *bunkers* refers to international aviation and international marine fuel depots, which are not included in a specific country's energy use statistics (or greenhouse gas emissions statistics).
Source: International Energy Agency, *Key World Energy Statistics 2015* (Paris: International Energy Agency, 2015), 30, www.iea.org/publications/freepublications/publication/KeyWorld_Statistics_2015.pdf.

world energy consumption contracted from 22 percent in 2005 to 16 percent in 2014, largely due to improved energy efficiency.[26]

Natural Resources and Pollution

Perhaps the largest aggregate impact that humans have on the biosphere is their carbon footprint (see Box 1.1), which has grown more than tenfold since 1960. The United States and China have the largest total national carbon footprints, with China emitting 27 percent of global carbon emissions, followed by the United States with 14 percent.[27] In 2013, the United States emitted about twice as much carbon dioxide (CO_2) as the entire continent of Africa.[28] China has a much smaller per capita footprint than the United States (6.2 tons per person in 2010 versus 17.6 tons in the United States,[29] although China's footprint has increased since then), but its population is more than four times as large. India accounts for about 9 percent of global CO_2 emissions, and its national carbon footprint is the third largest, but its per capita footprint is only about 1.6 tons per person.[30]

TABLE 1.1 **Projected World Energy Consumption (Quadrillion BTU) by Country Grouping, 2010–2040**

REGION	2010	2015	2020	2025	2030	2035	2040	AVERAGE ANNUAL PERCENTAGE CHANGE
OECD	**242**	**244**	**255**	**263**	**269**	**276**	**285**	**0.5**
Americas	120	121	126	130	133	137	144	0.6
Europe	82	82	85	89	91	93	95	0.5
Asia	40	41	43	44	45	46	46	0.5
Non-OECD	**282**	**328**	**375**	**418**	**460**	**501**	**535**	**2.2**
Europe and Eurasia	47	50	53	57	61	65	67	1.2
Asia	159	194	230	262	290	317	337	2.5
Middle East	28	33	37	39	43	46	49	1.9
Africa	19	20	22	24	27	31	35	2.1
Central and South America	29	31	33	35	39	42	47	1.6
World	**524**	**572**	**630**	**680**	**729**	**777**	**820**	**1.5**

Source: US Energy Information Administration (EIA), *International Energy Outlook 2013* (Washington, DC: EIA, 2013), 9, www.eia.gov/forecasts/archive/ieo13/pdf/0484(2013).pdf.

However, an energy sector transition is underway in many parts of the world, leading to an increase in the use of renewable energy. In 2014, renewables became the second largest source of electricity, behind coal. Energy efficiency improvements also helped to restrain the growth of energy demand in 2014 to just one-third of the level it otherwise would have been. According to International Energy Agency projections, energy demand is expected to grow at 1 percent per year to 2040, about half the average annual rate since 1990, due to increased energy efficiency in end uses and structural changes to the economy. CO_2 emissions from power generation are expected to grow at only one-fifth of the rate at which power output will increase between now and 2040, breaking the long-standing one-for-one relationship.[31]

Despite positive progress, efforts are not yet enough to move the world onto a pathway consistent with the 2°C climate goal (see Chapter 3). The years 2011–2015 have been the warmest five-year period on record, according to the World Meteo-

BOX 1.1 WHAT IS A CARBON FOOTPRINT?

A carbon footprint is a measure of the impact our activities have on climate change. Many of our daily activities cause emissions of greenhouse gases (GHGs). For example, we produce GHG emissions from burning gasoline when we drive, burning oil or gas for home heating, or using electricity generated from coal, natural gas, and oil. These are considered to be the *primary footprint*—the sum of direct emissions of carbon dioxide (CO_2) from the burning of fossil fuels for energy consumption and transportation. More fuel-efficient cars have a smaller primary footprint, as do energy-efficient light bulbs.

The *secondary footprint* is the sum of indirect emissions of GHGs during the lifecycle of products used by an individual or organization. For example, the GHGs emitted during the production of plastic for water bottles, as well as the energy used to transport the water, contribute to the secondary footprint. Products with more packaging will generally have a larger secondary footprint than products with a minimal amount of packaging.

***Source:* Maggie L. Walser, "Carbon Footprint," in *Encyclopedia of Earth,* ed. Cutler J. Cleveland, first published July 14, 2010, last revised April 5, 2013, www.eoearth.org/view/article/51cbed2c7896bb431f690448/.**

rological Organization, and 2015 was the warmest year for which observational records exist.[32] If present rates continue, global temperatures will rise by at least 2°C by the end of the century.[33]

The world's freshwater resources are also under serious stress. Increased water consumption, rising population, and climate change mean that about 80 percent of the world's population lives in countries with areas classified as having high levels of threat to water security.[34] About 3.4 billion people live in regions with absolute water scarcity.[35] Agricultural water use, mainly crop irrigation, accounts for about 70 percent of total global consumption and about 90 percent in developing countries, and estimates predict that global agricultural water demand will increase by 20 percent by the year 2050.[36] Industrial use accounts for about 20 percent of total water use and domestic uses for 10 percent.[37] The need to withdraw freshwater from surface and underground sources (e.g., lakes, rivers, reservoirs, aquifers, and wells) is expected to increase by more than 50 percent by 2050, with the bulk of the increase coming from developing countries.[38]

The convergence of population growth, rising demand for lumber and fuelwood, and the conversion of forests to agriculture have also put increasing pressure on the world's forests, especially in developing countries. At the beginning of the twentieth century, the world contained about five billion hectares of forested area; now fewer than four billion hectares remain.[39] Between 2000 and 2012, 2.3 million square kilometers of tree cover disappeared.[40] From 2010 through 2015, a net of about 6.6 million hectares of natural forests were lost annually.[41] Deforestation, in turn, has contributed to significant GHG emissions and the loss of biodiversity (the variety of living things), including the extinction of species and the loss of genetic diversity within species. Scientists began warning in the 1980s that the destruction of tropical forests, which hold an estimated 50 to 90 percent of all species, could result in the loss of one-fourth to one-half of the world's species within a few decades.

Biodiversity is not confined to the tropical forests, however, and humans are dramatically transforming virtually all of Earth's ecosystems. Despite the growing number of nature reserves, national parks, and other protected areas, including the addition of more than 6.1 million square kilometers since 2010, an amount roughly the size of Australia,[42] a recent UN report concluded that half of the world's richest biodiversity zones remain entirely unprotected.[43] The Millennium Ecosystem Assessment (see Box 1.2) estimated that between 10 and 50 percent of species are currently threatened with extinction, including 12 percent of bird species, 23 percent of mammal species, and 25 percent of conifer species (cone-bearing trees).[44]

Many of the world's major fisheries are overfished or on the verge of collapse. The declining marine catch in many areas, the increased percentage of overexploited fish stocks, and the decreased proportion of non–fully exploited species provide strong evidence that the state of world marine fisheries is worsening.[45] Because the waters and biological resources of the high seas belong to no nation, it is not surprising that overfishing has become a serious problem. The Food and Agriculture Organization of the UN (FAO) reports that "61 percent of commercially important assessed marine fish stocks worldwide are fully fished, 29 percent are overfished [and] about 90 percent of large predatory fish stocks are already depleted."[46] Nearly 30 percent of the world's marine fish stocks are considered overexploited or fished at biologically unsustainable levels.[47] Staples such as tuna, swordfish, Atlantic salmon, and even cod could soon be on the endangered list, crippling the economies they support (fishing provides some two hundred million jobs worldwide).[48] In addition, inefficient fishing practices waste a high percentage of each year's catch and cause severe environmental damage.[49] About twenty million metric tons of bycatch (unintentionally caught fish, seabirds, sea turtles, marine mammals, and other ocean life) die every year when they are carelessly swept up and discarded by commercial fishing operations.[50]

Marine environments are also under siege from land-based sources of marine pollution, believed to account for nearly 80 percent of the total pollution of the

BOX 1.2 WHAT IS THE MILLENNIUM ECOSYSTEM ASSESSMENT?

The Millennium Ecosystem Assessment examined the health of the world's ecosystems and the consequences of ecosystem change for human well-being. Sponsored by the UN and other international organizations, the assessment involved the work of more than 1,360 experts worldwide who conducted comprehensive reviews of current knowledge, scientific literature, and field data. Their findings, contained in five technical volumes and six synthesis reports, provide a state-of-the-art scientific appraisal of the condition and trends in the world's ecosystems and the services they provide (such as clean water, food, forest products, flood control, and natural resources) and the options to restore, conserve, or enhance the sustainable use of ecosystems.

The core findings of the assessment are that human actions are rapidly depleting Earth's natural resources and putting such strain on the environment that the ability of the planet's ecosystems to sustain future generations can no longer be taken for granted. At the same time, the assessment shows that with appropriate actions it is possible to reverse the degradation of many ecosystem services over the next fifty years, but the changes in policy and practice required are substantial and not currently underway.

The research was conducted from 2001 to 2005 and represents the most recent, globally comprehensive report of its kind. Assessment reports and information on its findings, history, operation, participants, and use by scientists and policymakers can be found on the Millennium Ecosystem Assessment website, www.millennium assessment.org.

oceans. The major land-based pollutants are synthetic organic compounds; excess sedimentation from mining, deforestation, or agriculture; biological contaminants in sewage; and excessive nutrients from fertilizers and sewage. Large quantities of plastic and other debris can be found in the most remote parts of the world's oceans. Plastic persists almost indefinitely in the environment and has a significant impact on marine and coastal biodiversity.[51] A study published in 2016 reported that, if present rates continue, by 2050 there will be more plastic in the world's oceans than fish (by weight).[52]

Human impacts on wetlands are also increasing. Wetlands cover about thirteen million square kilometers worldwide.[53] Different types of wetlands serve as important sources of drinking water, fish nurseries, natural irrigation for agriculture, water cleansing systems, protection against floods and storms, and natural sinks for CO_2. In the United States alone, wetlands provide approximately $23 billion

PHOTO 1.1 Wetlands provide habitat for a wide variety and large number of wildlife species, including the great blue heron. Courtesy Pamela Chasek.

worth of coastal area storm protection.[54] Wetlands are also some of the most important biologically diverse areas in the world, providing essential habitats for many species. Despite an international treaty, the Ramsar Convention, dedicated to their protection, wetlands are increasingly filled in or otherwise destroyed to make way for buildings and farms or damaged by unsustainable water use and pollution. Studies conclude that between 64 and 71 percent of the world's wetlands have been destroyed in the last hundred years and only 20 percent of the remaining wetlands lie within protected areas.[55] Given their ecological and economic importance, an influential 2012 report concluded: "There is an urgent need to put wetlands and water-related ecosystem services at the heart of water management in order to meet the social, economic and environmental needs of a global population predicted to reach 9 billion by 2050."[56]

Land degradation, water shortages, increasing demands for food, and other factors are combining to create negative feedbacks. Most of the unforested land available to meet current and future food requirements is already in production. Further expansion will involve fragile, marginal, and currently forested lands. As land becomes increasingly scarce, farmers face incentives to turn to intensive agriculture, including the use of dramatically higher levels of irrigation and chemicals. This, in turn, can contribute to soil erosion and salinization, deteriorating water quality, and land degradation.

Economic growth, expanding populations, rising demand, changing diets, urbanization, changes in weather patterns possibly linked to climate change, the use of food crops for biofuel, and certain agriculture policies, including subsidies in developed countries, are combining to raise food prices and increase the number of people vulnerable to starvation, severe hunger, and malnutrition. The FAO estimates that 805 million people, including 791 million in developing countries, live with undernourishment—an inability to take in enough calories over at least one year to meet dietary energy requirements.[57] Global food production must increase by 60 percent by 2050 just to meet increased demands due to population increases.[58] This includes the increasing demand for meat and fish among the growing number of middle-class consumers in China, India, and other developing countries (although per capita meat and fish consumption in these countries remains far below that in Australia, Europe, Japan, and North America). Because it takes many pounds of feed to produce a pound of animal meat or aquaculture fish, grains as feed for animals use a significant amount of resources and raise prices.[59] Meat production is also extremely water intensive. The production of one kilogram of beef requires an average of fifteen thousand liters of water compared with fifteen hundred liters of water needed to produce one kilogram of grain.[60] Food production costs have also increased in many areas, including the cost of seeds (partly because of patents and other intellectual property rights), fuel (for machinery and vehicles), fertilizers, pesticides, water, land, and labor. Weather variability, including from climate change, has also affected international food supply and prices.[61] Prominent examples include the historic heat waves, droughts (especially in California[62] and Australia), and storms in Australia, Brazil, Russia, the United States, and other critical food production areas over the last decade.

Biofuel production is another important factor. Biofuels are liquid renewable fuels such as ethanol (an alcohol fermented from plant materials) and biodiesel (a fuel made from vegetable oils or animal fats) that can substitute for petroleum-based fuels. Although potential future biofuels made from algae, seaweed, or plant waste would have significant economic and ecological benefits, the production of many current biofuels requires significant amounts of pesticides, fertilizer, water, and energy, and many experts do not consider them environmentally benign.[63] Manufacturing most of the biofuels currently in use also shifts valuable resources (e.g., land, water, labor, capital) away from the production of food crops into the production of feedstock for biofuels. For example, in 2012, about 31 percent (about 3,465 million bushels) of US corn was used in the production of ethanol.[64] Diverting land and corn from growing food for people or animals raises corn prices in global markets.[65]

Environmental quality in many urban areas continues to be a major problem, and the situation could worsen. Although cities provide significant economies of scale for environmentally friendly technology and practices, under current conditions in many parts of the world, increasing urbanization implies heavier water and air pollution and higher rates of natural resource consumption. Air pollution in many major urban areas is already at harmful levels, responsible for more than one million deaths a year,[66] and it continues to worsen in many urban areas in Asia and Africa. Hundreds of millions living in poverty in urban areas lack consistent access to clean water or electricity. Municipal waste systems in many cities cannot keep pace with urban expansion.[67] Although conditions have improved in some areas, an estimated 863 million people were living in slums in 2014, up from 776.7 million in 2000.[68]

It was only in 2008 that the world's urban population surpassed the rural population. By 2050, about 66 percent of the world's population, about 6.3 billion people, is expected to live in urban areas, a large increase from the 3.6 billion in 2011.[69] The number of cities with at least ten million inhabitants is projected to rise from twenty-eight in 2014 to at least forty-one in 2030[70] (see Table 1.2). The largest increases in urban populations are expected in the world's two poorest regions, South Asia and sub-Saharan Africa, where populations are projected to double within twenty years.[71]

The trends described in this section are some of the most important forces that shape global environmental politics. They have resulted from the intense economic development, rapid population growth, inefficient production, and unsustainable resource consumption prevalent in many parts of the world. This is not to say that population growth and economic development are necessarily harmful. Indeed, most would argue they are not. Rather, it is the manner in which much of this economic development occurred, one characterized by high levels of resource consumption and pollution, that produced these troubling changes in the global environment.

AN INTRODUCTION TO GLOBAL ENVIRONMENTAL POLITICS

Environmental problems do not respect national boundaries. Transboundary air pollution, the degradation of shared rivers, and the pollution of oceans and seas are just a few examples of the international dimensions of environmental problems. The cumulative impact that human beings have on the planet, together with an increased

TABLE 1.2 **The World's Twenty Largest Megacities, 2014**

RANK	MEGACITY	POPULATION (IN THOUSANDS)
1	Tokyo, Japan	37,833
2	Delhi, India	24,953
3	Shanghai, China	22,991
4	Mexico City, Mexico	20,843
5	São Paulo, Brazil	20,831
6	Mumbai, India	20,741
7	Kinki MMA, Japan	20,123
8	Beijing, China	19,520
9	New York–Newark, United States	18,591
10	Al-Qahirah, Egypt	18,419
11	Dhaka, Bangladesh	16,982
12	Karachi, Pakistan	16,126
13	Buenos Aires, Argentina	15,024
14	Kolkata, India	14,766
15	Istanbul, Turkey	13,954
16	Chongqing, China	12,916
17	Manila, Philippines	12,764
18	Lagos, Nigeria	12,614
19	Guangzhou, China	11,843
20	Kinshasa, Democratic Republic of Congo	11,116

Source: UN, *World Urbanization Prospects 2014* (New York: UN, 2015), 93.

understanding of ecological processes, means that the environment cannot be viewed as a relatively stable background factor. The interactions between economic development and the complex, often fragile ecosystems on which that development depends have become major international political and economic issues.

The sources, consequences, and actors involved in an environmental issue can be local, national, regional, or global. If the sources or consequences are global, or transcend more than one international region, or the actors involved in creating or addressing the problem transcend more than one region, then we consider the activity and its consequences to be a global environmental issue.[72] The main actors in international environmental politics are states (national governments), international organizations, environmental nongovernmental organizations (NGOs), corporations and industry groups, scientific bodies, and important individuals (see Chapter 2).

Global environmental issues can be analyzed in many ways. From the economist's point of view, environmental problems represent negative externalities—the unintended consequences or side effects of one's actions that are borne by others (and for which no compensation is paid). Externalities have always existed, but when the use of helpful but polluting technologies—such as coal-fired power plants, synthetic fertilizers, pesticides, herbicides, and plastics—expanded rapidly, the externalities they produced became serious global issues.

In this sense, the negative externalities that lead to environmental degradation are similar to the "tragedy of the commons." The ecologist Garrett Hardin observed that overgrazing unrestricted common lands, prior to their enclosure, was a metaphor for the overexploitation of Earth's common property: land, air, and water resources.[73] The root cause of overgrazing was the absence of a method for obliging herders to take into account the harmful effects that their own herds' grazing had on the other herders who shared the common land. Hardin recognized that air, water, and many other environmental resources, unlike the traditional commons, could not readily be fenced and parceled out to private owners who would be motivated to preserve them. Without sufficient knowledge or structures to restrain them, people (or states) will logically pursue their interest in utilizing the earth's common resources until they are destroyed, resulting in the tragedy of the commons. How to address externalities and the damage they inflict on environmental resources that, by their very nature, no one can own is a central challenge in global environmental politics.

Oran Young, a political scientist, groups international environmental problems into four broad clusters: commons, shared natural resources, transboundary externalities, and linked issues.[74] Young describes the commons as the natural resources and vital life-support services that belong to all humankind rather than to any one country. These include Antarctica, the high seas, deep seabed minerals, the stratospheric ozone layer, the global climate system, and outer space. They may be geographically limited, as in Antarctica, or global in scope, such as the ozone layer and climate system. Shared natural resources are physical or biological systems that extend into or across the jurisdiction of two or more states. These include nonrenewable resources, such as pools of oil beneath the earth's surface; renewable resources, such as migratory species of animals; and complex ecosystems that transcend national boundaries, such as regional seas and river basins.

Transboundary externalities result from activities that occur within the jurisdiction of individual states but produce results affecting the environment or people in other states. Transboundary externalities include the consequences of environmental accidents, such as the 1986 explosion at the Chernobyl nuclear power plant in the former Soviet Union or the accident in 2000 at a gold-processing plant in

Romania that released cyanide and heavy metals into a river system, killing fish and contaminating drinking water in parts of Romania, Bulgaria, Hungary, and Serbia. Transboundary externalities can also include transnational air pollution or the loss of biological diversity, caused in part by the destruction of tropical forests, which leads to species extinction as well as reduced potential for developing new pharmaceuticals. *Linked issues* refers to cases where efforts to deal with environmental concerns have unintended consequences affecting other issues and vice versa. The most common linked issues involve efforts to protect the environment and efforts to promote economic development or trade.

Different combinations of factors, including internal economic and political forces, foreign policy goals, and the impact of international organizations, NGOs, and corporations, can influence a state's policy preferences on different environmental issues (see Chapter 2). Because the actual costs and risks of environmental degradation are never distributed equally among states, some governments are less motivated than others to participate in international efforts to reduce environmental threats. States often possess different views about what constitutes an equitable solution to a particular environmental problem. Yet, despite their disparate interests, in order to address most international environmental issues, states must strive for consensus, at least among those that significantly contribute to, and are significantly affected by, a given environmental problem.

Consequently, an important characteristic of global environmental politics is the significance of veto power. For every global environmental issue, there exist one or more states whose cooperation is so essential to a successful agreement for coping with the problem that these states have the potential to block strong international action. When these states oppose an agreement or try to weaken it significantly, they become veto (or blocking) states and form veto coalitions.

The role of veto coalitions is central to the dynamics of bargaining and negotiation in global environmental politics. On the issue of a whaling moratorium, for example, four states, led by Japan, accounted for three-fourths of the whaling catch worldwide; they could therefore make or break the effectiveness of a global regime to save the whales. Similarly, the major grain exporters (Argentina, Australia, Canada, Chile, the United States, and Uruguay) were in position to block the initial attempts to reach consensus on a biosafety protocol under the Convention on Biological Diversity (CBD) for fear that the proposed provisions on trade in genetically modified crops were too stringent and would hamper grain exports (see Chapter 4).

Veto power is so important that powerful states are not free to impose a global environmental agreement on much less powerful states if the latter are strongly opposed to it and critical to the agreement's success. For example, industrialized countries could not pressure tropical-forest countries such as Brazil, Indonesia, and Malaysia to accept a binding agreement on the world's forests during the 1992 UN Conference on Environment and Development (UNCED; see Chapter 4). Comparatively weaker states can also use veto power to demand compensation and other forms of favorable treatment. This occurred during the expansion of the ozone-layer regime, when India and China led a coalition of developing countries that successfully demanded a financial mechanism that would provide resources to assist them in meeting the higher costs of using new non-ozone-depleting chemicals (see Chapter 3). Nevertheless, although some developing states can prevent an agreement or bargain for special treatment on some environmental issues, in general the major economic powers wield greater leverage because of their larger role in global production and consumption and their ability to provide or deny funding for a particular regime.

A related characteristic of global environmental politics is that the political dynamics within an issue area also often reflect issues involving international trade. The issue of international hazardous waste trading, for instance, is shaped by the relationship between the industrialized countries that seek to export waste as well as materials for recycling and the developing countries that are potential importers. Trade relations between tropical timber exporters and consuming nations are critical to the dynamics of tropical deforestation. Sometimes the trade patterns are so significant that they provide the producing/exporting countries or the importing countries with veto power.

Economic power, interests, and trade dynamics certainly affect state preferences, negotiating positions, and the outcome of bargaining on particular issues. Military power, however, is not particularly useful for influencing such outcomes. A country's ability to give or withhold economic benefits, such as access to markets or economic assistance, can persuade states dependent on those benefits to go along with that power's policy if the benefits are more important than the issue at stake in the negotiations. Thus, Japan and the Republic of Korea accepted international agreements on drift-net fishing and whaling because they feared loss of access to US markets. And Japan succeeded in ensuring the support of some small nonwhaling nations for its pro-whaling position by offering assistance to their fishing industries (see Chapter 4).

Although states are the most important actors, another characteristic of global environmental politics is that public opinion and environmental NGOs can also affect the creation, content, or implementation of international environmental policy. Public opinion, channeled through electoral politics and NGOs into national negotiating positions in key countries, has influenced certain aspects of the global bargaining on whaling, endangered species, hazardous wastes, persistent organic

PHOTO 1.2 Public opinion can play an important role in global environmental politics. Courtesy Kiara Worth, IISD/*Earth Negotiations Bulletin*, www.iisd.ca.

pollutants (POPs), and ozone depletion. NGOs have also provided important input to global negotiations and have been integral parts of some implementation strategies (see Chapter 2).

Different types of intergovernmental organizations (IGOs)—including large UN agencies, global and regional financial institutions, scientific organizations, and specialized agencies—play a variety of roles in global environmental politics. These roles include agenda setting, providing independent and authoritative information, helping to develop norms or codes of conduct (soft law) to guide action in particular environmental issue areas, convening and managing formal treaty negotiations, helping to implement global environmental treaties, providing funds, and influencing the environmental and development policies of particular countries (see Chapter 2).

Another set of critical venues for policy development are the large global conferences convened by the UN (see Box 1.3 and Chapter 6). The first of these conferences, the historic 1972 Stockholm Conference on the Human Environment, was responsible for placing global environmental concerns on the international agenda and set the stage for the creation of new international norms for environmental issues. The foundation of the conference was the growing realization that "many of the causes and effects of environmental problems are global: this is, beyond the jurisdiction and sovereignty of any nation-state. . . .Global frameworks and other institutions are necessary in order to help organize and coordinate international action."[75] Stockholm also marked the beginning of an explosive increase in NGOs and IGOs dedicated to environmental preservation, with an estimated hundred thousand such organizations formed in the subsequent twenty years.[76]

BOX 1.3 MAJOR UNITED NATIONS SUSTAINABLE DEVELOPMENT CONFERENCES

EARTH SUMMIT SERIES

1972	**UN Conference on the Human Environment (Stockholm Conference; Stockholm, Sweden)**
1992	**UN Conference on Environment and Development (Earth Summit; Rio de Janeiro, Brazil)**
2002	**World Summit on Sustainable Development (Johannesburg, South Africa)**
2012	**UN Conference on Sustainable Development (Rio de Janeiro, Brazil)**

UN GENERAL ASSEMBLY MILLENNIUM AND SUSTAINABLE DEVELOPMENT GOALS

2000	**UN Millennium Summit (UN Headquarters, New York)**
2015	**UN Sustainable Development Summit (UN Headquarters, New York)**

Twenty years later, in 1992, governments gathered for UNCED, often called the Earth Summit. In addition to adopting a global action program, Agenda 21 (referring to the twenty-first century), UNCED also produced two nonbinding sets of principles that shaped future developments—the Rio Declaration on Environment and Development and the Statement of Forest Principles.[77] Two major global treaties, the climate and biodiversity conventions, were negotiated independently of the UNCED process but on parallel tracks and officially adopted at the Earth Summit. They are often called the Rio Conventions. The Earth Summit launched a significant expansion of international environmental policy and treaty regimes. Over the next twenty-five years, new or strengthened conventions, protocols, and policy agreements emerged on climate change, biodiversity, desertification, mercury, POPs, biosafety, access to and benefit sharing of genetic resources, forests, and ozone depletion (see Chapters 3 and 4). Two additional global environmental conferences were held, one in 2002 in Johannesburg, South Africa, and the second in 2012 in Rio de Janeiro, which served to maintain attention on important issues and ideas in global environmental politics (see Chapter 6).

Perhaps the most critical venues for global environmental politics are the conferences and related meetings convened to negotiate, expand, and implement environmental policies in specific issues areas, including legally binding agreements (see

Box 1.4). Government representatives gather on a regular basis to examine and perhaps improve global policy to address biodiversity, climate change, endangered species, fisheries, forests, hazardous waste, ocean pollution, stratospheric ozone, toxic chemicals, wetlands, whales, and other issues. Preparing for and implementing the results of these conferences can also influence elements of domestic environmental

BOX 1.4 SELECTED GLOBAL ENVIRONMENTAL TREATIES SINCE 1970

1971	**Ramsar Convention on Wetlands of International Importance**
1972	**Convention on the Prevention of Marine Pollution by Dumping of Wastes and Other Matter (London Convention)**
1973	**Convention on International Trade in Endangered Species of Wild Fauna and Flora (CITES)**
1973	**International Convention for the Prevention of Pollution from Ships (MARPOL)**
1976	**Convention for the Protection of the Mediterranean Sea Against Pollution**
1979	**Convention on the Conservation of Migratory Species of Wild Animals**
1980	**Convention on the Conservation of Antarctic Marine Living Resources**
1985	**Vienna Convention for Protection of the Ozone Layer**
1987	**Montreal Protocol on Substances That Deplete the Ozone Layer**
1989	**Basel Convention on the Control of Transboundary Movements of Hazardous Wastes and Their Disposal**
1992	**UN Framework Convention on Climate Change (UNFCCC)**
1992	**Convention on Biological Diversity (CBD)**
1994	**UN Convention to Combat Desertification (UNCCD)**
1997	**Kyoto Protocol to the UN Framework Convention on Climate Change**
1998	**Rotterdam Convention on the Prior Informed Consent Procedure for Certain Hazardous Chemicals and Pesticides in International Trade**
2000	**Cartagena Protocol on Biosafety to the Convention on Biological Diversity**
2001	**Stockholm Convention on Persistent Organic Pollutants**
2001	**International Treaty on Plant Genetic Resources for Food and Agriculture**
2010	**Nagoya Protocol on Access to Genetic Resources and the Fair and Equitable Sharing of Benefits Arising from Their Utilization to the Convention on Biological Diversity**
2013	**Minamata Convention on Mercury**
2015	**Paris Agreement to the UN Framework Convention on Climate Change**

and even development policy. It is important, however, not to focus solely on the negotiations that create a particular treaty, as doing so can obscure the evolving constellation of binding rules, normative principles, institutions, operating procedures, review mechanisms, and implementation activities that compose environmental policy in a given issue area. Understanding global environmental politics, including environmental treaties and treaty conferences, requires understanding international regimes.

INTERNATIONAL REGIMES IN GLOBAL ENVIRONMENTAL POLITICS

International regime is the name given by scholars (and now some practitioners) of international policy to a system of principles, norms, rules, operating procedures, and institutions that actors create to regulate and coordinate action in a particular issue area of international relations. Principles are beliefs of fact, causation, and rectitude. Norms are standards of behavior. Rules are specific prescriptions or proscriptions for action. Operating procedures are prevailing practices for work within the regime, including methods for making and implementing collective choice. Institutions are mechanisms and organizations for implementing, operating, evaluating, and expanding the regime and its policy.[78]

Regimes are essentially international policy, regulatory, and administrative systems. A regime usually centers on one or more formal international agreements, but key elements can also include the relevant actions of important international organizations, parts of other interrelated international agreements, and accepted norms of international behavior among actors active in the issue area (including governments, international organizations, NGOs, multinational corporations, and others). These elements together form the entire suite of principles, norms, rules, and procedures that seek to govern and guide behavior on the particular issue.

Regimes of varying strength and effectiveness are found in most areas of international relations, including trade, finance, environment, human rights, communications, travel, and even security. As a result, regimes receive a good deal of theoretical and empirical attention from scholars of international relations, and this represents an important development in the study of international cooperation—especially into how, why, and under what circumstances states attempt to cooperate or create international institutions and what factors influence the success of such attempts.[79]

One important line of progenitor theories is marked by concern for the impact and mitigation of structural anarchy, especially the difficulty of establishing international cooperation.[80] (*Anarchy* in this usage does not mean chaos but the absence of hierarchy, specifically the lack of world government or other formal hierarchical structures to govern international politics.) A second line flows both from constitutionalist scholars who study treaties and the formal structure of international organizations, and from researchers employing the institutional process approach, which concentrates on examining how an organization's day-to-day practices, processes, and methods of operation influence outcomes.[81]

A third line of antecedents starts with the premise that despite structural anarchy, extensive common interests exist among states and their people and that scholars and statesmen must learn how these interests can be realized. Present in eighteenth-century enlightened optimism, nineteenth-century liberalism, and twentieth-century Wilsonian idealism, this view influenced in the 1970s a branch of legal and political scholarship concerned with world order and international law that argued that custom, patterned interaction and the needs and wants of civilian populations are important sources of international law and require the respect of states.[82]

Functionalism represents a fourth important line of predecessors. Functionalism, often associated with the work of David Mitrany, argues that the scholarly and political focus of international cooperation must center not on formal interstate politics but rather on providing opportunities for technical (nonpolitical) cooperation among specialists and specialized organizations to solve common problems.[83] Functionalists argue that such technical cooperation can begin a process in which increasing interdependence and spillover (technical management in one area begetting technical management in another) will present opportunities for organizing more and more government functions internationally and technically rather than nationally and politically—a process that will slowly erode or bypass domestic regulators in favor of peaceful global institutions.

Although attractively optimistic, functionalism proved inadequate to explain the totality of actions and outcomes in international relations in which states do not want to relinquish control and technological determinism did not respond automatically to most aspects of increasing interdependence. However, functionalist insights did influence several important theoretical approaches.[84]

Neofunctional integration theory critiqued and extended functionalism, arguing that gradual, regional integration is most important for understanding and creating effective international governance.[85] This approach also lost favor, particularly when Ernst Haas, formerly a leading proponent, argued that focusing exclusively on regional encapsulation had become inadequate for addressing new, turbulent issue areas of international relations characterized by high degrees of complexity, interdependence, and competing national interests, which we now know include environmental issues. Haas argued that the interplay of knowledge, learning, and politics is critical to understanding and managing such issue areas as well as the conduct and adaptability of international organizations created to address them.[86]

Research on transnational relations, which are nongovernmental interconnections and interactions across national boundaries, argued similarly that interdependence can fracture international politics into distinct issue areas and that states are neither the only important actors in international politics nor even totally coherent actors.[87] These insights culminated in complex interdependence, proposed by Robert Keohane and Joseph Nye as an alternative to realism as a paradigm for understanding international relations.[88]

The study of regimes resulted from these lines of inquiry. If international relations are increasingly interdependent, influenced by new types of actors and interactions, and fractured into issue areas across which power and interests vary, then how actors choose to manage these issue areas—the regimes they create to manage them—becomes important to the conduct and study of international politics.

States and other actors create regimes through multilateral negotiations. Negotiations take place when at least some states consider the status quo unacceptable or that negative consequences and high costs will occur if existing trends continue. Although reaching agreement on how to manage the problem is in a state's best interest, so is gaining as much as possible while giving up as little as possible. Nevertheless, the expected value of the outcome to each state, and hence the total value of the outcome, must be positive (or at least neutral), or else there would be no incentive to negotiate or to accept the outcome. In multilateral negotiations, states will not come to an agreement unless they believe they will be better off in some way than they would be with no agreement.[89]

Most regimes center on a binding agreement or legal instrument. For global environmental problems, the most common kind of legal instrument is a convention. A convention may contain all of the binding obligations expected to be negotiated, or it may be followed by a more detailed legal instrument, often called a protocol, which elaborates more specific norms and rules. Because the members of most international regimes are states, regime rules apply to the actions of states. These governments then assume responsibility for ensuring that companies and other actors within their jurisdiction change their behavior to the extent necessary for the country as a whole to be in compliance with the rules of the regime.

If a convention is negotiated in anticipation that parties will negotiate one or more subsequent elaborating texts, it is called a framework convention. Framework conventions usually establish a set of general principles, norms, and goals for cooperation on the issue as well as how members of the regimes will meet and make decisions. The latter usually takes the form of a regular Conference of the

Parties, an annual, biannual, or otherwise regularly scheduled gathering of all parties to the convention as well as interested observers (observers often include representatives from nonparty states, international organizations, NGOs, and industry groups). Framework conventions usually do not impose major binding obligations on the parties. A framework convention is then followed by the negotiation of one or more protocols, which spell out specific obligations on the overall issue in question or on narrower subissues.

A nonbinding agreement can form the centerpiece of a regime to the extent that it establishes norms that influence state behavior. This type of agreement is often referred to as soft law. Nonbinding agreements, codes of conduct, and guidelines for behavior exist for a number of global environmental problems, including land-based sources of marine pollution and sustainable forest management, with varying degrees of effectiveness. Some consider Agenda 21, the plan of action adopted at the 1992 Earth Summit, and the Sustainable Development Goals (SDGs) adopted in 2015 (see Chapter 6) as soft-law umbrella regimes for worldwide sustainable development because they outline goals and broad norms of behavior that countries have agreed to regarding a wide range of environmental and development issues. Although nonbinding agreements can influence state behavior to some extent, regimes based on legal instruments are usually more effective. That is why some countries become dissatisfied with a given nonbinding code of conduct or other soft-law mechanism and advocate for creating a legally binding agreement.

Global Environmental Regimes

Today, regimes exist on a wide variety of global environmental issues, from whale protection to climate change to hazardous wastes. Chapters 3 and 4 describe the development of and the challenges faced by some key global regimes. As these cases demonstrate, global environmental regimes can vary significantly in their history, purpose, rules, strength, and effectiveness.

Environmental regimes change over time, often expanding and becoming stronger but sometimes weakening or changing in scope. The whaling regime was created in 1946 to perpetuate commercial whaling by establishing international regulation, but it evolved into a ban on commercial whaling in 1985 (see Chapter 4). The regime that seeks to control marine oil pollution began with the 1954 International Convention for the Prevention of Pollution of the Sea by Oil, which established rules only for ships within fifty miles (eighty kilometers) of the nearest coast, allowing for significant and deliberate oil spillage outside this area.[90] This led some states in 1973 to create the International Convention for the Prevention of Pollution from Ships, also known as MARPOL or the Maritime Pollution Convention, which limits oil discharges at sea, prohibits them in certain sensitive zones, and sets minimum distances from land for the discharge of other pollutants. However, shipping interests in crucial maritime states opposed MARPOL so strongly that it did not enter into force until a decade later. States also negotiated the Convention on the Prevention of Marine Pollution by Dumping of Wastes and Other Matter (London Convention, 1972), which prohibited the dumping of specific substances, including high-level radioactive wastes, and required permits for others. It was the first marine-pollution agreement to accept the right of coastal states to enforce prohibitions against pollution and became an important forum for negotiating further controls on ocean dumping.

In another example of regime evolution, until the 1970s virtually all wildlife conservation treaties lacked binding legal commitments and, perhaps consequently, were ineffective in protecting migratory birds and other species. This changed when states adopted the 1973 Convention on International Trade in Endangered Species of Wild Fauna and Flora (CITES; see Chapter 4). It set up a system of trade sanctions and a worldwide reporting network to curb the traffic in endangered species and thus, by eliminating the market, to reduce the incentive to capture, kill, or harvest endangered plants and animals. Although effective in many instances, CITES also contains loopholes that allow states with interests in a particular species to opt out of the controls on it.

Many regimes are strengthened as efforts shift from creating an initial framework convention to negotiating and implementing specific protocols. For example, the regional regime controlling cross-border acid rain and air pollution in Europe began with the 1979 Convention on Long-Range Transboundary Air Pollution, which did not commit signatories to specific emissions reductions. States later strengthened the regime by adding eight protocols that financed the monitoring and evaluation of long-range air pollutants in Europe (1984) and mandated efforts to reduce sulfur emissions (1985 and 1994), nitrogen oxides (1988), volatile organic compounds (1991), heavy metals (1998), POPs (1998), and acidification and ground-level ozone (1999). The heavy metals and POPs agreements also represented significant expansions of the core mandate established by the original convention.

The ozone regime also began with a framework convention (see Chapter 3). The 1985 Vienna Convention for the Protection of the Ozone Layer did not require countries to control the chemicals that threaten stratospheric ozone; in fact it did not even mention these substances by name. The 1987 Montreal Protocol then required actual reductions in certain halons and chlorofluorocarbons (CFCs), the most prominent ozone-depleting substances (ODS). Then, in the late 1980s and 1990s, significant advances in scientific understanding of the threat, the discovery of alternative chemicals, and the use of innovative regime rules allowed governments to reach a series of agreements that now mandate the near complete phase-out of all ODS. As a result, the production of CFCs and most other ODS has been eliminated.

The agreement that created the climate regime, the 1992 Framework Convention on Climate Change (UNFCCC; see Chapter 3), also failed to impose binding targets and timetables for GHG emissions. It did call on industrialized countries to return emissions to 1990 levels but stated this as a nonbinding goal. Only with the adoption of the Kyoto Protocol in 1997 did industrialized countries agree to even modest reductions in their GHG emissions.

Some treaties and regimes, like the 2001 Stockholm Convention on Persistent Organic Pollutants and the Montreal Protocol, have very clear, binding controls (see Chapter 3); others do not. The 1992 Convention on Biological Diversity (CBD; see Chapter 4), for example, does not obligate parties to measurable conservation objectives but instead requires the development of national strategies for conserving biodiversity. Similarly, the 1994 UN Convention to Combat Desertification (UNCCD; see Chapter 4), which established a regime to address land degradation in the drylands, calls for countries to draw up integrated national programs in consultation with local communities.

Some regimes, such as the ozone regime, are considered successes. These regimes have not completely solved the environmental issues they address, and each contains loopholes, but the situation is far better than it was before they were created. However, many regimes have had only mixed successes at best. Nevertheless, negotiation of the central agreement and other aspects of the regime (such as the related activities of international organizations) provide greater opportunities for addressing the environmental issue in question than when no regime exists (either because negotiations failed or none were attempted).[91] Thus, even though the biodiversity and climate regimes have not come close to solving those problems—in fact each problem continues to accelerate, with potentially disastrous results—the situation would be far worse, and the prospects for future improvements more remote, if the regimes did not exist.

Evidence for this conclusion exists in issues that have no extant regimes or for which initial attempts to create a regime failed. For instance, several efforts to create some type of regime for the protection of coral reefs have failed to gain traction, and coral reefs continue to degrade rapidly around the world. Shark populations continue to fall, largely as a result of sharks killed as bycatch, to make shark-fin soup, and for use in commercial products, including cosmetics. Efforts to initiate binding global protections for most sharks have failed, although a broad conservation plan was agreed on in 2010 to protect several species under the auspices of the Convention on Migratory Species.[92] Many countries have laws protecting coastal mangroves, but many of these same countries also sanction their enclosure or even allow their removal if needed for coastal development or to create ponds for shrimp farms. Without an international regime leading all countries to adjust their behavior simultaneously, this situation is likely to continue, and mangroves (and the ecological and economic value they have) will continue to disappear.

Theoretical Approaches to International Regimes

Several major theoretical approaches have been used to explain how international regimes come into existence and why they change.[93] These include structural, game-theoretic, institutional-bargaining, and epistemic-community approaches. Each may help explain one or more international regimes, but none individually can account for all of the regimes described and analyzed in this book.

The structural, or hegemonic-power, approach holds that the primary factor determining regime formation and change is the relative strength of the state actors involved in a particular issue and that "stronger states in the issue system will dominate the weaker ones and determine the rules of the game."[94] This approach suggests that strong international regimes are a function of a hegemonic state that can exercise leadership over weaker states and that the absence of such a hegemonic state is likely to frustrate regime formation.

The structural approach can be viewed in two ways, one stressing coercive power, the other focusing on public goods. In the coercive-power variant, regimes are set up by hegemonic states that use their military and economic leverage over other states to bring them into regimes, as the United States did in setting up trade and monetary regimes immediately after World War II.[95] The second variant views the same postwar regimes as the result of a hegemonic power's adopting policies that create public goods, that is, benefits open to all states that want to participate, such as export markets in the United States and the establishment of the dollar as a stable currency for international payments.

However useful the structural approach has been to explain the creation of post–World War II economic systems, it cannot explain why global environmental regimes have been negotiated. In the 1970s and 1980s, the United States was not a military hegemon but part of a bipolar system with the Soviet Union. Beginning in the mid-1980s, the United States faced the rise of competing economic powers in Japan and Europe. Moreover, the European Union (EU), whose member states negotiate on global environmental issues as a single bloc, became the economic equal of the United States in the late 1990s. Finally, the United States did not seek to create many of these environmental regimes. From 1981 to 1993 and from 2001 to 2009, both crucial periods in the creation and expansion of most global environmental regimes, the United States had presidents ideologically hostile toward international environmental regulation; consequently, the United States did not take many lead positions (as the theory argues a hegemonic state must do). Thus, the creation and expansion of these regimes depended on wide consensus among a number of states, not on imposition by the United States.[96]

Another approach to understanding regime creation is based on game theory and utilitarian models of bargaining. In game theory, bargaining scenarios are examined under different conditions with regard to the number of parties involved, the nature of the conflict (zero-sum or non–zero-sum), and the assumptions that the actors are rational (they will try to pursue outcomes favorable to them) and interconnected in some way—that is, they cannot pursue their own interests independently of the choices of other actors. This approach suggests that small groups of states, or coalitions, are more likely to succeed in negotiating an international regime than a large number because each player can more readily understand the bargaining strategies of the other players. Political scientist Fen Osler Hampson took this approach into account when he analyzed the process of regime creation as an effort by a small coalition of states to form a regime by exercising leadership over a much larger number of national actors.[97]

Nevertheless, for an environmental regime to succeed, it must include all states that have a large impact on the issue, including potential veto states. Veto states follow their own interests (as all states do), so a veto state in a small group will likely be as prone to opposition as it would be in a large group of states. And if veto states are left outside the small group, they will still be in a position to frustrate regime formation when the regime is enlarged, or they may simply refuse to join the regime, limiting the regime's success.

Another approach is the epistemic-communities model, which emphasizes the impact of international learning and transnational networks of experts and bureaucrats, primarily on the basis of scientific research into a given problem, as a factor influencing the evolution of regimes.[98] This approach, advanced initially by political scientist Peter Haas to explain the creation of and compliance with the Mediterranean Action Plan, identifies intra-elite shifts within and outside governments as the critical factor in the convergence of state policies in support of a stronger regime. The shifts empowered technical and scientific specialists allied with officials of international organizations. These elites thus formed transnational epistemic communities, that is, communities of experts sharing common values and approaches to policy problems.

The importance of scientific evidence and expertise in the politics of many global environmental issues cannot be ignored. Indeed, a significant degree of scientific understanding and consensus has sometimes been a minimum condition for serious international action on an issue. The impetus for agreement in 1990 that the world should phase out CFCs completely came from incontrovertible scientific evidence that damage to the ozone layer was much greater than previously thought and that CFCs were largely responsible. The Kyoto Protocol was made possible, in part, by the Second Assessment Report of the Intergovernmental Panel on Climate Change, which confirmed that the earth's temperature was increasing and that there is a "discernible human influence" on climate.

However, although scientific elites have played supportive and enabling roles in certain environmental negotiations, on some issues they remained divided or even captured by particular government or private interests. And on other issues, such as the whaling ban, the hazardous waste trade, desertification, Antarctica, and the ocean dumping of radioactive wastes, scientists have contributed little to regime formation or strengthening. In some of these cases, scientific elites were not particularly influential in policy making, whereas in others key actors explicitly rejected scientific findings as the basis for decisions.[99]

The case studies presented in Chapters 3 and 4 also suggest that theoretical approaches based solely on a unitary actor model (one suggesting that state actors can be treated as though they are a single entity encompassing an internally consistent set of values and attitudes), ignoring the roles of domestic sociopolitical structures and processes, are likely to form poor bases for analyzing and predicting the outcomes of global environmental bargaining. Negotiating positions usually reflect domestic sociopolitical balances, and these can change when those balances shift. For example, after Barack Obama was elected president, the United States dramatically shifted its stance from opposing to supporting global negotiations that would elaborate a regime to reduce mercury emissions. Although the structure of an issue in terms of economic interests may indicate which states are most likely to join a veto coalition, domestic political pressures and bargaining can tip the balance for or against regime creation or strengthening. A fully complete theoretical explanation for global environmental regime formation or change must incorporate the variable of state actors' domestic politics.

A nuanced analysis of regime formation and strengthening, therefore, should link international political dynamics with domestic politics and view the whole as a two-level game. While representatives of countries are maneuvering the outcome of bargaining over regime issues, officials must also bargain with interest groups within their domestic political systems. Because the two processes often take place simultaneously, the arenas influence each other and become part of the negotiations at each level.[100]

A theoretical explanation for the formation of global environmental regimes must also leave room for the importance of the rules of the negotiating forum and the linkages between the negotiations on regimes and the wider relationships among the negotiating parties. The legal structure of the negotiating forum—the rules of the game regarding who may participate and how authoritative decisions are to be made—becomes particularly important when the negotiations take place within an already established treaty or organization.[101] The ozone and whaling cases illustrate how these rules can be crucial in determining the outcomes of the negotiations.

Economic and political ties among key state actors can also sway a veto state to compromise or defect. Particularly when the environmental regime under negotiation does not involve issues central to the economy of the states that could block agreement, the potential veto state's concern about how a veto would affect relations with states important for economic or political reasons sometimes makes possible the formation or strengthening of a regime.

PARADIGMS IN GLOBAL ENVIRONMENTAL POLITICS

Public policy and regimes are shaped not only by impersonal forces, such as science, technological innovation, and economic growth, but also by peoples', governments', and institutions' perceptions of reality. In times of relative stability, public policies and systems of behavior tend to flow in accordance with dominant paradigms, or sets of beliefs, ideas, and values. A dominant paradigm is challenged when contradictions appear between its assumptions and observed reality. If these contradictions are not resolved, eventually it gives way to a new paradigm through a process known as a paradigm shift.[102]

Because economic and environmental policy are intertwined in many ways, the paradigm that has dominated public understanding of environmental management during the period of rapid global economic growth in the last two centuries has been essentially a system of beliefs about economics. It has been referred to as the *exclusionist paradigm* because it excludes human beings from the laws of nature. It has also been called *frontier economics*, suggesting the sense of unlimited resources characteristic of a society living on an open frontier.[103]

In capitalist societies, this paradigm has rested primarily on two assumptions of neoclassical economics: the free market will tend to maximize social welfare, and there exists an infinite supply of both natural resources and sinks for disposing of the wastes that accrue from exploiting those resources—provided that the free market is operating efficiently. Humans will not deplete a resource, according to this worldview, as long as technology is given free rein and prices are allowed to fluctuate enough to stimulate the search for substitutes; in this way, absolute scarcity can be postponed indefinitely into the future.[104] Waste disposal is viewed as a problem to be cleaned up after the fact—but not at the cost of interference with market decisions.[105]

Because conventional economic theory is concerned with the allocation of scarce resources and nature is not considered a constraining factor, this paradigm considers the environment largely irrelevant to economics. (Despite a different economic and political ideology, the former Soviet Union and other communist states also shared this assumption.) The traditional international legal principles of state sovereignty (including control over resources within a state's borders) and unrestricted access to the planet's common resources, such as the oceans and their living resources, buttressed the exclusionist paradigm.

Sustainable Development: Rise of an Alternative Paradigm

In the 1960s, the dominant paradigm came under attack. The critique started in the United States and then spread to Europe and other regions. The 1962 publication of Rachel Carson's *Silent Spring,* which documented the dangers to human health from synthetic pesticides, marked the beginning of an explosion of popular literature about new threats to the environment, including radiation, lead, toxic wastes, and air and water pollution. The first mass movement for environmental protection, which focused on domestic issues including air and water pollution, developed in the United States in the late 1960s. Throughout this period, research and writing on environmental issues began to raise awareness that economic activity without concern for the environmental consequences carried high costs to society. Parallel changes in public concern about pollution also occurred in other industrialized countries. The burst of environmental concern in the United States led to the passage of a series of landmark pieces of legislation, including the National Environmental Policy Act of 1969, the 1970 Clean Air Act, the 1970 establishment of the US Environmental Protection Agency, and new rules to combat water pollution in 1972. These laws and those that built on them dramatically decreased air, water, and soil pollution in the United States. The National Environmental Policy Act also directed federal agencies to support international cooperation in "anticipating and preventing a decline in the quality of mankind's world environment."[106]

But the United States was not alone. As noted above, the first global environmental conference in history, the UN Conference on the Human Environment, convened in Stockholm in 1972. The motto of the Stockholm Conference, "Only One Earth," was a revolutionary concept for its time. The conference approved a landmark declaration and a 109-point action plan for advancing international environmental cooperation, including creating a new international organization, the UN Environment Programme (UNEP), to provide a focal point for environmental action and coordination of environmentally related activities within the UN system. In preparation for, or as a result of, Stockholm, environmental ministries and agencies were established in more than one hundred countries (most governments did not have such ministries before 1972). Stockholm also marked the beginning of the explosive increase in environmentally focused NGOs and IGOs dedicated to environmental preservation.

The rise of environmental consciousness in the 1960s and early 1970s attacked the dominant paradigm but did not produce a widely accepted set of alternative assumptions about physical and economic realities that could become a competing worldview. The essential assumptions of classical economics remained largely intact. Confronted with evidence that existing patterns of resource exploitation could cause irreversible damage, proponents of classical economics continued to maintain that such exploitation was still economically rational.[107]

Over time, however, an alternative paradigm that challenged the assumptions of classical economics began to take shape. Two of the intellectual forerunners of this paradigm were the *Limits to Growth* study, published by the Club of Rome in 1972, and *Global 2000: The Report to the President*, released by the US Council on Environmental Quality and the Department of State in 1980.[108] Each study applied global-systems computer modeling to the projected interactions among population, economic growth, and natural resources and concluded that if current trends continued, many ecosystems and natural resources would become seriously and irreversibly degraded and that these environmental developments would then have serious and negative economic consequences. Because each study suggested that economic development and population growth were on a path that would eventually strain the earth's carrying capacity (the total amount of resource consumption that the earth's natural systems can support without undergoing degradation), the viewpoint underlying the studies was generally referred to as the *limits-to-growth perspective.*

Defenders of the dominant paradigm, among them Herman Kahn and Julian Simon, criticized these studies for projecting the depletion of nonrenewable resources without taking into account technological changes and market responses. These critics argued that overpopulation would not become a problem because people are the world's "ultimate resource," and they characterized the authors of studies as "no-growth elitists" who would freeze developing countries out of the benefits of economic growth. They argued that human ingenuity would enable humanity to leap over the alleged limits to growth through new and better technologies.[109] These arguments found a following among those concerned about economic growth. The development of an alternative paradigm was then set back in the early 1980s, when the Reagan administration in the United States and the Thatcher government in the United Kingdom embraced policies consistent with the exclusionist paradigm.

Despite these political developments, knowledge about ecological principles and their relationship to economic development continued to spread. A global community of practitioners and scholars began to emerge, allied in the belief that ecologically sound policies should replace policies based on the exclusionist paradigm.

By the mid-1980s, *sustainable development* had emerged as the catchphrase of the search for an alternative paradigm, and the term was heard with increasing frequency at conferences around the world.[110] An important milestone was the 1987 publication by the World Commission on Environment and Development of *Our Common Future* (better known as the Brundtland Report, after the commission's chair, former Norwegian prime minister Gro Harlem Brundtland). The UN established the Brundtland Commission to examine the impact of environmental degradation and natural resource depletion on future economic and social development. The commission's report is considered a landmark in global environmental politics in part because it helped to define, legitimize, and popularize the concept of sustainable development. Drawing on and synthesizing the views and research of hundreds of people worldwide, it also codified some of the central beliefs of the emerging sustainable development paradigm.

The Brundtland Commission defined sustainable development as "development that meets the need of the present without compromising the ability of future generations to meet their own needs."[111] The central themes of its report criticized existing economic and social systems (and the dominant paradigm) for failing to reconcile those needs. It asserted that the earth's natural systems have finite capabilities and resources and that the continuation of existing economic policies carries the risk of irreversible damage to the natural systems on which all life depends.

The sustainable development paradigm emphasizes the need to redefine the term *development*. It posits that economic growth cannot continue at the expense of the planet's natural capital (its stock of renewable and nonrenewable resources) and vital natural support systems such as the ozone layer, biodiversity, and a stable climate. Instead, the world economy must learn to live off the interest of the planet's natural capital. That means reducing the amount of resources used per unit of gross national product (GNP), shifting from fossil fuels to renewable energy, and reusing and recycling rather than consuming and discarding resources. It implies a transition to sustainable systems of natural resource management, efforts to stabilize world population, and a more measured approach to consumption.

The sustainable development paradigm holds that future generations have an equal right to use our planet's natural resources—a concept known as intergenerational equity.[112] The approach also affirms the need for greater equity among and within nations. Highly industrialized countries such as the United States, which use a disproportionate share of the world's environmental resources, are seen as

PHOTO 1.3 Youth activists marching for intergenerational climate justice at the 2014 Climate March in New York City. Courtesy Pamela Chasek.

pursuing an unsustainable type of economic growth, as are societies in which grossly unequal distribution of land and other resources produces significantly negative impacts. To meet current and future needs, developing countries must meet the basic needs of the poor in ways that do not deplete the countries' natural resources, and industrialized countries must examine attitudes and actions regarding unnecessary and wasteful aspects of their material abundance.[113]

One of the main anomalies of the classical economic paradigm is its measure of macroeconomic growth, that is, GNP. Advocates of sustainable development note that although GNP is an effective measure of broad economic activity, it fails to reflect the physical capability of an economy to provide material wealth in the future or to take into account the relative well-being of the society in general. Thus, a country could systematically deplete its natural resources, erode its soils, and pollute its waters without that loss of real wealth and its long-term negative economic impact showing up in calculations of GNP. Moreover, the economic expense of trying to fix these problems would actually add to GNP.

In the second half of the 1980s, some economists began to study how to correct this anomaly in conventional accounting and to advocate for governments and international organizations to use alternatives to GNP, such as real net national product, sustainable social net national product, or index of sustainable economic welfare, which include changes in environmental resources as well as other indicators that measure human welfare.[114] Of particular importance is the annual UN Development Programme's (UNDP) *Human Development Report*, which uses human indicators to rate the quality of life in all countries by measures other than economic ones, including literacy, life expectancy, and respect for women's rights.[115] The Himalayan kingdom of Bhutan measures well-being not through GNP but through a Gross National Happiness Index that provides an overview of performance across nine domains: psychological well-being, time use, community vitality, cultural diversity, ecological resilience, living standard, health, education, and good governance.[116] The World Bank's work on national capital accounting[117] and the UN's System of Environmental-Economic Accounts[118] have helped to pioneer the inclusion of social and environmental aspects when assessing the wealth of nations. The Organization for Economic Cooperation and Development's Global Project on Measuring the Progress of Societies employs broader indicators than traditional GNP- or similarly based analyses.[119] The Environmental Sustainability Index ranks countries on twenty-one elements of sustainability covering natural resource endowments, past and present pollution levels, environmental management efforts, and contributions to the protection of the global commons.[120] The EU and its member states have developed and use a broad range of social and environmental indicators, often regrouped in sets of sustainable development indicators. The EU also promotes and supports the use of internationally recognized indicators in neighboring countries and developing countries.[121]

The use of these and related approaches reflects an increasing awareness that free markets alone often fail to ensure the sustainable use of natural resources. Because the market usually does not address externalities effectively, the approach argues that prices should reflect the real costs to society of producing and consuming a given resource or emitting pollution that harms people or the environment. Conventional economic policies, however, systematically underprice or ignore natural resources[122] as well as the costs of pollution and related externalities. Public policies that do not correct for these market failures tend to encourage pollution, more rapid depletion of renewable resources, wasteful consumption, and the degradation of environmental services (i.e., the conserving or restorative functions of nature; for example, the conversion of CO_2 to oxygen by plants and the cleansing of water by wetlands). Adjusting the markets to send such price signals and exchanging income taxes for green taxes are means to address this problem and examples of the polluter pays principle, endorsed by the 1992 Rio Declaration on

Environment and Development (see Chapter 6). Placing an upper limit on consumption is another method.[123]

The alternative paradigm gained significant credibility through the Earth Summit in June 1992. The Earth Summit presented the first post–Cold War test of whether the international community possessed the collective will and wisdom to develop sustainably and to improve the human condition. And it was the first significant opportunity for industrialized countries (sometimes referred to in those discussions as "the North") and developing countries ("the South") to hold formal discussions on how they might combine economic and social development concerns with those of environmental protection as governments struggled to put into action the concept of sustainable development.[124] The agreements reached in Rio essentially held that developing countries would try to put into practice more environmentally sound development policies if the industrialized countries agreed to provide the necessary support, that is, new and additional financial resources, technology transfer on concessional and preferential terms, and assistance with capacity building, education, and training. Yet, twenty-five years later, few countries have lived up to their Rio commitments or completely embraced the sustainable development paradigm.

Globalization and Sustainable Development

Within many powerful institutions in China, India, the United States, and other countries, ideas that appear to be descended from the exclusionist paradigm still tend to dominate some policies. Many corporations, government ministries dealing with trade and finance, leaders of particular political parties, and some officials at multilateral institutions support policies that contradict the requirements for sustainable development. Interest groups dominated by certain industries locked into old paradigms continue to determine many national political agendas, while the globalization of industry, finance, technology, and information potentially erode certain aspects of the powers held by national authorities.[125] Additionally, studies show that most of the explicit goals set out in international environmental agreements have not been met.[126]

Has the sustainable development paradigm failed? Only ten years after the Earth Summit, many delegates and observers were asking this question as they gathered in Johannesburg in September 2002 at the World Summit on Sustainable Development (WSSD). Convened to review the implementation of Agenda 21 and the other agreements adopted at the Earth Summit, the conference produced no definitive answer and, at best, mixed results. Although there were many official expressions of concern regarding the limited implementation of the UNCED agreements on sustainable development and the meeting outlined some broad action plans, delegates did not agree on many new substantive commitments, let alone new legally binding agreements.

During and since the WSSD, some have argued that the sustainable development paradigm has not failed but that its ascendancy has stalled because of the rise of what they see as a variation of the exclusionist paradigm: globalization.[127] Globalization is often identified with a number of trends, including a greater international movement of commodities, money, information, and people, as well as the development of economic and legal systems, infrastructures, organizations, and technology to allow this movement. Economic globalization means globe-spanning economic relationships. The interrelationships of markets, finance, goods, and services, and the networks created by transnational corporations are particularly important manifestations.

One can view globalization as a description and/or an organizing principle, goal, or paradigm. As a description, globalization is the name given to the increasing interconnectedness of global economic, social, transportation, and communications systems, although some also include the impacts of these networks and the economic and political conditions that support them. These interconnections and their impacts are real. At the same time, the prevalence of policy choices that favor increased economic interconnectedness and other aspects of globalization, and the arguments of those that support or oppose these policies, make it clear that globalization is also a paradigm for organizing international economic activity.

Supporters of the globalization paradigm advocate for the liberalization of international markets, including reducing trade and other national economic barriers, minimizing regulations on the market (especially in highly regulated developing countries), and granting rights to corporations to invest in any country with few restraints or conditions. Governments should not interfere with the free play of the market. Efforts to prioritize social, development, or environmental concerns will retard the pursuit of the economic growth that is required for such goals to be achieved. Critics of the globalization paradigm oppose these policies, arguing that they are incompatible with sustainable development, increasing global equity, and sovereign political control over economic and social policy.

Actions by powerful countries and corporations supported the ascendancy of the globalization paradigm in the 1990s and 2000s. Some argue that many senior US policymakers saw globalization as supplanting the need for international assistance and even the sustainable development paradigm. "Trade, not aid" became a Washington mantra during the George W. Bush administration. Even among US policymakers favorable to environmental and development objectives, the trade and globalization agenda tended to occupy the available political space and crowd out sustainable development concerns.[128] The same argument could be made about key policies in China, India, and Russia, among other large countries.

As governments prepared for the 2012 UN Conference on Sustainable Development (UNCSD or Rio+20), the concerns expressed about sustainable development and globalization in 2002 at WSSD resurfaced, although some of the language had changed. The UNCSD was charged with securing renewed political commitment for sustainable development, assessing progress and implementation gaps in meeting previously agreed-upon commitments, and addressing new and emerging challenges. In addition, the UN General Assembly called for the conference to focus on two themes: (1) a green economy in the context of sustainable development and poverty eradication and (2) the institutional framework for sustainable development.

A green economy, according to one prominent definition, is one focused on improved human well-being and social equity while significantly reducing environmental risks and ecological scarcities.[129] Discussions surrounding the green economy had become increasingly prominent during the preparatory meetings leading up to Rio+20. In a green economy, growth in income, employment, and social development is driven by public and private investments in economically productive activities that also reduce carbon emissions and pollution, enhance energy and resource efficiency, and prevent the loss of biodiversity and ecosystem services.[130]

During the last few years, the idea of a green economy has entered the mainstream of policy discourse. Traction for the concept has been aided by technological developments in key industries, disillusionment with the prevailing paradigm, and unease produced by the financial and economic crisis of 2008. These and other factors combined to create new interest in models and practices through which material wealth is produced without exacerbating environmental risks, resource scarcities, and social disparities.[131]

Some of the research and policy work on a green economy emphasizes the importance of internalizing environmental externalities in prices to send the right signals to producers and consumers—that is, to get the prices right. Other discussions focus on the importance of government actions that assist research, development, and deployment of new technologies in key sectors; finance infrastructure investments; provide supportive policy environments for green investments by the private sector; and ensure that green economy policies support employment and income generation for the poor.[132] Other discussions point toward the need for greater awareness within the private sector regarding the opportunities represented by the green economy and the importance of responding to government policy reforms and price signals through higher levels of financing and investment.[133]

Supporters of the green economy paradigm, like the sustainable development paradigm, believe it offers a way to pursue the economic aspirations of both rich and poor countries in a world that faces climate change, pollution, and ecological scarcity. A green economy can meet this challenge, they argue, by offering a development path that reduces carbon dependency, promotes resource and energy efficiency, and lessens environmental degradation. As economic growth and investments become less dependent on liquidating environmental assets and sacrificing environmental quality, both rich and poor countries can attain more sustainable economic development.[134]

During the Rio+20 process, however, the green economy paradigm met with resistance from some developing countries. Bolivia summed up the opposition, asserting that no single development model—whatever its color—should be imposed and that the rights of individual developing states to pursue development paths that reflect their own needs, resources, and history must be upheld.[135] Others warned that a green economy paradigm does not adequately consider development and equity issues or could be used by rich countries to justify unilateral trade measures against developing countries or as a new conditional standard that developing countries would have to meet in order to access aid, loans, and debt rescheduling and forgiveness.[136]

As a result of this debate, the final document adopted at the conference articulated the challenges in moving to an alternative economic paradigm:

> We affirm that there are different approaches, visions, models and tools available to each country, in accordance with its national circumstances and priorities, to achieve sustainable development in its three dimensions which is our overarching goal. In this regard, we consider green economy in the context of sustainable development and poverty eradication as one of the important tools available for achieving sustainable development and that it could provide options for policymaking but should not be a rigid set of rules. We emphasize that it should contribute to eradicating poverty as well as sustained economic growth, enhancing social inclusion, improving human welfare and creating opportunities for employment and decent work for all, while maintaining the healthy functioning of the Earth's ecosystems.[137]

So, are the globalization and sustainable development paradigms incompatible? Does globalization pose an impenetrable obstacle to effective global environmental policy? There are two primary arguments in this debate.

Supporters of globalization, as a paradigm or as a fact of international life, argue that it goes hand in hand with sustainable development and is beneficial for the environment because it is an engine of wealth creation. As societies become richer, the initial process of industrialization results in greater pollution. This happened in Europe and the United States and is happening now in many developing countries. As economic development continues, a point is eventually reached at which most material needs have been met and citizens enjoy general economic security, at least for a majority of the population. At this point, societies develop greater concern for pollution reduction and environmental protection, as Western Europe and the United States did. In addition, because of wealth creation, society has the economic and technical ability to implement the necessary measures to achieve these goals. Globalization, by delivering the development side of the sustainable development equation, can solve the economic and social problems that contribute to environmental degradation. Along these lines, poverty is seen as a critical component of environmental degradation, and environmentalists who oppose globalization are sometimes condemned as eco-imperialists for trying to deny poor countries the right to develop.[138]

The opposing argument sees both the globalization paradigm and most aspects of globalization in practice as contrary to sustainable development. In this view, globalization extends the exclusionist paradigm into all aspects of international economic relations, promoting and accelerating the overconsumption of natural resources and overproduction of waste on a global scale. It encourages the movement of capital, technology, goods, and labor to areas with high returns on investment without regard for the impact on the communities who live there or the environment. Globalization stretches the chains of production and consumption over great distances and across many locations, which increases the separation between sources of environmental problems and their impact. The division of labor associated with globalization increases the transport of raw materials, commodities, semiprocessed materials, parts, finished goods, and waste; requires greater energy consumption resulting in more pollution, including higher carbon emissions; and increases the risk of localized pollution problems and even major environmental accidents.[139] Critics also argue that globalization reinforces the sharp inequalities between developing and developed countries (see Chapter 6), or at least the inequalities between rich and poor, both nationally and internationally.

For example, the ready availability of so many different types of vegetables and fruits throughout the year is partly the result of a shift from subsistence farming in parts of many developing countries to intensive cash cropping and international trade, the wages and profits of which do not translate into sufficient food and social development in many local societies. Agribusinesses, not farmers, often reap the benefits and own the best-quality land. Chemical fertilizers and pesticides are relied on to produce uniform, export-quality produce; far fewer of these chemicals were needed to grow local and subsistence crops. Poor farmers of export crops also have perverse incentives or are even forced by economic circumstances to cultivate low-quality, marginal land, contributing to soil erosion, habitat destruction, and land degradation.[140] The produce must then be transported to international markets, creating additional environmental externalities.

In agriculture and many other markets, the reorganization of production under globalization has led to the creation of extended commodity chains that spread environmental impacts over many countries. For example, the production of cotton T-shirts can involve as many as six different countries, creating different types of pollution and environmental impacts in each one (see Box 1.5).

The exact relationship between globalization, sustainable development, and the environment is of course more complex than either of these two archetypal arguments. Each perspective contains elements of truth, and the specific impact of a particular aspect of globalization on a particular environmental issue depends on national and international economic and policy choices.

Will the exclusionist, globalization, sustainable development, or green economy paradigm dominate future political and economic perspectives? Will a hybrid emerge? Will policy continue to reflect elements of all of these approaches? Some argue that a future paradigm shift will not result from changing economic or political interests but rather require a "revolution of social consciousness and values."[141] Governments and, more important, people do not necessarily change entrenched behaviors when they become aware of the seriousness of a potential threat. Such behavioral change sometimes requires a broader societal shift.

Although globalization remains a powerful force, some signs point to sustainable development becoming fully mainstreamed in certain economic and political circles. The EU, for example, has formally recognized the need to change unsustainable consumption and production patterns and move toward a more integrated approach to policy making.[142] Political rhetoric often exceeds actual policy changes in this area, but some European and other governments (e.g., Costa Rica) do appear committed to achieving economic growth that is truly sustainable through relying increasingly on alternative energy, eliminating many toxic chemicals, improving energy efficiency, and integrating two additional emergent paradigms to help guide decision making on environment and human health issues: environment-security links and the precautionary principle.

Environmental Change as a Security Issue

The environment-security paradigm holds that environmental degradation and resource depletion can affect national security. The central idea is that climate change, resource depletion, and environmental degradation act as threat multipliers that augment other conditions known to cause violence among opposing groups

BOX 1.5 COMMODITY CHAINS

Globalization can produce extended commodity chains that spread environmental impacts. The production of cotton T-shirts provides an example of how the production and use of even a simple product can involve as many as six different countries, with different types of resource use, pollution, and environmental impacts created in each one.

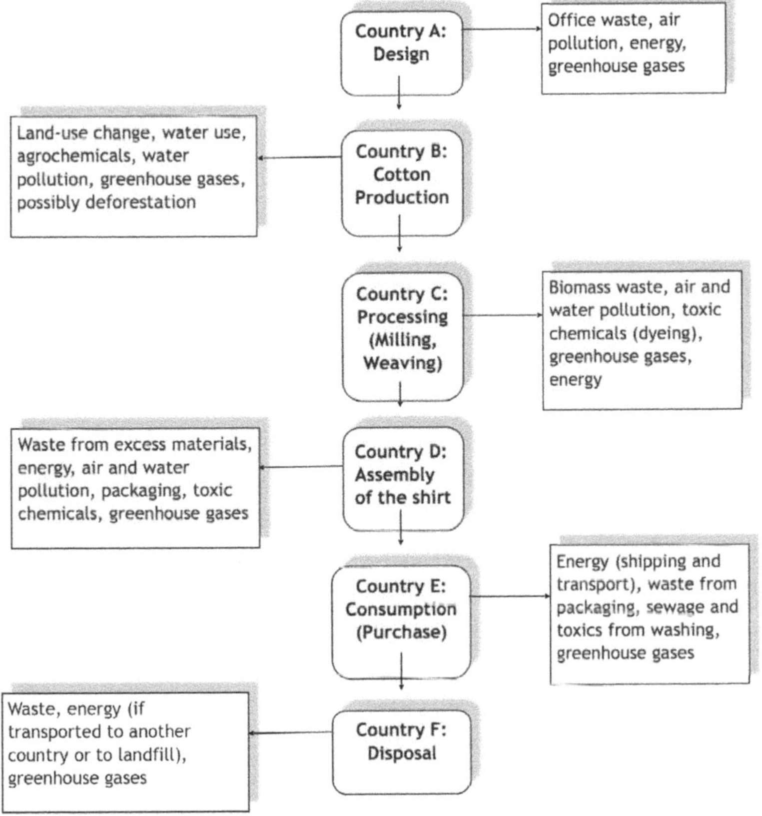

Source of information on commodity chains and waste chains: Ronnie D. Lipschutz, *Global Environmental Politics: Power, Perspectives and Practice* (Washington, DC: CQ Press, 2004), 124.

within a state or even among states. As argued by Thomas Homer-Dixon, who helped to pioneer our understanding of this issue, resource scarcity, ecosystem collapse, and other environmental problems can act as tectonic stresses, exacerbating existing political, social, or economic instability to the point that armed conflict occurs.[143] Environmental degradation can help cause or increase the impact of other problems known to contribute to violence within or among states, such as resource disputes, refugee movements, poverty, hunger, and weak governments.

For example, changing climate conditions contributed to the devastating ethnic conflict in Darfur, Sudan.[144] Environmental factors did not cause the violence, but they pushed other factors, including poverty, increasing ethnic and political divisions, and the territorial ambitions of certain groups, past the tipping point into widespread, systematic violence. The government and several rebel groups had opposed each other for years, reflecting the long-standing animosity that existed between elements of the Afro-Arab ethnic groups that dominate in the North and the non-Arab farming ethnic groups in the South as well as the territorial ambitions of particular actors. Over time, severe changes in rainfall patterns, increasing drought, and deteriorating soils caused many farmers to block off the remaining fertile land, fearing that shared use by the herders would ruin it. Many Arab herders were angry that they were not receiving their share of the land, leading to violent clashes, which were then used by some political leaders as excuses to widen the conflict.

In North America, the collapse of fisheries in northwestern Mexico contributed to the decision by some fishermen to become involved in drug smuggling and other crimes.[145] Similarly, overfishing and illegal fishing off the coast of Somalia contributed to the increase in piracy. Large criminal enterprises, many of which pose threats to local security, are responsible for 50–90 percent of illegal logging around the world.[146] In Haiti, massive deforestation (less than 2 percent of the nation remains forested) led to severely eroded hillsides, massive soil erosion and runoff, and declining water quality. This exacerbated the already difficult situation for rural farmers trying to work the country's mountainous terrain. Soil runoff from the mountains also polluted many of the nation's already overfished coastal areas, nearly eliminating fishing as a source of income. With no means to make a living in rural areas, the majority of Haitians moved to city slums, most living without clean water or proper sanitation, producing conditions that worsened the impact of the massive earthquake in 2010, which killed perhaps three hundred thousand and left at least one million Haitians homeless.[147]

US and European political, military, and intelligence communities have accepted certain aspects of the emerging paradigm that environmental degradation can lead to security concerns.[148] Of particular concern is climate change, which could produce huge numbers of refugees from flooded coastal areas, increase water and food scarcity, spread disease, and weaken economies in parts of the world that are already vulnerable, unstable, prone to extremism, or suffer significant cultural, ethnic, or economic divisions. Africa, for example, although "least responsible for greenhouse gas emissions, is almost universally seen as the continent most at risk of climate-induced conflict—a function of the continent's reliance on climate-dependent sectors (such as rain-fed agriculture) and its history of resource, ethnic and political conflict."[149] Similarly, with conditions in the Middle East already volatile, "climate change threatens to reduce the availability of scarce water resources, increase food insecurity, hinder economic growth and lead to large-scale population movements."[150]

Environmental degradation and the mismanagement of natural resources can fuel conflict among and within states and contribute to poverty and state failure. On the flip side, war and other security issues can affect the environment. Military spending absorbs government finances and policy attention that might otherwise be dedicated to environmental protection. Military operations, even in peacetime, consume large quantities of natural resources. Armed conflict itself produces habitat destruction, overexploitation of natural resources, and pollution. Civil wars in Africa, Asia, and Latin America have destroyed many hectares of forests and wetlands.

Armed conflict also has an impact on states' and regions' abilities to guard protected areas and enforce conservation regulations.[151] This is particularly true during civil war or in very weak states, where the breakdown of the rule of law, increased availability of weapons, and disrupted economic and agricultural production all affect environmental protection. In the Congo, for example, armed conflict since 1994 has severely impacted many nature reserves, including some designated as World Heritage sites. Governments, international organizations, and NGOs have faced huge obstacles as a result of the "proliferation of arms and ammunition; displaced people, military, and dissidents; a general breakdown of law and order; uncontrolled exploitation of natural, mineral and land resources by various interest groups; and the increased use of wild areas as refuges and for subsistence."[152] Anti-poaching patrols ceased in many areas for different periods, and increased poaching, harvesting game for food, and habitat destruction seriously affected wildlife populations in some parks. In parts of Bolivia, Colombia, Mexico, Peru, and other countries, rebel groups and drug traffickers, either on their own or in alliance, have sometimes prevented the enforcement of wildlife conservation, habitat protection, or deforestation laws by essentially controlling access to certain areas or bribing or intimidating inspectors and other officials.[153]

The environment and security paradigm replaces traditional analyses that assume that environmental degradation is irrelevant to a state's national security interests. This does not imply that the environment is more important than traditional security calculations, but it does argue that an analysis of factors that can negatively affect a state's security must include environmental degradation and resource mismanagement (much as the sustainable development paradigm argues that serious environmental degradation can negatively affect a state's economy). It is not clear, however, that increased awareness of this relationship will lead to new action to ward off resource collapse in vulnerable parts of Africa, Asia, Latin America, and the Caribbean. Nor is it clear that recognition of the serious security problems posed by climate change will lead to increased efforts to reduce GHG emissions.

The Precautionary Principle: A New Paradigm for Environmental Policy?

The exclusionist paradigm implies that economic policy calculations need not factor in resource scarcity and environmental degradation. If resource scarcity begins to occur, the market will respond by raising prices, which will reduce demand and spur the search for substitutes, thereby averting a crisis. Similarly, there is no need to consider or take steps to avoid environmental problems before they occur, as these can be remedied after the fact if the market demands it. The globalization paradigm argues that priorities should be placed on policies that accelerate global economic growth, as this will provide the resources for environmental protection.

Unfortunately, although these deductions make sense from a purely market perspective, they fail to account accurately for the physical limitations of the earth's biological and physical systems. It is true that prices will rise and incentives will exist to develop substitutes when scarcity becomes an issue, but for some environmental problems, these market forces will occur too late. Certain environmental impacts cannot be remedied once they occur, at least not on timescales relevant to human economic and political systems. If the ozone layer thins significantly, a rain forest gets destroyed, a coral reef dies, the climate system shifts to a different equilibrium, a species becomes extinct, or a human life is shortened by air, water, or toxic pollution, these changes will last, if not forever, then at least for a very, very long time.

Moreover, in some cases, environmental degradation actually increases incentives to exploit a particular resource. Declines in rhino and tuna populations increase their price and thus the interest of poachers. Water scarcity due to changes in weather patterns increases pressure on aquifers. Lower crop yields due to climate change can cause farmers to cultivate marginal land, clear forests to increase capacity, or increase the use of fertilizers or pesticides that have a net negative impact on the environment.

In other cases, operating under the exclusionist paradigm simply represents a poor economic decision. Sometimes, the impacts of pollution or environmental degradation cost far more than the economic benefits accrued from production. Deforestation in Haiti and some other areas is an example. For the country as a whole, the economic benefits of using the wood or cleared land are far fewer than the economic costs associated with the harm caused to fisheries, farming, and freshwater resources resulting from the severe erosion and runoff from hills and mountains that no longer have trees to hold the soil in place. In other cases, such as climate change or ozone depletion, the economic costs associated with the worst consequences of the problem are higher than the cost of taking steps to prevent them from occurring.

Those holding this position argue that in many situations, the best policy—from an environmental, human health, and economic point of view (and perhaps an ethical one as well)—is to avoid producing certain serious environmental problems in the first place. The difficulty, of course, is that the complexity of many environmental issues prevents clear calculations of an activity's environmental costs, while its economic benefits are usually quite clear. Thus, the lack of scientific certainty regarding the range, extent, and cost of environmental impacts from particular activities or products can prevent effective policy in the face of strong lobbying by economic interests.

The precautionary principle attempts to resolve this dilemma and provide guidance regarding the development of national and international environmental policy. The most widely used definition of the precautionary principle was set forth by governments in 1992 at the Earth Summit in Principle 15 of the Rio Declaration: "Where there are threats of serious or irreversible damage, lack of full scientific certainty shall not be used as a reason for postponing cost-effective measures to prevent environmental degradation."[154]

Those supporting the use of the precautionary principle argue that it leads to several main policy-relevant ideas:[155]

- The importance and efficacy of taking preventative action, when the lack of action might produce essentially irreversible, unwanted impacts on the environment or human health;
- The need to shift the burden of proof from those seeking to protect human health and the environment to those supporting a particular activity or product. Rather than forcing others to prove something is definitely harmful, which has traditionally been the case, now proponents of, for example, using a particular chemical would need to show it is not harmful;
- The need to keep science and rational arguments central to decision making involving health and environmental issues with the understanding that complete scientific certainty or unanimity regarding future harm is not required to make policy designed to protect the environment or human health from irreversible damage; and
- The importance of asking why we should risk irreversible or very serious harm for a particular product or activity.[156]

Several important global environmental statements and treaty regimes contain elements of the precautionary principle either explicitly or implicitly.[157] For example, the Ministerial Declaration from the Second International Conference on the Protection of the North Sea (1987) states, "In order to protect the North Sea from possibly damaging effects of the most dangerous substances, a precautionary approach is necessary which may require action to control inputs of such substances even before a causal link has been established by absolutely clear scientific evidence."[158] The Montreal Protocol on Substances That Deplete the Ozone Layer (1987) also endorsed the concept of precautionary policy, stating that parties to the agreement are "determined to protect the ozone layer by taking precautionary measures to control equitably total global emissions of substances that deplete it."[159]

The climate regime includes the concept of precaution as one of its central principles. Article 3 of the UNFCCC (1992) states:

> In their actions to achieve the objective of the Convention and to implement its provisions, the Parties shall be guided, *inter alia*, by the following: . . .
>
> The parties should take precautionary measures to anticipate, prevent, or minimize the causes of climate change and mitigate its adverse effects. Where there are threats of serious or irreversible damage, lack of full scientific certainty should not be used as a reason for postponing such measures.[160]

The 2000 Cartagena Protocol on Biosafety expressly allows parties to ban imports of genetically modified organisms, even where there is a "lack of scientific certainty due to insufficient relevant scientific information and knowledge" concerning health or environmental impacts.[161] The 2001 Stockholm Convention on Persistent Organic Pollutants defines the objective of the regime: "Mindful of the precautionary approach as set forth in Principle 15 of the Rio Declaration on Environment and Development, the objective of this Convention is to protect human health and the environment from persistent organic pollutants."[162] In addition, the treaty states that precaution should be used when considering additional substances to add to the control measures and that the lack of scientific certainty regarding the precise levels of a substance's toxicity or propensity for long-range transport and bioaccumulation shall not be grounds for failing to consider controlling it under the regime.

Local and national laws in a number of countries have also incorporated the principle. Most important is the EU announcement in 2000 stating that the precautionary principle will guide EU policy decisions on environmental and human health issues and is also a "a full-fledged and general principle of international law."[163]

Even though there is increasing reference to the precautionary principle in international politics, arguments exist that it should not be accepted as a principle of international law (on par with universally accepted principles such as sovereignty). Some argue that shifting the burden of proof means that decisions will not be based on scientific certainty but rather on "emotional and irrational" factors.[164] Others argue that precautionary actions will cost too much, harming companies and hindering economic development.[165] Some argue that applying the principle too broadly will require proving that something is totally safe, which is essentially impossible to prove in all situations.[166] Others note that its use in treaties or acceptance by international legal bodies as a guiding point of international law is not universal. For example, during the George W. Bush administration, the United States argued during several multilateral negotiations that the precautionary principle was not an accepted principle of international law that bound states to certain norms. Under this interpretation, references to precaution in treaties that the United States signed or ratified related only to the particular activity under discussion—not a general international legal principle applicable across all countries and issues.[167]

Other analysts, legal scholars, and policymakers dismiss these arguments. They believe that inclusion of the precautionary principle (or its key elements under another name) in so many international treaties, its status within the EU (which currently includes twenty-eight member countries), and its emergence in local and national laws in many countries prove that "the precautionary principle has evolved from being a 'soft law' 'aspirational' goal to its present status as an authoritative norm recognized by governments and international organizations as a firm guide to activities affecting the environment."[168]

Clearly the precautionary principle has become a part of many international environmental policies, having found its way into an increasing number of global regimes, influenced international decision making, and been more and more accepted in debates on national policies in multiple countries. Yet if the precautionary principle is a new dominant paradigm, why don't we see greater levels of international commitments with regard to climate change, biodiversity, forests, and fisheries?

Perhaps there is no real dominant paradigm. It appears that multiple paradigms exist today and compete for primacy. Elements of the exclusionist paradigm still influence some global, national, local, and corporate policies but so, too, do elements of the sustainable development paradigm and the precautionary principle.

At the same time, the totality of the evidence supports the thesis that we could be in a time of paradigm transition: from exclusionist premises to sustainable development and precaution. But the future is far from clear. As economies, populations, cities, energy production, and resource demands continue to grow, the paradigms that influence policy debates could go a long way toward determining what the world will look like.

CONCLUSION

Global environmental politics involves actions by, and interactions among, states, IGOs, and other actors that transcend a given region and that affect the environment and natural resources of multiple regions or the entire planet. The emergence of environmental issues in world politics reflects growing awareness of the cumulative stresses that human activities have on Earth's resources and life-support systems.

Much of global environmental politics focuses on efforts to negotiate and implement multilateral agreements or other mechanisms for cooperation to protect the environment and natural resources. Some of these agreements stand at the center of global environmental regimes of varying effectiveness that seek to govern or guide specific state behaviors regarding the environmental problem in question.

Legitimate differences in economic, political, and environmental interests make achieving unanimity among states responsible for, or directly affected by, an environmental problem a political and diplomatic challenge. One or more states often have the ability to block or weaken a multilateral agreement, and finding ways to overcome such blockage is a major concern. For a regime to form, veto states must be persuaded to abandon their opposition or at least to accept a compromise.

Other obstacles stem from socioeconomic paradigms that justify extensive, and sometitmes essentially unlimited, exploitation of nature and discount the impact of pollution and deteriorating ecosystems on economic and social well-being. Despite the weakening of these paradigms and widespread recognition of an alternative sustainable development paradigm, the rise of globalization and the resilience of aspects of the traditional paradigms have complicated the shift to potential new models centered on a green economy, incorporation of the precautionary principle, and global sustainable development.

Subsequent chapters in this book explore these and other key issues in global environmental politics. Chapter 2 examines the main actors in global environmental politics. States are the most important actors because they negotiate international legal instruments, create global environmental regimes, and adopt economic, trade, and regulatory policies that directly and indirectly affect the environment. At the same time, nonstate actors also play major roles. International organizations, treaty secretariats, NGOs, and multinational corporations help set the global environmental agenda, initiate and influence the process of regime formation, and carry out actions that directly affect the global environment.

Chapters 3 and 4 look at the development of ten important global environmental regimes: ozone depletion, hazardous wastes, toxic chemicals, climate change, biodiversity, trade in endangered species, forests, desertification, fisheries, and whaling. Each issue is analyzed with a focus on what occurred during different stages in the development of the regime and the role of veto coalitions and other major causal factors.

Chapter 5 examines obstacles to creating, implementing, and complying with environmental regimes and the means of effective implementation. The first two sections examine factors that make it difficult to create regimes with strong control measures and for states to implement them. The third section outlines methods to improve regime implementation, compliance, and effectiveness. The final section discusses options for increasing the financing available to help implement global environmental regimes. Because inadequate financial and technical resources and counterproductive economic incentives inhibit the ability of many countries to implement or expand environmental regimes, financial issues have been at the center of global environmental policy debates for many years and will continue to be for the foreseeable future.

Chapter 6 explains how the evolution of global environmental politics cannot be understood completely outside the context of the historic and current relationship between industrialized and developing countries and the other two pillars of sustainable development: economic development and social development. The final section looks at the Sustainable Development Goals (SDGs) adopted by the UN General Assembly in 2015 and how they may affect global environmental politics. Chapter 7 concludes our discussion with some thoughts on the past, present, and future of global environmental politics.

2

Actors in the Environmental Arena

States are the most important actors in global environmental politics. States adopt the broad economic, regulatory, trade, and development policies that affect the environment. They decide which issues receive formal consideration by the international community directly (through advocacy for international action on a particular issue) and indirectly (through membership in the governing councils of international organizations). States negotiate the international legal instruments that create and implement global environmental regimes. Donor states influence the effectiveness of these regimes and other environmental policies through aid programs and donations to implementation programs and multilateral banks.

But nonstate actors also exert significant and increasing influence on global environmental politics. Intergovernmental organizations (IGOs) help to set the global environmental agenda, initiate and mediate the process of regime formation, and cooperate with developing countries on projects and programs directly affecting the environment. Treaty secretariats influence agenda setting and financing issues that affect global environmental regimes. Nongovernmental organizations (NGOs) participate in agenda setting, attempt to influence negotiations on regime formation and expansion, and help shape the environmental policies of donor agencies. Multinational corporations influence state positions in regime negotiations and carry out actions that directly affect the global environment. This chapter examines the roles that these actors play in global environmental politics.

NATION-STATE ACTORS: ROLES AND INTERESTS

Perhaps the most important actions by state actors in global environmental politics concern the creation, implementation, and expansion of international environmental regimes. In regime negotiations, a state may play one of four roles: lead state, supporting state, swing state, or veto (or blocking) state. A lead state has a strong commitment to effective international action on the issue, moves the negotiation process forward by proposing options for an agreement, and attempts to win the support of other state actors.

A supporting state speaks in favor of a lead state's proposal in negotiations. A swing state has mixed incentives and, in exchange for its acceptance of an agreement, seeks a concession to its interests but typically not one that significantly weakens the regime. A veto state seeks to block a proposed environmental regime outright, tries to weaken it to the point that it cannot be effective, or refuses to join, thereby severely reducing the global or long-term effectiveness of the regime.

States sometimes change roles due to changes in government or strategic interests. The United States switched from a veto state that helped to block global negotiations on a mercury treaty for many years to a lead state that strongly supported efforts to start negotiations following the election of President Barack Obama, to a swing state during the later stages of negotiations. Canada shifted from a swing state in the climate negotiations under the liberal government of Paul Martin to a veto state under the conservative government of Stephen Harper to a likely swing state, but also a potential lead state, under Prime Minister Justin Trudeau. China and India switched from swing states during the first stages of the ozone negotiations (1983–1987) to leaders of a veto coalition of developing countries (1989–1990) to enhance their bargaining leverage, successfully refusing to join the agreement to phase out chlorofluorocarbons (CFCs) until the industrialized countries agreed to provide significant financial assistance to assist developing countries transition to less harmful chemicals and more advanced technology (see Chapter 3).

There may be more than one lead state on a given issue. For example, Canada and Sweden both played lead roles in initiating actions that led to negotiations on persistent organic pollutants (POPs). Sometimes a state steps forward to advance a policy that puts it clearly in the lead for a particular period, as Germany did with the climate-change issue in 1990 and Canada did with the fisheries issue in 1992. As issues develop over time, the role of lead state may shift from one state or combination of states to another. During some of the early ozone negotiations, Finland and Sweden played lead roles by submitting their own draft convention and heavily influencing a later draft put before the conference. In 1986, the United States stepped into the lead role by proposing a gradual 95 percent reduction in CFCs. In the early 1990s, the European Union (EU) emerged as the lead state in negotiations to phase out other ozone-depleting substances such as methyl bromide and hydrochlorofluorocarbons (HCFCs).

Lead states use a wide range of methods to influence other state actors on a global environmental issue, including (but not limited to) the following:

- Funding, producing, and/or calling attention to research that defines the problem and demonstrates its urgency, as when Canadian research revealed long-range dangers posed by POPs and when US-based research revealed a threat to the earth's protective ozone layer;
- Seeking to influence public opinion in target states, as Canada did when it supplied US tourists with pamphlets on the acidification of its forests and waters and instructed its Washington, DC, embassy to cooperate with US environmental organizations concerned about acid rain;
- Using its diplomatic clout to encourage an international organization to identify the issue as a priority, as when the United States and Canada persuaded the Organization for Economic Cooperation and Development (OECD) to take up the issue of protecting the ozone layer, African countries persuaded the United Nations (UN) to begin negotiations on a treaty to combat desertification, and Sweden and Canada led efforts to get various organizations to address POPs;
- Working with NGOs that can support its position in other countries and at international conferences, as the Alliance of Small Island States (AOSIS) did in its proposal to place quantitative limits on greenhouse gas (GHG) emissions in the Kyoto Protocol negotiations;
- Making a diplomatic démarche to a state that is threatening a veto role, as the United States did with Japan on African elephant ivory; or
- Pledging to commit financial or technical resources to addressing the problem, such as the incentives that industrialized countries provided in the Montreal Protocol and Stockholm Convention to gain critical developing-country participation.

Although economic, scientific, technological, and diplomatic resources cannot ensure that a lead state will prevail on an environmental issue, they constitute valuable assets for helping to create a regime. When a big power like the United States takes a lead role through scientific research, unilateral action, and diplomatic initiative, as it did on the issue of ozone protection, it helps to sway states that do not otherwise have clearly defined interests in the issue.

States play different roles on different issues. A lead state on one issue may be a potential veto state on another. Whether a state plays a lead, supporting, swing, or veto role in regard to a particular global environmental issue depends primarily on domestic political factors and the relative costs and benefits of the proposed regime. Another variable, which has been important in some cases, is potential international political consequences, including increased prestige or damage to a country's global image.

Domestic Political Factors

A state's definition of its interests with regard to a particular global environmental issue and its consequent choice of role depend largely on domestic economic and political interests and ideological currents. Whether a government opposes, supports, or leads on an issue often reflects the relative strength and influence of powerful economic and bureaucratic forces and domestic environmental constituencies. Ideological factors related to broader domestic political themes can also play prominent roles in the definition of interests.

Domestic economic interests are particularly prominent in promoting veto roles. When the Liberal Democratic Party dominated Japanese politics, for example, major trading companies generally received government support for their interests in whaling because of their close ties to the party.[1] Norway's fishing industry, which claims it suffered declining fish catches because of the international protection of whales, prevailed on its government to defend Norwegian whaling before the international community. The United States played swing or veto roles on certain climate-change and chemicals-related issues because of pressure from domestic oil, gas, automobile, and chemicals manufacturers and their supporters in Congress.

A state's position on a global environmental issue sometimes reflects the interests of dominant socioeconomic elites. In Indonesia, for example, a 2011 study found that seven conglomerates controlled more than nine million hectares of land, including large forest concessions that could remain exempt from any moratorium on forest clearing established under the country's Reducing Emissions from Deforestation and Degradation (REDD) program.[2] The extent of holdings could complicate Indonesia's efforts to reduce carbon dioxide (CO_2) emissions and biodiversity declines caused by logging and plantation development.

Government bureaucracies with institutional interests threatened by potential global action on a particular environmental issue often attempt to influence the adoption of swing or blocking roles. During the negotiation of the Montreal Protocol in the mid-1980s, officials in the US Departments of Commerce, Interior, and Agriculture, together with some members of the White House staff, sought to reopen basic questions about the scientific evidence and the possible damage to the US economy from imposing additional CFC controls to protect the ozone layer but were overruled.[3]

Taking a lead role on a global environmental issue becomes far more likely if there is little or no domestic opposition. The United States easily took a lead role on whaling, for example, because the US whaling industry had already been eliminated. Similarly, the absence of significant bureaucratic or business interest in opposing a ban on importing African elephant ivory made it easy for Washington to assume a lead role on that issue.

The existence of a strong environmental movement can be a decisive factor in a state's definition of its interest on an issue, especially if environmental interests compose a potential swing vote in parliamentary elections. The sudden emergence of West German and French bids for leadership roles on certain environmental issues in 1989 reflected in large part the upsurge of public support for strong environmental protection policies. In 1984, the Green Party won 8.2 percent of the vote for West German representatives to the European Parliament. In 1987, a Green Party coalition held nearly 10 percent of the seats in the Bundestag, the German parliament.[4] Polls taken in advance of the 1989 European Parliament election indicated a surge in environmentalist sentiment in Germany and France. These electoral developments contributed to the choice in 1989 by both countries to become part of the lead coalition proposing negotiations on a framework convention on climate change.

But a strong environmental movement does not guarantee that a state actor will play a lead or supporting role on a particular issue, particularly when it faces concerted opposition from well-connected economic and political interests. US environmental organizations are among the largest and best organized in the world, but they were unable to sway US policy regarding climate change during the George W. Bush administration or successfully lobby the Senate to ratify the Biodiversity, Basel, Rotterdam, or Stockholm Conventions.

Conversely, the absence of a strong environmental movement makes it more likely that a state will play a swing or veto role on an international environmental issue. For example, Japanese NGOs are relatively underdeveloped in comparison with those in North America and Europe, and the Japanese political system makes it difficult for interest groups without high-level political links to influence policy. The Japanese government therefore felt little domestic pressure to support environmental regimes on African elephants, whaling, and drift-net fishing. In contrast, US wildlife NGOs placed a great deal of domestic pressure on the US government to take strong positions on these issues.

The ideology or belief system of top policymakers can also shape a country's definition of its interest in an environmental regime. Although the United States had exported very little of its hazardous waste, the George H. W. Bush administration led the veto coalition against a ban on hazardous waste exports to developing countries because of its general opposition to regulatory intervention in national and international markets. The first Bush administration also helped to veto a proposal for industrialized states to set targets for per capita energy use because officials saw this as unwarranted state interference in consumer preferences.[5]

Comparative Costs and Benefits of Environmental Regimes

A second group of variables that affect perceptions of national interests regarding a global environmental issue involve the potential risks and costs of an environmental threat and the costs and benefits associated with the proposed regime.[6] Exceptional vulnerability to the consequences of environmental problems can drive countries to support, or even take the lead on, strong global action. Thirty-two small island states especially vulnerable to sea-level rise because of global warming formed AOSIS in November 1990 to speak with a single, more influential voice in the climate negotiations and became among the strongest proponents of international action to reduce GHG emissions. Sweden and Norway, which led the fight for the Convention on Long-Range Transboundary Air Pollution, are the major recipients of sulfur dioxide air pollution from other European countries, and their lakes and soils are also acid sensitive, causing the damage from acid rain to appear earlier and more seriously in those Nordic countries than in the United Kingdom or Germany. Canada pushed for strong action on POPs after the discovery that the chemicals tend to bioaccumulate in Arctic food chains and disproportionately affect Inuit communities in northern Canada.

The costs of implementing a given global environmental regime, which can differ dramatically from one country to another, also shape negotiation positions (see Chapter 5). The ozone negotiations provide several examples. Because of an early and unilateral ban on aerosols using CFCs, chemicals that deplete stratospheric ozone, the United States was ahead of members of the European Community (EC) and Japan in finding substitutes for CFCs in aerosol cans; it therefore joined Canada and the Nordic states in supporting such a ban, while the EC and Japan rejected it. The Soviet Union, fearful that it would be unable to develop new technologies to replace CFCs, opposed any globally mandated CFC cuts until 1987. China and India, which were minor producers at the time but already gearing up for major production increases (including a plan by India's chemical industry to export half its projected CFC production to the Middle East and Asia), feared that the transition to ozone-safe chemicals would be too costly without access to new, alternative technologies and refused to accept controls until industrialized countries agreed in 1990 to provide significant financial and technical assistance. Moreover, the perceived cost of eliminating the use of methyl bromide in agricultural applications, especially in California, caused the United States in 1995 to push successfully for a large exemption for such use as part of the agreement to phase out nearly all other uses of the chemical.[7]

PHOTO 2.1 Saudi Arabia and other countries that rely on oil exports have generally played swing or veto roles in climate negotiations. Courtesy Franz Dejon, IISD/*Earth Negotiations Bulletin*, www.iisd.ca.

Because achieving reductions in GHG emissions is easier and/or cheaper for some countries than others, the perceived economic impacts of implementation have also significantly affected the climate negotiations. For example, EU states are generally net importers of fossil fuels, and most have learned how to reduce energy use without compromising economic growth. Because the EU sees its cost of compliance as relatively modest, particularly given the economic costs associated with climate change, it has played a lead role in the negotiations. Meanwhile, other countries that rely on oil exports (e.g., Saudi Arabia) or utilize large domestic coal reserves (e.g., Australia, China, India, and the United States) have generally played swing or veto roles.

International Political and Diplomatic Considerations

States also consider potential benefits or costs to broader international interests when considering their position on a particular global environmental issue. A state may hope to gain international prestige by assuming a lead role, or it may decide against a veto role to avoid international opprobrium or damage to its relations with countries for which the environmental issue is of significantly greater concern.

Concern for national reputation or status in the international community was once confined largely to the area of international security. Beginning in the early 1990s, a few states began to regard leadership on the global environment as a means of enhancing their international status. In 1994, then EU environment commissioner Yannis Paleokrassas hailed the prospect of a region-wide carbon tax, which would give the EU a lead role in climate change and result in "the resumption of world environmental and fiscal leadership by the European Union," suggesting that the EU would gain a new kind of international prestige.[8]

At the 1992 Earth Summit, some observers believed the United States tarnished its image when it stood alone in rejecting the Convention on Biological Diversity (CBD). Germany and Japan, among other countries, shared US unhappiness concerning some provisions in the CBD but avoided a veto role for fear of damaging their prestige. A George H. W. Bush administration official later charged that Germany and Japan had departed from the US position in part to demonstrate their new status as emerging, independent world powers.[9]

A state's concern about how a veto role might affect its image sometimes focuses on a particular country or group of countries. In negotiations on controlling international trade in hazardous wastes, for example, the decision by France and the United Kingdom in 1989 to alter their position and not play a veto role stemmed in part from a broader national interest in maintaining close ties with former colonies in Africa. Japan chose not to block efforts to ban trade in African elephant ivory in 1989 largely because it feared damage to its relations with its most important trading partners, the United States and Europe. Canada ratified the Kyoto Protocol in 2002 in part to protect its "environmentally progressive international image,"[10] although it withdrew from Kyoto in 2011, when the conservative government of Stephen Harper, no longer concerned with this aspect of its international image, objected to its impact on the domestic oil and gas industry.[11]

Subnational Actors

National governments, despite their assertion of exclusive rights to act in international relations, are no longer the only governmental actors in global environmental politics. In recent years, many cities, states, and provinces have enacted their own environmental and energy policies, and these could have a major impact on global environmental problems, especially climate change. Although municipal and state governments are unlikely to usurp national government functions in regime strengthening, they can supplement national efforts, especially when national governments fail to act.

Cities are critical when it comes to climate action.[12] They generate 75 percent of all global GHG emissions. Roughly 54 percent of the world's 7.3 billion people currently live in cities, and by 2050 that number is expected to rise to around 70 percent of the world's population.[13] One of the largest attempts to initiate organized climate action across a large number of cities began in 2005 when a bipartisan group of 132 US mayors, frustrated by the Bush administration's rejection of the Kyoto Protocol, pledged that their cities would try to meet Kyoto's US target: a 7 percent reduction in GHG emissions from 1990 levels by 2014. The cities ranged from liberal Los Angeles, California, to conservative Hurst, Texas. By 2016, 1,060 mayors, representing large and small cities in all fifty states with a total population of nearly eighty-nine million had signed the Mayors Climate Protection Agreement.[14]

In July 2014, seventeen cities from nine countries formed the Carbon Neutral Cities Alliance, a collaboration of global cities committed and actively working to reducing GHG emissions by at least 80 percent by 2050 or sooner—the most ambitious GHG emission reduction targets undertaken by a group of cities. Alliance cities are among the first local governments to develop and implement strategies to mitigate GHG emissions to this extent while simultaneously committing to grow their local economies and improve the quality of life of their residents. The cities include Berlin, Germany; Boston, Massachusetts; Boulder, Colorado; Copenhagen, Denmark; London, United Kingdom; Melbourne, Australia; Minneapolis, Minnesota; New York, New York; Oslo, Norway; Portland, Oregon; San Francisco, California; Stockholm, Sweden; Sydney, Australia; Vancouver, Canada; Washington, DC; and Yokohama, Japan.[15]

Boston, for example, ranked as the most energy-efficient US city for the last four years, is reducing electricity demand by two hundred megawatts and supporting a citywide scale-up of solar technology, particularly for its municipal buildings. Buildings must report their energy use and complete regular assessments to help ramp up efficiency. Boston has also strived to bring the public on board to help the city meet its climate goals through actions ranging from bike weeks to personal carbon challenges.[16]

Since 2008, San Francisco has offered residents and businesses an incentive to install solar, and as a result, solar rooftops in the city have quadrupled. Zero-emission electric vehicles now make up half of the city's transit system, running on the San Francisco Public Utilities Commission's 100 percent GHG-free power. The city is the first large city to phase out petroleum diesel in its entire municipal fleet and replace it with renewable diesel in 2016.[17]

In 2014, New York Mayor Bill de Blasio announced that New York City was committing to reducing its GHG emissions by 80 percent from 2005 levels by 2050, starting with a plan to retrofit public and private buildings. Because nearly three quarters of New York City's GHG emissions come from energy used to heat, cool, and power buildings, building retrofits must be a key component of any large-scale

PHOTO 2.2 Former New York mayor Michael Bloomberg speaking in 2012 as mayors from around the world gathered in Rio de Janeiro for Rio+C40 to announce aggressive emissions reductions gains. Courtesy C40 Cities.

effort to reduce emissions.[18] The San Diego City Council voted unanimously to cut the city's GHG emissions by 50 percent and to have all electricity used in the city (the eighth largest in the United States) produced from renewable energy by 2035.[19]

According to the C40 Climate Leadership Group, a total of 228 city governments from around the world, representing 436 million people, have set targets for reducing GHG emissions. If they meet these targets, they will cumulatively save thirteen gigatons of CO_2 equivalent by 2050—more than twice what the United States emits in a year from energy-related sources.[20]

There has also been significant action to reduce GHG emissions at the US state level. By 2016, twenty states had official GHG emission reduction targets and even more had renewable energy standards that set deadlines for utilities to produce a certain percentage of their energy from renewable energy, such as wind, solar, hydro, and geothermal.[21] In 2015, Hawaii became the first state to mandate that all of its electricity be produced from renewable energy sources, setting a 2045 deadline. In 2016, Oregon committed to eliminating the use of electricity from coal-fired power plants by 2035 and requiring that utilities provide at least half of their customers' electricity from renewable sources by 2040.[22] The largest state in the United States, California, passed legislation in 2015 requiring utilities to purchase half of their power from renewable sources by 2030, with penalties for noncompliance. It also mandated efforts to double the energy efficiency of California's homes, businesses, and factories and provided new incentives for utilities to install additional charging stations for electric vehicles.[23] Minnesota has set a renewable energy standard of 27 percent by 2025, and by 2013 electricity produced from renewables had already reached 20.2 percent, mostly from wind energy.[24] Washington State reduced carbon emissions by 54 percent between 2005 and 2012 and produced 76 percent of its energy from renewables in 2013, primarily from hydro power.[25]

Nine Northeast and Mid-Atlantic states limit GHG emissions through a cooperative effort called the Regional Greenhouse Gas Initiative, the first mandatory, multi-state, market-based CO_2 emissions-reduction program in the United States. Connecticut, Delaware, Maine, Maryland, Massachusetts, New Hampshire, New York, Rhode Island, and Vermont require a 45 percent reduction in GHG emissions from power plants by 2020 relative to 2004 levels. Governor Chris Christie pulled New Jersey out of the initiative in 2011. Since the first auction of CO_2 allowances in September 2008, carbon emissions covered by the program in the nine states have dropped by almost one-third. In addition, the auctions have generated $1.3 billion in benefits, which has led to the creation of more than fourteen thousand new jobs and saved consumers $460 million in lower electric bills in 2012–2014.[26]

The United States is not the only country in which activities are taking place at the state and provincial levels. In May 2008, Australia's most populous state, New South Wales, announced that all government operations, including state-run schools, hospitals, and police stations, would be carbon neutral by 2020.[27] City council leaders from more than thirty cities in Great Britain pledged in 2015 to get 100 percent of their electricity from renewable sources by 2050.[28] In Canada, the province of British Columbia introduced a carbon tax, and Alberta is planning to do the same. All hospitals, schools, colleges, universities, and government agencies in British Columbia have been carbon neutral since 2010 with regard to their paper, fleet, and building emissions, and government agencies are also carbon neutral for their business travel.[29] Quebec started operating a cap-and-trade system in 2013 and a year later linked its system with that of California, thus creating the largest carbon market in North America and the first one in the world to be designed and operated by subnational governments in different countries.[30] In 2009, Ontario implemented the Green Energy and Green Economy Act, which contains provisions for a system of renewable energy feed-in tariffs, including wind, solar, micro-hydro, and biomass projects.[31]

INTERGOVERNMENTAL ORGANIZATIONS

The influence of IGOs on global environmental politics has greatly increased since 1972 (see Box 2.1). IGOs are formed by member states in order to achieve general and multiple purposes—for instance, the UN and various regional associations such as the Organization of American States (OAS)—or for more specific purposes—for instance, the Food and Agriculture Organization of the UN (FAO), World Health Organization (WHO), and International Civil Aviation Organization. IGOs range in size and resources, from the World Bank, which lends more than $42 billion and has a staff of nearly 12,000 and an operating budget of $2.5 billion, to the UN Environment Programme (UNEP), which has a professional staff of 853 and an annual budget for the 2016–2017 biennium of $687 million.[32]

BOX 2.1 PROMINENT INTERGOVERNMENTAL ORGANIZATIONS IN GLOBAL ENVIRONMENTAL POLITICS

Many intergovernmental organizations (IGOs) play important roles in different aspects of global environmental politics. These include but are not limited to the following:

African Development Bank
Asian Development Bank
Food and Agriculture Organization of the UN (FAO)
Global Environment Facility (GEF)
Inter-American Development Bank
International Monetary Fund (IMF)
International Maritime Organization
Intergovernmental Panel on Climate Change (IPCC)
International Tropical Timber Organization
Organization for Economic Cooperation and Development (OECD)
Organization of the Petroleum Exporting Countries (OPEC)
UN Development Programme (UNDP)
UN Environment Programme (UNEP)
UN Population Fund
UN Human Settlements Programme
World Bank
World Health Organization (WHO)
World Meteorological Organization (WMO)
World Trade Organization (WTO)

Although accountable to governing bodies composed of representatives of the member states, IGO staff can take initiatives and influence outcomes on global issues. IGO bureaucracies have varying degrees of independence, ability, and ambition, differing levels of which can affect regime negotiations and implementation. Senior staff at UNEP and the FAO must take their cues from their governing councils in setting agendas, sponsoring negotiations, and implementing development and environment programs. These governing councils include representatives from all governments that participate in the IGO and meet every one to three years to provide formal guidance to their respective organizations. At the World Bank, which depends on major donor countries for its funds, the staff nevertheless has discretion in planning and executing projects.

An IGO can seek to influence global environmental policy in several ways:[33]

- It may help determine which issues the international community will address through its influence on the agenda for global action.
- It can seek to convene international conferences.
- It can seek to influence negotiations on a global environmental regime by providing independent and authoritative information on a global environmental issue.
- It may develop norms or codes of conduct (soft law) to guide action in particular environmental issue areas.
- It may influence states' environmental and development policies on issues not under international negotiation but relevant to global environmental politics.
- It may affect the implementation of global environmental policies through the provision of funds.

No IGO influences global environmental politics by performing all of these functions. IGOs tend to specialize in one or more political functions, although one may indirectly influence another.

Setting Agendas and Influencing Regime Development

UNEP is the principal locus for agenda-setting activities in global environmental politics because of its mandate to catalyze and coordinate environmental activities and to serve as a focal point for such activities within the UN system (see Box 2.2). UNEP identifies global environmental issues requiring international cooperation. In 1976, for example, the UNEP Governing Council chose ozone depletion as one of five priority problems, and consequently UNEP convened a meeting of experts in Washington, DC, which resulted in adoption of the World Plan of Action on the Ozone Layer in 1977—five years before negotiations on a global agreement began. UNEP played a similar role in initiating negotiations on climate change. Along with the World Meteorological Organization (WMO), UNEP created the Intergovernmental Panel on Climate Change (IPCC) to study scientific and policy issues in preparation for negotiations on a global convention on climate change.

BOX 2.2 WHAT IS THE UNITED NATIONS ENVIRONMENT PROGRAMME?

The UN Environment Programme (UNEP) is the lead UN organization on environmental issues. Founded as a result of the UN Conference on the Human Environment in June 1972, UNEP's original mandate was to promote, catalyze, and coordinate the development of environmental policy within the UN system and internationally. UNEP's current mission is "To provide leadership and encourage partnership in caring for the environment by inspiring, informing, and enabling nations and peoples to improve their quality of life without compromising that of future generations."

UNEP assists the development and implementation of international environmental policy, helps to monitor and raise awareness of environmental issues, assists developing countries implement environmentally sound policies, promotes environmental science and information sharing and how they can work in conjunction with policy, seeks to coordinate UN environmental activities, and encourages sustainable development at the local, national, regional, and global level.

UNEP's headquarters is in Nairobi, Kenya, and it maintains offices and units in several other countries (such as the UNEP Chemicals office in Geneva, Switzerland, that houses the secretariats for the Basel, Rotterdam, and Stockholm Conventions). UNEP has a relatively small staff and budget compared with many UN organizations. This reflects its original mandate to act as a catalyst and coordinator rather than an on-the-ground manager of large programs like the UN Development Programme, UN Children's Emergency Fund, or World Health Organization. Nevertheless, UNEP has had notable successes, particularly in assisting the development, implementation, administration, and expansion of global environmental regimes.

***Source:* UNEP website, www.unep.org.**

UNEP has convened and managed the international negotiations that created most of the global environmental conventions of the past three decades, including the Convention on Migratory Species of Wild Animals (1979), the Vienna Convention for the Protection of the Ozone Layer (1985), the Montreal Protocol on Substances that Deplete the Ozone Layer (1987), the Basel Convention on the Control of Transboundary Movements of Hazardous Wastes and Their Disposal (1989), the CBD (1992), the Stockholm Convention on Persistent Organic Pollutants (2001), and the Minamata Convention on Mercury (2013). With the FAO, UNEP convened the negotiations that resulted in the 1998 Rotterdam Convention on the Prior Informed Consent Procedure for Certain Hazardous Chemicals and Pesticides in International Trade.

UNEP also influences the global environmental agenda by monitoring and assessing the state of the environment and disseminating that information to governments and NGOs. Along these lines, UNEP has established the Global Environmental Monitoring System/Water Programme, which provides authoritative, scientifically sound information on the state and trends of global inland water quality; the Global Resource Information Database, a global network of environmental data centers facilitating the generation and dissemination of key environmental information; and the UNEP World Conservation Monitoring Centre, which acts as the world biodiversity information and assessment center. UNEP is also part of the Global Earth Observation System of Systems, which works on comprehensive, coordinated, and sustained Earth observations.

UNEP has also undertaken a number of global assessments, including five Global Environmental Outlook assessments (since 1995), nine ozone assessments (since 1985), three mercury assessments (since 2002), the Global Biodiversity Assessment (1995), the Cultural and Spiritual Values of Biodiversity Assessment (1999), the Global Marine Assessment (2001 and 2007), the Millennium Ecosystem Assessment (2005), the Global International Waters Assessment (2006), and the International Assessment of Agricultural Knowledge, Science and Technology for Development (2008).

Former UNEP executive director Mostafa Tolba influenced environmental diplomacy through direct participation in negotiations. In informal talks with the chiefs of EC delegations during the negotiations on the Montreal Protocol, he lobbied hard for strong controls on CFCs.[34] At the critical ozone Conference of the Parties (COP) in 1990, he convened informal meetings with twenty-five environment ministers to push for a compromise on the contentious issue of establishing a formal mechanism for providing financial assistance and technology transfer (see Chapter 3). At the final session of the negotiations on the CBD, Tolba took over when talks gridlocked on key issues regarding the financing mechanism and virtually forced acceptance of a compromise text (see Chapter 4).

Tolba sometimes openly championed developing countries' concerns. During the final round of negotiations that created the Basel Convention, for instance, he fought for a ban on shipping hazardous wastes to or from noncontracting parties and for a requirement that exporters check disposal sites at their own expense. But

Tolba and the developing countries lost on both issues because they were opposed by the waste-exporting states (see Chapter 3).

Tolba's retirement and replacement with a new executive director, Elizabeth Dowdeswell, reduced UNEP's role in agenda setting for most of the 1990s. Although UNEP had its share of successes during this period, chronic financial problems, the absence of a clear focus, challenges associated with its Nairobi location, and management difficulties contributed to a reduction in UNEP's leadership in the international environmental policy-making process.[35]

Following the appointment of Klaus Töpfer as UNEP's executive director in 1998, donor countries demonstrated renewed faith in the organization and its work program by increasing their pledges to UNEP's Environment Fund. During Töpfer's tenure, UNEP developed the Global Earth Observation System of Systems; initiated the Strategic Approach for International Chemicals Management; improved the scientific base of UNEP; and created the Global Ministerial Environment Forum so that high-level discussions could examine existing environmental challenges, identify new and emerging issues, and set assessment priorities on a regular basis.[36]

Achim Steiner became UNEP's fifth executive director in 2006. In 2007 and in 2013 UNEP adopted medium-term strategies[37] that further streamlined its operations to focus on the following areas: climate change, disasters and conflicts, ecosystem management, environmental governance, chemicals and waste, resource efficiency (sustainable consumption and production), and environmental monitoring. Also under Steiner's tenure, following the 2012 UN Conference on Sustainable Development (UNCSD), the UN General Assembly adopted a resolution that provided for UNEP to receive secure, stable, and increased financial resources from the regular budget of the UN and opened the UNEP Governing Council to full participation by all UN member states, renaming it the UN Environment Assembly (UNEA) of UNEP.[38] UNEA had its first meeting in 2014.[39]

The UN Commission on Sustainable Development (CSD) also sought an agenda-setting role in global environmental politics during its twenty-year history. The CSD was created to review progress in the implementation of Agenda 21 and the Rio Declaration on Environment and Development and later was tasked with providing policy guidance to follow up the Johannesburg Plan of Implementation. The commission generated greater concern for some issues on the international sustainable development agenda, including sustainable consumption and production, freshwater resources, energy, and forests. A CSD recommendation to the UN General Assembly resulted in the establishment of the UN Open-Ended Informal Consultative Process on Oceans and the Law of the Sea, which meets annually to strengthen international cooperation on ocean-related issues.[40]

PHOTO 2.3 Former UNEP executive director Achim Steiner addressing the first session of the United Nations Environment Assembly of UNEP. Courtesy IISD/*Earth Negotiations Bulletin*, www.iisd.ca.

The CSD struggled, however, with moving beyond abstract debate and was unable to reach agreement on how to move beyond general discussion on energy, sustainable production and consumption, chemicals, wastes, and other key sustainable development issues. As a result, the 2012 UNCSD agreed to replace the CSD with the new High-Level Political Forum on Sustainable Development (see Chapter 7).[41]

Providing Independent and Authoritative Information

IGOs can also influence global environmental politics by providing independent and authoritative scientific information to states, other IGOs, the public, and the press. In very few cases are all scientific issues regarding a particular environmental issue completely understood and their future implications projected with confidence before international negotiations begin. Many environmental problems are so complex scientifically, with many different parameters, interrelations, and correlations that cannot easily be stated as precise causal relationships, that the substance of what is being negotiated, what is an appropriate trade-off, what is a reasonable fallback position, and what are effective outcomes can be difficult to define for many years.[42] At the same time, the probable consequences could be catastrophic. Therefore, states are left in the unenviable position of having to elaborate policies on issues rife with uncertainties.

The scientific community has always played a role in intergovernmental environmental treaty negotiations, going back to some of the earliest negotiations on oceans. Policymakers rely on scientists to present facts and projections about specific issues. As a result, international networks of cooperating scientists and scientific institutions have become actors in global environmental policy. Huge teams of scientists can review each other's work, perform integrated assessments, and generate ideas that far exceed the aggregation of each individual's particular knowledge.[43]

One of the first international bodies of scientists to provide independent and authoritative information to international negotiators was the Ozone Trends Panel. Organized by the National Aeronautics and Space Administration (NASA), and thus not an official IGO, the panel worked for sixteen months on a comprehensive scientific exercise that involved more than one hundred scientists from ten countries. The panel's March 1988 report made headlines around the world: ozone-layer depletion was no longer a theory; it was now substantiated by hard scientific evidence; and CFCs and other chemicals were implicated beyond a reasonable doubt. The report increased support for strengthening the Montreal Protocol, including a phaseout of CFCs. Additional scientific evidence in the subsequent five years helped efforts to further strengthen the regime and phase out other ozone-depleting chemicals (see Chapter 3).

The best-known example of an IGO providing authoritative scientific information is the IPCC. Established by the WMO and UNEP in 1988 at the request of the world's governments, the IPCC is charged with providing detailed reports based on available, peer-reviewed scientific information on key issues relevant to understanding climate change, its impacts, and potential response strategies. The first assessment report of the IPCC, released in 1990, served as the basis for negotiating the UN Framework Convention on Climate Change (UNFCCC). Since then, the IPCC has released four additional comprehensive assessment reports (1995, 2001, 2007, and 2014), as well as other reports on specific topics, involving the work of thousands of scientists from around the world. In 2007, the IPCC and former US vice president Al Gore were jointly awarded the Nobel Peace Prize for their efforts to augment and disseminate knowledge about human-made climate change and provide the foundation for measures needed to counteract such change.

There have been several attempts to use the IPCC model to create scientific bodies to serve other conventions. The Millennium Ecosystem Assessment, called for by former UN secretary-general Kofi Annan, examined the consequences of ecosystem change for human well-being and the scientific basis for action needed to enhance the conservation and sustainable use of those systems. The assessment was coordinated by UNEP and overseen by representatives of different conventions (the CBD, Convention to Combat Desertification [UNCCD], Ramsar Convention on Wetlands, and Convention on Migratory Species) as well as national governments, UN agencies, civil society representatives, and the private sector. More than thirteen hundred scientists and other experts from ninety-five countries were involved in its work between 2001 and 2005, evaluating an immense array of scientific literature and ultimately publishing five technical volumes.[44] To follow up on the Millennium Ecosystem Assessment, in April 2012 more than ninety governments agreed to establish the Intergovernmental Science-Policy Platform on Biodiversity and Ecosystem Services (IPBES). Open to all UN member states, the IPBES began work in 2014. It assesses the planet's biodiversity and ecosystem services and provides scientifically sound information to support more informed policy decisions.[45]

Developing Nonbinding Norms and Codes of Conduct

International organizations also influence global environmental politics by facilitating the development of common norms or standards for government behavior. Nontreaty measures, often called soft law, have been developed to help guide state behavior on environmental issues, including codes of conduct, declarations of principle, global action plans, and other international agreements that create new norms and expectations without the binding legal status of treaties.[46]

These nonbinding agreements are usually developed or negotiated by groups of experts representing their governments, usually through processes convened by IGOs. Many UN agencies contribute to these processes, although UNEP and FAO have been the most active with regard to environmental issues. Concerning the management of hazardous waste, for instance, a UNEP ad hoc working group of experts helped draft guidelines in 1984. In 1987, the same process produced guidelines and principles aimed at making the worldwide pesticide trade more responsive to the threats these substances pose to the environment and human health (see Chapter 3). UNEP also played an instrumental role in efforts to get countries to adopt standards limiting or prohibiting lead in gasoline.

Since 1963, the Joint FAO/WHO Food Standards Programme (via the Codex Alimentarius Commission) has developed food standards, guidelines, and codes of practice aimed at protecting the health of consumers and ensuring fair trade. The FAO also drafted guidelines on the environmental criteria for the registration of pesticides (1985).

The 1995 FAO Code of Conduct for Responsible Fisheries sets out principles and international standards of behavior for responsible practices with a view to ensuring the effective conservation, management, and development of living aquatic resources. It built on thirty years of FAO work on the issue (see Box 2.3). The FAO Committee on Fisheries (COFI), which consists of FAO member states, was established in 1965 and remains the primary global forum for considering major issues related to fisheries and aquaculture policy. Until the late 1980s, COFI focused on problems of coastal states in the development of their fisheries, but when the pressures of overfishing on global fish stocks became increasingly difficult to ignore, COFI and the FAO Secretariat began pushing more aggressively for new

BOX 2.3 WHAT IS THE FOOD AND AGRICULTURE ORGANIZATION OF THE UNITED NATIONS?

The Food and Agriculture Organization of the UN (FAO) leads international efforts to defeat hunger, advance agricultural productivity, and ensure food safety. It serves both developed and developing countries, acting as a neutral forum where nations meet to discuss issues, negotiate agreements, and create programs. FAO also serves as a source of knowledge and information, helping developing countries modernize and improve agriculture, forestry, and fisheries practices and ensure good nutrition for all. FAO work currently focuses on food security, natural resource management, forestry and fisheries, early warning of food emergencies, disaster recovery, food safety, bioenergy, and other issues. Since its founding in 1945, FAO has paid special attention to developing rural areas, home to 75 percent of the world's poor and hungry people.

Today, FAO has 194 member states, 2 associate members, and 1 member organization, the EU. Its headquarters are in Rome, and it has an extensive set of regional, subregional, and country offices. FAO works in partnership with institutions of all kinds—UN agencies, national governments, private foundations, large NGOs, grassroots organizations, companies, professional associations, and others. Some partnerships operate at the national level or in the field; others are regional or global in nature. The FAO's budget for 2016–2017, including program, project, and administration costs, is $2.6 billion.

***Source:* FAO website, www.fao.org.**

international norms for sustainable fisheries. The FAO Secretariat began collecting and analyzing data on global fish catch, issuing annual reviews on the state of the world's fisheries, and organizing technical workshops. These efforts helped to focus government and NGO attention on such issues as excess fishing capacity and fisheries subsidies. In 1991, COFI recommended that the FAO develop the concept of responsible fisheries in the form of a code of conduct, and the FAO Secretariat convened global negotiations. The resulting Code of Conduct for Responsible Fisheries is the most comprehensive set of international norms for sustainable fisheries management that currently exists and, despite not being legally binding, has influenced state and producer practices.

Soft-law agreements are often a good way to avoid the lengthy process of negotiating, signing, and ratifying binding agreements while also seeking to change international behavior. However, when soft-law regimes are adopted because key parties are unwilling to go beyond nonbinding guidelines, then the agreed-upon norms are usually not particularly stringent, and state compliance is likely to be uneven at best. The 1985 Code of Conduct on the Distribution and Use of Pesticides and the 1985 Cairo guidelines on international hazardous waste trade are examples of this pattern.

However, soft law sometimes gets turned into binding international law. For example, over time the principles included in a soft-law agreement may become widely regarded as the appropriate norms for a problem, and thus they are ultimately absorbed into treaty law. Alternatively, sometimes political pressures may arise from those dissatisfied with spotty adherence to soft-law norms, and thus these parties successfully advocate for international negotiations to turn a nonbinding agreement into a binding one.

Influencing National Development Policies

IGOs affect global environmental politics by influencing the environmental and development policies of individual states outside the context of regime negotiations. National policy decisions on how to manage forests, generate and use energy, increase agricultural production, allocate government resources, regulate pollution, and manage other economic, development, and environment issues determine how sustainable a country will be and the impact it will have on global environmental issues. IGOs can influence such policies in several ways:

- They provide financing for particular development projects, as well as advice and technical assistance that help shape the country's development strategy.
- They provide financing for environment-protection projects.

- They provide financing, technical assistance, training, and capacity building to create or improve government agencies.
- They undertake research aimed at persuading state officials to adopt certain policies.
- They provide targeted information to government officials, NGOs, the private sector, and the public.
- They focus normative pressure on states regarding sustainable development policy issues.

FAO, for example, is the world's principal repository of global fishery statistics. FAO compiles, collates, analyzes, and integrates fishery and aquaculture data and information, creating a range of information products that are relevant, timely, and easily available to users (in print and electronically). In agriculture, FAO works with countries to help farmers diversify food production, protect plant and animal health, market their products, and conserve natural resources. FAO provides farmers capacity building in integrated pest management to reduce their reliance on chemical pesticides. FAO also provides technical assistance and advice to help countries develop and improve national forest programs, plan and carry out forest activities, and implement effective forest legislation.

UNDP, with a budget of $5 billion annually, a staff of eight thousand worldwide, and liaison offices in 177 countries, is a large source of multilateral grant-development assistance (see Box 2.4). UNDP's current strategic plan focuses on helping countries build and share solutions in three main areas: sustainable development, democratic governance and peacebuilding, and climate and disaster resilience.[47] UNDP encourages countries to shift to sustainability, where economic growth benefits poor and marginalized groups and avoids irreversible environmental damage. Over the past four years, UNDP mobilized nearly $2 billion in funding for sustainable development.[48] UNDP also works to integrate issues of climate, disaster risk, and energy at the country level and focuses on building resilience and ensuring that development remains risk-informed and sustainable. UNDP maintains a $1.7 billion portfolio in climate-change adaptation, mitigation, and sustainable energy.[49]

UNDP has gone further than any other UN agency in calling for donor countries and developing-country governments to allocate resources for human development (health, population, and education) at particular levels as a norm in the context of what it calls "sustainable human development." Through its annual *Human Development Report*, which ranks nations according to their provision of these social services, UNDP pressures developing countries into devoting more of their budgets to these social sectors.

BOX 2.4 WHAT IS THE UNITED NATIONS DEVELOPMENT PROGRAMME?

UNDP is the UN's main economic development organization. Headquartered in New York, UNDP has offices in more than one hundred seventy countries and territories that work with national governments, IGOs, NGOs, and others to implement programs and build developing-country capacity to address local, national, and global development challenges. In each country office, the UNDP resident representative also normally serves as the coordinator of all UN development activities in that country. Through such coordination, UNDP seeks to ensure effective use of UN and international aid resources.

UNDP's networks helped to implement, link, and coordinate efforts to achieve the Millennium Development Goals (MDGs) and, in 2016 began work in support of the Sustainable Development Goals (SDGs). To achieve the SDGs and encourage global sustainable development, UNDP focuses on helping countries build and share solutions to the challenges of poverty reduction, crisis prevention and recovery, gender equality and women's empowerment, sustainable development, and inclusive and effective democratic governance. UNDP's annual *Human Development Report* contains updated global and national statistics while also focusing attention on key development issues. UNDP is among the largest UN agencies. The UNDP administrator is the third highest ranking member of the UN after the UN secretary-general and deputy secretary-general.

***Source:* UNDP website, www.undp.org.**

TREATY SECRETARIATS

Treaty secretariats are a specific type of IGO established by an international treaty to manage the day-to-day operation of the treaty regime.[50] Although most secretariats perform similar core functions, they vary considerably in their additional responsibilities, size, funding, degree of activism, autonomy, and relationships with other IGOs, secretariats, and treaties. Some of the larger secretariats, like the Climate Secretariat, have as many as five hundred members, whereas the Secretariat of the Convention on Migratory Species of Wild Animals has fewer than forty. Several secretariats, such as those for the ozone, biodiversity, and chemicals regimes, are part of UNEP. Some, like the Climate Secretariat, are administered by the UN Secretariat or other UN agencies.

Staffed by international civil servants, secretariats are located in different parts of the world, although several clusters exist due to host country willingness to provide financial or logistical support and the advantages of locating new secretariats near existing UN offices or other secretariats. The CBD Secretariat is located in Montreal, Canada; the Climate, Desertification, and Migratory Species Secretariats are in Bonn, Germany; the secretariats for the Convention on International Trade in Endangered Species of Wild Fauna and Flora (CITES) and the Basel, Rotterdam, and Stockholm Conventions are in Geneva, Switzerland; the Ramsar Convention on Wetlands Secretariat is in Gland, Switzerland; and the Ozone Secretariat is in Nairobi, Kenya.

The core tasks for nearly all treaty secretariats include the following:

- Arranging and servicing meetings of the COP and all subsidiary bodies;
- Preparing and transmitting reports based on information received from the COP and subsidiary bodies;
- Preparing reports on secretariat implementation activities for the COP;
- Ensuring coordination with relevant international bodies and NGOs;
- Liaising and communicating with relevant authorities, nonparties, and international organizations;
- Compiling and analyzing scientific, economic, and social data and information;
- Monitoring adherence to treaty obligations;
- Giving guidance and advice to parties; and
- Providing expert technical advice to parties.[51]

Increasingly, treaty secretariats are involved in raising funds for treaty implementation and awareness-raising activities and to provide training, capacity building, and technical assistance to developing countries. Secretariats can also create synergies by coordinating and cooperating with other secretariats. The need for close cooperation is obvious: integrated environmental systems are addressed by fragmented international management. For example, the success of the UNFCCC is directly conditioned by at least ten other international treaties, while the goals, operation, and impact of the CBD intersect with dozens of international wildlife, habitat, and pollution conventions.

Treaty secretariats may influence the treatment of global environmental issues in ways that are similar to the international organizations discussed earlier in this chapter. A secretariat's level of influence depends largely on its mandate, its funding, and the professional and personal ability and commitment of its staff. Essentially, however, treaty secretariats have two broad areas of impact:

1. Treaty secretariats can influence the behavior of actors by helping to change their knowledge and belief systems.
2. Treaty secretariats can influence political processes through the creation, support, and shaping of norm-building processes for issue-specific international cooperation.[52]

Treaty Secretariats as Knowledge Brokers

Environmental treaty secretariats embody the institutional memory of the regime they serve. A secretariat provides continuity for negotiations that stretch through numerous sessions over a period of years (including both the negotiation and the implementation of the treaty), during which there may be considerable turnover among government negotiators.[53] More specifically, they possess expert knowledge of various categories: technical and scientific knowledge on the problem, administrative and procedural knowledge (which they often generate themselves), and diplomatic knowledge useful when dealing with the complex interlinkages characteristic of international environmental regimes.[54]

As knowledge brokers, secretariats are in a position to manage the horizontal flow of information among national governments and the vertical flow of information among international organizations, national governments, and local stakeholders. This information can take the form of syntheses of scientific findings, such as the Ozone Secretariat's reports on the impact that HCFCs (chemicals controlled under the Montreal Protocol) have on climate change. Even though many secretariats do not have the means or the mandate for actual scientific research, they have the ability to collect and disseminate scientific knowledge. For example, the CBD Secretariat maintains close links with the scientific community through international scientific cooperative programs and the participation of secretariat staff in relevant scientific symposia. The secretariat gathers scientific information on different issues relevant to biodiversity conservation as well as on administrative, social, legal, and economic aspects of the related issues, such as access and benefit sharing. This knowledge is processed and made available through preparatory documents, the secretariat's website, periodic reports, a newsletter, and a comprehensive handbook.[55]

Knowledge and information management is another key role for treaty secretariats. The COP, its subsidiary bodies, national policymakers, NGO and corporate stakeholders, and other interested actors, such as the media, scientists, and members of civil society, draw on and interpret the information and documentation compiled and disseminated by the secretariat in their analytical, political, and scientific assessments and the related discourses.[56] The frequency of visits to and downloads from its website highlights the usefulness of the Climate Secretariat's role in information management. Website usage grew from 309,657 visits in 1999 to nearly 10 million in 2013. In 2013 alone, 3.8 terabytes (38,000 gigabytes) of information, including more than two million PDF documents, were downloaded.[57] The website contains information about the regime and ongoing negotiations, progress in implementing the climate agreements, official documents, and background data and other information on climate change.

Secretariats can also act as knowledge brokers by gathering, synthesizing, processing, and disseminating information to states and other actors.[58] They can convene expert panels and academic assessments, which can help to raise concern among external actors to the level needed to have an impact on political activity. For example, the Basel, Climate, Rotterdam, and Stockholm Secretariats hold online webinars and workshops on scientific, technical, and treaty implementation topics. Many secretariats promote the use of side events during meetings of the COP or the subsidiary bodies in which scientists and other nongovernmental experts share information with policymakers and with each other.

Marketing, a subset of knowledge brokering, moves beyond provision of technical information to the strategic use of information to shape shared opinions and understanding about political processes, norms, and/or institutions. It involves the deliberate selection of specific pieces of information and transforms that information to meet specific political ends. This information is then repeated across multiple political forums.[59] Many secretariats use their websites, press releases, and various social media accounts, including Facebook and Twitter, to market their knowledge to various communities.

Treaty Secretariats and the Political Process

Treaty secretariats can influence political processes through the creation, support, and shaping of norm-building processes for issue-specific international cooperation, such as the advance informed-agreement provisions in the Biosafety Protocol and the prior informed consent (PIC) procedure under the Rotterdam Convention. They can initiate conferences to follow up on treaties or to introduce relevant new topics to the parties. They are usually in charge of administering negotiations on the implementation or expansion of the regime. In this case, secretariat staff can exercise considerable influence "even when they are not key players during the negotiation stage."[60] For example, the Biodiversity Secretariat demonstrated a balanced and continuous effort to facilitate dialogues and negotiations on both the issues of biosafety and access to genetic resources and the fair and equitable sharing of benefits arising from their use, which contributed to the successful adoption of the Cartagena and Nagoya Protocols.

Secretariats can also influence the political process through capacity building, including such activities as assisting countries to comply with international rules, or shaping domestic policies through, for example, workshops, or providing formal or informal technical advice.[61] Secretariats provide basic informational materials on relevant conventions and their sociopolitical implications, such as those developed by the UNCCD Secretariat. The CITES Secretariat provides training materials for wildlife enforcement officers. The Rotterdam Convention Secretariat provides a training manual to explain the convention and its obligations to those responsible for the export of chemicals. The Ozone Secretariat conducts public outreach activities around World Ozone Day and notable anniversaries of the Vienna Convention and Montreal Protocol. Some secretariats provide booklets and games that explain the issues to children.

Some secretariats and their senior staff stick closely to their administrative and facilitative roles, performing only those tasks specifically assigned to them. Others, while also performing the normal administrative and facilitative roles, are more proactive. They seek to push the agenda, looking for new initiatives and trying to

PHOTO 2.4 The Ozone Secretariat conducted outreach activities to commemorate the thirtieth anniversary of the Vienna Convention under the slogan "Ozone: All there is between you and UV." Courtesy UNEP/Ozone Secretariat.

get governments to support and implement them.[62] Secretariats in the latter category benefit from skillful and charismatic leadership. UNEP Executive Director Tolba did this in the early years of the ozone regime—inviting, cajoling, and pressuring somewhat reluctant or disinterested governments to come back to the bargaining table to expand the regime, initiating ideas and advancing concerns that might have otherwise been overlooked, and pushing negotiators toward compromise solutions on difficult issues.[63] He played a similar role during negotiations that created the Basel Convention on hazardous wastes.

More often than not, however, the secretariat's role in regime negotiations is less overt and more facilitative—the important but often unrecognized, and sometimes pivotal, role of promoting a smooth process, which can be crucial in steering negotiations toward a successful outcome.[64] For example, the Climate Secretariat tends not to generate and broker analytical knowledge on climate change and related economic or regulatory policies; instead it mainly processes and administers factual information. In other words, the secretariat does not exert influence on the parties about whether a particular decision or action is politically desirable and should be taken in order to mitigate or adapt to climate change. Rather, it influences how things are done once parties have agreed that measures have to be taken.[65]

Nevertheless, it is important to note that treaty secretariats sometimes become more active players in global environmental politics than some governments and other actors may prefer. When secretariats move beyond fulfilling their basic functions and begin influencing global discourse through knowledge management, advancing the institutionalization or expansion of a convention, supporting particular proposals during negotiations, or proactively assisting in capacity building, they become stakeholders in their own right. Government officials occasionally upbraid secretariat officials for moving beyond a purely facilitative role, arguing that secretariats should not influence policy development.[66] At other times they are praised for acting in pursuit of the stated goals of the regime. Thus, in many respects, the most effective or legitimate role for a secretariat within a given issue area remains an open question.[67]

INTERNATIONAL FINANCIAL INSTITUTIONS

In terms of direct impact on the development and environmental policies of developing states, some of the most powerful IGOs are international financial institutions because of the amount of financial resources they transfer or loan to developing countries every year in support of particular projects and economic policies.

With regard to specific funding for environmental protection, the Global Environment Facility (GEF) plays a central role (see Box 2.5). Since 1991, the GEF has

BOX 2.5 WHAT IS THE GLOBAL ENVIRONMENT FACILITY?

The Global Environment Facility (GEF) is the largest international public funder of projects that address global environmental issues. It provides grants to developing countries and countries with economies in transition for projects in six focal areas: biodiversity, climate change, chemicals and waste, land degradation, international waters, and sustainable forest management. The GEF is also the designated financial mechanism for five global environmental agreements: the Convention on Biological Diversity (CBD); the UN Convention to Combat Desertification (UNCCD); the UN Framework Convention on Climate Change (UNFCCC); the Stockholm Convention on Persistent Organic Pollutants, and the Minamata Convention on Mercury. For each of these conventions, the GEF assists eligible countries meet their regime obligations under rules and guidance provided by the conventions and their Conferences of the Parties. The GEF is also associated with other regimes, including several global and regional agreements that address transboundary water systems and the Montreal Protocol on Substances that Deplete the Ozone Layer.

Originally a pilot program of the World Bank, governments agreed to restructure the GEF in 1994 and moved it out of the World Bank system. The decision to make the GEF an independent institution was designed in part to enhance the involvement of developing countries in the decision-making process and in the implementation of the projects. Since 1994, the World Bank has served as the trustee of the GEF trust fund and provided administrative services. In addition to the World Bank, the GEF has eighteen implementing partners, including UNDP, UNEP, FAO, other UN agencies, regional development banks, and NGOs, who work with national governments to implement GEF-funded projects.

The GEF Secretariat handles the organization's day-to-day operations. It is based in Washington, DC, and reports directly to the GEF Council and GEF Assembly. The GEF Council is the main governing body. It functions as an independent board of directors, with primary responsibility for developing, adopting, and evaluating GEF programs. Composed of representatives from sixteen developing countries, fourteen developed countries, and two countries with transitional economies, the council meets twice each year. All decisions are by consensus. The GEF Assembly includes representatives from all 183 member countries. It meets every three to four years and is responsible for reviewing and evaluating the GEF's general policies, operation, and membership. The assembly also considers and approves proposed amendments to the GEF Instrument, the document that established the GEF, and sets the rules by which the GEF operates.

Source: GEF website, www.gefweb.org.

provided new and additional grants and concessional funding to cover the "incremental" or additional costs associated with transforming a project with national benefits into one with global environmental benefits. GEF grants directly support actions to combat major environmental issues such as climate change, loss of biodiversity, polluted international waters, land degradation and desertification, and POPs, as well as to stimulate green growth.

The GEF has provided more than $14.5 billion in grants and mobilized more than $75.4 billion in co-financing for nearly four thousand projects in more than 183 countries. Through its Small Grants Programme, which provides grants of up to $50,000, the GEF has invested $450 million and leveraged similar levels of financing supporting more than 14,500 small grants directly to civil society and community-based organizations in more than 125 countries.[68]

The World Bank (see Box 2.6) has had the biggest impact on development and related environmental policies. Historically, the bank was driven by the need to lend large amounts of money each year; by a bias toward large-scale, capital-intensive, and centralized projects; and by its practice of assessing projects accord-

BOX 2.6 WHAT IS THE WORLD BANK?

The World Bank is the largest source of international financial and development assistance to developing countries. It is not a bank in the conventional sense but rather the largest of a group of related development institutions owned by more than 180 member countries. Together they provide commercial and low-interest loans, interest-free credits, and grants to developing countries for a wide array of purposes that include investments in education, health, public administration, infrastructure, financial and private-sector development, agriculture, and environmental and natural resource management.

The World Bank Group consists of a number of different institutions. The first, the International Bank for Reconstruction and Development (World Bank), was created by the United States and its allies in 1944 to facilitate post–World War II reconstruction. Over the years it was joined by four other institutions (the International Development Association, International Finance Corporation, Multilateral Guarantee Agency, and International Center for the Settlement of Investment Disputes), and their collective mandate changed to worldwide poverty alleviation and economic development. Established in 1944, the World Bank is the largest member institution of the World Bank Group, which is headquartered in Washington, DC. It has more than ten thousand employees in more than one hundred twenty offices worldwide. Since 1947 it has funded nearly 13,000 projects in 173 countries.

***Source:* World Bank website, www.worldbank.org.**

ing to a quantifiable rate of return (how the loan contributes to conventional gross national product calculations), while discounting longer-term, unquantifiable social and environmental costs and benefits. In the 1970s and 1980s, the World Bank supported schemes to colonize rain forests in Brazil and Indonesia, cattle-ranching projects in Central and South America, and tobacco projects in Africa that contributed to accelerated deforestation, and a cattle-development project in Botswana that contributed to desertification.[69]

In response to persistent, well-orchestrated pressure from NGOs, criticism by some prominent members of the US Congress, and calls for it to become part of the solution to global environmental problems rather than a contributor, the World Bank began a process of evolution in the late 1980s toward greater sensitivity to the environmental implications of its lending. These reforms included mandatory environmental assessment procedures and the public disclosure of these assessments in advance of project approval. In addition, the bank's board of executive directors mandated a series of sector-specific policies to guide World Bank investment in such areas as forestry and energy, including a ban on financing logging in primary tropical forests.[70]

Along with these policy reform efforts, the World Bank pursued structural changes and investment strategies intended to demonstrate a commitment to environmentally sustainable development. A separate environmental unit created in the 1980s evolved into a vice presidency for environmentally and socially sustainable development in the 1990s. By the mid-1990s, the bank had developed a portfolio of environment-sector projects, ranging from support for national environmental agencies to investments in national parks.[71] Many continued to criticize the bank, however, saying that its environmental reforms were merely efforts to deflect outside criticism, no major changes had occurred in the bank's overall performance, and lending imperatives tied to traditional models of economic growth continued to outweigh environmental considerations.[72]

In response to continued criticism, in 2001 the bank adopted a new strategy titled "Making Sustainable Commitments: An Environment Strategy for the World Bank." The strategy noted the need for mainstreaming "the environment into investments, programs, sector strategies, and policy dialogue."[73] The strategy placed the environment within the institution's poverty-reduction mission and highlighted three objectives: improving the quality of life, enhancing the quality of growth, and protecting the regional and global commons.[74] Yet, three years later, experts such as Frances Seymour from the World Resources Institute maintained that the World Bank still had not succeeded in mainstreaming sustainability into its operations. She argued that this resulted from three factors: bank staff continued to view environmental issues as a compliance issue, staff did not see environmental issues as integral to their operations, and populations affected by bank projects remained underrepresented.[75] Echoing these concerns, in 2008 the Independent Evaluation Group of the World Bank recommended that the bank remedy internal constraints, including poor knowledge, inadequate capacity, and insufficient coordination concerning environmental challenges.[76]

In June 2012 the World Bank released a new environment strategy for 2012 to 2022 aimed at enabling countries to pursue sustainable development.[77] The strategy identifies seven priority areas for the World Bank's engagement in environment projects: wealth accounting and ecosystem valuation, protection of oceans, pollution management, low-emission development, adaptation, disaster risk management, and small island states' resilience. Among other things, the strategy recognizes the growing role of the private sector in addressing sustainability concerns and the need to ensure that global markets promote sustainable development.

Environmental NGOs, including Friends of the Earth, expressed skepticism, warning that the strategy may be relying too much on private-sector interventions and market mechanisms. They argued that greater private-sector involvement in a project could lead to decreased capacity to monitor social and environmental impact. The Sierra Club noted that there was a lack of operational details in the strategy and that it, instead, focused on rhetoric and broad goals.[78] Others praised the strategy, noting that the current economic model, driven by unsustainable patterns of growth and consumption, is putting too much pressure on an already threatened environment.[79]

The World Bank is in the process of reviewing, updating, and strengthening its environmental and social policies that serve to protect vulnerable people and the environment in World Bank investment projects. On July 1, 2015, the bank began a third phase of consultations on the second draft of the proposed Environmental and Social Framework. The first draft had been released in 2014 and received immediate criticism from environmental and human rights NGOs. The 2015 proposal broadens the range of biodiversity concerns and adds provisions for the sustainable use of living natural resources (e.g., fisheries and forests). Climate-change considerations have been added, including requirements to estimate and reduce GHG emissions in bank-supported projects and to promote climate resilience. Assessments of social and environmental risk will be strengthened, ensuring that resources are targeted to high-risk projects. Finally, the draft framework includes Free, Prior, and Informed Consent for Indigenous Peoples and requires increased and ongoing stakeholder engagement.[80]

A group of nineteen NGOs immediately criticized the revised draft, saying the bank's proposed changes "will vastly weaken protections for affected communities and the environment at the same time as the bank intends to finance more high-risk projects" through governments in economically struggling regions. The groups say the new standards would shift too much responsibility to governments to police themselves and fail to require detailed procedures or budgets for the bank's oversight.[81] The consultations on this new policy continued into 2016.

The International Monetary Fund (IMF; see Box 2.7) was even slower than the World Bank and regional banks to acknowledge the need to take environmental considerations explicitly into account in its lending operations. It defined its role as limited to helping countries achieve a balance of payments and pay off their international debts. Only in 1991 did the IMF executive board consider for the first time the extent to which the IMF should "address environmental issues." It decided that the IMF should avoid policies that might harm the environment but that

BOX 2.7 WHAT IS THE INTERNATIONAL MONETARY FUND?

The fundamental mission of the International Monetary Fund (IMF) is to ensure the stability of the international monetary system. It provides policy advice and financing to countries in economic difficulties and also works with developing nations to help them achieve macroeconomic stability and reduce poverty. Founded in 1944 and headquartered in Washington, DC, the IMF is a specialized agency of the UN but has its own charter, governing structure, and finances. The highest decision-making body of the IMF, the Board of Governors, consists of one governor and one alternate governor for each of its 188 member countries. However, voting power among the governors is distributed based on the size of each country's share of the global economy. Thus, the United States, Japan, and EU countries wield primary influence. In December 2015, for example, Angola had 0.12 percent of the voting power, whereas the United States had 17.69 percent.

The work of the IMF focuses on three main areas: economic surveillance, lending, and technical assistance. Surveillance refers to the monitoring of economic and financial developments and the provision of policy advice, aimed especially at crisis prevention. The IMF also lends to countries with balance-of-payments difficulties, providing temporary financing and supporting policies aimed at correcting the underlying problems. It also provides low-income countries with loans aimed especially at poverty reduction. Finally, the IMF provides countries with technical assistance and training in its areas of expertise. In recent years, the IMF has employed elements of its surveillance and technical assistance work to help develop standards and codes of good practice as part of international efforts to strengthen the global financial system. Financing for IMF activities comes mainly from the money that countries pay as their capital subscription when they become members. The size of these payments also varies by the size of their economy.

Source: **IMF website, www.imf.org.**

it should not conduct research or build up its own expertise on the possible environmental consequences of its policies.[82]

Because the World Bank addresses environmental issues and supports an extensive work program on environmental and other sectoral issues, the executive board of the IMF decided early that the IMF should not duplicate the bank's work in this area. The IMF also believes that its mandate and expertise constrain its ability to address environmental issues to specific types of work. The IMF's involvement in environmental policy is thus limited to areas that have a serious and perceptible impact on a country's macroeconomic outlook. The IMF sees fiscal instruments (emissions taxes, trading systems, fuel taxes, and charges for water resources) as central to promoting greener growth. If applied effectively, the IMF argues that they reduce environmental harm, are cost-effective, and strike the right balance between environmental benefits and economic costs. For example, many countries subsidize the production and consumption of fossil fuels rather than charging to discourage their use or tax electricity use or vehicle sales in general rather than the pollution produced by certain types of power plants or vehicles.

The IMF promotes the use of environmentally oriented fiscal reform and the sustainable management of renewable resources, such as forests, through its analytical work, technical assistance to member countries, and outreach activities.[83] Yet these efforts can run into domestic obstacles. A country may not have a relevant and sufficiently detailed environmental action plan or national strategy. Even where they do exist, such plans or strategies are sometimes not specific enough to allow the IMF staff to consider their macroeconomic implications. Sometimes national authorities themselves are not fully committed to environmental objectives because of pressure from one or more interest groups or because these objectives conflict with short-run economic growth or with some other objective of the country's policymakers. Thus, the IMF argues, it can integrate environment into its policy dialogue only to the extent that member countries allow it to do so.[84]

In 2014 a new multilateral development bank entered the scene: the New Development Bank (NDB). Originally called the BRICS Development Bank, NDB is operated by the BRICS states (Brazil, Russia, India, China, and South Africa) as an alternative to the World Bank and IMF. The bank seeks to foster greater financial and development cooperation among these five emerging markets and other interested nations. Together, BRICS states comprise more than three billion people, nearly 42 percent of the world's population, cover more than one-quarter of the world's land area over three continents, and account for more than 25 percent of global gross domestic product (GDP).[85] South–South economic cooperation has expanded dramatically in recent years. Brazil now has more embassies in Africa than does the United Kingdom. China has become Africa's most important trading partner. The value of South–South trade now exceeds North–South trade by some $2.2 trillion—more than one-quarter of global trade. Low-income countries have also seen unprecedented growth in South–South foreign aid—with China, Brazil, and India all becoming larger donors.[86]

The rising economic strength of the BRICS has outpaced any increase in their voice at the World Bank and the IMF. This long-standing dissatisfaction with the World Bank and the IMF helped to push the BRICS to create a developing country–centered alternative to the existing global development financial institutions.[87] The NDB is headquartered in Shanghai and opened its doors in July 2015 with $50 billion to invest in public infrastructure. Unlike the World Bank, which assigns votes based on capital share, the NDB assigns each participant country one vote, and none have veto power. Although the NDB website lists sustainable development among the initiative's central purposes, it will take time to determine the actual impact that NDB will have on the environment.[88]

REGIONAL AND OTHER MULTILATERAL ORGANIZATIONS

Regional and other multilateral organizations play an increasing role in environmental politics. Some, such as the regional fisheries management organizations, are specific functional groups that take on environmental responsibilities out of necessity. Others have broad political and economic agendas that also include environmental issues. Still others have been specifically established to address environmental concerns.

The EU is the only regional organization whose decisions obligate its members. In the 1950s, six European countries decided to pool their economic resources and set up a system of joint decision making on economic issues. To do so, they formed several organizations, of which the European Economic Community was the most important (the name was eventually shortened to the European Community).[89] The group grew in size, and the 1992 Maastricht Treaty introduced new forms of cooperation among the then twelve members on issues such as defense, justice, and home affairs, including the environment. By adding this intergovernmental cooperation to the existing community system, the Maastricht Treaty created the EU. The EU is unique in that its now twenty-eight member states have set up common institutions to which they delegate some of their sovereignty so that decisions on specific matters, including agriculture, fisheries, and trade, can be made at the European level. Both individual EU member states and the EU itself, as a "regional economic integration organization," can ratify and join global environmental agreements.[90] During regime negotiations, EU states often negotiate as a single entity, giving their negotiating positions considerable importance.

In 2010, the EU adopted Europe 2020, a ten-year growth strategy that focuses on smart growth (developing an economy based on knowledge and innovation), sustainable growth (promoting a more resource-efficient, greener, and more competitive economy), and inclusive growth (fostering a high-employment economy delivering social and territorial cohesion). The strategy sets goals in the areas of employment, innovation, education, poverty reduction, and climate/energy. The 2020 targets included reducing GHG emissions by 20 percent compared with 1990 levels, increasing the share of renewables in final energy consumption to 20 percent, and increasing energy efficiency by 20 percent.[91] In 2014, the EU expanded their goals, pledging to achieve by 2030 at least a 40 percent reduction in GHG emissions compared with 1990 levels, an increase in the share of renewable energy to at least 27 percent, an increase in energy efficiency of at least 27 percent, improvement in the EU emissions trading system, and continuation of efforts to reach an 80 percent reduction in GHG emissions by 2050.[92]

The Organization of American States (OAS), one of the oldest regional organizations, was the first to hold a presidential summit specifically focused on the environment when it convened the Summit of the Americas on Sustainable Development in Bolivia in December 1996. The Department of Sustainable Development is the principal technical arm of the OAS General Secretariat that supports OAS member states in the design and implementation of policies, programs, and projects oriented to integrate environmental priorities with poverty alleviation and socioeconomic development goals, including integrated water management, energy and climate-change mitigation, risk management and climate-change adaptation, biodiversity and sustainable land management, and environmental law.

The fifth Summit of the Americas, in Port of Spain, Trinidad and Tobago, in 2009, focused on environmental sustainability, reaffirming the region's commitment to sustainable development and recognizing the adverse impacts of climate change on the region and the need to reduce GHG emissions.[93] The consensus statement issued at the sixth Summit of the Americas, in Cartagena, Colombia, in 2012, addressed, among other issues, the negative impacts of climate change, stating that the parties would mitigate natural disasters' "social, economic, and environmental impact by allocating resources and designing strategies geared to adaptation, risk management, and the creation of efficient prevention and response mechanisms."[94] The results of the seventh Summit of the Americas, in Panama City, Panama, in 2015, called for strengthening "hemispheric efforts geared toward making progress in the areas of sustainable development and climate change in order to counteract the impacts of climate change, increase the capacity for adaptation of communities and ecosystems vulnerable to climate change, and increase efforts to mitigate GHG emissions."[95]

The African Union includes the promotion of sustainable development as one of its official objectives. At its inaugural summit in mid-2001, the African Union adopted the New Partnership for Africa's Development (NEPAD) as a blueprint for the continent's future development. NEPAD's primary objectives are eradicating poverty in Africa, placing African countries on a path of sustainable growth and development, and halting the continent's marginalization in the globalization process. NEPAD recognizes the need to protect the environment not only for Africa's benefit but also for the many natural resources of global importance the continent holds, including a wide range of flora and fauna, paleoanthropological resources, and immense forests that act as carbon sinks. These resources could be degraded without support from the international community. Implicit in NEPAD's approach is the need for the developed world to support Africa's sustainable development for the sake of both Africans and the wider global community.

In 2013, the Assembly of African Union Heads of State and Government, in Addis Ababa, Ethiopia, adopted Agenda 2063, a vision and action plan to work together to build a prosperous and united Africa. Agenda 2063 calls on Africans to act with a sense of urgency on climate change and the environment; to ensure cost-effective, renewable, and sustainable energy to all African households and businesses; to implement sustainable forest management; and to develop equitable and sustainable use and management of water resources.[96]

Asia-Pacific Economic Cooperation (APEC) was formed in 1989 in response to the growing interdependence among Asia-Pacific economies. Although APEC's primary goal is to champion sustainable economic growth and free trade, its work includes consideration of three categories of environmental issues: air, atmospheric, and water pollution, especially those related to energy production and use; resource degradation; and demographic shifts, including food security and urbanization.

APEC held its first ocean-related ministerial meeting in South Korea in 2002, with the theme "Toward the Sustainability of Marine and Coastal Resources." During the meeting, ministers discussed sustainable fisheries, ocean science and technology, marine environmental protection, and integrated coastal management and adopted the Seoul Oceans Declaration. In September 2007, APEC leaders adopted a Declaration on Climate Change, Energy Security, and Clean Development, which supported a post-2012 international climate-change arrangement that "strengthens, broadens and deepens the current arrangements and leads to reduced global emissions of greenhouse gases."[97]

In 2011, member economies committed to reduce energy intensity in the region by 45 percent by 2030. In 2012, in Vladivostok, Russia, APEC leaders agreed to reduce tariffs on 54 environmental products to 5 percent or less by the end of 2015. The targeted products, from solar panels to wind turbines, account for approximately $600 billion in world trade.[98] In 2014, members agreed to work toward doubling the share of renewables in APEC's energy mix by 2030, including in power generation. Members have also endorsed rationalizing and phasing out fossil-fuel subsidies that encourage wasteful consumption.

Funded by a multiyear project under the APEC Energy Working Group, APEC has helped urban planners develop low-carbon model town plans for a series of cities throughout the Asia-Pacific region. These cities are reducing their carbon footprint by adopting emission-reduction targets and energy-efficient initiatives and expanding the use of solar panels and electric vehicles. APEC projects also support the development of smart electricity grids that enable sources of clean power to be seamlessly connected to existing structures and distributed to rural communities.[99]

The Group of 77 (G-77), which functions as the "negotiating arm of the developing countries" within the UN system, is an important international entity in environmental politics.[100] The G-77 was established in 1964 by seventy-seven developing countries at the end of the first session of the UN Conference on Trade and Development. Although its membership has grown to more than one hundred thirty countries, the original name was retained because of its historic significance. China, which has the status of associate member, also plays an influential role in the G-77. As the largest developing-country coalition in the UN, the G-77 provides the means for developing countries to articulate and promote their collective interests, enhance joint negotiating capacity in the UN system, and promote economic and technical cooperation.[101] Since the early 1990s, as more developing countries have become involved in the negotiation of multilateral environmental agreements (MEAs), the G-77 has played key roles in these negotiations.

The Organization for Economic Cooperation and Development (OECD) is also an actor on the international environmental stage. The OECD's thirty-four members include all of the major industrialized countries, plus Chile, Mexico, Israel, South Korea, and Turkey. The OECD has played a key role in promoting sustainable consumption and production within its member states and provides a great deal of background information and support on such issues as climate change, trade and environment issues, and transport and the environment.

States have created regional organizations explicitly to address environmental issues. One such organization is the Pacific Regional Environment Programme (SPREP).[102] Created in 1982, SPREP has developed a framework for environmentally sound planning and management suited to the Pacific island region. In order to improve and protect the environment, SPREP's action program aims to build national capacity in environmental and resource management. SPREP also provides capacity building, training, and support for member states to improve their ability to represent their interests in international negotiations and UN global conferences.

NONGOVERNMENTAL ORGANIZATIONS

The emergence of environmental issues as major concerns in world politics coincided with the emergence of NGOs as important actors in environmental politics.[103] Although business organizations are sometimes included in the UN definition of an NGO, we use the term here to denote an independent, nonprofit organization not beholden to a government or a profit-making organization.

NGO influence on global environmental politics stems from three principal factors. First, NGOs often possess expert knowledge and innovative thinking about global environmental issues acquired from years of focused specialization on the issues under negotiation. Second, NGOs are acknowledged to be dedicated to goals that transcend national or sectoral interests. Third, some NGOs often represent substantial constituencies within their own countries and thus can command attention from policymakers because of their potential ability to mobilize people to influence policies and even tight elections.

In the industrialized countries, most NGOs active in global environmental politics fall into one of three categories: organizations affiliated with international NGOs—that is, NGOs with branches in more than one country; large national organizations focused primarily on domestic environmental issues; and think tanks, or research institutes, whose influence comes primarily from publishing studies and proposals for action.

Some international NGOs are loose federations of national affiliates; others have more centralized structures. Friends of the Earth International, based in Amsterdam, is a confederation of seventy-five national independent affiliates, half of which are in developing countries, and two million members and supporters.[104] At an annual meeting, delegates democratically set priorities and select five or more campaigns on which to cooperate. Greenpeace is one of the largest international NGOs; it has offices in twenty-six countries covering operations in fifty-five countries and more than 2.8 million financial supporters and members.[105] Its international activities are tightly organized by a well-staffed headquarters (also in Amsterdam) and guided by issues and strategies determined at an annual meeting.

WWF (formerly known as the World Wildlife Fund and the World Wide Fund for Nature) is one of the world's largest and most experienced independent

PHOTO 2.5 Friends of the Earth Europe called for an energy revolution at the December 2014 Lima Climate Change Conference. Courtesy Kiara Worth, IISD/*Earth Negotiations Bulletin*, www.iisd.ca.

conservation organizations. Headquartered in Switzerland, WWF has five million members worldwide and works in one hundred countries. WWF's work has evolved from saving species and landscapes to addressing the larger global threats and forces that impact them. Recognizing that the problems facing the planet are increasingly complex and urgent, WWF's current strategy puts people at the center and organizes its work around six key areas: forests, marine, freshwater, wildlife, food, and climate.[106]

The European Environmental Bureau, organized in 1974, is now a confederation of more than one hundred fifty environmental citizen organizations based in thirty EU and neighboring states, representing more than fifteen million individual members and supporters. The bureau's vision is of a world in which all people of present and future generations are able to enjoy a rich, clean, and healthy environment; where prosperity and peace are secured for all; where responsible societies respect the carrying capacity of the planet and preserve it for future generations, including its rich biodiversity; and where effective environmental policies and sustainable development have priority over short-term objectives that only serve the current generation or certain segments of society.[107]

The second category of NGOs includes the big US environmental organizations, almost all of which have international programs. Some, such as the Sierra

Club, the National Audubon Society, and the National Wildlife Federation, were formed in the late nineteenth and early twentieth centuries around conservation issues. Others, including the Environmental Defense Fund and the Natural Resources Defense Council, arose in the early 1970s in an attempt to use legal, economic, and regulatory processes to affect national policy, with an initial focus on air and water pollution. These organizations also work on international issues, particularly on climate change, energy, rain forests, and ozone depletion. Other organizations with more specific agendas are also internationally active on their issues; among these are Defenders of Wildlife and the Humane Society.

Environmental think tanks, normally funded by private donations or contracts, rely primarily on their technical expertise and research programs to influence global environmental policy. A prominent example is the World Resources Institute, which publishes well-respected reports on specific issues. The International Institute for Environment and Development in London drew early attention to the connection between the environment and poverty in developing countries. In a few countries, government-funded but nevertheless independent institutes seek to influence both the policies of their own governments and international negotiations. The International Institute for Sustainable Development (IISD) of Canada and the Stockholm Environment Institute of Sweden have played such roles.

Unlike environmental NGOs in the North, environmentalism in developing countries grew out of what some of its founders saw as a "lopsided, iniquitous and environmentally destructive process of development" and is often interlinked with questions of human rights, ethnicity, and distributive justice.[108] Southern NGOs have tended to stress land use, forest management, fishing rights, and the redistribution of power over natural resources.[109] They also tend to be more critical of consumerism and uncontrolled economic development than their colleagues in the North. An increasing number of southern NGOs, especially those based in low-lying coastal areas or small islands, are concerned about climate change, and urban air and water pollution have also drawn increased attention in many countries. Some developing-country NGOs became involved in international policy issues through opposition to multilateral bank projects and government policies that displace villages or threaten forests and have tended to regard multinational corporations as enemies of the environment. Critical of their governments on environmental and sometimes other domestic policies, NGO members committed to environmental protection have often been harassed, subjected to political repression, and jailed. In some countries, however, they have acquired political legitimacy and a measure of influence on national environmental-policy issues.

India's environmental movement, which is representative of a number of developing countries, dates back to the Chipko movement, which started in the Garhwal

Himalaya in April 1973. Between 1973 and 1980, more than a dozen instances were recorded in which men, women, and children threatened to hug forest trees rather than allow them to be logged for export. Unlike environmentalists in the North, however, the Indian activists were not interested in saving the trees as an end in itself, but in using the forest for agricultural and household requirements.[110] Today, India has a large number of NGOs, ranging from the Center for Science and Environment, which researches, lobbies for, and communicates the urgency of development that is both sustainable and equitable, to the Wildlife Trust of India, which prevents destruction of India's wildlife, especially endangered species and threatened habitats. The Energy and Resource Institute (TERI) is the largest developing-country institution working toward sustainability. Not only does it have six offices in India, but it also has affiliated institutes and research bases in Europe, the United States, Africa, Japan, Malaysia, and the United Arab Emirates.

Some of the most important aspects of Brazil's environmental movement can be traced to the 1980s, when rubber tappers organized to resist destruction of the forests that supported them and that they had tended for decades. In 1989, after a cattle rancher murdered Chico Mendes, a key leader of the rubber tappers, popular support grew, and the Brazilian government began to take more meaningful action. The country set aside extractive reserves to protect forests where tapping and other sustainable extraction could continue. Today, there are numerous Brazilian NGOs that work with indigenous and local communities to end deforestation, promote forest certification, and protect local livelihoods,

In Sarawak, Malaysia, loggers cleared 2.8 million hectares, or 30 percent, of the forest between 1963 and 1985. Many of the timber licenses issued by the Sarawak government covered the customary land of the natives who depend on the forests for food and shelter. Beginning in early 1987, natives started erecting blockades across timber roads in an attempt to stop the logging.[111] Legal and illegal logging continues in Malaysia, Cambodia, and other countries, and protests and blockades against aggressive deforestation activities have produced serious disputes.[112]

The Green Belt Movement, based in Kenya, is an influential grassroots NGO that empowers communities, particularly women, to conserve the environment and improve livelihoods. Founded in 1977 by the late Wangari Maathai (under the auspices of the National Council of Women of Kenya), it aims to create a society of people who consciously work for the continued improvement of their environment. Programs include tree planting, biodiversity conservation, civic and environmental education, advocacy and networking, food security, and capacity building for women and girls. In 2004, Maathai received the Nobel Peace Prize for her efforts with the Green Belt Movement—the first Nobel Peace Prize given to an environmentalist.[113]

While many environmental and development battles continue to be fought at the community level in developing countries, some NGOs and coalitions in those countries also tackle a broader range of environmental and development issues. The Third World Network, for example, is an independent, nonprofit, international network of organizations and individuals involved in issues relating to development, the Third World, and North-South issues. Its mission is to bring about a greater articulation of the needs and rights of peoples in the Third World, a fair distribution of world resources, and forms of development that are ecologically sustainable and fulfill human needs. To this end, the Third World Network conducts research into economic, social, and environmental issues pertaining to the South, publishes books and magazines, organizes and participates in seminars, and represents southern interests and perspectives at international fora such as UN conferences and processes. Headquartered in Penang, Malaysia, the Third World Network also has regional offices in Ghana, Malaysia, Switzerland, and Uruguay and researchers located in Beijing, Delhi, Jakarta, Manila, and New York.[114]

International coalitions of NGOs working on a specific environmental issue have also become a means of increasing NGO influence. The Antarctic and Southern Oceans Coalition brings together more than thirty organizations seeking to maintain the Antarctic continent, its surrounding islands, and the great Southern Ocean as an unspoiled wilderness. The Climate Action Network has more than seven hundred member organizations in ninety countries that work to promote government and individual action to limit human-induced climate change.

Despite some inherent tensions among the missions of some northern and southern NGOs, there have been many instances of close North–South NGO cooperation. One example is the Pesticide Action Network, a network of more than six hundred NGOs, institutions, and individuals in more than ninety countries working to replace hazardous pesticides with ecologically sound alternatives. Five autonomous regional centers coordinate projects and campaigns. The Pesticide Action Network and partner groups from around the world lobbied for the creation and expansion of the Stockholm Convention on Persistent Organic Pollutants, and they provide technical and financial assistance to help developing countries eliminate toxic pesticides addressed by the treaty (see Chapter 3).

Another successful coalition is the International POPs Elimination Network (IPEN), which works for the global elimination of POPs on an expedited, yet socially equitable, basis. Founded by a small number of NGOs, IPEN was formally launched in June 1998 during the first session of formal negotiations on creating a global treaty to control and/or eliminate POPs. The network mobilized grassroots support for a global POPs treaty and leveraged the resources and created a forum for activists from around the world to participate in the negotiations. IPEN has since become a coalition of more than seven hundred public health, environmental, consumer, and other NGOs in 116 countries (including many groups involved in the Pesticide Action Network) and actively participates in all Stockholm Convention meetings. IPEN is also active in local efforts to combat toxic pollutants, with more than one hundred projects in fifty countries.[115]

One of the most important organizations through which NGOs influence environmental politics is the International Union for the Conservation of Nature and Natural Resources (IUCN). The IUCN is the world's oldest and largest global environmental organization, with nearly thirteen hundred government and NGO members and more than fifteen thousand volunteer experts in 185 countries. Its work is supported by almost one thousand staff in forty-five offices and hundreds of partners in public, NGO, and private sectors around the world.[116] Governed by a general assembly of delegates from its member organizations (states, government agencies, NGOs, and others) that meets every three years, the IUCN has had a major influence on global agreements on wildlife conservation. The IUCN has been successful in drafting environmental treaties and assisting in monitoring their implementation.

Influencing Environmental Regime Formation

NGOs can attempt to influence the development, expansion, and implementation of international regimes in various ways, such as the following:

- Raising public awareness about particular issues and conducting education campaigns;
- Influencing the global environmental agenda by defining a new issue or redefining an old one;
- Lobbying governments to accept a more advanced position on an issue;
- Proposing draft text to be included in conventions in advance of negotiations;
- Participating and/or lobbying in international negotiations;
- Generating media attention;
- Supporting ratification and implementation of an environmental treaty by the government in their host country;
- Bringing lawsuits to compel national action on an issue;
- Organizing consumer boycotts to pressure international corporations;
- Providing reporting services;
- Assisting implementation of the regime, particularly in developing countries; and
- Monitoring the implementation of conventions and reporting to the secretariat and/or the parties.

One example of an NGO influencing the global environmental agenda is the role played by WWF and Conservation International in creating the demand for banning commerce in African elephant ivory. In particular, the groups published a detailed report on the problem, circulating it to the parties to CITES, and engaged in public education campaigns.

Pressing for changes in the policy of a major actor is sometimes the best way for NGOs to influence an international regime. In efforts to protect the ozone layer, during the late 1970s a group of US environmental organizations lobbied for a domestic ban on aerosols and the regulation of CFCs. Because they later lobbied for a total phaseout of CFCs before negotiations on the Montreal Protocol began, they contributed to US international leadership on this issue. Similarly, three US NGOs working with pro-treaty biotechnology firms influenced the Clinton administration's decision to reverse the Bush administration's position and sign the CBD (although the United States still has not ratified the treaty).[117]

Greenpeace's monitoring of and reporting on the toxic waste trade was a key factor in encouraging a coalition of countries to push for a complete ban on North–South waste trade under the Basel Convention. The Inuit Circumpolar Conference, an NGO representing 150,000 Inuit of Alaska, Canada, Greenland, and Chukotka (Russia), participated in negotiations that produced the Stockholm Convention on Persistent Organic Pollutants, and their stories concerning the dangers that toxic chemicals pose for the future of their people put a human face on the need to eliminate POPs.

Although effective consumer boycotts are rare in international environmental politics (they are more common on local and national issues), an NGO-organized boycott of Icelandic products because of Iceland's pro-whaling stand, including protests at fast-food and supermarket chains that sold fish caught by Iceland's fishing fleet, contributed to a temporary two-year halt to that country's whaling.[118] Other notable NGO-led boycotts include Mitsubishi making concessions on forest policy following a campaign spearheaded by Rainforest Action Network, and Shell agreeing to dispose of its offshore Brent Spar oil platform on land (rather than dumping it at sea as originally planned).[119]

NGOs can influence international regimes in a more specialized way by circulating ideas for inclusion in a convention or amendment and circulating it in advance of the negotiations in the hope that a national delegation will include it among their proposals. In exceptional cases, this strategy can even include developing an entire draft convention. The Convention Concerning the Protection of the World Cultural and Natural Heritage, signed in 1972 in Paris, was based on a draft produced by IUCN. CITES, adopted in 1973, was the result of an IUCN initiative that went through three drafts over nearly a decade.[120]

NGOs have become especially active and well organized in lobbying at international negotiations. The COPs to most environmental conventions permit NGO observers, enabling NGOs to be involved in the proceedings. Certain NGOs specialize in the meetings of particular conventions and over the years have acquired a high level of technical and legal expertise. The Humane Society of the United States has been lobbying at meetings of the International Whaling Commission (IWC) since 1973, and Greenpeace has been active in the COP to the London Convention since the early 1980s and the Basel Convention since its inception. The Climate Action Network is active in climate-change negotiations. IPEN is an active participant during negotiations related to the Stockholm Convention on POPs and the Rotterdam Convention on PIC.

NGOs also influence international conferences through staging protests and attracting media attention. Greenpeace has staged many actions, including suspending banners protesting forest destruction and inaction on climate change. SustainUS and other youth, indigenous peoples, and women climate activists regularly stage protests at climate-change negotiations. Climate Action Network presents "The Fossil of the Day" awards during UN climate-change negotiations. Members vote for countries judged to have done their "best" to block progress in the negotiations.

PHOTO 2.6 "Fossil of the Day," hosted by Climate Action Network, presents awards to countries perceived as "blocking progress in the climate negotiations." Courtesy IISD/*Earth Negotiations Bulletin*, www.iisd.ca.

NGOs also influence international conferences by providing scientific and technical information and new arguments to delegations. In the process leading up to the whaling moratorium, NGOs supplied factual information on violations of the whaling convention as well as scientific information not otherwise available to the delegations.[121] In some circumstances, NGOs have a particularly strong influence on a key delegation's positions, an example being the 1991–1992 biodiversity negotiations when WWF-Australia and other NGOs were consulted on major issues in the convention before the Australian delegation adopted positions.[122] The Foundation for International Environmental Law and Development (FIELD) has assisted AOSIS in climate-change negotiations, providing AOSIS with advice and legal expertise, enabling the alliance to wield greater influence in the climate negotiations.[123] Greenpeace provided a great deal of technical support to African countries that supported a ban on the dumping of hazardous wastes in developing countries during the negotiation of the Basel Convention.

NGOs can also provide useful reporting services during global environmental negotiations and related conferences. Since 1972, NGOs at selected UN-sponsored environmental conferences have published *ECO*, which provides a combination of news stories and commentary. The *Earth Negotiations Bulletin*, published by IISD, has provided objective reports of many different environment and development negotiations since 1992.[124] Countries cannot easily or effectively report about ongoing negotiations on their own. Were a government to attempt to provide such information, the reports would likely be perceived as biased. If the UN or a formal secretariat published daily reports, they would have the status of official documents, and member governments would have difficulty agreeing on their content, style, and tone. However, because the NGO community, including impartial research institutions like IISD, is already providing the information, governments and international organizations have little incentive to step in.[125]

NGOs can sometimes assist governments in implementing the provisions of environmental regimes. This can include offering assistance in drafting national legislation, providing technical and scientific assistance on relevant issues, and brokering the provision of essential financial support. NGOs can also influence regime formation by monitoring compliance with an agreement once it goes into effect. Investigation and reporting by NGOs can put pressure on parties that are violating provisions of an agreement. They can demonstrate the need for a more effective enforcement mechanism (or for creation of a mechanism where none exists) or help build support for further elaboration or strengthening of the existing regime rules.

This NGO function has been especially important with regard to the CITES and whaling regimes. The international Trade Records Analysis of Flora and Fauna in Commerce (TRAFFIC), a joint wildlife-trade monitoring program of WWF and IUCN, plays a vital role in supplementing the CITES Secretariat in monitoring the compliance of various countries with CITES bans on trade in endangered species.[126] The World Resources Institute and other NGOs in the United States and the EU produce detailed reviews of national climate action plans. Greenpeace's aggressive reporting of hazardous wastes dumped in violation of the Basel Convention helped build support for a full ban on international shipping of such wastes to non-OECD countries.

BUSINESS AND INDUSTRY

Private business firms, especially multinational corporations, are important and interested actors in global environmental politics. Their core activities, although often essential, consume resources and produce pollution, and environmental regulations can directly affect their economic interests. Corporations also have significant assets for influencing global environmental politics. They have good access to decision makers in most governments and international organizations and can deploy impressive technical expertise on the issues in which they are interested. They have national and international industrial associations that represent their interests in policy issues, as well as significant financial and technical resources that are important for developing solutions.

Corporations often oppose national and international policies that they believe will impose significant costs on them or otherwise reduce expected profits. Indeed, at times corporations have worked to weaken proposed or existing global environmental policies, including those on ozone protection, climate change, whaling, hazardous wastes, chemicals, and fisheries. Corporations sometimes support an international agreement if it will create weaker regulations on their activities than the regulations they expect to be imposed domestically.

At the same time, however, corporate interests vary across companies and sectors, and some corporations have supported creating strong national and international environmental policy. For example, companies that market substitute products or processes for an environmentally harmful activity or whose economic interests will be harmed by further environmental degradation lobby governments and IGOs for greater environmental protection. Corporations without a direct economic interest in an issue might support environmental policies to enhance their reputation, to attract attention from potential customers, or when senior leaders believe such action is simply the right thing to do.

Similarly, corporations in countries with existing strong domestic regulations on an activity with a global environmental dimension tend to support international agreements that will impose similar standards on competitors abroad. For example, on fisheries-management issues, the US and Japanese fishing industries are more strictly regulated on various issues of high-seas fishing, particularly quotas on bluefin tuna and other highly migratory species, than other Asian fishing states (Republic of Korea, China, Taiwan, and Indonesia); their respective fishing industries therefore pushed the United States and Japan to take strong positions on regulation of high-seas fishing capacity in FAO negotiations in 1998.

A particular industry's interests regarding a proposed global environmental regime are often far from monolithic. On ozone, climate change, biodiversity, and fisheries, industries have been divided either along national lines or among industry sectors or subsectors. When companies see a positive stake in a global environmental agreement, they can dilute the influence of other companies that seek to weaken it. In 1992, the Industrial Biotechnology Association opposed the biodiversity convention because it feared the provisions on intellectual property rights would legally condone existing violations of those rights.[127] But the issue was not a high priority for most of the industry, and two of its leading member corporations, Merck and Genentech, believed the convention would benefit them by encouraging developing countries to negotiate agreements with companies for access to genetic resources. After those companies joined environmentalists in calling for the United States to sign the convention in 1993, the Industrial Biotechnology Association came out in favor of signing it.[128]

Similarly, US industries seeking to promote alternatives to fossil fuels began lobbying at UNFCCC meetings in 1994 to reduce the influence of pro–fossil fuel industries, which had previously monopolized industry views on the issue. Similarly, because global insurance companies are concerned about the increased hurricane and storm damage that significant climate change would likely cause, they support GHG emissions reductions and have tried to raise awareness among corporations regarding the dangers of climate change, including by conducting research projects on its negative economic consequences as well as the future impacts of storms and floods.[129]

Influence on Regime Formation

Business and industry affect global environmental regimes by influencing regime formation and by undertaking business activities that either weaken a regime or contribute to its effectiveness. To influence the formation of regimes, corporations attempt to do the following:

- Shape the definition of the issue under negotiation in a manner favorable to their interests;

- Fund and distribute targeted research and other information supportive of their interests;
- Initiate advertising campaigns to influence public opinion;
- Persuade individual governments to adopt a particular position on a regime being negotiated by lobbying it in its capital; and
- Lobby delegations to the negotiating conference on the regime.

Corporations had great success during the issue-definition phase associated with creation of the International Convention for the Prevention of Pollution of the Sea by Oil (1954). The major oil companies and global shipping interests (most of which the oil companies owned directly or indirectly) were the only actors with the technical expertise to make detailed proposals on maritime oil pollution. The technical papers submitted by the International Chamber of Shipping, comprising thirty national associations of ship owners, and the Oil Companies International Marine Forum, representing the interests of major oil companies, defined the terms of the discussion[130] and ensured that the convention would be compatible with oil and shipping interests—and quite ineffective in preventing oil pollution of the oceans. That degree of success in defining an issue is unlikely to recur in the future because governments and NGOs now have more expertise on issues being negotiated; furthermore, NGOs are better organized and more aggressive.

In most global environmental issues, corporations have relied on their domestic political clout to ensure that governments do not adopt strong policies adversely affecting their interests. The domestic US industry most strongly opposed to a ban on hazardous waste trade, the secondary-metals industry, helped persuade US officials to block such a ban in the negotiation of the Basel Convention. And on ozone depletion, Japan agreed to a phaseout of CFCs only after some of its largest electronics firms agreed they could eliminate their use.

For many years, industrial lobbies in the United States succeeded in reducing the executive branch's flexibility in climate-change negotiations. Some of the most powerful trade associations launched the Global Climate Information Project in 1997. Through a multimillion-dollar print and television advertising campaign, the project cast doubt on the desirability of emissions controls in the Kyoto Protocol, then entering the final stages of negotiation, by arguing that such controls would raise the price of gasoline, heating oil, and consumer goods and reduce the competitiveness of American businesses. An alliance of business and labor interests succeeded in persuading the US Senate to vote 95–0 for a resolution stating that the United States should not participate in a climate treaty that would require US GHG reductions without similar commitments from large developing countries or that would result in serious harm to the US economy.[131]

Industry associations have been actively involved in influencing negotiations on several other global environmental regimes. Sometimes, industries with particular technical expertise or relatively unchallenged influence over the issue have been part of a key country's delegation. For example, the Japanese commissioner to the IWC has generally been the president of the Japanese Whaling Association.[132] US and Canadian food manufacturers have participated on US delegations to the FAO's Codex Alimentarius Commission, which sets international food standards.[133] The Israeli delegation to some ozone-layer negotiations included officials from a methyl bromide manufacturer during key negotiations on expanding controls on the chemical.[134] The Global Climate Coalition, an industry group, worked closely with the delegations from the United States and Saudi Arabia during the negotiation of the UNFCCC.

Like NGOs, representatives of corporate interests lobby negotiations by providing information and analysis to the delegations most sympathetic to their cause. For example, at different times during the climate-change negotiations, coal and oil interests actively advised the US, Russian, and Saudi delegations on how to oppose or weaken proposals that they believed would harm the fossil-fuel industry.[135] Industry groups had a particularly strong presence at the negotiating sessions for the Cartagena Protocol on Biosafety, with eight industry groups represented at the first round of negotiations in 1996 and twenty such groups from many different countries present at the final meetings in 1999.[136] Individual corporations, among them Monsanto, DuPont, and Syngenta (formerly Novartis and Zeneca), also sent their own representatives to many of the meetings. Chemical manufacturers actively participate in meetings of the Stockholm and Rotterdam Conventions, submitting information and speaking during the negotiations as well as meeting with particular delegations.[137]

Corporations may facilitate or delay, strengthen or weaken global environmental regimes by actions that directly affect the environment. They may take these actions unilaterally or based on agreements reached with their respective governments. Such actions can be crucial to a government's ability to commit itself to a regime-strengthening policy.

For example, the US chemical industry delayed movement toward an international regime for regulating ozone-depleting CFCs in the early 1980s, in part by reducing their own research efforts on CFC substitutes following the election of President Ronald Reagan, whose administration generally opposed additional environmental regulations.[138] Later, after developing effective substitutes, DuPont gave impetus to an accelerated timetable for a CFC phaseout by unilaterally pledging to phase out their production of CFCs ahead of the schedule already agreed on by the Montreal Protocol parties. In 1989, Nissan and Toyota pledged to eliminate

CFCs from their cars and manufacturing processes as early as the mid-1990s. In 1992, Ford Motor Company pledged to eliminate 90 percent of CFC use from its manufacturing processes worldwide by the end of that year and to eliminate all CFCs from its air conditioners and manufacturing by the end of 1994.

Early in the climate-change negotiations, the Japanese auto industry, which accounted for 20 percent of Japan's CO_2 emissions, adopted a goal of improving fuel efficiency by 8.5 percent by 2000, encouraging the Japanese government to commit to stabilize national CO_2 emissions at 1990 levels by 2000.[139] More recently, numerous corporations around the world have pledged to reduce their GHG emissions and to improve their environmental accounting.[140]

Industry and Nonregime Issues

Corporations can also have significant influence on a global environmental issue when no binding international regime governs the issue. For example, the agrochemical industry once enjoyed strong influence on the FAO's Plant Protection Service, which was responsible for the organization's pesticide activities. The industry's international trade association even had a joint program with the FAO to promote pesticide use worldwide until the 1970s.[141] This influence was instrumental in carrying out the industry's main strategy for avoiding binding international restrictions on sales of pesticides in developing countries. Instead of binding rules, the FAO drafted a voluntary code of conduct on pesticide distribution and use between 1982 and 1985 in close consultation with the industry.

In 1991, at the request of UNCED Secretary-General Maurice Strong, Swiss industrialist Stephan Schmidheiny enlisted forty-eight corporate chief executives from all over the world to set up the Business Council for Sustainable Development to support the objectives of the Earth Summit. The group issued a declaration calling for changes in consumption patterns and for the prices of goods to reflect environmental costs of production, use, recycling, and disposal.[142] In January 1995, the business council and the World Industry Council for the Environment, an initiative of the International Chamber of Commerce, merged into the World Business Council for Sustainable Development, which has become a coalition of more than two hundred international companies committed to sustainable development via the three pillars of economic growth, ecological balance, and social progress. With members from thirty-five countries and more than twenty major industrial sectors, the World Business Council for Sustainable Development addresses a range of issues, including corporate social responsibility, access to clean water, capacity building, sustainable livelihoods, harmonization of trade law with MEAs, and development of public–private partnerships in key areas of sustainable development, including energy and climate.[143]

CONCLUSION

State and nonstate actors play key roles in the creation and implementation of national and international environmental policy. State actors play the primary roles in determining the outcomes of issues at stake in global environmental politics, but nonstate actors—IGOs, treaty secretariats, NGOs, and corporations—influence the policies of individual state actors toward global environmental issues as well as the international negotiation process itself. Whether a state adopts the role of lead state, supporting state, swing state, or veto state on a particular issue depends primarily on domestic political factors and on the relative costs and benefits of the proposed regime. But international political-diplomatic consequences can also affect the choice of role.

IGOs, especially UNEP, have played important roles in regime formation by helping to set the international agenda and by sponsoring and shaping negotiations on global environmental regimes and soft-law norms. The Bretton Woods institutions (World Bank and IMF) and certain UN agencies, particularly UNDP and FAO, influence state development strategies through financial, development, and technical assistance. IGOs also can influence state policy through research and advocacy of specific norms at the global level. Treaty secretariats, a subset of IGOs, can influence the behavior of political actors by acting as knowledge brokers and through the creation, support, and shaping of intergovernmental negotiations and cooperation.

NGOs influence environmental regimes by defining issues, swaying the policies of governments, lobbying at intergovernmental negotiations, providing information and reporting services, proposing convention text, and monitoring the implementation of agreements. They have also sought to change the policies and structure of major international institutions, such as the World Bank and the World Trade Organization (WTO; see Chapter 6), with varying degrees of success. They have been more successful when the target institution depends on funding from a key state that the NGOs can influence and less successful when the institution is relatively independent or has no tradition of permitting NGO participation in its processes.

Corporations also influence regime creation and expansion. Business and industry groups utilize technical expertise, privileged access to certain government ministries, and political clout with legislative bodies in attempts to either weaken or strengthen particular aspects of a regime. They can also directly affect the ability of the international community to meet regime goals by their own actions. They are able to maximize their political effectiveness in shaping the outcome of a global environmental issue when they can avert negotiations on a binding regime altogether.

3

The Development of Environmental Regimes:

Stratospheric Ozone, Hazardous Waste, Toxic Chemicals, and Climate Change

The development of global environmental regimes generally involves five interrelated processes or stages: agenda setting and issue definition, fact finding, bargaining on regime creation, regime implementation, and regime review and strengthening. The length of time each stage takes can vary greatly. The stages are also not always distinct; the issue-definition stage often overlaps with the fact-finding stage, which may, in turn, overlap with the bargaining stage; the implementation stage continues during the regime-review stage. Nevertheless, examining negotiations through these stages provides a framework that reduces some of the complexities of multilateral negotiations to a more manageable level for understanding and analysis.

Agenda setting and issue definition involve bringing the issue to the attention of the international community and identifying the scope and magnitude of the environmental threat, its primary causes, and the type of international action required to address the issue. An issue may be placed on the global environmental agenda by one or more state actors, by an international organization (usually at the suggestion of one or more member states), or by a nongovernmental organization (NGO). The actors that introduce and define the issue often publicize new scientific evidence or theories, as they did for ozone depletion, fisheries, and toxic chemicals. Issue definition may also involve identifying a different approach to international action on a problem, as it did for whaling, desertification, hazardous waste, and trade in endangered species.

Fact finding involves studying the science, economics, policy, and ethics surrounding the issue. This is done both to improve understanding of the issue and to build international consensus on the nature of the problem and the most appropriate international actions to address it. Fact-finding efforts in different issue areas vary from well-developed to nonexistent. Sometimes an intergovernmental organization (IGO) can bring key actors together in an attempt to establish a baseline of facts on which they can agree, as the United Nations Environment Programme (UNEP) did in building support for negotiations on persistent organic pollutants (POPs). Sometimes states create a scientific body to review existing information and develop comprehensive consensus reports, as governments did when they created the Intergovernmental Panel on Climate Change (IPCC) prior to the start of global negotiations. When successful fact finding and consensus building do not occur before negotiations begin, scientific facts are more likely to be challenged by states opposed to international action. This occurred early in international discussions regarding the ozone layer. However, fact-finding efforts can be agreed on later in the process, even after negotiations begin, potentially resulting in greater consensus regarding the science and possible policy approaches (something that also occurred in the development of the ozone regime). At the same time, debates concerning key scientific and related facts can sometimes continue for years, even after a regime has been created, as we see in some aspects of the whaling regime.

The regime-creation stage involves bargaining among nation-states (with other actors sometimes playing important roles) on the goals and content of global policy to address the issue. The fact-finding stage often shades into this bargaining stage. Meetings ostensibly devoted to establishing the scope and seriousness of the problem may also include attempts to delineate or discuss policy options.

The nature of global environmental politics means that regime proponents face difficult questions during the bargaining process. To be truly effective, a regime to mitigate a global danger such as ozone depletion or climate change must eventually have the participation of all states that contribute significantly to the problem. However, at some point, negotiators must determine whether to go ahead with a less-than-optimal number of signatories or to accommodate veto-state demands. These can be difficult decisions. Can the regime successfully address the problem without the participation of particular nations? Will the agreement be successful if it has universal support but is weakened by compromises with veto states?

The outcome of the bargaining process depends in part on the bargaining leverage and cohesion of the veto coalition. Veto states can prevent the creation of a strong international regime by refusing to participate in it, or they can weaken it severely by insisting on significant concessions. In certain cases, an agreement may form without key members of the veto coalition and thus remain relatively ineffective, as in the Kyoto Protocol. In other cases, as happened with forests, a regime cannot be created. In some cases, as in the ozone regime, an effective regime can form or be strengthened through difficult compromises among veto and lead states or when veto states change their position after receiving a particular concession, in response to new scientific information, as a result of changes in their domestic politics, or in response to new technological developments and economic incentives.

Successful regime building does not end with the signing or ratification of a global environmental convention. Once established, a regime must be implemented. Most regimes also contain important provisions for parties to review and, if they choose, to augment its effectiveness. In the review and strengthening stage, which exists in parallel with regime implementation, parties negotiate if and how to make the central provisions clearer or more stringent, how to improve implementation, and/or how to expand the scope of the regime. Regime strengthening may occur because new scientific evidence becomes available, political shifts take place in one or more major states, new technologies make addressing the environmental issue less expensive, or the existing regime is ineffective in bringing about meaningful actions to reduce the threat.

The process of regime review and strengthening takes place within the processes mandated by the regime's central convention. The most important elements usually involve formal agreement by the convention's Conference of the Parties (COP) to strengthen or expand binding rules, normative codes of conduct, or regime procedures. This type of regime strengthening usually takes one of three forms.

First, the COP can adopt a new treaty, usually called a protocol, which establishes new, concrete commitments. Examples of this convention-protocol approach include when parties to the 1985 Vienna Convention for the Protection of the Ozone Layer adopted the 1987 Montreal Protocol and the parties to the 1992 United Nations Framework Convention on Climate Change (UNFCCC) adopted the 1997 Kyoto Protocol. Parties to the 1979 Convention on Long-Range Transboundary Air Pollution, a regional treaty covering the Northern Hemisphere, have adopted eight protocols that address particular types and sources of pollution.

As noted in Chapter 1, a framework convention does not establish detailed, binding commitments, usually because negotiators could not reach agreement on such measures. Rather, framework conventions typically acknowledge the importance of the issue, mandate further study and information sharing, encourage or require the development of national or regional plans to address the threat, and create a COP for further consideration of the issue. Protocols to a framework convention are entirely new treaties and must be ratified by a certain number of states, as specified in the protocol, to enter into force. Only countries that opt in via formal ratification are bound by the terms of the new protocol. Thus, the United

States ratified and is obligated to implement the UNFCCC but did not ratify and is not obligated to abide by the Kyoto Protocol.

The two-stage convention-protocol approach allows the international community to establish the institutional and legal framework for future work even when agreement does not exist on the specific actions to be taken. However, the convention-protocol approach has been criticized for taking too much time. For example, after the UNFCCC was signed, it took five years to negotiate the Kyoto Protocol and then more than seven years for the protocol to enter into force. Yet the two-stage approach is often a negotiating necessity. The weaker framework convention is chosen not as a preferred option by lead states but because it represents the limit of what veto states will accept.

In the second type of regime strengthening, a COP formally amends the treaty, changing or adding provisions in the main text or binding annex. Examples include expanding the lists of chemicals controlled in the ozone regime, uplisting species such as the African elephant in the Convention on International Trade in Endangered Species of Wild Fauna and Flora (CITES), and establishing a moratorium on commercial whaling by the International Whaling Commission (IWC). Regime strengthening by formal amendment normally requires reaching decisions by consensus, with all parties agreeing; if that is not possible, some treaties allow approval by vote (usually a two-thirds or three-fourths supermajority of those present and voting). In most cases, states must then formally ratify the amendment, in a process similar to ratification of the original treaty. States that choose not to ratify the amendment are not bound by it.

In a few regimes, certain amendments do not require formal ratification to become binding commitments; however, in most of these treaties, parties have a period of time during which they can opt out if they do not wish to be bound by the amendment. For example, CITES and the IWC allow amendment by two-thirds and three-fourths majorities, respectively, but both have opt-out provisions for amendments. The Stockholm Convention allows each party to choose (at the time it joins the regime) if it will be immediately bound when additional toxic chemicals are added to the regime or if it wants to preserve its right to opt in by formally ratifying the amendment each time controls are placed on a new chemical. These types of opt-out and opt-in arrangements allow changes to take effect, at least for some parties, without long ratification delays, but if they are not designed or managed effectively, they risk creating confusing situations in which many different parties are subject to many different sets of rules.

In the third type of regime strengthening, some treaties allow the COP to mandate important new or stronger actions without a formal amendment or protocol procedure. These mechanisms exist to allow parties to change regime terms or technical details rapidly in response to new information and without the delays produced by ratification requirements. Many regimes allow the COP to make binding decisions on matters related to regime implementation, operation, or other issues, provided that the decisions do not alter the text of the treaty. In most cases these decisions are reached by consensus (albeit sometimes with some states not perfectly happy), but some regimes allow for supermajority votes if consensus cannot be reached.

Other regimes go even further, allowing COP decisions to alter particular types of binding control measures. For example, the Montreal Protocol allows the Meeting of the Parties (MOP) to adjust the targets and timetables for chemicals already controlled by the regime. (There is no functional difference between a COP and a MOP. Most treaties use the term *COP* but some protocols, such as agreements created under another treaty that has its own COP, use *MOP*.) Such decisions should be reached by consensus, but if all efforts at consensus fail, the treaty allows voting approval by a supermajority, although no vote has yet been held on these issues. New ozone-depleting chemicals can be added to the Montreal Protocol only by formal amendments, which require ratification. However, once a chemical is listed in the treaty, this innovative adjustment mechanism allows parties to strengthen the protocol's controls rapidly in response to new scientific information and technological developments. The Basel Convention allows substantive decisions to be made by a two-thirds majority of those present and voting, without any opt-out provision for those who oppose it. The Stockholm Convention provides for the COP to change certain technical annexes and other aspects of the convention without requiring formal ratification by parties (although changes to other aspects of the convention require either formal amendment with ratification or opt-in or opt-out provisions). The Rotterdam Convention allows its COP to add to the list of chemicals covered by its prior informed consent (PIC) procedure, although a consensus of all parties at the meeting is required; there are no provisions for voting.

In this chapter and Chapter 4, we analyze ten different environmental regimes. This chapter discusses the ozone, hazardous waste, toxic chemicals, and climate regimes. These regimes all seek to prevent the production, use, emission, and/or improper management of specific substances that endanger the environment and human health. As such, they can all be considered pollution-control regimes, which feature specific rules to limit particular substances from entering the environment. Chapter 4 shifts the discussion to regimes that address shared natural resources: physical or biological systems that extend into or across the jurisdictions of two or more states. In that chapter, we examine the biodiversity, endangered species, forests, desertification, ocean fisheries, and whaling regimes.

These ten regimes span a wide range of issues, actors, interests, political circumstances, and effectiveness. For each case, we outline the environmental issue, delineate key stages in the regime's development, and discuss the role of lead and veto coalitions in shaping the outcomes of bargaining. Their respective content, development, and impact reveal important similarities and differences in regime politics and help us understand why states sometimes do or do not cooperate effectively on global environmental issues.

STRATOSPHERIC OZONE DEPLETION

Ozone is a pungent, slightly bluish gas composed of three oxygen atoms (O_3). Ninety percent of naturally occurring ozone resides in the stratosphere, the portion of the atmosphere ten to fifty kilometers (six to thirty miles) above the earth. Commonly called the ozone layer, stratospheric ozone helps to shield the earth from ultraviolet radiation (UV). Even though only about three of every ten million molecules in the atmosphere are ozone, the ozone layer absorbs all of the deadly UV-C radiation and most of the harmful UV-B radiation emitted by the sun. (*UV-B* and *UV-C* denote electromagnetic radiation of different wavelengths.) Therefore, destruction of the ozone layer would be catastrophic, and significant depletion would be very harmful. Increased UV radiation would cause many more skin cancers and eye cataracts, weaken immune systems, reduce crop yields, harm or kill single-cell organisms, damage aquatic ecosystems, and speed the deterioration of certain plastics and other human-made materials, among other serious impacts.[1] The environmental importance of stratospheric ozone contrasts with that of ground-level ozone, a harmful air pollutant that contributes to respiratory problems and damages plants. Most ground-level ozone is produced by the interaction in sunlight of chemicals from factory and automobile emissions.

In the 1970s, scientists discovered that certain human-made chemicals, called chlorofluorocarbons (CFCs), posed a serious threat to stratospheric ozone.[2] CFCs release chlorine atoms into the stratosphere that act as a catalyst in the destruction of ozone molecules. Created in the 1920s to replace flammable and noxious refrigerants, CFCs are inert, nonflammable, nontoxic, colorless, odorless, and wonderfully adaptable to a wide variety of profitable uses. By the mid-1970s, CFCs had become the chemical of choice for coolants in air-conditioning and refrigerating systems, propellants in aerosol sprays, solvents in the cleaning of electronic components, and the blowing agent for the manufacture of flexible and rigid foam. Scientists later discovered that other chemicals were also ozone-depleting substances (ODS), including halons (a very effective and otherwise safe fire suppressant), carbon tetrachloride, methyl chloroform, and methyl bromide. Each of these substances can release chlorine or bromine atoms into the stratosphere, which then destroy ozone molecules.[3]

The economic importance of these chemicals, especially CFCs, made international controls very difficult to establish.[4] The absence of firm scientific consensus on the nature and seriousness of the problem, antiregulatory campaigns by corporations producing or using CFCs, concerns for the cost of unilateral regulation, worries on the part of developing countries that restricting access to CFCs would slow economic development, and opposition by the then European Community (EC) prevented effective action for many years.

The definition and agenda-setting stage of the ozone-depletion issue began in 1977 and continued until the early 1980s. The fact-finding process also lasted many years because scientific estimates of potential depletion fluctuated from the late 1970s to the late 1980s, and no evidence had yet emerged in nature confirming the theory and laboratory findings. Indeed, when the bargaining process formally began in 1982, the exact nature of the threat was unclear even to proponents of international action.[5]

The United States, which at that time accounted for more than 40 percent of worldwide CFC production, took a lead role in the negotiations in part because it had already banned CFC use in aerosol spray cans, which accounted for a large percentage of total use at that time, and wanted other countries to follow suit and in part because of concern among key actors in the State Department, Environmental Protection Agency, and Congress.[6] However, for an international ozone-protection agreement to succeed, it was essential that all states producing and consuming CFCs join the regime. Thus, the EC, which opposed controls, constituted a potential veto coalition because its member states also accounted for more than 40 percent of global CFC production (exporting one-third of that to developing countries). West Germany supported CFC controls, but the EC position was effectively controlled by the other large producing countries—France, Italy, and the United Kingdom—which doubted the science, wanted to preserve their industries' overseas markets, and wished to avoid the costs of adopting substitutes. Japan, also a major producer and user of CFCs, supported this position.

Large developing countries, including Brazil, China, India, and Indonesia, formed another potential veto coalition. Their bargaining leverage stemmed from their potential to produce very large quantities of CFCs in the future—production that, if it occurred, would eviscerate the effectiveness of any regime.[7] Although most developing countries did not play an active role early in the regime's development, they eventually used this leverage to secure a delayed control schedule and precedent-setting provisions on financial and technical assistance (FTA).

Although negotiations began with an explicit understanding that only a framework convention would be discussed, in 1983, the lead states (the United States, Canada, and the Nordic states) proposed adding binding restrictions on CFC production to the potential treaty. The veto coalition, led by the EC, steadfastly rejected negotiations on such regulations. Thus, the ozone regime's first agreement, the 1985 Vienna Convention for the Protection of the Ozone Layer, affirmed the importance of protecting the ozone layer and included provisions on monitoring, research, and data exchanges but imposed no specific obligations to reduce the production or use of CFCs. Indeed, the convention did not even mention CFCs by name. However, because of a late-stage lead-state initiative, the negotiators agreed to resume talks if further evidence emerged supporting the potential threat.[8]

Only weeks after nations provisionally agreed on the Vienna Convention, British scientists published the first publicly available reports about the Antarctic ozone hole.[9] Publication of its existence galvanized proponents of CFC controls, who argued that the hole justified negotiations to strengthen the nascent regime (despite the lack of firm evidence linking the hole to CFCs until 1989).[10] Thus, faced with domestic and international pressure, the veto states returned to the bargaining table in early 1986. These negotiations concluded in September 1987 with agreement on the Montreal Protocol.

During these negotiations, the lead states—a coalition that now included Canada, Finland, Norway, Sweden, Switzerland, and the United States—initially advocated a freeze, followed by a 95 percent reduction, in production of CFCs over a period of ten to fourteen years. The industrialized-country veto coalition—the EC, Japan, and the Soviet Union—eventually proposed placing a cap on production capacity at current levels. However, because many manufacturers outside the United States possessed significant excess production capacity, even if a cap was imposed, European producers likely would still be able to increase their actual output of CFCs. Lead states responded with a series of counterproposals before eventually proposing a 50 percent cut as a final offer during the last stages of the negotiations. After stating for months that it could not accept more than a 20 percent reduction, the EC relented and accepted the compromise proposal in the final days of the negotiations.

The 1987 Montreal Protocol on Substances that Deplete the Ozone Layer mandated that industrialized countries freeze and then reduce by 50 percent their production and use of the five most widely used CFCs by 2000. Production of three key halons would be frozen on the same terms. Developing countries were given ten extra years to meet each obligation, allowing them to increase their use of CFCs before taking on commitments. Instrumentally, this grace period helped gain agreement from a potential developing-country veto coalition, which argued they deserved access to these important chemicals. Substantively, creating two control schedules was recognition that industrialized countries had emitted almost all of the CFCs in the atmosphere to that point and that developing countries needed access to these important chemicals to aid their economic development. As such, the grace period reflects the principle of common but differentiated responsibilities (CBDR), which has since become a mainstay of international environmental politics. The principle states that all countries have a common responsibility to address global environmental issues but that some countries have special responsibilities to act first or enact more measures because of their larger contribution to the problem or their access to greater financial and technological resources to address it.

The protocol also included important provisions establishing scientific and technological assessment panels to provide parties with independent and authoritative information, requiring parties to report on their ODS production and use, banning trade in CFCs and halons with countries that did not ratify the agreement, creating provisions for reviewing the effectiveness of the regime, and strengthening controls through amendments and adjustments. As noted above, the innovative provision for adjustments allows parties to strengthen controls on chemicals already controlled under the protocol by a decision of the MOP. The MOP meets annually and is the supreme decision-making body of the regime, composed of all countries that have ratified the protocol. Unlike formal amendments, adjustments do not require ratification by countries but instead become binding on all parties immediately after adoption.

The ten-year evolution of the EC position from rejecting all discussion of control measures to proposing a production cap to accepting a compromise 50 percent reduction target reflected several factors: disunity within the EC (Belgium, Denmark, the Netherlands, and West Germany supported CFC regulations), the personal role played by UNEP Executive Director Mostafa Tolba, diplomatic pressure by the United States, pressure from European NGOs, and reluctance of the EC to be seen as the culprit should negotiations fail. The evolution of the lead-state position from seeking a near 95 percent cut to accepting a 50 percent cut reflected the need to include EC countries in the protocol. Understanding that a regime without countries responsible for 40 percent of global production could not succeed, lead states concluded that it was better to compromise at 50 percent cuts (even though these carried far higher adjustment costs for the lead states, as they had already taken most of the lost-cost reduction measures, whereas the Europeans had done almost nothing) in the hope that these cuts could be strengthened in the future, rather than to create a regime without the EC.

The 1987 Montreal Protocol is widely considered a historic achievement in global environmental politics. Six factors stand out:

- It was the first treaty to address a truly global environmental threat.
- The protocol required significant cuts in the production and use of several very important chemicals, central to economic activity in key industries.
- The final agreement was reached in the absence of clear scientific proof concerning the problem, making it perhaps the first prominent example of application of the precautionary principle in a global environmental treaty (even if that precise term does not appear in the treaty).
- The design and effectiveness of key architectural elements of the protocol have influenced aspects of later environmental treaties, including the control measures, reporting requirements, assessment panels, differentiated responsibilities for developing countries, and review procedures.
- The protocol contained clear, innovative, and effective mechanisms for expanding and strengthening the treaty in response to new scientific information.
- The protocol has been a significant success, something that cannot be said of other global environmental agreements.

At the same time, the original Montreal Protocol (before its significant expansion in the 1990s; see Box 3.1) addressed only five CFCs and three halons (ignoring, at least for the time being, other known ODS); required that these chemicals be reduced, not eliminated; neglected to require that CFC alternatives not damage the ozone layer; included no provisions for independent monitoring of ODS production and use; and contained no real provisions for providing FTA to developing countries to help them implement the regime. Thus, while hailing the initial protocol as a great success, some of those most worried about the problem doubted the new agreement would be sufficient to truly safeguard the ozone layer over the long term.[11]

Regime Strengthening

Within months of the adoption of the Montreal Protocol in late 1987, scientists announced that their initial research suggested that CFCs were likely responsible for creation of the ozone hole, which continued to grow larger every year, although natural processes peculiar to Antarctica contributed to its severity. Studies during the next two years confirmed these findings. In March 1988, satellite data revealed that stratospheric ozone above the heavily populated Northern Hemisphere had also begun to thin. In 1989 the regime's Scientific Assessment Panel concluded that

BOX 3.1 OZONE REGIME MILESTONES

1920	In the late 1920s, Thomas Midgley significantly improves the process of synthesizing chlorofluorocarbons (CFCs), leading to new formulations and their eventual widespread use as refrigerants, in air-conditioning, and as aerosol propellants.
1974	Scientists F. Sherwood Rowland and Mario Molina publish their discovery that CFCs could deplete stratospheric ozone.
1976	The US National Academy of Sciences releases a report confirming the scientific credibility of the CFC-ozone depletion hypothesis.
1978	The United States bans the use of CFCs in aerosol spray cans, about 40 percent of US CFC consumption at that time.
1982	Negotiations begin on a global treaty.
1985	British scientists publish discovery of the Antarctic ozone hole.
1985	Vienna Convention for the Protection of the Ozone Layer is adopted.
1986	Negotiations begin on a protocol to restrict ozone-depleting chemicals.
1987	Montreal Protocol on Substances that Deplete the Ozone Layer is adopted.
1989	Ozone regime's Scientific Assessment Panel concludes that peer-reviewed scientific research has confirmed that CFCs are depleting stratospheric ozone.
1990	London Amendment and Adjustment mandates the phaseout of all CFCs and halons, as well as several other ozone-depleting substances, and creates the Multilateral Fund.
1992	Copenhagen Amendment and Adjustment adds binding controls on hydrochlorofluorocarbons (HCFCs) and methyl bromide, accelerates the phaseout schedules on CFCs and halons, establishes the Implementation Committee, and creates essential use exemptions.
1995	Parties agree to phase out methyl bromide with exemptions for critical agricultural uses and quarantine and preshipment applications.
1997	Parties agree to accelerate the methyl bromide phaseout schedule.
1999	Parties agree to accelerate controls on CFCs and halons in developing countries.
2007	Parties agree to accelerate the phaseout of HCFCs.
2015	Parties agree to use the Montreal Protocol to address hydrofluorocarbons and begin negotiations on a possible amendment in 2016.

the world's scientific community had reached broad agreement that CFCs were indeed depleting stratospheric ozone.[12]

This period also saw significant changes in the economic interests of key actors. After strenuously objecting to national and international CFC controls in the 1970s and most of the 1980s, in 1988 DuPont announced that it would soon be able to produce CFC substitutes. DuPont was followed by other large chemical companies, including several in Europe. Now that they could make substitutes, the major CFC manufacturers changed their position. They no longer opposed a CFC phaseout but lobbied instead for an extended transition period and against controls on hydrochlorofluorocarbons (HCFCs), a class of CFC substitutes that deplete ozone but at a significantly reduced rate (see Box 3.2).[13] In response to these scientific and economic changes and to increased pressure from domestic environmental lobbies, the EC abruptly shifted roles.[14]

By June 1990, when the second MOP to the Montreal Protocol convened in London, EC states had assumed a lead role in the difficult negotiations that significantly strengthened the ozone regime. The resulting agreement, the 1990 London Amendment and Adjustment, was historic in its own right, requiring that parties completely phase out the production and use of the original eight CFCs and halons, carbon tetrachloride, and all other CFCs and halons by the year 2000 and methyl chloroform by 2005.[15]

Because the long-term success of the ozone regime also depended on getting large developing countries to participate, a second historic achievement in London was the creation of the Multilateral Fund for the Implementation of the Montreal Protocol. The first such fund established under an environmental agreement, the Multilateral Fund assists developing countries and "countries with economies in transition" in implementing the protocol.[16] The fund addressed demands by many developing countries, especially China and India, which had refused to join the regime until it included specific provisions for financial assistance, especially with regard to gaining access to the new alternatives to CFCs. The Multilateral Fund meets the incremental costs to developing countries of implementing the control measures (the increased cost associated with producing or using ODS alternatives) and also finances the development of national plans, capacity building, technical assistance, training, information sharing, and operation of the fund's secretariat. The Multilateral Fund is replenished every three years. An executive committee made up of seven donor and seven recipient countries is the decision-making body that approves proposals from developing countries, and a free-standing secretariat provides administration. Replenishment levels are negotiated by the MOP. The total budget for the 2015–2017 triennium is $507 million.[17] Since its establishment,

BOX 3.2 CHEMICALS CONTROLLED BY THE MONTREAL PROTOCOL

- **Chlorofluorocarbons (CFCs): Inert, long-lived, nontoxic, noncorrosive, nonflammable, and extremely versatile chemicals widely used (until phaseout by the Montreal Protocol) in refrigeration and air-conditioning systems, in spray cans as aerosol propellants, to make flexible and rigid foams (e.g., seat cushions and Styrofoam), in solvents, and in many other applications. The five most widely used CFC formulations were controlled under the original 1987 Montreal Protocol. The remaining CFCs were regulated under the 1990 London Amendment.**
- **Halons: Used primarily in fire extinguishing systems and first controlled under the 1987 Montreal Protocol.**
- **Carbon tetrachloride: Used primarily as a solvent or cleaning agent but also in fire extinguishers and as an industrial chemical, including in the creation of refrigerants. First controlled under the 1990 London Amendment.**
- **Methyl chloroform: Also used primarily as a solvent. First controlled under the 1990 London Amendment.**
- **Hydrochlorofluorocarbons (HCFCs): Originally developed in the 1950s for air conditioning but not widely used until reformulations were introduced in 1989 as replacements for CFCs. Although much less destructive than CFCs, HCFCs also contribute to ozone depletion and are greenhouse gases (GHGs). First controlled under the 1992 Copenhagen Amendment.**
- **Methyl bromide: A powerfully toxic pesticide and insecticide used in agriculture, especially for high-value crops; fumigating structures to kill pests, especially termites; and quarantine treatment of shipping containers and agricultural commodities awaiting export. First controlled under the 1992 Copenhagen Amendment.**
- **Hydrobromofluorocarbons: Not widely used but added to the Montreal Protocol under the 1992 Copenhagen Amendment to prevent new uses.**
- **Bromochloromethane: A new ozone-depleting substance that some companies sought to introduce to the market in 1998. Added to the Montreal Protocol in the 1999 Beijing Amendment for immediate phaseout to prevent its use.**
- **Hydrofluorocarbons (HFCs): Developed as replacements for CFCs, HFCs are used primarily in air-conditioning systems. HFCs do not deplete stratospheric ozone but are powerful GHGs. In 2015, countries agreed to develop policies under the Montreal Protocol to manage and reduce the use of HFCs.**

the fund has disbursed more than $3.1 billion to support about seven thousand projects in 145 countries and is widely considered a key ingredient in the success of the ozone regime. The existence and effectiveness of the fund has made it easier, both politically and economically, for many developing countries to accept a series of agreements to accelerate ODS phaseout schedules. The fund gave them confidence that financial assistance would be available to assist them in implementing the new controls.[18]

Parties strengthened the regime again in 1992 at the MOP4 in Copenhagen. Acting again in response to evidence of accelerating ozone-layer depletion and progress in the deployment of CFC substitutes, parties accelerated the existing phaseout schedules; added controls on methyl bromide, a toxic fumigant used in agriculture and once the second most widely used insecticide in the world by volume; and agreed to phase out hydrochlorofluorocarbons (HCFCs), the less ozone-depleting CFC substitute, by 2030.[19] The 1992 MOP also created two other important regime elements. Parties established the Implementation Committee, which examines cases of possible noncompliance and makes recommendations to the MOP aimed at securing compliance.[20] The MOP also created "essential use exemptions" that allow a party to propose continued use of certain ODS for specific purposes beyond the final phaseout date if it believes that no viable alternatives exist. The MOP must then formally approve the uses and amounts proposed by the party. While providing a loophole, the inclusion of exemptions was a way to overcome the lowest-common-denominator problem (see Chapter 5) and appease potential veto states from blocking the introduction of faster phaseout dates.

By the conclusion of the 1992 negotiations, the European Union (EU) and United States had largely reversed the roles they played during the 1970s and 1980s. This became even clearer the following year, when the EU led the first in a series of attempts to accelerate the HCFC controls. Opposing them was a veto coalition that included the United States (the key lead state in the 1970s and 1980s), Australia, China, and India, which argued that further restrictions on HCFCs would not reduce damage to the ozone layer enough to justify the extra economic costs; would punish firms that had made significant and good-faith investments in HCFC technologies, preventing them from recouping their investment; increase the use of hydrofluorocarbons (HFCs), which, although not ozone depleting, are potent greenhouse gases (GHGs); and detract attention and resources from other measures to protect the ozone layer. Although parties agreed in 1999 to a modest strengthening of the HCFC controls, this stalemate continued until 2007.

A similar division developed with respect to methyl bromide. Since the early 1990s, NGOs had called for a rapid phaseout of methyl bromide because of its threat to both human health (as a toxic pesticide) and the ozone layer (as an ODS). Many industrialized countries, including the United States and the EU, had taken steps domestically to limit, and in some cases phase out, methyl bromide and supported regulating it under the protocol. However, the United States helped champion a loophole that allowed parties to continue using methyl bromide for critical agricultural uses even after its official phaseout date. This procedure gives the requesting country more latitude in defining what constitutes a critical use than countries have when requesting essential-use exemptions for CFCs and halons. The United States pushed for this new loophole in response to domestic lobbying from influential agricultural interests, particularly in California. The EU and other lead states on the methyl bromide issue reluctantly accepted this new exemption as the price for securing veto-state agreement to phase out most other uses of methyl bromide and in the hope that the adjustment procedure would provide opportunities to speed up the control schedule in the future.[21]

This strategy proved correct when parties agreed in 1997 that industrialized countries would phase out methyl bromide by 2005 and developing countries by 2015 (see Table 3.1). Potential veto states within the developing-country coalition accepted the new requirements, which far exceeded the previous commitment that only required a freeze, in part because the agreement included language enabling them to receive financial assistance earmarked for methyl bromide projects from the Multilateral Fund and because, like the United States, they knew that if necessary, they could exercise the exemption for critical agricultural uses.

Although control measures and multilateral fund replenishments draw the most attention, parties have also strengthened the ozone regime via less glamorous but impactful improvements in reporting and information sharing. Tightening certain technical details, such as reporting, can sometimes serve to reduce an environmentally harmful act through means other than direct regulations.

For example, an unintended consequence of the ozone regime was creation of a global black market in CFCs. So in 1997, parties developed a new licensing system and provisions for targeted information exchanges that made it more difficult to sneak CFCs across borders under false pretenses. Similarly, in 1999, parties agreed to report on the amount of methyl bromide used in their country for quarantine and preshipment applications, how it was applied, and measures taken to control its release into the environment. Prior to its control under the protocol, methyl bromide was widely used to clean shipping containers and other items in order to limit the spread of invasive species. These quarantine and preshipment uses are another large but less controversial exempted use of methyl bromide. Parties recognized (after a push by lead states) that mandatory reporting on the amounts

TABLE 3.1 **Montreal Protocol Chemical Controls**

CHEMICALS	DEVELOPED COUNTRIES' PHASEOUT SCHEDULE*	DEVELOPING COUNTRIES' PHASEOUT SCHEDULE*
Chlorofluorocarbons (CFCs)	Phase out by 1996	Phase out by 2010
Halons	Phase out by 1994	Phase out by 2010
Carbon tetrachloride	Phase out by 1996	Phase out by 2010
Methyl chloroform	Phase out by 1996	Freeze by 2003 at average 1998–2000 levels, reduce by 30% by 2005 and 70% by 2010, and phase out by 2015
Hydrobromofluorocarbons (HBFCs)	Phase out by 1996	Phase out by 1996
Hydrochlorofluorocarbons (HCFCs)	Reduce by 35% by 2004, 75% by 2010, 90% by 2015, and phase out by 2020, allowing 0.5% for servicing purposes during the period 2020–2030	Freeze by 2013 at average 2009–2010 levels; Reduce by 10% by 2015, 35% by 2020, and 67.5% by 2025, and phase out by 2030, allowing for an annual average of 2.5% for servicing purposes during the period 2030–2040
Methyl bromide	Phase out by 2005	Freeze by 2002 at average 1995–1998 levels, reduce by 20% by 2005, and phase out by 2015
Bromochloromethane	Phase out by 2002	Phase out by 2002

Note: This table represents the controls as amended and adjusted by the parties through the 2015 Meeting of the Parties.

*Exemptions exist for continuing production and consumption of small amounts for essential uses or for laboratory and analytical uses of some ozone-depleting substances after the phaseout date, and larger exemptions exist for critical agricultural and quarantine and preshipment uses of methyl bromide.

used for these purposes would provide information useful for discouraging unnecessary or excessive applications and for detecting unapproved diversion of methyl bromide to other uses.

In September 2007, parties marked the twentieth anniversary of the protocol by returning to Montreal for MOP19. In a surprising development, countries agreed to accelerate the HCFC phaseout by a full decade and augment the interim cuts. This agreement, heralded worldwide in environmental policy circles, represented an important accomplishment for addressing both ozone depletion and climate change (as noted, HCFCs are powerful GHGs). It was also the most significant strengthening of ODS controls in a decade and revealed new attitudes on the part of former veto and swing states, with the United States suddenly switching to a lead position on accelerating the HCFC phaseout, emphasizing the positive climate aspects of the move. In an example of the political interlinkages that can arise in environmental politics, in addition to protecting the ozone layer, the United States apparently wanted a climate victory in the ozone negotiations to buttress its image and negotiating position in the parallel climate-change talks.

China, the biggest producer of HCFCs, and India, a longtime opponent of accelerating the HCFC phaseout in developing countries, shifted from veto states to swing states. China is the world's leading manufacturer of air conditioners that use HCFC-22 as a refrigerant. After initially blocking the agreement, China eventually agreed to the new requirements in exchange for political commitments that the next replenishment of the Multilateral Fund would include substantially more funding for HCFC alternatives, which it did. Australia, India, Russia, and other former veto or swing states also relented and chose not to block the agreement. Despite their concerns about the feasibility and cost of speeding up HCFC elimination, they eventually accepted lead-state arguments in support of the new HCFC controls. The potential veto states also did not want the blame for scuttling a deal on the protocol's anniversary.[22] As noted by an observer at the talks, "An agreement on HCFCs was therefore timely and served several interests. Many developing-country delegates saw new policy commitments on HCFCs as a way to ensure continued availability of funding. . . . Industrialized countries saw an agreement on accelerated phaseout of HCFCs as an easy win for climate, [and one that included] action by both developed and developing countries."[23]

The 2007 Montreal Adjustment marked the last major strengthening of regulations on substances that deplete stratospheric ozone. However, subsequent MOPs continued to review, develop, and expand the regime in other ways. As noted above, every three years parties negotiate the replenishment level for the Multilateral Fund. The MOP also reviews work by the Multilateral Fund annually, outlining priorities and adjusting policy as needed. Each year parties review essential-use nominations, which have declined significantly, including critical-use exemptions for methyl bromide.

Finally, parties have recently agreed, after years of debate, to use the ozone regime to address HFCs—potent GHGs invented as replacements for CFCs. Because HFCs are not an ODS, they do not naturally fall under the purview of the Montreal

Protocol. A coalition of lead states, which includes many small island developing states, Canada, Mexico, and the United States, had repeatedly proposed amending the protocol and placing controls on HFCs. Supported by the EU, Norway, Switzerland, and others, they argued that parties to the Montreal Protocol have a responsibility to address HFCs, as these substances might not exist were it not for the treaty's controls on CFCs and HCFCs. Such an amendment would also allow developing countries to receive support from the Multilateral Fund to reduce HFC use and emissions. Their proposals had been blocked repeatedly by a coalition of veto states, led by India, Iran, Kuwait, Saudi Arabia, and others. These states argue that the Montreal Protocol cannot legally address chemicals that do not directly affect the ozone layer; HFCs are needed for economic development, especially as HCFCs are phased out; many alternatives are more expensive; HFC alternatives are not effective in all applications in very high temperature countries; implementing controls on HFCs would take resources away from eliminating HCFCs and methyl bromide; funding for the conversion from HFCs to alternatives would require iron-clad assurances regarding large replenishments of the Multilateral Fund and its use for HFCs; and addressing non-ODS climate issues under the ozone regime complicates the climate negotiations and represents a way for industrialized countries to delay additional binding commitments in the climate regime.[24] However, in 2015, parties reached a general agreement that they could address these concerns while using the ozone regime as a vehicle to manage and reduce the use of HFCs, although the specific goals and methods for controlling HFCs remain to be decided.[25]

The Ozone Regime Today

The ozone regime is widely considered the most successful global environmental regime. The protocol currently mandates the elimination of ninety-six chemicals. The ozone regime has eliminated nearly all production and use of new CFCs, halons, carbon tetrachloride, and methyl chloroform.[26] Despite the exemptions (and perhaps even because of them, as exemptions help keep potential veto states in the regime), methyl bromide production has declined drastically. Although recycling is allowed and exemptions exist for using small amounts of CFCs and halons for approved essential uses and larger amounts of methyl bromide for critical agricultural and quarantine and preshipment applications, their use for these purposes has also declined significantly.[27] HCFC reductions are proceeding in rough accordance with the control schedule. As a result, the atmospheric abundance of all major ODS except HCFCs is declining, as is the amount of chlorine and bromine in the stratosphere, and ozone depletion has largely stabilized.[28] "Because Argentina, Brazil, China, the EU, India, Indonesia, and Thailand, among many other countries, did not take meaningful action to reduce CFCs and other ODS until they joined the Montreal Protocol, and because key ODS alternatives were invented or commercialized in response to controls established by the protocol, these declines [in ODS production, use, and atmospheric abundance] must be attributed to the impact of the ozone regime."[29]

The Ozone Secretariat calculates that without the Montreal Protocol, global CFC consumption would have reached about three million tons in 2010 and eight million tons by 2060, resulting in as much as 50 percent depletion of the ozone layer by 2035.[30] By preventing the increases in UV radiation that would have occurred from this depletion, studies indicate that the Montreal Protocol prevented tens of millions of cases of fatal skin cancer and many more millions of cases of nonfatal skin cancer and eye cataracts, as well as significant damage to plants and ecosystems, including many food crops, and negative impacts on aquatic organisms.[31]

Because most ODS are potent GHGs, the ozone regime has also delivered substantial climate benefits. Just the reductions in CFC and halon emissions prior to 2000 prevented the equivalent of approximately 25 billion metric tons of carbon dioxide (CO_2) emissions—or several times as much as the initial targets of the Kyoto Protocol.[32] The 2007 agreement to speed up the phaseout of HCFCs will eliminate

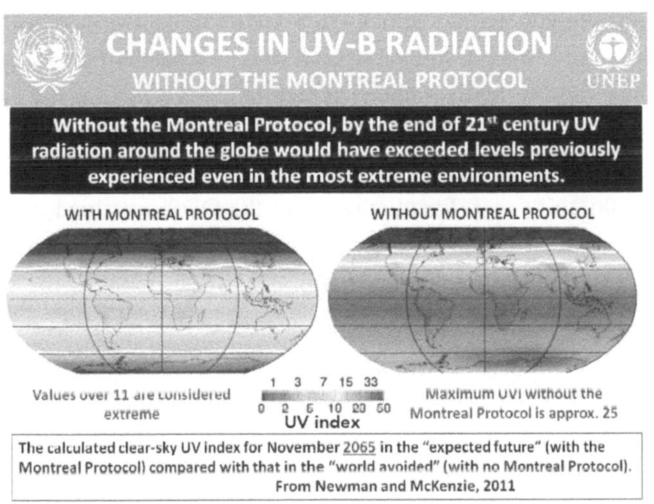

PHOTO 3.1 The Montreal Protocol's Environmental Effects Assessment Panel reported in 2015 that the protocol's success in preventing large increases in UV radiation has now been quantified. *Source:* Presentation by Janet Bornman, Min Shao, and Nigel Paul, "Report of the Environmental Effects Assessment Panel" to the 36th Open-ended Working Group of the Parties to the United Nations Montreal Protocol, 20–24 July 2015, Paris, France. Images on this slide were taken from Paul Newman and Richard Lloyd McKenzie, "UV Impacts Avoided by the Montreal Protocol," *Photochemical and Photobiological Sciences* 10, no. 7 (April 2011): 1152–1160.

the equivalent of the CO_2 produced by millions of cars. Overall, the Montreal Protocol is estimated to have averted GHG emissions equal to more than 135 billion metric tons of CO_2,[33] and any future agreement on HFCs would avert even more.

Despite its many successes, stratospheric ozone levels in general terms remain lower than before CFCs started attacking them, and the Antarctic ozone hole remained near its worst levels as late as 2015.[34] The regime is on pace to reverse this, but doing so requires overcoming a number of challenges.[35] These include completing the total phaseout of CFCs in all developing countries, including essential-use exemptions for metered-dose inhalers; implementing and funding the complete transition away from HCFCs; and ensuring that HCFCs are not replaced by substances with high global-warming potential or other harmful environmental impacts. Parties must also eliminate methyl bromide, which remains an important and contentious challenge despite reductions in the use of critical-use and quarantine and preshipment exemptions. Parties must also deploy substitutes for the few remaining exempted uses of halons, eliminate illegal trade in ODS, prevent the commercial development of new ODS, address HFCs, and continue to provide funding to assist some developing countries in meeting these challenges. Each task includes a different set of hurdles, and success is not guaranteed.

Another critical challenge is effectively managing ODS currently contained in wastes and implementing and funding ODS destruction: "Every kilogram of ODS produced since the 1920s but not yet vented to the atmosphere lies trapped somewhere waiting to escape. Many millions of tons of CFCs remain in old or discarded refrigerators, air-conditioners, insulating foam, and dozens of other products and wastes, collectively known as 'ODS Banks.' A hundred thousand tons of ODS enter the waste stream every year. Eventually, all of the ODS contained in these banks that we do not capture and recycle or destroy will reach the atmosphere."[36] Currently, ODS leakage from banks represents the largest threat to the ozone layer when one factors in the ozone-depleting properties of each chemical.[37] Many developing countries lack the regulatory infrastructure, financial resources, expertise, and equipment to manage or destroy ODS banks in an environmentally sound manner, especially given the immense volume of older refrigerators and air conditioners in use around the world or already in the waste stream. "Addressing ODS banks will require difficult choices regarding resource allocation. Failing to act could lead to unnecessary emissions, while focusing too many resources on ODS banks might preclude effective action in other important areas."[38]

Explaining the Ozone Regime

Four sets of large-scale causal factors shaped development of global ozone policy: the necessity of accommodating veto states, advancing scientific knowledge and increasing consensus about that knowledge, changing patterns of economic interests among the major actors, and the extant development of the regime:[39]

1. As with other regimes discussed in this volume, one major factor affecting the development, timing, and content of the ozone regime is that all countries with significant existing or potential ODS consumption had to be included in the regime for it to succeed. This required lead states to compromise with veto states during key stages of the regime's development.
2. Advancing scientific knowledge led to discovery of the threat, galvanized epistemic networks and certain policymakers, changed public opinion, increased concern about the environmental and economic costs of inaction, undercut arguments by control opponents, and, at different times, significantly enhanced prospects for strengthening the regime.[40]
3. The economic interests of the major actors, including lead and veto states, influenced development of the ozone regime in several different ways. Not surprisingly, economic interests tied to CFCs and other ODS often prevented stronger controls. Yet, during several crucial periods, the development of effective ODS substitutes altered economic interests, helping parties strengthen the regime, most significantly in 1990 and 1992. In addition, the creation and successful operation of the Multilateral Fund significantly impacted the calculations of many developing countries, turning veto and swing states to regime supporters in 1990 and enhancing prospects that developing countries would accept strong control measures in 1992, 1995, 1997, 1999, and 2007.[41]
4. Regime design matters.[42] The existence and framework of the Vienna Convention allowed governments to press forward quickly and effectively on a binding protocol. Provisions of the Montreal Protocol allowed governments to strengthen it far more rapidly than would have been possible otherwise. In particular, the requirements to review the effectiveness of the control measures, the mandates for comprehensive scientific and technical assessments, the ability for parties to adjust existing controls through MOP decisions, and the generally effective operation of the Multilateral Fund all created significant opportunities for strengthening the regime relatively quickly in response to new developments.[43]

The history of global ozone policy illustrates how human activity can upset important global environmental systems, the role that veto coalitions can play in weakening regime rules, how states sometimes shift roles, and the potential impact on global environmental policy of changing domestic politics, advancing scientific knowledge, technological innovations, changing economic interests, and particular sets of regime rules. The impact of these factors can vary significantly over time and from case to case, however, and the future is far from certain. Nevertheless, if countries fully implement all of the requirements in the ozone regime (still an "if") and address ODS banks, then the ozone layer over most of the earth could fully recover around 2050, with the more extensive depletion above Antarctica recovering later this century.

HAZARDOUS WASTE

Hazardous wastes are discarded materials that can damage human health or the environment. This includes wastes that consist of or contain heavy metals, toxic chemicals, infectious medical wastes, and corrosive, flammable, explosive, or radioactive substances. Estimates vary, but several billion tons of hazardous wastes are generated each year, although the precise figure is unknown.[44] Industrialized countries generate the majority of this waste, but quantities have increased rapidly in certain developing countries. Most hazardous waste remains in the country in which it was produced, but some is shipped across international boundaries for a variety of reasons. Most of this movement is among Organization for Economic Cooperation and Development (OECD) countries, but an increasing amount of waste, especially electronic waste (e-waste), gets exported to developing countries.

In the 1970s and 1980s, laws regulating hazardous waste disposal grew in OECD countries, and many individual firms began to seek cheaper sites for disposal.[45] As a consequence, North–South hazardous waste shipments began to increase significantly. Developing countries or firms within them, particularly the poorer states in Africa, Central America, South Asia, and the Caribbean, were tempted by offers of substantial revenues for accepting wastes but lacked the technology or administrative capacity to dispose of them safely. Some of this trade was legal, but much was not, with the wastes entering countries covertly as a result of bribes to corrupt officials or labeled as something else. In some cases, businesses interested in recycling products containing hazardous materials (such as the ship-breaking industry in South Asia and parts of the e-waste industry) circumvented import rules or ignored or obstructed domestic environmental and human-health regulations.

During this period several notorious cases of illegal dumping occurred. In one, the cargo ship *Khian Sea* went to sea in 1986 in search of a disposal site for fourteen thousand tons of incinerator ash containing high levels of lead, cadmium, and other heavy metals. The ash came from incinerators in Philadelphia and had previously gone to New Jersey, but New Jersey refused to accept any more after 1984. The ship spent almost two years at sea, looking for a place that would accept its cargo, during which its name changed twice. In January 1988, it dumped four thousand tons of ash in Haiti; it dumped the remaining ten thousand tons in November at different spots in the Atlantic and Indian oceans.

The issue-definition stage began in 1984 and 1985, when a UNEP-organized working group of legal and technical experts developed a set of voluntary guidelines on the management, disposal, and trade of hazardous wastes (which became the Cairo Guidelines). Designed primarily to assist governments in developing and implementing national policies for managing hazardous wastes, the guidelines also specified notification and consent of the receiving state prior to the export of hazardous waste and verification by the exporting state that the receiving state had disposal requirements at least as stringent as those of the exporting state.

These soft-law guidelines did not satisfy some key actors, most notably African states that received the bulk of illegal hazardous waste exports. Some of these states characterized trade in hazardous waste as a form of exploitation of poor and weak states by rich countries and businesses and sought to define the issue as a problem requiring an outright ban rather than soft-law guidelines or regulations allowing some shipments. This characterization drew support from NGOs and some officials in industrialized states, particularly in Europe.

The bargaining stage began in 1987, when UNEP, at the request of governments comprising UNEP's Governing Council, organized formal negotiations to control international trade in hazardous wastes (see Box 3.3).[46] During the next eighteen months, major differences emerged between African lead states and industrialized countries that were swing and veto states. African states wanted a total ban on waste exports and export-state liability when illegal traffic did occur, in part because many developing countries did not possess the administrative, financial, or technical ability to enforce a ban on their own. Waste-exporting states wanted a convention that would permit the trade, providing that importing countries were notified and agreed to accept it—something known as a prior informed consent or PIC regime.

During the final round of negotiations in March 1989, the veto coalition, led by the United States, took advantage of the fact that some poor countries wished to continue accepting wastes and stated that ban supporters had to accept a PIC regime or get no treaty. At the time, the United States exported only about 1 percent of its hazardous wastes (although this was a large amount by weight), mostly to Canada and Mexico, but it led the veto coalition largely because of an ideological position that rejected limitations on its right to export and practical concerns regarding implementing the proposed treaty. The Organization of African Unity proposed language to ban waste exports to countries that lacked the same level of facilities and technology as the exporting nations and to require inspection of

BOX 3.3 BASEL CONVENTION MILESTONES

1987 **UN Environment Programme (UNEP) adopts the Cairo Guidelines on Waste Trading.**

1987 **UNEP convenes negotiations aimed at creating a treaty to ban or control the international trade of hazardous waste.**

1989 **Basel Convention is adopted.**

1991 **Twelve African countries adopt the Bamako Convention.**

1992 **Basel Convention enters into force.**

1994 **A Greenpeace publication documents a thousand cases of illegal toxic waste exports.**

1995 **Basel Ban Amendment is formally adopted.**

1998 **Fourth meeting of the Conference of the Parties (COP4) adopts Annexes VIII and IX to the convention, further clarifying which wastes the convention regulates.**

1999 **Protocol on Liability and Compensation is adopted.**

2002 **Parties establish the first prioritized plan for implementing the convention.**

2008 **COP9 adopts technical guidelines for the environmentally sound management of mobile phones and establishes Partnership for Action on Computer Equipment.**

2011 **COP10 adopts an updated strategic plan for implementing the convention through 2021 that includes specified goals and performance indicators.**

2013 **Basel, Rotterdam, and Stockholm Conventions hold their first fully coordinated COPs, including simultaneous and separate COP sessions over a two-week period.**

2015 **COP12 again meets in coordination with the Rotterdam and Stockholm COPs. Parties approve additional technical guidelines, augment partnership programs and the environmentally sound management working group, and extend the synergies process.**

disposal sites by UN inspectors, but key industrialized countries rejected these proposals.[47]

The 1989 Basel Convention on Control of Transboundary Movements of Hazardous Wastes and Their Disposal prohibited the export of hazardous wastes to countries with less-advanced storage and disposal facilities unless the importing state had detailed information on the waste shipment and gave prior written consent.[48] Agreements between signatory and nonsignatory states were permitted, although they needed to conform to the terms of the convention. Critics charged that the convention did not go further than existing regulations in most industrialized countries—regulations that had already failed to curb legal or illegal waste traffic. They also noted that the convention lacked precision on key definitions, such as *environmentally sound* and even *hazardous wastes,* and contained no liability provisions to deter illegal dumping or provide cleanup costs.[49]

International Waste Policy Outside the Basel Convention

In April 1989, soon after the formal adoption of the Basel Convention and three years before it entered into force, thirty mostly industrialized countries (not including the United States) pledged to dispose of most of their wastes at home and to ban the export of hazardous wastes to countries that lacked the legal and technological capacity to handle them.[50] Later in 1989, the EC reached a separate agreement, after extended negotiations, to ban waste shipments from its countries to sixty-eight former European colonies in Africa, the Caribbean, and the Pacific. The EC had sought an exception for exports to countries with adequate technical capacity, but developing countries insisted on a total ban.[51]

In 1991, twelve African states signed the Bamako Convention on the Ban of the Import into Africa and the Control of Transboundary Movement and Management of Hazardous Wastes within Africa. Twenty-five countries have ratified the agreement to date. In 1992, Costa Rica, El Salvador, Guatemala, Honduras, Nicaragua, and Panama adopted the Regional Convention on the Transboundary Movement of Hazardous Wastes. In 1995, South Pacific governments, Britain, and France signed the Waigani Convention, which banned the importation of hazardous and radioactive wastes into more than a dozen South Pacific countries. These regional agreements, combined with other unilateral and multilateral policies, initially created stronger hazardous waste mechanisms outside the Basel Convention than within it.

Regime Strengthening: The Ban Amendment and the Liability Protocol

In May 1992, after receiving ratification from the required twenty countries (Article 35), the Basel Convention entered into force, three years after negotiations concluded. It was a weak regime, with limited binding rules and without ratification by any of the major waste-exporting states that composed the veto coalition during the negotiations. In less than two years, however, growing demands for stronger action helped lead states strengthen the regime.

By early 1994, more than one hundred countries had passed domestic legislation banning the import of hazardous wastes, although not all of them had the administrative capacity to do so unilaterally.[52] This development shows an important potential consequence of a global environmental regime: the strengthening of relevant domestic law. Some of the credit must also go to Greenpeace, which published and publicized a report documenting one thousand cases of illegal toxic waste exports.[53] Even the United States, although not a party to the regime, signaled it would support a ban on hazardous waste exports if the ban exempted scrap metal, glass, textiles, and paper, which are widely traded for recycling.[54]

Building on these developments, at COP2 a broad coalition, including the Group of 77 (G-77), pressed for adopting a complete ban on hazardous waste exports from OECD countries to non-OECD countries, including those exported for recycling.[55] They argued that shipments of recyclables often were not for recycling but for dumping and that the OECD countries would never reduce their creation of wastes as long as they could ship some to developing countries. Australia, Canada, Germany, Japan, the Netherlands, the United Kingdom, and the United States countered that any ban should exempt recyclables. China and a number of Central and Eastern European states came out in favor of the G-77 proposal. Greenpeace, demonstrating the impact that NGOs can have within certain regimes at certain times, also made an important contribution by releasing a seven-year study of more than fifty recycling operations in non-OECD countries that provided concrete evidence of widespread dumping of hazardous wastes falsely labeled and shipped as recyclables as well as many other shipments of recyclables that had not been recycled at all but just dumped in developing countries.[56]

Despite intensive lobbying by waste-exporting countries, particularly in support of allowing bilateral agreements on hazardous waste exports for recycling, the G-77 remained firm, agreeing to negotiate only on the timetable for implementing a ban. Confronted with non-OECD unity, the veto coalition began to divide, with some withdrawing their opposition. The veto coalition was also weakened because several of its members, including the United States, had not ratified the Basel Convention and, as nonparties, remained technically outside the decision-making process. They could speak in opposition to the ban, but their views did not officially count and they could not vote if matters came to that. When debate ended, COP2 approved the ban. Countries opposed to the ban obtained nothing more than a delay in its full implementation.

One year later, at COP3, parties significantly strengthened the decision by adopting the ban as a formal amendment to the convention (COP2 had approved the ban in a far less legally binding form). The Ban Amendment prohibits export of hazardous wastes for final disposal or recycling from countries listed in Annex VII of the convention (which currently includes all of the industrialized-country parties) to non–Annex VII countries. The Ban Amendment does not prevent a developing country from receiving hazardous wastes from an industrialized country because they can do so by joining Annex VII. However, as of early 2016, the Ban Amendment still had not received sufficient ratifications to enter into force.[57]

A central reason inhibiting ratification of the Ban Amendment is its prohibition on exports of wastes intended for recovery and recycling. Many industrialized countries, as well as an increasing number of developing ones (including China and India), have significant economic interests in maintaining the trade in wastes for recycling—including ships, electronics, scrap metal, glass, cardboard, paper, and some chemicals. As a result, not only has the Ban Amendment not entered into force, but also the total amount of waste shipments rose sharply during the first decade of the convention's existence, especially wastes intended for recycling. Although recycling in theory is environmentally benign, this activity in certain industries in many developing countries releases air and water pollutants, toxic chemicals, and heavy metals into local environments and the workers.

To remedy this situation, the COP authorized technical working groups to draw up lists of banned and exempted wastes. COP4 approved the first of these lists; in doing so, it diffused industry arguments that nobody knew what the ban was banning. Supporters of the Ban Amendment hoped that the new lists would speed its ratification and implementation. Although this did not occur, many countries that have not ratified the Ban Amendment still support the lists, as they provide greater clarity to other elements of the convention. Beginning in 2011 at COP10, parties have taken a series of decisions that support the overall purpose of the amendment. These include requiring new PIC procedures and use of precise custom codes, updating criteria for classifying particular material as hazardous, and assisting developing countries to improve their capacity to monitor and trace shipments of hazardous wastes. These measures have enhanced prospects that the central purpose of the Ban Amendment can be more widely implemented through other regime mechanisms and may even enhance prospects for further ratifications. As a result, some observers believe that the amendment has already had an impact on domestic law and attitudes in many countries even without entering into force.[58]

In December 1999, COP5 adopted the Basel Protocol on Liability and Compensation, which addressed developing countries' concerns that they lack sufficient funds and technologies to prevent or cope with the consequences of illegal dumping or accidental spills. The protocol establishes provisions for determining liability and compensation for damage resulting from the legal or illegal transnational movement of hazardous wastes. Seventeen years later, however, the liability protocol has not received the ratifications necessary for it to enter into force.

Regime Strengthening: Action Plans, Regional Centers, and Technical Guidelines

Concerned that the Basel Convention was having little practical effect, parties began to identify and review regime priorities and to assist implementation activities. First, in 2002, COP6 established a prioritized action plan for implementing the convention through 2010 that emphasized the environmentally sound management of specific, priority waste streams such as lead-acid batteries, polychlorinated biphenyls (PCBs), used oil, electronics, and obsolete pesticides. This first strategic plan was a success in providing guidance to parties, the secretariat, regional centers, IGOs, NGOs, and corporations regarding the regime's priorities, but developing countries did not implement some actions because of inadequate funding.[59]

COP6 also created a compliance mechanism to review instances where parties, individually or collectively, might have failed to operate in accordance with regime provisions and to make recommendations to improve implementation. Modeled somewhat on the procedure in the Montreal Protocol, the inclusion of a compliance mechanism under the Basel Convention is significant, as similar efforts have not succeeded under the Stockholm Convention (see below).

Parties also strengthened the Basel Convention Regional Centers and affirmed their role in facilitating implementation of the convention in developing countries by building capacity, educating the public, collecting data, reporting, promoting environmentally sound waste management, easing the transfer of cleaner production technologies, and helping to train customs officials. There are now fifteen such centers located in different parts of Africa, Asia, Eastern Europe, and Latin America.

In 2006, an egregious incident of hazardous waste dumping in Côte d'Ivoire served to highlight the original purpose of the convention and the dangers associated with hazardous waste. An old chemical tanker carrying more than four hundred metric tons of heavily contaminated wash water (water used to clean its holds) sailed to Nigeria to deliver a different cargo and then docked in Abidjan, a port city of five million people and the economic capital of Côte d'Ivoire. Under the cover of night, the contaminated wastewater was transferred to tanker trucks belonging to a local company, which then dumped it at sixteen different open-air sites around the city, many near water supplies or fields growing food. At least fifteen people died, thousands were hospitalized, and over a hundred thousand sought medical treatment, overwhelming local hospitals. Many fishing, vegetable, and small livestock activities were halted, associated businesses closed, and workers laid off. Protests erupted over suspicions of (unproven) government corruption in the scandal.[60] The incident highlighted the absence of effective tracking systems for the transboundary movement of hazardous waste and the concern that these shipments, both legal and illegal, might be producing more environmental damage than recognized.

Continuing the effort to strengthen the regime by prioritizing certain activities, in 2011, COP10 adopted an updated action plan and strategic framework for 2012 to 2021 that, for the first time, includes specific goals and performance indicators to measure progress in implementing the Basel Convention. Many delegates "said this was long overdue, stressing that without concrete goals and indicators, it is very difficult to measure progress" and that the new system "will increase transparency and accountability around implementation."[61] However, as they had for many years, developing countries again expressed concerns regarding the lack of adequate financial and technical resources. In their view, the implementation of the strategic framework, including the guidelines on the environmentally sound management of wastes and the steps to stop illegal traffic, would largely depend on the provision of sufficient FTA and related efforts to strengthen the Basel Convention Regional Centers.[62]

The practical impact of the Basel Convention has been strengthened significantly through the development and updating of nonbinding technical guidelines designed to assist industry and governments in managing hazardous waste in an environmentally sound manner. Guidelines are now in place for more than twenty different types of hazardous wastes, including waste oil, biomedical and healthcare wastes, POPs, individual chemicals such as PCBs, obsolete ships, and mobile phones. New or updated guidelines are considered at each COP. The development of technical guidelines provides an important example of effective regime strengthening even when new binding rules are not created.

In a related initiative, parties created the Framework for the Environmentally Sound Management of Hazardous Wastes and Other Wastes. This initiative seeks to develop a common understanding of what environmentally sound management encompasses, tools to support and promote the implementation of environmentally sound management of waste by companies and countries, and strategies to implement environmentally sound management. In 2015, COP12 expanded the initiative's ESM (Environmentally Sound Management) Expert Working Group, which collects information, develops draft manuals and facts sheets, holds regional meetings, and pursues other practical measures.[63]

Regime Strengthening: E-Waste

E-waste comprises discarded, broken, or obsolete electronic devices, including computers, printers, monitors, televisions, phones, and CD, DVD, and MP3 players, as well as their parts and components. Globally, e-waste generation is growing

PHOTO 3.2 A pile of imported computer housings in Guiyu, a town in southern China that is known as one of the world's most notorious destinations for e-waste. Courtesy Basel Action Network, www.flickr.com/photos/basel-action-network/9263493998/.

by about forty million tons a year.[64] Some EU states have life-cycle requirements on certain electronic items, but most countries do not.

E-waste often contains hazardous materials, including heavy metals such as lead, cadmium, and beryllium and a variety of toxic chemicals, including certain flame retardants. Processing e-waste, particularly in developing countries, can yield important resources but can also cause serious pollution and health problems if proper care is not taken to protect workers and prevent release of the pollutants into the environment via direct dumping, poorly designed and operated landfills, open-pit burning, or incinerator exhaust and ashes. A 2015 report published by UNEP found that 90 percent of the world's e-waste is illegally traded, dumped, or improperly disposed of each year.[65]

The immense scope of the e-waste issue was largely unforeseen when countries negotiated the original convention. Parties initiated serious discussions of the growing problem in 2006, approving the Nairobi Declaration, which states that parties will work to promote awareness of e-waste, clean technology, and green design; encourage information exchange from developed to developing countries; improve relevant waste management controls; and prevent and combat illegal traffic.[66]

Two years later, at COP9 in 2008, parties took more concrete steps, adopting specific technical guidelines and an overall guidance document for the environmentally sound management of used and end-of-life mobile phones. The guidelines address design considerations relevant to reducing hazardous waste; the collection, refurbishment, and recycling of used and end-of-life mobile phones; the transboundary movement of collected phones; and the management of hazardous waste from end-of-life mobile phones. The guidelines built on the Mobile Phone Partnership Initiative, launched in 2002, in which manufacturers and service providers partnered with the Basel Convention to develop and promote the environmentally sound management of end-of-life mobile phones. The guidelines were updated again in 2011.

COP9 also established the Partnership for Action on Computer Equipment (PACE), which was patterned after the mobile-phone process. The PACE working group provides a forum for dialogue among governments, industry, NGOs, and academic experts; develops technical guidelines for environmentally sound repair, refurbishment, and recycling of computer equipment and components; offers expert advice and participation in relevant initiatives; and works with the Basel Convention and parties to promote effective action.[67] Although some expressed concern that involving companies would weaken these efforts, others believed that the concerns for market image, financial interests, and technical expertise of many computer and electronic companies could form the basis for productive partnerships on e-waste as they had for the mobile-phone experience. In 2015, COP12 extended the PACE mandate and requested that the PACE working group develop work plans for implementing concrete actions at the regional and national levels.

Addressing other types of e-waste has proven more challenging. In 2015, parties adopted technical guidelines on many categories of e-waste but only on a provisional basis and with explicit statements that national laws supersede these nonbinding guidelines. Despite broad agreement on the danger of e-waste and more than a decade of detailed discussion on the draft guidelines, significant disagreements remained between countries that want the guidelines to allow for robust domestic markets in, and exports or imports of, electronic equipment for reuse, repair, or recycling and other countries, including many in Africa and Latin America, and environmental NGOs that see aspects of such trade as waste dumping.[68] These differences capture a difficult issue within the waste regime: how to allow countries to pursue legitimate reuse, repair, and recycling strategies for a variety of hazardous waste, including e-waste, while also promoting and ensuring environmentally sound management and preventing activities that claim to be reuse and recycling but are actually waste dumping.

Synergies

The technical guidelines and partnerships are part of a new emphasis on the environmentally sound management of the entire life cycle of hazardous substances—production, use, emissions, waste management, and disposal—and enhancing coordination among actors and initiatives to improve effectiveness and augment resources. Along these lines, the synergies initiative seeks more effective global policy on hazardous chemicals and wastes by enabling the Basel, Rotterdam, and Stockholm Conventions—and their COPs, secretariats, regional centers, and subsidiary bodies—to coordinate or even combine certain implementation and administration activities.[69] Supporters believe this will substantially improve the efficiency and effectiveness of all three conventions, enhance information exchange, direct more resources to implementation activities, and yield other benefits, including "advantageous synergies unavailable if the three processes remain entirely distinct."[70] The initiative and a series of specific recommendations have been formally approved, after much debate, by the three COPs. Since 2013, the three conventions have held coordinated COPs; established joint secretariat services with regard to information management, public awareness, budget cycles, and common administrative functions; initiated cooperative use of regional centers; and begun work to synchronize reporting requirements and coordinate other activities.[71]

PHOTO 3.3 Rolph Payet, from the Seychelles, is the first executive secretary of the joint secretariat of the Basel, Rotterdam, and Stockholm Conventions. Courtesy Kiara Worth, IISD/*Earth Negotiations Bulletin*, www.iisd.ca.

Moving Forward

The current global regime for managing hazardous waste and controlling its international movement is quite different from the original weak regime created in 1989. The expanded Basel Convention has helped to eliminate some of the worst forms of toxic-waste dumping, improved the management of hazardous wastes, and established frameworks, guidelines, and partnerships that could portend more improvements in the future. The evolution of the Basel Convention shows how veto power can dissipate when faced with a strong coalition that includes developing countries and some OECD countries. The information, publicity, and political pressure generated by several NGOs, especially Greenpeace and the Basel Action Network, also played an important role. Once the hazardous waste trade issue became a political symbol uniting developing countries, it overcame the leverage of waste exporters on some (but not all) key issues. And once the regime branched out toward efforts to help reduce the creation of certain wastes and improve the management of all wastes (through technical guidelines, partnerships, promoting environmentally sound management, and other initiatives), it expanded its network of supporters and increased its relevance.

Yet the hazardous waste regime faces many challenges. Although promising policy initiatives and economic incentives have emerged to promote more effective management, recycling, and disposal of hazardous waste, several of the central goals of the regime—to reduce the amount of hazardous waste produced, limit its movement, and induce its environmentally sound management—remain difficult to achieve at the global level. Indeed, both the production and the transboundary movement of hazardous waste continue to grow. This trend is difficult to address given the increasing industrialization of many developing countries. For example, a UN study predicts that by 2020 e-waste from discarded computers will be five times higher than in 2007 in India and two to four times higher in China and South Africa; e-waste from televisions will be 1.3 to 2 times higher in China and India; and e-waste from mobile phones will be seven times higher in China and eighteen times higher in India.[72]

In addition, the Ban Amendment and Liability Protocol have not received sufficient ratifications to enter into force, although some countries believe the Ban Amendment could receive sufficient ratification as early as 2017.[73] Furthermore, the United States, one of the largest producers of hazardous waste, still has not ratified the Basel Convention. Several issues, such as the export of hazardous wastes for recycling, e-waste, illegal dumping, and the dismantling of ships, continue to require significant attention.

Finally, parties must grapple with the challenge of securing sufficient funding to support key regime priorities. Delegates have told observers that efforts spent creating and revising the technical guidelines matter little to a developing country that lacks the financial resources or cadres of technically trained personnel to administer and enforce them.[74] As the Basel Convention approaches the twenty-fifth anniversary of its entry into force, addressing these challenges will determine the long-term impact of the hazardous waste regime.

TOXIC CHEMICALS

The development and use of chemicals for commercial purposes accelerated significantly after World War II. Of the millions of chemical substances known in industry and scientific research, tens of thousands have been produced for regular use in the industrial, agriculture, and service sectors. Since the 1960s, more than one hundred thousand chemicals have been registered for commercial use in the EU alone,[75] and around the world more than 248,000 different chemical products are commercially available.[76] A major center of economic activity, the global chemicals industry engages in more than $3 trillion of business annually.[77] Most of this activity remains in industrialized countries, but production and use of all types of chemicals are rising rapidly in developing countries.[78] Indeed, China leads the world in combined chemical purchases and sales.[79]

Many chemicals enter the market and become widely used before systematic assessments are made,[80] and detailed analyses of the potential impacts on human health and the environment exist for only a small number of these substances.[81] Not all chemicals are hazardous, of course, but toxic chemicals are produced or used in virtually every country in the world. Toxic chemicals include poisons, carcinogens, teratogens (affecting offspring), mutagens (affecting genes), irritants, narcotics, and chemicals with dermatological effects. Toxins are released into the environment through the normal use of certain products (e.g., pesticides and fertilizers), industrial and manufacturing practices that involve or produce hazardous chemicals, leakage from wastes, mismanagement, accidents, and intentional dumping. Once they have been dispersed into the environment, the complete cleanup of many toxic chemicals is difficult, sometimes impossible, and their harmful effects can continue for many years.

The issue-definition phase for toxic chemicals began in the 1960s, when concern started to grow about potentially negative impacts from pesticides and other chemicals. Instrumental in this process were both groundbreaking publications, especially Rachel Carson's *Silent Spring,* and high-profile accidents, such as the 1968 tragedy in Kyushu, Japan, in which thirteen hundred people were poisoned after eating rice contaminated with high levels of PCBs.[82] In the late 1960s and early 1970s, new risk assessments led some industrialized countries to adopt domestic regulations on a relatively small set of hazardous chemicals. The United States, for example, banned dichlorodiphenyltrichloroethane, commonly known as DDT, in 1972 and initiated controls on PCBs in 1976.[83] During this period, the OECD became one of the first international organizations to address toxic chemicals, focusing on information exchange and improving scientific understanding and policy measures among its members.

Stimulated in part by discussion on hazardous chemicals at the 1972 United Nations Conference on the Human Environment in Stockholm,[84] governments adopted several multilateral agreements in the 1970s and early 1980s to help protect oceans, regional seas, and rivers from dumping and pollution.[85] In 1976, UNEP created the International Register of Potentially Toxic Chemicals to gather, process, and distribute information on hazardous chemicals. The Food and Agriculture Organization of the UN (FAO) and UNEP led development of both the 1985 International Code of Conduct for the Distribution and Use of Pesticides and the 1987 London Guidelines for the Exchange of Information on Chemicals in International Trade. Unfortunately, many developing countries lacked the regulatory infrastructure that would enable them to use the information made available through these initiatives.[86]

In 1989, amendments to the FAO Code of Conduct and the UNEP London Guidelines created a voluntary PIC procedure to help countries, especially developing countries, learn about chemicals that had been banned or severely restricted in other countries so that they could make informed decisions before they allowed them as imports. Although the voluntary PIC system was seen as a victory for NGOs, which had long called for its adoption, and for developing countries, because they hoped it would assist them in identifying and regulating such imports, many of its supporters also believed that a voluntary system would eventually prove insufficient.[87]

The fact-finding stage, in general terms, began during the formal preparations for the 1992 Earth Summit in Rio, during which governments agreed to devote an entire chapter in Agenda 21 to chemicals. Among other actions, Agenda 21 called on states to create a mandatory PIC procedure and to improve coordination among the many national agencies and international organizations working on chemicals and related issues. To this end, governments created the Intergovernmental Forum on Chemical Safety in 1994 to address coordination among governments and the Inter-Organization Programme for the Sound Management of Chemicals in 1995 to address coordination among international organizations (see Box 3.4).[88] The fact-finding process continued in these bodies.

BOX 3.4 ROTTERDAM AND STOCKHOLM CONVENTIONS MILESTONES

1976 UN Environment Programme (UNEP) creates International Register of Potentially Toxic Chemicals.

1985 Food and Agriculture Organization (FAO) Council adopts International Code of Conduct for the Distribution and Use of Pesticides.

1987 UNEP Governing Council adopts London Guidelines for the Exchange of Information on Chemicals in International Trade.

1989 Amendments to FAO Code of Conduct and UNEP London Guidelines create a voluntary prior informed consent (PIC) procedure for trade in toxic chemicals trade

1992 Agenda 21, adopted by the Rio Earth Summit, calls on governments to create a mandatory PIC procedure by 2000 and improve coordination among both national governments and international organizations working on chemical issues.

1994 Intergovernmental Forum on Chemical Safety (IFCS) created to enhance coordination among governments.

1995 Inter-Organization Programme for the Sound Management of Chemicals (IOMC) created to coordinate efforts among international organizations.

1995 UNEP's Governing Council calls for international assessment of twelve persistent organic pollutants (POPs), known as the dirty dozen.

1995 The Intergovernmental Conference to Adopt a Global Programme of Action for Protection of the Marine Environment from Land-Based Activities calls for a legally binding treaty targeting the dirty dozen.

1996 Formal negotiations begin on potential global PIC convention.

1996 A UNEP/IFCS working group, established by the IOMC, concludes that scientific evidence supports international action to reduce risks posed by POPs.

1997 UNEP's Governing Council authorizes formal negotiations to create global POPs treaty.

1998 Rotterdam Convention on the Prior Informed Consent Procedure for Certain Hazardous Chemicals and Pesticides in International Trade adopted.

1998 Formal negotiations begin on potential POPs treaty.

2001 Stockholm Convention on Persistent Organic Pollutants adopted. These POPs include (1) pesticides: aldrin, chlordane, DDT, dieldrin, endrin, heptachlor, mirex, and toxaphene; (2) industrial chemicals:

continues

BOX 3.4 ROTTERDAM AND STOCKHOLM CONVENTIONS MILESTONES *continued*

	hexachlorobenzene and polychlorinated biphenyls; and (3) unintentionally produced POPs: dioxins and furans.
2004	**Stockholm and Rotterdam Conventions enter into force.**
2007	**POPs Review Committee concludes first set of evaluations and formally recommends parties add substances to the Stockholm Convention.**
2008	**Working group established by the Basel, Rotterdam, and Stockholm Conventions' COPs submit formal synergies proposal.**
2009	**Perfluorooctane sulfonate (PFOS), chlordecone, hexabromobiphenyl, hexabromodiphenyl ether and heptabromodiphenyl ether, alpha hexachlorocyclohexane, beta hexachlorocyclohexane, lindane, pentachlorobenzene, and tetrabromodiphenyl ether/pentabromodiphenyl ether added to Stockholm Convention; parties give final approval to synergies initiative.**
2011	**Endosulfan added to Stockholm Convention. Aldicarb, alachlor, and endosulfan added to the Rotterdam Convention.**
2013	**Basel, Rotterdam, and Stockholm Conventions hold first fully coordinated COPs and identify concrete areas where synergies could be achieved. Hexabromocyclododecane added to Stockholm Convention. Azinphos-methyl, pentabromodiphenyl ether, octabromodiphenyl ether, and PFOS added to Rotterdam Convention.**
2015	**Pentachlorophenol, hexachlorobutadien, and polychlorinated naphthalenes added to Stockholm Convention. Methamidophos added to the Rotterdam Convention.**

Governments then asked UNEP and the FAO to convene global negotiations with the goal of adopting a binding PIC procedure. The result was the 1998 Rotterdam Convention on the Prior Informed Consent Procedure for Certain Hazardous Chemicals and Pesticides in International Trade, which mandates that parties export certain toxic chemicals only with the informed consent of the importing party.[89]

During this period, concern began to grow regarding a particular set of toxic chemicals known as persistent organic pollutants, or POPs. Scientists and policymakers usually define POPs as possessing four key characteristics: toxicity, persistence, bioaccumulation, and long-range environmental transport.

POPs are toxic. Although extensive variations occur across substances, species, and exposures, the observed or suspected impacts of POPs on wildlife and humans include reproductive disorders, birth defects, cancers, developmental impairment, damage to central and peripheral nervous systems, immune system impairment, and endocrine disruption.[90]

POPs are stable and persistent compounds that resist photolytic, chemical, and biological degradation. This means that once released into the environment, most POPs remain toxic for years before breaking down.

POPs bioaccumulate. Once ingested, they are readily absorbed by, and remain in, the fatty tissue of living organisms. Over time, POP concentrations can build up in animals and people, potentially reaching ten thousand times the background levels found in the surrounding environment. Fish, birds, mammals, and humans can absorb high concentrations of POPs quickly if they eat multiple organisms in which POPs have already accumulated. Mammals, including humans, can then pass these chemicals to their offspring through breast milk.

Finally, POPs can engage in long-range transport across national borders and have been found in ecosystems, waterways, animals, and people thousands of kilometers from the nearest location of their production, use, or release. POPs travel through air currents, waterways, migrating animals, food chains, and a process known as the grasshopper effect, in which POPs released in one part of the world can, through a repeated process of evaporation and deposit, be transported through the atmosphere to regions far away from the original source (see Figure 3.1).

FIGURE 3.1 **Migration of Persistent Organic Pollutants**

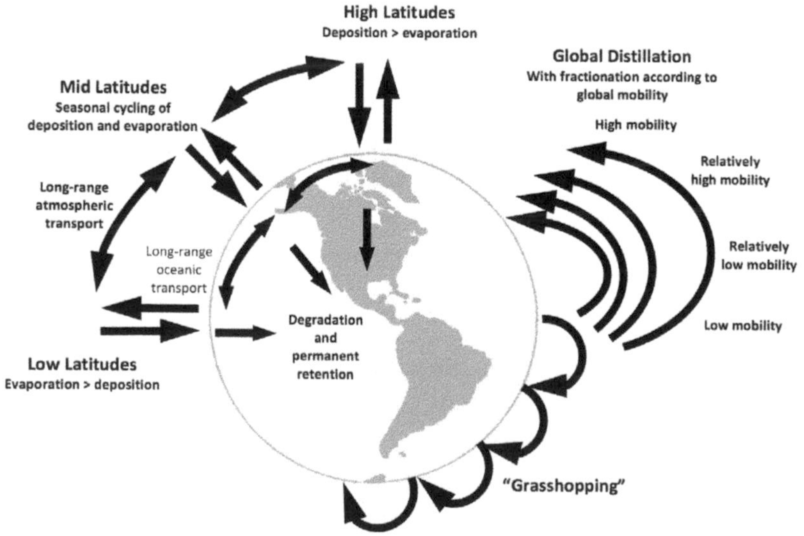

In the 1980s and 1990s, Canada and Sweden played lead roles in the issue-definition and fact-finding phases by both supporting POPs research and putting POPs on the agenda of several international forums. Much of this work had been initiated after scientific studies found very high levels of certain POPs in the Arctic, including in wildlife and even in the breast milk of Inuit women in northern Canada, thousands of miles from the nearest source of emissions.[91] These findings and subsequent studies added a normative component to the issue-definition phase because POPs were now seen as a threat to the food chain, and thus the cultural survival, of the Inuit.[92]

The issue-definition phase reached a turning point in May 1995, when UNEP's Governing Council called for an international assessment of twelve POPs known as the dirty dozen: the pesticides aldrin, chlordane, DDT, dieldrin, endrin, heptachlor, mirex, and toxaphene; the industrial chemicals PCBs and hexachlorobenzene (which is also a pesticide); and two unintentionally produced substances, dioxins and furans, which are created when certain substances burn or through particular industrial activities. UNEP acted in response to growing scientific data regarding the transnational movement and toxicity of POPs, increasing evidence of POPs in various food chains, and the cumulative political efforts of the lead states, NGOs, and representatives of the Inuit and other indigenous peoples whose traditional food sources were becoming contaminated by POPs. Organizations and initiatives with foci outside of chemicals also called for negotiations, revealing the important impact that action in multiple venues can have on initiating or advancing the fact-finding or negotiation stages.

In response to UNEP's call, the Inter-Organization Programme for the Sound Management of Chemicals established a working group to proceed with fact finding. In June 1996, the working group concluded that scientific evidence supported international action to reduce the risks posed by POPs. In February 1997, UNEP's Governing Council endorsed this conclusion and authorized formal negotiations aimed at creating a global POPs treaty.

The fact-finding process continued in eight regional workshops on POPs that UNEP and the Intergovernmental Forum on Chemical Safety convened in preparation for the negotiations. More than 138 countries participated in the workshops, which greatly increased awareness of POPs issues, particularly in developing countries and countries with economies in transition. Preparations also included convening preliminary meetings and studying previous negotiating processes on chemicals and specific aspects of the Rotterdam Convention, the Aarhus POPs Protocol to the Convention on Long-Range Transboundary Air Pollution, the Montreal Protocol, and other initiatives to see what lessons could be learned.[93]

The bargaining stage officially began in June 1998 and lasted three years. Individual sessions included five official weeklong meetings of the Intergovernmental Negotiating Committee, the main negotiating body; two meetings of the Criteria Expert Group, which focused on developing procedures for identifying and adding new chemicals to the treaty; a weeklong negotiation (officially called a consultation) and other meetings and communications focused exclusively on FTA; numerous formal contact groups; and countless intersessional communications and informal consultations.

During the negotiations, the EU, Canada, NGOs, and representatives of northern indigenous peoples played lead roles in supporting a strong regime. The POPs negotiations were notable for the prominent role given to the Inuit and other northern indigenous peoples to speak to delegates and the press concerning the threats that POPs posed to their health and their cultural heritage of subsistence hunting and fishing.

Countries playing potential veto roles shifted according to the specific issue in question. Interestingly, no governments opposed creating controls on the dirty dozen. The issue-definition and fact-finding phases, combined with other efforts that took place before the negotiations, produced a ringing endorsement at the first session of the Intergovernmental Negotiating Committee of the need for global regulations. This reflected not only a general acceptance of the science regarding POPs but also the relatively modest adjustment costs, given that industrialized countries had already established significant controls on the dirty dozen.

The EU and NGOs also supported creating controls on chemicals beyond the dirty dozen (as was done in the regional Aarhus POPs Protocol). The veto coalition opposing this view, which included many developing countries, the United States, and Japan (supported by companies that made or used the chemicals), argued successfully that starting with twelve on which consensus existed provided the best opportunity for creating a new regime.

Although agreement existed on the need to phase out the rest of the dirty dozen, Australia, Brazil, China, India, Indonesia, the United States, and other countries stated that they needed individual exemptions for specific uses of certain chemicals, at least for a short period. For example, Russia, the United States, and other countries noted that because PCBs were once widely used in electrical transformers and other equipment, and even though new equipment using PCBs was no longer produced, hundreds of thousands of tons of PCBs were still in use in existing equipment around the world. Australia and China supported the continued use of mirex to control termites, including in telephone poles, in remote areas. Botswana and China supported continued use of chlordane to protect wooden dams and certain other structures from insects. Other parties argued they would need small amounts of aldrin for use as an insecticide during the transition to alternatives. More broadly, African countries and health-related NGOs advocated strongly for some type of broad exemption for DDT because its use was essential for battling mosquitoes that spread malaria, a position that quickly gained near-universal support.[94]

To address these concerns and overcome potential veto-state positions on individual POPs, negotiators agreed on the concepts of acceptable purposes and specific exemptions, although different views existed on which chemicals or uses deserved exemptions and how they should be administered. This followed, in general terms, what had occurred a decade earlier during expansion of the ozone regime: when parties strengthened that regime by agreeing to eliminate CFCs and halons, and later methyl bromide, they included allowances for various types of exemptions to address the specific concerns of potential veto states.

Going into the negotiation stage, governments knew they would need to create provisions for providing FTA to developing countries to help them implement the regime as well as a mechanism for adding new chemicals to strengthen the agreement.[95] Industrialized and developing countries disagreed strongly on the mechanism for providing financial assistance. Countries also disagreed about possible procedures for adding new chemicals, if the treaty should include a noncompliance procedure, and institutional links to other treaties. Resolving these and other issues required difficult and detailed negotiations. The resulting 2001 Stockholm Convention on Persistent Organic Pollutants seeks to protect human health and the environment by eliminating or reducing the production, use, trade, and emission of POPs.[96] All parties must eliminate the production and use of aldrin, chlordane, dieldrin, endrin, heptachlor, hexachlorobenzene, mirex, PCBs, and toxaphene; restrict the production and use of DDT to what is needed for disease-vector control and when there are no suitable and affordable alternatives; and minimize the release of dioxins and furans into the environment.[97]

The treaty divides POPs into three categories, according to their source and the type of control measures placed on them. Substances slated for elimination are addressed in Article 3 and listed in Annex A. Substances whose production and use will be severely limited, like DDT, are addressed in Article 3 and listed in Annex B. POPs produced inadvertently, as unintentional by-products of other activities, are addressed in Article 5 and listed in Annex C. Because the complete elimination of Annex C substances is often technically impossible, parties agree to take specific steps to "minimize and where feasible eliminate" their emission by seeking to apply the relevant "best available techniques" and "best environmental practices," including those spelled out in annexes to the convention (see Appendix A).

To ensure an effective phaseout process, parties must also ban the import or export of all POPs controlled under the convention (except for narrowly defined purposes or environmentally sound disposal), promote the use of the best available technologies and practices for reducing emissions and managing POP wastes, and take steps to prevent the development and commercial introduction of new POPs. Parties must also develop national implementation plans; report on the production, import, and export of controlled POPs; and review the effectiveness of the convention at regular intervals.

In addition to the broad health-related exemption granted for DDT, the treaty includes a specific exemption for PCBs that allows countries to maintain existing equipment containing PCBs until 2025. The convention also allows any party to produce and use certain POPs for delineated acceptable purposes. The convention also created a category of country-specific exemptions that permit specific parties to continue using small amounts of specific POPs for specific purposes for specific amounts of time. Each party when ratifying the treaty must indicate which country-specific exemptions it will claim (e.g., using mirex for termite control). The exemption then lasts for five years, no questions asked. After that, an extension for another five years must be specifically granted by the COP.[98]

As seen in the ozone case, an important factor in the long-term effectiveness of an environmental regime is the process it contains for increasing the scope and strength of its environmental protections in response to new information or technological developments. The Stockholm Convention established specific scientifically based criteria and a step-by-step procedure for identifying, evaluating, and adding chemicals to the treaty (Article 8 and Annexes D, E, and F). This critical feature, which sought to ensure the convention's relevance beyond the dirty dozen, took a long time to develop. During negotiations, the EU advocated a process emphasizing the precautionary principle and allowing for the addition of chemicals relatively easily and quickly. The United States, Japan, Australia, and others wanted more sovereign control and a more regimented mechanism that required explicit risk analyses and clear evidence of existing harm before the COP could add a chemical.

The agreed-upon process represents a working compromise between these views, incorporating elements of risk analysis according to set criteria, use of experts, precaution, flexibility, and sovereign control by the parties (see Figure 3.2).[99] Under the treaty, any party may nominate a chemical for evaluation. A POPs Review Committee (POPRC), made up of thirty-one experts nominated by parties, then works on behalf (and under the oversight) of the COP to examine the nominated chemical in detail. The POPRC first determines whether the substance can be considered a POP under the terms of the treaty by examining if its toxicity, persistence, bioaccumulation, and potential for long-range environmental transport meet the specific criteria set out in the convention. If a substance meets the POPs criteria, the committee then drafts a risk profile to evaluate whether future emis-

FIGURE 3.2 **Process for Adding New Chemicals to the Stockholm Convention**

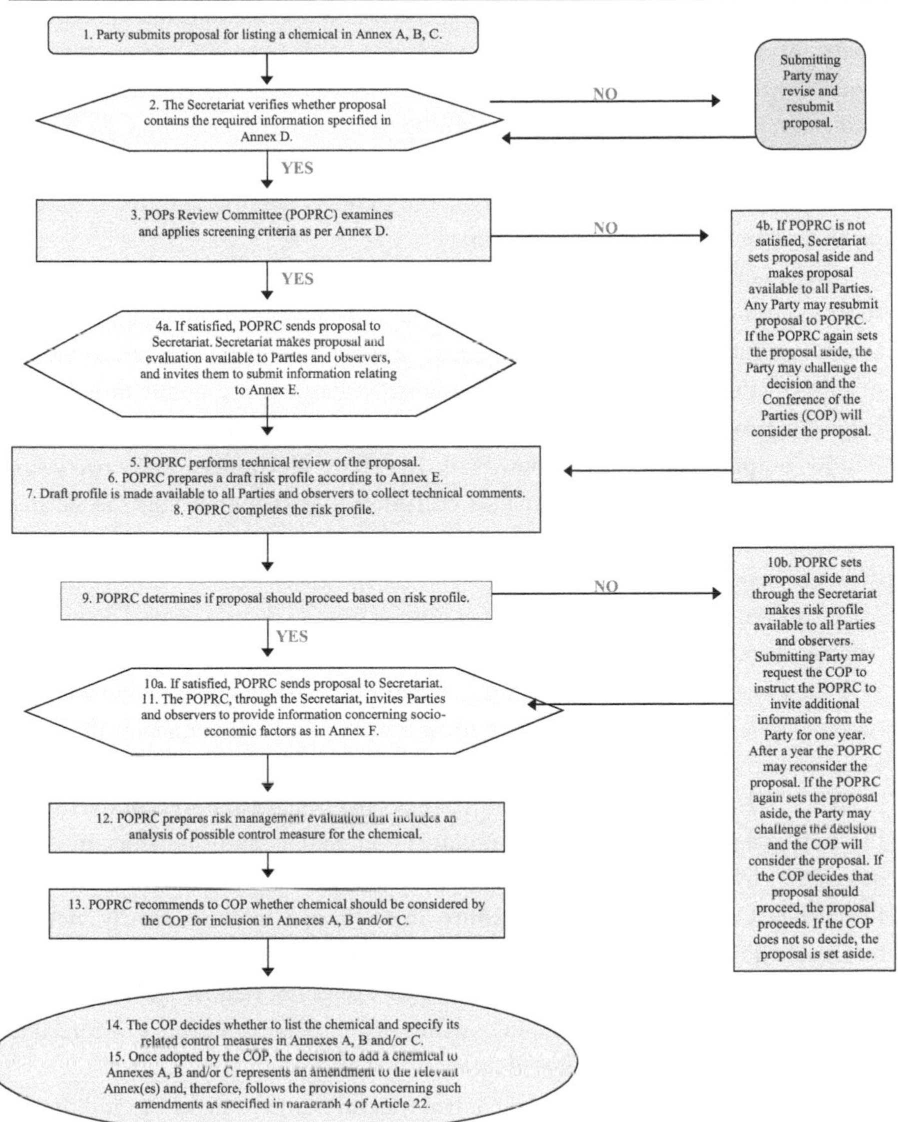

sions of the substance would produce significant adverse environmental or human-health impacts. If the POPRC determines it would, the committee develops a risk-management evaluation that assesses the relevant costs and benefits of international controls. Finally, based on these analyses, the POPRC decides to recommend or not to recommend that the COP consider controlling the substance under the convention. In carrying out these interrelated tasks, the POPRC is instructed to employ the specific scientific criteria for identifying and evaluating candidate POPs (as set out in Annex D of the convention), to follow specific information requirements for developing a risk profile for candidate POPs (Annex E), to consider socioeconomic impacts of controlling a POP in developing the risk-management evaluation (Annex F), and to include a strong perspective of precaution. Each stage (criteria, risk profile, risk-management evaluation) typically takes one year, but some chemicals progress more slowly if the POPRC requires additional time to gather and review relevant information.

As demanded by the EU, precaution informs the process in that the absence of strict scientific certainty does not prevent the COP from controlling a potentially hazardous substance.[100] At the same time, sovereign control is preserved, as demanded by the United States and other countries. Parties must nominate a POP to begin the process. All parties can submit comments and suggest changes to the POPRC outputs before they become final. The COP, which meets every two years, reviews the POPRC's recommendation, considers socioeconomic issues associated with potential listing, and holds final decision-making authority regarding controls and exemptions.[101]

To prevent a very small number of countries from preventing global action, the convention allows for voting if all efforts to reach consensus on the listing of a new POP have been exhausted. A three-fourths majority of parties present and voting is required to add a chemical (the EU votes as a unit, so its vote counts for the number of its member states, which currently stand at twenty-eight, even if they are not present). This last-ditch procedure, which has only been used once, contrasts with the Rotterdam Convention, which requires complete consensus. Thus, in 2013, opposition by Sudan, and only Sudan, prevented the addition of fenthion to the Rotterdam Convention's PIC procedure, even though fenthion clearly met the technical and procedural criteria. At the same time, the opt-in/opt-out procedure in the Stockholm Convention means that a vote does not remove a country's sovereign right to produce and use a POP within its borders, as it cannot be forced to ratify, and thus comply with, the addition of that chemical.

As noted above, to organize the control measures and to make the addition of chemicals more orderly, the convention establishes three annexes that group substances by the type of restrictions placed on them. New chemicals slated for elimination go into Annex A, those to be restricted go into Annex B, and unintentionally produced substances go into Annex C. This means that adding chemicals requires changing only the relevant annex, not amending the main body of the convention. However, states could not agree whether additions to the annexes should be immediately binding on all parties or subject to formal ratification (amendments to the main text require ratification). In a compromise, they created what are referred to as opt-in and opt-out provisions. Countries that ratify the treaty can choose to be an opt-in party, which means they are not required to address a chemical added to an annex unless they formally ratify the change;[102] otherwise the addition automatically applies to them unless they object within one year (the so-called opt-out provision). While potentially confusing, the entire package makes it easier to add chemicals and speeds the implementation of the new controls.[103]

Another critical feature of the convention is the financial mechanism that assists developing countries and countries with economies in transition in meeting their treaty obligations. Under the convention, industrialized countries must provide new financial resources, albeit at unspecified levels, and promote the transfer of technical assistance. Although all negotiators acknowledged the importance of providing FTA, very different views existed regarding the proper level and delivery mechanisms. Most developing countries strongly supported creating a new standalone financial institution patterned after that developed under the Montreal Protocol. They opposed designating the Global Environment Facility (GEF) as the financial mechanism because of concerns about the GEF's willingness to address POPs as a priority area and to follow directions from the Stockholm Convention COP on POPs-related issues. The G-77 also insisted that all FTA be new and additional to current programs so that POPs-related activities did not result in less FTA in other areas. Donor countries strongly supported using the GEF, stating that doing so would reduce administrative costs, provide parties with important expertise, and produce synergies because new FTA programs could be bundled and augmented with existing programs in other forums, such as the Rotterdam and Basel Conventions.

In the final compromise, industrialized countries agreed to provide FTA to assist countries to implement the convention and to promote the transfer of relevant technology.[104] The amounts of money and other assistance were unspecified, but they must represent new resources, rather than funds redirected from existing development or environmental assistance programs. The GEF was designated as the main financial mechanism, although only on a provisional basis. The COP gives instructions to and receives reports from the GEF with regard to its role in the financial mechanism, reviews the GEF's performance on a regular basis, and has the option to stop using the GEF entirely or as the main conduit for financial assistance. In response to the concerns expressed during the negotiations, the GEF subsequently created a dedicated chemicals focal area and POPs program, and donor countries have earmarked hundreds of millions of dollars expressly for chemicals during subsequent GEF replenishments.

The Stockholm Convention entered into force in 2004. It currently has one hundred eighty parties. Most countries and all of the major producers and users of toxic chemicals have ratified the convention except Israel, Malaysia, and the United States. Although the George W. Bush administration supported the treaty and intended to push for its ratification by the Senate, the terrorist attacks on September 11, 2001, put the White House on a war footing, allowing a few opponents in the Senate to block consideration of the treaty out of concern for how the regime might expand.[105] Yet this may have been a tactical error: as a nonparty, the United States may speak at the COPs, but its voice does not count in actual decision making, and it cannot serve as a member of the POPRC.

Regime Expansion: Adding New Chemicals

The regime-strengthening process began almost as soon as the convention was signed. In May 2005, COP1 adopted important decisions on the budget, financial mechanism, operation of the POPRC, and other issues necessary for the regime to operate. Six months later, the POPRC held its first meeting. The committee addressed several operational issues, such as developing procedures for handling confidential information and delineating procedures for the participation of additional experts. POPRC1 then began considering the first set of chemicals proposed by parties for possible inclusion in the convention, including the pesticide lindane and the industrial chemical perfluorooctane sulfonate (PFOS), which were still produced and used in several countries (see Box 3.5). The POPRC adopted risk profiles for these substances in 2006, and in 2007 it approved risk-management evaluations and formally recommended that the COP consider adding these substances to the convention. It completed the same process for four other chemicals in 2008.

Anticipation was high prior to COP4 in 2009, as participants and observers wondered if parties would be able to reach agreement to expand the regime. During the debate, the country that had nominated a POP acted as the lead state on that substance, with support from different parties depending on the substance. In some instances, parties work together as a coalition but choose a particular party to make the formal nomination for political reasons. For example, nominations coming from a developing country might carry more influence with other developing countries or countries in a certain region.

The EU, Norway, Switzerland, and several other countries strongly supported listing all nine substances. Veto states varied depending on which countries opposed listing the chemical or insisted on specific exemptions or certain acceptable purposes. Veto states were empowered to the extent that they were willing to prevent consensus on listing a chemical unless certain exemptions were allowed; if they could credibly claim they would not ratify an amendment (in theory this only works for countries that produce or use sufficient quantities of a substance to

BOX 3.5 INFORMATION ON SELECTED PERSISTENT ORGANIC POLLUTANTS ADDED TO THE STOCKHOLM CONVENTION

- **Chlordecone: once widely used as an agricultural pesticide (nominated by the EU; added in 2009).**
- **Endosulfan: broad-spectrum insecticide, still widely used in India when nominated (nominated by the EU; added in 2011).**
- **Hexabromobiphenyl: industrial chemical used as a flame retardant, mainly in the 1970s (nominated by the EU; added in 2009).**
- **Hexabromocyclododecane: flame retardant produced in China, Europe, Japan, and the United States and used in building insulation, electronic and electric equipment, automobiles, and upholstered furniture (nominated by Norway; added in 2015).**
- **Lindane: broad-spectrum insecticide for treating seeds, soils, plants, animals, and people, whose production had decreased prior to its addition to the convention, although a few countries still produced and used it (nominated by Mexico; added in 2009).**
- **Pentabromodiphenyl ethers: used in polychlorinated biphenyl products and as a fungicide, flame retardant, and chemical intermediate and also produced unintentionally during combustion and as an impurity in certain solvents and pesticides (nominated by Norway; added in 2009).**
- **Pentachlorophenol: once used as a pesticide and disinfectant and still used as a wood preservative when added to the convention, including for telephone poles in some countries and especially in fiberboard and particle boards in India (nominated by the EU; added in 2015 but only after a vote).**
- **Perfluorooctane sulfonate, its salts, and perfluorooctane sulfonyl fluoride: still produced and widely used in several countries when added to the convention and found in electric and electronic parts, firefighting foam, photo imaging, hydraulic fluids, and textiles (nominated by Sweden; added in 2009).**

threaten the effectiveness of the controls); or if they were willing to withhold support on an unrelated issue if their position was not adopted. In the end, COP4 added nine chemicals to the convention (see Appendix A), with certain exemptions and acceptable purposes included for five (see Table 3.2). This significantly strengthened the regime only five years after the treaty entered into force.

The debates at COP4 revealed key issues that have been repeated in successive debates about adding chemicals. An important issue for some chemicals is the

TABLE 3.2 **Indicative Exemptions Under the Stockholm Convention (as of January 2016)**

CHEMICAL	ANNEX*	YEAR ADDED	SPECIFIC EXEMPTIONS / ACCEPTABLE PURPOSES
Endosulfan and its related isomers	A	2011	**Production:** As allowed for the parties listed in the register of specific exemptions **Use:** Crop–pest complexes as listed in accordance with the provisions of Part VI of Annex A
Hexabromocyclododecane	A	2013	**Production:** As allowed by the parties listed in the register of specific exemptions **Use:** Expanded polystyrene and extruded polystyrene in buildings in accordance with the provisions of Part VII of Annex A
Hexabromodiphenyl ether and heptabromodiphenyl ether (commercial octabromodiphenyl ether)	A	2009	**Production:** None **Use:** Articles in accordance with the provisions of Part IV of Annex A
Lindane	A	2009	**Production:** None **Use:** Human health pharmaceutical for control of head lice and scabies as second-line treatment
Pentachlorophenol and its salts and esters	A	2015	**Production**: As allowed for the parties listed in the register of specific exemptions **Use**: For utility poles and cross-arms in accordance with the provisions of Part VIII of Annex A
Perfluorooctane sulfonate, its salts, and perfluorooctane sulfonyl fluoride	B	2009	**Production:** For the use below **Use:** Acceptable purposes and specific exemptions in accordance with Part III of Annex B
Polychlorinated naphthalenes	A & C	2015	**Production**: For the use below **Use**: Production of polyfluorinated naphthalenes, including octafluoronaphthalene
Tetrabromodiphenyl ether and pentabromodiphenyl ether (commercial pentabromodiphenyl ether)	A	2009	**Production:** None **Use:** Articles in accordance with the provisions of Part IV of Annex A

*Annex A requires eliminating production and use. Annex B requires restricting production and use to listed purposes. Annex C requires taking specific measures to minimize and, where feasible, eliminate emissions of substances produced as unintentional by-products of combustion or industrial processes.

Source: Chart adapted from Stockholm Convention Secretariat, "The New POPs Under the Stockholm Convention," http://chm.pops.int/TheConvention/ThePOPs/TheNewPOPs/tabid/2511/Default.aspx.

annex in which they could be placed. Lead states usually push for inclusion of chemicals in Annex A, which mandates elimination. Some states pushed for one or two chemicals to be placed in Annex B, which establishes restrictions but no near-term elimination. Parties can also disagree on the category of potential exemptions that should be applied to a chemical. Lead states usually argue that only a limited number of specific, time-limited exemptions be allowed. Other states support the more lenient acceptable purpose category, which allows larger and less controlled levels of exempted use. Finally, many of the most contentious listing issues can become interrelated. For example, a veto state could offer to relent on listing or acceptable purposes for one chemical in exchange for the creation of more special exemptions for another substance or a compromise on issues related to FTA.

The nomination of new chemicals by parties and subsequent action by the POPRC and the COP prove that the procedures for adding new substances work. It also confirms that lead states intend to nominate and support consideration of additional chemicals in accordance with the precautionary principle. Indeed, additional chemicals are under review, and more nominations are expected.[106] At the same time, potential obstacles have been revealed. As noted by participants and observers, in 2008 the POPRC and COP moved "from considering what are commonly referred to as 'dead' chemicals to those 'live' chemicals that are still in use in many parts of the world."[107] By creating the POPRC, the Stockholm Convention had attempted to separate the scientific and technical consideration of nominated POPs, which are the purview of the POPRC, from the political concerns of parties, which are discussed by the COP. In essence, the POPRC addresses whether the convention can control a substance. Then the COP decides if it should. The lines can blur, however, because the convention asks the POPRC to include certain socioeconomic considerations in the risk-management evaluation phase. This was not an important issue on most of the substances that the POPRC considered at its early meetings, but the shift to evaluating toxic chemicals still in widespread production and use presents a new challenge. Since 2008, some POPRC members have taken positions that reflect their country's economic and political views as much as a technical evaluation of the POP's toxicity, persistence, bioaccumulation, long-range environmental transport, and consequential risks to human health and the environment. This has produced some strong exchanges during these POPRC meetings and even some contentious votes.[108]

Ultimately, several live chemicals have been added to the Stockholm Convention despite strong opposition during POPRC and COP deliberations, including PFOS in 2009, endosulfan in 2011, and pentachlorophenol in 2015. Indeed, India's veto position forced a vote in 2015 on the addition of pentachlorophenol, something that had never before occurred in the COP (as noted, a few votes have taken place in the POPRC). Ninety parties voted to add pentachlorophenol, two opposed, and eight abstained.[109]

It is now clear that efforts to continue strengthening the Stockholm Convention have the resources to overcome veto states, either by addressing their concerns via exemptions or by resorting to a vote if their demands are seen as too extreme or their brinkmanship negotiating tactics backfire (as India's appeared to have with regard to pentachlorophenol).[110] However, countries are not required to ratify the addition of particular chemicals, and several important countries have not (see below). Moreover, voting could weaken support for the regime among countries that consistently lose votes in the POPRC or the COP or that worry that they could wind up on the losing end in the future. For these reasons, several countries, including China, India, Russia, and the United States, expressed regret that votes had been taken.

However, there is some evidence that the convention can impact countries that do not ratify a particular chemical by reinforcing or even accelerating global market forces or by impacting national political and regulatory mechanisms. For example, at the time of its listing, endosulfan was still used as a pesticide in some countries, particularly India. The Indian government tried to prevent its addition to the control measures but finally relented when agreement was reached on a

PHOTO 3.4 India votes against adding pentachlorophenol to the Stockholm Convention in 2015. Courtesy Kiara Worth, IISD/*Earth Negotiations Bulletin*, www.iisd.ca.

broad set of exemptions. However, the final decision to list endosulfan led to domestic pressure within India (from both environmentalists and manufacturers of alternatives) to eliminate the production and use of this pesticide, showing that the Stockholm Convention can "play an important agenda-setting role that can help influence domestic decision-making even in the presence of particular economic interests."[111]

Financial and Technical Assistance

Although the convention established general mandates, it also required the COP to take action to implement and strengthen the provisions on FTA. COP1 and COP2 took a number of important procedural steps, but the discussions revealed that the split between donor and recipient countries present during the convention's negotiation had not dissipated. By COP4 in 2009, the suite of intersecting issues on financial resources and technical assistance had become complex.[112] Among other issues, the parties needed to review reports on the operations and extant effectiveness of the financial mechanism, particularly the GEF; decide if the regime should keep the GEF as the principal entity of the financial mechanism; and, if so, provide updated guidance to the GEF regarding how the COP wanted it to operate in supporting the convention; review needs-assessment reports on the potential costs for developing countries to implement the regime; make decisions in response to this information, including preferences for POPs-related funding levels in the next round of negotiations on replenishing the GEF; and select regional centers through which capacity building and technical assistance would flow.

Further complicating matters, the bargaining strategies of many participants caused these and other issues to become interlinked. This is not uncommon during global environmental negotiations, but it forced delegates to search for a complex package deal that almost prevented decisions on issues on which there was no disagreement. For example, many developing countries would not allow a decision on the listing of additional chemicals until a satisfactory resolution was reached on the package of FTA issues. The EU attempted to include noncompliance as part of the overall compromise package. China, India, and others essentially refused to consider a package that included a noncompliance procedure. Some countries dug in their heels on issues relating to certain chemicals in an attempt to get movement on other chemicals or on an unrelated issue.

In the end, these linkages produced a stalemate that almost derailed the meeting, something that would have prevented adding the first set of new chemicals. Finally, after 4:00 am on Saturday (the meeting was supposed to end at 6:00 pm on Friday), long after the interpreters had left the building, a final compromise allowed the COP to adopt a package of decisions that added nine new chemicals and reaffirmed the GEF as the principal entity for the financial mechanism.[113] COP4 also called on donors to take the funding-needs assessment of developing countries, as revealed in their Stockholm Convention national implementation plans, and the listing of new chemicals in the convention into full consideration during the fifth replenishment of the GEF. It requested that the GEF continue its efforts, called for by previous COPs, to streamline the processes for applying for and receiving financial assistance.

One year later, in May 2010, global negotiations for the fifth GEF replenishment concluded, with thirty-five donors agreeing to provide the GEF with $4.34 billion to support GEF activities from July 1, 2010, to June 30, 2014, a 54 percent increase above the 2006–2010 level. Of the total replenishment, $425 million was dedicated to the chemicals focal area.[114] The GEF reported that its Stockholm Convention–related funding during this period would focus on reducing POP releases, "in particular PCB phase-out and disposal, and removal and disposal of obsolete pesticides . . . [and] making headway on the reduction of releases of unintentionally produced dioxins and furans from industrial and non-industrial sources."[115] Pilot projects to address the newly added POPs would also be supported, as would the updating of National Implementation Plans, issues that developing countries had highlighted during the previous COP.

One year later, parties finished a review of the GEF's work to see if it fulfilled the terms of the agreement it had signed with the COP to act as the main financial mechanism for the regime. COP5 agreed to continue the GEF's role and finalized terms of reference for a study that will inform the next official review of the financial mechanism. This process of developing countries expressing concern, the COP providing instructions to the GEF, the GEF providing reports, the COP re-endorsing the role of the GEF, and, most important, developed-country parties earmarking hundreds of millions of dollars for the chemicals focal area during GEF replenishments has repeated itself.

Since 2001, the GEF has allocated more than $900 million to POPs projects in more than 135 countries. The GEF has also leveraged more than $2.4 billion of additional funding—from governments, the private sector, international organizations, foundations, and NGOs—to support POPs projects.[116] In 2013 and 2015, the COP agreed that the GEF should continue its role as the main financial mechanism, although detailed reviews would continue.

Concrete measures to advance the provision of effective technical assistance have included the creation of Stockholm Convention regional and subregional centers in Algeria, Brazil, China, Czech Republic, India, Iran, Kenya, Kuwait, Mexico, Panama, Russia, Senegal, South Africa, Spain, and Uruguay. These centers, some of which also act as Basel Convention Regional Centers, serve as official nodes for capacity building, information sharing, training, technology transfer, and technical assistance. Some have accessed the international, regional, and national financial and technical resources and expertise to develop effective programs, whereas others have not. COPs review the operation of these centers with uneven results.

Although significant progress has been made by the COP, the GEF, the parties, and other actors to develop and deploy resources and mechanisms for FTA, concerns remain that not enough funds are being earmarked for POPs projects and that too little time and money is spent actually reducing emissions of POPs. Going forward, the COP will continue to review the GEF, regional centers, and other international organizations regarding their impact and cost-effectiveness. At the same time, political preferences of the donors for the GEF, and of many developing countries for the centers, may leave the current architecture unchanged for many years.

Creating Networks

In 2009, COP4 endorsed establishment of a global DDT partnership, the Global Alliance. This network of stakeholders—including doctors, health agencies, international organizations, NGOs, national governments, corporations, and scientists—works to develop and deploy more effective and cost-efficient alternative products, methods, and strategies to control malaria than the use of DDT. COP4 also created the PCB Elimination Network to strengthen efforts to phase out equipment containing PCBs. Members include experts from multiple treaty secretariats, international organizations, governments, NGOs, research institutions, and industry. The network exchanges information, evaluates PCB use, supports pilot programs in developing countries, promotes improved techniques for managing PCBs, and develops recommendations for further action.

These alliances both seek to identify gaps in existing initiatives, improve coordination among relevant actors, catalyze new action, and take advantage of the global scale of the Stockholm Convention for awareness raising and information sharing. The networks, which might not exist without the convention, demonstrate how regimes can enhance the impact of their formal regulations by developing "initiatives that coordinate and support multi-sector action among governments, corporations, non-governmental organizations (NGOs) and other stakeholders to achieve common goals."[117]

Synergies

For several years, Switzerland, the EU, and others have pushed the concept of creating formal coordination among the three main chemical and waste conventions to achieve synergies and reduce costs. As noted above, in 2005 and 2006, the Basel,

Rotterdam, and Stockholm COPs established a joint working group on synergies to examine the issue, develop background materials, and draft recommendations. Although this process was far from complete, by 2007, the joint working group had clarified key concepts, purposes, and potential outcomes of the process, helping to transform the "concept of synergies from a nebulous norm into a series of practical actions, such as adopting a streamlined reporting system, which parties see as being beneficial."[118] At COP3, parties to the Stockholm Convention strongly supported the initiative—unlike at previous COPs, where developing countries expressed significant concern that the process would divert attention and resources away from technical assistance. The final proposal of the working group was considered first, by virtue of the calendar, by the Basel and Rotterdam COPs. In May 2009, POPs COP4 gave the final approval needed to begin the groundbreaking initiative.

In 2010, parties convened an extraordinary simultaneous meeting of the COPs to the Basel, Rotterdam, and Stockholm Conventions (Ex-COP). The Ex-COP adopted a single omnibus decision on synergies that outlined the intention to offer joint services, organize joint activities, synchronize budget cycles, conduct joint audits, coordinate or combine many managerial functions, coordinate review arrangements, develop joint clearinghouse and other information and communications activities, and establish a new executive secretary to oversee the secretariats of all three conventions.

In 2013, the three conventions held their COPs on successive days as well as an Ex-COP in a busy two-week period in Geneva and reviewed and advanced the synergies agenda. In 2015, the COPs again met together, and similar meetings are scheduled for 2017. The joint meetings have had mixed results. Positive impacts include reduced costs[119] and, more substantively, the ability for parties to consider issues that link two more of the conventions in an integrated fashion at the same time rather than considering one aspect at one COP and another at a different COP several months later. (POPs wastes, financial assistance, and regional centers are three examples.) However, holding meetings at the same time creates large and complex agendas and taxes the physical and mental stamina of delegates and secretariat staff. This has led to unnecessarily hurried activity at the end of the meetings as well as potential misunderstandings or mistakes. It has also allowed countries to deploy veto and brinkmanship negotiation tactics across treaties by, for example, refusing to allow agreement on a particular issue in the Basel Convention unless their positions were reflected in a decision on an unrelated issue in the Stockholm Convention.[120]

More broadly, certain operational elements within the three convention secretariats and regional centers have already merged, especially within the joint secretariat location in Geneva. The secretariat has stated that this has already yielded financial savings associated with administration and meeting costs, some integrated information and implementation activities at the regional level, and co-financing opportunities via the GEF, but the larger challenge of effectively integrating programs to improve the environmentally sound management of chemicals and wastes on a global basis will be the true test.[121]

Noncompliance Procedures

Creating effective noncompliance procedures has proven a difficult task for most environmental regimes. The Montreal Protocol is one of the very few regimes possessing a working procedure for examining potential cases of state noncompliance. Article 17 of the Stockholm Convention states that the COP will develop "mechanisms for determining noncompliance with the provisions of this Convention and for the treatment of Parties found to be in noncompliance." The EU and Switzerland have attached significant importance to developing a robust noncompliance procedure and play a strong lead role on the issue. Other industrialized countries and some developing countries attach less importance to the issue, acting as potential swing states. Another group of developing countries, often led by China and India, constitutes a powerful veto coalition. They link implementation and effectiveness to the provision of financial resources and argue that a noncompliance procedure can only be developed after such assistance has been provided. They emphasize that any procedure related to compliance should not be punitive but assistance oriented and focus on identifying obstacles to effective compliance in a given party so that additional assistance can be targeted effectively.

Attempts to resolve these differences during negotiation of the convention failed, leading to the compromise language in Article 17, which, unlike nearly all of the other parts of the convention requiring action by the COP, carried no deadline. COP1 created an open-ended working group on noncompliance to allow delegates the opportunity to consider the issue in detail. However, discussions at successive COPs have yielded little substantive progress (and sometimes generated heated debates) beyond a preliminary draft text covered with square brackets and alternative formulations supported by different groups. (Square brackets are used to indicate portions of a draft document on which parties do not agree.) Although parties seem to agree that the noncompliance mechanism for the POPs regime should be facilitative rather than punitive, differences remain on other fundamental issues, including the ultimate objective and underlying principles of the noncompliance procedure, how to initiate action on potential cases of noncompliance (some countries reject giving either the secretariat or other parties the authority to initiate the procedure), whether the provision of specific levels of FTA can be evaluated under the noncompliance mechanism, and the composition and decision-making processes for the compliance committee.

Successes and Challenges

The global regime for toxic chemicals has expanded significantly since governments adopted the Stockholm Convention in 2001. As of early 2016, one hundred eighty countries have ratified the convention. Fourteen new chemicals have been added. Production, use, and emissions of controlled POPs have declined, as has the use of specific exemptions for the original dirty dozen. The POPRC continues to evaluate candidate POPs nominated by parties. The GEF has created a dedicated chemicals focal area, distributed more than $900 million for chemicals projects, and helped to mobilize more than $2.4 billion in additional co-financing. Regional centers serve as nodes for capacity building and technical assistance. Technical guidelines have been developed to help measure and reduce dioxin and furan emissions as well as emissions from POPs waste. Global networks have been created to speed deployment of alternatives to DDT and the phaseout of PCBs. Awareness regarding the production, use, and impacts of toxic chemicals has increased within many national governments. The synergies initiative has produced cost savings and augmented productive coordination within the Basel, Rotterdam, and Stockholm Conventions.

At the same time, and like all of the other regimes discussed in this book, the Stockholm Convention faces significant challenges. Perhaps the most important is continuing to address live chemicals. The regime has taken the first, difficult steps in this direction, particularly in the POPRC and COP debates on PFOS, endosulfan, and pentachlorophenol. However, many more POPs exist, and concern is rising over a new class of endocrine disruptors that may affect humans at low doses over long periods and might be found in some brands of everyday products, including plastics, pesticides, and detergents.[122] The United States, Israel, and Malaysia, each a producer and consumer of toxic chemicals, are not yet parties to the Stockholm Convention, and a number of important parties—including Argentina, Australia, Bangladesh, China, India, Korea, New Zealand, Russia, and Venezuela—have not ratified the control measures on some of the chemicals added to the treaty.[123] Voting within the POPRC or the COP could also weaken support for the regime among those countries that lose or among other actors concerned for protecting the principle of sovereignty in that their economic interests could be affected by future votes. Working to ensure that the use of voting and the opt-in/opt-out structure does not create situations in which key countries remain outside the regime with regard to individual POPs, and thus weaken the treaty's global impact, remains a key challenge.[124]

Exemptions represent another challenge. Acceptable purpose and country-specific exemptions might be political necessities that overcome the lowest-common-denominator problem by establishing asymmetrical controls, but they can weaken the impact of listing a particular chemical, especially if the country in question both produces and consumes the substance. Although countries have retired most exemptions for the original dirty dozen, some chemicals added to the convention carry larger lists of acceptable purposes and country-specific exemptions. For the regime to be effective over the long term, the COP must prevent parties from renewing these exemptions and reduce acceptable uses, especially if there is evidence of nontoxic alternative substances or practices. This could represent a significant challenge, however, if parties "find it difficult to stand in opposition to renewal of another's exemption if they themselves are hoping to find support for continuing an exemption."[125]

Another challenge, common to all environmental regimes, is the need for more financial and technical resources to assist some developing countries in their transition away from the use of toxic chemicals and to improve the management of those that remain. Although donor countries and the GEF have significantly increased assistance and hopes remain that the Consultative Process on Financing Options for Chemicals and Wastes will yield increased efficiencies and funding levels, further regime strengthening and effective implementation will require the availability and proper application of sufficient FTA for some states and some substances.

Finally, the synergies initiative presents important challenges and opportunities. Establishing effective, institutionalized coordination, collaboration, and selective consolidation among the Stockholm, Rotterdam, and Basel Conventions will not be easy, but it is a necessary step toward establishing environmentally sound, implementable controls on all aspects of the life cycle of toxic chemicals. Effective implementation of the synergies initiative will enhance the effectiveness of the conventions, promote cost-savings at the national and secretariat level, allow more resources and attention to shift toward implementation, raise the profile of chemicals and wastes issues within countries, and provide more opportunities for regime expansion in the future. If effective, elements of the synergies initiative could help address several obstacles to effective environmental policy, which will be discussed further in Chapter 5, including poorly designed, uncoordinated, or contradictory regimes; overburdened national bureaucracies; and inadequate resources. At the same time, as seen at the 2015 COPs, synergies allow countries to play veto roles across treaty regimes and introduce time constraints and other complexities that can inhibit progress. The synergies initiative has advanced considerably, and attempts to coordinate implementation and funding activities, and the tone and outputs of the COPs in 2017 and beyond could reveal a great deal regarding the long-term impact of this process.

CLIMATE CHANGE

Climate change is the prototype of a global commons issue. The earth's climate system affects all nations, and broad international cooperation is required to mitigate global warming. The release of heat-trapping GHGs from human activities, especially the burning of fossil fuels and deforestation, is intensifying the natural greenhouse effect and warming the planet. The earth's average temperature in 2015 was already 1.02°C above the preindustrial average between 1850 and 1900. Without a reduction in emissions that contribute to climate change, the earth's average temperature is projected to rise another 3.7°C to 4.8°C over the next hundred years.[126]

Developing an effective regime to mitigate climate change has been complicated by the multiple sources of GHG emissions, by scientific uncertainties regarding the precise scope and timing of future impacts, and by the need to address the development needs of developing countries. Perhaps most important, however, is that fossil fuels remain central to nearly every nation's economy; the policy changes required to reduce GHG emissions raise difficult questions about who should bear the short-term economic costs and how to allocate the potential long-term benefits. Even to stabilize the amount of CO_2 in the atmosphere (which would not reduce the warming caused by emissions already in the atmosphere) would require cutting current emissions by roughly one-half or more. That would necessitate major increases in energy efficiency and conservation and a switch from coal and oil to natural gas and renewable energy, all of which would affect powerful economic and political interests.

GHG emissions from the burning of fossil fuels account for roughly 78 percent of total world GHG emissions.[127] Deforestation and methane emissions contribute most of the rest. Fossil-fuel burning has increased atmospheric concentrations of CO_2 by 26 percent since 1959 (see Figure 3.3). The top twenty emitters of CO_2 in 2012, led by China (27 percent) and the United States (14 percent), account for about 61 percent of the world's emissions (see Table 3.3). This is down from 77 percent in 2010, as emissions from developing countries have increased and some key industrialized countries, including the United States, Canada, Germany, Italy, the United Kingdom, and France, have decreased their emissions, although developed countries' per capita emissions remain higher than those of most developing countries (see Table 3.4).

Scientists have long known that the buildup of CO_2 in the atmosphere can cause climate change. The first scientific article suggesting that atmospheric temperatures will rise as atmospheric CO_2 concentrations increase was published in 1896.[128] A research article in 1938 argued that CO_2 levels were climbing and might be responsible for raising global temperatures.[129] However, the process of issue

FIGURE 3.3 **Atmospheric Concentration of Carbon Dioxide at Mauna Loa, Hawaii, 1959–2014**

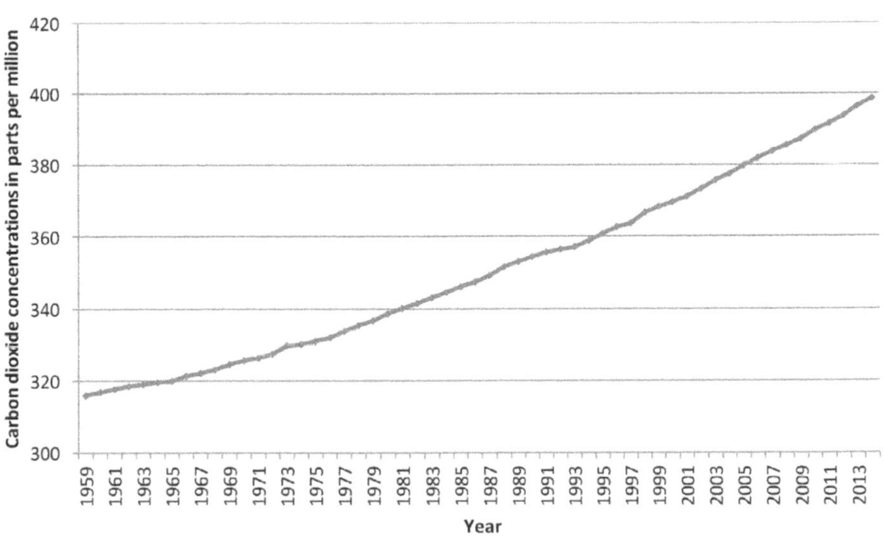

Source: NOAA Earth System Research Laboratory, ftp://aftp.cmdl.noaa.gov/products/trends/co2/co2_annmean_mlo.txt.

definition did not really begin until the mid-1980s. The World Meteorological Organization (WMO) and UNEP took the first major step by organizing a conference that produced a scientific consensus statement that global warming was a serious possibility.[130] In 1986, WMO, the National Aeronautics and Space Administration (NASA), and several other agencies issued a three-volume report concluding that climate change was already taking place at a relatively rapid rate.[131]

The fact-finding process coincided with the issue-definition stage. In 1988 WMO and UNEP, at the request of member states, organized the IPCC in an attempt to establish a common factual basis for negotiations that would focus on policy options. The First Assessment Report of the IPCC, approved in August 1990, affirmed global warming as a serious threat. The report predicted that if states continue to pursue business as usual, the global average surface temperature would rise at a rate unprecedented in human history. However, although the first IPCC report, which like all IPCC reports was based on peer-reviewed publications in scholarly journals, showed increasing scientific consensus on climate change, it failed to establish consensus on the economics of the problem—one of the key points of contention during subsequent negotiations.

This case study focuses on the negotiations of the climate regime in four rounds. It does not look at the extensive work done by other subsidiary bodies under the convention.[132]

TABLE 3.3 **Top Twenty Emitting Countries by Total Fossil-Fuel Carbon Dioxide (1,000 Metric Tons of Carbon), 2012**

COUNTRY	1990 EMISSIONS	2010 EMISSIONS	2012 EMISSIONS	PERCENTAGE CHANGE 1990–2012	PERCENTAGE CHANGE 2010–2012
China	658,554	2,247,534	2,625,730	299%	14%
United States	1,326,725	1,497,865	1,396,791	5%	-7%
India	188,344	564,474	611,226	225%	8%
Russia	565,901	460,551	491,840	-13%	6%
Japan	319,704	310,481	342,270	7%	9%
Germany	276,425	207,966	199,716	-28%	-4%
South Korea	65,901	153,580	166,679	153%	8%
Iran	61,954	156,730	164,498	166%	5%
Saudi Arabia	58,646	134,653	137,878	135%	2%
Canada	122,739	141,402	137,820	12%	-3%
Indonesia	41,032	129,970	129,988	217%	0%
Mexico	104,907	127,127	129,942	24%	2%
United Kingdom	156,481	134,498	128,494	-18%	-5%
South Africa	90,963	123,229	125,742	38%	2%
Brazil	56,966	114,419	122,082	114%	6%
Italy	115,925	111,252	102,369	-12%	-9%
Australia	79,943	99,685	101,147	27%	1%
France	108,576	98,879	93,713	-14%	-6%
Ukraine	174,988	76,294	93,713	-49%	14%
Thailand	26,134	81,614	88,044	237%	7%
Total Top 20	4,600,808	6,972,203	7,384,352	61%	6%
Global Total	6,144,000	9,138,791	9,666,501	57%	6%

Sources: T. A. Boden and T. J. Blasing, *Record High 2010 Global Carbon Dioxide Emissions from Fossil-Fuel Combustion and Cement Manufacture* (Oak Ridge, TN: Carbon Dioxide Information Analysis Center, Oak Ridge National Laboratory, 2012), http://cdiac.ornl.gov/trends/emis/prelim_2009_2010_estimates.html; T. A. Boden, G. Marland, and R. J. Andres, *Global, Regional, and National Fossil-Fuel CO2 Emissions* (Oak Ridge, TN: Carbon Dioxide Information Analysis Center, Oak Ridge National Laboratory, US Department of Energy, 2013), http://cdiac.ornl.gov/trends/emis/meth_reg.html; T. A. Boden, G. Marland, and R. J. Andres, *National CO2 Emissions from Fossil-Fuel Burning, Cement Manufacture and Gas Flaring: 1758–2006* (Oak Ridge, TN: Carbon Dioxide Information Analysis Center, Oak Ridge National Laboratory, 2009), http://cdiac.ornl.gov/trends/emis/tre_tp20.html.

TABLE 3.4 **Top Twenty Carbon Emitters Ranked by Per Capita Carbon Emissions (Metric Tons), 2011**

PER CAPITA EMISSIONS RANK	OVERALL EMISSIONS RANK	NATION	CARBON DIOXIDE PER CAPITA (METRIC TONS)
10	10	Saudi Arabia	5.11
13	2	United States	4.54
15	17	Australia	4.43
20	11	Canada	3.84
21	4	Russia	3.44
24	7	South Korea	3.3
35	5	Japan	2.54
38	12	South Africa	2.51
40	6	Germany	2.40
44	8	Iran	2.12
49	14	United Kingdom	1.96
55	1	China	1.8
56	16	Italy	1.79
64	22	Ukraine	1.7
76	18	France	1.45
89	21	Thailand	1.24
97	13	Mexico	1.07
121	9	Indonesia	0.63
125	15	Brazil	0.61
137	3	India	0.46

Source: T. Boden, B. Andres, and G. Marland, *Ranking of the World's Countries by 2011 Per Capita Fossil-Fuel CO2 Emission Rates* (Oak Ridge, TN: Carbon Dioxide Information Analysis Center, Oak Ridge National Laboratory, US Department of Energy, 2013), http://cdiac.ornl.gov/trends/emis/top2011.cap.

Round 1: The United Nations Framework Convention on Climate Change

The first round of climate negotiations began in February 1991 under the auspices of the Intergovernmental Negotiating Committee for a Framework Convention on Climate Change, which had been created by the UN General Assembly to draft a global treaty. In the beginning, the energy culture of states generally determined whether a state would join a lead-state or veto-state coalition with regard to GHG emissions targets and timetables. Initially, three groups of states existed:[133]

- States with few indigenous fossil-fuel resources and relatively dependent on imported energy: This group included Japan and many European states, including Denmark, Finland, France, Italy, the Netherlands, and Sweden.
- States with large supplies of cheap energy resources and a culture of highly inefficient energy use: This group included Brazil, Canada, China, India, Mexico, Russia, and the United States.
- States highly dependent on fossil-fuel exports for income: This group included the Arab oil states, Australia, Norway, and, initially, the United Kingdom.

The initial coalition of lead states (Finland, the Netherlands, Norway, and Sweden) squared off with the United States, as leader of the veto coalition, first on whether to hold global negotiations on climate change and then on whether the negotiations should seek to produce a protocol containing specific obligations on emissions. The lead states wanted to negotiate a framework convention in parallel with negotiations for a protocol limiting emissions to be completed no later than a year after the convention. The United States insisted on holding talks only on a framework convention, with no parallel negotiations on protocols, arguing that regulating carbon emissions would require major changes in fossil-fuel consumption and, consequently, lifestyles and industrial structure. In October 1990, Japan broke rank with the United States on the issue by committing itself to stabilizing its GHG emissions at 1990 levels by 2000. That left the United States and the Soviet Union alone among industrialized countries rejecting a target and timetable for controlling GHG emissions.[134]

The EC became the key lead state in the negotiations by virtue of its previous announced commitment to lower its joint CO_2 emissions to 1990 levels by 2000. Australia, Austria, Denmark, Germany, Japan, the Netherlands, and New Zealand also committed themselves to reducing their emissions by 2000 or 2005.

Had binding commitments for controlling GHG emissions been included in the text, developing countries' agreement would have been crucial. The large, rapidly industrializing countries (Brazil, China, and India) already accounted for 21 percent of global emissions in 1989 (about the same as the United States), and as their economies grew, their emissions levels would certainly rise. Because they viewed fossil fuels as a vital component of their success as potential industrial powers, they formed a potential veto coalition.[135]

The negotiating session in February 1992 ended without resolution of the issue of a stabilization target and timetable. British, Dutch, German, and other EC member governments sent officials to Washington, DC, in an unsuccessful effort to persuade the United States to go along with a binding commitment to stabilize emissions at 1990 levels by 2000. In April 1992, President George H. W. Bush personally called Prime Minister Helmut Kohl of Germany and asked him to drop his government's demand for the stabilization commitment in return for Bush's participation in the upcoming Earth Summit. Bush announced his decision to attend the Rio conference only after the final draft text of the convention was completed without reference to binding commitments to controlling GHGs.[136]

In June 1992, 154 countries signed the UNFCCC at the Earth Summit in Rio. The convention required Annex I parties (forty industrialized countries) to take steps aimed at reducing their GHG emissions in 2000 to "earlier levels"—a phrase interpreted by the EC to mean 1990 levels—but did not commit governments to hold emissions to a specific level by a certain date. Nor did it address emissions-reduction targets after 2000. But the text did provide for regular review of the adequacy of the commitments.

The UNFCCC entered into force in March 1994, after ratification by the minimum-necessary fifty states.[137] Although the veto power exercised by the United States and, to a lesser extent, Russia prevented inclusion of binding targets and timetables in the UNFCCC, it could not prevent efforts to begin negotiations on a binding protocol. The EC issued a statement upon signing the convention calling for an early start on negotiation of an agreement with binding targets and timetables. Germany joined with an international network of NGOs and the Alliance of Small Island States (AOSIS) to press for a significant strengthening of the regime (see Box 3.6).

Round 2: The Kyoto Protocol

The first COP to the UNFCCC convened in Berlin in March 1995 and immediately addressed the issue of regime strengthening. In addition to its work on initiating implementation of the UNFCCC, the COP agreed to negotiate, by the end of 1997, quantitative limits on GHG emissions beyond 2000. The COP created a new subsidiary body, the Ad Hoc Group on the Berlin Mandate, to conduct the negotiations (COPs often place large and potentially divisive issues into separate subsidiary bodies that can meet more frequently). However, the COP could not agree if the new limits on GHG emissions should represent real reductions from current levels, as opposed to simply reduced levels of future emissions, or which countries would be subject to the new commitments. The EU supported a commitment of substantial reductions, but the JUSCANZ group (Japan, the United States, Canada, Australia, and New Zealand), which constituted a new veto coalition, opposed negotiations for reduced emissions.

AOSIS played a lead role by submitting the first draft of the protocol. The EU maintained its lead-state role by tabling a proposal to reduce emissions of the three main GHGs (CO_2, methane, and nitrous oxide) from 1990 levels by at least 7.5

BOX 3.6 CLIMATE CHANGE MILESTONES

1988	World Meteorological Organization and UN Environment Programme, at the request of member states, organize the Intergovernmental Panel on Climate Change (IPCC).
1990	IPCC's First Assessment Report affirms that global warming is a serious threat.
1991	Formal negotiations for a climate convention begin under the auspices of the Intergovernmental Negotiating Committee for a Framework Convention on Climate Change.
1992	United Nations Framework Convention on Climate Change (UNFCCC) is signed in Rio de Janeiro, Brazil.
1994	UNFCCC enters into force.
1995	First meeting of the Conference of the Parties (COP) convenes in Berlin.
1995	IPCC's Second Assessment Report affirms the human influence on climate change.
1997	Kyoto Protocol is adopted in Japan, requiring industrialized countries to reduce their greenhouse gas (GHG) emissions.
2001	IPCC's Third Assessment Report concludes that temperature increases over the twenty-first century could be significantly larger than previously thought and that the evidence for human influence on climate change is stronger than ever.
2005	Kyoto Protocol enters into force.
2007	IPCC's Fourth Assessment Report says there is strong certainty that most of the observed warming of the past half-century is due to human influences.
2007	Bali Action Plan is adopted, including negotiating tracks to be pursued under the Ad Hoc Working Group on Long-Term Cooperative Action (convention track) and the Ad Hoc Working Group on Further Commitments for Annex I Parties Under the Protocol (protocol track).
2009	Copenhagen Accord is adopted, calling on participating countries to pledge specific actions they will undertake to mitigate GHG emissions.
2010	UNFCCC COP establishes the Green Climate Fund as a mechanism to assist developing countries in adaptation and mitigation practices to counter climate change.
2011	Ad Hoc Working Group on the Durban Platform for Enhanced Action (ADP) is established by the UNFCCC COP to develop a protocol, another legal instrument, or an agreed-upon outcome with legal force under the convention applicable to all parties.
2012	Doha Amendment to the Kyoto Protocol is adopted, setting up a second commitment period from 2013 to 2020.

continues

BOX 3.6 CLIMATE CHANGE MILESTONES *continued*

2013 **Parties adopt a decision establishing the Warsaw International Mechanism on Loss and Damage, and the Warsaw REDD+* Framework—a series of seven decisions on REDD+ finance, institutional arrangements, and methodological issues.**

2014 **Parties establish the Lima work program on gender and adopt the Lima Ministerial Declaration on Education and Awareness-Raising.**

2014 **IPCC's Fifth Assessment Report says that warming of the climate system is unequivocal; human influence on the climate system is clear; increasing GHG emissions and consequential global warming will likely produce severe, pervasive, and irreversible climate-change impacts but these impacts can be reduced by significantly limiting future emissions.**

2015 **UNFCCC COP21 adopts the Paris Agreement, the first-ever universal, legally binding climate agreement.**

*** REDD+ stands for reducing emissions from deforestation and degradation in developing countries, including conservation.**

percent by 2005 and by 15 percent by 2010. The EU proposal allowed some EU member countries, such as Germany, to undertake deeper emissions reductions and poorer EU states to accept lower targets, provided the overall EU reduction reached 7.5 percent. In sharp contrast, the United States proposed stabilizing emissions of six GHGs at 1990 levels by 2008–2010 for all Annex I parties.

The United States also proposed allowing countries to meet their targets through emissions trading with other parties. Countries able to exceed their emissions-reduction requirements would be able sell those excess reductions, or credits, to a country that was having trouble meeting its targets. In theory, this would allow countries with relatively inexpensive options to make more reductions while allowing countries with only very expensive options to do less. If the system worked, it would encourage greater technological innovation (as some countries sought to sell credits for profit) while allowing the world as a whole to achieve the same GHG reductions at a lower cost.

The EU did not oppose the concept of emissions trading but objected to the US proposal because it established few conditions for how the trading would occur. The EU and many developing countries were particularly concerned that the US proposal would assign emissions reductions to Russia and former Soviet bloc states in Central and Eastern Europe. These emissions were referred to as "hot air" because these countries' emission levels were already down more than 30 percent from 1990 as a result of the closure of many obsolete plants following the collapse of communism and the ongoing restructuring of their economies. Because emissions-reduction and trading levels would be pegged to 1990 levels, these countries would be able to sell emissions-reduction credits for emissions that no longer existed (hot air). This would allow parties buying the hot air to meet their reduction targets on paper but without actually reducing GHG emissions. Some developing countries also objected because countries purchasing credits would be able to delay serious efforts to transition away from fossil fuels. Other parties argued the proposed protocol should allow parties to fulfill only a certain percentage of their required reductions through trading.

Australia introduced another important issue: differentiation. It argued that because its economy depended far more heavily on exports of fossil fuels (coal) than the average Annex I party, it should not have to reduce its emissions as much as other countries. The demand for differentiation became another way for the veto coalition to seek to reduce its costs for complying with a possible targets-and-timetables agreement by allowing some states to justify lower targets.

As parties gathered for COP3 in Kyoto in 1997 (the planned deadline for adopting a protocol), differences between lead and veto states had grown. The United States, which had previously supported equal reductions for all industrialized-country parties, endorsed the concept of differentiation to accommodate the greater economic burdens that equal reductions would impose on certain states. The US delegation also took the position that it could not accept any emissions reductions unless large developing countries also agreed to binding emission reductions—a condition mandated by a unanimous vote in the US Senate. This proposal was unacceptable to developing countries.

Following a week and a half of intense negotiations, delegates finally adopted the Kyoto Protocol.[138] The protocol required industrialized-country parties to reduce their collective emissions of six GHGs (CO_2, methane, nitrous oxide, HFCs, perfluorocarbons, and sulfur hexafluoride) by at least 5.2 percent below their 1990 levels between 2008 and 2012. Countries had different requirements within this collective mandate, ranging from a 10 percent increase for Iceland (which already had very low emissions because of its reliance on geothermal and hydroelectric power) to 8 percent reductions for the EU and most of the countries in Eastern Europe. Switzerland and Canada had 8 and 6 percent reductions, respectively. Russia and New Zealand only had to freeze emissions. Australia could increase emissions by 8 percent. The United States agreed to a 7 percent reduction but won a concession that the three newer GHGs (HFCs, perfluorocarbons, and sulfur hexafluoride) would be calculated from a 1995, rather than a 1990, baseline. The presence of so many different requirements made the overall target less ambitious and was the first in a number of developments that limited the protocol's impact.

The US proposal for a formal commitment by developing countries to control and eventually reduce their emissions was dropped after China, India, and other developing-country parties attacked it, making clear that they constituted a broad and firm veto coalition on the issue and would not compromise. Arguing for the importance of upholding the principle of common but differentiated responsibilities (CBDR), these delegations even rejected an opt-in position that would have provided for voluntary adoption of an emissions target by non–Annex I parties.

Provisions in the Kyoto Protocol stated that it could enter into force only after ratification by fifty-five parties, including enough Annex I countries that their collective emissions represented at least 55 percent of the CO_2 emissions from Annex I countries in 1990. Designed to ensure that the protocol would have a meaningful impact if it entered into force, the requirement also provided bargaining leverage for industrialized countries, which could withhold ratification in exchange for compromises on particular issues. Thus, although most developing countries and small island states ratified immediately, many Annex I parties signaled their intention to use subsequent COP meetings to address remaining concerns and negotiate more favorable terms before they ratified.

By 2001, the protocol had still not entered into force. President George W. Bush announced in March 2001 that he would not seek US ratification of the agreement: "I oppose the Kyoto Protocol because it exempts 80 percent of the world, including major population centers such as China and India, from compliance, and would cause serious harm to the U.S. economy," he wrote, also citing what he called "the incomplete state of scientific knowledge of the causes of, and solutions to, global warming."[139] Although the protocol could enter into force without the United States, it would need the ratification of at least all members of the EU, as well as Canada, Japan, and the Russian Federation.

By mid-2004, Russia had become the focus of attention. With more than 120 countries having ratified already—including more than thirty Annex I parties representing 44 percent of that group's 1990 emissions—the 55 percent was now tantalizingly close, even without US involvement. If Russia, which represented 17.4 percent of the 1990 emissions of Annex I countries, signed on, the treaty would enter into force. In the end it was Russia's desire for admission into the World Trade Organization that provided the final incentive. The EU had told Moscow that it would support Russia's admission only after it ratified Kyoto.[140] On November 18, 2004, Russia ratified the protocol, which then entered into force on February 16, 2005.[141]

Round 3: The Copenhagen Accords

Yet even before the Kyoto Protocol entered into force, significant attention had already turned to the question of what would happen when the first commitment

PHOTO 3.5 Greenpeace Youth greeting delegates at the Bonn Climate Change Talks in June 2009, highlighting that decisions negotiated at this meeting will determine the outcome of the upcoming Copenhagen Climate Change Conference and the fate of numerous people around the world. Courtesy IISD/*Earth Negotiations Bulletin*, www.iisd.ca.

period ended in 2012 and the process of regime review and strengthening began anew. Article 3.9 of the protocol provides for commitments for subsequent periods for Annex I parties. Neither the precise nature nor the duration of such commitments is specified. Many believed that negotiations on a successor regime to the Kyoto Protocol's first commitment period would have to begin in 2008 to avoid a gap between the first commitment period and subsequent commitment periods (many believed a gap between commitment periods would create counterproductive uncertainty and complications for countries and industry). Negotiations on a successor agreement were expected to take at least two years, and the new agreement's entry into force could take at least another two years. Yet achieving consensus on the nature of such an agreement—including its goals and requirements, burden sharing, inclusion of developing countries, and means to ensure participation by both the United States, among the world's largest per capita emitters of GHGs, and China, the world's largest total GHG emitter—was not easy.

Negotiations began in 2005 and lasted until COP15 in Copenhagen in 2009. During this period, the internal composition of the lead state and veto state coalitions as well as other negotiation dynamics underwent several transitions. The EU was weakened by internal divisions and economic realities, making it more difficult for it to play a strong lead-state role. China became a key potential veto state due to its increasing economic strength and new status as the largest GHG emitter. This development hardened the US position, as another potential veto state, that China must take on binding obligations to reduce emissions. The G-77 became increasingly fragmented on climate policy, splitting into different groups on different issues according to vulnerability to climate change, rates of economic development, levels of GHG emissions, and oil exports. G-77 and China subcoalitions played different roles (lead state, swing state, or veto state) depending on which issue was under discussion. These coalitions included:

- BASIC: This coalition of Brazil, South Africa, India, and China plays a central role in climate negotiations (including those that resulted in the 2009 Copenhagen Accords) due to their fast-growing economies, increasing geopolitical status, and attempts to forge common positions on several key issues.
- Least-Developed Countries: These forty-eight countries focus on defending their interests, especially with regard to vulnerability and adaptation to climate change.
- AOSIS: These forty-two island and low-lying states are most vulnerable to sea-level rise and play the role of lead states in pushing for deep cuts in GHG emissions.
- Organization of Petroleum Exporting Countries (OPEC): These twelve countries have economies that rely heavily on fossil-fuel extraction and export and oppose measures to reduce GHGs that would significantly impact their economies. They also advocate for financial compensation to offset any adverse impacts.
- Bolivarian Alliance for the Peoples of Our America (ALBA): Consisting of Venezuela, Cuba, Bolivia, Nicaragua, Ecuador, Dominica, Antigua and Barbuda, and St. Vincent and the Grenadines (countries listed in the order they joined), this coalition pushes for developed countries to pay their climate debt and commit to steep emission cuts.
- Central American Integration System (SICA): This coalition pushes for greater recognition as one of the most vulnerable regions to the impacts of climate change.
- Central Asia, Caucasus, Albania, and Moldova (CACAM): This coalition represents these countries' interests as non–Annex I countries with economies in transition.
- Coalition of Rainforest Nations: This coalition strongly favors mechanisms that would pay developing countries to preserve large forests as carbon sinks.

- African Group: This coalition supports large GHG cuts and payments to developing countries to mitigate and adapt to climate change.

In addition to the fragmentation of the G-77, several developed-country subgroups were added into the mix. The Umbrella Group is a loose coalition of non-EU developed countries that formed following the adoption of the Kyoto Protocol. Although there is no formal list of members, the group is usually made up of Australia, Canada, Japan, New Zealand, Kazakhstan, Norway, the Russian Federation, Ukraine, and the United States. This coalition has sometimes served as a veto coalition to EU proposals. The Environmental Integrity Group, formed in 2000, comprises Liechtenstein, Mexico, Monaco, the Republic of Korea, and Switzerland—countries that do not caucus with either the EU or the Umbrella Group. The growing number of coalitions has created more complex negotiations as more and more countries seek substantive participation in the small contact groups that often hammer out the final deals, closed off from NGOs and the media.

The first challenge was to begin formal negotiations. After two years of deliberations and the release of the IPCC Fourth Assessment Report one month before, delegates attending COP13 in 2007 in Bali, Indonesia agreed on a process for reaching a comprehensive framework agreement for the post-2012 period in Copenhagen, Denmark, in December 2009. At the heart of the Bali Action Plan were negotiating tracks to be pursued under both the UNFCCC and the Kyoto Protocol. Two processes were necessary because a working group established under the Kyoto Protocol could not consider commitments for developing countries (non–Annex I parties) or include Annex I countries that had not ratified the Kyoto Protocol, namely, the United States. These issues could only be discussed under the UNFCCC. Two tracks meant that all types of potential future regime policies could be discussed by all of the relevant countries.

The two working groups met eight times in 2008 and 2009 as they tried to overcome a host of obstacles. Many of the most difficult issues revolved around broad policy questions concerning the post-2012 period: Should the new commitments be legally binding or voluntary? Which countries would have to reduce their GHG emissions? What targets and timetables should be established? Should these be short-term or long-term targets, or both? Should the controls address GHG emissions in general, like Kyoto, or should they include action on specific sources of emissions, like cement production or deforestation? What types and levels of new technology transfer and financial assistance, if any, should be provided to developing countries? Should developing countries be required to adopt particular commitments in exchange for such assistance? Should the new agreement take the form of a new protocol, an extension of the Kyoto Protocol, an amendment to the convention, or some other agreement? How should the regime balance actions to mitigate climate change and those to help countries adapt to it?

When delegates arrived in Copenhagen, they had more than two hundred pages of draft text before them—the output of the two working groups. Despite the preparatory work, however, negotiators were unable to resolve many of the core issues. One critical disagreement concerned the legal form of a Copenhagen outcome. The proposal by the industrialized countries for a single new agreement that combined the outcomes from the Kyoto and convention track negotiations was strongly opposed by developing countries, which stated that they would not allow "Kyoto to be killed."

The developing countries' position reflected, in part, their concern that the core principle of CBDR must not be undermined or abandoned.[142] The disagreement reflected a negotiating dynamic that emerged in 2002, when European countries began pressing for action from developing countries. For the first decade of the regime, from 1991 to 2001, the negotiations focused almost exclusively on developed countries' emissions. The basic axis during this period was the EU-US split. Although developing countries engaged in these debates, the negotiations focused primarily on what developed countries would do.[143] However, in their second decade, the negotiations became increasingly about potential developing countries' commitments, dividing the climate-change talks over the principle of CBDR.

Several related and problematic obstacles involved the world's two biggest GHG emitters and most powerful veto states: the United States and China. The United States insisted that a future agreement contain commitments by both developed and developing countries. China, supported by India, refused to accept any binding commitment to limit its emissions, even if they were differentiated. Meanwhile, most of the Annex I parties with Kyoto targets were unwilling to accept a second round of targets unless both the United States and the major emerging economies, in particular China, agreed to do their share under a legally binding global agreement.[144]

During the final days of the talks, in an extraordinary process, a very small group of heads of state and other high-level representatives from the major economies, including China and the United States, and main UNFCCC negotiating groups reached consensus on a framework agreement, the Copenhagen Accord.[145] Indeed, these negotiations were so private that when US President Barack Obama announced the text to the media as the Copenhagen outcome, most delegations had not yet seen it. When it was presented to the plenary for adoption, a long and acrimonious debate ensued over the document's status. A relatively small number of delegations, led by ALBA, blocked formal adoption of the agreement, calling the process that produced it "untransparent and undemocratic" because the text of the

PHOTO 3.6 Heads of state from the BASIC countries during informal consultations in Copenhagen in 2009. From left to right in circle: South African President Jacob Zuma (back of head), Chinese Premier Wen Jiabao, Indian Prime Minister Manmohan Singh (in turban), and Brazilian President Luiz Inácio Lula da Silva (front right). Courtesy Leila Mead, IISD/*Earth Negotiations Bulletin*, www.iisd.ca.

Copenhagen Accord had been developed by a small group, appearing "out of nowhere, with expectations that it would then be automatically approved by all parties."[146] In the end, rather than formally adopt the Copenhagen Accord, the COP agreed to merely take note of it.

In retrospect, the Copenhagen Accord represented a creative compromise that avoided a breakdown of the climate regime. The nonbinding agreement set forth a long-term, aspirational global goal of limiting temperature rise to no more than 2°C, established a process for recording voluntary mitigation targets and actions of both developed and developing countries, and agreed to increase funding for mitigation and adaptation by developing countries, including fast-start money for the 2010–2012 period approaching $30 billion and a goal of mobilizing $100 billion per year by 2020.[147] By 2010, more than one hundred forty countries had endorsed the accord, and more than eighty countries had submitted emissions targets and mitigation actions as called for by the accord.

By establishing a process for listing both developed-country targets and developing-country actions, the Copenhagen Accord satisfied US demands for symmetry. By establishing only political commitments for developing countries, it satisfied China's rejection of legally binding obligations. And by focusing on a political rather than a legal outcome, it postponed the decision about whether to continue the Kyoto Protocol.[148]

Round 4: The Paris Agreement

The first challenge after Copenhagen was to restore the diplomatic trust that had been lost as a result of the secretive negotiations. Many agreed that without a positive, balanced outcome at the next COP, there would be little chance of achieving meaningful global action on climate change and restoring trust in the UNFCCC and the Kyoto Protocol.[149]

Negotiations continued on two parallel tracks after Copenhagen, and the divisions that plagued the previous round of negotiations continued through four more meetings. When the COP convened in Cancun in December 2010, the Mexican hosts mapped out and carefully followed a transparent, multipronged process that gave parties the opportunity to bring forward their views and, in the final days, seek compromise text, particularly on the crunch issues of mitigation, monitoring, reporting and verification, international consultation and analysis, and a second commitment period under the Kyoto Protocol.[150]

The resulting Cancun Agreements included formal affirmation of the IPCC-recommended global target to limit global warming to 2°C above preindustrial levels; agreement to scale up mitigation efforts to work toward a global goal in 2011 to substantially reduce global emissions by 2050; establishment of an Adaptation Committee to enable enhanced action on adaptation and promote increased finance, technology, and capacity building; confirmation of the $30 billion fast-start pledges under the Copenhagen Accord and the newly established Green Climate Fund; and establishment of a Technology Mechanism to improve technology transfer and development.[151] These decisions added a number of new subsidiary bodies to the climate regime (see Figure 3.4). Although the substantive outcome was viewed by many as far from perfect and Bolivia went as far as to oppose the adoption of the Cancun Agreements because they would not reduce emissions sufficiently to prevent climate change,[152] most participants left Cancun with restored confidence in the UNFCCC process.[153] However, many also acknowledged that the meeting's achievements represented only a small step forward.[154]

The following year negotiators gathered in Durban, South Africa, hoping to turn a corner and make more substantial progress.[155] Delegates agreed to the Durban Platform for Enhanced Action, which launched a new negotiating process to develop a protocol or other agreement that would include all parties and address the post-2020 period.[156] The new negotiating body, the Ad Hoc Working Group on the Durban Platform for Enhanced Action (ADP), marked a sea change in the post-Kyoto negotiations. This was the first time that negotiations would take place

FIGURE 3.4 **Subsidiary Bodies Under the United Nations Framework Convention on Climate Change**

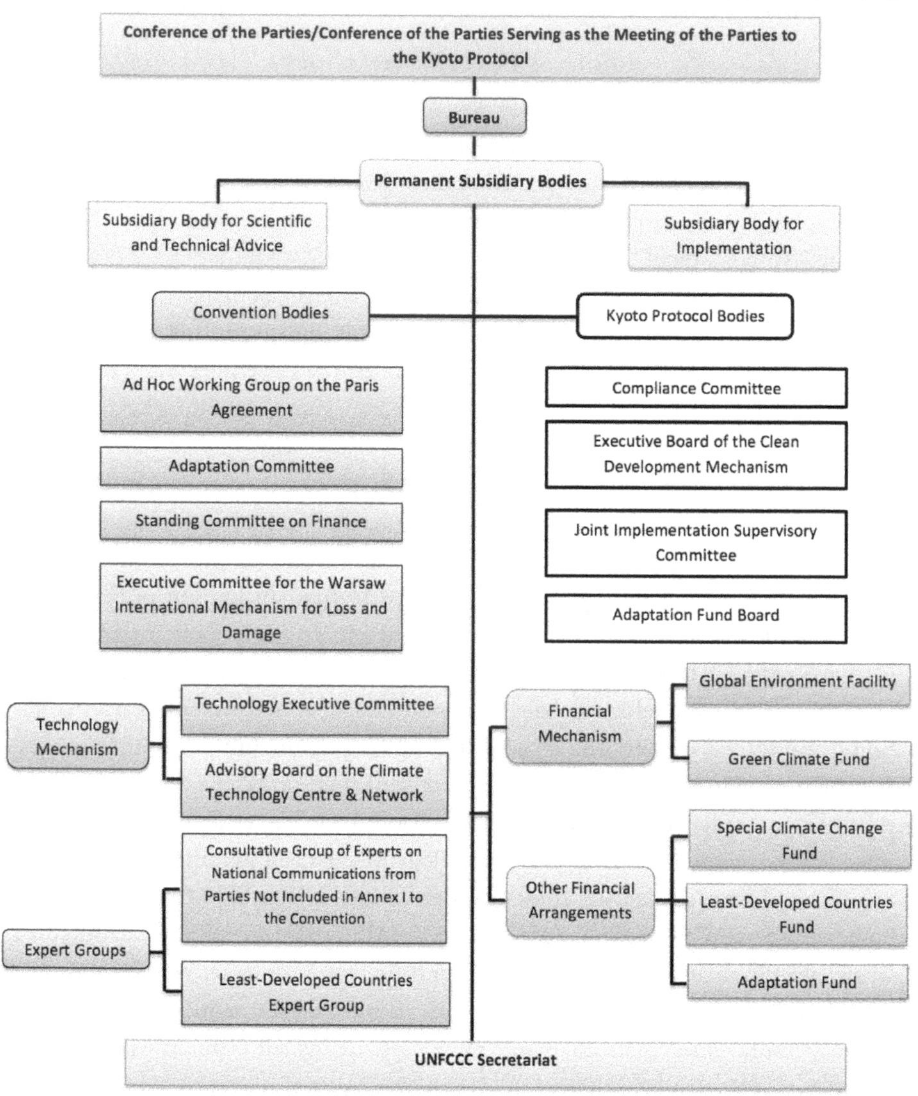

Adapted from UNFCCC Secretariat, http://unfccc.int/files/inc/graphics/image/png/unfccc_bodies_large.png.

on a single track. They also agreed in principle to extend the Kyoto Protocol so there would be no gap in commitment periods between 2012 and 2020.

One year later, and mere weeks before the end of Kyoto's first commitment period, governments met in Doha, Qatar, in 2012. By this time it was clear that the kind of top-down commitments contained in the Kyoto Protocol might not be the answer. The first commitment period under Kyoto included binding targets for thirty-seven industrialized countries, but while many already accepted the fact that the United States would never ratify the protocol, they did not expect that some of the key Kyoto Protocol parties—Japan, Canada, New Zealand and Russia—would jump ship by refusing to take on commitments in the second commitment period. This, coupled with the fact that under the Kyoto Protocol major developing countries with growing GHG emissions, such as China and India, did not have commitments, meant that in 2012, the Kyoto Protocol only covered about 15 percent of global GHG emissions.[157]

With this backdrop, governments approved The Doha Climate Gateway, which called for adopting a new universal global climate agreement by 2015 to cover the post-2020 period. To address the period before 2020, parties to the Kyoto Protocol adopted an amendment to the protocol that established the Kyoto Protocol's second commitment period from 2013 until 2020. This keeps Kyoto operational as a transitional measure. A total of 144 instruments of acceptance are required for the Doha Amendment to enter into force.[158]

The ADP met for twelve sessions after Doha, culminating in Paris in 2015. Under the ADP, delegates addressed two work streams: the first focused on a 2015 agreement and the second addressed pre-2020 ambition. The parallel work streams came out of the decision in Durban: the only way that many developing countries, especially India and China, would agree to launch negotiations under the convention on a new agreement containing a second commitment period would be if developed countries increased their ambition before 2020. Progress toward a new agreement was seen by many as an indication of whether the UNFCCC was still relevant and able to take the necessary action to combat climate change.[159]

Although the ADP negotiations had an underlying North–South dynamic with regard to responsibilities for both GHG mitigation and adaptation funding, they also featured a plethora of regional and interest groups. In addition to the thirteen groups listed earlier, several new groups formed during this round of negotiations. Armenia, Kyrgyzstan, and Tajikistan (which were later joined by Afghanistan) formed the Group of Mountain Landlocked Developing Countries in 2010 to highlight issues unique to their nations, including significant vulnerability to transportation costs and food insecurity. In 2012, Colombia, Costa Rica, Chile, Peru, Guatemala, and Panama created the Association of Independent Latin American and Caribbean States (AILAC). AILAC's platform calls for these and other countries to stop waiting for emissions reductions or financial support from wealthy countries and cooperate among themselves to launch ambitious low-carbon economic development at home and abroad. Also in 2012 the Like-Minded Developing Countries (LMDCs) formed to support maintaining CBDR, a core principle of the UNFCCC, meaning that developed countries must act first because they have done the most to create the problem of climate change.[160]

The ADP worked in several phases. During 2013, the focus was on fact-finding and improving delegates' understanding of the key elements of the 2015 agreement (adaptation, mitigation, technology, finance, capacity building, and transparency) and defining the scope, structure, and design of the new agreement. In December 2013, in Warsaw, COP19 agreed to ask member states to publicly outline what post-2020 climate actions they intended to take under a new international agreement, known as their intended nationally determined contributions (INDCs). Although some expressed concern that the 2015 agreement was developing into a purely bottom-up arrangement, meaning that states would delineate the extent and nature of their contributions, others saw this as a step forward. What seemed to be lacking, argued some, were top-down commitments and a pledge-and-review mechanism to assess the patchwork of national contributions to determine if they represented emission reductions substantial enough to stay within the 2°C target.[161]

Perhaps the biggest breakthrough in the climate negotiations took place outside of the UNFCCC negotiating chambers. In November 2014, US President Barack Obama and Chinese President Xi Jinping made a historic joint announcement on climate change, emphasizing their personal commitment to a successful climate agreement in Paris and marking a new era of multilateral climate diplomacy as well as a new pillar in their bilateral relationship. They agreed that climate change is one of the greatest threats facing humanity and that their two countries have a critical role to play in addressing it. They also expressed determination to move ahead decisively to implement domestic climate policies, to strengthen bilateral coordination and cooperation, and to promote sustainable development and the transition to green, low-carbon, and climate-resilient economies.[162] This announcement ended the long-standing game of GHG chicken between the United States and China, in which each of them was waiting for, and demanding that, the other take responsibility and develop plans for large, long-term GHG reductions.[163] Each country also feared that the other might blame them for a failure in Paris. By taking their public pledge together, a significant hurdle on the road to Paris was removed.

Meanwhile, the ADP met three times in 2014 before COP20 in Lima, where governments continued to clarify positions and operationalize the INDCs. By October, countries had made progress in elaborating the elements of a draft negotiating text under the first work stream. The Lima Call for Climate Action[164] was adopted in December 2014 and set the stage for the final bargaining phase to begin. But the question of how differentiation would be reflected in the Paris agreement was far from resolved. For example, most developing countries, in particular the

LMDCs, maintained that there should be differentiation, both in the 2015 agreement and the INDCs, in accordance with parties' obligations under the convention and reflecting the principles of CBDR and equity. On the other side, the United States advocated differentiation in accordance with CBDR and respective capabilities in line with varying national circumstances. The LMDCs also strongly opposed the formulation "parties in a position to do so" in relation to providing financial and technical support to developing countries for the preparation and implementation of their INDCs, arguing that such language disrupts convention-based bifurcation, effectively dismantling the wall between Annex I and non–Annex I parties.[165]

The bargaining phase began in earnest in February 2015 in Geneva, when delegates developed a negotiating text based on the elements annexed to Decision 1/CP.20 (Lima Call for Climate Action). The ADP worked through the elements text section by section, with parties proposing additions in places where they felt their views were not adequately reflected. The final eighty-six-page Geneva negotiating text covered all key substantive areas of the ADP's mandate, from adaptation to finance, technology, capacity building, mitigation, and transparency.

Negotiations continued in June and September. Delegates worked on streamlining and consolidating the text on the new climate agreement as well as negotiating text for decisions related to both work streams. In October, at the final meeting before Paris, there was a setback. The co-chairs had issued a revised text as a basis for further negotiations that many found unbalanced and unacceptable. Dissatisfied with this text, parties engaged in a text recompilation exercise, followed by a painstaking process of streamlining and clustering. Many of the compromises reached at the June and September sessions disappeared, as parties returned to positions expressed in Geneva eight months earlier.[166] The outcome was a significantly larger negotiating text, comprising a thirty-one-page draft agreement and twenty-page draft decision text on the first work stream, both with multiple options and a wide range of contrasting ideas. The text on the second work stream was included in a separate eight-page document. So although many welcomed the restoration of parties' ownership of the text, even more worried that delegates in Paris had been saddled with an impossible task.[167]

After the debacle in Copenhagen and the years spent rebuilding trust, many felt that the Paris Climate Change Conference in December 2015 could not afford to fail. Yet there were also concerns that the alternative to a failed conference would be a watered-down or meaningless agreement. After difficult negotiations under the ADP during the first week and under the French presidency of the COP during the second week, parties adopted the Paris Agreement by consensus during a dramatic session on December 12, 2015. In the end, many agreed that the outcome in Paris met or even exceeded expectations.

PHOTO 3.7 Celebrating the adoption of the Paris Agreement: French Ambassador Responsible for Climate Negotiations Laurence Tubiana; UNFCCC Executive Secretary Christiana Figueres; UN Secretary-General Ban Ki-moon; COP 21/CMP 11 President Laurent Fabius, foreign minister, France; and President François Hollande, France. Courtesy Kiara Worth, IISD/*Earth Negotiations Bulletin*, www.iisd.ca.

The 2015 Paris Climate Agreement represents an evolution in climate governance and a change in the UNFCCC COP process. At the center of the Paris Agreement are five-year cycles: each nationally determined contribution (NDC) cycle is to be more ambitious than the last and a global stocktake will inform collective efforts on mitigation, adaptation, and support will occur midway through the contribution cycle, every five years after 2023. Through these five-year cycles, parties are to "ratchet up" efforts to limit the increase in global temperature to "well below 2°C above preindustrial levels and to pursue efforts to limit the temperature increase to 1.5°C above pre-industrial levels." To track progress, parties are bound to a transparency framework, which represents the legally binding portion of the agreement, alongside an obligation to undertake and communicate their NDCs. The Paris Agreement also anchors, strengthens, and creates institutions and mechanisms, particularly for means of implementation. The decision supporting the agreement identifies modalities to be created or established for several new mechanisms, such as the new Paris Committee for Capacity Building and the mitigation and sustainable development mechanism, and to account for public climate finance.[168]

The agreement also represents an evolution in how parties address differentiation. The agreement builds on the compromise in Lima, which drew from the 2014

US–China joint announcement on climate change, that adds the element of "in light of different national circumstances" to the end of the familiar CBDR and respective capabilities. It makes no explicit mention of the annexes of the convention, the historic harbingers of differentiation, but only developed and developing countries, with subtle realignments in various sections. The NDCs represent, as US Secretary of State John Kerry called them, a "monument to differentiation": each country determines its "fair contribution" according to its respective capabilities and in light of its "different national circumstances."[169]

Finally, to make the Paris Agreement acceptable to the United States, it had to be written in such a way that President Obama could accept it without seeking congressional approval.[170] In 1997 the US Senate had refused to ratify the Kyoto Protocol, and the political climate in 2015 did not look any better. As a result, the Paris Agreement is a treaty under international law, but only certain provisions are legally binding. Meeting that test precluded binding emission targets and new binding financial commitments, much to the dismay of many NGOs, AOSIS, and the least-developed countries. Poorer countries had pushed for a legally binding provision requiring that rich countries appropriate a minimum of at least $100 billion a year to help them mitigate and adapt to climate change. In the final deal, that $100 billion figure appears only in a preamble, not in the legally binding portion of the agreement. So why did these countries accept it? Perhaps because, as UN Secretary-General Ban Ki-moon said, there was "no Plan B" if the deal fell apart.[171]

Why else did Paris succeed? According to some, the foundation of the Paris Agreement was actually laid in the Copenhagen Accord. After failing to gain formal acceptance in Copenhagen, the key elements of the agreement had been largely adopted the following year as part of the Cancun Agreements and had been reflected in other decisions leading up to Paris. So countries knew at least the broad outlines of what they were getting.

Second, by Paris the positions of several key developing countries, including China and Brazil, had changed. In Copenhagen, Cancun, and Durban, these countries had still hoped for an indefinite continuation of the Kyoto Protocol. Although no formal decision was ever made not to continue Kyoto, by Paris everyone seemed to have accepted that the next phase of the climate-change regime would be a single agreement applicable to all parties. The joint announcement by the United States and China in 2014 heralded this shift and gave many observers confidence that Paris could succeed where Copenhagen had failed.[172] Credit is also due to the role of NGOs, especially youth activists, who continually challenged governments to take strong action to prevent catastrophic climate change.

Round 5: Beyond Paris

The Paris conference gave new hope to the UN climate-change process and to environmental multilateralism. However, parties must still finalize important aspects of the new agreement and then effectively implement its provisions. In Paris, countries agreed only on the basic structure of the new climate-change regime—the cycle of NDCs, reporting, review, stocktaking, and updating. Now, they must elaborate more detailed rules for how the Paris Agreement will work in practice, including rules for reporting and review, international emissions trading, and a host of other issues.[173]

The Paris Agreement will not, on its own, solve climate change. At best, the NDCs announced as part of the agreement will, according to scientists, cut global GHG emissions by about half of what is necessary to prevent a 2°C temperature increase. But the Paris deal could represent the moment at which, because of a shift in global economic policy, the inexorable rise in planet-warming carbon emissions that started during the Industrial Revolution begins to level out and eventually decline.[174]

CONCLUSION

The ozone, hazardous waste, toxic chemicals, and climate regimes demonstrate how both state and nonstate actors can come together to address transboundary and atmospheric pollution problems. Each regime establishes binding controls, including in some cases specific targets and timetables, to limit emissions of specific substances. Each also demonstrates how regimes can strengthen over time but that such strengthening does not necessarily lead to fundamental success.

Whether a regime succeeds in addressing an environmental threat depends on the strength of the regime and the degree to which parties comply with its core provisions. Negotiating a strong global environmental regime almost always depends on inducing one or more key states in a veto coalition to go along with one or more of the core proposed provisions of the regime. By *strong*, we mean an agreement that mandates actions expected to have an impact on the problem and includes obligations or norms that make it sufficiently clear that parties can be held accountable for implementing them. In these four cases, numerous issues affected the negotiations. New scientific evidence helped move veto states on some issues (ozone and POPs) but far less on other issues (climate change). International political considerations played a role in the Basel Convention, where French and British desires to maintain close relations with former colonies factored into their views on the hazardous waste trade. Domestic political and ethical concerns played a key role in making Canada a lead state in the POPs negotiations. Perceptions of economic interests changed significantly in the ozone regime, allowing for rapid strengthening, whereas perceptions of economic interests in some countries slowed efforts to strengthen the climate regime.

Regime formation also requires leadership by one or more states committed to defining the issue and proposing policies to address it. In these cases, states motivated by particular vulnerabilities played lead roles: African countries on hazardous waste; Canada and some European countries on POPs; and AOSIS on climate change. However, only in the ozone case did arguably the most powerful state, the United States, play a lead role.

The ozone and climate regimes are often compared by scholars and policymakers because they have important similarities. Both address the earth's atmosphere. Both attempt to prevent changes to a critical natural system. Each addresses a system that exists within a dynamic equilibrium but has certain tipping points. This means that human action can impact the ozone layer and global climate system to a certain degree without changing either significantly, but once these impacts reach a certain level, it becomes essentially impossible to prevent significant negative changes to these systems or to reverse the changes (or fix the problem) for a very long time.

Both regimes started with framework conventions that established important goals, norms, institutions, and procedures. Governments then negotiated protocols that specified binding emissions reductions. Each has been significantly influenced by scientific bodies and economic interests. Both regimes impact important economic sectors, and their control measures faced significant opposition from powerful national and international interests. Both include references to the importance of addressing their issues in a precautionary manner. Both follow the principle of CBDR by mandating that industrialized countries address the issue first because they were responsible for creating the problem and have the necessary resources to address it. Each includes provisions for developing countries to receive FTA to help them meet their regime obligations.

The two regimes are also interrelated. Many of the chemicals that deplete the ozone layer and the substances developed to replace them are also powerful GHGs. Thus, by reducing CFC emissions, the ozone regime helped to address climate change, but by promoting certain CFC substitutes, such as HFCs, the ozone regime complicated matters and actually contributed to GHG emissions.

Yet, in other ways, the ozone and climate regimes are quite different. The ozone regime is widely considered to be among the most effective examples of international environmental policy. The climate regime has slowed the growth of GHG emissions, but global emissions have still increased significantly since 1990, serious impacts of climate change are already being observed, and despite the 2015 Paris Agreement, it is possible that catastrophic changes could still occur in the future.

The regimes have also developed at very different speeds. Governments concluded negotiations on the framework treaty for the ozone regime in 1985, eleven years after the discovery that CFCs might threaten stratospheric ozone. Scientists discovered that increasing GHGs could warm the atmosphere one hundred years before the UNFCCC was adopted. The ozone regime quickly expanded its scope, has strong and effective control mechanisms, and covers all major emitters of ODS. The climate regime has developed at a far slower pace, and only in 2015 did it include commitments designed to prevent the earth warming more than 2°C.

Although both regimes establish targets, in the ozone regime, all industrialized countries must meet essentially the same standards, whereas in the climate regime, different countries have established different levels of commitments to reduce emissions. Finally, governments have expanded and strengthened the ozone regime, primarily because of scientific consensus and the availability of substitutes for ozone-depleting chemicals. In contrast, although the IPCC has provided the scientific consensus that climate change is occurring and renewable energy technologies (including wind, solar, and geothermal) are increasingly available and cost-efficient, many governments have not taken significant action, in part because of concerns for the short-term costs associated with reducing the use of fossil fuels that contribute most to CO_2 emissions.

These differences reflect a variety of factors, including characteristics of the issue area; the evolution of scientific consensus; the identity and interests of the major actors, especially the lead and veto states; the design of the respective regimes; the evolution of economic and political interests; and the presence or absence of well-known obstacles to effective cooperation (see Chapter 5). This contrasts somewhat with global regimes that address the conservation of natural resources. Chapter 4 examines six regimes for natural resource conservation and management and how they differ from pollution-control regimes. The conclusion to Chapter 4 reviews and compares all ten case studies presented in Chapters 3 and 4.

4

The Development of Environmental Regimes:

Natural Resources, Species, and Habitats

Like the pollution-control regimes described in Chapter 3, regimes designed to conserve natural resources must overcome conflicts among states' economic and political interests, concerns for protecting state sovereignty, and different opinions regarding the importance of the precautionary principle and the principle of common but differentiated responsibilities (CBDR) and how to implement these principles. Moreover, natural resources regimes face the additional challenge of trying to protect resources and species that are of international importance but exist within the boundaries of sovereign states or beyond the boundaries of any state.

The regimes described in this chapter focus on shared natural resources: physical or biological systems that extend into or across the jurisdictions of two or more states. Shared natural resources include nonrenewable resources (for example, underground pools of oil or waterways) subject to the jurisdiction of two or more states, renewable and biological resources (fish stocks, birds, mammals), and complex ecosystems (forests, regional seas, river basins, coral reefs, and deserts).[1] Many shared natural resources exist in or pass through the commons or the jurisdictional zones of two or more states. Many highly migratory fish and marine mammals, including whales, move through the waters of several coastal states as well as the waters that are part of the high seas, beyond a country's exclusive economic zone (EEZ), the two-hundred-mile territorial waters under the jurisdiction of individual states.[2] Shared resources may also link states far removed from each other geographically, as in the case of migratory birds and other species.

The international management of natural resources must also address transboundary externalities that arise when activities that occur within the jurisdiction of an individual state produce results that affect the welfare of those residing in other states.[3] Such situations involve a very difficult question, one central not only to environmental but also to human rights and humanitarian issues: when does the international community have a legitimate interest, right, or obligation to seek significant changes in the domestic affairs of individual states because the activities occurring within their jurisdictions pose severe threats to the well-being of others or to international society as a whole? For example, should states still have unfettered rights to cut huge tracts of their forested land for timber or agriculture because these forests benefit the entire world as biodiversity reserves and as carbon sinks that mitigate climate change? Do countries have a right to try to change how other states manage ecosystems with rich biological diversity because the loss of particular plants and animals could prevent the discovery of new drugs that might cure cancer or other diseases around the world? Do states have the right to tell other states to stop killing, buying, and selling endangered species because extinction is now a global concern? Should the ethical perspectives of a large group of countries regarding whales, elephants, or turtles affect the activities of a smaller set of countries that do not share these views?

In addition to national sovereignty issues, efforts to negotiate regimes to deal with biodiversity, endangered species, forests, fish stocks, and land management may also have consequences for particular economic development strategies or efforts to promote free trade. Are states free to impose restrictions on imports from other countries if their production involves practices that are unacceptable on environmental grounds, such as catching shrimp in a way that endangers sea turtles? Should a country be prevented from developing a tropical timber industry, which could have major short-term economic benefits, because of the consequences of biodiversity loss?

Finally, pollution-control regimes, such as those for ozone and persistent organic pollutants (POPs), often include clear and measurable targets and timetables. Many natural resources regimes, especially those for biodiversity and desertification, do not lend themselves to those types of rules. Effective protection and management of natural resources often require complex sets of new policies that seek to address factors that threaten the resource. It is also often more difficult to develop effective indicators to measure implementation or to determine the impact of the regime.

The six cases examined in this chapter highlight different aspects of international natural resource management. The Convention on Biological Diversity (CBD) highlights North–South contrasts in the distribution of biodiversity resources and how natural resource management can conflict with particular economic, social, and political interests. The Convention on International Trade in

Endangered Species of Wild Fauna and Flora (CITES) also seeks to protect endangered species but is faced with the challenge of combating a globalized black market in those species. The desertification regime faces the challenge of reducing land degradation that impacts environmental sustainability and economic and social development. The forests case raises the question of whether legally binding treaties are always the solution for global environmental problems. The fisheries regime illustrates the importance and difficulty of managing resources that move between areas of national jurisdiction and the global commons. The International Convention for the Regulation of Whaling demonstrates how significantly regimes can change and what happens when politics and economics reduce the effectiveness of a regime and throw its purpose into question.

BIODIVERSITY LOSS

Biological diversity, or biodiversity, is most often associated with the earth's vast variety of plants, animals, and microorganisms, but the term encompasses diversity at all levels, from genes to species to ecosystems to landscapes. Approximately 1.75 million species have been identified, mostly small creatures such as insects. Many scientists believe that there could be as many as thirteen million species, although individual estimates range from three million to one hundred million. Ecosystems are another aspect of biodiversity. In each ecosystem, including those that occur within or among forests, wetlands, mountains, deserts, and rivers, living creatures interact with each other as well as with the air, water, and soil around them; in this way, they form an interconnected community. Biodiversity also includes genetic differences within species, such as different breeds and varieties, as well as chromosomes, genes, and genetic sequences (DNA).

The International Union for Conservation of Nature and Natural Resources (IUCN), in its Red List of Threatened Species, assesses species' extinction risks as Least Concern, Near-Threatened, three progressively escalating categories of Threatened (Vulnerable, Endangered, and Critically Endangered), and Extinct. By March 2014, IUCN had assessed 71,576 mostly terrestrial and freshwater species: 860 (1 percent) were extinct or extinct in the wild, and 21,286 (30 percent) were threatened, with 4,286 (6 percent) deemed critically endangered. The percentages of threatened terrestrial species ran from 13 percent (birds) to 41 percent (amphibians and gymnosperms). Of 6,041 marine species assessed, 16 percent are threatened and 9 percent are near-threatened, most by overexploitation, habitat loss, and climate change.[4] The overarching driver of species extinction is human population growth and increasing per capita consumption, which in turn lead to the main proximate causes—climate change, habitat destruction, pollution, and invasive species. How long these trends continue, their rate, and their geographic distribution will dominate the scenarios of species extinction and challenge efforts to protect biodiversity.[5]

Despite general acknowledgment of the importance of biodiversity and its value to the well-being of future generations, attempts to create an effective global regime for conserving biodiversity have suffered from differences concerning the definition of the problem, the application of the principle of national sovereignty versus that of the common heritage of humankind,[6] resistance to strong legal obligations by a veto coalition of developing states whose territories hold most of the world's biodiversity, and inconsistent support from the United States and several other key industrialized states.

In 1987, concern about the rate of species extinction led the governments that comprise the United Nations Environment Programme's (UNEP's) Governing Council to create a working group of experts to study the potential for an umbrella convention to rationalize activities in biodiversity conservation. As the group began the process of issue definition in 1990, the idea of a biodiversity convention became entangled in North–South struggles over plant genetic resources and intellectual property rights. The debate took shape around the ownership of genetic resources, with southern states arguing for explicit state sovereignty over the genetic resources within their borders and northern states arguing the view, previously accepted under international law, that these resources form part of the "common heritage of [hu]mankind." Some developing countries insisted that genetic resources belong to the states in which they are located and that access should be based on a "mutual agreement between countries." They also argued for the inclusion of provisions for noncommercial access to biotechnologies based on plant genetic resources found in the South as a central element in any biodiversity convention. Most industrialized countries initially opposed the inclusion of biotechnology in the convention and attempted to define the scope of the regime to include only the conservation of biodiversity in the wild and mechanisms to finance such efforts.[7]

Formal negotiations on what would become the CBD were completed in five sessions from July 1991 to May 1992. One hundred fifty-three countries signed the convention in June 1992, and the convention entered into force on December 29, 1993. To date, 196 countries are now parties to the CBD.[8] Notably, the United States is not a party to the convention, although the Clinton administration signed the convention in June 1993 (see Box 4.1).[9]

The resulting regime has three objectives: the conservation of biological diversity, the sustainable use of its components, and the fair and equitable sharing of benefits arising out of the use of genetic resources. Parties are obligated to inventory

BOX 4.1 CONVENTION ON BIOLOGICAL DIVERSITY MILESTONES

1987	UN Environment Programme's (UNEP's) Governing Council creates a working group of experts to study an umbrella convention to rationalize activities in biodiversity conservation.
1991	Negotiations on the Convention on Biological Diversity (CBD) begin.
1992	One hundred fifty-three countries sign the CBD at the Earth Summit in Rio de Janeiro, Brazil.
1993	CBD enters into force.
1995	Working Group on Biosafety is established by the Conference of the Parties (COP) to elaborate a protocol on biosafety.
2000	Cartagena Protocol on Biosafety is adopted.
2002	Global target for significantly reducing the rate of biodiversity loss by 2010 is adopted.
2003	Cartagena Protocol enters into force.
2004	COP7 establishes the Working Group on Access and Benefit Sharing.
2004	COP7 adopts the Akwé: Kon Guidelines for cultural, environmental, and social impact assessments and the Addis Ababa Principles and Guidelines for sustainable use.
2005	Ad Hoc Group on Liability and Redress holds first meeting.
2010	COP10 adopts the Strategic Plan 2011–2020 and the Aichi Biodiversity Targets.
2010	Nagoya–Kuala Lumpur Supplementary Protocol on Liability and Redress to the Cartagena Protocol on Biosafety is adopted.
2010	Nagoya Protocol on Access to Genetic Resources and the Fair and Equitable Sharing of Benefits Arising from Their Utilization is adopted.
2012	Intergovernmental Science-Policy Platform on Biodiversity and Ecosystem Services is established.
2014	COP12 creates a Subsidiary Body for Implementation to improve compliance with the convention.
2014	Nagoya Protocol enters into force.

and monitor biodiversity, incorporate the concepts of conservation and sustainable development into national strategies and economic development, and preserve indigenous conservation practices. The convention takes a comprehensive, rather than sectoral, approach to the conservation of biological diversity and the sustainable use of biological resources, and this has proven to be an implementation challenge. The fact that the treaty encompasses socioeconomic issues, such as the sharing of benefits from the use of genetic resources and access to technology, including biotechnology, has also led to implementation challenges. In order to implement and strengthen the CBD regime, the Conference of the Parties (COP) has made decisions requiring implementation actions by parties and negotiated protocols to establish concrete commitments on biosafety and the sharing of benefits from the use of genetic resources.

Regime Strengthening

Implementation decisions under the CBD have been less focused than in some of the other major global environmental regimes. This reflects the more diffuse nature of the regime's rules and norms, the absence of a strong lead-state coalition, the absence of an enforcement mechanism, and a general lack of political will. However, the COP has made progress in both identifying global conservation priority areas and developing work programs on conservation and/or sustainable use in particular sectors.

The COP's first approach to implementation was the development of seven work programs in critical areas that sustain biodiversity and provide critical ecosystem services: mountain regions, dry and subhumid lands, marine and coastal areas, islands, inland waters, agricultural systems, and forests.[10] These programs are the main instruments that CBD parties use to achieve the commitments contained in the convention. They include guidelines for national implementation, often recommending reforms of national laws, policies, or administrative practices. The work programs also identify tasks for furthering implementation at the international level (for instance, assigning tasks to the CBD COP and subsidiary bodies with a view to the further refinement of CBD provisions or concepts) as well as opportunities for collaboration between the CBD and other international instruments or processes.[11]

However, the overall coherence of the programs of work has been obscured, according to some observers, by the "convoluted, repetitious and disorderly drafting of CBD COP decisions."[12] This is an obstacle for national officials who are responsible for implementing the convention. Furthermore, in a treaty that relies on national implementation, there is no mechanism to systematically and effectively monitor implementation at the national level. The COP does not even review national reports but, rather, offers conclusions on the basis of the secretariat's syntheses of reports submitted by parties.[13]

Lack of effective implementation was clearly demonstrated in the international community's failure to meet the global target of significantly reducing the rate of biodiversity loss by 2010. The COP adopted this target in 2002, and it was later endorsed by the World Summit on Sustainable Development (WSSD) and incorporated into the Millennium Development Goals (MDGs).[14] The 2010 *Global Biodiversity Outlook* provided scientific evidence that the global target was not met. In particular, the authors noted the following:

- Species that have been assessed for extinction risk are on average moving closer to extinction. Amphibians face the greatest risk, and coral species are deteriorating most rapidly in status. Nearly one-quarter of plant species are estimated to be threatened with extinction.
- The abundance of vertebrate species fell by nearly one-third on average between 1970 and 2006, with especially severe declines in the tropics and among freshwater species.
- Natural habitats in most parts of the world continue to decline in extent and integrity.
- Extensive fragmentation and degradation of forests, rivers, and other ecosystems have also led to loss of biodiversity and ecosystem services.
- Crop and livestock genetic diversity continues to decline.
- The five principal pressures directly driving biodiversity loss (habitat change, overexploitation, pollution, invasive alien species, and climate change) are either constant or increasing in intensity.[15]

The causes of these failures include the insufficient scale of action to implement the convention, insufficient integration of biodiversity issues into broader policies, insufficient attention to the underlying drivers of biodiversity loss, and insufficient inclusion of the real benefits of biodiversity (and the costs of its loss) within economic systems and markets.[16]

In response to this failure, in October 2010 the COP adopted renewed commitments in the Strategic Plan for Biodiversity 2011–2020,[17] which calls for effective and urgent action this decade. The Strategic Plan is supported by the twenty Aichi Biodiversity Targets to be met by 2020 at the latest (see Appendix B). In 2014, *Global Biodiversity Outlook 4*, which was released as part of COP12 in the Republic of Korea, examined progress toward the Aichi targets.[18] The report noted that some of the areas that have witnessed progress include an increase in protected areas, access and benefit-sharing of resources, promotion of sustainable use, slowing down of loss of some forest habitats like the Brazilian Amazon, and restoration efforts of degraded ecosystems, especially forests and wetlands, among others. For the majority of the targets, however, the report noted that additional efforts will be required to meet the 2020 deadline, including the following:

- Although global rates of deforestation are declining, they remain alarmingly high. The total area of land remaining in natural or semi-natural conditions has shown a downward trend in recent decades and would decline further by 2020 if recent trends continue (Target 5).
- Nitrogen and phosphorus pollution continues to pose a very significant threat to biodiversity and ecosystem services globally (Target 8).
- The percentage of reefs rated as threatened increased by 30 percent from 1997 to 2007. Overfishing and destructive fishing methods are the most pervasive threats, affecting around 55 percent of reefs. One-quarter of reefs are affected by coastal development and pollution from land, including nutrients from farming and sewage. Around one-tenth suffer from marine-based pollution (Target 10).
- The protection of those species most in decline is not on track to be achieved. Despite individual success stories, the average risk of extinction for birds, mammals, amphibians, and corals shows no sign of decreasing (Target 12).
- Substantial efforts are required if the goal of restoration of at least 15 percent of ecosystems is to be met. A number of parties have set targets related to ecosystem restoration. For example, Belarus, Belgium, Brazil, Dominica, the European Union (EU), Japan, Malta, and the United Kingdom have set targets to restore at least 15 percent of degraded lands (Target 15).[19]

The report concluded that what is needed is a package of actions, such as a legal or policy framework, socioeconomic incentives, public and stakeholder engagement, and an overall substantial increase in total biodiversity-related funding to reverse the loss of biodiversity.[20]

Cartagena Protocol on Biosafety

Biosafety refers to a set of precautionary practices that seek to ensure the safe transfer, handling, use, and disposal of living modified organisms (LMOs) derived from modern biotechnology. By the early 1990s, most countries with biotechnology industries had domestic biosafety legislation in place, but there were no binding international agreements regarding genetically modified organisms that cross national borders. Biotechnology, particularly its agricultural applications, was a highly controversial issue. Policy responses varied widely in different legal orders, the most well-known example being the contrasting approaches of the United States and the EU, with the latter calling for a precautionary approach toward modern biotechnology. In 1999, several European governments joined European environmental nongovernmental organizations (NGOs) in calling for a moratorium on the import of genetically modified foods. Although the moratorium ended in 2004, it provoked a World Trade Organization (WTO) dispute between the United States and the EU, which was decided in favor of the United States in 2006.[21]

Parties to the CBD began negotiations on the biosafety protocol in 1996. A powerful veto coalition emerged, called the Miami Group, which included the world's major grain exporters outside of the EU (Argentina, Australia, Canada, Chile, the United States, and Uruguay). The veto coalition argued that trade restrictions in the protocol would harm the multibillion-dollar agricultural export industry, that imprecision in several key provisions would create uncertainty and difficulties implementing the treaty, that countries would be able to block imports based on their own criteria rather than on sound scientific knowledge, and that the increased documentation required under the protocol would create unnecessary and costly bureaucratic procedures.[22] Participation in the regime by at least some veto states was deemed important to the agreement's future success, so crafting acceptable compromises proved difficult.

In January 2000, governments finally reached an agreement and adopted the Cartagena Protocol on Biosafety.[23] The protocol entered into force in September 2003 and requires parties to take precautionary measures to prevent LMOs from causing harm to biodiversity and human health. The protocol has since been supplemented by the 2010 Nagoya–Kuala Lumpur Supplementary Protocol on Liability and Redress to the Cartagena Protocol on Biosafety,[24] which provides international rules and procedures on liability and redress for damage to biodiversity resulting from LMOs. The supplementary protocol has not yet entered into force.[25]

The successful implementation of the Cartagena Protocol depends on the interplay of economic interests. One example of this is the difficulty parties had in reaching agreement on documentation requirements for bulk shipments of LMOs intended for food, feed, and processing (LMO-FFPs). In order to adopt the protocol, negotiators put off an agreement on this issue; according to Article 18.2(a) of the protocol, parties are required to decide on the detailed requirements for such documentation within two years of entry into force. At the second Meeting of the Parties (MOP) in 2005, exporting countries expressed concern that labeling shipments that might include LMOs could interfere with trade. Apart from fears that many commodity producers did not have the capability to account for small amounts of LMOs that a shipment might contain, there was widespread concern that stricter documentation requirements could prove costly, restrict market access, and have a negative impact on countries that rely heavily on agricultural exports. Meanwhile, importing countries wanted to set up documentation requirements that would state which LMOs actually were included in a shipment rather than a longer list of LMOs that might be included. Many developing-country importers, particularly African parties, stressed that documentation without guidance regarding which LMOs were most likely contained in the shipment posed significant capacity challenges to importing states to detect and monitor the content of incoming shipments.[26] New Zealand and Brazil played the role of veto states, later joined by Mexico, Paraguay, and Peru, and expressed serious objections to establishing any rule that would affect commodity trade in general.[27]

At MOP3 in Curitiba, Brazil, in 2006, Brazil shifted positions and, because of its role as host country, played the role of lead state by preparing drafts and promoting compromise to demonstrate its commitment to a successful outcome of the meeting. Under Brazil's leadership, parties agreed on a compromise package that balanced the interests of importing and exporting states as well as of developed- and developing-country parties. The Curitiba Rules request parties to take measures to ensure that documentation accompanying LMO-FFPs in commercial production clearly states that the shipment contains LMO-FFPs in cases where the identity of the LMO is known. In cases where the identity of the LMO is not known, the Curitiba Rules still allow documentation to state that the shipment may contain one or more LMO-FFPs, and they acknowledge that the expression "may contain" does not require a listing of LMOs of species other than those that constitute the shipment.

The rules were reviewed at MOP7, held in the Republic of Korea in 2014. The African Group wanted to develop a stand-alone document to accompany LMO-FFPs, which importing developing countries have traditionally viewed as a necessity for informed decision making on LMO imports. A number of other countries, including Brazil, Ecuador, the EU, Honduras, Japan, New Zealand, Paraguay, the Philippines, South Africa, and Uruguay, disagreed. Bolivia, Moldova, Norway, Peru, and Qatar suggested keeping the item under review and collecting additional experiences during the third review of the protocol's effectiveness. The EU suggested, and many parties agreed to, compromise text, which states that further review of the need for a stand-alone document is not required, unless a subsequent COP/MOP decides otherwise in light of the experience gained. The compromise was accepted.[28] Although this decision effectively suspends further discussions on the most controversial items relating to LMO-FFPs, several developing-country parties indicated that making decisions on imports of LMO-FFPs will remain a challenge in the absence of additional guidance.[29]

Considering that large agrobusinesses and other economic interests, backed in most cases by their governments, did not want any agreement at all, the Cartagena Protocol is a historic achievement. For the first time under international law there is a requirement that countries take precautionary measures to prevent LMOs from causing harm to biodiversity and human health. Furthermore, at MOP5 in 2010 a new phase in the international regulation of biotechnology began: one that focuses on cooperation in managing the risks associated with LMOs rather than on the struggle between those who see biotechnology as a solution for many of the world's pressing problems and those who oppose it because they consider the risks of LMOs greater than the benefits.[30] At the same time, however, to date only one member of the original veto coalition (Uruguay) has ratified the Cartagena Protocol, leaving many of the world's top grain exporters outside the regime, a situation that hinders the regime's overall effectiveness.

Access and Benefit Sharing

Genetic resources from plants, animals, and microorganisms are used for a variety of purposes, ranging from basic research to consumer products to medicines. Those using genetic resources include research institutes, universities, and private companies operating in many different economic sectors, including pharmaceuticals, agriculture, horticulture, cosmetics, material science, and biotechnology. For example, calanolide A, a compound isolated from the latex of the tree *Calophyllum lanigerum var. austrocoriaceum* found in the Malaysian rain forest, is used as a treatment for HIV-1.[31] An appetite suppressant has been derived from species of Hoodia, succulent plants indigenous to southern Africa and long used by the San people to stave off hunger and thirst.[32]

Since the CBD's entry into force in 1993, developing countries have called for an increased focus on the convention's third official objective: fair and equitable sharing of benefits arising from the use of genetic resources.[33] This issue involves how companies, collectors, researchers, and others gain access to valuable genetic resources in return for sharing the benefits of this access with the countries of origin and with local and indigenous communities. In 2004, the COP mandated that the Working Group on Access and Benefit Sharing elaborate an "international regime on access to genetic resources and benefit-sharing." In 2008, the COP agreed on a schedule of meetings to complete negotiations before 2010.[34]

Sharp divisions between the lead countries (the providers of genetic resources) and the veto coalition (user countries) plagued the access and benefit-sharing negotiations. The Group of Like-Minded Megadiverse Countries (LMMC), formed in 2002, took the lead on behalf of provider countries. The megadiverse countries are primarily tropical countries that possess rich varieties of animal and plant species, habitats, and ecosystems. Up to 70 percent of the world's biological diversity is located in the megadiverse countries, which include Bolivia, Brazil, China, Colombia, Costa Rica, Democratic Republic of Congo, Ecuador, India, Indonesia, Kenya, Madagascar, Malaysia, Mexico, Peru, Philippines, South Africa, and Venezuela. The LMMC, with the African Group, claimed that the current distribution of benefits was unfair and sought to change it. Those regarded as user countries (i.e., those with industries that commercialize genetic resources)—mostly industrialized countries—were quite content with the status quo, in which access to genetic resources was arguably free.

After seven years of negotiations, parties adopted the Nagoya Protocol Access to Genetic Resources and the Fair and Equitable Sharing of Benefits Arising from Their Utilization in October 2010 in Nagoya, Japan. In a move that many criticized for its lack of transparency, the Japanese COP presidency convened a secret meeting of the African Group, Brazil, the EU, and Norway in order to produce a draft to be considered by ministers. This enraged many delegations, in particular the Like-Minded Asia-Pacific and Latin American and Caribbean group members who felt excluded from this key meeting. Others, however, believed that the Japanese-brokered meetings—for better or worse—had produced an agreement that would have been impossible otherwise, as negotiations had ground to a halt.[35]

The final compromise text was characterized by many as a "masterpiece in creative ambiguity." Instead of resolving outstanding issues by crafting balanced compromise proposals—an endeavor that would have failed—the most contentious references were either deleted from the text or replaced by short and general provisions that allowed for flexible interpretation (but possibly also too wide a berth for implementation).[36]

Particularly contentious issues included the following:

- Whether the scope of the protocol would extend beyond genetic resources to biological resources more generally;
- How the holders of traditional knowledge related to genetic resources would be involved in procedures of access to such knowledge;
- How far countries will cooperate with one another when there are allegations of illegal uses;[37] and
- Whether the scope of the protocol would extend to genetic resources acquired prior to the protocol's entry into force.

On the first point, some developed countries had insisted that derivatives of genetic resources be excluded from the protocol and instead negotiated in bilateral contracts. Developing countries, on the other hand, tried to ensure that derivatives, such as naturally occurring biochemicals, were included.[38] The final text states that the protocol shall apply to "genetic resources" and to the "benefits arising from the utilization of such resources,"[39] which includes research and development on the genetic and/or biochemical composition of genetic material. Research on the properties of extracts and molecules from plants, for example, and their development and commercialization as ingredients in pharmaceuticals or cosmetics will now have to meet access and benefit-sharing requirements.

With respect to the treatment of traditional knowledge, some developed countries had argued that traditional knowledge relating to genetic resources should be addressed by the World Intellectual Property Organization. However, others argued that leaving out traditional knowledge made little sense, as it is often used alongside genetic resources, and doing so would significantly reduce the benefits for developing countries and local communities.[40] The protocol states that its rules apply to "traditional knowledge associated with genetic resources within the scope of the Convention and to the benefits arising from the utilization of such knowledge."[41]

Along these lines it is worth noting that another group that holds traditional knowledge played an important role in the negotiations—women. The Like-Minded-in-Spirit Group of Women, a group of female delegates, including representatives from governments, NGOs, indigenous and local communities, civil society, and industry, was formed in November 2009 to incorporate a gender perspective in the access and benefit-sharing regime. This group became the first platform to ensure that women's voices are heard and their contribution is fully recognized in the CBD. As a result of their efforts, references to the important role that women play in access and benefit sharing and biodiversity conservation and the need for the full participation of women in all levels of policy making and implementation appear throughout the agreement.

On international cooperation, developed countries had argued that the protocol should focus on compliance with national legislation instead of creating international regulations. However, because only about twenty-five developing countries had legislation on access and benefit sharing in place, it was argued that such a requirement would further weaken the effectiveness of the protocol.[42] The final text encourages transboundary cooperation and provides that each party shall take "appropriate, effective and proportionate legislative, administrative or policy measures" to provide that genetic resources and traditional knowledge used within their jurisdiction have been accessed in accordance with "prior informed consent and that mutually agreed terms have been established."[43]

To resolve the question of sharing benefits from new and continuing uses of genetic resources acquired prior to the entry into force of the protocol—one of the

PHOTO 4.1 The Like-Minded-in-Spirit Group of Women was formed to ensure that women's voices are heard and their contribution was fully recognized in the Nagoya Protocol negotiations. Courtesy Franz Dejon, IISD/*Earth Negotiations Bulletin*, www.iisd.ca.

key demands of the African Group—delegates also resorted to creative ambiguity. Although there is no direct reference to this issue, a provision envisages creation of a global multilateral benefit-sharing mechanism to address benefit sharing in transboundary situations or situations where it is not possible to grant or obtain prior informed consent. Such a mechanism, once established, could cover benefits arising from genetic resources acquired outside the framework of the CBD.[44]

The Nagoya Protocol entered into force on October 12, 2014, and by early 2016 had seventy parties. In the end, however, the main strength of the Nagoya Protocol is also its weakness: the creative ambiguities could lead to differing interpretations at the national level, create legal uncertainties, and hinder implementation. Depending on how these issues are addressed, the protocol may or may not become a powerful tool for a more balanced implementation of the CBD's three objectives.[45]

Moving Forward

Although parties have made progress on important issues, the biodiversity regime remains weak. The complexity of the biodiversity crisis, the multiple levels at which it can be addressed (e.g., ecosystem, species, genes), the North–South contrasts in the distribution of biodiversity, and the many ways that biodiversity protection can conflict with important economic, social, and political interests make reaching agreement on action-enforcing language a contentious process. Numerous work programs, working groups, and subsidiary bodies have served to increase the number of meetings each year and decrease parties' focus on strengthening and implementing the convention.

A few steps have been taken to address these and other issues. The Strategic Plan for Biodiversity 2011–2020[46] serves as the framework for revising, updating, and implementing National Biodiversity Strategies and Action Plans, which are the key national-level implementation plans.[47] At COP12 in 2014, delegates also agreed to create a Subsidiary Body for Implementation to improve compliance with the convention.

In addition, the Intergovernmental Science-Policy Platform on Biodiversity and Ecosystem Services (IPBES) was established in 2012 to serve as an interface between the scientific and the policy communities to synthesize, review, assess, and critically evaluate relevant information and knowledge generated worldwide by governments, academia, scientific organizations, NGOs, and indigenous communities. It is hoped that IPBES will be able to provide scientifically credible and independent information that takes into account the complex relationships among biodiversity, ecosystem services, and people. Thus, this could assist the CBD in achieving the Aichi Targets and slow down the decline in biodiversity and ecosystem services.[48]

Effective strengthening of the biodiversity regime will depend, in part, on greater commitments by states with significant economic, political, or biodiversity resources. Some European states have been active in trying to strengthen the regime, but without greater clout—and the support of developing countries as well as the United States, which remains a nonparty to the regime—the convention could remain unfocused and ineffective.

INTERNATIONAL TRADE IN ENDANGERED SPECIES

Although the CBD was adopted in 1992 to conserve biodiversity in general, concern about the impacts of trade on endangered species of plants and wildlife dates back to the early 1960s. Today, international trade in wildlife is estimated to be worth billions of dollars annually and to include hundreds of millions of plant and animal specimens. The trade ranges from live animals and plants to a vast array of products derived from them, including foods, leather goods, musical instruments, timber, tourist curios, and medicines. The level of exploitation of some animal and plant species is high, and their trade, together with other factors such as habitat loss, can deplete their populations and even bring some close to extinction.[49]

Because the trade in wild animals and plants crosses national borders, international cooperation is required to regulate it and prevent certain species from overexploitation and event extinction.

CITES, which was adopted in 1973, was conceived in the spirit of such cooperation. The treaty combats overexploitation of wild animals and plants by delineating threatened species, establishing rules regarding their trade, and imposing trade sanctions against violators.[50] CITES is really an umbrella regime containing a multitude of smaller regimes within regimes that address specific species. Under this umbrella, proponent and veto coalitions vary across the specific agreements on individual species (or groups of species) and often cross traditional North–South divisions.[51]

CITES currently protects roughly fifty-six hundred species of animals and thirty thousand species of plants. A COP meets every two to three years to decide how to regulate trade in species in different degrees of danger. CITES divides threatened species into three categories, with various levels of controls for each category. Species listed in Appendix I are threatened with extinction and are not to be traded except for scientific or cultural endeavors. Species listed in Appendix II, although not yet endangered, are considered to be affected by international trade that, if left unregulated, would endanger them. Before a country can allow exports of an Appendix II species, a scientific authority must determine that the proposed export will not be detrimental to the survival of the species. The decision to list a particular species in Appendix I or II requires a vote by the parties. Species listed in Appendix III are listed voluntarily by range states (states within which the species live) seeking cooperation in the control of international trade, and they do not require a vote. As of early 2016, Appendix I lists more than 930 species; Appendix II lists more than 34,400, and Appendix III lists more than 140.[52]

All 182 member parties are required to adopt national legislation that corresponds to the species listings of CITES. They have to designate two authorities on a domestic level: a management authority and a scientific authority. The scientific authority advises the management authority, which is in charge of issuing permits and certificates in keeping with the CITES appendices. These authorities work with customs offices, police departments, and other appropriate agencies to record species trading and report to CITES. Thus, the operation and enforcement of CITES can be compromised when national and local officials do not, or cannot, enforce it.

CITES has three main operational bodies: the Standing Committee, the Animals Committee, and the Plants Committee. The Standing Committee oversees and helps to coordinate the workings of other bodies with policy guidance and budget management. The Animals and Plants Committees work between COPs and report to the COP about their respective mandates. The main implementation tool used by these bodies to monitor CITES's effectiveness is a review of significant trade, a process whereby the bodies evaluate trade data pertaining to specific species, delving deeper if they notice anything out of place. However, CITES's capacity to actually reduce illegal trade using this process is minimal. The review of significant trade relies on data reported by countries through government agencies; these statistics include information only on legal trading. Because one of the major causes of species loss is illegal trading, these statistics do not reflect or have much of an effect on the illegal movement of species and their derivatives.

The more than thirty thousand plant species protected under CITES's three appendices compose 85 percent of all of the species covered by the treaty. The collection of certain rare or commercially desirable plant species poses a major threat to their survival in the wild. Examples include trees that produce high-quality lumber (e.g., big leaf mahogany, Brazilian rosewood), herbs for medicinal use (e.g., American ginseng, goldenseal), and unusual, exotic ornamental species, such as orchids, cacti, and cycads. For example, Brazilian rosewood produces a highly prized wood. Its red-brown timber is attractive, heavy, and strong, as well as highly resistant to insect attack and decay. Of more importance, however, is its high resonance—ideal for the production of musical instruments (see Box 4.2). The tree is also harvested for the construction of high-quality furniture and for its oils and resins. Brazilian rosewood was listed on CITES Appendix I in 1992, making trade in its timber illegal. Nevertheless, deforestation in its native habitat and illegal logging continued, and mature trees with thick trunks are now very rare.[53]

Another example is the African cherry (*Prunus Africana*), which is found in mountainous tropical forests in central and southern Africa and Madagascar. For centuries it has been harvested for its hard and durable timber as well as for its bark, which has medicinal properties and is used to treat malaria, fever, kidney disease, urinary tract infections, and, more recently, prostate enlargement. As long as all of the bark is not removed, the tree can bear repeated harvests and has been used sustainably for hundreds of years. Indigenous knowledge maintained that, postharvest, bark grows back more quickly on the side of the tree that faces the sunrise, and it was also believed that medicine made from this east-facing bark would heal a patient faster. Thus, traditionally, only one side of the tree was stripped, yielding about 55 kilograms (121 pounds) of bark. But when completely stripped, a large tree may yield up to a metric ton of bark—worth considerably more on the international market. Harvest limits and protective folklore have therefore given way to market demand, and the African cherry appears to be in steep decline, despite its inclusion in CITES Appendix II.[54]

In recent years, CITES has focused on combating illegal wildlife trade, which has become one of the largest sources of criminal earnings in the world—ranking

BOX 4.2 GUITARS, THE CONVENTION ON INTERNATIONAL TRADE IN ENDANGERED SPECIES OF WILD FAUNA AND FLORA, AND THE LACEY ACT

Each party to the Convention on International Trade in Endangered Species of Wild Fauna and Flora (CITES) must pass domestic laws that implement the treaty. In the United States, Congress has passed multiple such laws, of which the Lacey Act is the most relevant to CITES. Under the Lacey Act, it is unlawful to import or export fish, wildlife, or plants that are taken in violation of state or foreign law, including all species protected by CITES. In 2008, Congress amended the Lacey Act to include a wider variety of prohibited plants and plant products, including illegally logged woods, such as Madagascar ebony, which is threatened due to overexploitation combined with slow growth of the species

On November 17, 2009, as part of an investigation into the illegal trade of ebony wood from Madagascar, US federal agents raided the Gibson Guitar Corporation's Nashville, Tennessee, manufacturing facility. One of the largest guitar manufacturers in the world, Gibson is known for such iconic instruments as the Les Paul electric guitar, John Lennon's acoustic-electric dreadnought, banjos, mandolins, and even pianos under the Baldwin name. Gibson had purchased fingerboard blanks that consisted of sawn boards of Madagascar ebony from an exporter who did not have authority to export Madagascar ebony. Two years later, on August 24, 2011, agents raided Gibson again, seizing pallets of ebony and rosewood fingerboards imported from India. In August 2012, Gibson agreed to pay a $300,000 fine and donate $50,000 to the National Fish and Wildlife Foundation to promote the protection of endangered hardwood trees to settle the charges that it had illegally imported Madagascar ebony. In return, the government deferred prosecution for criminal violations of the Lacey Act.

In a 2015 study on the effectiveness of the Lacey Act, Jeff Prestemon of the US Forest Service found that the amount of imported wood covered by the act dropped by as much as 70 percent and prices rose 30 to 60 percent from 2008 to mid-2013. Although direct impacts on deforestation rates have not been evaluated, Prestemon's economic models offer a straightforward means to estimate the impact of legislation on trade in endangered species.

Sources: **James McKinley Jr., "Famed Guitar Maker Raided by Federal Agents,"** ***New York Times,*** **August 31, 2011; "Gibson Guitar to Pay $300,000 for Violating Lacey Act with Illegal Timber Imports from Madagascar," mongabay.com, August 6, 2012, http://news.mongabay.com/2012/0806-gibson-doj-lacey.html; James McKinley Jr. "Gibson Guitar Settles Claim over Imported Ebony,"** ***New York Times,*** **August 6, 2012; J. P. Prestemon, "The Impacts of the Lacey Act Amendment of 2008 on US Hardwood Lumber and Hardwood Plywood Imports,"** ***Forest Policy and Economics*** **50 (2015), 31–44.**

alongside trafficking of drugs, people, and weapons. According to UNEP, illegal wildlife trade is estimated to be worth $50 billion to $150 billion per year. The illegal fisheries catch is valued at $10 billion to $23.5 billion a year globally, and illegal logging, including processing, is valued at $30 billion to $100 billion.[55]

Demand for illegal wildlife is ubiquitous and growing (see Table 4.1). Illicit wildlife trade ranges in scale from single-item, local bartering to multi-ton, commercialized exports of animals and plants. Wildlife contraband may include live pets, hunting trophies, fashion accessories, cultural artifacts, ingredients for traditional or fanciful medicine, wild protein for human consumption (or bushmeat), and other products. Some of the most lucrative illicit wildlife commodities include tiger parts, elephant ivory, rhino horn, and exotic birds and reptiles. Although there is no distinct criminal profile that describes wildlife poachers and traffickers, illicit wildlife trade networks often involve a combination of local hunters, regional middlemen, wildlife experts, criminal entities (that sometimes include terrorists and drug traffickers), global suppliers, front companies, online retailers, corrupt officials, and consumers willing to purchase such contraband.[56]

The Internet has contributed to the growth of the illegal wildlife trade, providing an unprecedented technological platform for a burgeoning, undocumented trade in endangered animals, alive and dead (see Box 4.3). The ability to scan the globe for buyers or sellers without leaving one's office, to mask one's identity with increasingly sophisticated technology and software, and to buy and sell online without ever having to meet even a middleman are just three aspects of Internet-based endangered-species crime that challenge the abilities of national and international law enforcement officials. In addition, many national laws aimed at regulating wildlife trade to ecologically sustainable levels do not yet address aspects of illicit Internet sales, and some countries have few laws governing Internet commerce at all. Even where laws exist, enforcement is often inadequate because officials do not have the capacity to address Internet crime or because they are not focused on online trafficking in wildlife. One such case is the African elephant.

African Elephants

The case of African elephants illustrates CITES's efforts to curb species loss and exemplifies the difficulties inherent in negotiations among numerous parties. The fact-finding stage led to the African elephant's listing under CITES Appendix II in 1977 (see Box 4.4). Beginning in the early 1980s, African elephant populations began to decline precipitously, falling from 1.3 million in 1979 to 625,000 in 1989.[57] In 1985, CITES established a system of ivory export quotas in the countries with elephant herds. Declines continued, however, and a study sponsored by WWF and

TABLE 4.1 **Selected Illicit Wildlife Trade and Estimated Retail Value in US Dollars**

Elephants	$2,200 per kilogram of ivory[1]
Rhinos	$66,000 per kilogram of rhino horn[2]
Snakes	$235,175 per liter of snake venom[3]
Big Cats	$1,300–$35,000 per tiger or snow leopard skin;[4] up to $70,000 for tiger remains[5]
Bears	$200,000 per pound of bear bile[6]
Sharks	$400 per pound of shark fin[7]
Reptiles (often live)	$10,600 per iguana;[8] $4,400 per komodo dragon;[9] $4,000 per ploughshare tortoise;[10] $10,000 per tortoise from Madagascar;[11] $20,000 per golden coin turtle[12]
Fish	$200,000 per Asian arowana fish (dragon fish)[13]
Great Apes (often live)	$40,000 per baby gorilla;[14] $45,000 per orangutan[15]
Birds	$31,000 per black cockatoo[16]

Source: For this and other information, see "Endangered Animals and Wildlife Prices," Havoscope, www.havocscope.com/black-market-prices/animals-wildlife/.

1 UNEP, *UNEP Yearbook: Emerging Issues in Our Global Environment* (Nairobi: UNEP, 2014), 26, www.unep.org/yearbook/2014/PDF/UNEP_YearBook_2014.pdf.

2 Ibid.

3 P. Vijian, "Smugglers Deliver Deadly Bite into Snake Population," *Bernama*, August 27, 2011.

4 Bryan Walsh, "How U.S. Soldiers Are Fueling the Endangered Species Trade," *Time*, Ecocentric Blog, February 27, 2012; Bhalin Singh, "Plight of the Bengal: India Awakens to the Reality of Its Tigers—and Their Fate," Mongabay.com, June 6, 2010.

5 Rhett Butler, "Laos Emerges as Key Source in Asia's Illicit Wildlife Trade," *Yale Environment 360*, February 26, 2009.

6 Victoria Kim, "Woman Staying in Los Angeles Accused in Bear Bile Importation," *Los Angeles Times*, March 28, 2009.

7 John Berman and Sarah Rosenberg, "'Sharkwater': Turning the Page on 'Jaws'," ABC News Nightline, October 26, 2007.

8 "Man 'Steals Iguanas in Fake Leg'," *BBC News*, September 22, 2007.

9 "Komodo Dragon Costs Rp 40 M on Black Market," *Jakarta Post*, March 23, 2011.

10 David Adam, "Monkeys, Butterflies, Turtles . . . How the Pet Trade's Greed is Emptying South-East Asia's Forests," *Observer*, February 21, 2010.

11 Hannah McNeish, "Madagascar's 'Tortoise Mafia' on the Attack," *BBC News*, June 27, 2011.

12 Feargus O'Sullivan, "Threatened Species on the Menu Worldwide," *The National*, July 17, 2011.

13 Associated Press, "7 Charged in LA with Smuggling Endangered Fish," *Houston Chronicle*, May 11, 2010.

14 Miguel Llanos, "Baby Gorilla on Black Market for $40,000 Is Rescued," MSNBC, October 11, 2011.

15 Diana Wright, "Domestic Black Market for Endangered Wildlife Thrives in Indonesia," Mongabay.com, September 18, 2005.

16 Carolyn Barry, "Australia's Wildlife Blackmarket Trade," *Australian Geographic*, August 16, 2011.

Conservation International concluded that African elephants were being harvested at a rate far exceeding that considered sustainable. This rate of loss, driven primarily by the international trade in ivory, led to increasing calls to place African elephants in Appendix I of CITES and establish a worldwide ban on trade in African elephant ivory.

BOX 4.3 ENDANGERED SPECIES ONLINE

Website monitoring is vital to understand the level and scope of illegal wildlife trade online. The Trade Records Analysis of Flora and Fauna in Commerce (TRAFFIC), a wildlife trade monitoring network, began, in January 2012, to closely track websites in China for key illegal wildlife products and to search for related code words used for these products. By the end of September 2014, they had increased their search from fifteen websites to twenty-five, from five items to eight (ivory, rhino horn, tiger bone, hawksbill sea turtle shells, pangolin scales, leopard bones, Saiga antelope horn, and hornbill casques), and from twelve code words to sixty-four.

In their first month of monitoring, TRAFFIC found almost thirty thousand advertisements for illegal wildlife products, a figure that rose to more than fifty thousand in the next two months but dropped again in April 2012 to around thirty thousand after TRAFFIC contacted and shared the monitoring results with website managers, several of whom immediately deleted the identified advertisements. This number has since stayed stable thanks to cooperation with e-commerce platforms, website managers, and enforcement authorities. However, social media platforms, which allow dealers to select their audiences and thus protect their privacy, remain a challenge for monitoring.

Examples of Advertisements for Illegal Wildlife Products Posted on Social Media in One Month

SOCIAL MEDIA ACCOUNT	IVORY TUSKS	IVORY SEGMENTS	RHINO HORNS OR HORN PIECES	HELMETED HORNBILL CASQUE	IVORY ITEMS
Dealer 1	60+	100+	10		Thousands
Dealer 2	2	54		25	Hundreds
Dealer 3	26	70+	50+	21	Hundreds
Dealer 4	5	11			Hundreds
Dealer 5	7	11	15		Hundreds
Dealer 6	15	30+	2		Hundreds
Total	**115+**	**276+**	**77+**	**46+**	**Thousands**

Source: **Xiao Yu and Wang Jia, *Moving Targets: Tracking Online Sales of Illegal Wildlife Products in China* (Cambridge, UK: TRAFFIC, February 2015), www.traffic.org/storage/China-monitoring-report.pdf.**

BOX 4.4 CONVENTION ON INTERNATIONAL TRADE IN ENDANGERED SPECIES OF WILD FAUNA AND FLORA MILESTONES ON ELEPHANTS

1963	Eighth International Union for the Conservation of Nature and Natural Resources (IUCN) General Assembly, held in Nairobi, Kenya, calls for the creation of an international convention to regulate export, transit, and import of rare or threatened wild species or the skins and trophies thereof.
1964–1971	IUCN sends out successive drafts of the convention for review by governments.
1972	UN Conference on the Human Environment, held in Stockholm, proposes that a plenipotentiary conference be convened as soon as possible to prepare and adopt a convention on export, import, and transit of certain species of wild animals and plants.
1973	Plenipotentiary Conference to Conclude an International Convention on Trade in Certain Species of Wildlife, hosted by the United States in Washington, DC, convenes February 12–March 2, 1973.
1973	Convention on International Trade in Endangered Species of Wild Fauna and Flora (CITES) is adopted on March 3, and twenty-one countries sign the convention.
1975	CITES enters into force on July 1.
1977	African elephants are listed under CITES Appendix II.
1985	CITES establishes a system of ivory export quotas in countries with elephant herds.
1989	CITES parties vote to place all African elephant herds in Appendix I.
1997	Conference of the Parties (COP) approves limited sales of ivory. COP approves similar sales in 2002 and 2004.
2007	In response to reports of increased illegal trade in ivory, COP bars additional proposals for ivory trade for nine years following one more one-off sale it schedules for 2008.
2008	One-off sale of 108 tons of ivory takes place in November with a total profit of nearly $15.5 million to Botswana, Namibia, South Africa, and Zimbabwe.
2010	Tanzania and Zambia propose another one-off ivory sale and to downlist some African elephant populations to Appendix II; the proposal fails to get enough votes.
2013	COP agrees to revise rules for trade in elephants and elephant products, including on employing DNA analysis, monitoring ivory stockpiles, controlling live-elephant trade, and dealing with countries that are persistently involved in illegal trade, but is unable to resolve differences on other key issues to stop illegal trade in ivory and other elephant products.
2014	Forty-six countries adopt the London Declaration, agreeing to tackle the illegal wildlife trade that is killing thousands of elephants, rhinos, and other endangered species each year.

The bargaining stage began at the seventh CITES COP in October 1989, when an odd international coalition consisting of Austria, the Gambia, Hungary, Kenya, Somalia, Tanzania, and the United States initiated an effort to list the African elephant in Appendix I and ban trade in ivory products entirely. Another unlikely coalition, uniting foes in southern Africa's struggle over apartheid (Botswana, Malawi, Mozambique, South Africa, Zambia, and Zimbabwe), opposed the listing. Underlying their resistance was the fact that several southern African herds had grown in the 1980s as a result of conservation efforts financed through limited hunting of elephants and commercial trade of elephant parts. Despite this resistance, a two-thirds majority of all CITES parties voted to place all African elephant herds in Appendix I.[58] The southern African states lodged reservations against the ban and announced plans to sell their ivory through a cartel, with the proceeds to be used to finance conservation.[59]

It was Japan, however, not the African states, that determined the viability of the regime. In 1989, the worldwide ivory market was worth an estimated \$50 million to \$60 million annually. Japan dominated this market, importing more than 80 percent of all African ivory products, making it the potential leader of an effective veto coalition.[60] As the major consumer nation, Japan had been expected to enter a reservation, allowing a significant portion of the ivory market to remain viable and effectively vetoing the ban. However, facing heavy pressure from the United States, the European Community (EC), and national and international NGOs, Japan eventually decided not to oppose the ban. World prices for raw ivory eventually plunged by 90 percent.[61]

In the 1990s, three southern African countries (Botswana, Namibia, and Zimbabwe) called for ending the ivory trade ban, proposing that the African elephant be downlisted from CITES Appendix I to Appendix II. Their efforts were unsuccessful at CITES meetings in 1992 and 1994.[62]

At COP10 in June 1997, in Harare, Zimbabwe, the three southern African range states, with support from Japan, again proposed a split downlisting of the elephant populations in their countries. The resulting debate was long and acrimonious. The three range states argued that their herds had grown to a combined total of about 150,000 and that their inability to exploit the herds commercially was costing them revenues that could be used to increase their conservation budgets. The United States and other parties feared that even partial easing of the trade ban would result in a new flood of illegal trade in ivory and cited deficiencies in enforcement and control measures in the three African countries and Japan that had been identified by the CITES panel of experts. They pointed out that, without adequate controls in place, it would be extremely difficult to track where elephant tusks originated.

In the end, a committee of nineteen CITES members worked out a compromise under which each of the three states could get permission to sell a strictly limited experimental quota of ivory under a stringent set of conditions.[63] A heavily regulated one-time sale of ivory from these countries was also approved after monitoring deficiencies were adequately addressed. All experimental sales went to Japan, with all funds obtained by the sale to be invested in elephant-conservation efforts.[64]

At COP12 in 2002, Botswana, Namibia, and South Africa proposed another limited sale of ivory. This proposal was accepted after the establishment of strict monitoring and verification conditions. In 2004, at COP13, Namibia proposed a two-thousand-kilogram annual quota of raw ivory, in addition to the trade of worked ivory, leather, and hair products. The proposal involving raw ivory was rejected, but Namibia was allowed to participate in trade in leather and hair products and noncommercial trade in worked ivory amulets known as *ekipas*.[65]

At COP14 in 2007, TRAFFIC reported that illegal trade in ivory had increased since 2005 and implicated the countries of Cameroon, China, the Democratic Republic of Congo, Nigeria, and Thailand as the major players. Four proposals on African elephants were also presented. After negotiations, an all-African consensus was reached that kept the allowance of the one-off sale approved at COP12, along with the trade in leather, hair products, and *ekipas* approved at COP13. In addition, Botswana, Namibia, South Africa, and Zimbabwe received permission to have a one-off sale of raw ivory that had been registered in government stocks prior to January 31, 2007.[66] The decision also bars additional proposals for ivory trade for nine years following the one-off sale and allows the Standing Committee to stop the agreed-upon trade if noncompliance arises. The Standing Committee was also tasked with proposing a decision-making mechanism for ivory trade in time for consideration at COP16 in 2013 and requested the secretariat to establish a specific fund for African elephants.[67]

In July 2008, at the fifty-seventh meeting of the CITES Standing Committee, delegates gave the go-ahead for the one-off sale of ivory and agreed that China could join Japan as an approved bidder on the ivory. Combined, Botswana, Namibia, South Africa, and Zimbabwe were allowed to sell 108 tons.[68] The secretariat visited all four African countries to verify the quantity and legality of ivory stocks before allowing the sale to proceed. The sale took place in October and November 2008 with a total profit of nearly $15.5 million to the four southern African states.[69]

Nevertheless, by May 2012, elephant poaching levels were reportedly the worst in a decade.[70] At COP16 in 2013, delegates revised and modernized the rules of the game for the trade in elephants and elephant products, including through addressing e-commerce, employing DNA analysis, monitoring ivory stockpiles, controlling live-elephant trade, and dealing with countries that are persistently involved in illegal trade in ivory. However, COP16 did not resolve the debate on one-off ivory sales. Participants disagreed strongly on the impact and wisdom of such sales as a strategy to protect elephants. Proponents laud one-off sales as a way of funding conservation efforts and fulfilling demand through controlled means, whereas opponents see them as stimulating demand and increasing incentives for poaching and black markets. Although CITES programs to assess the impact of these sales, such as Monitoring the Illegal Killing of Elephants and Elephant Trade Information System, found no clear connection between the sales and illegal markets, several delegates pointed to the limited number of one-off sales as providing insufficient evidence for such a conclusion. Parties remained split on whether to even discuss a potential CITES decision-making mechanism to standardize decisions on whether and when to allow one-off sales, with some countries opposing any move toward allowing such sales. As a result, the COP postponed the decision on one-off ivory sales until COP17, in South Africa in September 2016.[71]

Despite these efforts, the global poaching trade is at its highest in decades, with tens of thousands of African elephants killed every year—more than one hundred

PHOTO 4.2 On the morning of June 19, 2015, in Times Square, New York City, the US Fish and Wildlife Service, with wildlife and conservation partners, hosted its second ivory crush event. One ton of ivory seized during an undercover operation, plus other ivory from the New York State Department of Environmental Conservation and the Association of Zoos and Aquariums, was crushed. Courtesy Kelsey Williams/US Fish and Wildlife Service, https://www.flickr.com/photos/usfwshq/18962965111/in/album-72157652312709464/.

thousand between 2011 and 2014. The slaughter outstrips the rate at which elephants can reproduce, and some experts warn that there could be as little as five years left to save elephants from extinction in the wild.[72] In 2014, forty-six countries adopted the London Declaration, agreeing to tackle the illegal wildlife trade that is killing thousands of elephants, rhinos, and other endangered species each year. At that meeting in London, Botswana, Chad, Ethiopia, Rwanda, and Uganda also launched an elephant protection initiative.[73] A number of countries, including Belgium, China, France, Hong Kong, Kenya, the United Kingdom, and the United States, have held symbolic ivory crushes and ivory burnings to raise awareness.[74]

Controlling International Trade in Endangered Species

The case of African elephant ivory illustrates several distinctive features of the CITES regime. First, CITES is actually an umbrella regime enveloping a multitude of mini regimes across which states' political and economic interests vary from species to species. These mini regimes, while sharing a common organizational structure, are all characterized by an individual set of developmental stages, lead states, and coalitions that often consist of unusual alliances. Veto coalitions can be led by producer nations, consumer nations, or a coalition of both, as is the case with elephant ivory. In addition, not all producer or consumer nations share the same interests. In the elephant case, range states split over listing, largely reflecting differences in the viability of central versus southern African elephant populations.

Second, the role that science plays in the listing of species can also vary by species. Although logically associated with the issue-definition and fact-finding stages, scientific knowledge can also play an important role in bargaining and regime strengthening (as seen in the ozone case in Chapter 3). The case of African elephants demonstrates an important scientific role in issue definition and fact finding, via the documentation of the initial population crashes, as well as in the bargaining and regime-strengthening stages, via the documentation of different population trajectories for southern and eastern African elephant populations.

Third, although scientific knowledge can inform debates, economic and political factors often determine specific outcomes. Strong commercial interests on the part of consumer nations or issues such as national sovereignty may lead nations to oppose listings or other conservation measures despite strong evidence of declining populations.

Finally, the impact that a CITES listing has on controlling population declines also varies by species. A CITES listing can be ineffective in stopping overexploitation, particularly if important trading countries file a reservation to the listing, trade is predominantly domestic rather than international (e.g., trade in Chinese tigers and tiger parts), factors other than trade are more important in driving population loss (e.g., habitat loss), or monitoring is difficult because of the type of product traded (e.g., sawn wood or plant extracts).

Overall, CITES has produced mixed results. CITES, like the whaling and ozone cases, illustrates the effectiveness of bans or prohibitions as a mechanism for regulating activities that threaten the environment, natural resources, or wildlife. However, it is weakened by powerful commercial interests, new technologies, and the ability of parties to opt out of regulation by entering reservations on particular species. At the same time, the threats to endangered species continue to multiply, and a black market for trade in endangered species continues to proliferate, driven by both greed and poverty, presenting significant challenges to many endangered species even if they are already part of the CITES regime.

FORESTS

The issue of forests is unique among these case studies in that it continues to defy the creation of a comprehensive global regime. The main reasons for this are linked to the complexity of the issue and the successful efforts of a veto coalition. As in several other cases, the makeup of a veto coalition changed over time, but only in this issue has the veto coalition changed so much in both membership and rationale yet still blocked the adoption of a global treaty. However, over time the demands for a binding global treaty have decreased, and the broader discussions on global forest policy appear to have moved beyond this impasse.

Over the past twenty-five years, the earth lost 3.1 percent of its forested area, dropping from 4.1 billion hectares to just under 4 billion hectares. In a very positive sign, the deforestation rate slowed by more than 50 percent between 1990 and 2015 (see Table 4.2). This change reflects both decreased deforestation in some countries and significantly increased plantation and other new forested areas in

TABLE 4.2 **Global Forest Area Change, 1990–2015**

YEAR	FOREST (1,000 HECTARES)	ANNUAL CHANGE (1,000 HECTARES)	ANNUALIZED CHANGE*
1990	4,128,269		
2000	4,055,602	–7,267	–0.18
2005	4,032,743	–4,572	–0.11
2010	4,015,673	–3,414	–0.08
2015	3,999,134	–3,308	–0.08

*Calculated as the compound annual growth rate.

Source: Food and Agriculture Organization of the UN (FAO), *Global Forest Resources Assessment 2015* (Rome: FAO, 2015).

other countries. It appears that net forest area change has stabilized over the past decade. This is an important development given the fact that wood removals in 2011 are about 200 million cubic meters higher per year than in 1990 and human populations have grown during this period by about 37 percent.[75]

An estimated 1.3 billion people—nearly 20 percent of humanity—rely on forests and forest products for their livelihoods, with the majority living on less than $1.25 a day. The most recent evidence, drawn from more than three hundred communities living in or near forested areas in twenty-four developing countries, suggests that the contribution of forests to household incomes in such areas is surprisingly large—28 percent. This is roughly the same as earnings from agriculture.[76]

Forests provide a number of important ecosystem services. Ecosystem services are any positive benefit that an ecosystem, such as a forest, provides to people, including the production of food and water; the control of climate and disease; nutrients and crop pollination; and even spiritual and recreational benefits.[77] For example, forests are vital for climate regulation and help maintain the fertility of the soil, protect watersheds, and reduce the risk of natural disasters. The five most forest-rich countries (the Russian Federation, Brazil, Canada, the United States, and China) account for more than half of the total global forest area. The losses from deforestation every year—about the size of Greece—account for 12–20 percent of the global greenhouse gas (GHG) emissions that contribute to global warming. At the same time, forests absorb about 15 percent of the planet's GHG emissions.[78] Forests are also home to about 80 percent of the world's remaining terrestrial biodiversity.[79]

Most forests are cut down to provide land for food and cash crops. Other causes of deforestation and forest degradation include overharvesting (of both industrial wood and fuelwood), overgrazing by livestock (which degrades the soil and has other impacts), insect pests and diseases (which are expanding their range because of climate change), fires, storms, and air pollution. Wood is essential for construction and a host of other uses. Timber exports are a source of foreign exchange for many countries. Deforestation is linked to both global markets and local needs. For example, 65 percent of the total primary energy supply in Africa comes from solid biomass, including firewood and charcoal harvested from local forests.[80]

Although cutting trees and clearing forests make perfect sense to those engaged in these practices, they have a negative impact on many people. As trees disappear, forest dwellers, often the poorest and most vulnerable members of society, are deprived of their homes and livelihoods. Fuelwood and other forest products become harder to obtain. Flooding results, land is eroded, and lakes and dams are filled with silt. With fewer trees to soak up carbon dioxide (CO_2) from the atmosphere, the risk of climate change increases. As plant and wildlife species become extinct, biological diversity is reduced.[81]

Countries have discussed forest-policy issues within the UN system since the end of World War II.[82] The Food and Agriculture Organization of the UN (FAO) was the principal global forum for the discussion of international forestry issues from the mid-1940s until 1971, when the FAO established the Committee on Forestry. Since its first session in 1972, this committee has met regularly at two-year intervals to review forestry problems of "an international character."[83] Forest industries and the restoration of timber supplies were prominent topics of early conferences and remain on the committee's agenda along with logging and the marketing and use of forest products.

The launch of international forest governance can be traced to the 1980s, when accelerating trade and a globalizing environmental movement contributed to concern about the loss of tropical forests (see Box 4.5).[84] Other milestones in the global dialogue on forest policy include the adoption of the International Tropical Timber Agreement in 1983 and the establishment of the International Tropical Timber Organization in 1986. These initiatives sought to promote international trade in tropical timber, the sustainable management of tropical forests, and the development of forest industries. The organization's membership represents 90 percent of world trade in tropical timber and 80 percent of the world's tropical forests.

The Tropical Forestry Action Plan (TFAP) was launched in 1985 to address tropical forest loss and advocate the economic benefits of forestry by promoting development aid to agroforestry, wood-based energy production, industrial timber development, and forest conservation. TFAP was eventually abandoned, however, for failing to meet these ambitions and for being too slow, centralized, and narrow in scope.[85]

The 1992 UN Conference on Environment and Development (UNCED or Earth Summit) marked a turning point in the international forest-policy dialogue. Negotiations on forests in the Preparatory Committee were polarized. The developed countries, which had called for a forest convention in 1990, argued that forests should be seen as a global commons because all humanity has a stake in their conservation. On the other side, the Group of 77 (G-77) claimed that forests are sovereign national resources to be used in line with national development objectives. With rejection of a treaty by the G-77 dooming negotiations on a formal convention, delegates instead negotiated two non–legally binding agreements on forests: the Forest Principles[86] and Chapter 11 of the outcome document, Agenda 21, titled "Combating Deforestation."[87]

During the UNCED negotiations on the Forest Principles, the United States and Canada tried to link the principle of the sovereignty of countries over their

BOX 4.5 UNITED NATIONS FOREST POLICY MILESTONES

1971 Food and Agriculture Organization of the UN (FAO) establishes the Committee on Forestry to bring together heads of forest services and other senior government officials to identify emerging policy and technical issues, to seek solutions, and to advise FAO and others on appropriate action.

1983 International Tropical Timber Agreement (ITTA) adopted, responding to concern over the fate of tropical forests. The agreement gave equal importance to conservation and trade.

1985 At FAO's World Forestry Congress in Mexico in June 1985, the Tropical Forestry Action Plan (TFAP) was adopted as the new international framework for forest-related action. The majority of the TFAP initiatives had collapsed by 1995.

1986 International Tropical Timber Organization is created as an intergovernmental organization promoting the conservation and sustainable management, use, and trade of tropical forest resources.

1992 UN Conference on Environment and Development (Earth Summit) adopts the Non-Legally Binding Authoritative Statement on Principles for a Global Consensus on the Management, Conservation, and Sustainable Development of All Types of Forests (Forest Principles).

1994 ITTA, 1994 adopted as successor agreement to the ITTA. ITTA, 1994 established the Bali Partnership Fund to assist producing members to make the investments necessary to enhance their capacity to implement a strategy for achieving exports of tropical timber and timber products from sustainably managed sources.

1995 UN establishes the International Panel on Forests (IPF) under the Commission on Sustainable Development (CSD), with a two-year mandate to pursue consensus on coordinated proposals for action to support the management, conservation, and sustainable development of forests.

1997 UN establishes the Intergovernmental Forum on Forests, under the CSD, with a three-year mandate to follow up on the work of the IPF and identify the possible elements of international forest arrangements and mechanisms, including a legally binding instrument on forests.

2000 Upon the recommendation of the CSD, the UN establishes the UN Forum on Forests (UNFF) to promote the management, conservation, and sustainable development of all types of forests and to strengthen long-term political commitment to this end.

continues

BOX 4.5 UNITED NATIONS FOREST POLICY MILESTONES *continued*

2006	**Negotiations conclude on ITTA, 2006 as a successor agreement to ITTA, 1994. ITTA, 2006 focuses on the world tropical timber economy and the sustainable management of forests.**
2007	**UNFF completes negotiations on, and the UN General Assembly adopts, the Non-Legally Binding Instrument on All Types of Forests to strengthen political commitment and action to implement sustainable management of all types of forests and to provide a framework for national action and international cooperation.**
2011	**ITTA, 2006 enters into force.**
2015	**The International Arrangement on Forests, including UNFF, the Collaborative Partnership on Forests, the UNFF Global Forest Financing Facilitation Network, and the UNFF Trust Fund, are renewed until 2030.**

own forest resources with the principles of national responsibility and global concern for forests. Canada, with huge forest resources under rapid development, proposed the principle that forests are of interest to the international community, that international standards should be implemented in forest management, and that targets and time frames should be included in national forestry plans. But Malaysia and India, as veto states, saw these formulations as an effort to establish the legal principle that forests are "global commons," or part of the "common heritage of [hu]mankind," a status that might eventually give industrialized countries the right to interfere in the management of the tropical-forest countries' resources.[88]

The final version of the Forest Principles only hints that forests are a global environmental issue and omits both the idea of international guidelines for forest management and all references to trade in sustainably managed forest products. It gives blanket approval to the conversion of natural forests to other uses. Developed countries widely regarded the agreement as worse than no declaration at all because it appeared to legitimize unsustainable forest-management policies.[89] The Forest Principles and Chapter 11 of Agenda 21 both reaffirmed the rights of sovereign nations to use their forests in accordance with their national priorities and policy objectives. The Rio agreements also stress the cross-sectoral nature of forests and point out that forests simultaneously provide a wide range of socioeconomic benefits and environmental values and services.

The Forest Principles agreement and the North–South confrontation over the issue seemed to shut the door on global negotiations on forests. By 1995, however, a series of lower-profile international meetings and initiatives, including several joint North–South collaborations, began a new process of maneuvering over sustainable forest management.[90] The result was agreement to begin the next phase of fact finding and bargaining.

Interim Solutions

With Canada and Malaysia acting as lead states, the UN Commission on Sustainable Development (CSD) established the Intergovernmental Panel on Forests (IPF) in 1995. The IPF was given a two-year mandate to build consensus on priority issues in five interrelated categories: implementation of UNCED decisions related to forests at the national and international level; international cooperation in financial assistance and technology transfer; scientific research, forest assessment, and development of criteria and indicators for sustainable forest management; trade-and-environment issues relating to forest products and services; and international organizations and instruments, including the possibility of a forests convention.[91]

By the time the IPF completed its work in February 1997, it had developed more than one hundred proposals for action on issues related to sustainable forest management.[92] These recommendations, however, did not effectively leverage changes in forest-management policies and practices. The IPF created no mechanism for reporting or follow-up on the recommendations, further limiting their impact on policy.

In addition, the debate about the need for a global forest convention remained as polarized as it was in 1992, although there was now a new alignment of country preferences. Malaysia and Canada, the lead states, supported elements of a convention in the hope that a global agreement on sustainable forestry could provide the basis for an officially sponsored, international ecolabel system for wood products that would be more amenable to their timber industries than other proposed or existing certification systems.[93]

The EU still officially supported the negotiation of a binding treaty. Some of its key member states (France, Germany, and Italy) had long been the staunchest supporters of a global forest treaty. But by 1996 some environmental groups and aid agencies in EU member states had begun to oppose a binding agreement, in part because they saw that no new money would be forthcoming to support it.[94]

Some developing countries, including Costa Rica, Indonesia, Papua New Guinea, and the Philippines, had changed their position to support a convention in the hope that it would generate new sources of development assistance for forests.

There was also some movement from the African countries in favor of a convention. However, the major South American countries remained firmly opposed.[95]

The United States, which had supported a convention in Rio, now opposed it and so became one of the leaders of the veto coalition. The influence of the corporate sector, which opposed a convention on the grounds that it would be interventionist and regulatory, was largely responsible for this shift.[96] Japan, which had endorsed a convention at UNCED without actively supporting it, now opposed the idea, as did Australia and New Zealand. The forest convention issue thus shows how different states—and the timber industry in different countries—can share the same political and economic interests (in this instance, freedom from third-party certification by a system that the industry didn't trust) but come out on opposite sides of the issue because of differing assessments of the situation.

In the end, the IPF was unable to agree on recommendations for a global forest convention. Instead, in June 1997, the UN General Assembly (UNGA) established an Intergovernmental Forum on Forests (IFF) under the auspices of the CSD.[97] In other words, governments supported the need for dialogue but could not advance matters further than the status quo.

The IFF, which concluded its work in February 2000, was charged with promoting and facilitating implementation of the IPF's proposals for action; reviewing, monitoring, and reporting on progress in the management, conservation, and sustainable development of all types of forests; and considering matters left pending by the panel, particularly trade, finance, technology transfer, and a possible forest convention. The same issues that stymied the IPF continued to prove difficult for the IFF. Canada did not give up its aim of securing agreement on a global forest convention, but the veto coalition of industrialized and developing states opposed to negotiating a forest treaty doomed the Canadian effort. Delegates finally agreed to recommend to the CSD that the UN establish an intergovernmental body called the UN Forum on Forests (UNFF) and, within five years, "consider with a view to recommending the parameters of a mandate for developing a legal framework on all types of forests." The language is sufficiently obscure that the lead and veto coalitions both felt they had achieved a successful outcome to the negotiations.

United Nations Forum on Forests

The UN Economic and Social Council (ECOSOC) established the UNFF in 2000 with the goal of promoting "the management, conservation and sustainable development of the world's forests, and to strengthen long term political commitment to this end."[98] The Collaborative Partnership on Forests was also established to support the work of the UNFF and its member countries and to foster increased cooperation and coordination on forests.[99] When discussion on a forests convention or other international arrangement on forests resumed at UNFF5 in May 2005, the session was supposed to review the effectiveness of the current international arrangement on forests, including the UNFF itself, and also to consider whether negotiations on a global forest convention could be initiated. However, many of the most ardent proponents of a global forest convention were already conceding that a consensus was unlikely to emerge for any type of legally binding agreement.[100] The coalitions that had emerged in 1997 remained largely unchanged in 2005, and the debate appeared as polarized as ever. There was agreement that the global forest agenda had made some progress under the UNFF and that deforestation and forest degradation continued at an unsustainably high rate, but there was no consensus on how to proceed.

Developing countries, although divided on the need for a treaty, were united in their call for industrialized countries to implement commitments related to financial resources, capacity building, and technology transfer, which they saw as critical to advancing the management, conservation, and sustainable development of all types of forests.[101] Canada, the EU, Malaysia, and Switzerland continued to act as lead states, although they recognized that a treaty might not be possible and started to look for alternative proposals. The veto coalition, led by Brazil, continued to oppose a treaty, calling instead for the continuation and strengthening of the UNFF and the Collaborative Partnership on Forests. Several compromise proposals began to emerge. Some countries called for a non–legally binding voluntary code of conduct with clear overarching goals and a limited number of targets. Canada, Switzerland, and the United States, among others, supported this proposal, but Brazil and others rejected quantifiable goals and argued that the 1992 Forest Principles were a code of conduct. Negotiations on targets and timetables began, but although there was tentative agreement about goals and the possibility of negotiating a voluntary code, there was no consensus on the details. NGOs argued that members had engaged in policy talks for too long while deforestation continued unabated and unchallenged. They argued that governments must adopt clear, measurable targets; provide the necessary resources to implement actions to achieve them; and ensure broad participation of NGOs and indigenous peoples.

In the end, countries recognized that without the support of two key players in the veto coalition—the country with the largest timber industry (the United States) and the country with the world's largest tropical forest (Brazil)—no treaty would be possible. Other options were put on the table, but there was still no consensus on the adoption of targets, a voluntary code of conduct, or the consideration of a treaty in the future. With no agreement possible, delegates agreed to reconvene at UNFF6 in 2006 to try, yet again, to reach consensus on an international arrangement on forests.

UNFF6 finally secured the next step in strengthening the international arrangement on forests by deciding to develop a voluntary instrument. To this end, delegates agreed on four global objectives on forests:

- Reversing the loss of forest cover and increasing efforts to prevent forest degradation;
- Enhancing forest benefits and their contribution to international development goals;
- Increasing the area of protected forests and areas of sustainably managed forests; and
- Reversing the decline in official development assistance (ODA; foreign aid) for sustainable forest management.

They also agreed to continue the work of the UNFF at least through 2015 and to conclude and adopt at its seventh session "a non–legally binding instrument on all types of forests."[102] So, fourteen years after the Earth Summit, the idea of a binding forest treaty seemed to have disappeared off the agenda, despite the efforts of a few staunch supporters, including the Canadians. Most countries seeking a legally binding treaty had no intention of abandoning the UNFF, with many stating that a voluntary instrument was a good first step toward securing a more binding agreement.

Nine months later, UNFF7 completed negotiation of a non–legally binding instrument covering all types of forests, which the UNGA endorsed and adopted in December 2007.[103] The instrument sets out a framework for accomplishing the global objectives on forests and defines its overall purpose as the following:

- To strengthen political commitment and action at all levels to implement effectively sustainable management of all types of forests and to achieve the shared global objectives on forests;
- To enhance the contribution of forests to the achievement of the internationally agreed-upon development goals, including the MDGs, in particular with respect to poverty eradication and environmental sustainability; and
- To provide a framework for national action and international cooperation.

UNFF7 also adopted a focused, multiyear program of work from 2007 to 2015, during which period the forum would meet biannually to review implementation of the non–legally binding instrument, sustainable forest management, the global objectives on forests, and the IPF/IFF proposals for action.[104]

The effectiveness of this International Arrangement on Forests (IAF; see Box 4.6) was reviewed at UNFF11 in 2015, at which time governments were supposed

BOX 4.6 WHAT IS THE INTERNATIONAL ARRANGEMENT ON FORESTS?

The current International Arrangement on Forests is composed of the following:

- **UN Forum on Forests: the UN intergovernmental body charged with promoting the management, conservation, and sustainable development of all types of forests and strengthening long-term political commitment to this end**
- **UNFF Secretariat: the UNFF director and administrative officers based in New York**
- **Collaborative Partnership on Forests (CPF): an informal, voluntary arrangement among fourteen international organizations and secretariats with substantial programs on forests**
- **UNFF Global Forest Financing Facilitation Network: designed to mobilize and enhance access to financial resources for forests**
- **UNFF Trust Fund: covers travel support for representatives from developing countries to attend meetings**

The members of the CPF are the following:

- **Center for International Forestry Research**
- **Convention on Biological Diversity Secretariat**
- **Food and Agriculture Organization of the UN**
- **Global Environment Facility (GEF Secretariat)**
- **International Tropical Timber Organization**
- **International Union for the Conservation of Nature and Natural Resources**
- **International Union of Forest Research Organizations**
- **UN Convention to Combat Desertification (UNCCD Secretariat)**
- **UN Development Programme**
- **UN Environment Programme**
- **UNFF Secretariat**
- **UN Framework Convention on Climate Change (UNFCCC Secretariat)**
- **World Agroforestry Centre**
- **World Bank**

to consider a full range of options, including a legally binding instrument on all types of forests. However, in the lead-up to the meeting, it became increasingly apparent that governments no longer had an appetite to negotiate a forests treaty.[105] Even the previous lead coalition, Canada, the EU, Malaysia, and Switzerland, did not mention a treaty as the future for the IAF. So after twenty years of arguing about whether to have a treaty or not, governments moved on and focused instead on the UNFF's future. Most governments agreed that UNFF should continue and realized that this was an opportunity to shape the body's future.

So at UNFF11, governments adopted a resolution on the IAF beyond 2015 as well as a ministerial declaration. The declaration highlights how sustainable forest management is vital to addressing development challenges—from poverty eradication and economic growth to food security and climate-change mitigation and adaptation. UNFF11 delegates decided to strengthen the overall IAF and ensure its coherence with the post-2015 development agenda and the Sustainable Development Goals (SDGs; see Chapter 6). They also agreed to extend the mandate of UNFF and the IAF to 2030, defined IAF objectives and components, and outlined the strategic direction for the arrangement. Finally, countries also strengthened the forum and its secretariat and agreed to develop a strategic plan for the IAF (2017–2030) with quadrennial programs of work. Beginning in 2017, the forum will meet annually, with an increased focus on monitoring, assessing, and reporting on implementation of the forest instrument, mobilizing resources, and sharing technical advice.[106]

It is important to remember that UNFF is just one of many platforms for addressing global forest issues. Forest issues have also been discussed in other conventions, like the CBD, CITES, the UN Framework Convention on Climate Change (UNFCCC), and the UN Convention to Combat Desertification (UNCCD). Forest governance involves a variety of actors: governments and international organizations such as FAO, UNEP, the UN Development Programme (UNDP), and the World Bank. There are also different certification systems, such as the Forest Stewardship Council (FSC) (see Chapter 6) and the Pan European Forest Certification.

Hence, forest issues are covered by many fora and involve a number of actors at the international level, showing both the importance of forest issues but also fragmentation in their governance.[107] The challenge for UNFF for the next fifteen years may be one of coordinating these multiple instruments, addressing issues that fall between the cracks of these other fora, focusing on new innovative policy issues, addressing the drivers of deforestation, promoting sustainable forest management, and implementing the SDGs.

The forests case demonstrates that it is not always possible to negotiate a treaty to address a global environmental issue. In fact, with deforestation slowing and sustainable forest management increasing without a treaty, it may not be necessary. This case also demonstrates that coalitions have the ability to shift significantly over time as a result of changing perceptions of the problem and changing and competing economic interests. Given the track record of the other natural resources treaties addressed in this chapter and the challenges in both negotiating and implementing a treaty, governments have finally determined that a global, legally binding instrument on forests may not be the best solution and that it is time to move on.

DESERTIFICATION AND LAND DEGRADATION

Desertification and land degradation affect the lives of two billion people living in drylands in more than 110 countries and cost approximately $490 billion per year.[108] Much of this affected population is already poor, and experts estimate that by 2030 the demand for energy in these areas will rise by 50 percent, the demand for food will rise by 45 percent, and the demand for water will rise by 30 percent. It is also expected that desertification and land degradation will drive seven hundred million people out of their homes because they will no longer be able to feed themselves or have access to sufficient water.[109]

Given these facts, land degradation and desertification can be considered issues requiring immediate international attention. Yet, they had never been priority issues on the global environmental agenda, despite efforts by many African countries since the 1970s. Indeed, desertification was put on the 1992 UNCED agenda only because African countries persisted. When the desertification convention became the first treaty to be negotiated after UNCED, some looked at it as a test of whether developed-country governments had the political will to follow up on some of the Agenda 21 commitments of greatest interest to developing countries and whether desertification and land degradation would finally become a priority issue.

Complexity, vagueness, and disagreement on whether desertification was indeed a global problem plagued the issue-definition stage. UNEP and most specialists defined desertification as sustained land degradation in arid, semiarid, and dry subhumid areas resulting mainly from adverse human impact (see Box 4.7).[110] But the term *desertification* evokes images of deserts advancing and destroying productive land, whereas scientists have found no evidence to support claims that the Sahara is expanding at an alarming rate.[111] Foes of a convention exploited that fact: at one point in the UNCED negotiations, the United States proposed that negotiators discard the term *desertification* and suggested substituting *land degradation*. Some donor countries objected to the designation "global" because they thought it might

BOX 4.7 DRYLANDS FACTS

- **The total population of the world's drylands is 2.1 billion. Drylands are home to almost one of every three people living in the world today.**
- **The majority of the world's dryland population is in developing countries.**
- **Drylands support 50 percent of the world's livestock.**
- **Drylands comprise 44 percent of all cultivated land.**
- **Plant species endemic to drylands make up 30 percent of the plants under cultivation today.**
- **The largest dryland areas are in Australia, China, Kazakhstan, Russia, and the United States.**
- **At least 99 percent of the surface area of six countries (Botswana, Burkina Faso, Iraq, Kazakhstan, Moldova, and Turkmenistan) is classified as drylands.**
- **Drylands store 46 percent of the planet's carbon inventory.**

Source: **UNCCD, *Desertification: A Visual Synthesis* (Bonn: UNCCD, 2012).**

imply that treaty-implementation efforts would be eligible for Global Environment Facility (GEF) funding.[112]

African countries encountered other problems in defining desertification. First, desertification does not involve resources or life-support systems of global interest, unlike other environmental issues on which major global treaties have been negotiated. It affects countries not suffering from desertification only because it threatens the economies and societies of many other countries. Second, a bewildering array of natural and social factors have an impact on land degradation in drylands, including overpopulation, climatic cycles, social and economic structures, poor pastoral or agricultural practices, bad government and donor policies, and North–South economic relations. It was difficult, therefore, to articulate in a simple and clear way either the nature of the problem or the international actions needed to address it.

In addition, for many African countries, there is a strong link between poverty alleviation and desertification control. Consequently, the African countries' definition of the problem emphasized the need for additional funding but for as-yet-unidentified activities. These countries hoped that a desertification convention would help them gain access to additional funding.[113] It was unclear to many developed countries exactly why such assistance should be provided.

Finally, the African countries' attempt to define the desertification issue was hampered because the earlier UNEP Plan of Action to Combat Desertification, launched in 1977, was generally acknowledged as a failure. A UNEP evaluation of the plan had blamed the failure on African governments and the donor community for not giving the issue priority and for gross mismanagement. UNEP had found that only $1 billion of the $9 billion provided by donor agencies from 1978 to 1983 had been spent directly on projects in the field.[114]

When the issue of creating a desertification convention was first raised during the UNCED process, only France, with its historic ties to Africa, expressed support for the idea. Most industrialized countries and the World Bank argued that the primary problems were the macroeconomic policies of African governments (such as levying excessive taxes on agriculture and failing to grant enforceable property rights) and that policy reforms, better planning, and more popular participation would achieve better results than a new international program or formal agreement.[115]

Despite these problems in the definition of desertification, UNCED put it on the global agenda because of African persistence and because the United States unexpectedly supported the African position. After opposing a desertification convention throughout the negotiations leading up to the Earth Summit, the United States shifted its position in Rio, backing language calling for a convention in the hope of winning African support on forests and on other issues in Agenda 21.[116] Other industrialized countries then followed suit, and the call for a desertification convention became part of Agenda 21.[117]

Negotiations began in May 1993 and were completed in fifteen months. A formal fact-finding process was attempted through an information-sharing segment at the first session of the Intergovernmental Negotiating Committee, but the process focused primarily on socioeconomic strategies for slowing and reversing desertification and on reports from individual countries rather than on the scientific understanding of the problem. That process produced general agreement on the importance of such strategies as the integration of arid and semiarid areas into national economies, popular participation in antidesertification efforts, and land-tenure reform.[118] As a result, the convention would be the first to call for affected countries to provide for effective participation by grassroots organizations, NGOs, and local populations in the preparation of national action programs.[119]

The bargaining stage revolved not around commitments to environmental conservation actions but around financial, trade, institutional, and symbolic issues. The African countries were the lead states and presented detailed draft language for every section of the convention, some of which was accepted as the basis for negotiation.

Differences over financial resources and the financial mechanism nearly caused the negotiations to collapse. As in other global negotiations, some members of the G-77 and China demanded commitments to "new and additional" financial resources and creation of a special fund for desertification as the centerpiece of the convention.

Industrialized countries acted as a united veto coalition in rejecting provisions for new and additional financing, agreeing only to ensure "adequate" financial resources for antidesertification programs. The developed countries felt they bore no responsibility for desertification, unlike ozone depletion and climate change, and were therefore unwilling to accept binding obligations to increase their financial assistance to the affected countries.[120] They insisted that existing resources could be used more effectively.

The deadlock on a funding mechanism was broken only after the United States proposed the Global Mechanism under the authority of the COP, to be housed within an existing organization, which would improve monitoring and assessment of existing aid flows and increase coordination among donors. Developing countries remained dissatisfied because such a mechanism would not increase development assistance to African and other countries suffering from desertification. They ultimately accepted the Global Mechanism because it was the only compromise acceptable to donor countries.[121]

The UNCCD was opened for signature in October 1994 and entered into force on December 26, 1996. Today, 195 countries and the EU are parties.[122] The convention recognizes the physical, biological, and socioeconomic aspects of desertification, the importance of redirecting technology transfer so that it is demand-driven, and the importance of local populations in efforts to combat desertification. The core of the convention is the development of national and subregional/regional action programs by national governments in cooperation with donors, local populations, and NGOs.

Implementing and Strengthening the Convention

The UNCCD faced significant challenges during its first six years. These included establishing and operationalizing the Global Mechanism and reconciling the convention's emphasis on bottom-up approaches with involvement at all levels by all relevant actors with the logistical requirements for operating an effective international coordinating body. At the national level, challenges included assisting countries affected by desertification develop effective action programs in conjunction with donor countries, international organizations, local communities, and NGOs.[123]

Between 1997 and 2003, the COP set up institutional mechanisms to enable effective implementation of the convention. This work and the lack of a dedicated financing mechanism in the convention meant that the first five COPs spent time on procedures and institutions rather than on substance. During this period, the COP established two subsidiary bodies: the Committee on Science and Technology and the Committee for the Review of the Implementation of the Convention. After a long-fought battle, the convention designated the GEF as the financial mechanism for the convention once the GEF agreed to establish a program to fund projects to combat desertification.

It took ten years for the convention to make the transition from awareness raising to implementation, but by 2005 it appeared as though crucial building blocks required for success were in place. Eighty-one affected countries had submitted national action programs, synergies had been developed with the climate change and biodiversity conventions, new initiatives were under way, and there seemed to be a growing understanding in the international community that the MDGs could not be achieved without addressing the root causes of rural poverty, many of which were brought on or exacerbated by desertification and drought.[124]

When COP7 convened in Nairobi in 2005, however, delegates resumed the acrimonious debates on many of the same issues that had plagued the convention since its negotiation. To some extent, this reflected the fact that, unlike the other treaties discussed in this chapter, desertification does not involve concerns for preserving natural resources. Many of the political problems in this regime, the only multilateral environmental agreement (MEA) driven by developing countries, stem from the fact that land degradation is not a priority issue for donor governments. As one developing-country official put it, the "scorching breath of the desert is not readily felt by the prosperous public of the rich North."[125]

The tone in Nairobi was also shaped by the critical report of the UN Joint Inspection Unit (an external oversight body). In 2003, parties had requested the Joint Inspection Unit to review the activities of the UNCCD Secretariat. The report confirmed, among other things, that the convention had a major identity crisis: "In the course of the review, it appeared to the inspectors that from the outset there has been a lack of common understanding and recognition of the Convention in its true and proper perspective."[126] The report stated that it seemed unclear whether the convention is environmental, developmental, or both and whether it concerns problems of a purely local or a global nature. "The very name of the Convention may perhaps be misleading since the fundamental problem is one of land degradation, of which desertification is a key element. The failure and/or unwillingness to recognize the Convention in its proper perspective have inevitably led to undesirable consequences."[127] The Nairobi meeting ended with agreement that, in response to the Joint Inspection Unit's report, parties should adopt a long-term strategic plan for implementation of the convention at the next COP. Although many admitted this was not a panacea to the UNCCD's problems, they also hoped that it would help to strengthen the regime.

The strategic plan was adopted in 2007 at COP8 in Madrid. The plan strives to link the work programs of the convention's institutions to a common vision, clarifies their mandates and methods of work, and institutionalizes a results-based management approach. It also sets out operational objectives on issues, including awareness raising, policies, improving the flow of science and technology, and capacity building, and further defines the coordination and respective mandates of the secretariat and the Global Mechanism so as to enhance coordination and integration. The strategic plan, in effect, also expanded the UNCCD's mandate by including land degradation:

> To provide a global framework to support the development and implementation of national and regional policies, programmes and measures to prevent, control and reverse desertification/land degradation and mitigate the effects of drought through scientific and technological excellence, raising public awareness, standard setting, advocacy and resource mobilization, thereby contributing to poverty reduction.[128]

The Science-Policy Nexus

Since the convention's inception, the role of science has been marginalized. In its initial institutional architecture, scientific and technological input was predominantly channeled to the COP through its subsidiary Committee on Science and Technology and a roster of independent experts nominated by the parties. However, the science and technology committee's large and diverse membership renders it rather unwieldy. Different people attend each meeting, and the discussions rarely include detailed, focused, and meaningful exchanges on specific scientific issues. Government representatives, many of whom lack the training or expertise to engage in substantive scientific debates, typically dominate the meetings. Committee sessions are also often marred by procedural quarrels, resulting in low-profile, nonauthoritative outputs with little relevance for either the COP or the scientific community.[129]

In short, the UNCCD process lacks an efficient operational mechanism to process and channel practical and scientific expertise for political decision makers. The COP fails to tap the information potentially available from the scientific community, which in turn is unable to draw the attention of the parties to the scientific aspects of the issues on the COP's agenda.[130]

To address this problem, in 2007, the COP called for scientific-style conferences. Three such conferences have been held so far (see Box 4.8). Although these

BOX 4.8 UNITED NATIONS CONVENTION TO COMBAT DESERTIFICATION MILESTONES

1977 UN Conference on Desertification adopts the Plan of Action to Combat Desertification.

1991 Forty African environment ministers meeting in Abidjan, Côte d'Ivoire, call for a desertification convention to be included in Agenda 21.

1992 Chapter 12 of Agenda 21 calls on the UN General Assembly to establish a committee to elaborate a convention to combat desertification.

1994 UN Convention to Combat Desertification (UNCCD) is adopted in Paris.

1996 UNCCD enters into force.

1997 First meeting of the Conference of the Parties (COP) and first meeting of the Committee on Science and Technology is held in Rome.

2002 First meeting of the Committee to Review Implementation of the Convention is held.

2007 Strategic Plan is adopted in response to the Joint Inspection Unit report.

2009 UNCCD convenes first Scientific Conference to consider the theme "Biophysical and Socio-economic Monitoring and Assessment of Desertification and Land Degradation, to Support Decision Making in Land and Water Management."

2012 Rio+20 outcome document, *The Future We Want*, recognizes the need for urgent action to reverse land degradation and commits to striving to achieve a land degradation–neutral world in the context of sustainable development (paragraph 206).

2013 UNCCD convenes second Scientific Conference under the thematic topic of "Economic Assessment of Desertification, Sustainable Land Management and Resilience of Arid, Semi-arid and Dry Sub-humid Areas."

2013 COP11 establishes a working group to develop a science-based definition of land-degradation neutrality in arid, semi-arid, and dry subhumid areas.

2015 UNCCD convenes third Scientific Conference on "Combating DLDD [Desertification, Land Degradation, and Drought] for Poverty Reduction and Sustainable Development: The Contribution of Science, Technology, Traditional Knowledge and Practices."

2015 The 2030 Agenda for Sustainable Development includes Target 15.3 in the Sustainable Development Goals: "by 2020, combat desertification, and restore degraded land and soil, including land affected by desertification, drought and floods, and strive to achieve a land-degradation neutral world."

conferences enabled scientists to participate in the work of the UNCCD, it still proved difficult to translate the scientific presentations into decisions taken by the COP. To address this continued shortcoming, some parties called for an independent scientific body, outside the immediate UNCCD process, similar in form and function to the Intergovernmental Panel on Climate Change (IPCC). However, given the 2012 establishment of the Intergovernmental Science-Policy Platform on Biodiversity and Ecosystem Services and its decision to launch a work program on land degradation and restoration, the UNCCD decided to forgo the IPCC model and instead establish a science-policy interface and the Scientific Knowledge Brokering Portal to enhance the UNCCD as a global authority on desertification, land degradation, drought, and sustainable land management.[131]

Land-Degradation Neutrality

On the ground, implementation of the convention has been fraught with difficulties. The parties' obligations and the convention's expectations for parties are not quite clear; the robust financial and political capital necessary for its implementation is still not in place; the major tool for on-the-ground implementation, the National Action Plans, are irrelevant to mainstream, international development cooperation; and most donors choose to address issues related to land degradation bilaterally rather than under the framework of the convention.[132] There is also little meaningful involvement of local communities in defining, identifying, monitoring, and responding to desertification, even though such participation is a UNCCD centerpiece.[133] These constraints, combined with its dryland-restricted mandate, mean that the UNCCD is hindered from assuming global responsibility for land degradation. As a result, there is no clear indication that any significant amount of dryland degradation has been successfully reversed during the lifetime of the UNCCD.[134]

The need for a shift in focus of the UNCCD paved the way for the emergence of the concept of land-degradation neutrality, first introduced as "zero net land degradation" in a background paper prepared for COP10 in 2011. This led to a proposal at Rio+20 (the 2012 UN Conference on Sustainable Development [UNCSD]), which was eventually included in the outcome document, *The Future We Want*, to recognize the need for urgent action to reverse land degradation and to achieve a land degradation–neutral world in the context of sustainable development.[135] Land-degradation neutrality also became a part of the SDGs and the 2030 Sustainable Development Agenda adopted by the UNGA in 2015 (see Chapter 6). Target 15.3 states: "by 2020, combat desertification, and restore degraded land and soil, including land affected by desertification, drought and floods, and strive to achieve a land-degradation neutral world."[136]

PHOTO 4.3 Participants from Civil Society Organizations at the twelfth meeting of the UN Convention to Combat Desertification (UNCCD) Conference of the Parties in Turkey. The UNCCD was the first convention to call for affected countries to provide for effective participation by grassroots organizations, nongovernmental organizations, and local populations. Courtesy Franz Dejon, IISD/*Earth Negotiations Bulletin*, www.iisd.ca.

At COP12 in 2015, the UNCCD agreed to a formal scientific definition of land-degradation neutrality and to align the UNCCD's goals and parties' action programs with the SDGs. The UNCCD's definition of land-degradation neutrality is a "state whereby the amount and quality of land resources, necessary to support ecosystem functions and services and enhance food security, remains stable or increases within specified temporal and spatial scales and ecosystems."[137] Target 15.3 would be achieved by: (1) managing land more sustainably, which would reduce the rate of degradation; and (2) increasing the rate of restoration of degraded land, so that the two trends converge to give a zero net rate of land degradation.

On the face of it, this is a compelling proposition. Governments commit to ensuring that the rate of restoration at least equals the rate of degradation. Food production and ecosystems are maintained, thus also contributing to political and economic stability. Furthermore, land rehabilitation of up to twelve million hectares of degraded land a year could help close the carbon emissions gap by 25 percent by 2030, thus helping to mitigate climate change.[138]

But not everyone agrees. Some critics argue that this initiative essentially gives governments and powerful interests the right to degrade land as long as they can rehabilitate an equivalent area elsewhere. The assumption appears to be that the area within which neutrality must be achieved is either the nation-state or the natural borders of an ecosystem. However, as some critics say, one banked hectare might not be of the same quality as a hectare that is lost, and the ecosystem services provided by the restored hectare may not be as valuable as that provided by the degraded land. The proposed voluntary reporting could become a meaningless exercise of data manipulation to show zero loss, when in fact productive resources are still diminishing.[139]

The next challenge will be to actually operationalize the target.[140] According to the UNCCD, an estimated $2 billion will be needed every year to support actual restoration activities. They hope that this can be mobilized through the Land Degradation Neutrality Fund that will be in operation by the end of 2016 and with diverse sources of financing, including from the private sector. The Ankara Initiative, which was announced during COP12 and is valued at $5 million from Turkey and an estimated $3 million to be sourced from the GEF, will provide the initial support for these activities.[141]

Moving Forward

Unlike other regimes, the UNCCD's implementation has not been hindered by issues of national sovereignty or scientific uncertainty. In fact, the knowledge and technical skills exist to halt desertification, land degradation, and drought, but political and economic factors have determined whether the expertise is ever put into practice. Implementation has proven difficult because of the nature of the problem, lack of political commitment, and bureaucratic mistrust, often demonstrated by the developed countries, which serve as a veto coalition exploiting the power of the purse. With the UN's adoption of the SDGs, which include a goal on land and a target on land-degradation neutrality, the UNCCD has a new focus and direction for the next fifteen years. COP12 in 2015, situated as it was between the UNGA's adoption of the SDGs and the UNFCCC's adoption of the Paris Agreement, was seen as a watershed event, ensuring that the convention would achieve greater relevance in the global sustainable development agenda, not only through SDG Target 15.3 but also through the convention's relevance beyond arid lands and the relationship between land-degradation neutrality and climate-change mitigation.[142] Whether the UNCCD becomes more relevant and receives increased political commitment and financial support from some donor parties and the private sector remains to be seen. The convention also needs to maintain a delicate balance between the global goal of land-degradation neutrality and its original focus on the needs at the local level. However, twenty years after the convention's entry into force, this new focus and direction may indeed brighten the future of the first sustainable development convention.

FISHERIES DEPLETION

For centuries, the ocean's bounties were viewed as limitless. But for the past three decades, the world's marine fisheries have been in crisis—overexploited to the point that the most valuable fish stocks have been depleted and some virtually eliminated. Nearly 30 percent of the world's marine fish stocks are considered overexploited or fished at biologically unsustainable levels.[143] The biggest declines are in key commercial species such as flounder, sole, turbot, halibut, cod, hake, redfish, haddock, and bass. Pelagic fish, including tuna and mackerel, which live near the surface, are also in decline. Because fishing fleets can overexploit one fishery and then move on to another, and because fleets continued to catch high levels of lower-value fish even after depleting the most desirable stocks, the fisheries crisis was disguised for many years by the continuing increase in the total global catch figures, which grew from 16.8 million tons in 1950 to a peak of 86.4 million tons in 1996. Since then, the global catch has leveled off, amounting to 82.6 million tons in 2011 and 79.7 million tons in 2012.[144] The percentage of fish stocks caught within biologically sustainable levels declined from 90 percent in 1974 to 71.2 percent in 2011 (see Figure 4.1). Thus, in 2011, 28.8 percent of fish stocks were being fished at biologically unsustainable rates.[145]

FIGURE 4.1 **Global Trends in the State of World Marine Fish Stocks, 1974–2011**

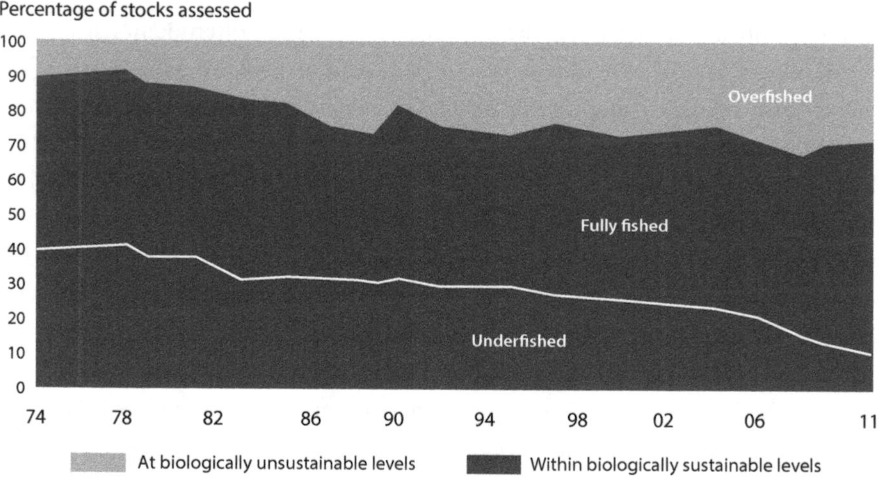

Notes: Dark shading within biologically sustainable levels; light shading at biologically unsustainable levels. The light line divides the stocks within biologically sustainable levels into two subcategories: fully fished (above the line) and underfished (below the line).

Source: FAO, *State of the World Fisheries and Aquaculture* (Rome: FAO, 2014), 37, www.fao.org/3/d1eaa9a1-5a71-4e42-86c0-f2111f07de16/i3720e.pdf.

The growing global demand for fish; an excess of fishing vessels—partly driven by subsidies (for boats, fuel, equipment, and fish catches, depending on the country) estimated at up to $35 billion per year, equivalent to around one-fifth of the industry's overall revenue; increasingly effective fishing technologies; larger nets and storage capacity; and a lack of new or alternative opportunities are all contributing to a race to fish. This is depleting many coastal fisheries and causing fishing fleets to look farther and fish deeper into international waters. New species and areas are being targeted as traditional stocks become exhausted. Only the deepest and most inaccessible parts of the ocean are yet to feel pressure.[146] Inadequate regulations on catch and enforcement and illegal, unreported, and unregulated fishing also contribute to the fisheries crisis.

The FAO estimates that three billion people derive 20 percent of their animal protein from fish or fish products and that fisheries and aquaculture combined, including ancillary industries such as processing, marketing, and distribution, support the livelihoods of 660 to 820 million people, which is approximately 10–12 percent of the world's population.[147] These benefits are threatened as fish continue to be harvested at unsustainable levels. The World Bank estimates that mismanagement of fisheries represents an annual loss of $50 billion to the global economy, in large part to the detriment of developing countries.[148]

Fishery resources are found either under national jurisdiction or in international waters, and often in some combination of the two. This situation complicates the politics of forming a regime. So too does the fact that countries with distant-water fishing fleets (China, Japan, Poland, the Republic of Korea, Russia, Spain, and Taiwan) are responsible for the majority of the catch in international waters, providing them with the potential for effectively vetoing a global agreement to address overfishing.

Of the global fish catch, 95 percent is taken within the two-hundred-mile EEZs that are under the national jurisdiction of individual coastal states. But some important fish stocks, such as cod and pollock, straddle EEZs and adjacent areas of the high seas. Highly migratory fish stocks, especially tuna and swordfish, move long distances, passing through both the high seas and the EEZs of multiple coastal states each year. These straddling and highly migratory fish stocks are particularly important on the Challenger Plateau off the coast of New Zealand, off Argentina's Patagonian Shelf, off the coasts of Chile and Peru, in the Barents Sea, off the coast of Norway, in the Bering Sea, in the Sea of Okhotsk, in the South Pacific Ocean, and on the Grand Banks of Newfoundland outside Canada's two-hundred-mile nautical zone. As many straddling stocks and highly migratory fish stocks have dwindled, coastal and distant-water states each blame overfishing by the other group as the cause.

Negotiation of the UN Fish Stocks Agreement

The first binding global agreement to address overfishing is often referred to as the UN Fish Stocks Agreement.[149] Not surprisingly, the agreement arose from conflicts over straddling and highly migratory fish stocks. Canada was the lead state in putting the issue of a global management regime for these stocks on the political agenda.

Canada was motivated to push for formal agreement limiting the freedom of distant-water fishing fleets to exploit these stocks because of a dispute with the EC, especially Spain, about the Spanish fleet's overfishing of the stocks on the Grand Banks outside Canada's EEZ. The regional fisheries management organization responsible for regulating fishing in the Grand Banks area, both within Canada's EEZ and on the high seas, is the Northwest Atlantic Fisheries Organization (NAFO),

BOX 4.9 SELECTED FISHERIES CONSERVATION MILESTONES*

1992 **UN Conference on Environment and Development (UNCED) calls for negotiation of an agreement to conserve highly migratory fish stocks and straddling fish stocks in Chapter 17 of Agenda 21.**

1993 **UN Conference on Straddling Fish Stocks and Highly Migratory Fish Stocks opens in New York.**

1995 **UN adopts the UN Agreement for the Implementation of the Provisions of the United Nations Convention on the Law of the Sea of 10 December 1982 Relating to the Conservation and Management of Straddling Fish Stocks and Highly Migratory Fish Stocks (Fish Stocks Agreement).**

1995 **Food and Agriculture Organization of the UN (FAO) adopts the international Code of Conduct for Responsible Fisheries.**

1999 **FAO adopts three international plans of action on reducing incidental catch of seabirds in longline fisheries, conservation and management of sharks, and the management of fishing capacity.**

2001 **Fish Stocks Agreement enters into force.**

2001 **FAO adopts the International Plan of Action to Prevent, Deter and Eliminate Illegal, Unreported and Unregulated Fishing.**

2006 **First review conference for the Fish Stocks Agreement convenes.**

2010 **Second review conference for the Fish Stocks Agreement convenes.**

2016 **Third review conference for the Fish Stocks Agreement convenes.**

***Not including Regional Fisheries Management Organizations (RFMOs)**

founded in 1979. From 1986 to 1990, NAFO failed to enforce high-seas catch limits agreed to by the organization on most of the straddling stocks because the EC had exercised its right to opt out of the regional quotas; Canada, therefore, appealed to the broader international community to adopt a global policy governing the problem.

During the negotiations in preparation for the 1992 Earth Summit, Canada proposed language calling for recognition of the special interests of coastal states in highly migratory stocks and stocks that straddle national EEZs and international waters. The Europeans, as veto states, disagreed, producing a diplomatic deadlock on the issue. The issue remained unresolved until the conference in Rio, when the United States brokered a compromise. The result was an agreement to hold an intergovernmental conference under UN auspices "with a view to promoting effective implementation of the provisions of the Law of the Sea on straddling and highly migratory fish stocks." The Europeans agreed to that formula because its diplomats believed the Convention on the Law of the Sea guaranteed the sovereign right of states to fish on the high seas. Canada hoped that the need for conservation would trump that traditional sovereign right.

The UN Conference on Straddling Fish Stocks and Highly Migratory Fish Stocks opened in July 1993 under the authority of the UNGA. The main conflict of interest was between the seventy coastal fishing states and the ten distant-water fishing states. The coastal states, led by the like-minded caucus (Argentina, Australia, Canada, Chile, Iceland, New Zealand, Norway, and Peru), accused the distant-water fishing states of abusing their right to fish to the detriment of straddling stocks. The veto coalition was composed of distant-water fishing states, led by the European Commission (on behalf of its distant-water fishing states),[150] Japan, and the Republic of Korea, which argued that mismanagement of national fisheries by coastal fishing states was just as much to blame for the most serious problems of stock depletion.[151] Both sides were only half right, a conclusion based on the Canadian–EC case: the evidence is clear that there was gross mismanagement and overfishing within the Canadian EEZ and that from 1986 to 1989 the Spanish and Portuguese fleets were consistently catching several times the EC's NAFO allocation of groundfish (demersal fish) catch.[152]

As they had during the UNCED negotiations, the like-minded caucus proposed a legally binding agreement that would prescribe conservation rules for high-seas fishing that affected straddling stocks and highly migratory stocks. Coastal states also objected to proposed international rules that would limit their freedom to manage their EEZs. Distant-water fishing states called for nonbinding conservation guidelines that would apply equally to coastal state fisheries and the high seas. They had long argued that the regulation of fishing practices on the high seas should be left to regional or subregional organizations.

Both groups of states were, in a sense, separate veto coalitions that were prepared, at least initially, to block agreement on measures needed to conserve stocks effectively. The United States, which is both a coastal fishing state and a distant-water fishing state, was in a pivotal position. Initially, the United States was ready to join with the distant-water fishing states to oppose a binding convention because of its close historic ties with Europe and Japan on Law of the Sea issues. The United States had clashed with Canada and other coastal states during the negotiations on the Law of the Sea treaty. But in 1994, officials in the White House and the National Oceanic and Atmospheric Administration with strong commitments to conservation intervened after lobbying by NGOs. As a result, the United States came out for a binding agreement and began playing the role of lead state.

One of the US contributions to the text was a proposal that the precautionary approach to fishing be applied by requiring the adoption of reference points (target levels of fishing effort aimed at conserving fish stocks) and measures for rebuilding the stocks, including reduced fishing efforts, if the reference points are exceeded. Canada resisted the application of precautionary reference points within fisheries under national jurisdiction, along with other conservation requirements, as a violation of national sovereignty. The United States pushed Canada and the like-minded caucus to accept certain basic conservation principles and guidelines for their application to straddling stocks on the high seas and within areas under national jurisdiction, but the issue remained unresolved after four negotiating sessions in April 1995.

The like-minded caucus also pressed for coastal states to have the right to board and inspect fishing vessels in international waters, which they argued was necessary to ensure compliance with international conservation measures. Traditionally, the enforcement of legal obligations on the high seas was the responsibility of the flag state (the state in which the vessel was registered), and distant-water fishing states wanted to maintain the status quo. The United States again sided with the like-minded caucus in supporting wider latitude for high-seas inspection by states other than the flag state under certain circumstances. The distant-water fishing states resisted until the last session.

Before the negotiations could be completed, tensions between Canada and the EU escalated dramatically over Spanish fishing for turbot, allegedly in violation of NAFO quotas. In September 1994, the thirteen members of NAFO voted to reduce the annual allowable catch of rapidly declining stocks of turbot by 38 percent and reallocated much of the EU share of the quota to Canada. The EU used its right to opt out of the quota and set its own, much higher, unilateral quota. In response, in February 1995, the Canadian fisheries minister warned that Canada would not let EU vessels "devastate turbot the way it devastated other ground fish stocks."[153] In

March 1995, Canadian ships aggressively pursued and seized or cut the nets of Spanish trawlers outside the Canadian EEZ.

The Canadian actions angered the EU and temporarily polarized the conference. The March–April 1995 round of negotiations was still deadlocked on the issue of the right of coastal states to board ships on the high seas that they suspect of having violated a regional fisheries conservation measure. The draft agreement allowed wider latitude for such high-seas boarding and inspection than the distant-water fishing states were prepared to accept.

However, as tensions eased, a Canadian–EU agreement reached immediately after that round may have contributed to a successful conclusion of the negotiations. Canada agreed to give the EU the same quota as Canada, instead of one-fifth of the Canadian quota that had been authorized by NAFO. Canada also dropped charges against the Spanish trawler it had seized and repealed legislation authorizing such actions in international waters. In return, the EU agreed to a new regime of independent inspectors onboard every EU ship in the NAFO area to ensure that conservation rules were being followed.[154]

In the fifth and final negotiating session in August 1995, distant-water fishing states were still resisting high-seas boarding and the precautionary approach to fisheries management. The distant-water fishing states had agreed to boarding and inspecting in principle, but there were still differences about whether the regional fisheries management organizations had to reach agreement on procedures governing such boarding and inspecting: Canada insisted that it would not require prior agreement on procedures by the organizations, whereas Japan and the Republic of Korea insisted on regional agreement as a precondition for boarding and inspection. A compromise was ultimately adopted: states that were parties to regional fisheries management organizations could board and inspect vessels on the high seas of parties to the Fish Stocks Agreement suspected of violating regional conservation measures without prior regional agreement, but only if the regional organization had failed to adopt procedures for such boarding and inspection for two years prior to the boarding.

As discussed in Chapter 1, the precautionary principle states that the lack of scientific certainty should not be used as a reason for postponing or failing to take effective conservation measures if inaction could produce significant environmental harm. Japan was concerned that coastal states would use the precautionary approach as an open license to adopt moratoria on fishing as the new management norm and was reluctant to see the principle enter into a binding international agreement. But Japan finally accepted the precautionary approach, perhaps because it did not want to be blamed for the collapse of the negotiations.[155]

Implementation Challenges

After receiving ratifications from the required thirty signatories, a process that took nearly six years, the UN Fish Stocks Agreement entered into force in December 2001. By early 2016, eighty-three countries had ratified the treaty, but only five of the top ten fishing states (Chile, India, Japan, Russia, and the United States) and the EU are parties to the agreement. China has signed but not ratified and remains a nonparty. Many of the other most important fishing states, including Malaysia, Mexico, Peru, Thailand, and Vietnam, also remain nonparties. Although these countries' support was not needed for the Fish Stocks Agreement to enter into force, their compliance is essential if the treaty is to be effective.

The agreement represents a major step forward in global cooperation for conservation of fish stocks, but it does not effectively address three key global management issues. First, the regional fisheries management organizations that make decisions on management measures such as catch quotas normally allow member states simply to opt out of the decision if they don't like it—the weakness that prompted Canada's original push for a new regime. The second problem is overcapacity in the global fishing fleet. Although the agreement calls for states to take measures to "prevent or eliminate excess fishing capacity," it does not spell out this obligation or set up a mechanism for implementation. Finally, the agreement does not apply to all fish stocks under national jurisdiction but only to those referred to in the title, or approximately 20 percent of the global fish catch.

States have created several nonbinding agreements to supplement the Fish Stocks Agreement and the regional fisheries management organizations. In October 1995, governments adopted an international Code of Conduct for Responsible Fisheries, which provides principles and standards applicable to the conservation, management, and development of all aspects of fisheries, such as the capture, processing, and trade of fishery products, as well as fishing operations, aquaculture, fisheries research, and the integration of fisheries into coastal-area management. To support implementation of the code of conduct, the FAO Technical Guidelines for Responsible Fisheries were elaborated.[156]

The FAO then developed international plans of action addressing specific issues in implementing the code of conduct. The 1999 International Plan of Action for the Management of Fishing Capacity aims to reduce excess fishing capacity in world fisheries. The 2001 International Plan of Action to Prevent, Deter and Eliminate Illegal, Unreported and Unregulated Fishing recommends good practice and calls upon states to adopt national plans of action to combat illegal, unreported, and unregulated fishing (see Box 4.10).[157] Although voluntary instruments can be useful, their nonbinding nature significantly impedes their effectiveness. Thus far,

BOX 4.10 ILLEGAL, UNREPORTED, AND UNREGULATED FISHING

Illegal, unreported, and unregulated (IUU) fishing is a global threat to sustainable fisheries and marine biodiversity. IUU fishing includes fishing that is against the laws and regulations of a country or an international agreement; misreporting catches to the relevant national or regional authority; or fishing in a way that undermines management efforts to conserve marine species and ecosystems. IUU fishing occurs globally and is thought to account for up to 30 percent of catches in some areas. However, because these catches are not recorded, the exact amounts are hard to quantify.

IUU fishing has enormous consequences. Not only are these poachers decimating valuable fish populations, they are also killing tens of thousands of marine animals as bycatch and destroying habitats through their unregulated use of damaging and illegal fishing practices. Annual global economic losses due to IUU fishing are estimated to be between $10 billion and $23 billion, representing eleven million to twenty-six million tons of fish.

IUU fishing is often an organized criminal activity. For example, a pirate vessel may be owned by a company in the Caribbean that is then owned by someone in Europe or Asia; it may have a Russian skipper and a crew from the Philippines or China; and it may be flagged to Togo. IUU fishing boats use various strategies to evade detection and apprehension and often disguise the origin of their illegal catch so well that the fish is often sold legitimately into consumer markets in Japan, the EU, and the United States.

To combat IUU fishing, countries and international organizations have emphasized the importance of enhanced port state control. In 2009, the FAO Conference approved the FAO Agreement on Port State Measures to Prevent, Deter and Eliminate Illegal, Unreported and Unregulated Fishing. The agreement aims to prevent illegally caught fish from entering international markets by requiring foreign vessels to provide advance notice and request permission for port entry. Port country officials will then conduct regular inspections in accordance with universal minimum standards, and offending vessels will be denied use of port or certain port services and information shared through new international networks.

***Sources:* "Pirate Fishing," Environmental Justice Foundation, www.ejfoundation.org/oceans/issues-pirate-fishing; FAO, *Agreement on Port State Measures to Prevent, Deter and Eliminate Illegal, Unreported and Unregulated Fishing* (Rome: FAO, 2009), http://www.fao.org/fileadmin/user_upload/legal/docs/037t-e.pdf; and "Fishing Problems: Pirate Fishing," WWF, http://wwf.panda.org/about_our_earth/blue_planet/problems/problems_fishing/fisheries_management/illegal_fishing/.**

efforts to achieve the fine balance between encouraging widespread and international participation and the effective implementation of the guidelines and measures outlined in these voluntary instruments have not been that successful.

In 2006, the UN held a review conference to assess implementation of the Fish Stocks Agreement. The conference recommended an urgent reduction in the world's fishing capacity to levels commensurate with the sustainability of fish stocks, urgent strengthening of the mandates of regional fisheries management organizations to implement modern approaches to fisheries, integrating ecosystem considerations into fisheries management, developing a legally binding instrument on minimum standards for port-state measures and a comprehensive global registry of fishing vessels, expanding assistance to developing countries, and maintaining a continuing dialogue to address concerns raised by nonparties, including issues related to boarding fishing vessels and inspections.[158]

The review conference convened again in 2010. This meeting focused on the role of flag states and agreed to develop criteria for assessing flag-state performance and to address the persistent failure of flag states to carry out their responsibilities. Progress was also made on deep-sea fisheries, with adoption of an EU proposal on establishing long-term conservation and management measures in accordance with the 2008 FAO International Guidelines on Deep-Sea Fisheries in the High Seas. This strengthened the agreement's principle of promoting the protection of habitats of special concern. However, the lack of state compliance with the agreement's provisions still constitutes an impediment to the recovery of such stocks, as well as associated and dependent species and habitats of special concern.

The review conferences also demonstrated that much has changed since the treaty's 1995 adoption. Parties and nonparties alike now accept certain principles of the treaty, such as the ecosystem and precautionary approaches to management, that were agreed to only after long hours of negotiations in 1995. These discussions also revealed a shift in dynamics from the original negotiations, which had been divided between the distant-water fishing states and the coastal states. In 2010, the divide was between the lead coalition of parties and a potential veto coalition of nonparties, whose continued refusal to ratify the agreement threatens the status of remaining fish stocks.[159] The review conference resumed again in May 2016.[160]

The history of the fisheries regime includes several particularly interesting features. One of the key factors in the agenda-setting phase, at least for one important actor, Canada, was less a concern for conservation of straddling and highly migratory fish stocks than it was Canada's desire to stop the EU from unilaterally determining its catch levels in the Grand Banks fishery. In the original negotiations, two different veto coalitions—the like-minded caucus of coastal states and the major distant-water fishing states—initially opposed key provisions of the regime. The

US shift from veto state to lead state proved a major factor in overcoming the resistance of these two veto coalitions and gave greater impetus to the adoption of innovative conservation measures. And the willingness of Canada to use physical force on the high seas in its dispute with the EU, with the result that the EU agreed to onboard inspectors on the high seas, helped put the issue of boarding and inspecting in a different light for key veto states. Finally, the refusal to ratify the agreement by some of the main fishing states (such as China and Peru, to name a few) continues to impede the regime's effectiveness.

WHALING

The history of global policy to safeguard whales illustrates the transformation of an international regime from one that allowed virtually unregulated exploitation to a framework for global conservation despite resistance from a strong veto coalition. Despite this transformation, however, the international whaling regime has been at a crossroads for more than a quarter of a century. The balance of power in the regime's decision-making body, the International Whaling Commission (IWC), rests narrowly with the states favoring a whaling ban. The veto coalition, empowered by its ability to exit the regime at any time, remains strong. Although advances in monitoring whale populations offer the prospect of developing biologically sound management systems, desires to uphold national sovereignty and strong emotions on both sides of the issue endanger the regime.

Emotions and concerns for national sovereignty influence the global debate on whaling far more than scientific analysis or national economic interests (whaling no longer represents a significant economic enterprise on a global or even national basis). For some governments and many environmental NGOs, whaling is seen as both an act of unnecessary human cruelty to an intelligent species and a powerful symbol of environmental overexploitation. To whaling states, harvesting whales represents the right to preserve cultural traditions, maintain coastal livelihoods, and exercise national sovereignty.

Humans have hunted whales for thousands of years. Increases in technology and the size of whaling fleets, particularly in the nineteenth and twentieth century, reduced whale populations significantly. In 1946, whaling nations established the International Convention for the Regulation of Whaling. The convention prohibited killing certain endangered whale species, set quotas and minimum sizes for whales caught commercially, and regulated whaling seasons. The convention was not, however, an environmental regime but a club of whaling nations designed to manage the catch. The regime's designated decision-making body, the IWC, met in secret each year to haggle over quotas set so high that far more whales were being killed annually under the new regime than before the regulations had gone into effect. Indeed, the total number of whales killed more than doubled between 1951 and 1962. The IWC also had no power to enforce its regulations on the size of catch or even its ban on killing endangered species. Although the major whaling nations were members of the IWC, many developing countries, including Brazil, Chile, China, Ecuador, Peru, and the Republic of Korea, refused to join or abide by its restrictions. Some allowed pirate whalers, often financed by sales to Japan, to operate freely.

The process of fact finding and consensus building played virtually no role in relations among IWC members. Scientific knowledge was usually subordinated to political and economic interests. The IWC's scientific committee routinely produced data and analyses supporting continued commercial exploitation, and no outside international organization existed that could facilitate a different framework for decisions based on scientific facts. Given this situation, it is not surprising that by the 1960s the survival of the largest species, the blue whale, was in doubt; finback stocks were dwindling; and many other species were experiencing population declines as whalers filled their quotas with younger and smaller whales.

Increasing public awareness of the diminishing stocks, including the potential extinction of blue whales, coincided with the emerging environmental movement to turn the tide against commercial whaling. The plight of the whales seized the imagination of many Americans, who were beginning to learn more about the intelligence of cetaceans, and the new awareness led to broad popular support for meaningful protection. Responding to the 1969 Endangered Species Act, the United States declared eight whale species endangered in 1970 and began to take the lead in defining the whaling issue internationally.[161]

Placing the issue of whaling in the context of the broader international environmental agenda, the United States first proposed an immediate moratorium on commercial whaling at the 1972 UN Conference on the Human Environment. Adopted by fifty-two of the countries attending the conference, the proposal signaled strong international support for a moratorium. However, because it had not been generated through the IWC, it carried no force within the whaling regime itself. In the IWC, the whaling states (Chile, Iceland, Japan, Norway, Peru, and the Soviet Union) not only constituted a powerful veto coalition (that could even choose to leave the regime if they wished) but also held a near majority. A proposal for a whaling moratorium was defeated in the IWC by a vote of six to four, with four abstentions.

Seeing the need to change the whaling regime itself, the United States, Sweden, and other lead states took advantage of the fact that the IWC does not limit membership to whaling nations and sought to overwhelm the veto coalition by recruiting nonwhaling states into the commission. Thus, rather than trying to transform the regime by building consensus within the IWC, lead states simply sought to assemble the three-fourths majority required to institute a whaling ban. To this end, between 1979 and 1982, the anti-whaling coalition recruited the Seychelles and a number of other developing states, most of which viewed the whaling issue from the perspective that the oceans and their natural resources are the common heritage of humankind.[162]

The United States also sought to weaken the veto coalition by threatening economic sanctions. It used domestic legislation to ban imports of fish products and to deny fishing permits within the United States' two-hundred-mile EEZ to countries that violated international whale-conservation programs. This action put pressure on Chile and Peru, both heavily dependent on US fishing permits and markets, to comply with whale conservation programs.

By 1982, enough developing-country nonwhaling nations had joined the IWC to tilt the balance decisively. A five-year moratorium on all commercial whaling, to take effect in 1985, passed twenty-five to seven, with five abstentions. Four of the veto-coalition states (Japan, Norway, Peru, and the Soviet Union), which accounted for 75 percent of whaling and almost all consumption of whale meat and other whale products, filed formal reservations to the moratorium but chose not to defy it openly when it went into effect (see Box 4.11).

Japan, Norway, and the Soviet Union ended their commercial whaling by the 1987–1988 whaling season. Soon after, however, Japan, Iceland, and Norway unilaterally began to practice what they called scientific whaling. Article VIII of the convention states that countries are able to issue special permits to kill whales for scientific research purposes. Article VIII gives responsibility for setting and regulating these catches to individual governments, not the IWC. It also states that the scientific information produced by the special permit whaling should be presented, at least annually, to the IWC.

Most IWC members found no scientific merit in this whaling because it kills hundreds of minke whales annually and is conducted by commercial ships. However, other economic and political interests weakened the ability of the United States and other countries to pressure whaling states to end the practice. For example, to avoid a probable Japanese retaliation targeting US fish exports, the United States decided not to ban imports of $1 billion in Japanese seafood annually as retaliation for Japan's whaling, instead choosing the lesser sanction of denying the Japanese permission to fish in US waters.

Although the scientific whaling programs allowed some whaling to continue, veto states had their sights set on the larger target of repealing the whaling moratorium. At the 1990 IWC meeting, after the United States had led a majority of IWC members in blocking a proposal to allow limited commercial whaling in the Atlantic and instead extended the moratorium for another year, Iceland, Japan, and

BOX 4.11 INTERNATIONAL WHALING COMMISSION MILESTONES

1946	**International Convention for the Regulation of Whaling is adopted.**
1972	**United States proposes an immediate moratorium on commercial whaling at the UN Conference on the Human Environment.**
1979	**Indian Ocean Sanctuary establishes moratorium on factory ship whaling (except for minke whales).**
1982	**International Whaling Commission (IWC) approves a five-year moratorium on all commercial whaling.**
1987	**Japan begins scientific whaling.**
1990	**IWC extends moratorium for another year.**
1992	**IWC extends the moratorium. Iceland leaves the IWC.**
1994	**IWC establishes the Southern Ocean Whale Sanctuary.**
2002	**Iceland rejoins the IWC.**
2010	**Australia institutes proceedings before the UN International Court of Justice (ICJ) against Japan's scientific whaling program in the Antarctic.**
2014	**The ICJ rules against Japan, agreeing with Australia that Japan's scientific research program is masking a commercial whaling venture in the Antarctic.**
2014	**IWC passes a New Zealand–sponsored resolution that incorporates more rigorous standards for scientific whaling permits.**
2015	**Japan resumes scientific whaling in the Antarctic.**

Norway threatened to leave the IWC if the moratorium was not overturned at the next meeting. When the IWC voted to retain the moratorium in 1992, Iceland followed through with the threat, leaving the IWC, although it returned in 2002.

In 1993 Japan and Norway prepared another attempt to end the whaling ban. In advance of the IWC meeting, both governments spent large amounts of money and effort in nonwhaling countries to promote the position that minke whales were no longer endangered and that whaling villages, severely impoverished by the moratorium, were being denied the right to pursue a cultural tradition.[163] In addition, Japan induced six Caribbean IWC members to support its position by providing funds for new fishing vessels and paying their annual IWC membership fees.[164]

Yet, despite these efforts, the IWC again voted to extend the whaling moratorium for another year.

Over the objections of the veto states, the IWC strengthened the regime in 1994 by adopting a no-catch area (even for scientific whaling) for all whales inhabiting waters below 40 degrees South latitude. The action created the Southern Ocean Whale Sanctuary, an Antarctic whale sanctuary that could protect up to 90 percent of the estimated 3.5 million remaining great whales. The sanctuary is reviewed and open to change every ten years; changes require a 75 percent majority. The whaling nation most affected by the vote was Japan, which was taking three hundred minkes from the Antarctic annually, ostensibly for scientific purposes. Japan and Norway continued to defy both the whaling moratorium and the provisions for a no-catch area.[165]

Adopting the whaling moratorium and creating a no-catch area suggests a strong regime for the protection for whales. Although certainly reducing the number of whales killed each year, the regime's impact has been severely weakened by outright defiance of the whaling moratorium, incursions into the whale sanctuaries (in both the Southern and the Indian Oceans), and the use of loopholes such as scientific whaling—all by nations that have strong environmental records on many other issues.

Norway registered a formal reservation to the moratorium at the time of its passage, stating that this allowed it to ignore the ban. Despite significant international pressure, Norway has conducted commercial whaling outside the control of the IWC throughout the moratorium, capturing approximately 10,412 whales each year between 1993 and 2014.[166] Iceland set its own conservation limits but significantly increased these quotas in 2009 and caught 745 whales between 2006 and 2014.[167] Iceland and Norway, however, whale within their own waters (EEZs). Japan is the only country whaling in international waters. Japan has conducted its whaling operations mostly under the banner of scientific whaling, with 15,093 whales captured since 1987, although the number of whales has decreased in recent years, largely a result of weather conditions and sabotage acts by NGO activists like Sea Shepherd Conservation Society[168] (see Figure 4.2).

Japan defends its whaling by pointing to the large amount of scientific data it has generated. Some of these data, including stomach contents and reliable estimates of age, cannot be collected without killing the whales. Nevertheless, many scientists contend that, although the data are collected using a high degree of scientific rigor, the resulting information does not provide new and important information relevant to the management of stocks but instead largely supports previous knowledge.[169]

FIGURE 4.2 **Scientific Whaling and Commercial Catches Under Objection, 1986–2014**

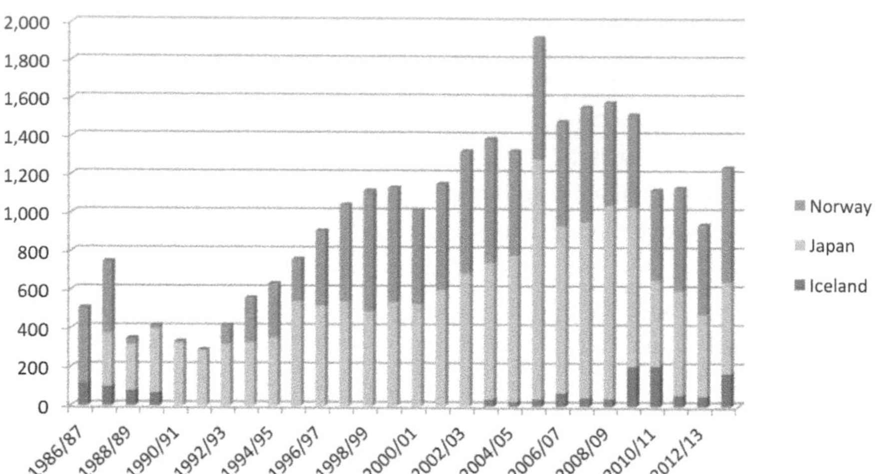

Note: In 1987–1988, Iceland had a scientific whaling permit, and Japan and Norway caught whales in objection to the moratorium. Beginning in 1993–1994, Japan did all of the scientific whaling, and Norway continued to catch whales in objection to the moratorium. Iceland did not kill any whales from 1989 to 2003 but resumed whaling in 2003, after rejoining the International Whaling Commission in 2002.
Source: "Special Permit Catches Since 1985," IWC, http://iwcoffice.org/table_permit.

Over the years, the lead states on whale conservation have included Australia, New Zealand, the United States, the twenty-eight EU member countries,[170] and the so-called Buenos Aires group of thirteen countries from Central and South America. This coalition opposes the resumption of any commercial whaling and supports sanctuaries that also prohibit scientific whaling. Their position is that the convention needs modernization that will, among other things, remove language that allows members to unilaterally issue special permits to kill whales for research purposes.[171]

The key veto states have been Iceland, Japan, and Norway, but their coalition has grown steadily since the 1990s. This expansion was engineered largely by Japan, which engaged in what opponents label as vote buying—that is, building support for its position on whaling through foreign aid and paying IWC membership fees. The head of Japan's Fisheries Agency confirmed this practice, but government officials subsequently denied it.[172] The veto coalition asserts that whales should be managed just like other marine living resources and that opposition to whaling is contrary to the convention because its purpose is to "provide for the proper conservation of whale stocks and thus make possible the orderly development of the whaling industry."[173] They believe that the moratorium and the establishment of the Southern Ocean Whale Sanctuary were adopted without a recommendation from the IWC's Scientific Committee that such measures were required for conservation purposes. These positions were set out in a resolution, called the St. Kitts and Nevis Declaration, adopted by a vote of thirty-three in favor and thirty-two against, with one abstention, at the IWC annual meeting in 2006.[174]

Regime Strengthening

The fact that certain actors effectively ignore regime rules raises concerns about the IWC's future. The deep and "seemingly irreconcilable philosophical and political divisions" between the veto coalition and the lead states have led many to refer to the IWC as a dysfunctional regime.[175] In 2006, after almost a quarter century of the polarized views dominating and hampering its work, the IWC began to explore how to overcome this conflict. After a series of intersessional working group meetings from 2008 to 2010, the result, a Proposed Consensus Decision to Improve the Conservation of Whales, was presented at the sixty-second meeting of the IWC, held in Morocco in June 2010.[176] After two days of private negotiations, delegates were unable to reach consensus on the moratorium, the number of whales that might be taken, special-permit whaling, indigenous whaling, sanctuaries, and trade. Japan said the key stumbling block for them was the demand by the EU and the Buenos Aires Group of Latin American countries that Japan end its Antarctic whaling program within a set time frame. For Japan, agreeing to reduce its quota from 935 whales in 2010 to 200 in ten years' time represented a significant step forward that ought to have been sufficient to its opponents.[177]

As discussions were suspended, the Japanese delegate noted that, although many IWC members emphasized the importance of conservation and management based on science, public opinion against whaling was not based on science. In Japan's view, the two divergent positions on whaling should be mutually acceptable, and IWC members must be willing to accept that different views exist in order to avoid a continued impasse and restore the IWC.[178]

Meanwhile, on May 31, 2010, expressing frustrations with the IWC, Australia instituted proceedings before the UN International Court of Justice (ICJ) against Japan, alleging that

> Japan's continued pursuit of a large scale programme of whaling under the Second Phase of its Japanese Whale Research Programme under Special Permit in the Antarctic ("JARPA II") [is] in breach of obligations assumed by Japan under the International Convention for the Regulation of Whaling ("ICRW"), as well as its other international obligations for the preservation of marine mammals and marine environment.[179]

Australia requested the court to order that Japan "(a) cease implementation of JARPA II; (b) revoke any authorisations, permits or licences allowing the activities which are the subject of this application to be undertaken; and (c) provide assurances and guarantees that it will not take any further action under the JARPA II or any similar programme until such programme has been brought into conformity with its obligations under international law."[180]

On March 31, 2014, the ICJ ruled against Japan, agreeing with Australia that Japan's scientific research program masked a commercial whaling venture in the Antarctic. The ICJ ordered a temporary halt to the activities, largely involving fin, humpback, and minke whales, finding that the Japanese Whaling Research Programme under Special Permit in the Antarctic (JARPA II) is "not in accordance with three provisions of the Schedule to the International Convention for the Regulation of Whaling."[181] The ICJ's ruling, however, only applied to Japan's activities around Antarctica, not in the northwest Pacific. Not even a month after the ICJ's ruling, Japan announced that it would resume limited scientific whaling in the northwest Pacific.[182]

At the IWC Scientific Committee meeting in May 2014, the Japanese government tried to discuss its scientific whaling data, thereby undermining the ICJ ruling. At its sixty-fifth meeting in Slovenia, in September 2014, the IWC passed a New Zealand–sponsored resolution that incorporates more rigorous standards for scientific permits, as prescribed by the ICJ ruling. Resolution 2014–5 was passed by a vote of thirty-five votes in favor and twenty against with five abstentions. It calls on the IWC Scientific Committee to determine whether the design and implementation of a country's program are reasonable in relation to achieving the stated scientific research objectives, whether the research is likely to lead to improvements in whale conservation and management, whether the research objectives could be achieved by nonlethal means, whether the scale of lethal sampling is reasonable in relation to the program's stated research objectives, and other matters the committee considers relevant. The resolution also calls for the Scientific Committee to revise its review procedure for lethal research proposals.[183]

The other big votes at the meeting were on a proposal for a South Atlantic whale sanctuary (where whaling would be prohibited) and a proposal by the Japanese government to introduce a new kind of "small type coastal whaling," where such whaling would be treated like aboriginal subsistence whaling under the IWC. Aboriginal subsistence whaling is a category reserved for indigenous communities with a history of whaling, under a separate special quota system. Both of these proposals failed to pass. One of the most contentious discussions was about Greenland's whaling. Whaling in Greenland is supposed to be for subsistence purposes, with a quota that fulfills the cultural and nutritional needs of the indigenous com-

PHOTO 4.4 Whaleman Foundation Founder Jeff Pantukhoff leads a rally at the White House to stop all commercial and scientific whaling by Japan, Norway, and Iceland. Copyright Chris Guinness/Whaleman Foundation.

munity. However, the number of whales hunted in Greenland has been controversial because meat has been found for sale in supermarkets and restaurants, including in Denmark. Because Greenland is an autonomous region within Denmark, it is represented by Denmark at the IWC. Greenland submitted a proposal for a subsistence hunt that was to include endangered species such as fin and humpback whales. The other EU parties to the IWC were lobbied by Denmark and, as a result, voted in favor of the Greenland proposal. As a result, Greenland was permitted to hunt 207 whales per year for four years.[184]

In June 2015, Japan submitted new plans for scientific whaling in the Antarctic. Although the IWC's Scientific Committee concluded that there is no justification for Japan to kill whales for research purposes, Japan resumed its scientific whale hunt in December 2015.[185] Meanwhile, Norway and Iceland continued their commercial whale hunting into the 2015 season.

Over the years, the IWC has evolved from a whalers' club, which created quotas based on the power of the competing economic interests of whaling nations, into an international body divided into whaling and anti-whaling states in which "reliance on arguments grounded in moral beliefs have decreased the . . . whaling states' commitment to the process of collective decision making."[186] This shift in discourse has been driven by strong emotions. Both groups feel entirely justified in refusing to compromise for fear of an outcome undesirable to their side.[187] Pro-whaling countries fear losing their sovereign right to take ocean resources in international waters outside territorial limits. There is concern that the moratorium on whaling is the first step down a slippery slope whereby certain depleted fish stocks will become off-limits. On the other hand, anti-whalers fear that any exception to the moratorium will degenerate into an open season on whales. For anti-whaling nations and NGOs, whaling is emblematic of the short-sighted degradation of the planet. They argue that whaling is inexcusably cruel and endangers an already scarce species, compounding the threats whales face from global warming, noise and chemical pollution, physical strikes by ships, and net entanglements.[188]

Coalition building on both sides has been characterized more by political maneuvering than by a process that values fact finding and consensus building. Science appears to have played a marginal role in decision making, with its credibility diminished by the practice of commercial whaling being carried out under the banner of scientific whaling, even after the ICJ ruled against Japan's scientific whaling program. With no end in sight for this deadlock, the future effectiveness of the IWC remains in the balance.

CONCLUSION

The environmental regimes discussed in Chapters 3 and 4 show that the negotiation of a strong global environmental regime almost always depends on inducing one or more key veto states to go along with one or more of the core proposed provisions of the regime. By a strong or effective regime, we mean an agreement that mandates actions that can reasonably be expected to have an impact on the problem if they are implemented and that includes obligations or norms that make it sufficiently clear that parties can be held accountable for implementing them. Whether a regime succeeds in addressing an environmental threat depends, of course, on how strong the regime is and on the degree to which parties comply with its core provisions. Success in overcoming the impact of veto states in global environmental negotiations usually results from one or more of the following five developments:

1. A veto state changes its own understanding of the problem because of new scientific evidence.
2. A veto state changes its position because its economic interests have changed.
3. A veto state has a change of government, and the new government has a different policy toward the issue.
4. A veto state comes under effective domestic political pressure to change its policy.
5. A veto state fears negative reactions from other governments or adverse international opinion, which it regards as more important than its interest in vetoing a specific provision of the regime.

As Table 4.3 shows, in some of these cases one or more veto states either agreed to the central obligation proposed by the lead-state coalition or accepted the regime in general, despite earlier rejection.

TABLE 4.3 **Veto States and Regime Creation or Strengthening**

ISSUE*	KEY VETO STATES	BASIS OF VETO POWER	VETO STATE CONCESSION
Ozone depletion	European Community	Percentage of chlorofluorocarbon production	Agreeing to 50 percent cut; agreeing to phaseout
Hazardous waste trade	United States, European Union, Japan	Percentage of exports	Agreeing to ban exports
Toxic chemicals	Developing countries that use DDT for malaria control	Percentage of use of DDT; global support for increased malaria control	Acceptance of elimination of DDT but with blanket exception for disease control; acceptance of regular reviews on continued need for DDT
Climate change	United States	Percentage of carbon dioxide emissions	Agreeing to stabilization goal**
Biodiversity loss	United States	Percentage of financing of Global Environment Facility; biotechnology	Signing the agreement**
African elephant ivory	Japan, southern African states	Percentage of imports (Japan); elephant herds (southern African states)	No reservation to CITES uplist
Forests	Brazil and Latin American countries, United States	Percentage of the world's forests; largest timber industry	No agreement
Desertification	European Community, United States	Percentage of official development assistance	Agreeing to create the Global Mechanism as a funding mechanism
Fisheries depletion	European Commission, Japan, and the Like-Minded Caucus	Percentage of global catch of straddling and highly migratory stocks	Agreement to precautionary reference points and new enforcement measures
Whaling	Japan and Norway	Percentage of catch	Acceptance of ban on whaling against depleted populations

*This chart outlines one aspect of the veto coalition situation for each case as a point of comparison.

**In both of these cases, veto state power has not totally been overcome because, although the United States in each case made certain concessions in the negotiations, the result was a much weaker treaty.

New scientific evidence helped move veto states on some issues (ozone depletion, climate change, and POPs) but has been secondary or irrelevant in others (whaling, hazardous waste trade, desertification, and African elephants). International considerations were primary in several cases. Japan's concern with economic and diplomatic ties with other major trading nations and its international image helped tilt its stance on the ivory ban. French and British desire to maintain productive relations with former colonies factored into their policy on the hazardous waste trade. The leading distant-water fishing states dropped their resistance to key provisions in the Fish Stocks Agreement in part because they did not want to appear to be blocking the first major global agreement on sustainable fishing. Changing economic interests or new political strategies concerning how to pursue those interests can also lead veto states to change position. The United Kingdom and France dropped their opposition to phasing out chlorofluorocarbons (CFCs) in part because their chemical industries invented substitutes. Several veto states in the forest negotiations changed positions when they believed they might secure a treaty that would preserve market access or secure new sources of multilateral funding.

In some cases, domestic political developments played a key role in facilitating agreement. The Obama administration in the United States and the Justin Trudeau administration in Canada pursued significantly different and more productive national and international policies on climate change than their predecessors. Concern about POPs in the Inuit communities of northern Canada pushed Canada to the forefront of the negotiations to ban certain types of these substances.

Regime formation usually requires leadership by one or more states committed to defining the issue and proposing and supporting strong international policy. Sometimes that role is played by states motivated by particular vulnerability (African countries on the hazardous waste trade and desertification; small island states on climate change) and sometimes by a state that has an advantageous legal or economic situation (the original US call for a phaseout of CFCs).The absence of lead states seeking to strengthen the regime is a major factor, along with the presence of veto states, why the language in the conservation provisions of the biodiversity treaty remains largely advisory rather than binding.

Lead and veto states are not all equal. Lead states with greater diplomatic clout, economic resources, or negotiating skill outperform those with fewer resources. In the case of desertification, although African countries form an active lead-state coalition, their weak political and economic influence has contributed to the ineffectiveness of the regime. The impact of a veto state depends on its ability to keep the regime from being effective. This can vary from issue to issue, and sometimes states that usually have less political or economic influence can have significant veto power if, for example, they have a large distant-water fishing fleet or are the main home to particular species. In general, however, the states and coalitions with the largest economies and populations (such as Brazil, China, India, the EU, and the United States) are the most potent potential veto states.

Overall, as these cases show, the United States has greater diplomatic influence on other state actors and intergovernmental organizations than any other state, although the EU as a unit is comparable and China and India are rivaling both. When the United States has taken the lead, as it did on ozone depletion, whaling, and the African elephant, the result has been a much stronger regime than otherwise would have been established. In the case of the Fish Stocks Agreement, the lead role played by the United States was crucial to agreement on conservation norms for the high seas and within EEZs. On the other hand, when the United States has been a veto state, as in the Basel Convention, the Biodiversity Convention, and the Kyoto Protocol, the result is a significantly weaker regime.

In the case of biodiversity, efforts by a coalition of veto states have combined with several other factors—the complexity of the issue, lack of high levels of media interest, less domestic lobbying by environmental NGOs, and a poorly designed regime with a proliferation of working groups—to prevent the regime from becoming significantly stronger and more effective over time. These reasons have also contributed to the biodiversity convention receiving far less high-level political attention in major states than do the ozone or climate treaties.

In the case of climate change, the adoption of the Paris Agreement was only possible by avoiding the top-down requirements for emissions reductions, which proved problematic in the Kyoto Protocol, and allowing countries to determine their own GHG emissions reductions. This enabled both China and the United States, as the largest GHG emitters and veto states, to accept the agreement in December 2015.

As indicated in the cases examined in these two chapters, the international community has been able to negotiate an impressively large number of agreements to reduce environmental threats. Many of these regimes have also grown significantly since the creation of their first agreement. Governments continue to meet and negotiate new pollution controls (as in the ozone and chemicals treaties), list new species (CITES), and even negotiate entirely new protocols within the regime (the Liability Protocol under the Basel Convention, the Kyoto Protocol, the Cartagena Protocol on Biosafety, and the Nagoya Protocol on Access and Benefit Sharing) or new types of agreements that accept political realities while offering a framework for potential success, such as the 2015 Paris Agreement.

Global environmental regimes now include conventions that enjoy nearly universal participation and have the potential to affect economic development strategies, production technologies, and even domestic political processes in ways supportive of long-term sustainable development. However, as these cases also demonstrate, not all of these agreements have been successful. Serious obstacles exist to negotiating strong, global environmental treaties. Moreover, negotiating a strong treaty on paper does not mean it will be effective in practice. All of the regimes discussed in these chapters face serious implementation challenges, including compliance, financing, technology transfer, and effective translation of regime rules into national policy. The next chapter focuses on these challenges.

5

Effective Environmental Regimes: Obstacles and Opportunities

Environmental issues are an important part of international relations. Countries have negotiated more than 280 major multilateral environmental agreements (MEAs)—international agreements focused on environmental protection[1]—and more than 1,150 multilateral and 1,500 bilateral agreements that contain at least some provisions addressing the environment.[2] However, simply negotiating an agreement does not guarantee environmental protection.

The most important measure of the effectiveness of an environmental regime—the extent to which it produces measurable improvements in the environment—is a function of three factors. First is regime design, particularly the strength of the key control provisions aimed at addressing the environmental threat, but also the provisions on reporting, monitoring, regime strengthening, noncompliance, and financial and technical assistance (FTA). Second is the level of implementation, the extent to which countries and, to a lesser extent, international organizations adopt formal legislation and enact other regulations to implement the agreement. Third is compliance, the degree to which countries and other actors actually observe these regulations and the extent to which their actions conform to the explicit rules, norms, and procedures contained in the regime.[3]

This chapter examines some of the factors that inhibit or promote effective international environmental regimes. The first section outlines obstacles that can make it difficult to create and implement effective regimes with strong, binding control measures. These obstacles primarily relate to factors at the international level. The second section looks at variables that inhibit effective implementation and compliance. These primarily concern national-level issues. The third section outlines potential avenues to improve compliance. The final section discusses options for increasing the financing available to implement global environmental regimes.

OBSTACLES TO CREATING STRONG ENVIRONMENTAL REGIMES

One can distinguish eight major categories of obstacles that can inhibit creation of strong and effective global environmental regimes: (1) systemic or structural obstacles that stem from the structure of the international system, the structure of international law, and the structure of the global economic system; (2) a lack of necessary and sufficient conditions—in particular, public or official concern, a hospitable contractual environment, and capacity; (3) lowest-common-denominator problems; (4) time-horizon conflicts; (5) obstacles that stem from common characteristics of global environmental issues; (6) obstacles that result from the interconnections of environmental issues, including potential conflicts among solutions; (7) regime-design difficulties; and (8) changing views on how to apply the principle of common but differentiated responsibilities (CBDR).[4] Of course, when we think about these categories, it is important to see them as broad, indicative, and heuristic rather than exhaustive and exclusive (see Box 5.1). The categories and individual causal factors are interrelated, and their individual and relative impacts vary significantly across countries and issue areas. They also do not prevent effective policy; they simply make it more difficult to achieve.

BOX 5.1 PROMINENT OBSTACLES TO CREATING STRONG AND EFFECTIVE ENVIRONMENTAL REGIMES

SYSTEMIC OBSTACLES

- **Anarchical structure of the international political system**
- **Incongruence of global political and ecological systems**
- **Incongruence of fundamental principles of international law and fundamental requirements for effective environmental policy**
- **Certain aspects of the structure of international economic systems**

THE ABSENCE OF NECESSARY CONDITIONS

- **Inadequate concern**
- **Inhospitable contractual environments**
- **Insufficient capacity**

continues

BOX 5.1 PROMINENT OBSTACLES TO CREATING STRONG AND EFFECTIVE ENVIRONMENTAL REGIMES *continued*

LOWEST-COMMON-DENOMINATOR PROBLEMS

- **Strength and effectiveness of an environmental treaty depends on securing the agreement, participation, and compliance of veto states**

TIME-HORIZON CONFLICTS

- **Time-consuming process of global policy development and implementation**
- **Incongruent timescales among environmental systems and political and corporate systems**

CHARACTERISTICS OF GLOBAL ENVIRONMENTAL ISSUES

- **Links to important economic and social activities and interests**
- **Unequal adjustment costs**
- **Scientific complexity and uncertainty**
- **Different core beliefs**
- **Large number of actors**

INTERCONNECTIONS AMONG ENVIRONMENTAL ISSUES

- **Successfully addressing one problem can require addressing one or more separate but interrelated problems**
- **Solutions to one problem may exacerbate another problem**

REGIME-DESIGN DIFFICULTIES

- **Effective regime design is difficult**
- **Other political and economic issues influence regime design**

CONFLICTING VIEWS ON THE PRINCIPLE OF COMMON BUT DIFFERENTIATED RESPONSIBILITIES

- **Global economic and ecological developments have altered how some countries seek to operationalize key paradigms**

Systemic Obstacles

Some impediments to creating strong global environmental regimes result from inherent elements of the global political, ecological, legal, and economic systems. One of the broadest is the anarchical structure of international politics. Anarchy, as used here, means the absence of hierarchy, specifically the absence of a world government with recognized authority to maintain order and make rules. For thousands of years, notable statesmen, philosophers, historians, and political scientists have argued that aspects of this structure have broad consequences for international relations.[5] In particular, states tend to believe they can rely only on self-help to ensure their safety, states usually attempt to balance the power of other states through alliances and armaments, states prefer independence over interdependence, and states often find it difficult to achieve effective international cooperation.[6]

The last consequence is perhaps the most relevant to environmental regimes. Just as in security or economic issues, system structure places pressures on state actors that can make it difficult to create effective environmental regimes (although to a far lesser extent than in security issues). Strong states sometimes attempt to dictate terms to weaker states. States worry that other countries might face fewer costs from an agreement (even if both sides benefit environmentally) or that others might gain more economically or politically.[7] For example, the administration of George W. Bush refused to seek ratification of the Kyoto Protocol in part due to concern for its relative economic impacts, arguing that the United States would suffer competitively if it reduced greenhouse gases (GHGs) but China did not.

States can fail to agree when some fear others might double-cross them by not fulfilling regime obligations or paying their share of the costs.[8] States sometimes try to free-ride and enjoy the benefits produced by others without contributing their fair share, for example, by continuing to emit a certain pollutant when others have agreed to stop, the fear of which can scuttle an agreement or render it ineffective.[9] States sometimes have incentives to pursue policies that appear rational on their own but that result in harming or destroying a common-pool resource, resulting in a "tragedy of the commons."[10] A current example is depletion of ocean fisheries. Many countries allow fishing fleets to catch as much fish as they can in international waters, which is good for them individually in the short run, even as the resource is depleted for everyone in the long run. States sometimes fail to locate mutually advantageous policies because of suspicions, a lack of information, market failure,[11] or misperception of the motives, intentions, or actions of other governments.[12] Governments can also compromise environmental negotiations by linking them to unrelated international or domestic political, security, and economic issues.

Another systemic or structural obstacle is the lack of congruence among the global political and ecological systems. The structure of the global political system, which comprises independent sovereign states, is incongruent with ecological systems and not well suited to address complex, interdependent, international environmental problems whose causes, impacts, and solutions transcend unrelated political boundaries. Pollution released into the air or water spreads easily to other countries. Chlorofluorocarbons (CFCs) deplete the ozone layer without respect to

PHOTO 5.1 Members of the Global Indigenous Peoples' Caucus greeted delegates to the fifth meeting of the Stockholm Convention Conference of the Parties. Courtesy Brad Vincelette, IISD/ *Earth Negotiations Bulletin*, www.iisd.ca.

which country released them. Persistent organic pollutants (POPs) released in the United States or Mexico affect people, animals, and ecosystems in northern Canada. Some of the mercury released from coal-fired power plants in China, India, Indonesia, and other countries becomes absorbed and concentrated in ocean species eaten by people all over the world. High-seas fisheries and atmospheric chemistry are outside the political control of any one state.

This structural conflict has affected negotiations on global and regional commons issues—such as the atmosphere (ozone depletion and climate change) and the high seas (fisheries and whales)—as well as negotiations on problems when air and water pollution cross national borders. For example, upwind and downwind states can hold different views regarding appropriate rules to control air pollution, as was apparent in efforts to develop specific protocols to the Convention on Long-Range Transboundary Air Pollution and in the US–Canada acid rain negotiations. Similar problems exist in the management of transboundary waterways. Of the more than two hundred sixty river basins around the world, one-third of them are shared by more than two countries, and nineteen major river basins are shared by five or more states.[13] This significantly complicates efforts to manage pollution, overfishing, and sustainable use. For example, ten African countries rely on the Nile River and its tributaries. Cooperative management efforts date back to 1902, but pollution, potential overuse, and other disputes threaten the river's health.

Egypt has at times even threatened military action against upstream countries Sudan, Ethiopia, and Uganda for actions or proposals that it perceives as illegal or excessive diversions of water from the Nile.[14]

A similar conflict exists between the foundations of international law and the requirements for effective international environmental policy. Perhaps the most fundamental principle of international law is sovereignty. States have nearly unassailable control over activities within their borders, including the use of natural resources. At the same time, however, legitimate actions within one country can create environmental problems for another. Consequently, effective international environmental policy often requires limiting what a state does within its own borders.

This conflict is embodied in Principle 21 of the 1972 Stockholm Declaration, often cited as one of the most important foundations of modern international environmental law. It reads, "States have, in accordance with the Charter of the United Nations and the principles of international law, the sovereign right to exploit their own resources pursuant to their own environmental policies, and the responsibility to ensure that activities within their jurisdiction or control do not cause damage to the environment of other states or of areas beyond the limits of national jurisdiction."[15] This principle later became Principle 2 of the 1992 Rio Declaration, but with the words "and developmental" inserted before "policies," making it even more self-contradictory.

Overcoming the inherent tension captured in this principle is one of the most fundamental challenges of global environmental politics. Many states strongly resist regime provisions that, although beneficial to the environment, compromise their national sovereignty. For example, many of the most controversial proposals during negotiation of the Convention on Biological Diversity (CBD) involved potential restrictions on state control over genetic resources within their borders.[16] The debate over a forest convention has been strongly affected by states wanting to ensure that they maintain clear sovereignty over their forest resources. Concerns about potential infringements on national sovereignty led to the inclusion of veto clauses that allow each party to block third-party adjudication under the Basel Convention.[17] China, India, and the United States argued for many years that efforts to curtail GHG emissions should not hamper their right to economic growth or use of domestic coal reserves.

Some argue that elements of the international economic system present an inherent, structural impediment to creating and implementing strong and effective global environmental policy.[18] Different discussions along these lines point to the system's emphasis on resource extraction, globalization, free trade, lowest-cost production, high levels of consumption and consumerism, and, especially, the failure to include the economic and other costs produced by environmental degradation in the cost of activities and products that cause the degradation.

Some aspects of these arguments seem well founded. For example, few of the economic costs associated with the environmental and human-health impacts of using toxic chemicals or burning coal or gasoline are included in their price. These costs are passed on to society as a whole, rather than paid by the actors actually producing the pollution. Thus, there is little economic incentive for an individual company to reduce pollution when everyone pays its costs. There is an increasing consensus among a variety of theorists and politicians from across the political spectrum regarding the need to include the economic costs of environmental degradation into the larger economic system, although they often reach different conclusions about how to accomplish this.

Many also agree that the emphasis placed by certain international economic forces on developing countries to maximize resource extraction, pay off foreign debts, and industrialize as quickly as possible has produced serious environmental problems. The ultimate impact of free trade and economic integration on certain aspects of the environment also faces scrutiny, particularly when domestic environmental laws, such as the European Union (EU) ban on Canadian fur imports from animals caught in leg-hold traps, are overruled by free-trade rules under the World Trade Organization (WTO)[19] (see Chapter 6).

Yet it is probably too simplistic to assert that the global economic system only inhibits strong environmental regimes. Indeed, when properly harnessed, these same forces can support effective regimes. For example, in the expansion of the ozone regime, the global economic system supported the introduction of more environmentally friendly technology into developing countries much more quickly than many had expected. The financial power amassed by the global insurance industry supports stronger action on climate change. Free-trade rules and economic integration have likely improved overall energy efficiency in Europe. Introducing carbon taxes and similar measures, while lowering other taxes, appears to increase demand for clean energy[20] and to decouple increased economic growth from increased GHG emissions.[21] Thus, the key may be to examine, case by case, how economic interests and systems run counter to, or support, the goals or operation of particular environmental policies rather than reflexively assume that they necessarily inhibit effective environmental regimes.

The Absence of Necessary Conditions: Concern, Contractual Environment, and Capacity

As discussed by Peter Haas, Robert Keohane, and Marc Levy, effective environmental regimes require three necessary conditions.[22] First, there must be adequate levels of concern within governments, and perhaps among the public at large, so that states devote resources to examine and address the problem and implement potential solutions. Environmental problems compete with many economic, security, and social issues for space on national and international agendas. Concern must exist for the issue-definition, fact-finding, bargaining, and regime-strengthening phases to occur and be successfully completed.

Second, there must be a sufficiently hospitable contractual environment so that states can gather together, negotiate with reasonable ease and costs, make credible commitments, reach agreement on new policies, and monitor each other's behavior in implementing those policies. In other words, if too many of the negative consequences of system structure, such as fears of cheating or free riding, are present, or if transaction costs (time, money, and effort involved in negotiating a treaty) are too high, then creating strong agreements is difficult.

Third, states must possess the scientific, political, economic, and administrative capacity to understand the threat, participate in creating the global regime, and then implement and ensure compliance with the regime's principles, norms, and rules. Capacity is essentially a measure of the necessary scientific, administrative, economic, and political resources a country possesses to address a particular issue, as well as the physical and political ability to deploy those resources effectively.

Concern, contractual environment, and capacity are not obstacles themselves. The presence of each is a necessary but insufficient condition. Thus, it is their absence that significantly inhibits, if not prevents, the creation and implementation of strong environmental regimes. The concepts are easy to oversimplify, but concern, contractual environment, and capacity encapsulate important, even critical, causal factors and are interconnected with many of the other issues discussed in this chapter.

Lowest-Common-Denominator Problems

Once states begin negotiations to create or strengthen a global environmental regime, an obstacle can emerge: the lowest-common-denominator problem.[23] This problem is a result of how international environmental negotiations work, the requirements for effective international environmental policy, the structural obstacles outlined above, the varying levels of national concern for particular environmental issues, the need for consensus, and the presence of veto states.

All states are sovereign entities and can choose whether or not to join an environmental agreement. However, because active participation by many countries is required to address global environmental problems, the countries most concerned often need support from countries with far less interest. Thus, an environmental treaty can be only as strong as the least cooperative state allows it to be. The regime's overall effectiveness, thus, is undermined by the compromises made in persuading these states, the veto states, to participate.

For example, during negotiation of the 1991 Protocol on Environmental Protection to the Antarctic Treaty, which protects Antarctica from possible mineral exploitation, opposition from the United States resulted in a fifty-year moratorium rather than the initially proposed permanent protection. As discussed in Chapter 3, from 1977 to 1989, the European Community (EC) acted as a veto state, forcing lead states to accept much weaker rules in the 1985 Vienna Convention and 1987 Montreal Protocol than they had sought. During the Stockholm Convention negotiations, countries critical to its long-term success insisted on specific exemptions so that they could continue to use small amounts of certain POPs, even though the convention called for eliminating all production and use of these substances. This process has repeated itself as parties have added chemicals to the convention. The lowest-common-denominator problem has affected the climate regime for many years. All of the major emitters of GHGs must cooperate for the regime to succeed. For many years, China, India, and the United States were reluctant to take actions to curb their domestic emissions. This limited the ability of Europe, the Alliance of Small Island States (AOSIS), and other lead states to move forward with an aggressive emissions-reduction agreement.

Decision-making procedures that require consensus on key issues also create lowest-common-denominator problems because they allow one or more states to block agreements that would strengthen a regime, even if the vast majority of countries support the change. For example, in 2015, Sudan was the only country that objected to adding the pesticide fenthion to the prior informed consent (PIC) procedure that operates under the Rotterdam Convention. Despite being inconsequential to the success of the PIC procedure overall, Sudan prevented the addition of fenthion, even after being told by other African countries that listing would provide easy access to more information and not prevent its use.[24] At the same meeting, India was the only country that objected to, and thus prevented, the listing of trichlorfon. Guatemala and India prevented the listing of the severely hazardous pesticide formulation of paraquat dichloride, despite strong statements of support for listing by other Latin American countries, all African countries, and the EU member states, among others. Cuba, Kazakhstan, Kyrgyzstan, Russia, and Zimbabwe prevented the listing of chrysotile asbestos, despite a large number of interventions in support of a proposed listing[25] and calls by the World Health Organization (WHO) not only for its listing but also for more countries to ban the substance.[26]

Voting procedures can overcome this type of lowest common denominator. However, in situations in which a regime allows voting (such as the Convention on International Trade in Endangered Species of Wild Fauna and Flora [CITES], whaling, and POPs on some issues), states whose participation is essential to success can create lowest-common-denominator problems by threatening not to participate if the regime is strengthened by a vote. There can also be political costs to forcing a vote. Most treaties have language emphasizing consensus, and once a norm has been established against voting, countries are reluctant to use the voting rules, even in the presence of overwhelming majorities, for fear of harming the contractual environment or creating resentment or mistrust that might harm regime implementation. For example, the Montreal Protocol allows for voting, but it has never been used, even when as few as two countries disagreed. Perhaps as a result, however, a norm developed that a single country will not block consensus. In other cases, such as the CBD, the United Nations Framework Convention on Climate Change (UNFCCC), and the UN Convention to Combat Desertification (UNCCD), the voting rules have not yet been adopted, and as a result, all decisions must be taken by consensus, creating even more lowest-common-denominator agreements.

Time-Horizon Conflicts

Another category of obstacles relates to the incongruent timescales of policy development and environmental issues. The process to create and implement effective global environmental policy is neither easy nor speedy. It often operates, as one long-time observer noted, like a slow boat.[27] The international agenda must be set, negotiations convened, appropriate policies identified, strong agreements reached, implementation strategies agreed to, treaties ratified, national and international policies implemented and reported on, environmental problems monitored, and international policies revised in light of new data and lessons learned. The common practice of starting with a framework convention and adopting subsequent protocols adds even more time. Enough governments must ratify the convention and protocols so that they can enter into force and be effective.

Each step in this process can be time-consuming. As discussed in Chapter 3, the environmental problems posed by hazardous waste shipments were identified in the 1970s, but the Basel Convention did not come into effect until 1992, and the Ban Amendment still requires additional ratifications to take effect. The United Nations Convention on the Law of the Sea, a complex treaty that contains provisions on most aspects of maritime law, took nearly ten years to negotiate and another twelve to receive sufficient ratifications to enter into force. The International Convention for the Prevention of Pollution from Ships (MARPOL) experienced a ten-year time lag from its negotiation to its entry into force, despite the decades of collaborative efforts on oil pollution leading up to it.

Knowledge of the greenhouse effect goes back more than one hundred fifty years. Joseph Fourier, a French mathematician and physicist, discovered in 1824

PHOTO 5.2 Youth delegate Hilary Bowman holds up a T-shirt that says, "You have been negotiating all my life. You cannot tell me that you need more time" at the sixteenth meeting of the UN Framework Convention on Climate Change Conference of the Parties in Cancun. Courtesy Leila Mead, IISD/*Earth Negotiations Bulletin*, www.iisd.ca.

that gases in the atmosphere likely increase the surface temperature of the earth. In 1859, John Tyndall, an Irish physicist, explained the ability of various gases, including carbon dioxide (CO_2) and water vapor, to absorb radiant heat, proving that the earth's atmosphere has a natural greenhouse effect. In 1896, Svante Arrhenius, a Swedish scientist, published an article suggesting that temperatures would rise 5°C if atmospheric CO_2 doubled. In 1960, Charles Keeling published data clearly showing that CO_2 levels were rising. Nevertheless, formal negotiations on the UNFCCC did not begin until 1991. Scientists discovered the threat to the ozone layer in 1974, but negotiations did not begin until 1982, the first binding controls did not come into force until 1988, developing countries did not have to phase out most uses of CFCs until 2010, and hydrochlorofluorocarbons (HCFCs) will not be phased out until 2030.

Yet environmental issues do not wait for the policy process. As negotiations continue, more species become extinct, forests are cut down, land is degraded, GHGs are emitted into the atmosphere, toxic chemicals are released, and hazardous wastes are not properly managed, making it even more difficult to create and implement effective regimes.

Time-horizon conflicts also stem from an incongruence of environmental systems and political and corporate systems: most political and corporate reward systems operate on much shorter timescales than environmental issues. Addressing environmental problems effectively often requires an informed, long-term perspective. However, because the most serious consequences of many environmental problems will not occur for many years (or this appears to be the case, even if it is later proven incorrect), policymakers and other actors sometimes find it difficult to create or implement policies that carry short-term costs even if these actions will prevent higher costs in the future. In addition, environmental issues often do not develop in linear, predictable patterns nor do their impacts occur simultaneously in all regions and in all countries. This can mask their global impact or cause some actors to remain less concerned about addressing them immediately.

At the same time, however, policymakers often have shorter time horizons. Major political figures in the United States, for example, face elections every two years (members of the House of Representatives), four years (president and governors), or six years (senators). Most corporations release reports on their revenues, costs, and profits every three months—reports that can significantly affect their stock price and executive compensation. Thus, even if every political figure and corporate leader wanted to address an environmental issue, the time horizons for their most immediate approval processes (elections and quarterly reports) are not in tune with the long-term perspective required.

Biodiversity loss and climate change are obvious examples of issues that are affected by time-horizon conflicts. Efforts to add additional substances to the POPs regime also face this problem. Although thousands of chemical spills occur each year,[28] sometimes resulting in exposure to POPs and other toxic substances, the most widespread threats posed by many chemicals, including potential impacts on reproductive health, may only occur in the future as a result of long-term exposure from their slow accumulation in humans and the environment.[29] Preventing these impacts requires accepting certain current costs for likely, but future, benefits, something that history indicates is not easy.

Time-horizon conflicts are increasingly important because some environmental issues likely possess critical tipping points beyond which effective policy becomes far more difficult and perhaps impossible. The point at which enough CO_2 enters the atmosphere so that significant climate change will be impossible to avoid becomes closer each year, and avoiding it requires peaking global emissions soon, perhaps within a decade.[30] Fish stocks may decline gradually but can collapse rapidly once too many fish have been taken. Stocks then take many years to recover, if they recover at all. Once cut, many tropical forests cannot recover into the same ecosystems. Land and water can become so contaminated with radioactivity or toxic chemicals that it is unusable for decades or longer. Coral reefs take centuries to grow. The fact that aspects of the climate, fish stocks, biodiversity, and other problems are potentially nearing critical tipping points could enhance the urgency of reaching effective agreements, but it also represents an obstacle beyond which truly effective policy may not be possible.

Characteristics of Global Environmental Issues

Another set of obstacles stems from common characteristics inherent in global environmental problems. Although they are certainly not unique to environmental issues and have impacts that are both interconnected and vary across countries and issue areas, these characteristics are important elements of global environmental politics and have the capacity to exacerbate many of the other obstacles outlined in this chapter. As noted above, these categories should be seen as indicative and heuristic rather than exhaustive and exclusive.

One of the most critical characteristics is that environmental issues are inextricably linked to important economic and political interests. Environmental issues, and therefore environmental negotiations, are not independent of other economic and political activities and interests. Indeed, environmental issues exist because of these activities and interests. Environmental problems are produced as externalities of individuals, corporations, and nations pursuing other goals and interests. They result from important local, corporate, national, and international economic and political activities, such as energy production, mining, manufacturing, farming, fishing, transportation, resource consumption, livestock husbandry, urbanization, weapons production, and military conflict.

Few, if any, individuals or organizations harm the environment as an end in itself. People do not get up in the morning, leave their homes, and announce, "I intend to pollute today." What people do say is, "I intend to manufacture, to produce energy, to farm, to drive my car to work." Environmental degradation is a consequence of these otherwise legitimate pursuits. The fact that many of these activities could be pursued successfully while doing less harm to the environment does not erase the links among the issues.

Creating strong international environmental regimes, therefore, often requires addressing economic, social, and security interests that are important to certain countries or interest groups. Regardless of whether these interests are justified, the links create obstacles to effective action. The presence of important economic interests can lower relative concern, make veto states more determined, and cause powerful domestic economic actors to lobby for their views. They can also enhance fears of free riding, create more opportunities for positional bargaining, and otherwise harm the contractual environment.

There are many examples of the obstacles posed by the links between environmental problems and economic interests. Protecting the earth's remaining biodiversity requires addressing the economic and political pressures that cause habitat destruction, something that has been impossible to achieve in a binding global agreement. In the Nagoya Protocol negotiations, developing countries called for fair and equitable sharing of benefits arising from the use of genetic resources with the countries of origin and with local and indigenous communities, whereas foreign companies, collectors, researchers, and other users who profit greatly from derivatives of these resources preferred the status quo, where they could gain access essentially for free. Addressing climate change requires significant changes in fossil-fuel consumption. Complete protection of the ozone layer requires a near total phaseout of methyl bromide emissions, something that major agricultural and shipping interests, including those in the United States, have been hesitant to do. Combating deforestation in some developing countries would have a significant impact on their timber industry. Addressing the serious decline in fisheries will affect the economies of both distant-water fishing states and coastal states.

Economic links even impact scientifically based regime procedures. For example, as discussed in Chapter 3, the Stockholm Convention tasks the thirty-one members of the Persistent Organic Pollutants Review Committee with determining, on the basis of available scientific information, if a nominated chemical meets the criteria for being considered a POP and then evaluating if the risks it poses to human health or the environment meet the criteria required for adding the chemical to the treaty's control regime. Information related to economic and social issues are to be considered later in the process and especially by the full Conference of the Parties (COP). However, concerns for national economic and political interests have increasingly affected the work of the committee, complicating and delaying decisions that should have been based entirely on scientific information.[31] Similarly, the analogous technical subsidiary body under the Rotterdam Convention, the Chemical Review Committee, has also seen increasing politicization of what was designed to be a science-based committee.[32]

Sometimes the linkages are particularly difficult to argue against, even for strong proponents of an environmental regime. For example, the total elimination of the POP dichlorodiphenyltrichloroethane (DDT) would prevent its use as an inexpensive tool in the battle against malaria. Even those countries most committed to addressing POPs under the Stockholm Convention agree that this use of DDT should continue (although with methods that reduce its environmental impact) while alternative products and processes are developed. Similarly, although strongly agreeing in 2009 that the toxic chemical perfluorooctane sulfonate (PFOS) should be eliminated as part of the expansion of the Stockholm Convention, the United States and Switzerland also successfully argued that an exception should be granted so that small amounts of the substance can be used in certain medical devices until replacements are developed. During negotiation of the mercury treaty, governments accepted arguments by African countries, supported by information provided by WHO, that they should be allowed to continue using a very effective and low-cost preservative for vaccines that contains trace amounts of mercury.[33]

A second characteristic, and one closely linked to the first, is unequal adjustment costs. Addressing an environmental problem means changing the economic, political, and/or cultural activities that ultimately cause the problem. Making these changes, or adjustments, can produce many benefits, but they also carry different economic and political costs in different countries. These variations can reflect differences in a country's contribution to the problem, level of economic development, national enforcement capabilities, existing regulations, resource base, trade profile, method of energy production, and transportation policy; the political and economic influence of an industry within a country; and a host of other factors.

Large variations in adjustment costs in countries essential to a regime act as obstacles to creating a strong regime. Indeed, they are part of the reason that veto coalitions form. In addition to concerns about the costs they will bear, states often also consider potential positional advantages or disadvantages produced by the relative costs to be borne by other states. Thus, states may reject solutions that ask them to bear a larger burden than other states. Alternatively they may demand special compensation for joining the regime, which in turn can weaken the regime.

Unequal adjustment costs exist in all of the regimes outlined in Chapters 3 and 4, and addressing their impact is a critical and difficult part of global environmental politics. During negotiation of the Kyoto Protocol, many governments argued that their different levels of industrialization, energy profiles, transportation infrastructures, core industries, and even local temperatures made adhering to one set of mandatory reductions in CO_2 emissions inherently unfair. As a result, the Kyoto Protocol contained no mandatory reductions of CO_2 emissions for developing countries and different, modest targets for developed countries. The issue of unequal adjustment costs continues to pose challenges for the climate regime and is reflected in the variation of nationally determined contributions submitted as part of the 2015 Paris Agreement. Although using renewable energy sources to replace fossil fuels will reduce CO_2 emissions, create new jobs, reduce air pollution, and produce far greater long-term benefits for most countries and the planet as a whole, some countries, regions, and companies that rely heavily on fossil fuels will experience higher costs during the transition than those that do not. Controls on carbon emissions also mean enormous adjustment for states whose economies depend on exporting oil, natural gas, or coal, including Australia, Canada, Russia, Saudi Arabia, and the United States.

Different governments consistently seek to exclude certain substances from the toxic chemicals regime or press for special exemptions, arguing that a particular industry using the substance would bear higher and unfair burdens if forced to comply with the same standards as companies in other countries that do not use the substance. China, India, Indonesia, and others objected to rules requiring them to install state-of-the-art devices to prevent mercury emissions from existing coal-fired power plants in part because they would face higher costs than the United States and the EU, where such devices were already common.[34] Iceland, Japan, Norway, and other countries that permit whaling argue that the economic, cultural, or scientific adjustment costs of stopping all whaling would place unfair burdens on particular groups. Some developing countries express concern that efforts to protect biodiversity will include attempts to prevent their use of biodiverse areas for traditional types of economic development—costs most industrialized countries would not bear.

A third obstacle is that environmental issues often involve significant scientific complexity and uncertainty regarding their scope, severity, impact, or time frame. Scientific complexity can challenge the capacity of government bureaucracies to understand the problem and design and implement effective solutions. Scientific uncertainty about an environmental problem can undermine concern and, perhaps most important, allow other, more certain economic or political interests to be prioritized. Uncertainty and complexity can lead different states to perceive payoffs differently, perhaps reducing incentives to risk cooperation and increasing incentives either to free ride or to ignore the problem altogether, thereby harming the contractual environment.

For example, opponents of strong policies to mitigate climate change emphasize not only the costs of such an agreement (including the links to important economic interests and unequal adjustment costs) but also what they argue are important uncertainties regarding the severity of the problem (the vast majority of scientists and the Intergovernmental Panel on Climate Change do not share this view). Uncertainty about the impacts of long-term, low-level exposure to toxic chemicals inhibits the chemicals regime from expanding more quickly, despite increasing evidence that causes many experts to express significant concern. Biodiversity loss, biosafety, and ozone depletion are some of the other issues for which scientific complexity and uncertainty slowed or prevented the creation of strong regimes.

Fourth, states and groups within states sometimes possess different core religious, cultural, or political beliefs and values relevant to environmental issues. Such conflicting beliefs and values can limit the creation of sufficient transnational concern, block potential policies, cause some actors not to participate, and necessitate compromises that weaken the resulting regime. For example, as discussed in Chapter 4, some groups in Iceland, Japan, and Norway have strong cultural links to whaling. They do not view it as a moral issue and thus reject international attempts to curtail their whaling as inappropriate foreign intrusion on their rights and beliefs. Some individuals in Asia believe products from endangered animal species, such as rhino horn, have important medicinal properties. Even though no corroborating scientific evidence exists, this creates a market for certain endangered species and their products and undercuts international controls designed to protect them. Some political ideologies treat economic development and freedom from government regulations as higher priorities than environmental protection and resist cooperative solutions that they believe would restrict economic or personal freedom.

Fifth, large numbers of actors must cooperate to create and implement effective global environmental policy, a characteristic of environmental issues that increases the impact of other obstacles, including system structure, lowest-common-denominator issues, and time-horizon conflicts. Social science has long acknowledged that reaching cooperative solutions to common problems becomes more difficult as the number of actors increases. More actors mean more heterogeneity of interests. The larger the number of actors, the more likely that an agreement, if concluded at all, will be partial in at least one of three ways: (1) covering only some of the agenda topics, (2) leaving some disagreement latent in an ambiguous text, or (3) being signed and accepted only by some states. In addition, the risk of suboptimal outcomes, or lowest-common-denominator agreements, seems to increase as the number of actors increases.[35]

Large numbers can also increase incentives for noncompliance because of reduced fears of detection, particularly if the short-term adjustment costs are high or uneven. Large numbers can be particularly dangerous to the success of a regime that seeks to protect the commons, such as the oceans or atmosphere, which all can use but no one controls. If some states fear that others will cheat, they may believe they face a use-it-or-lose-it scenario that compels them to use the resource, leading to its more rapid degradation.[36] The situation is compounded in cases in which many states need to control many private actors in order for the environmental policy to succeed. CITES faces obstacles with compliance because the number of potential violators is so large, especially with the advent of Internet sales of endangered species and their products. An immense number of ships can violate ocean pollution and fishing agreements. Thousands of companies in countries around the world work with toxic chemicals or create hazardous waste. The huge number of GHG emissions sources complicates global policy making.

Interconnections Among Environmental Issues

Environmental issues do not exist in isolation. Causes, impacts, consequences, and solutions are often interconnected in surprising ways. Sometimes these connections can inhibit successful action. This is the case when one environmental problem exacerbates another, making the problem more difficult to solve because long-term success in that issue also requires effectively addressing the other issue. For example, climate change threatens millions of species with extinction, making the preservation of biodiversity more difficult. Coral reefs face serious threats from warming seas, increased runoff from land degraded by deforestation, and pollution released by industrial facilities. Solving one threat to a reef will not save it unless the others are also solved. Deforestation and land degradation are major contributors to biodiversity loss, through habitat destruction, and to climate change, through the release of CO_2 into the atmosphere and because deforested land can no longer act as carbon sinks by absorbing CO_2 from the air. Thus, effective long-term global policies on biodiversity or climate change will also require action to combat the destruction of tropical forests and land degradation.

Interconnections also create obstacles if addressing one environmental problem exacerbates another. For example, replacing coal-fired power plants with nuclear power plants decreases GHG emissions but creates the potential for immense environmental problems if radiation is released as a result of a natural disaster (as happened in the aftermath of the tsunami that hit Japan in 2011), an accident at the plant (as occurred at the Chernobyl nuclear power plant in Ukraine in 1986), a terrorist attack, or a leak from the storage of nuclear waste. Dams help address climate change by producing electricity without burning fossil fuels, but some also produce harmful environmental impacts such as riparian habitat loss, erosion, loss of river animal and fish populations, and potential declines in water quality. Biofuels can be used to replace gasoline and reduce GHGs, but some biofuels, such as those made from corn or other crops requiring good soil, divert land from food production, often require significant quantities of water and fertilizer, and use large amounts of energy to gather, transport, and refine into fuel.[37]

Several chemicals developed to replace ozone-depleting substances (ODS) and thus safeguard the ozone layer exacerbated other environmental problems. As outlined in Chapter 3, companies developed HCFCs and hydrofluorocarbons (HFCs) as substitutes for CFCs. These chemicals proved crucial to protecting the ozone layer while requiring relatively small changes to the huge refrigeration and air-conditioning industries. Unfortunately, most HCFCs and HFCs are far stronger GHGs than the CFCs they replaced. Thus, their invention and increased use, which occurred only as part of global attempts to protect the ozone layer, augmented climate change. Similarly, when China replaced halons, the fire suppressants that are also powerful ODS, it did so in part by using firefighting foam mixes that included PFOS. As outlined in Chapter 3, in 2009, parties to the Stockholm Convention added PFOS to the list of chemicals slated for elimination, but China and others argued successfully that an exemption should be granted for use in firefighting foam because it would not be economical to phase out this fire-control substance so soon after eliminating halons. Thus, one solution to the problem of halons as ozone-depleting chemicals exacerbated the problems of toxins in the environment and complicated policy discussions under the Stockholm Convention.

Regime-Design Difficulties

Another obstacle to strong, effective global environmental regimes is sometimes the design of the regime itself. As Ron Mitchell puts it, "Regime design matters."[38] Regime rules inappropriate to an issue are unlikely to work. Control measures and reporting requirements that are too complex or vague might not be implemented correctly. Treaties without enough flexibility cannot be adjusted in response to new scientific findings. Treaties with too much flexibility might be changed so often that some governments and industries, frustrated with the inability to make long-term plans, may begin to leave or ignore the regime.

Regime design is difficult. All of the issues outlined in the previous sections can inhibit the design of an effective regime. The process requires a nuanced understanding of the science of the environmental issue, including its causes and consequences, how it interacts with other issues, and how it will evolve over time; the economic and social activities that give rise to the problem and will be affected by it; how to address the issue so that a long-term solution is environmentally, economically, and politically possible; and how to design the solution in the form of an international regime that can be implemented effectively at the national level. This last point is often overlooked. No matter how well-meaning a treaty's intention or how strong its control provisions, it will not yield measurable environmental benefits if states do not implement it.

Equally important is the fact that regimes are negotiated more than they are designed—and negotiated by people and governments with concerns that might run counter to the requirements for a perfectly crafted environmental regime. Environmental treaties are not designed by a small group of experts whose only goal is to eliminate a global environmental problem. In reality, treaties result from negotiations involving hundreds of government representatives from different types of ministries whose collective job is to address the environmental issue but whose individual instructions also reflect concerns for other national and international economic and political goals.

Delegates operate within frameworks established by instructions and briefing books given to them by their governments. People from different parts of the government with different perspectives participate in creating these frameworks. In the United States, for example, although Environmental Protection Agency officials might see the negotiations as a means to address the environmental issue, trade officials might want to make sure that a tough stand in the negotiations does not affect relations with a crucial trading partner or upset relationships important to an upcoming trade negotiation. State Department officials might object to a particular regime component, even if it would be very effective, for fear that it will set a precedent that could be demanded in negotiations on other issues. Congressional staff and White House domestic political advisers might not want policies that would upset key political allies or donors to political campaigns. Budget officials might insist on limiting provisions of FTA. None of this is improper—each person is simply attending to his or her government responsibility—but it does point out how these underlying complexities produce pressures that can influence national negotiation positions away from consensus on optimal regime design.

Consequently, government goals in global environmental negotiations are often broader than just addressing a specific environmental issue. Some developing countries might try to use the negotiations to obtain development assistance masked as environmental investments. Donor countries might try to limit financial obligations in general or to funnel assistance through the Global Environment Facility (GEF) because they think doing so will save money or that they might be able to influence GEF activities more easily than a stand-alone fund. Some governments might push against a particular principle—for example, the precautionary principle—because they do not want it to be accepted as a general principle of international law. Some might try to build global scientific networks as a means to increase scientific training in their countries. Others might push for a strong noncompliance regime because they support strong international adjudication procedures in general. Some countries might have disagreements with particular international organizations, nongovernmental organizations (NGOs), or other governments that affect their negotiating positions.

Thus, environmental regime design should not be seen as the equivalent of blueprints drawn by a small group of brilliant architects who specialize in building hospitals and have been given the time and money to create an outstanding facility that will address one particular disease. They are more like blueprints drawn by a group of several hundred architects who specialize in different types of design and who have been assigned the group task of designing a hospital to address a set of diseases. Plus, many of the architects have other jobs and must make sure that parts of the planned hospital can also be used as a bank, training facility, research center, school, police station, courthouse, travel agency, or construction company. Moreover, they do not agree on which of these other uses is the most important, they do not have enough land or money to construct a building that could do all of these things well, not all of them are particularly good architects, and they do not have a great deal of time before the diseases spread and more people start to die. Creating and implementing effective global environmental policy is challenging.

Changing Views on the Principle of Common but Differentiated Responsibilities

As discussed in Chapter 1, paradigms influence how environmental issues are viewed and potential policies developed and evaluated, but these paradigms are neither static nor universally shared. Paradigms can be challenged or replaced by alternative paradigms (e.g., the shift from frontier economics and the exclusionist paradigm to limits to growth and sustainable development). The internal definition of a paradigm or conceptions of how it should be put into practice can also change or come into dispute. To some extent, that has happened with the principle of CBDR.

The principle states that all countries have a common responsibility to address global environmental issues but also differentiated responsibilities to act depending on their contribution to the problem or greater financial and technological resources to address it. In many regimes (as shown in Chapters 3 and 4), this principle is reflected by providing developing countries with (1) more time to implement required control measures (e.g., in the ozone and climate regimes) or other provisions that provide them greater flexibility or exemptions (the POPs regime); and (2) FTA and capacity-building provisions to help them implement regime rules (nearly all global regimes include these, although with varying degrees of specificity and effectiveness). Broad acceptance of CBDR and how to operationalize it within regime operations made some negotiations easier in that it provided a rubric to follow and allowed some discussions to take on elements of bilateral negotiations between industrialized and developing countries, which, although difficult, is theoretically easier than negotiations involving many different groups.

CBDR remains an accepted principle and paradigm in global environmental politics, but a number of developments have caused some countries to change their view regarding how it should be operationalized in specific agreements—from a principle centered on a single division between developing and industrialized countries to one that is more nuanced. These developments include the rapid economic rise of some large developing countries, especially China; the increasing contribution of these countries to many global environmental problems; improved understanding of the environmental vulnerabilities that different countries face;

PHOTO 5.3 Members of the Freedom from Debt Coalition demand that countries commit to finance climate adaptation and mitigation at the twenty-first meeting of the UN Framework Convention on Climate Change Conference of the Parties in Paris. Courtesy Kiara Worth, IISD/*Earth Negotiations Bulletin*, www.iisd.ca.

and the vast differences in the economic resources available to different states classified as developing countries—for example, Brazil, Kuwait, and China versus Malawi, Haiti, and Bangladesh). Although observations regarding these developments are empirically correct, their introduction has complicated negotiations on climate change, mercury, chemicals, and other issues.

In climate change, for example, the UNFCCC and the Kyoto Protocol created differentiated obligations for developed and developing countries based on CBDR. The Kyoto Protocol, in particular, followed CBDR in establishing binding GHG reduction obligations only for industrialized countries. The United States refused to join the Kyoto Protocol in part because it did not establish binding GHG provisions on China and other large developing countries. Since then, China's economy has grown significantly, and its GHG emissions are now by far the largest in the world. This created demands by some countries, including some developing countries, for China and other large developing countries to control their emissions as part of the new climate agreement, with the understanding that industrialized countries still have to take the lead.

During the negotiation of the Minamata Convention, the United States stated clearly that application of the CBDR principle should not be based simply on whether a county was classified as developed or developing. This sentiment was echoed in different ways by delegates from the EU, Japan, and several other developed countries. As a result, no clear division was created for obligations to reduce mercury emissions solely on the basis of development status. During the negotiation of the Stockholm Convention, governments rejected the creation of separate control schedules for developing countries when adding new chemicals, agreeing that an extended timeline, like the one in the ozone regime, would simply shift the production and use of these chemicals to developing countries. As outlined in Chapter 3, the regime instead creates common restrictions with certain exemptions for which all countries can apply. In creating these exemptions, parties take into account the situation of developing counties on a case-by-case basis, a more nuanced application of CBDR. In accordance with the traditional paradigm, developing countries in both the mercury and chemicals regimes can access FTA to implement different aspects of the treaties.

Although CBDR remains an important component of global environmental agreements, it is no longer always operationalized purely through a simple division of the world into two groups of countries. Although this can perhaps lead to more effective policy in the long run, it can also pose an obstacle as it creates more coalitions, more options, and more disagreements about when and how the principle of CBDR should be operationalized.

OBSTACLES TO EFFECTIVE NATIONAL IMPLEMENTATION OF AND COMPLIANCE WITH GLOBAL ENVIRONMENTAL REGIMES

Treaties contain many different types of obligations. The most important are sometimes referred to as substantive obligations, particularly obligations to cease or limit a specific activity such as GHG emissions, CFC production, or the release of certain toxic chemicals. Also important are a variety of procedural obligations, such as monitoring and reporting requirements. Compliance refers to whether countries adhere to the mandatory provisions of an environmental convention and the extent to which they follow through on the steps they have taken to implement these provisions.[39]

Global environmental regimes employ a variety of mechanisms to promote implementation and compliance. These include using binding rules instead of voluntary measures; providing eligible countries with FTA to build capacity and help them to fulfill specific regime obligations; requiring regular reporting by the parties; allowing for independent evaluation and public availability of such reports; reviewing regime implementation and effectiveness; calling noncomplying parties to account publicly; providing incentives; creating formal noncompliance procedures that have the potential to establish penalties or provide assistance; augmenting public education and raising awareness; sharing information; creating focused implementation programs that involve cooperation among the private sector, NGOs, international organizations, and governments; and using NGOs and international organizations to monitor compliance. Of course, not all regimes employ each measure, and their success varies significantly across regimes and among parties.

Most countries that sign and ratify an international convention do so with the intention of complying with its provisions.[40] Nevertheless, complete compliance sometimes turns out to be politically, technically, administratively, or financially impossible, even when a government remains committed to the regime, especially with regard to provisions that allow for interpretation. Sometimes compliance becomes sufficiently difficult that a state decides to focus time, effort, and resources in other areas; that is, compliance is still possible, but a state chooses to reduce its effort to comply because of other priorities.

As attention turned from creating new global environmental regimes to implementing and strengthening existing ones, implementation and compliance became and remain important issues. In addition to the general obstacles outlined above, the literature on international environmental agreements suggests that noncompliance can be traced to several different types of factors, including inadequate translation of regime rules into domestic law; insufficient capacity or commitment to implement, administer, monitor, or enforce relevant domestic policy; misperception of the relevant costs and benefits; the costs of compliance; inadequate FTA; poorly designed regimes; and the large number of environmental conventions and the confusing and uncoordinated web of requirements they have produced (see Box 5.2).[41] As with the discussion of the obstacles to creating strong and effective regimes, these categories of implementation obstacles overlap significantly and are extremely interrelated. They are not listed in order of importance because their impacts vary from country to country and issue to issue. Indeed, scholars and national officials have many different opinions about which obstacles are most important overall or most relevant to particular issue areas.

Inadequate Translation of Regime Rules into Domestic Policy

Some states are unable to or choose not to adopt the domestic legislation necessary to implement and fully comply with an international agreement. This can include failing to adopt some or all of the needed regulations or adopting poorly crafted regulations. For instance, Peter Sand noted that "the main constraint on the implementation of CITES in each Party has been the need to create national legislation. Although this is an obligation under [CITES], several countries have not complied. . . . Others have only incomplete legislation."[42]

BOX 5.2 OBSTACLES TO EFFECTIVE NATIONAL IMPLEMENTATION

- **Inadequate translation of regime rules into domestic policy**
- **Insufficient capacity or commitment to implement, administer, monitor, or enforce domestic policy**
- **Misperception of relevant cost and benefits**
- **Costs of compliance**
- **Inadequate or poorly targeted financial and technical assistance**
- **Poorly designed regimes**
- **Many regimes, little coordination**

The failure to enact domestic law can stem from a variety of factors. Sometimes domestic economic or political opposition that failed to block a country from negotiating or signing a particular treaty can nevertheless prevent the country from ratifying it. If national ratification depends on approval by a legislative branch, as in the United States, then treaty ratification, and consequently, the translation of international regime rules into domestic law, can be prevented by interest groups or lawmakers opposed to its goals or means, by politicians seeking leverage to achieve other political ends, by an overburdened legislative agenda, or by conflicts over resource allocations. For example, since the 1990s, opposition from powerful interest groups and key senators has prevented the US Senate even from holding formal ratification votes on several key treaties, including the Biodiversity, Basel, Rotterdam, and Stockholm Conventions.

Even when a treaty is ratified, interest groups or the political opposition might still manage to prevent or weaken the necessary implementing legislation. Weak legislative and bureaucratic infrastructures or a lack of expertise on the issue can also prevent effective regulations from becoming law. The chemicals and wastes treaties, for example, require relatively sophisticated knowledge about toxic substances and their commercial uses, trade, and environmentally sound management to enact all of their provisions effectively into domestic law. Inefficient legislative procedures or political or economic instability also can keep states from fully or accurately enacting necessary domestic legislation. Finally, in democracies with nonintegrated federal structures, the federal government may not always have the jurisdiction to implement international environmental agreements completely at the state or provincial level. For example, in Belgium, each of the autonomous regions must separately adopt environmental legislation. In Canada, the provinces, not the federal government, control some aspects of environmental policy.[43]

Insufficient Capacity or Commitment to Implement, Administer, Monitor, or Enforce Domestic Policy

It is not enough simply to enact laws and regulations. They must also be effectively implemented, administered, monitored, and enforced. Doing so requires sufficient issue-specific skills, knowledge, technical know-how, legal authority, financial resources, enforcement capacity, and commitment at the individual and institutional levels. Insufficient capacity is a particular problem for some developing countries, but it exists in all parts of the world and varies from issue to issue and country to country.

Examples of capacity problems inhibiting compliance are unfortunately common. Many countries, including industrialized countries, lack the budgets, trained personnel, or commitment needed to enforce or otherwise comply fully and effectively with the rules established by CITES to control trade in endangered species.[44] Compliance with the CBD has been hindered by a lack of national capacity to manage protected areas and to control the impact of development projects. Russia did not comply with its obligations under the ozone regime for several years because its government temporarily lacked the capacity to stop the black-market production and export of CFCs. Full compliance with the Stockholm Convention includes locating, identifying, managing, and destroying stockpiles of obsolete pesticides in an environmentally sound manner, something beyond the technical and financial ability of many countries. Brazil, Indonesia, and some other countries have not demonstrated the consistent ability to prevent illegal logging and deforestation.[45] African countries continue to express concern that they are sometimes unable to prevent unwanted shipments of obsolete pesticides and products, toxic chemicals, and potentially hazardous wastes from enferring their countries, despite relevant provisions in the Basel and Rotterdam Conventions.[46] Several countries in Asia, Africa, and Central and South America express concern for their ability to prevent the use of mercury in illegal, small-scale gold-mining operations.[47]

Similarly, some states that want to comply might not act effectively because they do not know what is happening domestically. Two principal sets of factors affect states' abilities to monitor compliance with, and the effectiveness of, domestic environmental laws: (1) whether states have adequate feedback mechanisms, such as on-site monitoring, reporting requirements, inspections, complaint mechanisms, and close working relationships with relevant NGOs; and (2) the number and size of the potential violators whose conduct the government must monitor.[48]

For example, the relatively high level of compliance with the Montreal Protocol results not only from the widely accepted science on ozone depletion and changing economic interests but also the manageable number of facilities that produce the chemicals and require monitoring. Monitoring compliance with CITES, however, remains difficult in part because the number of potential violators is very large.

A lack of respect for the rule of law by particular groups within some countries is an important contributing factor. This problem tends to arise more often in countries where severe economic pressures, political instability, and patterns of corruption lead particular groups, government officials, or the general public to ignore elements of the legal system. For example, sections of the Central African Republic, Democratic Republic of Congo, and several other African countries are relatively lawless, making it difficult to preserve their significant biodiversity, forest, and ecosystem resources. Illegal deforestation in Bolivia, Brazil, Colombia, Indonesia, and other countries reflects not only lack of government capacity but also indifference to the law by those clearing the land.[49] In some countries, systematic corruption, extreme poverty, and the absence of a meaningful democratic process cause many people to feel alienated from the law-making apparatus, undermining their respect for the law, including regulations on wildlife conservation.[50] Similarly, the epidemic of illegal logging in national parks in Indonesia following the 1998 financial crisis resulted, at least in part, in a breakdown of law and order combined with economic pressures in the affected areas.[51]

Misperception of Relevant Costs and Benefits

A related obstacle is a lack of understanding regarding the full set of economic costs and benefits of pursuing environmental goals. Many analyses indicate that even if policymakers wish to ignore nonmonetary concepts relating to environmental and human-health protections, purely economic arguments support certain environmental protections. However, such arguments often do not win in domestic policy discussions. Businesses that would need to stop or change particular operations or incur economic costs make their case clearly in policy debates. Less clear, however, are the economic benefits of protecting natural resources; reducing human health impacts from pollution; using energy, water, and material resources more efficiently; and creating green jobs. These are often obscured by the importance placed on short-term adjustment costs (which could be substantial for certain actors), insufficient analysis of economic changes that will occur if more environmentally benign technology or practices are required, and a failure to include the negative economic impacts of environmental degradation.

For example, arguments in the late 1970s that eliminating CFCs from aerosol spray cans would be extremely costly proved inaccurate when new processes and products actually saved consumers money. Global efforts to remove lead from fuel have yielded annual economic benefits of approximately $2.4 trillion via the associated improvements in IQ, reductions in cardiovascular diseases, introduction of pollution-control devices (some are not usable on cars and trucks using leaded fuel), and other health and social benefits.[52] Forestry and logging in Kenya actually cost that country roughly $60 million in 2010 because the economic costs produced by deforestation, especially the impact on the quality and availability of fresh water, far surpassed the economic benefits from logging.[53] The National Academy of Sciences estimated that burning fossil fuels costs the United States about $120 billion a year in health costs, mostly from the health impacts and premature deaths caused by air pollution.[54] The United Nations Environment Programme (UNEP) calculates the negative cost of air pollution to the world's most advanced economies plus India and China to be $3.5 trillion per year due to health impacts and lives lost.[55]

More broadly, a groundbreaking 1997 study estimated the economic value of ecosystem services provided by natural ecosystems in the form of fresh water, cleaner air, pollination, food production, recreation, waste treatment, and other outputs at $16 trillion to $54 trillion per year.[56] A 2014 update to this study estimated land-use changes that negatively affected ecosystem services cost the global economy $4.3 trillion to $20.2 trillion each year from 1997 to 2011.[57] The Economics of Ecosystems and Biodiversity (TEEB) project is a major international initiative to study and publicize the global economic benefits of preserving biodiversity and healthy ecosystems.[58] A 2012 TEEB report highlighted how short-term economic gains from draining wetlands for farming, building, or excessive water use, or wetlands degradation from excessive releases of fertilizers and pollutants in their watersheds, threaten the far larger and many billions of dollars' worth of economic and environmental benefits these wetlands provide in preserving water quality, providing habitats and nurseries for fisheries, conserving biodiversity, and mitigating climate change (via carbon storage in peatlands, mangroves, and tidal marshes).[59] A 2012 report by UNEP's Finance Initiative in collaboration with a number of asset owners, investment managers, and information providers showed that consideration of the economic impact of environmental degradation and the depletion of natural resources has the potential to lower a country's sovereign debt rating, denoting the purchase of that country's bonds as a greater risk and increasing the interest rate a country might have to offer to attract buyers.[60]

An increasing number of large-scale studies conclude that efforts to reduce GHG emissions would prevent significant economic costs associated with sea-level rise, changes in rainfall patterns, droughts, more extreme weather, and an increase in the range of tropical diseases and other health problems.[61] A study by researchers from the European Commission, GEF, McKinsey & Company, Rockefeller Foundation, Standard Chartered Bank, and other organizations estimates that without mitigation and adaptation efforts, climate change will soon carry significant economic costs and could, under certain scenarios, cost some nations up to 19 percent of their gross domestic product (GDP) as early as 2030.[62] This includes Southeast Asia and the Middle East, where, in the absence of effective global action to limit GHG emissions, temperatures could become so high that their negative impacts on human health and labor capacity would significantly decrease economic output.[63]

Also, although many understand that some actors will suffer economic costs when countries seek to reduce GHG emissions, less widely acknowledged are the larger and broader economic benefits that many studies conclude will result from these efforts, particularly those associated with increased energy efficiency, fewer health problems from air pollution, reduced oil and gas imports, and the creation of new jobs in solar, wind, and geothermal industries.[64] At the national and global level, the economic benefits of reducing GHG gases appear to outweigh the economic costs. A report issued in 2016 by the International Energy Agency showed that global GDP grew in both 2014 and 2015 even as GHG emissions leveled off.[65] A report by the World Resources Institute, also released in 2016, found that over the last fifteen years GDP has gone up in twenty-one countries while their individual and collective emissions of GHGs have fallen or peaked.[66]

Looking ahead, at least 5 percent of global electricity consumption, and the associated GHG emissions, could be saved every year by transitioning to efficient lighting, action that would entail short-term costs but also result in annual worldwide energy savings of over $110 billion.[67] Methane vented or leaked from oil and gas systems represents about 20 percent of the anthropogenic release of GHGs and $27 billion to $60 billion a year in lost revenue.[68] A UN-commissioned study estimated that concerted efforts to address climate change and sustainable development would create 20 million additional jobs in the renewable-energy sector by 2030 and that a worldwide transition to make all buildings energy efficient would create 2 to 3.5 million more green jobs in Europe and the United States alone, with the potential much higher in developing countries.[69] Several studies conclude that investments in green infrastructure projects stimulate national economies and pay for themselves in energy savings, new jobs, and reduced costs associated with the impacts of pollution.[70] A 2015 study concluded that investments in low-carbon initiatives to improve public transportation, energy-efficient buildings, and waste disposal in cities could yield $16.6 trillion in financial savings by 2050 and avoid 3.7 gigatons of CO_2 emissions annually, which is more than India's current emissions.[71]

Costs of Compliance

Even if the long-term benefits are clear, implementation and compliance do require resources. Therefore, compliance with international environmental agreements is affected by the costs of such compliance relative to the country's level of economic development, current economic situation, resource base, and budgetary preferences. Affluent countries experiencing relatively strong economic growth are historically far more willing and able to comply with environmental regulations than poorer states or states with economies that are growing slowly or not at all. States with low per capita incomes are generally reluctant to commit significant funds to comply with commitments to reduce global threats, even if doing so is in the country's long-term interest, because such compliance would likely come at the expense of spending for economic and social development. Even in wealthy countries, competing economic and budgetary preferences or concerns about national economic rivals can inhibit implementation and compliance.

Countries experiencing economic and financial difficulties might refuse or become unable to comply with global environmental agreements. The Russian Federation, for example, did not immediately comply with the 1996 phaseout of CFCs because of its critical economic situation at the time.[72] Budget cuts often impact the ability of countries to combat illegal trade in endangered species under CITES, monitor trade under the Rotterdam Convention, or prevent the trade of hazardous waste or manage it effectively under the Basel Convention. More broadly, the global financial crisis that began in 2008 contributed to the failure by donor countries to meet collective, nonbinding pledges of financial support for broad sustainable development goals and increased the difficulty of reaching agreements in negotiations on the provision of financial support for implementing specific MEAs, including the POPs and mercury negotiations.[73]

Inadequate or Poorly Targeted Financial and Technical Assistance

Many global environmental regimes—including those for ozone, climate, biodiversity, desertification, toxic chemicals, and mercury—contain specific measures for providing FTA to developing countries and thus help these countries fulfill their obligations. Developing countries consistently argue that implementation and compliance with specific elements within some environmental regimes, including, for example, the Montreal Protocol and Stockholm Convention, depend on the provision of adequate FTA. For some developing countries, such measures are indeed critical to their ability to comply with the regime; for others, they provide an important boost; for some the political importance of assistance is as

PHOTO 5.4 An NGO campaign, Act Now for Climate Justice, called for delivering climate finance at the twenty-first meeting of the UN Framework Convention on Climate Change Conference of the Parties in Paris. Courtesy Liz Rubin, IISD/*Earth Negotiations Bulletin*, www.iisd.ca.

important as its economic impact. Outside the ozone regime, however, one can argue that the provision of FTA has not reached levels that ensure effective compliance across the globe, although increased funding is becoming available under the GEF and the UNFCCC, including the Green Climate Fund, the Least Developed Countries Fund, and the Adaptation Fund. At the same time, rapid economic development in some developing countries, the increasing gap between the least-developed countries (LDCs) and the newly industrialized developing countries, and the impact that the global financial crisis had on the economies of donor countries have complicated the provision of financial assistance.

Poorly Designed Regimes

A party's failure to comply with a regime sometimes reflects problems with the regime itself. As discussed above, regime design matters. Control measures and reporting requirements that are too complex or too vague allow states to make honest or intentional errors when translating them into domestic law. Regimes that do not pay attention to states' abilities to implement them, the relative costs of compliance, the importance of reporting and monitoring, the interconnections among environmental issues, or the provision of targeted and effective FTA are vulnerable to failure. Implementation and compliance, to some extent, are also a function of regime design.

Vague, weak, or poorly designed regime components can result from simple mistakes, lowest-common-denominator compromises, or intentional negotiating strategies designed to produce imprecise requirements that allow states significant choice regarding which, if any, concrete actions they will take. Regardless of the reason, if a treaty does not contain clear, implementable requirements, parties often have trouble translating the vague language into domestic rules or regulations, or parties can choose to interpret the vague requirements in ways that produce few adjustment costs. The language in the biodiversity and desertification conventions and their related compliance challenges illustrate this point. Although the treaties require countries to develop national plans, there is little guidance regarding how to enable these plans to actually be effective in conserving biodiversity or combating desertification.

Many Regimes, Little Coordination

Another obstacle to effective implementation and compliance is the sheer number of environmental treaties and other policy initiatives and the confusing and uncoordinated web of requirements, norms, and guidelines they include. Because all parties, particularly developing countries, have finite financial, technical, and human resources available, the more complex and confusing the total set of policies needed to implement treaty obligations, the more likely compliance will suffer.

If one counts agreements that expand or alter the provisions of a treaty, countries have created hundreds of multilateral and bilateral environmental accords over the past fifty years. After trade (broadly defined), environment is now the most common area of international rule making.[74] It is not uncommon to hear government officials at international meetings note the sheer number of environmental agreements and initiatives as a potential implementation obstacle.[75]

Each environmental regime, as well as many other international environmental policy initiatives, has its own set of control measures, policy guidelines, reporting requirements, monitoring systems, assessment mechanisms, implementation procedures, meeting schedules, financing requirements, and review procedures. In addition, nearly all of these regimes and initiatives exist independently of each other. As such, they sometimes place uncoordinated and confusing obligations on states that are difficult to fulfill. One example is reporting requirements that sometimes conflict, or at least remain uncoordinated, in their schedules, procedures, units of analysis, and required methods and formats. This was an issue within the ozone regime for many years and remains an issue within the chemicals and wastes sector, which includes three major treaties and many more international policy initiatives and organizations, although efforts are under way to remedy the problem.

In addition, some regimes establish contrary rules or incentives. For example, HFCs were considered a replacement for CFCs under the ozone regime but are also GHGs subject to controls under the climate regime. Some closely related regimes have uncoordinated membership and regulatory gaps that potentially impede effectiveness. As discussed in Chapter 3, several treaties and other international initiatives exist to address hazardous waste and toxic chemicals, including the global Basel, Rotterdam, and Stockholm Conventions, amendments to these conventions, and regional agreements. Although efforts continue to increase coordination, different ratification patterns exist within and among treaties. Some countries have pledged to fulfill obligations under some agreements and amendments but not others. This pattern has become more pronounced as parties continue adding chemicals to the Stockholm Convention and some countries opt out of the new controls, allowing certain chemicals or certain parts of their life cycles to escape global control.[76]

OPPORTUNITIES TO IMPROVE EFFECTIVE IMPLEMENTATION AND COMPLIANCE

Several options exist to strengthen compliance with global environmental agreements. No single option, however, can address all of the obstacles discussed in this chapter. Furthermore, whether these options or incentives can actually lead a government to comply depends on the willingness of states and other actors to take action. However, existing experience with global environmental regimes, academic research, and deductive logic indicate that regime implementation, compliance, and effectiveness can be improved (see Box 5.3).

BOX 5.3 OPPORTUNITIES TO IMPROVE EFFECTIVE IMPLEMENTATION AND COMPLIANCE

- **Raise awareness and concern**
- **Create market incentives**
- **Eliminate counterproductive subsidies**
- **Build domestic capacity**
- **Improve the effectiveness of financial and technical assistance**
- **Augment coordination among regimes and conventions**
- **Improve monitoring and reporting**
- **Consider sanctions**
- **Generate publicity**

Raise Awareness and Concern

An important factor in improving national implementation and compliance is elevating awareness, concern, and knowledge among government elites and the general public regarding environmental issues, including their negative human health and economic impacts. For each issue discussed in Chapters 3 and 4, sufficient expert knowledge exists on key aspects of the problem to demonstrate the scientific seriousness of the issue; the availability of technological, economic, and policy tools to address it; and the long-term environmental, human-health, and economic benefits of doing so.

Significant obstacles remain to implementing solutions, however, in part because many public officials and large elements of the public remain unaware of the near-term threats posed by environmental issues, including to human health, and the large gaps that exist between the policy goals agreed to at the international level and actual state of many environmental conditions.[77] Even less awareness appears to exist regarding the significant negative economic costs of environmental degradation, despite an ever increasing number of expert studies (including those outlined above in the subsection titled "Misperception of Relevant Costs and Benefits"). This lack of awareness means that concern for environmental issues often remains relatively low compared with other economic or political interests. The effectiveness of, and compliance with, international environmental regimes likely cannot increase significantly until officials in more countries acknowledge these facts and raise the priority of environmental issues or until elevated public concern forces them to do so.

Create Market Incentives

As already discussed, many economic forces at work today still reward rather than punish unsustainable activity because the local and global costs of pollution and unsustainable resource use carry little or no economic costs to those responsible. There is broad agreement that using market forces to reward environmentally friendly activities would greatly assist implementation of environmental treaties and the pursuit of the Sustainable Development Goals (SDGs).

Important technologies that are essential to sustainable development become profitable if the environmental and health costs are included in the price of unsustainable options. Clean energy is the most obvious example. Wind, solar, and geothermal energy sources are all likely economically superior to fossil fuels if one includes the full costs of the health impacts of the air pollution from fossil fuels, the climate impacts of their CO_2 emissions, and the broader environmental and national security impacts of development, extraction, and transportation. Placing a price on CO_2 emissions, therefore, is widely seen as a critical step toward addressing climate change.[78] The same can be said for addressing most aspects of air and water pollution, rapacious resource use, and some types of deforestation.

Establishing market prices (through taxes, permits, incentives, tradable emission credits, or other measures) for pollution and unsustainable activity can reward efficiency and emission avoidance, encourage innovation, create a level playing field for nonpolluting and sustainable technology options, induce the use of low-emission and zero-emission technologies, and reduce the overall, system-wide cost of sustainable economic growth. Any negative, systemic economic impact of the additional costs could be offset by tax reductions in other areas, such as income taxes or sales taxes on particularly sustainable products or services.

Countries can exploit market forces on their own, through agreements with neighbors or trading partners, or through international agreements. Individual regimes, UNEP, the United Nations Development Programme (UNDP), World Bank, International Monetary Fund (IMF), and other institutions could expand efforts to raise awareness of the broad benefits of employing market mechanisms and perhaps provide incentives. However, efforts by one or a group of countries to use market forces for environmental purposes can run afoul of the WTO if they affect free trade (see Chapter 6). Broad agreement exists that the global trade regime need not stand in the way of more ambitious national and international environmental policy, including market mechanisms, to address climate change or other issues, but the precise frameworks need additional clarification.[79] Similarly, it is not always clear under which circumstances a country can exclude or tax certain imports for environmental reasons or when a country with a particular type of pollution tax relevant to the manufacture of certain products can introduce a tariff on the import of similar products that carry a price advantage because the country of its manufacture has no such tax. This could be particularly relevant to climate change, as some political figures in the EU and the United States have called for consideration of tariffs on goods imported from countries without GHG-reduction policies.[80]

Eliminate Counterproductive Subsidies

One method for increasing the use of green energy and the sustainability of agriculture, forestry, and fisheries is eliminating subsidies that support fossil-fuel production and consumption, incentivize unsustainable farming practices, and contribute to the degradation of forests, aquifers, and fish stocks. The period from the 1960s through the 1980s saw a rapid, worldwide expansion of subsidies for natural resource production. Although some reductions in subsidies given to agriculture and fisheries occurred in the 1990s and early 2000s, the scale of environmentally harmful subsidies in the energy, road transport, water use, fishing, and agricultural sectors remains staggering.

For example, a 2014 IMF report concluded that governments spent $267 billion in 2013 on direct subsidies that reduced the price that consumers paid for gasoline, diesel fuel, heating oil, and other petroleum products; $112 billion on natural gas subsidies; and $5 billion on coal subsidies.[81] The International Energy Association estimates that Iran spent $84 billion, Saudi Arabia spent $62 billion, and India spent $47 billion on subsidies for fossil fuels in 2013, while Venezuela subsidized 92 percent of the consumer cost of using fossil fuels.[82] Official US government reports show that the US federal and state governments provide billions each year in direct and tax-related subsidies to the coal, gas, and oil industries.[83] Around the world, few consumers pay the full costs associated with using clean water, and a variety of subsidies (including for boat construction, fuel, and equipment) contribute to overfishing in the world's oceans.[84]

Despite the overall financial and environmental advantages of ending such subsidies, governments keep such policies in place in response to political pressure from key interest groups. The WTO Agreement on Subsidies and Countervailing Measures attempts to discipline the use of subsidies, but it concentrates only on subsidized imports that hurt domestic producers. It will take a concerted effort to fashion the necessary national and international consensus needed to end, or even severely limit, subsidies impeding conservation. Doing so, however, would make compliance far easier. Actions contrary to many global environmental policies would no longer enjoy artificial economic support, and billions of dollars that currently subsidize environmental degradation would be available to support environmental protection and sustainable economic practices.

Build Domestic Capacity

Improved compliance sometimes requires programs that strengthen the capacity of developing countries to implement environmental conventions. It also requires commitment by developing countries so that the assistance provided helps to develop permanent infrastructure.

Governments and international organizations recognize this need. GEF projects on biodiversity and climate change focus on capacity building or integrate capacity-building components into investment projects. Capacity-building activities also exist within many regimes. For example, the CITES capacity-building strategy trains the trainers in a country by holding seminars and providing training materials.[85] The ozone regime supported significant capacity building through its Multilateral Fund. The Basel and Stockholm Conventions regional centers act as nodes for capacity-building programs on issues relating to hazardous wastes and toxic chemicals.

Despite these efforts, many of which are successful, productive, additional, well-targeted capacity building can still augment regime compliance and effectiveness. Areas of particular need include environmental assessment and analysis, monitoring, regulatory infrastructure, enforcement, science education, public awareness, and the use and maintenance of a wide variety of environmentally friendly technologies. Capacity building can also increase government concern for an issue by expanding awareness of the issue within the bureaucracy and increasing the number, skills, and visibility of people working on the issue. At the same time, experience shows the importance of ensuring that the funds provided actually go to relevant capacity building.

Improve the Effectiveness of Financial and Technical Assistance

The line between capacity building and other types of FTA is largely an artificial one. In general, however, capacity building refers to permanent improvements in the ability and self-sufficiency of a country, whereas FTA refers to help with specific implementation and compliance activities. As noted above, effectively targeted FTA remains one of the most important avenues for improving compliance and regime effectiveness. Key areas include obtaining access to new products and processes; technology transfer; developing new or expanded implementation plans, legislation, and regulations; purchasing scientific, monitoring, and communications equipment; financing individual implementation projects; properly disposing of hazardous wastes and toxic chemicals; and introducing substitute technologies.

The mere availability of increased or better-targeted FTA is not a panacea. More effective compliance requires assistance targeted toward the most important needs, monitored to avoid waste, provided conditionally in stages to promote real action, continually assessed and reviewed so that procedures can be improved, and coordinated within and across regimes to achieve synergies and avoid duplication and unintended negative consequences.

Augment Coordination Among Regimes and Conventions

The broadest issue areas in global environment politics involve multiple, overlapping global and regional regimes, international organizations, and soft-law guidelines and procedures. Indicative examples include the atmosphere (ozone, climate, and regional air pollution agreements); chemicals and wastes (the Basel, Rotterdam, and Stockholm Conventions; various regional treaties; and the Strategic

Approach to International Chemicals Management); biodiversity, wildlife, and habitat protection (CBD, CITES, Ramsar Convention, the Convention on Migratory Species, and a host of wildlife-specific treaties); oceans (the Law of the Sea, the London Convention, and MARPOL); and fisheries (the Fish Stocks Agreement, the Food and Agriculture Organization Code of Conduct for Responsible Fisheries, and numerous regional fisheries agreements and third-party certification programs). In addition, some conventions span several issue areas. The UNCCD, for example, contains provisions that address biodiversity, climate change, forests, and freshwater resources.

Improved coordination among treaties and organizations would improve regime implementation and compliance by (1) helping to remove obstacles produced by the lack of coordination (outlined above); (2) allowing more effective use of limited resources; (3) avoiding unnecessary duplication of tasks; (4) potentially creating opportunities where efforts for joint initiatives could improve reporting, monitoring, environmental assessments, financing, and implementation; and (5) potentially strengthening treaty secretariats so they can manage the coordination and perform other functions more effectively.

The potential for improved coordination is broadly recognized. UNEP has repeatedly addressed the issue, and environmental ministers have discussed it in a variety of fora. The United Nations Conference on Environment and Development (UNCED), World Summit on Sustainable Development (WSSD), and first United Nations Environment Assembly all endorsed the concept. A variety of secretariats consult regularly. As noted in Chapter 3, a formal initiative to increase coordination in the chemicals sector is well under way. But more can be done. Some countries are pushing for enhanced coordination as a way to reduce duplicated secretariat and other bureaucratic costs so that available resources can be targeted to implementation programs that achieve measurable environmental results. Opportunities for enhanced coordination that have received particular attention and exhibit promise include examining and eliminating regulatory gaps and conflicts, coordinating reporting schedules and formats, co-locating secretariats and relevant international organizations that work in related issues, integrating certain operations within co-located secretariats, coordinating the scheduling of the COPs of related regimes, supporting ratification to remove membership gaps, integrating appropriately related implementation activities, and establishing common regional centers and other programs for capacity building and the provision of FTA.

Improve Monitoring and Reporting

Monitoring and reporting on environmental issues and regime implementation are essential components of regime effectiveness. Without regular and accurate monitoring and reporting by parties, it is difficult: to assess the baseline, trends, and current status of an environmental problem; to assess current levels of regime implementation; to identify specific instances or patterns of noncompliance or ineffectiveness; and to develop potential solutions. Studies on institutional effectiveness indicate that regimes employing systems of regular monitoring and reporting have better national domestic implementation and compliance than those that do not.[86]

Most environmental regimes require parties to submit data and reports on issues related to the environmental problem as well as on their implementation of the regime. Secretariats often compile this information and make it available to other parties and the public. Unfortunately, not all countries submit the required data and reports, and significant variations exist in the quality and timeliness of those that do. In addition, because most countries rely on existing national systems to gather information for regime reporting, the reports sometimes define, estimate, and aggregate the required data in different ways, making comparisons and analyses difficult.

Efforts to emphasize and improve national reporting and associated monitoring, combined with the ability of secretariats and COPs to review, publicize, and act on the information in a timely fashion, will likely increase regime compliance and effectiveness. In addition to stronger provisions within regimes, another method to achieve these goals is to increase the coordination and integration of the monitoring and reporting requirements among related regimes. For example, observers believe that regular and harmonized reporting from parties to the Basel, Rotterdam, and Stockholm Conventions (particularly if this occurs as part of the effort to augment coordination) could allow for far more accurate assessments of global levels and trends in the production, use, generation, transport, management, and disposal of toxic chemicals, hazardous waste, and e-waste. It would also make it easier to monitor progress in implementing these conventions and improve the ability to direct FTA to areas where they would have the most impact.[87] Furthermore, harmonized reporting could help reduce the overall volume of reporting requirements, which could free up human and financial resources to improve implementation.

Another method is to expand formal and informal relationships with NGOs, intergovernmental organizations, academics, and industry to help monitor environmental issues and regime implementation and compliance. For example, in addition to government reporting, several major private-sector actors and NGOs have monitored aspects of compliance with the Montreal Protocol, including illegal ODS trade.[88] The Carbon Disclosure Project has been instrumental in getting companies to track their CO_2 emissions. International NGOs, such as the Trade Records Analysis of Flora and Fauna in Commerce (TRAFFIC), work closely with the CITES Secretariat to monitor wildlife trade. Established in 1976, TRAFFIC employs more than one hundred people in thirty countries and assists in criminal investigations and enforcement actions; provides expertise for creating, reviewing, and improving wildlife-trade legislation; and works with wildlife consumers, producers, and managers to help dissuade unsustainable and illegal trade.[89] The International Fund for Animal Welfare supports INTERPOL wildlife law and enforcement training. International Fund for Animal Welfare–sponsored trainings have reached more than sixteen hundred law enforcement officers, customs officials, and other authorities in thirty countries around the globe.[90]

Consider Sanctions

Improving compliance may require additional sticks (sanctions) as well as more carrots (capacity building, FTA, and other incentives). Sanctions—such as trade restrictions, tariffs, fines, or prohibitions on receiving FTA—could be used against parties found to be in willful noncompliance with regime rules. Sanctions could also punish countries that choose to remain outside of a particular regime in an effort to discourage free riders. To be effective, sanctions must be credible and potent. States in conscious violation of a treaty or measures adopted by an MEA must be convinced not only that they will face penalties for the violation but also that the costs of the violation will exceed the gains expected from it.[91]

The ozone regime includes such provisions, prohibiting parties from exporting or importing ozone-depleting chemicals or products that use them to or from nonparties. CITES and the Basel Convention also include the possibility of sanctions as a potential punishment for noncompliance. However, little support appears to exist among most governments for expanding the use of sanctions as a remedy for treaty violations. Some argue they would make sense in situations such as illegal, unreported, and unregulated fishing, where sanctions (in this example, curbs on fishing rights or imports) could be directly related to the failure to comply with a treaty. Many developing countries, however, oppose the potential use of sanctions, arguing that such sanctions violate national sovereignty and, equally important, could be used as a disguised form of trade protectionism and would violate international trade agreements under the WTO (see Chapter 6).

Generate Publicity

Fear of negative publicity has sometimes proven to be an incentive for treaty compliance. Environmental conventions could create mechanisms through which negative publicity would become a more prominent consequence of refusal to participate in a global regime or failure to implement specific provisions.[92] The Internet, social networking, global television networks, and modern telecommunications make it easier, cheaper, and faster than ever to collect and distribute information, and evidence exists that such campaigns can have an impact in some cases. Countries go to significant lengths to deny or explain implementation lapses during many COPs and to avoid potential embarrassments in meeting reports, which shows they might be sensitive to systematic exposures. Norway lost money and public support when the EU boycotted Norwegian fish products because of Norway's position on whaling. Iceland stopped whaling for two years because of a public campaign of negative publicity and boycotts. Negative publicity can also be used to expose and deter corporate noncompliance with national laws. In Europe and the United States, for example, environmental groups sometimes act as important watchdogs, reporting violations of environmental regime rules to the public, national authorities, and regime secretariats.

Positive publicity might also improve compliance, and some diplomats argue that efforts should be made to publicize regime compliance or special achievements more effectively.[93] Beyond individual regimes, several broader efforts, such as the Environmental Performance Index, rank countries according to various environmental and sustainability criteria.[94] Supporters of such initiatives hope that these types of measures can replace, or at least augment, traditional gross national product rankings and that countries will take steps to attempt to rise in the rankings, or at least avoid being placed near the bottom.

INCREASING FINANCIAL RESOURCES FOR IMPLEMENTING GLOBAL ENVIRONMENTAL REGIMES

The issue of financial resources has been at the center of global environmental politics for many years and will continue to be for the foreseeable future. Improving regime compliance almost always requires additional financial and technical resources. More broadly, the successful expansion and implementation of MEAs, including those for climate, biodiversity, desertification, fisheries, and chemicals, require transitions to environmentally sound technologies and new strategies for natural resource management. As noted above, although these technologies and strategies could (and in many cases likely will) yield long-term economic benefits, such transitions require investment in the short run to implement, to ease the transition for those hardest hit, and to overcome resistance from powerful economic and political interests.

Most developing countries consider financial assistance to be an economic or political necessity to agree to new global environmental commitments and implement existing obligations. Some countries simply do not have the resources to effectively implement MEAs.[95] For others, such as India or South Africa, financial assistance provides valuable economic support so that resources can flow to other social needs. Financial assistance also provides some developing countries, including those with large and growing economies, with important political assistance, easing domestic objections regarding adjustment costs. Such measures also support the CBDR principle and represent a prerequisite to developing-country participation in MEAs, especially those that address problems caused originally or primarily by industrialized countries.

On the other hand, many donor countries face financial and political challenges that limit their ability to fund large new initiatives or make significant new commitments to assist developing countries in implementing existing programs. Many donor countries also want both to target assistance to specific actions that will have permanent impacts and to take into account the large economic differences among developing countries when creating and implementing FTA programs.[96]

The Montreal Protocol was the first regime in which the provision of financial assistance was a central issue in the negotiations. It demonstrated that donor and recipient countries participating in a global environmental regime could devise a financial mechanism that equitably distributes power and effectively links financial assistance with compliance.

The biodiversity, climate, desertification, and chemicals regimes use the GEF as their financial mechanism. As discussed in Chapter 2, the grants and concessional funds disbursed by the GEF complement traditional development assistance by covering the additional costs (also known as agreed-upon incremental costs) incurred when a national, regional, or global development project also targets global environmental objectives. Despite the fact that in 2014 donors pledged $4.43 billion to fund its operations through 2018, the GEF is unlikely to receive sufficient resources from donor countries to fund the entire amount required for developing countries to achieve full compliance with the biodiversity, desertification, and chemicals conventions. In addition, although official development assistance (ODA) levels rose in the last decade after falling in the 1990s, most of this money was directed toward traditional development activities, not toward implementing global environmental priorities. Indeed, the total investment needed to fulfill current environmental regime obligations and achieve the broad aims of the SDGs is already many times higher than total current ODA levels. In addition, the global recession that started in 2008 put tremendous pressure on national budgets. Major donors' aid to developing countries fell by nearly 3 percent in 2011, breaking a long trend of annual increases dating back to 1997.[97] Although one could argue that a workable coalition of industrialized countries, international organizations, and fast-growing developing countries possesses the resources,[98] and many statements are made regarding promises for the future, countries do not always have the interest to make the necessary investments on a systematic basis.

So what potential sources exist that could provide the necessary financial resources for implementing global environmental regimes? This section outlines several possibilities proposed by government officials, NGOs, or other experts in different international fora (see Box 5.4). Each is theoretically possible, but each faces obstacles before it could become policy.

BOX 5.4 OPPORTUNITIES TO INCREASE FINANCIAL RESOURCES FOR IMPLEMENTING GLOBAL ENVIRONMENTAL REGIMES

- **Multilateral and bilateral assistance focused on the Sustainable Development Goals**
- **Development of revenue from regime mechanisms**
- **Pollution taxes**
- **Exchange of debt obligations for sustainable development policy reforms and investments**
- **Green global trade and investment**
- **Public-private partnerships**
- **South–South financing and investment**
- **Triangular cooperation**

Multilateral and Bilateral Assistance Focused on the Sustainable Development Goals

Existing ODA and loan-guarantee programs, which dwarf environmental funding in size, could systematically apply resources to programs that also enhance environmental goals and help to achieve the SDGs that were adopted in 2015 (see Chapter 6). Overall ODA flows would not necessarily need to be reduced or enlarged, but governments and international financial institutions such as the World Bank would funnel aid to proven programs with shared environmental and development goals. Programs focused on energy production or industrialization would support only projects that produce or use green energy rather than oil or coal, employ significant energy-conservation measures, and emit low levels of pollution. Many developing countries have tremendous renewable energy resources, including outstanding conditions for cost-efficient solar power plants in large sections of

Africa, the Arab states, and parts of Pakistan and India. Excellent resources for constructing geothermal facilities exist in East Africa and the Pacific Rim, including Indonesia, the Philippines, and the west coasts of Mexico, Central America, and South America. Significant wind-power resources exist in many developing countries.

Similarly, cleaning and redeveloping brownfields—former industrial properties containing hazardous substances, pollutants, or contaminants—would enjoy priority over clearing land for construction or agriculture. Projects that would clear tropical forests or place roads into or near protected areas would not be funded, nor would products that use or produce toxic chemicals. Reuse and recycling projects would be emphasized over mining projects or production processes that require large amounts of raw materials. Funding would increase to countries that followed these types of guidelines in their own policies and decrease to countries that continued business as usual. Sustainable agriculture that produces food for local consumption on a regular basis would receive priority over boom-and-bust industrial export agriculture that consumes significant quantities of water and fertilizer and can leave countries as net importers of food. Energy-efficiency projects that train people in this increasingly profitable industry, which both saves money and reduces GHG emissions, would be supported over other types of job-training programs.

Donors or recipients wishing to focus all or part of their ODA programs on health and social issues could effectively pursue these goals while also promoting the social bases of sustainable development, including basic health and nutrition, vaccinations, family planning, land preservation, and education (especially for women and girls). Indeed, better health and education are widely shown to contribute to smaller, healthier families, higher incomes, and less stress on the environment and natural resources.

Development of Revenue from Regime Mechanisms

Environmental regimes have the potential to develop mechanisms to capture certain cost savings that result from environmental protection or to collect fees from services or permits. For example, one potential source of financing for greater energy efficiency, zero-GHG-emission energy sources, technological innovation, and technological diffusion is GHG emissions trading.

By making emissions reduction a potential profit source, the competitive nature of market capitalism is employed to combat climate change. In 1990, the United States established one of the first national systems for emissions trading for meeting sulfur dioxide emissions targets in the electric-power sector as a means to reduce acid rain. The EU Greenhouse Gas Emission Trading Scheme commenced operation in January 2005 as the world's largest multicountry, multisector GHG emissions–trading scheme worldwide.[99] State and regional GHG-trading schemes have been developed in the United States and other countries, including the Regional Greenhouse Gas Initiative (see Chapter 2), and California and Quebec linked their CO_2 trading systems in 2014.[100] As national and international systems expand, a small percentage of each auction or transaction could go into a fund for investing in clean-energy options in the poorest developing countries.

The central challenge to deploying an effective emissions trading system is designing and then continually improving the system so that it works at both the business and the environmental levels. The success of emissions-trading programs in the United States for sulfur emissions argues that this is possible, although maintaining an effective and efficient trading system for CO_2 presents a more difficult challenge. The EU Greenhouse Gas Emission Trading Scheme experienced difficulties for the first few years because an excess of permits drove prices too low. However, some of these problems have been fixed (the system is designed to be adjusted if needed), and the system expanded to cover emissions from more types of sources.

The climate regime already includes a mechanism for raising revenues, and possibilities exist in other regimes. The Clean Development Mechanism allows industrialized countries to implement GHG emissions–reduction projects in developing countries and receive salable, certified emissions-reduction credits, which can be counted toward meeting their Kyoto targets. The climate regime's Adaptation Fund receives proceeds from the equivalent of a 2 percent tax on the proceeds of Certified Emission Reductions issued under the Clean Development Mechanism projects.[101] The Green Climate Fund finances low-emission and climate-resilient development in developing countries, projects that limit and reduce GHG emissions, and activities that help vulnerable societies adapt to the unavoidable impacts of climate change.[102]

Pollution Taxes

Many ideas exist for state, regional, national, or even coordinated international taxes or user fees to penalize polluters, encourage the use of green technologies and practices, or raise money for sustainable development. Taxes would be levied on activities harmful in their own right or that produce negative externalities. A common proposal is a carbon tax, a tax on fossil fuels or GHG emissions. A successful example is the excise tax on CFCs enacted by the United States to help implement its obligations under the ozone regime. The tax raised several billion dollars for the US Treasury and acted as a significant incentive for companies to speed their transition to alternatives.[103]

Some taxes could be set quite low but still raise large sums through their aggregate impact. The impact on the poor of larger taxes meant to help change market behavior could be offset by related cuts in income or sales taxes or other programs, such as the rebates provided as part of the carbon tax in the Canadian province of British Columbia.[104] Some existing green taxes and proposals seek to be revenue neutral. Others propose that governments use at least some of the revenue to support sustainable development and environmental protection.

In proposals for coordinated action, countries would impose similar taxes on pollution or other activities and then pool or use the money individually to finance sustainable development and environmental regimes.[105] For example, in the early 1990s, the EU called for a tax on air fuel used for international flights to raise funds for environmental projects.[106] In 2009, during the climate-change negotiations, the group of LDCs proposed that developed countries should accept a compulsory levy on international flight tickets and shipping fuel to raise billions of dollars to help the world's poorest countries mitigate and adapt to climate change. The aviation levy, which proponents claim would increase the price of long-haul fares by less than 1 percent, could raise $10 billion a year.[107] An Ecuador-led initiative proposed a 3–5 percent tax on oil exported to industrialized countries that would likely raise $40 billion to $60 billion annually, which would be used to finance climate mitigation and adaptation activities in developing countries.[108] Another well-known proposal is to tax large-scale speculative currency trading. A levy of just 0.005 percent could generate $15 billion a year for environmental projects if enacted in countries through which most of such trading takes place. Larger levies, which have been proposed, would raise even more and potentially discourage such speculation, which some argue presents an unnecessary threat to the stability of national currencies.[109] Other possibilities include taxes on certain types of energy production, fossil fuel–powered transportation, the production of certain toxic chemicals or hazardous waste, and the release of heavy metals and air and water pollutants into the environment. In addition to raising funds for implementing globally agreed-upon environmental goals, the taxes would create additional economic deterrents to unnecessary pollution.

Many practical and political issues exist concerning the adoption and administration of such taxes, and the system would be subject to significant concerns about free riders. In addition, some national governments might fear that they would lose revenue, that the money raised in their countries would be wasted on inefficient international projects, that the taxes would be used to create slush funds for use by international organizations outside their control, or that the mechanism could contribute to other losses of sovereign control. The US Congress, for example, passed legislation in 1999 making it illegal for the United States to participate in global taxes.[110] Although a national tax, albeit one enacted in concert with other governments and administered domestically with proceeds distributed only by the United

States, might pass muster against this legislation and meet at least some of the concern expressed by other countries, it would still face formidable political obstacles.

Exchange of Debt Obligations for Sustainable Development Policy Reforms and Investments

Debt obligations create incentives for developing countries to exploit their natural resources at unsustainable rates and use budgetary resources for debt payments at the expense of sustainable development programs. Implementing aggressive debt-relief programs in concert with agreements by the debtor country to use a specific amount of the savings for environmental programs offers the potential to tap a source of funds for problems largely neglected by most assistance programs, such as programs needed to combat desertification in Africa.

Several initiatives in this direction have been developed in the past two decades. Under pressure from poor countries and NGOs in September 1996, the World Bank and the IMF launched the Initiative for Heavily Indebted Poor Countries (HIPCs), which helps the poorest and most heavily indebted countries escape from unsustainable debt and focus more energy on building the policy and institutional foundation for sustainable development and poverty reduction.[111] In 2005, the HIPC initiative was supplemented by the Multilateral Debt Relief Initiative, which allows for 100 percent relief on eligible debts from three multilateral institutions—the IMF, the World Bank, and the African Development Fund—for countries completing the HIPC initiative process. In 2007, the Inter-American Development Bank also decided to provide additional debt relief to HIPCs in the Western Hemisphere.

In 2005, leaders of the world's eight leading industrialized countries agreed to cancel the debt of eighteen of the world's poorest nations and to increase aid to, and investment in, Africa.[112] The pledge helped some of the countries that were eligible for the HIPC or Multilateral Debt Relief Initiatives but could not participate because of the domestic exigencies and the structural adjustments required by the program. Several broad alliances of religious, charitable, environmental, and labor groups (the best known being the Jubilee Network) continue to advocate for debt cancellation.[113] Although the HIPC, G-8, and other initiatives represent significant steps, public and private debt levels remain an impediment to successful environmental protection and sustainable development in many developing countries.

Green Global Trade and Investment

A variety of options exist for reducing trade barriers and removing subsidies to enhance the global availability of, and investment in, goods and services that benefit sustainable development. As discussed in Chapter 6, the relationship between trade and the environment is complex. However, efforts to remove tariffs and other trade barriers that reduce the flow or increase the price of green energy technologies (such as solar panels) or products that enhance energy or water efficiency increase the cost of sustainable development and take resources away from other efforts. As noted above, reducing counterproductive subsidies would have similar benefits. Addressing these issues has been a priority for some countries as part of WTO negotiations and other bilateral and multilateral trade negotiations but with only mixed success.

Public-Private Partnerships

Public-private partnerships (PPPs) are increasingly promoted as a way to finance environment and development projects, potentially including the SDGs. Although there is no universally agreed-upon definition, PPPs are often described as a medium- or long-term contractual arrangement between the state and a private-sector company; an arrangement in which the private sector participates in the supply of assets and services traditionally provided by government, such as hospitals, schools, prisons, roads, bridges, tunnels, railways, water and sanitation, and energy; and an arrangement involving some form of risk sharing between the public and private sectors.[114] The financial crisis of 2008 brought about renewed interest in PPPs. Facing constraints on public resources, while recognizing the importance of

PHOTO 5.5 NGOs demand governments end fossil-fuel subsidies at the June 2015 Bonn Climate Change Conference. Courtesy Leila Mead, IISD/*Earth Negotiations Bulletin*, www.iisd.ca.

investment in infrastructure to help their economies grow, governments increasingly turned to the private sector as an additional source of funding.[115]

When they work well, PPPs give governments and international organizations access to new resources (financial, technical, infrastructural). Civil society networks gain access to increased public and private funding, as well as in-kind and technical support. And businesses get access to risk and expectations management, market and community development expertise, contracts, and positive publicity.[116] Many UN summits and UN initiatives, including the Global Compact, have stressed the importance of PPPs.[117] Although not a PPP per se, the Basel Convention has developed initiatives on mobile phones and computer waste involving companies, NGOs, international organizations, and governments that contain similar elements (see Chapter 3).

However, PPPs do not always work well and may have inherent drawbacks. One study found that government financing of PPP projects is twice as expensive as it would have been had the government borrowed money from private banks or issued bonds.[118] Another found that less than 50 percent of PPPs have mechanisms for measuring effectiveness.[119] There are also concerns that "the least effective partnerships include weaker and poorer African countries, which arguably need successful projects the most"[120] and about transparency and accountability given that corporations can have incentives to keep information confidential in order not to give away competitive advantages. Finally, some studies question the overall effectiveness of many PPPs—potentially the most important metric—and conclude that their overall effect to date has been inconclusive.[121]

South–South Financing and Investment

South–South cooperation (SSC) is another form of financial assistance that has gained popularity. It can be defined as an exchange of knowledge and resources in the political, economic, social, cultural, environmental, or technical domain among governments, organizations, and individuals in two or more developing nations. It can take place on a bilateral, regional, subregional, or interregional basis. SSC is guided by the principles of respect for national sovereignty, equality, nonconditionality, noninterference in domestic affairs, national ownership and independence, and mutual benefit.[122] Through exchanges of experiences and the pooling and sharing of resources, SSC can foster self-reliance among developing countries, open new channels of communication, strengthen economic ties, and lead to more effective and better coordinated environmental and development policies.[123]

Recent developments in SSC have taken the form of increased volume of South–South trade, South–South flows of foreign direct investment, movements toward regional integration, technology transfers, sharing of solutions and experts, and other forms of exchanges.[124] For example, South–South trade in renewable energy equipment and services is growing faster than North–South renewable energy trade.[125] SSC was employed in pursuit of the Millennium Development Goals (MDGs) and is also included in the outcome documents of the WSSD, the Third International Conference on Financing for Development, and the 2030 Agenda for Sustainable Development (see Chapter 6).[126]

SSC can arguably be more sustainable than traditional North–South cooperation because the developing countries involved should share more mutual interests and be more adaptable to changing national circumstances. However, in practice, there is still no shared understanding on the overall nature of SSC or how it should relate to North–South cooperation. Several different and sometimes divergent interpretations of SSC have been expressed within and among developing countries. Some argue that SSC should be discussed as a complement to North–South cooperation; others argue that the two models must always be part of separate discussions due to the principle of CBDR;[127] and still others, usually donor countries, seek to insert references to all types of activity, including SSC, into regime discussions of FTA, believing that developing countries in a position to do so should have nearly the same responsibility to provide assistance as industrialized countries.[128]

Triangular Cooperation

Triangular cooperation is another form of assistance that seeks to bring together the providers of development assistance, partners in SSC, and international organizations to share knowledge and implement projects that support sustainable development.[129] Triangular cooperation occurs when traditional donor countries and international organizations facilitate SSC through the provision of funding, training, project management, technological systems, and other forms of support. When successful, triangular cooperation enhances aid efficiency, builds synergies between traditional and emerging donors, builds the capacity of donor agencies in developing countries, and improves the quality of SSC.[130] Along with PPPs and SSC, increased triangular cooperation has been referenced in the outcome documents of the WSSD, the Third International Conference on Financing for Development, and the 2030 Agenda for Sustainable Development.[131]

Triangular cooperation also carries risks, however, that must be addressed. These include lowering quality standards if emerging donors do not have the experience and capacity to provide high-quality development assistance; programs that reflect the experiences and preferences of the donors rather than the beneficiary countries' actual needs, priorities, and strategies; and high transaction costs because three groups of actors (instead of two as in traditional cooperation) must agree on common goals, standards, and procedures and create the legal, institutional, and budgetary conditions required for successful implementation.[132]

The scale of triangular cooperation is not yet to the scale of traditional North–South cooperation or even SSC. Yet, it reflects the fact that sources of finance are changing and some developing countries are losing their status as recipients of traditional development assistance and becoming donors. It also offers traditional donors the opportunity to scale up aid programs by joining forces with new donors and then to switch to supporting the new donors as they take on progressively larger roles. Triangular cooperation, if properly implemented, can accelerate this process and thereby enrich the system of international development cooperation.[133]

CONCLUSION

The effectiveness of an environmental regime, that is, the extent to which it produces measurable improvements in the environment, is a function of regime design, particularly the strength of the key control provisions aimed at addressing the environmental threat, as well as the level of implementation (the extent to which countries adopt domestic regulations to enact the agreement) and compliance (the degree to which countries conform to these regulations and other regime rules and procedures). Many factors can inhibit or promote the effectiveness of an environmental regime. Among the most fundamental are eight broad sets of obstacles that can make it difficult to create or strengthen regimes so they contain strong and effective control measures:

1. Structural or systemic obstacles that arise from the structure of the international system, the structure of international law, and the structure of the global economic system;
2. The lack of sufficient concern, hospitable contractual environments, or necessary capacity;
3. Lowest-common-denominator problems;
4. Time-horizon conflicts;
5. Obstacles that stem from the characteristics of global environmental issues themselves, including the inherent links among environmental issues and important economic and political issues, unequal adjustment costs, scientific complexity and uncertainty, the presence of different core values and beliefs, and the involvement of large numbers of actors;
6. Obstacles that stem from the interconnections among environmental issues;
7. Regime-design difficulties; and

8. Changing realities in the global economic and ecological systems that have created new and sometimes conflicting views regarding how to apply the principle of CBDR.

Once regimes are created, certain factors can negatively influence national compliance with their requirements. These include inadequate translation of regime rules into domestic law; insufficient capacity or commitment to implement, administer, monitor, or enforce policies; misperception of relevant costs and benefits; high costs of compliance; inadequate or poorly targeted FTA; poorly designed regimes; and the sheer number of international environmental agreements and the lack of coordination among them.

Despite these obstacles, options exist to strengthen compliance with environmental agreements. Among the most important are elevating concern, creating market incentives, eliminating counterproductive subsidies, augmenting domestic capacity, increasing and more effectively targeting technical and financial assistance, emphasizing and supporting improved reporting and monitoring, enhancing coordination among regimes and conventions, applying sanctions, and employing positive and negative publicity.

Issues of financial resources, including the politics and provision of financial assistance, are central issues in global environmental politics. Given the political and economic obstacles preventing significant increases in financing for environmental regimes, as well as the potentially large amounts needed to assure their effectiveness, it is necessary for MEAs to seek alternative sources for such resources. This chapter outlined several ways to increase funding for global environmental regimes, including focusing existing bilateral and multilateral assistance on projects directly supportive of environmental regimes and sustainable development, developing revenue from regime mechanisms such as emissions trading, creating new revenue streams from pollution taxes, canceling debts owed by poor countries or exchanging them for tangible sustainable development actions, and greening global trade and investment. PPPs, SSC, and triangular cooperation also have potential to increase funding.

In spite of daunting obstacles to the creation and effective implementation of international environmental agreements, successful examples do exist. Examining the obstacles to creating strong agreements and options for increasing compliance provides insights into additional tools for creating effective global environmental policy.

6

Environmental Politics and Sustainable Development

As the case studies in this book demonstrate, global environmental politics cannot be studied in a vacuum. Environmental issues are inextricably linked with economic and social issues. Increased awareness, improved scientific understanding, the number of countries involved in the negotiation of environmental treaties, and the relationship among environmental protection, economic development, and social development—the three dimensions or pillars of sustainable development—all contribute to the current global environmental landscape.

North–South economic issues are a crucial element of the political context of global environmental politics. In spite of the growth of many emerging economies, including Brazil, China, India, and South Africa, to name a few, many developing countries still perceive global economic relations as fundamentally inequitable. This often shapes their policy responses to global environmental issues and their negotiating strategies.

Developing countries insist that the industrialized countries, because of their historical dominance in the production and consumption of ozone-depleting substances (ODS), combustion of fossil fuels, and production of toxic chemicals and hazardous wastes, should bear the responsibility for solving environmental problems. More generally, they identify the high levels of consumption in industrialized countries as a key cause of global environmental degradation. For example, according to the United Nations Development Programme (UNDP), there are more than nine hundred cars per thousand people of driving age in the United States and more than six hundred in Western Europe but fewer than ten in India. Domestic per capita water consumption in the richest countries averages 425 liters a day, more than six times the average of 67 liters per day in the poorest countries.[1] The average person in an industrialized country, like the United States, accounts for nearly four times the carbon dioxide (CO_2) emissions of someone in China or India and nearly thirty times that of someone in Kenya. The average British citizen accounts for as much greenhouse gas (GHG) emissions in two months as a person in a least-developed country (LDC) generates in a year.[2] Chinese per capita emissions are rising rapidly, but many of these emissions relate to the production of products for consumption in the United States and Europe. Therefore, many developing countries argue that industrialized countries in the North must adopt more sustainable consumption and production patterns and significantly reduce the use of natural resources and fossil fuels before the South follows suit.

This chapter looks at global environmental politics within the context of sustainable development, with a focus on three elements in this complex relationship: North–South relations, social development, and economic development and trade. It concludes with a section on the UN's new sustainable development agenda and the Sustainable Development Goals (SDGs), which attempt to bring the global environment and development agendas together and operationalize the concept of sustainable development.

NORTH–SOUTH RELATIONS AND SUSTAINABLE DEVELOPMENT

Historically, developing countries perceived global environmental issues as a distinctively North–South issue and, sometimes, as an effort to sabotage their development aspirations. This perspective emerged back in 1971 at a seminar held in Founex, Switzerland, which laid the groundwork for the 1972 Stockholm Conference on the Human Environment. The Founex Report that resulted from the conference was the first paper to identify key environment and development objectives and relationships and the policy and conceptual differences separating developed and developing countries.[3] The tone and substance of the report foreshadowed what soon became the South's rhetoric for more than forty years at global environmental conferences and regime negotiations. The Founex Report provides critical testimony that these interests (1) have remained largely unchanged over time and (2) lie at the heart of today's global politics of sustainable development.[4] As the Founex Report puts it:

> The developing countries would clearly wish to avoid, as far as feasible, the [environmental] mistakes and distortions that have characterized the patterns of development of the industrialized societies. However, the major environmental problems of the developing countries are essentially of a different kind.

> They are predominantly problems that reflect the poverty and very lack of development in their societies. . . . These are problems, no less than those of industrial pollution, that clamor for attention in the context of the concern with human environment. They are problems which affect the greater mass of mankind. . . . In [industrialized] countries, it is appropriate to view development as a cause of environmental problems. . . . In [the southern] context, development becomes essentially a cure for their major environmental problems.[5]

Although many developing-country officials, particularly in environment ministries, recognize the seriousness of environmental degradation and how it negatively affects their economic future, the viewpoints expressed in the Founex Report help explain why many developing countries often regarded global environmental regimes as largely unrelated to their core concerns and even suspiciously—as a means by which industrialized countries will maintain control or even gain new control over resources and technology located in the South.

The 1972 Stockholm Conference on the Human Environment treated the environment as part of the broader development process in order to allay these concerns. This helped focus discussion on specific problems facing developing countries and implied that additional financial resources would be sought, primarily through existing development assistance channels.[6] Along these lines, the resulting Stockholm Declaration and Action Plan specifically noted (in Recommendations 102–109) that environmental concerns should not be a pretext for discriminatory trade policies or reduced access to markets and that the burdens of environmental policies of industrialized countries should not be transferred to developing countries. Recommendation 109, in particular, called on states to ensure that concerns of developed countries with their own environmental problems should not affect the flow of assistance to developing countries and that this flow should be adequate to meet the additional environmental requirements of such countries.[7]

Emergence of Sustainable Development

In the wake of the Stockholm Conference, the UN raised international environmental awareness through governments, nongovernmental organizations (NGOs), and the world's business and scientific communities. However, environmental and development issues were often addressed separately and in a fragmented fashion. Stockholm successfully brought international attention to the need for cooperation on environmental problems but did not resolve any of the inherent tensions in linking environmental protection with social and economic development.[8]

In 1983 the UN General Assembly (UNGA) established an independent commission to formulate a long-term agenda for action on the broad issues of environment and development. Chaired by Norway's environment minister, Gro Harlem Brundtland, the commission conducted fifteen public hearings over three years at locations around the world. Both governments and civil society participated in the hearings. The commission's 1987 report, *Our Common Future*, stressed the need for development strategies in all countries that recognized the limits of natural ecosystems to regenerate themselves and to absorb waste products. Recognizing "an accelerating ecological interdependence among nations,"[9] the commission emphasized the link between economic development and environmental issues and identified poverty eradication as a necessary and fundamental requirement for environmentally sustainable development. In addition, the report noted that the goals of economic and social development must be defined in terms of sustainability in all countries: developed or developing, market-oriented, or centrally planned.[10] It also determined that a series of rapid transitions and policy changes would be required, including keeping population levels in harmony with the ecosystem, reducing mass poverty, increasing equity within and among nations, increasing efficiency in the use of energy and other resources, reorienting technology, and merging environment and economics in decision making.[11]

The Brundtland Report also called on the UNGA to convene an international conference to review progress made and promote follow-up arrangements. This conference became the 1992 Earth Summit (formally known as the UN Conference on Environment and Development [UNCED]), which achieved a pact, underpinned by a set of core principles that had their origins in the Brundtland Report, among countries of the North and countries of the South that linked environmental and developmental concerns.

The Rio Principles

On the twentieth anniversary of the Stockholm Conference, governments gathered in Rio de Janeiro, Brazil, to move the sustainable development agenda forward. The 1992 Earth Summit attracted greater official and unofficial interest than had the Stockholm Conference. The summit and the preparatory work that preceded it showed there were still significant differences between developed and developing countries on many environmental issues. Each group provided different inputs to the agenda-setting process. Developed countries wanted to focus on ozone depletion, global warming, acid rain, and deforestation. Developing countries preferred exploring the relationship among sluggish economic growth, consumption levels, and production patterns in developing countries and the economic policies of the developed countries. They emphasized that an "environmentally healthy planet was impossible in a world that contained significant inequities."[12]

The major output of the Earth Summit was the global plan of action for sustainable development, called Agenda 21. Agenda 21 demonstrated an emerging consensus on the issues affecting the long-term sustainability of human society, including domestic social and economic policies, international economic relations, and cooperation on issues concerning the global commons. The summit also produced the Rio Declaration on Environment and Development, which led to the institutionalization of several principles that have roots in Stockholm but have become features of nearly all post-Rio global environmental treaties and politics: additionality, common but differentiated responsibilities (CBDR), and the polluter pays principles.

The first of these principles is additionality, which is not explicitly stated in the Rio Declaration but underlies most of Agenda 21 as well as the climate-change, ozone, and persistent organic pollutants regimes. The principle of additionality arose out of the South's concern that environmental issues would attract international aid away from traditional development issues. Developing countries were concerned that instead of raising new funds for addressing global environmental issues, the North and international financial institutions would simply divert resources previously targeted for development toward the environment. Thus, the principle of additionality sought to ensure that new monies would be made available to deal with global environmental issues.[13]

Despite assurances given to the South, however, this principle suffered a setback soon after the Earth Summit during the negotiation of the desertification convention. Early in these negotiations, it became clear that the industrialized countries were not going to make new funds available. This dismayed developing countries, particularly those in Africa, and became a major source of contention during the negotiations. Ultimately, the Global Mechanism was established under the 1994 UN Convention to Combat Desertification (UNCCD), its role essentially being to use existing resources more efficiently to meet the action needs of the convention (see Chapter 4).[14] Even though in 2002 the Global Environment Facility (GEF) decided to include land degradation as a new work area, the fact that the UNCCD regime began without new and additional financial resources to combat desertification damaged the principle of additionality.[15]

The principle of additionality and the southern demands for "new and additional" funding for developing countries' implementation of environmental agreements were also harmed by sharp reductions in official development assistance (ODA) in the 1990s. In response, developing countries started to use the threat of retreating from previous consensus agreements on environmental issues as leverage against the donor countries. For example, at the Earth Summit +5 (the 1997 Special Session of the UNGA to review the implementation of Agenda 21 and the other Rio agreements), the Group of 77 (G-77) and China refused to oppose proposals by oil-exporting states to delete all references to reducing consumption of fossil fuels. This tactic failed, however, to shake the veto exercised by donor countries on targets for ODA.[16]

Commitments made at the March 2002 UN Conference on Financing for Development reversed the ODA declines. In 2005, donors also committed to increase ODA at the Group of Eight summit in Gleneagles, Scotland,[17] and at the UN Millennium +5 Summit.[18] These pledges, combined with other commitments, implied an increase in aid from nearly $80 billion in 2004 to more than $135 billion in 2014. ODA has increased by 66 percent in real terms since 2000, when the Millennium Development Goals (MDGs) were adopted (see Figure 6.1). Yet, although ODA reached an all-time high in 2014, it still represented only 0.3 percent of combined gross national income.[19]

In 2014, the largest donors were the United States, the United Kingdom, Germany, France, and Japan. However, Denmark, Luxembourg, the Netherlands, Norway, Sweden, and the United Kingdom were the only countries to exceed the UN's ODA target of 0.7 percent of gross national income (see Box 6.1).[20] Moreover, environmental aid from both bilateral and multilateral aid agencies remains a small percentage of this figure. According to the Organization for Economic

FIGURE 6.1 **Net Official Development Assistance from Organization for Economic Cooperation and Development Countries, 1992–2014**

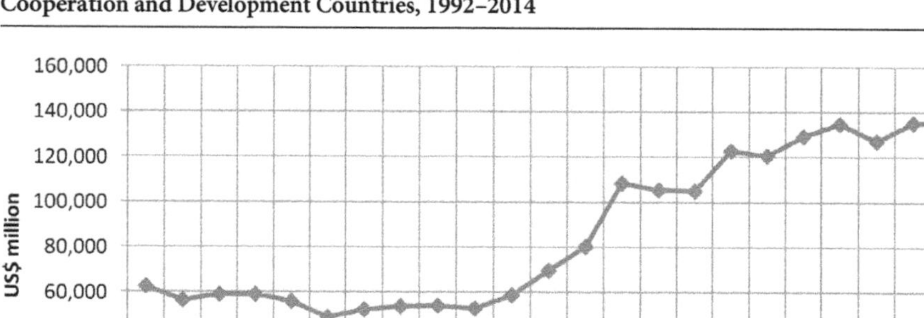

Source: Organization for Economic Cooperation and Development DAC Statistical Tables, http://stats.oecd.org/qwids/.

BOX 6.1 THE 0.7 PERCENT OFFICIAL DEVELOPMENT ASSISTANCE TARGET*

The best known international target in the aid field is raising official development assistance (ODA) to 0.7 percent of donors' gross national income. The target grew out of a proposal by the World Council of Churches in 1958 to transfer 1 percent of donor countries' incomes to developing countries. But it had a major problem: governments had no means of programming or even predicting the private element of capital flows, which in many years are more than half of the total.

This drawback stimulated efforts to define a separate subtarget for official flows. The Dutch economist Jan Tinbergen led this work as chairman of the UN Committee on Development Planning in 1964. Tinbergen estimated the capital inflows that developing economies needed to achieve desirable growth rates and proposed a target for official flows—both concessional (grants and subsidized loans) and nonconcessional—of 0.75 percent of gross national product (GNP) to be achieved by 1972. Some but not all developed countries accepted this target, but without the date, at the second meeting of the UN Conference on Trade and Development (UNCTAD) in 1968.

This idea was then taken up by the Pearson Commission, which was appointed by World Bank President Robert McNamara in 1968. The commission's 1969 report proposed that ODA "be raised to 0.70% of donor GNP by 1975 and in no case later than 1980."† After lengthy negotiations, this proposal was formally recognized in October 1970 in UN General Assembly Resolution 2626 (XXV), although most donor countries expressed reservations: "Each economically advanced country will progressively increase its official development assistance to the developing countries and will exert its best efforts to reach a minimum net amount of 0.7% of its gross national product" by the mid-1970s.

The new target gained acceptance, with exceptions. The United States made clear that, although it supported the aims of the resolution, it did not subscribe to specific targets or timetables. Switzerland was not a UN member at the time and did not adopt the target. All other developed countries have accepted it, at least as a long-term objective, and it has been repeatedly re-endorsed at international conferences. However, in 2014 only Sweden, the United Kingdom, Norway, Denmark, and Luxembourg achieved the target.‡ Finland achieved it once, in 1991. The Netherlands dropped below the target in 2013 for the first time since 1975.§ No other developed country has met the 0.7 percent target.

*** This information is excerpted from OECD, "History of the 0.7% ODA Target," 2010, www.oecd.org/dac/aidstatistics/45539274.pdf.**

† Lester B. Pearson (Chairman), *Partners in Development—Report of the Commission on International Development,*" (New York: Praeger, 1969), 18.

‡ "Development Aid Stable in 2014 but Flows to Poorest Countries Still Falling," Organization for Economic Cooperation and Development (OECD), April 8, 2015, http://www.oecd.org/dac/stats/development-aid-stable-in-2014-but-flows-to-poorest-countries-still-falling.htm.

§ OECD, *Development Cooperation Report: Mobilizing Resources for Sustainable Development* (Paris: OECD Publishing, 2014), 337.

Cooperation and Development (OECD), out of $187 billion of total bilateral and multilateral ODA in 2013, only 2.84 percent ($5.345 billion) was targeted for environmental aid.[21] So although there have been new and additional financial resources, the current and projected levels of ODA still fall far short of the estimates of what is necessary to achieve internationally agreed-upon environmental goals.[22]

Developing countries also believe that the North should bear the financial burden of measures to reverse ecological damage. This is a key component of the principle of CBDR. This principle states that global environmental problems are the common concern of all nations, and all nations should work toward their solution (common responsibilities), but responsibility for action should be differentiated in proportion to the responsibility for creating the problem and the financial and technical resources available for taking effective action (differentiated responsibilities). Because some nations have a greater and more direct responsibility for creating environmental problems, they have a greater responsibility to address them.

The CBDR principle enjoys broad support among developing countries and has been explicitly acknowledged in nearly all international environmental agreements since the mid-1980s. It is reflected in specific regime rules, such as the different requirements for industrialized and developing countries under the Montreal Protocol (as discussed in Chapter 3, developing countries are given additional years before they must phase out particular chemicals), the absence of developing-country commitments to reduce GHG emissions in the Kyoto Protocol, and provisions to provide developing countries with financial and technical assistance (FTA) to help them implement the ozone, climate, biodiversity, hazardous waste, and chemicals regimes.

At the same time, as discussed in Chapter 5, important differences exist regarding how countries believe the CBDR principle should influence global environmental policy both in general and on specific issues. Developing countries emphasize historical responsibilities for causing global environmental problems, the large disparities in current per capita contributions (e.g., in per capita GHG emissions or resource consumption), and their need to devote resources to lifting millions of people out of extreme poverty and underdevelopment. It would be unfair, counterproductive, and perhaps immoral, they maintain, for developing countries to devote scarce resources to combating global environmental problems at the expense of addressing development. Thus, many southern states argue that the CBDR principle not only demands that industrialized countries should take far more significant action earlier than developing countries and provide greatly increased FTA but also that developing countries should take on commitments only to the extent that they receive sufficient FTA to allow them to implement the requirements under a global regime without having a negative impact on their economic development. This means, for example, that the FTA must meet the extra, or incremental, costs for using alternatives to the ozone-depleting chemicals or coal-fired power plants that industrialized countries used during their economic development.

In contrast, although most industrialized countries allow that historical responsibility is relevant to policy discussions, they also emphasize the common responsibility of all countries to contribute to solving global environmental problems, which implies a need for developing countries to avoid duplicating the unsustainable historical development patterns of the industrialized world. They also point out that some developing countries are currently among the most important contributors to particular environmental problems and that it will be simply impossible to address these issues, in particular climate change, mercury pollution, and deforestation, if these developing countries do not act and act soon. Thus, many industrialized countries maintain that, although it is appropriate for them to act first and to provide FTA, developing countries must also take action; particular levels of FTA are not a precondition for developing countries to take responsible action; and developing countries experiencing rapid levels of economic growth or that have large impacts on particular environmental problems have more responsibility to act than other developing countries with regard to those problems.

These differences have been on full display in the climate negotiations. The United States and some other countries have argued that certain developing nations should agree to take significant action to reduce their GHG emissions from burning fossil fuels (e.g., China and India) and deforestation (e.g., Brazil and Indonesia). Many developing countries rejected these arguments, citing their low per capita emissions, their need for energy and economic development, inadequate FTA provisions, and the responsibility of industrialized countries for creating the problem.

The third principle is the polluter pays principle, which seeks to ensure that the economic and other costs of environmental action should be borne by those who create the need for that action. As with other Rio principles, the South has argued that the polluter pays principle has been steadily diluted. They point to an increasing pattern of pushing treaty implementation steadily southward, including in the climate, desertification, and biodiversity regimes, by seeking relatively fewer changes in behavior patterns in the North and relatively more in the South, even though northern behavior gave rise to most of the problems in the first place.[23]

Another consistent theme in developing-country views of global environmental issues is the inequality in governing structures of international organizations such as the World Bank, which allows a minority of donor countries to outvote the rest of the world. Developing countries have demanded that institutions that make decisions on how to spend funds on the global environment should have a democratic structure, that is, one in which each country is equally represented. Thus, developing countries did some of their toughest bargaining in environmental negotiations when they resisted the donor countries' proposed governance structure for the GEF (see Chapter 2).

The South also has demanded that the transfer of environmental technologies on concessional or preferential terms be part of environmental treaties. In the Montreal Protocol negotiations, for instance, developing states requested a guarantee from industrialized countries that corporations would provide them with patents and technical knowledge on ODS substitutes. This has also been a major issue in the climate-change and chemicals negotiations. Although significant investments involving the latest technologies have occurred in some developing countries in the climate and ozone sectors, the outright transfer of patents has not.

Needless to say, developing countries remain frustrated with global environmental politics, an attitude clearly related to convictions that the global economic system remains unfairly skewed in favor of advanced industrialized countries. On the one hand, some argue that the concept of sustainable development has allowed developing countries to incorporate long-standing concerns about economic and social development into the environmental agendas; by doing so, they have influenced the nature of global environmental discourse.[24] On the other hand, the South claims that it has seen few benefits from its continuing involvement in global environmental politics. Much of North–South environmental relations in the twenty-four years since the Earth Summit have focused on what the South sees as the North's failure to deliver what was promised or implied at Rio: new and additional financial resources, technology transfer, and capacity building.

THE SOCIAL PILLAR OF SUSTAINABLE DEVELOPMENT

The social development pillar or dimension of sustainable development addresses access to resources and opportunities, social justice, equity, participation, and empowerment. A strong social pillar means that all development sectors are stronger, whether it is agriculture, infrastructure development, management of natural resources, or rural and urban development. A weak social pillar means weakness in other sectors as well.

Developing-country concerns with social development, globalization, and other issues such as the HIV/AIDS pandemic led to a greater focus on the social development dimension of sustainable development as the millennium approached. There was growing recognition that the world was failing to achieve most of the goals for a more sustainable society set out in Agenda 21 and elsewhere. HIV/AIDS rolled back life expectancies in some countries to pre-1980 levels, and the number of people living with the disease approached the forty million mark. The world's population climbed above 6.1 billion in 2000, up from 5.5 billion in 1992—a significant increase in just eight years. The total number of people living in poverty dropped slightly—from 1.3 to 1.2 billion—but most of the gains were in Southeast Asia, and virtually no progress was made in sub-Saharan Africa, where almost half of the population lived in poverty. At least 1.1 billion people still lacked access to safe drinking water, and 2.4 billion lacked adequate sanitation.[25]

The world was also experiencing increasing globalization. Some viewed globalization as a threat, others as an opportunity. Many policymakers and industrialists in the developed world and some in developing countries were (and remain) positive about the phenomenon. However, many living in developing countries and a variety of NGOs worried that environmental and labor standards were in a race to the bottom and that social and economic disparities were being exacerbated. They were concerned that developing countries would eliminate or ignore environmental and labor standards in their efforts to attract foreign direct investment. There was a fear that if a host country demonstrated that it did not have strict pollution standards and did not condemn child labor or support an eight-hour work day, it would attract more corporate investment.[26]

In a speech delivered to the UNGA in April 2000 to launch the Millennium Report, then UN secretary-general Kofi Annan tackled the globalization issue. Observing that the opportunities provided by this phenomenon were being distributed unequally, he called for a candid debate on the positive and negative consequences of globalization and for discussions about how to make globalization work for all people in all countries. "How can we say that the half of the human race which has yet to make or receive a telephone call, let alone use a computer, is taking part in globalization?" he asked.[27]

The Millennium Assembly

The UNGA designated its fifty-fifth session, in September 2000, as the Millennium Assembly and held a Millennium Summit of world leaders to address the pressing challenges facing the world's people in the twenty-first century. At the Millennium Assembly, world leaders agreed to a far-reaching plan to support global development objectives for the new century. The world's leaders reaffirmed their commitment to work toward peace and security for all and a world in which sustainable development and poverty eradication would have the highest priority. Set against a backdrop of widespread concern about the social and ecological implications of globalization, the Millennium Assembly placed the relationship among poverty, environmental decline, and economic development firmly in the international spotlight.[28]

The following year, Secretary-General Annan presented his report, titled *Road Map Towards the Implementation of the United Nations Millennium Declaration* (UN document 56/326). The report's annex delineates eight development goals containing eighteen targets and forty-eight indicators, which are commonly known as the MDGs (see Box 6.2). The first seven goals were directed toward eradicating poverty in all its forms: halving extreme poverty and hunger, achieving universal primary education and gender equality, reducing the mortality of children under five by two-thirds and maternal mortality by three-quarters, reversing the spread of HIV/AIDS, halving the proportion of people without access to safe drinking water, and ensuring environmental sustainability. The final goal outlined measures for building a global partnership for development. The goals, targets, and indicators were developed following consultations held among members of the UN Secretariat and representatives of the International Monetary Fund (IMF), the OECD, and the World Bank in order to harmonize reporting on the development goals in the Millennium Declaration and the international development goals.

BOX 6.2 THE MILLENNIUM DEVELOPMENT GOALS

All UN member states pledged to do the following by 2015:

1. ERADICATE EXTREME POVERTY AND HUNGER

- **Reduce by half the proportion of people living on less than a dollar a day**
- **Reduce by half the proportion of people who suffer from hunger**

2. ACHIEVE UNIVERSAL PRIMARY EDUCATION

- **Ensure that all boys and girls complete a full course of primary schooling**

3. PROMOTE GENDER EQUALITY AND EMPOWER WOMEN

- **Eliminate gender disparity in primary and secondary education, preferably by 2005, and to all levels of education no later than 2015**

4. REDUCE CHILD MORTALITY

- **Reduce by two-thirds the mortality rate among children under five**

5. IMPROVE MATERNAL HEALTH

- **Reduce by three-quarters the maternal mortality ratio**

6. COMBAT HIV/AIDS, MALARIA, AND OTHER DISEASES

- **Halt and begin to reverse the spread of HIV/AIDS**
- **Halt and begin to reverse the incidence of malaria and other major diseases**

continues

BOX 6.2 THE MILLENNIUM DEVELOPMENT GOALS *continued*

7. ENSURE ENVIRONMENTAL SUSTAINABILITY

- **Integrate the principles of sustainable development into country policies and programs and reverse the loss of environmental resources**
- **Reduce by half the proportion of people without sustainable access to safe drinking water**
- **Achieve a significant improvement in the lives of at least one hundred million slum dwellers by 2020**

8. DEVELOP A GLOBAL PARTNERSHIP FOR DEVELOPMENT

- **Develop further an open trading and financial system that is rule-based, predictable, and nondiscriminatory. This target includes a commitment to good governance, development, and poverty reduction—both nationally and internationally.**
- **Address the special needs of the least-developed countries. This includes tariff- and quota-free access for their exports, enhanced debt relief for heavily indebted poor countries, cancellation of official bilateral debt, and more generous official development assistance for countries committed to poverty reduction.**
- **Address the special needs of landlocked countries and small island developing states**
- **Deal comprehensively with the debt problems of developing countries through national and international measures in order to make debt sustainable in the long term**
- **In cooperation with developing countries, develop decent and productive work for youth**
- **In cooperation with pharmaceutical companies, provide access to affordable essential drugs in developing countries**
- **In cooperation with the private sector, make available the benefits of new technologies—especially information and communications technologies**

Source: "Millennium Development Goals," UN, www.un.org/millenniumgoals.

After a slow start, the MDGs gained tremendous currency, primarily in development circles, but increasingly in related trade and finance spheres. Many actors counted on the MDGs to galvanize disparate and sometimes competing development agendas. Increasingly, stakeholders viewed the MDGs as a powerful political tool to hold governments and international institutions accountable. One reason for this is that the Millennium Declaration and its MDGs clarified the shared and individual roles and responsibilities of key stakeholders. The declaration set out the responsibilities of governments to implement various specific goals and targets. It instructed the network of international organizations to marshal their resources and expertise in the most strategic and efficient way possible to support and sustain the efforts of partners at global and country levels. And it urged citizens, civil-society organizations, and the private sector to bring to the table their unique strengths for motivation, mobilization, and action.[29]

Successes and Challenges in Implementing the Millennium Development Goals

There is broad agreement that the MDGs both provided a focal point for governments on which to hinge policies and ODA to alleviate poverty and improve the lives of poor people and served as a rallying point for NGOs to hold governments and the UN system accountable. In fact it could be argued that the MDGs saved the lives of millions and improved conditions for many more. As the 2015 MDG Report indicated:

- Extreme poverty declined significantly. In 1990, nearly half of the population in the developing world lived on less than $1.25 a day; that proportion dropped to 14 percent in 2015 (MDG 1).
- Globally, the number of people living in extreme poverty declined by more than half, falling from 1.9 billion in 1990 to 836 million in 2015 (MDG 1).
- The proportion of undernourished people in the developing regions fell by almost half since 1990, from 23.3 percent in 1990–1992 to 12.9 percent in 2014–2016 (MDG 1).
- The primary school net enrollment rate in developing regions reached 91 percent in 2015, up from 83 percent in 2000 (MDG 2).
- In Southern Asia, only 74 girls were enrolled in primary school for every 100 boys in 1990. In 2015, 103 girls were enrolled for every 100 boys (MDG 2).
- In 2015 women made up 41 percent of paid workers outside the agricultural sector, an increase from 35 percent in 1990 (MDG 3).
- The number of deaths of children under five declined from 12.7 million in 1990 to almost 6 million in 2015 globally (MDG 4).
- The maternal mortality ratio declined 45 percent worldwide since 1990, including declines of 64 percent in Southern Asia and 49 percent in sub-Saharan Africa (MDG 5).
- New HIV infections fell by approximately 40 percent between 2000 and 2013, from an estimated 3.5 million cases to 2.1 million (MDG 6).

- Over 6.2 million malaria deaths were averted between 2000 and 2015, primarily of children under five in sub-Saharan Africa (MDG 6).
- Between 2000 and 2013, tuberculosis prevention, diagnosis, and treatment interventions saved an estimated 37 million lives. The tuberculosis mortality rate fell by 45 percent (MDG 6).
- Since 1990, 2.6 billion people have gained access to improved drinking water and 2.1 billion people have gained access to improved sanitation. Globally, 147 countries have met the drinking water target, 95 countries have met the sanitation target, and 77 countries have met both (MDG 7).
- The proportion of urban population living in slums in the developing regions fell from approximately 39.4 percent in 2000 to 29.7 percent in 2014 (MDG 7).[30]

Nevertheless, the MDGs were criticized for being too narrow. The eight MDGs failed to consider the root causes of poverty or gender inequality, many of the underlying environmental issues, or the holistic nature of development. The goals made no mention of human rights, nor specifically addressed economic development. The MDGs were considered goals for only developing countries to achieve, with financial assistance from industrialized states.[31]

In addition, although significant achievements were made on many of the MDG targets, progress was uneven across regions and countries. Millions of people were left behind, especially the poorest and those disadvantaged because of their sex, age, disability, ethnicity, race, or geographic location. About eight hundred million people still live in extreme poverty and suffer from hunger. Over one hundred sixty million children under age five are stunted (inadequate height for their age) due to malnutrition. Fifty-seven million primary school age children are not in school. About sixteen thousand children die each day before celebrating their fifth birthday, most from preventable causes. The maternal mortality ratio in the developing world is fourteen times higher than that in developed countries. In 2015, one in three people (2.4 billion) still had insufficient sanitation facilities, including 946 million who still practice open defecation. More than 880 million people are estimated to be living in slum-like conditions in the world's cities.[32]

Perspectives on the MDGs and their implementation differ. Some argue that the MDGs form just another set of international development goals in a long history of nations setting and failing to achieve such goals. Others argued that there needed to be a greater link between the MDGs and the environment. In an influential article, Jeffrey Sachs and Walter Reid argued that development goals cannot be achieved and sustained without sound environmental management. Similarly,

PHOTO 6.1 During the UN Sustainable Development Summit in 2015, the UN even used toilet paper to raise awareness about the unmet sanitation Millennium Development Goal. Courtesy IISD/ *Earth Negotiations Bulletin*. www.iisd.ca.

environmental goals cannot be achieved without development. Yet the world underinvests in both, and developing and developed countries tend to overlook the policy link between poverty reduction and the environment.[33]

ECONOMIC DEVELOPMENT AND TRADE

The third pillar or dimension of sustainable development is economic development. The relationship between the global economy and the natural environment goes a long way toward explaining the evolution of global environmental politics. The global economy changed dramatically over the past seventy years. The post–World War II global economy of the 1950s and 1960s included a sharp divide between developed or industrialized countries in the North and developing countries in the South. At that time, developed countries accounted for 90 percent of world manufacturing output and 90 percent of exports.[34] In addition to this imbalance in production and exports, there was an imbalance in living standards and political power.

By 1974, encouraged by a surge in commodity prices and the Organization of Petroleum Exporting Countries' (OPEC's) successful manipulation of oil supplies in the early 1970s, developing countries attempted to restructure the global economic system. The South called for a bold but largely unrealistic plan, the New International Economic Order, a list of demands for the redistribution of wealth, which would include a new system of international commodity agreements, a unilateral reduction of barriers to imports from developing states into industrialized countries, the enhancement of developing countries' capabilities in science and technology, increased northern financing of technology transfer, and changes in patent laws to lower the cost of such transfers.[35]

After the late 1970s, however, the New International Economic Order faded from the global political agenda as economic trends turned against the South. Some officials in the North consequently felt even more strongly that it could disregard southern demands for change. Yet, although some northern observers might have considered the New International Economic Order agenda "discredited,"[36] it remained unfinished business for much of the South and was still considered a goal "very much worth pursuing."[37]

In the 1980s, commodity prices, debt, and trade issues shaped the economic picture in developing countries. Falling commodity prices devastated the economies of countries heavily dependent on commodity exports. Between 1980 and 1991, the price of a weighted index of thirty-three primary commodities exported by developing countries, not including energy, declined by 46 percent.[38] Meanwhile, heavy debt burdens, taken on at a time when commodity prices were high and northern banks were freely lending dollars from Arab oil revenues, siphoned off much of the foreign exchange of many developing countries. By 1995, the total external debt of the LDCs was $136 billion, a sum that represented 112.7 percent of their GNP that year.[39]

But the global economy was also changing. In 1994 the OECD countries' (industrialized) share of global gross domestic product (GDP) was 83 percent. By 2004, it was down to 80.5 percent. By 2014 it was 62.6 percent.[40] During this same period, OECD countries' share of exports declined from 73 percent to 59 percent of the global total[41] as new production, trade, and finance patterns emerged. Spurred by the revolution in information technology, trade liberalization, economic reforms, the demise of the Soviet Union, the opening of China, and the increased movement of capital and technology from developed to developing countries, the global economy nearly tripled in size from 1994 to 2014, increasing from $27 trillion to $78 trillion.[42] Although this economic growth reached practically every region of the world, a handful of large developing countries—led by China, India, and Brazil—accounted for a major share of global growth. Other emerging economies, such as Indonesia, Mexico, Russia, Turkey, and Vietnam, also grew at a rapid pace. This enabled developing countries to expand their share of the global GDP, fueling speculation that the world's economic balance of power has shifted away from the United States and Europe toward Asia and Latin America.[43]

However, despite the growth of some economies, the income gaps between and within the industrialized and developing worlds did not narrow. Europe and North

America, which represent 15 percent of the world's population, control 69 percent of the world's wealth (see Figure 6.2a and Figure 6.2b). Furthermore, the bottom half of the global population own less than 1 percent of total wealth. In sharp contrast, the richest 10 percent hold 87 percent of the world's wealth, and the top percentile alone account for 48.2 percent of global assets.[44] In fact, according to Oxfam, 80 billionaires have the same amount of wealth as the bottom half of the planet—3.674 billion people.[45]

Much of the economic growth in the emerging economies resulted from an expanded emphasis on international trade and investment in adherence with neoliberal economics—a political-economic movement, increasingly prominent since 1980, that deemphasizes or rejects government intervention, believing that progress and even social justice can be achieved through economic growth, which in turn requires freer markets. For example, neoliberals argue that the best way to protect the environment is by overcoming poverty through increased privatization, foreign direct investment, and free trade. As a result, the institutions managing the global economy (by promoting freer trade and international capital flows) have grown stronger, while those promoting social equity, poverty alleviation, and environmental cooperation remain weak.[46] The barriers to trade and investment began to fall, and the belief that poor countries could grow themselves out of poverty by boarding the liberalization express train took on an almost religious force—at least in many economic and policy circles within rich countries.[47] In other words, it was believed that if poorer countries supported trade liberalization, many of their economic development problems would be solved.

Yet many industrialized countries did not adhere to this philosophy in practice. During the early 1990s, trade barriers erected by industrialized countries against imports of manufactured and processed goods from developing countries increased even as most developing countries (under pressure from international financial institutions) were lowering their barriers to imports.[48] Tariffs on certain sectors of particular interest to developing countries, including agriculture, textiles, clothing, fish, and fish products, tended to be the highest in industrialized countries, limiting market access.[49] Furthermore, new kinds of nontariff barriers to trade (such as antidumping and countervailing duty actions), export-restraint agreements (such as the Multi-Fiber Arrangement), and direct subsidies were used to protect industries in the industrialized countries against imports from developing countries.

At the same time, trade liberalization raised concern among environmentalists regarding its potential impact on the earth's ecosystems and on governments' development choices. Many environmental NGOs see liberalization as driving the demand for greater consumption of natural resources and creating pressures to

FIGURE 6.2A **Global Population Distribution, 2014**

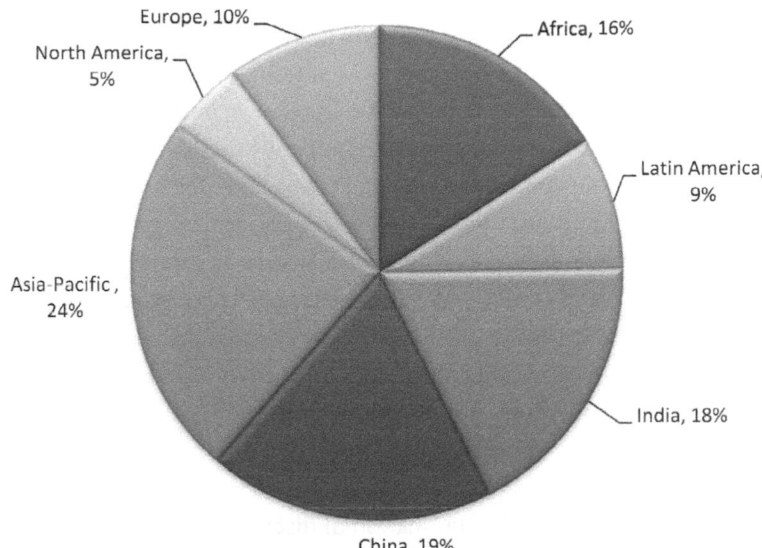

Source: United Nations Department of Economic and Social Affairs Population Division, *World Population Prospects: The 2015 Revision—Key Findings and Advance Tables* (New York: UN, 2015).

FIGURE 6.2B **Global Wealth Distribution, 2014**

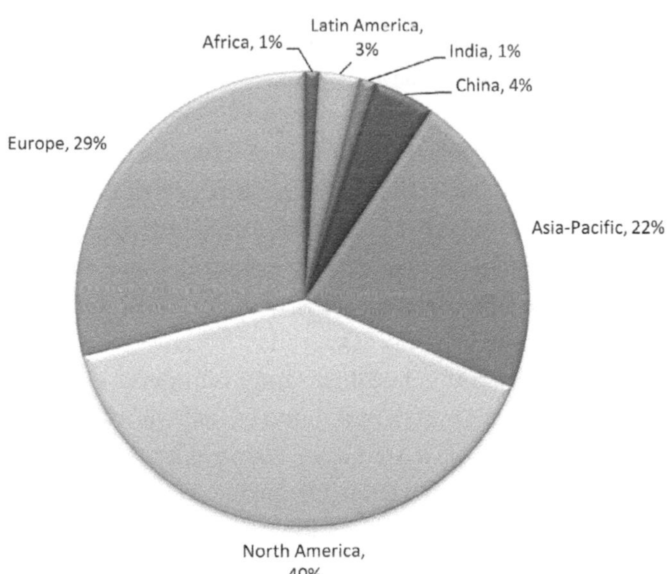

Source: Credit Suisse Research Institute, *Credit Suisse Global Wealth Databook, 2014* (Zurich, Switzerland: Credit Suisse Research Institute, 2014).

dismantle environmental regulations.[50] The global trade system evolved for decades without much thought about its impact on the environment. When the General Agreement on Tariffs and Trade (GATT), the central pillar of the international trading system, was negotiated just after World War II, there was no mention of the word *environment.* For the next forty years, trade officials and their environmental counterparts pursued their respective agendas on nearly parallel tracks that rarely, if ever, intersected. Little attention was paid to potential connections between trade liberalization and environmental protection. The wake-up call for environmentalists occurred after the United States banned tuna from Mexico and Venezuela because their fleets did not meet US standards for minimizing dolphin kills in tuna fishing. In 1991, the GATT declared the US ban illegal under the rules of international trade. US environmentalists were alarmed that a national environmental law could be overturned by the GATT and began serious efforts to address the environmental implications of international trade policy.[51]

The GATT and the World Trade Organization (WTO) constitute a regime that seeks to promote a common set of international trade rules, a reduction in tariffs and other trade barriers, and the elimination of discriminatory treatment in international trade relations.[52] The WTO, which governments created in 1995, has the mandate to rule on a broad spectrum of issues, from trade in goods and services to intellectual property rights, including issues affecting human health, the use of natural resources, and the protection of the environment.

The preamble to the treaty that established the WTO recognized that the organization should ensure "the optimal use of the world's resources in accordance with the objective of sustainable development."[53] This was a last-minute victory for environmentalists, although the statement is nonbinding. With this in mind, and with a desire to coordinate policies in the field of trade and the environment, when trade ministers approved the treaty and the other results of the Uruguay round of trade negotiations in Marrakech, Morocco, in April 1994, they also decided to begin a WTO work program on trade and environment. Their decision established the WTO's Committee on Trade and Environment (CTE) and ensured that the subject would have a place on the WTO agenda.

In November 2001, the WTO held its fourth ministerial conference in Doha, Qatar, and ministers agreed to set a new round of trade-liberalization negotiations in motion. They had attempted to start a new round of trade negotiations two years earlier, at the third ministerial conference in Seattle, Washington, but were unable to agree on the agenda amid protests by thousands of environmental, labor, and human rights activists against the WTO and its policies. The Doha Ministerial Declaration launched a broad-based round of multilateral trade negotiations on nine topics, eight of which were supposed to be completed as a single undertaking by 2005: implementation, agriculture, services, industrial tariffs, subsidies, anti-dumping, regional trade agreements, and the environment. The declaration contained more language on both economic development and environmental issues, including fishing subsidies, than any of its predecessors.

However, WTO member states failed to complete their negotiations in 2005, and the trade talks were formally declared to be at an impasse at the end of 2011. Soon after, a "small package" was agreed to at the ninth ministerial meeting in Bali in December 2013, built around trade facilitation (reducing the cost of trading, smoothing customs procedures, reducing red tape, and enhancing efficiency and transparency). This was the WTO's first multilateral pact in nearly twenty years. Although many were quick to note that the package agreed to in Bali represented just a fraction of the outstanding issues in the Doha round of negotiations—and skirted the most difficult ones—trade officials hoped that the achievement in Indonesia would have a much greater systemic value: that of reinstating confidence in the WTO's negotiating abilities.[54]

Two years later, at the tenth Ministerial Conference in Nairobi in December 2015, the WTO adopted the Nairobi Package, which contained ministerial decisions on agriculture, cotton, and issues related to LDCs. These included a commitment to abolish export subsidies for farm exports, which WTO Director-General Roberto Azevêdo hailed as the "most significant outcome on agriculture" in the organization's twenty-year history,[55] and preferential treatment for LDCs in the service sector and in the criteria for determining whether exports may benefit from trade preferences.[56] Despite these achievements, the text of the ministerial declaration showed that members were unable to overcome profound differences in other key areas:

> We recognize that many Members reaffirm the Doha Development Agenda, and the Declarations and Decisions adopted at Doha and at the Ministerial Conferences held since then, and reaffirm their full commitment to conclude the DDA [Doha Development Agenda] on that basis. Other Members do not reaffirm the Doha mandates, as they believe new approaches are necessary to achieve meaningful outcomes in multilateral negotiations. Members have different views on how to address the negotiations.[57]

Many countries have been so frustrated by the Doha stalemate that they have been negotiating bilateral and regional trade deals. For example, the United States concluded the Trans-Pacific Partnership with Japan, Vietnam, and nine other countries in early 2016 after seven years of negotiations. The United States and the European Union (EU) began negotiating the Transatlantic Trade and Investment

Partnership in 2013. China has signed many bilateral and regional agreements and in 2012 launched negotiations on a proposed a sixteen-country trade deal that would include India and Japan. Although regional agreements can be useful, they threaten to segregate the world into overlapping trading blocs with different rules, including for environmental protection. And most of these agreements—in which countries agree to eliminate tariffs for products made within the trading bloc—do not include the world's LDCs.[58]

According to some observers, it has become clear that the Doha negotiations are paralyzed because neither developed economies like the United States and the EU nor developing countries like China and India are willing or able to make fundamental concessions. At the start of the Doha round, American and European officials committed to producing a trade agreement that would promote development in poorer countries without asking them to reduce import barriers to the same extent as industrialized nations. But as developing countries, particularly China, began exporting far more than they were importing, wealthier countries started demanding that they also lower import barriers and cut subsidies to their farmers. Not surprisingly, China and India refused, insisting on sticking with the original principles.[59] Others put the blame on the developed countries, arguing that OECD countries are "keen to abandon the Doha Development Round . . . simply

PHOTO 6.2 NGOs calling on governments not to abandon the Doha Development Agenda at the World Trade Organization's tenth Ministerial Conference in December 2015. Photo © WTO. Courtesy Admedia Communication.

because the developed countries were not willing to give up on the massive agricultural subsidies that distort global trade."[60]

The following subsections examine some of the key issues along the trade-and-environment nexus, specifically, the relationship between environmental treaties and the WTO, how environmental issues have been dealt with in the dispute-settlement process, ecolabeling, standards and certification, subsidies and the environment, and liberalizing trade in environmental goods and services.

The Relationship Between Multilateral Environmental Agreements and the World Trade Organization

More than twenty multilateral environmental agreements (MEAs) incorporate trade measures to help them achieve their goals.[61] This means that the agreements use restraints, trade in particular substances or products, either among parties to the treaty, between parties and nonparties, or both. Although this represents a relatively small number of MEAs, they include some of the most important, including the Convention on International Trade in Endangered Species of Wild Fauna and Flora (CITES); the Montreal Protocol; the Basel, Rotterdam, and Stockholm Conventions; and the Cartagena Protocol on Biosafety. Under all of these treaties, trade in the specified products (e.g., endangered species, ODS, hazardous wastes, toxic chemicals, or genetically modified organisms) is banned or restricted among parties or between parties and nonparties (see Box 6.3).

Trade-restricting measures in an environmental agreement may serve one of two broad purposes. First, they may control a type of trade perceived to be a source of the environmental damage that the convention seeks to address. CITES, which requires import and export licenses for trade in endangered species, is a good example. The Basel Convention seeks to restrict or ban the movement and trade of hazardous waste, seeing such movement as a source of environmental harm. The Rotterdam Convention calls on parties to notify other parties before they export certain substances and allows parties to ban certain imports because the trade of toxic substances to countries unaware of their potential for harm can lead to environmental damage.

Second, environmental agreements may include trade measures as a means to ensure regime participation, compliance, and effectiveness. Some regimes use trade measures as an additional incentive to join and adhere to the MEA by barring nonparties from trading in restricted goods with parties. Nonparties to the Basel Convention, for example, cannot ship certain wastes to any party, nor can they import it from them. Some, like the Montreal Protocol, have provisions that allow parties to impose trade sanctions on countries found to have significantly violated regimes rules (to date, this has not been used in the ozone regime). Some

BOX 6.3 SELECTED MULTILATERAL ENVIRONMENTAL AGREEMENT TRADE MEASURES

CONVENTION ON INTERNATIONAL TRADE IN ENDANGERED SPECIES OF WILD FAUNA AND FLORA (CITES)

- Trade restrictions are invoked against parties and nonparties to protect listed species of animals and plants threatened with extinction and endangerment.
- A permit-and-listing system is used to prohibit the import or export of listed wildlife and wildlife products unless a scientific finding is made that the trade in question will not threaten the existence of the species.

MONTREAL PROTOCOL ON SUBSTANCES THAT DEPLETE THE OZONE LAYER

- Trade in ozone-depleting substances (ODS) with nonparties is prohibited unless the nonparty has demonstrated its full compliance with the control measures under the protocol.
- Trade provisions are used to encourage the phaseout of ODS and to discourage the establishment of pollution havens, in which parties shift their manufacturing capabilities to nonparties.

BASEL CONVENTION ON THE CONTROL OF TRANSBOUNDARY MOVEMENTS OF HAZARDOUS WASTES AND THEIR DISPOSAL

- Trade measures are used to limit the market for the transboundary movement and disposal of hazardous waste between Organization for Economic Cooperation and Development (OECD) and non-OECD countries.
- Parties must not permit hazardous waste or other wastes to be traded with a nonparty unless that party enters into a bilateral, multilateral, or regional agreement.

ROTTERDAM CONVENTION ON THE PRIOR INFORMED CONSENT PROCEDURE FOR CERTAIN HAZARDOUS CHEMICALS AND PESTICIDES IN INTERNATIONAL TRADE

- Parties can decide, from the convention's agreed-upon list of chemicals and pesticides, which ones they will not import.
- When trade in the controlled substances does take place, labeling and information requirements must be followed.
- If a party decides not to consent to imports of a specific chemical, it must also stop domestic production of the chemical for domestic use, as well as imports from nonparties.

CARTAGENA PROTOCOL ON BIOSAFETY

- Parties may restrict the import of some living modified organisms as part of a carefully specified risk-management procedure.
- Living modified organisms that will be intentionally released into the environment are subject to an advance informed-agreement procedure, and those destined for use as food, feed, or processing must be accompanied by identifying documents.

use trade restrictions as a means to enhance regime effectiveness, again by restricting trade in certain controlled substances (as a means to reinforce controls on production and use). This prevents leakage, that is, situations where nonparties or parties with exemptions simply increase production of a restricted good and ship it to the parties that have restricted their own production.[62]

The potential problem with using trade measures in MEAs is that they might conflict with WTO rules. An agreement that says parties can use trade restrictions against some countries (nonparties) but not against others (parties) could violate Articles I, III, and XI of the GATT (provisions addressing most-favored nations and national-treatment principles, as well as provisions on eliminating quantitative restrictions). Free-trade advocates worry that countries might use trade-restricting measures in an MEA as a means to seek economic gain or to reward friends and punish enemies rather than to protect the global environment. Environmentalists worry that countries affected by MEA trade restrictions might challenge their legitimacy before the WTO, which could weaken the MEA.

Most analysts argue that the latter is not particularly a problem when both countries involved are parties to the MEA. In such cases, both countries have voluntarily agreed to be bound by the MEA's rules, including the use of trade measures as spelled out in the agreement. However, problems can arise when the agreement spells out objectives only and leaves it to the parties to make domestic laws to achieve them. The Nagoya Protocol to the Convention on Biological Diversity (CBD) leaves it up to national governments to determine if changes are necessary to national patent laws for applicants to disclose the use of any traditional knowledge or genetic resources used in their invention. Although WTO members have expressed hope that disputes among parties might be settled within the MEAs themselves, a party complaining about the use of such nonspecific trade measures could choose to take its case to the WTO.[63]

The situation is further complicated if a party to an MEA uses trade measures in the agreement against a nonparty but both countries are WTO members. Here, the nonparty has not voluntarily agreed to be subject to the MEA's trade measures. As with party-to-party measures, the trade-restricting party may be violating the nonparty's rights under WTO rules, but here the nonparty might take the matter to the WTO even if the measures are spelled out specifically in the MEA.

This raises the crucial question of which regime, the MEA or the WTO, should be accorded primacy when they conflict. The relationship between the WTO and MEA trade measures has been part of the WTO CTE's agenda since its creation in 1995. The discussions, which are mandated by paragraphs 31 and 32 of the Doha Ministerial Declaration, address two main themes: the relationship between existing WTO rules and the specific trade obligations set out in MEAs and the collaboration between the WTO and MEA secretariats.[64] Thus far, the CTE has not made much progress on these issues, largely as a result of the overall state of the Doha round of trade negotiations. It remains to be seen if they can achieve an outcome that will equally benefit trade, the environment, and development.

Environmental Issues and the World Trade Organization Dispute Settlement System

Environmental policy increasingly affects, and is affected by, economic and trade policy. Consequently, it is not surprising that disputes between trade liberalization and environmental protection have increased in both number and diplomatic prominence. Indeed, the first case heard by the WTO Dispute Settlement Body involved an environmental dispute.[65]

An increasing number of domestic and international policies seek to regulate or restrict trade as a tool to address environmental problems. Such laws have been called environmental trade measures and include import prohibitions, product standards, standards governing production of natural resource exports, and mandatory ecolabeling schemes.[66] Exporters disadvantaged by such environmental measures sometimes charge that the policies are actually intended to protect domestic producers from foreign competition. Sometimes the exporting countries bring such complaints to the WTO's dispute-resolution panels.

The United States has taken the lead in defending the right to use environmental trade measures for domestic and international environmental objectives and has been the target of cases brought before WTO dispute panels. The United States used trade restrictions in conjunction with its lead-state efforts to end commercial whaling, to protect dolphins from being killed by tuna fishermen, to protect marine mammals from destructive drift nets, and to support CITES. For example, US threats to ban South Korean fish products from the US market and prohibit Korean fishing operations in US waters helped to persuade South Korea to give up both whaling and drift-net operations in the Pacific Ocean.[67] The United States banned wildlife-related exports from Taiwan in 1994 after that country violated CITES by failing to control imports of rhino horn and tiger bone. In 2015, the United States announced sweeping bans to trading ivory in the hopes of protecting the increasingly endangered African elephant. Although environmentalists see these as justifiable protections, less-powerful countries view the United States as throwing its weight around.

When a country believes that an environmental trade measure unfairly restricts market access, it can file a complaint, and a GATT/WTO dispute-resolution panel has the authority to determine whether a particular trade measure is or is not compatible with the GATT trade rules. The panels consist of trade specialists from three or five contracting parties with no stake in the issue and who have been agreed to by both parties to the dispute. Dispute panel rulings are normally submitted to the WTO Council (which includes all parties to the agreement) for approval. Decisions carry real weight. If a country fails to bring its law into conformity with the decision, other states are allowed to implement retaliatory trade measures. This is more threatening to small countries than large trading countries such as the United States. Few small countries will risk taking significant retaliatory measures on their own against the United States or the EU, as these could prove counterproductive.[68]

Domestic US laws that use trade measures to pursue environmental goals have been challenged before the GATT/WTO dispute-resolution panels on several occasions. The first panel decision, on the US–Mexican tuna–dolphin dispute, helped to shape the politics of trade-and-environment issues.

In 1991 Mexico filed a complaint with the GATT charging that a US embargo against Mexican yellowfin tuna was a protectionist measure put in place to benefit the US tuna industry. The embargo had been imposed under an amendment to the 1972 Marine Mammal Protection Act, which allowed for the use of trade sanctions against countries that killed too many dolphins while catching tuna (the Mexican fleet killed dolphins at twice the rate of the US fleet). The Mexican complaint to the GATT argued that the amendment was simply a measure to protect the US tuna fleet and that US measures should not be allowed to apply to activities by other countries in international waters (where most tuna is caught). More broadly, Mexico, supported by Venezuela, asked why it should forgo export earnings and a low-cost source of protein for its own people to reduce the incidental impact on a marine mammal that was not an endangered species.[69]

The GATT panel ruled that the US ban was a violation of the GATT because it was concerned only with the process of tuna fishing rather than with the product. It also ruled that Article XX of the GATT, which allows trade restrictions for human health or the conservation of animal or plant life, could not justify an exception to that rule because the article does not apply beyond US jurisdiction, that is, in international waters. This was a historic decision. It also reflected the tendency of most trade specialists to view restrictions on trade for environmental purposes as setting dangerous precedents that could harm the world trade system. That eight governments or agencies spoke against the US tuna ban before the panel and not one party spoke for it may also have had an influence.[70]

After the victory, Mexico hoped its products would reach American markets without prejudice; it was mistaken. For a while, it looked like the United States would impose the labeling standard established by the subsequent 1995 Agreement on the International Dolphin Conservation Program—no dolphins killed or seriously injured. In fact, the US Department of Commerce was ready to modify its labeling criteria accordingly until national conservation groups launched a massive public relations campaign against the proposed new standard. The groups claimed that tuna fishing using the purse seine method, regardless of the modifications, continued to adversely affect dolphins in the eastern Pacific Ocean. Eventually no changes were made, and the United States continued to exclude tuna fished with purse seine nets from its dolphin-safe label.[71]

Frustrated with Washington's failure to comply with the bilaterally agreed-upon tuna labeling standard and what it saw as a de facto embargo on its tuna products, Mexico requested consultations with the United States at the WTO in October 2008. Mexico argued that, although it can legally import its tuna products into the United States, without the label it cannot, in reality, sell its products there. In essence, Mexico invoked the WTO Agreements in support of a successful MEA, in particular of its sustainable fishing practices provisions.[72] On September 8, 2011, the WTO ruled that the US dolphin-safe labeling practice for tuna products—which was meant to inform consumers on the use of dolphin-friendly fishing practices—was unnecessarily trade restrictive and thus WTO illegal. However, the three-member panel disagreed with Mexico that the label also discriminated against Mexican tuna on the basis of nationality.

Both the United States and Mexico appealed, and in May 2012, the WTO's highest court ruled that the US dolphin-safe label violates WTO law by discriminating against Mexican tuna. However, rather than a ruling against dolphins, the Appellate Body largely sided with the arguments of pro-dolphin groups. The point of criticism was not necessarily the high standards used vis-à-vis Mexican products but rather the low standards used vis-à-vis all other products. The judges specifically criticized the low standards for being unable to guarantee that non-Mexican products eligible for the label were, in fact, fished in a dolphin-safe manner.[73]

Two other environmental complaints that have been brought under WTO dispute settlement rules are worth noting because of their precedent-setting nature. In the Venezuela reformulated-gasoline case, Venezuela and Brazil claimed they were discriminated against by a US Environmental Protection Agency rule under the Clean Air Act that required all refineries to make cleaner gasoline using the 1990 US industry standard as a baseline. Because fuel from foreign refineries was not as clean in 1990 as that from US refineries, the importing countries were beginning their cleanup efforts from a different starting point. In 1997, the WTO panel ruled in favor of Venezuela and Brazil, and the Environmental Protection Agency revised its rules.[74]

In a second case, in January 1997, India, Malaysia, Pakistan, and Thailand charged that a US ban on the importation of shrimp caught by vessels that kill endangered migratory sea turtles violated WTO rules that no nation can use trade restrictions to influence the (fishing) rules of other countries. The United States argued that relatively simple and inexpensive turtle-excluder devices (TEDs) can be placed on shrimp trawlers to save the turtles. To implement the US Endangered Species Act, the US Court of International Trade, in response to a lawsuit brought by an NGO, the Earth Island Institute, ruled in December 1995 that in order to export mechanically caught marine shrimp to the United States, countries that trawl for shrimp in waters where marine turtles live must, from June 1996, be certified by the US government to have equipped their vessels with TEDs. TEDs have been mandatory on all US shrimp trawlers since December 1994. If properly installed and operated, TEDs, while minimizing loss of the shrimp catch, permit most sea turtles to escape from shrimp trawling nets before they drown. The United States argued that the trade measure was necessary because sea turtles were threatened with extinction and the use of TEDs on shrimp nets was the only way to effectively protect them from drowning in shrimp nets.

In April 1998, the WTO dispute-settlement panel held that the US import ban on shrimp was "clearly a threat to the multilateral trading system" and consequently was "not within the scope of measures permitted under the chapeau of Article XX." The United States appealed the decision. In October 1998, the appellate body found that the US ban legitimately related to the "protection of exhaustible natural resources" and thus qualified for provisional justification under Article XX(g). This decision represented a step forward for the use of unilateral trade measures for environmental purposes. But the decision also found that the US import ban was applied in an unjustifiably or arbitrarily discriminatory manner and cited seven distinct flaws in the legislation. It found, for example, that the requirement that exporters adopt "essentially the same policy" as that applied by the United States had an unjustifiably "coercive effect" on foreign countries. It also found that the United States had not seriously attempted to reach a multilateral solution with the four complaining countries and that the process for certification of turtle protection programs was not "transparent" or "predictable."[75]

The ruling left open the possibility that a unilaterally imposed trade ban in response to foreign environmental practices could be implemented in compliance with the GATT. But some trade law experts believed the procedural criteria in the ruling were unrealistic. The case once again underlined the question of whether a WTO panel, which lacks both environmental expertise and mandate, should pass judgment on trade measures for environmental purposes.

In response to the appellate body decision, the United States adjusted its policy. The revised guidelines still prohibit the import of shrimp harvested with technology adversely affecting the relevant sea turtle species. But instead of requiring the use of TEDs, it allowed the exporting country to present evidence that its program to protect sea turtles in the course of shrimp trawling was comparable in effectiveness with the US program. The guidelines note, however, that the Department of State is not aware of technology as effective as the TED.[76]

Ecolabeling, Standards, and Certification

Ecolabels—labeling products according to environmental criteria by governments, industry, and NGOs—help consumers exercise preferences for environmentally sound production methods, such as wood harvested from sustainably managed forests rather than clear-cutting, fish caught from sustainable fisheries, or tuna caught with methods that do not kill large numbers of dolphins. Although some ecolabels are conferred by product firms themselves or by trade associations, the ones with the most credibility are third-party ecolabels awarded by independent entities that use clear and consistent criteria to evaluate the process and production methods by which a product is made, grown, or caught. Some governments sponsor ecolabel programs, but some of the most important are private, voluntary schemes. Third-party ecolabels have already demonstrated their potential for attracting the attention of producers where international policy making has failed, as shown by the case of the Forest Stewardship Council (FSC) and timber products.

Certification and labeling became an international issue after the establishment in 1993 of FSC, an independent NGO that created the world's first third-party ecolabeling scheme for wood products. By 1995, FSC had begun setting standards for sustainable forest management and criteria for potential certifiers to meet and had released a label to show that a product has been certified by FSC standards—harvesting trees in a way that protects water, soil, indigenous rights, and wildlife, as well as ensuring reforestation and good community and labor relations. FSC hoped to create a market for certified forest products among consumers and to use that market to leverage more sustainable forest management. Today, FSC's governing body comprises more than eight hundred member organizations and individuals equally divided among environmental, social, and economic voting chambers. FSC members include environmental organizations such as WWF, Greenpeace, and Friends of the Earth, as well as companies such as IKEA and Home Depot.

FSC has the support of a large and growing number of companies that have united themselves in various countries into buyers' groups committed to selling only independently certified timber and timber products. This unprecedented alliance resulted in arguably greater levels of dialogue and progress than the formal international negotiations on forests and began to change forest-management practices worldwide. As of January 2016, more than 186 million hectares of forested land were FSC certified in eighty countries around the world—the equivalent of more than 10 percent of the world's production forests. FSC works with one hundred fifty thousand small holders around the world and is increasingly working with indigenous groups who live in and around certified forests.[77]

Similarly, the London-based Marine Stewardship Council (MSC) has developed a standard for sustainable and well-managed fisheries and uses a product label to recognize and reward environmentally responsible practices. Consumers concerned about overfishing can choose seafood products that have been independently assessed against the MSC standard and labeled to prove it. The MSC was developed in 1997 by WWF, an environmental NGO, and Unilever, the world's largest buyer of seafood. It has operated independently since 1999. As of 2015, 265 fisheries had been certified, representing more than 12 percent of global wild fisheries' production for human consumption. Nearly one hundred fisheries have been added in the previous three years alone. Another forty to fifty fisheries are currently undergoing assessment. Worldwide, more than twenty thousand seafood products bear the blue MSC ecolabel, ranging from fresh, frozen, smoked, and canned fish to fish-oil dietary supplements. This amounts to more than $4.8 billion in global annual sales, all of which can be traced back to certified sustainable fisheries.[78] However, it is worth noting that the annual world trade in fish and fishery products is about $136 billion,[79] and MSC proponents understand there is a very long way to go to ensure sustainable fish production.

In addition to FSC and the MSC, there are more than four hundred different types of ecolabels. The large number can certainly confuse consumers regarding which systems are the most valid (see Figure 6.3). Although FSC, MSC, and some other initiatives have proven quite successful, ecolabeling systems do have the potential to be unfair and discriminatory. Consequently, labeling and related issues are under discussion within several WTO bodies.[80]

FIGURE 6.3 **Examples of Ecolabels**

Forest Stewardship Council

WaterSense

Marine Stewardship Council

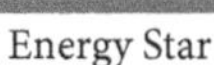
Energy Star

EU Ecolabel

In May 2012, the WTO's highest court issued its first-ever ruling on ecolabeling. The court ruled that the US dolphin-safe label violates WTO law by discriminating against Mexican tuna. The judgment was immediately lambasted by environmentalists and US consumer advocates who saw the judgment as an attack on US dolphin protection. The judges specifically criticized the US law for being unable to guarantee that non-Mexican products eligible for the label were, in fact, fished in a dolphin-safe manner. Thus, the label violated the WTO's Technical Barriers to Trade Agreement, which states that regulations must be implemented in a nondiscriminatory manner, treating foreign products no less favorably than domestic products. With this ruling, other labels, such as those pertaining to organic food, may have entered the realm of WTO law.[81]

Some countries are hostile to particular private ecolabeling schemes because they threaten to reduce markets for a domestic industry guilty of unsustainable practices. Both developed and developing countries have also expressed more justifiable concerns about some ecolabeling schemes that appear skewed in favor of domestic producers and against foreign competitors. This type of ecolabeling scheme conveys an advantage to a domestic industry by virtually mandating a particular technology or production process, ignoring that another technology or process may be equally or more environmentally sound and more suitable in the country of origin. The transparency of official and private voluntary ecolabeling schemes and the ability of affected exporters to participate in their development is yet another North–South issue in the WTO.

Subsidies and the Environment

Another important issue on the trade-and-environment agenda is what the CTE calls "the environmental benefits of removing trade restrictions and distortions"—a diplomatic euphemism for eliminating subsidies that harm the environment. A subsidy may be defined as any government-directed intervention that, whether through budgeted programs or other means, transfers resources to a particular economic group. Subsidies distort markets by sending signals to producers and consumers that fail to reflect the true costs of production, thus misallocating financial and natural resources. Subsidies on goods traded internationally also give unfair advantages to exports that are subsidized over others.

Subsidies can have negative impacts on the environment, especially in the commodity sectors (e.g., agriculture, forests, fossil fuels, fisheries, and mining). They draw more investment into these sectors and exacerbate the overexploitation of land, forests, water, and fish. They also reduce the cost of particular practices, products, or technologies that harm the environment, such as flood irrigation, mining, fossil-fuel extraction and use, or excessive use of pesticides.[82]

Fisheries subsidies are one of the factors that have led to massive overfishing (see Chapter 4). Estimated at $35 billion per year worldwide[83] (roughly 25 percent of the value of global fish catches), fishing subsidies not only negatively affect the world's fish stocks but also harm developing countries as they confront the excess capacity exported from the mostly depleted fisheries of richer countries. The global fishing fleet ballooned in the past forty years, and government subsidies (for boats, fuel, materials, or fish catch) contributed to this growth.[84]

Since the establishment of the WTO, some members have focused on the elimination of fisheries subsidies as possibly the greatest contribution the multilateral trading system could make to sustainable development. In particular, the lead-state coalition known as the Friends of Fish (Argentina, Australia, Chile, Colombia, Costa Rica, Ecuador, Iceland, New Zealand, Norway, Pakistan, Peru, Philippines, United States) have pointed to the win-win-win nature of such action: good for the environment, good for development, and good for trade. Their major argument is that subsidies are at least partly responsible for the alarming depletion of many fish stocks because much of the money is spent on commissioning new vessels or enhancing the efficiency of older boats.[85] But a veto coalition consisting of heavily subsidizing members (the EU, Japan, and South Korea) have argued that the empirical evidence that eliminating subsidies would benefit the environment was still weak. Japan and South Korea insisted that poor fisheries management, rather than subsidies, was the root cause of stock depletion.

The Doha Ministerial Declaration explicitly called for negotiations aimed at clarifying and improving WTO rules on fisheries subsidies. At the December 2005 WTO ministerial conference in Hong Kong, governments called on the WTO Negotiating Group on Rules to "strengthen disciplines on subsidies in the fisheries sector, including through the prohibition of certain forms of fisheries subsidies that contribute to overcapacity and over-fishing."[86] Since 2005, however, progress has been minimal. At the 2015 WTO ministerial conference in Nairobi, governments were once again unable to clinch a deal on fisheries subsidies. However, a group of WTO members did release a ministerial statement on fisheries subsidies pledging to reinvigorate WTO work in order to achieve ambitious and effective disciplines on fisheries subsidies, a move welcomed by conservation groups.[87]

Liberalizing Trade in Environmental Goods and Services

The final trade-and-environment issue to be discussed here is that of liberalizing trade in environmental goods and services. The 2001 Doha Ministerial Declaration instructs WTO members to negotiate the reduction or elimination of tariff and nontariff barriers on environmental goods and services. The WTO emphasizes that these negotiations will facilitate trade and economic development because domestic purchasers will be able to acquire environmental technologies from foreign companies at lower costs. The environment will benefit because of the wider availability of less-expensive products and technologies, which in turn will improve the quality of life by providing better access to clean water, sanitation, and clean energy. Finally, the liberalization of trade in environmental goods and services will help developing countries obtain the tools they need to address key environmental priorities as part of their ongoing development strategies.[88]

So what are environmental goods and services? And which ones should be the targets for easing trade restrictions? These are not straightforward issues. According to the OECD, "the environmental goods and services industry consists of activities which produce goods and services to measure, prevent, limit, minimize or correct environmental damage to water, air and soil, as well as problems related to waste, noise and ecosystems. This includes cleaner technologies, products and services that reduce environmental risk and minimize pollution and resource use."[89] Total global trade in environmental goods reached roughly $955 billion in 2012, according to US data, with tariffs on some products as high as 35 percent.[90]

Although it is useful to understand what these categories are, they have not been universally accepted by all WTO members. Indeed, the difficulty of defining environmental goods and services for the purposes of reducing trade barriers has plagued the negotiations. Many states have provided lists of proposed environmental goods for tariff reductions. Proposals put forward thus far cover several broad categories, including air pollution control, renewable energy, waste management, water treatment, environmental technologies, and carbon capture and storage.

A breakthrough came in July 2014 when a group of countries accounting for nearly 90 percent of global trade in environmental goods announced that they would negotiate an Environmental Goods Agreement. By May 2015, these countries had a compiled list of more than six hundred fifty tariff lines and more than two thousand products. Although the compiled product list has not been publicly available, the nominations cover a range of environmental categories, including goods related to cleaner and renewable energy (solar panels, wind turbines), energy efficiency, air pollution control (soot removers and catalytic converters), environmental monitoring and analysis (air and water quality monitors), and solid and hazardous waste management (waste incinerators, crushing and sorting machinery, and wastewater treatment [filters and disinfection equipment]), among others.[91]

The initial Environmental Goods Agreement group—including Australia, Canada, China, Costa Rica, the EU, Hong Kong, Japan, Korea, New Zealand, Norway, Singapore, Switzerland, Chinese Taipei, and the United States—were joined in 2015 by Iceland, Israel, and Turkey. Several officials had hoped to hammer out key points of the Environmental Goods Agreement deal in time for the WTO's tenth ministerial conference in December 2015. However, members ran into difficulties in early December over the list of goods. With talks scheduled to resume in 2016, participants hope to clinch a deal in the near future.[92]

The negotiations on reducing trade barriers for environmental goods and services could have an impact on several MEAs. Their outcome could affect the availability of technologies to replace ODS and persistent organic pollutants under the Montreal Protocol and Stockholm Convention, respectively. They could improve the availability of technologies for the environmentally sound management of hazardous wastes under the Basel Convention or reduce mercury emissions under the Minamata Convention. They could increase the availability and lower the cost of green energy and energy-efficiency technologies to help countries implement their commitments under the UN Framework Convention on Climate Change (UNFCCC) Paris Agreement. Trade liberalization could also contribute toward fulfilling the technology-transfer mandates contained in the UNFCCC and similar provisions in other MEAs.

The Outlook for Trade and Environment

Many of the issues described in this chapter are likely to remain on the trade-and-environment agenda for many years, including the relationship between trade rules and MEAs, ecolabels, reduction of fisheries, energy and agricultural subsidies, and liberalization of trade in environmental goods and services. The roles that developing countries and NGOs play within the context of the WTO will continue to evolve, as will the emphasis given to the relationship between trade and environment.

BALANCING THE ENVIRONMENTAL AND SUSTAINABLE DEVELOPMENT AGENDAS

For decades, governments, NGOs, the UN system, and other actors have been trying to operationalize sustainable development and determine just how to balance its three dimensions. Although the Brundtland Commission and the Rio Earth Summit put sustainable development on the international agenda, the environmental, social development, and economic development agendas have still not coalesced into a single sustainable development agenda.

The World Summit on Sustainable Development

These issues came to a head at the World Summit on Sustainable Development (WSSD) in Johannesburg, South Africa, in 2002, held ten years after the Rio Earth Summit to map out a detailed course of action for the further implementation of

Agenda 21. The summit produced three key outcomes. The first was the Johannesburg Declaration, a pledge by world leaders to commit their countries to the goal of sustainable development. The second was the Johannesburg Plan of Implementation, which set out a comprehensive program of action for sustainable development, including quantifiable goals and targets with fixed deadlines. Third, the summit produced nearly three hundred voluntary partnerships and other initiatives to support sustainable development.

Yet, among all of the targets, timetables, and partnerships agreed on at Johannesburg, there were no silver-bullet solutions to aid the fight against poverty and a deteriorating natural environment. In fact, as an implementation-focused summit, Johannesburg did not produce a particularly dramatic outcome—no agreements emerged that led to new treaties, and many of the agreed-upon targets had already been agreed on at the Millennium Assembly and other meetings—and did not carry the legal status of a binding treaty. As then UN secretary-general Kofi Annan told the press on the summit's last day, "I think we have to be careful not to expect conferences like this to produce miracles. But we do expect conferences like this to generate political commitment, momentum and energy for the attainment of the goals."[93]

The United Nations Conference on Sustainable Development

Ten years later, in June 2012, the eyes of the world turned to Rio for another global event. The UN Conference on Sustainable Development (UNCSD, also referred to as Rio+20) sought to secure renewed political commitment for sustainable development, assess both the progress made to date and the remaining gaps in implementing the outcomes of the major sustainable development summits, and address new and emerging challenges. Delegates pursued these goals under the umbrella of the two conference themes: a green economy in the context of sustainable development and poverty eradication (see Chapter 1), and the institutional framework necessary for sustainable development.

With regard to the institutional framework for sustainable development, Rio+20 took a step that will affect sustainable development policy for years to come: the call for defining a set of SDGs to help provide a "concrete approach that delivers means for measuring—in accordance with the contexts and priorities of each country—both advances as well as bottlenecks in efforts to balance sustained socioeconomic growth with the sustainable use of natural resources and the conservation of ecosystem services."[94] With the MDGs expiring in 2015, the UN and governments had already begun discussions on what would come next and guide international development policy for the subsequent fifteen years. Many agreed that the MDG experience demonstrated that when concrete objectives exist to

PHOTO 6.3 The UN projected the seventeen Sustainable Development Goals on its headquarters building during the Sustainable Development Summit in September 2015. Courtesy Pamela Chasek.

guide the international community toward a collective goal, it becomes easier for governments, international organizations, NGOs, foundations, and interested corporations to work together to reach them.

Supporters also believed that the SDGs approach would generate additional benefits and could play a useful role in guiding public policies. In the end, the Rio+20 outcome document, titled *The Future We Want,* agreed that countries would collectively develop "sustainable development goals [that] should be action oriented, concise and easy to communicate, limited in number, aspirational, global in nature and universally applicable to all countries while taking into account different national realities, capacities and levels of development and respecting national policies and priorities.[95]

The Sustainable Development Goals

The UN began the process of developing the SDGs (also known as the Global Goals for Sustainable Development) in early 2013. Unlike the MDGs, which were crafted by a group of UN experts under the guidance of the UN secretary-general, the SDGs were negotiated by governments in an Open Working Group that met thirteen times between March 2013 and July 2014. Although governments knew that it would be inherently difficult to negotiate a set of goals as concise as the MDGs, they had a larger agenda. The SDGs were intended both to be universal—in other words, an agenda that recognizes shared national and global challenges among all countries (not just developing countries)—and to offer a paradigm shift away from outdated development assumptions of the past.

Following the conclusion of the Open Working Group in July 2014, a process was established to reach final agreement on the SDGs and the broader post-2015 development agenda. These negotiations began in January 2015 and concluded in early August 2015 with the provisional adoption of the document *Transforming Our World: The 2030 Agenda for Sustainable Development*. The agenda, with the SDGs and targets as the cornerstone, also contains a declaration and sections on means of implementation, follow-up, and review.[96]

The 2030 Agenda for Sustainable Development was formally adopted at a summit of heads of state and government at UN Headquarters in New York in September 2015. Already, numerous governments, UN agencies, international organizations, and NGOs are adjusting their programs and plans to conform to the SDGs.

The 17 SDGs and 169 targets (see Box. 6.4) seek to end poverty and hunger and achieve sustainable development in its three dimensions by promoting inclusive economic growth, protecting the environment, and promoting social inclusion. The SDGs also encompass human rights, gender equality, women's and girls' empowerment, and peaceful and inclusive societies. And, as often repeated throughout the negotiations, unlike the MDGs, the SDGs are supposed to ensure that no country or person is left behind. The MDGs did not have to deal with these challenges because they focused on economic and social issues in developing countries and gave limited attention to the structural causes of poverty and sustainable development, including inequality, pollution, and resource scarcity.

Like the MDGs and previous sustainable development action plans and programs, the SDGs have been subject to criticism. Some governments and NGOs

BOX 6.4 THE SUSTAINABLE DEVELOPMENT GOALS

1. **End poverty in all its forms everywhere**
2. **End hunger, achieve food security and improved nutrition, and promote sustainable agriculture**
3. **Ensure healthy lives and promote well-being for all at all ages**
4. **Ensure inclusive and equitable quality education and promote lifelong learning opportunities for all**
5. **Achieve gender equality and empower all women and girls**
6. **Ensure availability and sustainable management of water and sanitation for all**
7. **Ensure access to affordable, reliable, sustainable, and modern energy for all**
8. **Promote sustained, inclusive, and sustainable economic growth, full and productive employment, and decent work for all**
9. **Build resilient infrastructure, promote inclusive and sustainable industrialization, and foster innovation**
10. **Reduce inequality within and among countries**
11. **Make cities and human settlements inclusive, safe, resilient, and sustainable**
12. **Ensure sustainable consumption and production patterns**
13. **Take urgent action to combat climate change and its impacts (taking note of agreements made by the UN Framework Convention on Climate Change)**
14. **Conserve and sustainably use the oceans, seas, and marine resources for sustainable development**
15. **Protect, restore and promote sustainable use of terrestrial ecosystems, sustainably manage forests, combat desertification and halt and reverse land degradation, and halt biodiversity loss**
16. **Promote peaceful and inclusive societies for sustainable development, provide access to justice for all, and build effective, accountable, and inclusive institutions at all levels**
17. **Strengthen the means of implementation and revitalize the global partnership for sustainable development**

Source: UN, *Transforming Our World: The 2030 Agenda for Sustainable Development* (New York: UN, 2015), http://sustainabledevelopment.un.org/content/documents/7891 TRANSFORMING%20OUR%20WORLD.pdf.

have complained that seventeen goals are too unwieldy to implement or sell to the public as policy priorities. Some critics argue that the 169 specific targets are a recipe for failure: an agenda adopted with great fanfare in September 2015 only to be quickly forgotten, sitting on a bookshelf, gathering dust.[97] Others have noted that the number of SDGs and derivative targets show what happens when a bureaucratic process runs out of control: "The organisers sought to consult as widely as possible, with the result that each country and aid lobbyist got a target for its particular bugbear. . . . Something for everyone has produced too much for anyone."[98]

Many others believe that the number of goals is necessary because they reflect the complexity and interconnectedness of today's social, economic, and environmental challenges. From this perspective, it is better to have seventeen goals and numerous targets that include action on women's empowerment, climate change, the environment, good governance, and peace and security, for example, than fewer goals that do not address these issues. To achieve truly sustainable development, these challenges must be addressed in an integrated way. It does not make any sense to try to reduce extreme poverty while ignoring the role that the environment and good governance play in building prosperity.[99]

As for the wide-ranging consultations, unlike the MDGs, the SDGs are deliberately the product of a more grassroots process, which began with input from a broader range of advocacy groups, everyday citizens, and governments than ever before, marking a paradigm shift.[100] Furthermore, the political inclusivity of the negotiating process and the breadth of the resulting goals recognize that governments alone cannot achieve sustainable development. It requires the participation of businesses and civil society as well as the political commitment of world leaders.

Other questions about the SDGs and the 2030 Agenda remain. Although the SDGs are universal and therefore apply to all countries, there are ongoing debates regarding what this means in practice. Developing countries consistently stress that, although the SDGs are universally relevant to all countries, the roles and responsibilities in their implementation should be differentiated with respect to national realities, capacities, levels of development, policies, and priorities, reflecting the principle of CBDR.[101] There are also questions regarding financing and the relationship between public and private sources of finance and whether the developed countries will bear most of the cost.

The Addis Ababa Action Agenda

There is no doubt that the question of financing the implementation of the SDGs was front and center during their negotiation and the formulation of the 2030 Agenda. However, delegates did not delve into this in depth until the final negotiating session because there was, in parallel with the negotiations of the 2030

Agenda, another set of negotiations leading up to the third International Conference on Financing for Development (FfD3), which took place in Addis Ababa, Ethiopia, in July 2015.

Ffd3 followed two previous conferences on financing for development, which took place in Monterrey, Mexico, in 2002 and in Doha, Qatar, in 2008. The former, which adopted the Monterrey Consensus, was the first UN-sponsored summit-level meeting to address key financial and related issues pertaining to global development.[102] The 2008 conference adopted the Doha Declaration, which recognized that mobilizing financial resources for development and the effective use of all of those resources were central to the global partnership for sustainable development.[103] FfD3 was convened to assess the progress made in the implementation of the Monterrey Consensus and the Doha Declaration, address new and emerging issues, reinvigorate and strengthen the financing for development follow-up process, and support the UN development agenda beyond 2015.[104]

The resulting Addis Ababa Action Agenda (AAAA) includes more than one hundred measures that will, if implemented, result in policies to enable and direct financial investments by both the public and private sectors to meet an array of sustainable development challenges.[105] Areas of focus include commitments to direct finance to social protection, invest in sustainable and resilient infrastructure, improve access to technology, assist the poorest countries, cooperate on tax issues, and address illicit financial flows that take resources away from development. Notably, in the AAAA, countries committed themselves to pursue the equal rights and opportunities of women and girls in the economy.[106]

With regard to the financing needs to achieve the 2030 Agenda, which could amount to trillions of dollars annually, the AAAA presents a policy framework that attempts to realign financial flows with sustainable development. It calls for mobilizing public finance, setting appropriate public policies and regulatory frameworks, unlocking the transformative potential of people and the private sector, and incentivizing changes in consumption, production, and investment patterns in support of sustainable development. To this end, the AAAA reiterates that countries have primary responsibility for their economic and social development, while committing the international community to create an enabling environment for development. The AAAA goes beyond the 2002 Monterrey Consensus to fully take into account the policy requirements for realizing all three dimensions—economic, social, and environmental—of sustainable development in an integrated manner to help support the implementation of the SDGs. The AAAA also emphasizes that development and dissemination of technology, as well as capacity building, are key means of implementation for the 2030 Agenda, and it incorporates each of the means of implementation targets of the SDGs.[107]

Although the 2030 Agenda recognizes that the full implementation of the AAAA is critical for the realization of the SDGs, not everyone was pleased with the outcome in Addis Ababa. Members of civil society complained that the AAAA did not sufficiently tackle structural injustices in the current global economic system and ensure that development finance is people centered and protects the environment. As they said, "We regret that the negotiations have diminished the FfD mandate to address international systemic issues in macroeconomic, financial, trade, tax, and monetary policies, while also failing to scale up existing resources and commit new financial ones."[108] Similarly, others noted that although developing countries managed to inscribe references to international coordination and financial and technical support in areas like fighting corruption and illicit finance, scaling up infrastructure investments, and knowledge and technology transfer, developed countries often pushed back firmly against the creation of new and potentially costly institutional mechanisms and partnerships for the SDGs.[109] This could make it more difficult for developing countries to mobilize sufficient tax and other revenues to put toward their own sustainable development.

CONCLUSION

The evolution of global environmental politics cannot be understood completely outside the context of the three dimensions of sustainable development. The perception held by many developing countries that global economic relations are fundamentally inequitable often shapes their policy responses to global environmental issues and related negotiating strategies. As the linkages between environmental issues and economic and social development have multiplied, the boundaries of global environmental politics have broadened and now sometimes include the politics of economic and social development. The difficulty of sorting through environmental and development priorities carries through to the trade arena, where it has been challenging for countries to achieve a broadly acceptable balance between free trade and environmental protection within the context of the WTO, including on issues as diverse as endangered-species protection, fisheries subsidies, and environmental goods and services, to name but a few.

Despite the apparent tension among economic, social, and environmental goals in both developed and developing countries, many respected observers argue that in the long run economic health depends on social and ecological health. The SDGs may mark a coordinated effort toward realizing a world where people, planet, prosperity, peace, and partnership come together. Through the SDGs, all countries pledge to take action both within their own borders and in support of wider international efforts. For the first time, a UN development plan recognizes the interlinkages among sustainability of ecosystem services, poverty eradication, economic development, and human well-being.

However, one has to ask if the new global goals actually have the potential to operationalize sustainable development. Although the goals contain elements of the three dimensions of sustainability, most of them are still presented using a silo approach—that is, they are addressed as separate elements, mostly in isolation from each other. However, in practice many goal areas will overlap, many targets may contribute to several goals, and some goals may actually conflict. Because the SDG framework does not reflect interlinkages and cannot ensure that development takes place within sustainable levels of resource use at either the global or regional scale, it is possible that the framework as a whole may not be internally consistent—and as a result not be sustainable.[110]

Nevertheless, as the preamble to *Transforming Our World: The 2030 Agenda for Sustainable Development* states, "We are resolved to free the human race from the tyranny of poverty and want and to heal and secure our planet." It continues, "We are determined to take the bold and transformative steps which are urgently needed to shift the world onto a sustainable and resilient path. As we embark on this collective journey, we pledge that no one will be left behind."[111]

If the public and policymakers accept and work toward this new sustainable development agenda, it is possible that the economic, social, and cultural changes will be made to support sustainable development at the community, national, and global levels. If this premise is correct, then the key questions might be, "Do governments have the political will to make this shift?" and "Do the people of the world have the will to accept, or even demand, the necessary change?"[112]

7

The Future of Global Environmental Politics

As 2015 began, many agreed that it would be a big year for the environment and sustainable development. At United Nations (UN) Headquarters in New York, governments were finalizing negotiations on what would become the 2030 Agenda for Sustainable Development, including the Sustainable Development Goals (SDGs). Climate negotiators knew they needed to reach consensus on a new agreement by year's end in Paris or risk the demise of the UN Framework Convention on Climate Change (UNFCCC). Other officials were planning to gather in July in Addis Ababa, Ethiopia, for the Third International Conference on Financing for Development to seek agreement on the means to implement the SDGs and the new sustainable development agenda. There was also a full complement of conferences and meetings to review implementation and perhaps strengthen existing multilateral environmental agreements (MEAs) on biodiversity, endangered species, migratory species, desertification, ozone depletion, toxic chemicals, and hazardous wastes. Finally, negotiations were in the planning stages on potential new agreements on hydrofluorocarbons (HFCs) under the Montreal Protocol and on marine biodiversity in areas beyond national jurisdiction under the UN Convention on the Law of the Sea.

Yet amidst this flurry of activity, concern remained that environmental multilateralism was waning. Nearly forty-five years after the UN first addressed the human environment at the Stockholm Conference and nearly twenty-five years after the first Rio Earth Summit, the optimism surrounding the promise of a paradigm shift to sustainable development had faded for some, and others had become downright pessimistic. The excitement of negotiating new treaties had been replaced by implementation battles over financial and technical assistance (FTA), accountability, additionality, the application of the principle of common but differentiated responsibilities (CBDR), and other issues. As revealed by the *Global Environment Outlook* report, the fifth issued by the UN Environment Programme (UNEP), multilateral environmental policy had failed to reverse, or even slow down, many of the most threatening global environmental trends, including climate change and biodiversity loss. As the report states:

> Neither the scope of environmental policy nor the speed of its implementation has been sufficient. Efforts to reduce the pressures from the underlying drivers—including enhanced resource efficiency and climate mitigation measures—may have resulted in moderate successes but have fundamentally failed to reduce environmental problems on a global scale.[1]

At the same time, the stakes continue to increase. In addition to the global macrotrends presented in Chapter 1, the economic costs of environmental degradation continue to grow. Many global environmental regimes still require significant change, in particular economic and social development strategies and production techniques, to be effective. Aspects of globalization and trade liberalization create incentives that negatively impact the effectiveness of certain global environmental policies. The ambitious global environmental agenda is arguably in danger of being overwhelmed by economic and political forces that, in their current form, threaten the health of the planet.

This concluding chapter examines the challenges of global environmental governance in a changing international system and how the institutional structure has evolved to meet these challenges. We conclude by returning to the concepts of paradigm shift as we look toward the future.

GLOBAL ENVIRONMENTAL GOVERNANCE IN A CHANGING INTERNATIONAL SYSTEM

Since the 1970s, the world has seen an unprecedented level of international activity and cooperation on environmental issues.[2] More governments and nonstate actors are active participants in environmental politics than in any other global issue area. The proliferation of MEAs represents an achievement in international diplomacy. However, activity does not necessarily produce success, cooperation does not necessarily lead to effective action, and past accomplishments do not necessarily mean greater achievements in the future. What occurs in the future will depend in part on how global environmental politics intersects with the complex realities of the twenty-first century.

The first of these complex realities involves the broad changes in the international system. The East–West Cold War politics that dominated the 1972 Stockholm Conference were replaced by a North–South dynamic at the 1992 Rio Earth Summit after the Cold War had come to an end. At the Earth Summit, there was a simple grand bargain: poor countries would become more environmentally sustainable if the rich countries would pay most of the costs.[3] This was codified in many MEAs, including the Montreal Protocol, the UNFCCC, the Convention on Biological Diversity (CBD), the Stockholm Convention on Persistent Organic Pollutants, and the UN Convention to Combat Desertification (UNCCD). Today, another transition is taking place. The simple, two-sided world of rich countries and poor countries no longer exists. Consequently, MEAs are struggling to determine which countries should take which actions and who should provide and receive FTA.

The past twenty years has seen the rapid development of emerging economies, led by China, Brazil, India, and Indonesia (see Table 7.1). China has surpassed Japan and all European countries to become the second largest national economy, has the second largest defense budget (after the United States), consumes the most natural resources, and emits the most greenhouse gases (GHGs). In 1974 Organization for Economic Cooperation and Development (OECD) member states made up 78 percent of the world's gross domestic product (GDP), but by 2014 this had dropped to 62.6 percent. As a result, the old model of OECD countries taking action first and paying the incremental costs for developing countries' action may no longer make sense. In fact, many countries considered to be developing have larger GDPs than some OECD countries. For example, according to the World Bank, in 2014, Bangladesh's GDP of $172.9 trillion was larger than OECD member Hungary's GDP of $138.3 trillion, and Sudan's GDP of $73.8 trillion was larger than OECD member Luxembourg's GDP of $64.9 trillion. In fact, there are forty-five developing countries with GDPs bigger than OECD member Slovenia's GDP of $48.6 trillion.[4]

Yet great inequalities remain. For example, if you add the top five non-OECD countries (China, Brazil, India, Russia, and Indonesia) to the thirty-four OECD countries, these thirty-nine countries represent 85 percent of the world's GDP. The forty-eight least-developed countries (LDCs), as designated by the UN,[5] comprise more than 880 million people (about 12 percent of the world's population) but represent only 1 percent of the world's GDP.[6] And the more than one hundred countries remaining contribute just 14 percent of the world's GDP.

Large disparities also exist among and within developing countries. The LDCs' annual average per capita income is measured at less than $905, with some countries, such as Malawi, as low at $250—less than $1 a day. On the other end of the

TABLE 7.1 **Top Twenty Countries Ranked by Gross Domestic Product, 1994 and 2014**

RANK	COUNTRY	1994 GDP ($ TRILLIONS)	RANK	COUNTRY	2014 GDP ($ TRILLIONS)
1	United States	7,308.8	1	United States	17,419.0
2	Japan	4,850.3	2	China	10,354.8
3	Germany	2,206.0	3	Japan	4,601.5
4	France	1,401.6	4	Germany	3,868.3
5	United Kingdom	1,140.5	5	United Kingdom	2,988.9
6	Italy	1,096.0	6	France	2,829.1
7	Canada	576.0	7	Brazil	2,346.1
8	China	562.3	8	Italy	2,141.2
9	Brazil	558.1	9	India	2,048.5
10	Spain	529.1	10	Russia	1,860.6
11	Mexico	527.3	11	Canada	1,785.3
12	Republic of Korea	458.7	12	Australia	1,454.7
13	Russia	395.1	13	Republic of Korea	1,410.4
14	Netherlands	374.3	14	Spain	1,381.3
15	India	333.0	15	Mexico	1,294.7
16	Australia	332.8	16	Indonesia	888.5
17	Switzerland	291.9	17	Netherlands	879.3
18	Argentina	257.4	18	Turkey	798.4
19	Belgium	246.2	19	Saudi Arabia	746.2
20	Sweden	226.1	20	Switzerland	701.0

Note: Gross domestic product (GDP) at purchaser's prices is the sum of gross value added by all resident producers in the economy plus any product taxes and minus any subsidies not included in the value of the products. It is calculated without making deductions for depreciation of fabricated assets or for depletion and degradation of natural resources. Data are in current US dollars. Dollar figures for GDP are converted from domestic currencies using single-year official exchange rates.

Source: World Bank Databank, http://data.worldbank.org/indicator/NY.GDP.MKTP.CD.

spectrum is Qatar (technically a developing country), with annual average per capita income as high as $92,000.[7]

Nevertheless, the per capita income of nearly all developing countries, including the BRICS countries (Brazil, Russia, India, China, and South Africa) is considerably below the OECD average (see Table 7.2). As a result, these countries continue to argue that the principle of CBDR is still valid because changes in GDP do not

TABLE 7.2 **Average Gross National Income Per Capita (in US Dollars) in Select Countries and Groupings, 2014**

Norway	$103,630
Qatar	$92,200
United States	$55,200
OECD Average	$38,832
Russia	$13,220
Brazil	$11,530
Turkey	$10,830
World Average	$10,787
China	$7,400
South Africa	$6,800
India	$1,570
LDC Average	$844
Malawi	$250

Source: "GNI Per Capita, Atlas Method (current US$), December 22, 2015," World Bank, http://data.worldbank.org/indicator/NY.GNP.PCAP.CD/countries.

negate historical responsibilities for causing global environmental problems, the large disparities in current per capita contributions (e.g., in per capita GHG emissions or resource consumption), and their need to devote resources to lifting billions of people out of extreme poverty. In contrast, most industrialized countries agree that historical responsibility and current per capita emissions are relevant to policy discussions, but they also emphasize the common responsibility of all countries to contribute to solving global environmental problems, which implies a need for developing countries to avoid duplicating the unsustainable historical development patterns of the industrialized world.

A second reality is the proliferation of stakeholders and potentially influential actors—including countries, evolving coalitions of countries, international organizations, nongovernmental organizations (NGOs), corporations, foundations, states and provinces, large cities, and others—and the consequential difficulty of creating and imposing top-down, system-wide policies. The 1992 model was based on the concept of a top-down global deal negotiated by governments through a consensus-seeking process in which a relatively small number of large countries or country coalitions (e.g., the Group of 77 [G-77]) had consistent influence across issue areas.[8] The current model is far more bottom up, voluntary, and leader driven across different stakeholder groups.[9] In today's multipolar world, many countries and shifting coalitions have different sets of cross-cutting interests on different issues and pursue them diligently. This makes it more difficult to achieve the broad consensus required in most environmental regimes to strengthen control measures, particularly if consensus by all parties is required (see Chapter 5). Moreover, outside of the European Union (EU), the most powerful countries and coalitions—including China, India, Russia, and the United States—do not provide global environmental leadership on many issues. In addition, although many corporations see tremendous economic opportunity in sustainable products and practices, the current system is also one in which some powerful economic interests and corporations still wield significant influence opposing new and stronger global environmental agreements. We can see negative impacts of this in the chemicals regimes when one or more states stall or prevent consensus due to the influence of a particular industry (see Chapter 3). In the United States, powerful industrial concerns have prevented ratification of the three chemicals conventions (Basel, Stockholm, and Rotterdam) and the CBD, worked to build doubt among the public about the basic science of climate change, and negatively affected American implementation of the Montreal Protocol with regard to eliminating methyl bromide.

On the positive side, we can see many encouraging results of this phenomenon. International organizations and environmental NGOs play key roles in agenda setting and regime implementation. As noted in Chapter 2, many states, cities, municipalities, and large businesses across the United States, Canada, and elsewhere are reducing GHG emissions even when their national governments refuse or are unable to do so. More nonstate actors have become part of norm-setting and norm-implementing institutions and mechanisms in global governance, which denotes a possible shift from purely intergovernmental regimes to more public–private and private–private global policy making.[10] These include the chemical and waste reduction and management partnerships developed in cooperation with the chemicals and waste regimes (as described in Chapter 3), and the ecolabeling initiatives developed by NGOs, manufacturers, and retailers (as described in Chapter 6). For example, collaboration between environmental groups and timber-trading companies in the Forest Stewardship Council (FSC) has led to timber certification that incentivizes sustainable forestry practices around the world. Informational side events at climate, biodiversity, and other MEA conferences are often the most attended and dynamic sessions. Governments, local authorities, NGOs, business and industry innovators, indigenous peoples, scientific and research communities, and many other groups participate in these panel discussions and events. They share best practices, research breakthroughs, innovations, and success stories, which then spread around the world at the subnational level. However, these types of initiatives are no panacea if global environmental governance is ineffective, nor can they replace the ability of effective governments to enact and implement policy at the national level. Environmental action by private and subnational public actors cannot and should not seek to replace state action but rather should work in tandem.[11]

A third reality is the fragmentation of global environmental issues. Far from a holistic, precautionary, and nonincremental approach, which was once deemed a requirement for global environmental governance, environmental policy is instead fragmented into a series of separate and unequal regimes.[12] This has resulted in conflicting agendas, inconsistencies, and competing demands for resources. In the ozone regime, as described in Chapter 3, connections with the response to climate change have come to the fore, notably in dealing with HFCs. Some countries have argued that because HFCs are GHGs, not ozone-depleting chemicals, they should only be dealt with under the climate regime. Others have argued that because the increase in the use of HFCs came about as a result of the ozone regime, and because the climate regime lacks specific and binding targets and timetables for reducing specific GHGs, they should be dealt with under the Montreal Protocol.[13] Only recently have governments agreed to seek a solution, and there is no certainty that a long-term, effective agreement will occur. The biodiversity, desertification, and forest regimes are also major stakeholders in the evolving commitments under the climate-change regime regarding land-use change and forests. Efforts to conserve endangered species of sharks take place both under the Convention on International Trade in Endangered Species of Wild Fauna and Flora (CITES) and the Convention on Migratory Species. Although the three chemicals and wastes conventions now share a secretariat and convene their Conferences of the Parties (COPs) at the same time, this process is not without its detractors (see Chapter 3), and no other cluster of MEAs has even been this successful. Within nations, different ministries often advocate for different domestic policies and negotiating positions at the global level that reflect their particular interests with respect to agriculture, business development, energy, foreign affairs, trade, and other issues rather than a holistic approach to sustainable development. Across international organizations, including within the UN system, multiple organizations address similar environmental and development issues, sometimes in pursuit of competing goals and often without effective coordination and collaboration, which yields wasteful competition and duplication. Thus, while debates over global environmental governance and sustainable development reflect the need for more synergistic policy development and implementation, responsibility for negotiating and implementing solutions to global environmental problems remains fragmented across both MEAs and government ministries.[14]

PHOTO 7.1 Johanne Fischer (Food and Agriculture Organization of the UN) presented a review of the implementation of the International Plan of Action for the Conservation and Management of Sharks at the first meeting of signatories to the Memorandum of Understanding on the Conservation of Migratory Sharks in 2012. Courtesy IISD/*Earth Negotiations Bulletin*, www.iisd.ca.

A fourth reality is the need for universality. Although there are many definitions of universality, in the environmental arena it often refers to recognition of the interconnectedness of national and global environment and development challenges and universal commitments to address them. Many environmental challenges, such as illegal trade in wildlife, are global issues, due to the interconnectedness of the global marketplace. Sustainably managing and protecting global public goods, such as biodiversity and the climate, entail global responsibility and concerted multinational cooperation.[15] Such issues are universal in that they affect everyone, regardless of wealth or income, gender or race, and need to be addressed by all countries, both individually and collectively, or the resulting policies will not be effective.

Several years before the 1992 Rio Earth Summit, a shift occurred in participation patterns at intergovernmental environmental negotiations. Negotiations for the Montreal Protocol on substances that deplete the ozone layer, which began in 1986, were open to all countries. However, the most active initial participants were representatives of countries whose industries had a stake in the outcome, along with a few representatives whose interests represented developing-country concerns. Participation in the Montreal Protocol negotiations expanded when discussions turned to financing mechanisms, and this broader participation model became the norm beginning in the early 1990s during the negotiations of the UNFCCC and CBD.

But universal participation in negotiations, which is needed and positive if it builds a truly global consensus, does not always mean universal ratification and implementation, which are required so that key countries do not remain outside a regime. For example, as noted in Chapter 3, although the negotiation of the Kyoto Protocol was open to all parties to the UNFCCC, the largest per capita GHG emitter, the United States, participated in the negotiations but never ratified the treaty, and major developing countries with growing GHG emissions, such as China and India, did not have commitments. As a result, by the end of the first commitment period in 2012, the Kyoto Protocol covered only about 15 percent of global GHG emissions, thus failing to slow down global warming.[16] Similarly, and also discussed in Chapter 3, a number of large countries have not ratified, and thus need not implement, the control measures on all of the toxic chemicals added to the Stockholm Convention. As outlined in Chapter 4, multiple countries are key actors in weakening attempts to protect global fisheries. Addressing global environmental issues requires universal participation in policy creation and implementation by all of the major actors or it will not succeed.

A fifth reality is that despite its flaws, the intergovernmental negotiating process itself is still a necessity. "Getting action in the United Nations," a diplomat once complained, "is like the mating of elephants. It takes place at a very high level, with an enormous amount of huffing and puffing, raises a tremendous amount of dust and nothing happens for at least 23 months."[17] Many who see the need for urgent action on environmental problems are skeptical of entrusting complete responsibility to the slow and often cumbersome, "huffing-and-puffing" multilateral negotiating process within the UN. As discussed in Chapter 5, environmental problems do not wait patiently while governments negotiate. When governments did not adopt a successor agreement to the Kyoto Protocol in Copenhagen in 2009, the earth's average temperature continued to rise for another six years before the Paris Agreement was adopted in 2015. Even with the Paris Agreement, however, the current promises to reduce emissions are still likely to lead to warming of 2.7°C to 3°C above preindustrial levels, breaching the 2°C threshold that scientists say is the limit of safety, beyond which the effects—droughts, floods, heat waves, and sea level rise—are likely to become catastrophic and irreversible.[18]

Although not every MEA has been negotiated within the UN system, since 1972 the UN or one of its specialized agencies—primarily UNEP—has been recognized as the main venue for addressing global and regional environmental issues.

Although there are frustrations inherent in this process and governments are not the only important actors (see the discussion above and in Chapter 2), the international system is still centered on states. Yet, governments seldom surrender decision-making authority to a supranational body. As a result, the international community is still forced to employ the slow method of intergovernmental negotiation as the primary tool in addressing global environmental issues.[19]

THE CONTINUING EVOLUTION OF GLOBAL ENVIRONMENTAL GOVERNANCE

Since Rio+20 in 2012, in particular, global environmental institutions have sought to evolve and improve their ability to address environmental and sustainable development concerns, albeit not always successfully. The MEAs, their secretariats, and the associated COPs have taken a variety of actions, some in response to the realities outlined in the previous section. UNEP, the main international organization in global environmental affairs, saw its governance structure changed and its financial situation somewhat improved as a result of Rio+20, and it has also pursued internal improvements. The UN as a whole has evolved to embrace sustainable development as a central theme as a result of the adoption of the 2030 Agenda for Sustainable Development and the SDGs and is making associated governance changes. This section highlights key aspects of the ongoing evolution of global environmental governance.

Evolution of Multilateral Environmental Agreements

As we have seen, after the momentum created by the 1972 Stockholm Declaration, the attention to environmental issues and the commitment to taking normative action led governments to adopt numerous agreements to address specific environmental issues. During this first phase, which spanned the 1970s and 1980s, more than a hundred global and regional MEAs were adopted. However, the sector-by-sector approach followed by most of the early MEAs ignored the interdependence of environmental issues and the need for an ecosystem approach to the preservation of environmental quality. Moreover, the early MEAs generally failed to adequately integrate environmental standards into economic development policies, thereby ignoring a concern that was expressed in the Stockholm Declaration.[20] Nearly all of the agreements also lacked meaningful mechanisms to hold states accountable for breaching an obligation to respect and protect the environment. In general, the conservation approach adopted in most of the MEAs from this period can be considered more "utilitarian than ecological."[21]

The environmental conventions and agreements adopted during the second phase, starting just before the 1992 Rio Declaration and continuing through the Minamata Convention on Mercury in 2013, reflected a greater willingness within the international community to respond to scientific evidence regarding the significant and even irreversible environmental threats to human health and the environment created by ozone-depleting chemicals, GHG emissions, overfishing, deforestation, toxic chemicals, mercury emissions, loss of biodiversity, and other damaging human activities.[22] This led to another spate of negotiations that resulted in the UNFCCC, CBD, UNCCD, Stockholm Convention, Rotterdam Convention, and Minamata Convention, and expansion of the Montreal Protocol and CITES, to name but a few of the MEA developments during this second phase. Although the effectiveness of these agreements has varied, their creation and, in many cases, expansion represent important achievements in global environmental governance.

More recently there has been a third phase, which has overlapped with the latter part of the second phase and is concerned with implementation and effectiveness. Even with so many MEAs on the books, true success stories are few and far between. The evolution of the system of global environmental governance, as demonstrated in this volume, shows that, although progress has been made in establishing a network of treaty obligations and soft law, "the main challenge remains how to guarantee at the global level that the regulatory system of human activities is systematically aligned with natural and ecological systems that govern life on the planet."[23] So it is logical that the latest phase of global environmental governance is focused on implementation. Moving forward, environmental negotiations are likely to continue to focus on implementation, monitoring, and compliance to ensure that existing MEAs are actually making a difference on the ground rather than just the creation of new agreements.

A critical issue in implementation is compliance, the degree to which countries actually comply with the rules they establish to put the international regime into action in their countries. In general, international environmental law suffers from a serious deficit of enforcement mechanisms. Unlike international trade or human rights law, there is no dispute settlement body or international court of the environment. Implementation of international environmental standards is largely left up to national governments that enact domestic laws and, in some cases, soft international enforcement mechanisms such as noncompliance procedures that permit "some level of moral and political suasion to be applied to states unwilling or unable to respect the standards set in the multilateral treaties to which they are parties."[24]

So a major question being addressed within MEAs is whether new provisions or significant reform of international institutions is required to improve the quality and effectiveness of national implementation of global environmental governance. On the one hand, there is a discernible trend toward broader acceptance of an enhanced role of international institutions in the supervision and implementation of environmental law. On the other hand, significant resistance persists with regard to delegating enforcement powers. Many countries even object to delegating significant monitoring responsibilities on domestic implementation, especially when the proposal impacts a state's perceptions of its sovereign right to manage natural resources and pursue economic and social development strategies of its own choosing.[25] As a result, there is no simple solution to this problem. The trend toward concentrating on implementation is clear, but ready solutions, especially on the issues of compliance and the need for more effective FTA (as discussed in Chapter 5), are difficult to foresee.

In response to worries about fragmentation, some governments and other actors are seeking greater collaboration among existing MEAs, and positive trends are emerging. The Basel, Stockholm, and Rotterdam Conventions, as described in Chapter 3, embarked on a "synergies" process in 2007 that resulted in a decision taken by all three COPs in 2010 to enhance coordination and cooperation.[26] This has resulted in a joint secretariat, joint meetings of the COPs of the three conventions, and increased coordination in certain implementation activities and, in some cases, the provision of FTA. This synergies process has helped parties improve the use of available resources through more coordinated national policy frameworks and institutional mechanisms for regulating chemicals and wastes, reduce the costs of implementing the conventions, better coordinate technical assistance activities, make more efficient use of financial resources to support developing countries' implementation of the conventions, and develop a more integrated, life-cycle approach for the environmentally sound management of chemicals and wastes.[27] The synergies process was facilitated by the fact that the three conventions address related issues and all three were already at least partially administered by UNEP and had secretariats located in Geneva (the Rotterdam Convention is co-administered by UNEP and the Food and Agriculture Organization of the UN [FAO] and also has an office in Rome).

UNEP is also trying to create better cooperation and coordination among six biodiversity-related conventions.[28] Although the process is not nearly as developed as the initiative underway among the Basel, Stockholm, and Rotterdam Conventions and is also hindered by different secretariat locations and administrative arrangements, the formative efforts are indicative of a trend. So, too, is the decision by parties to the Montreal Protocol to consider using that treaty, including its Multilateral Fund and Technology and Economic Assessment Panel, to facilitate reductions in the use of HFCs, which are also addressed in the climate regime. The Global

Environment Facility (GEF) also attempts to fund projects that have co-benefits in multiple issue areas, such as projects in the chemicals focal area that also address hazardous waste because they improve life-cycle management or projects that seek to protect a forested area as a biodiversity preserve but that also provide climate benefits because a healthy forest acts as a sink for carbon dioxide (CO_2).

Evolution of the United Nations Environment Programme

As described in Chapter 2, UNEP is the lead UN organization on the environment. Since UNEP's establishment in 1972, the UN institutional framework for environmental issues has grown in its size and complexity, with an increasing number of UN institutions, agreements, meetings, reports, and actors connected to environmental issues. Although governments had discussed reform options for years with limited success, the agenda for Rio+20 included consideration of the institutional framework for sustainable development as one of its two main agenda items, and some governments and NGOs hoped that this would provide the impetus for substantial UNEP reform.

There were two main camps among those advocating reform. One side included institutional reformists who wanted to improve the current system of treaty regimes and international institutions. The other side included those who believed far deeper changes were necessary, possibly including the creation of a UN Environment Organization, and replacing UNEP with this more powerful organization. Many in the first group focused on strengthening key institutions in specific issue areas and negotiating stronger and more effective global regimes. Increased coherence and coordination among the goals and processes of the major global environmental, financial, trade, and development institutions and systems were also a priority.[29] Some also supported elevating the precautionary principle to an official guiding principle of global environmental policy.

In the second group, France, Germany, and the EU spearheaded support to create a UN Environment Organization with the status of an official specialized UN agency, a status that UNEP did not have. They argued that this would increase the availability of financial resources and provide a more efficient and effective structure for governance and leadership. Some governments and NGOs also argued that this model could be the first step in an active effort to bring all of the environmental treaties together under a single roof. Other proposals were even more ambitious, such as creating a world environment agency (or a more robust UN Environment Organization) that would be modeled on and intended to counterbalance the World Trade Organization (WTO). Some proposed that this organization could operate as a type of global environmental legislature, entrusted with setting international standards on certain issues and given the authority to enforce them against laggard countries, similar to the WTO's ability to judge whether domestic laws and regulations violate global trading rules and order changes.[30]

After intense debate in Rio in 2012, the final agreement fell short of creating a UN Environment Organization or transforming UNEP into a specialized agency (and far short of establishing an organization with legislative or WTO-like authority).[31] Rio+20 did agree, however, to allow all countries to be part of UNEP's Governing Council (instead of only fifty-eight members) as well "as other measures to strengthen its governance as well as its responsiveness and accountability to member states" and to have "secure, stable, adequate and increased financial resources from the regular budget of the United Nations and voluntary contributions to fulfill its mandate."[32] Instead of UNEP becoming an umbrella organization for MEAs, the outcome merely encourages parties to MEAs to consider further measures to enhance coordination and cooperation,[33] which in practice supports efforts such as the synergies initiative.

The first universal Governing Council, renamed the UN Environment Assembly (UNEA) of UNEP, convened in 2014, under the overarching theme "Sustainable Development Goals and the Post-2015 Development Agenda, Including Sustainable Consumption and Production." If UNEP's leadership on a number of core themes is relatively well acknowledged, the institutional implications of an upgraded UNEA—as the UN General Assembly's (UNGA's) subsidiary organ charged with safeguarding the global sustainability agenda—are still being processed within the UN system. The sensitivities around the SDG discussions at the first UNEA, where lines were repeatedly drawn to remind delegates not to "preempt the outcome of the post-2015 process in New York," exemplified the tricky balancing act that UNEP must perform to hold its own in an increasingly competitive institutional environment.[34]

The first UNEA called for the full integration of the environmental dimension into the sustainable development agenda, acknowledging that a healthy environment is an essential requirement and key enabler for sustainable development. The first UNEA also appealed for ambitious universal implementation of the SDGs and inclusive social and economic development in harmony with nature. By trying to position itself at the center of efforts to integrate the economic, environmental, and social dimensions of sustainable development, UNEP wants to ensure that it is not left behind in the shift from the Millennium Development Goals (MDGs) to the SDGs. Thus, in its second forty years, UNEP must demonstrate that it can add to its traditional roles, including that of assisting with the creation and implementation of MEAs. UNEP must now also provide leadership in implementing the environmental dimension of sustainable development within the UN system and create

PHOTO 7.2 The First UN Environment Assembly of the UN Environment Programme took place in June 2014 in Nairobi. Courtesy IISD/*Earth Negotiations Bulletin,* www.iisd.ca.

coherent and accurate monitoring and evaluation frameworks to provide a credible platform for action on the SDGs.

From the Commission on Sustainable Development to the High-Level Political Forum on Sustainable Development

Rio+20 also set in motion a major change in the intergovernmental body charged with addressing sustainable development at UN Headquarters in New York. The Commission on Sustainable Development (CSD), as described in Chapter 2, was established as the UN focal point for follow-up to the 1992 Earth Summit and successive global sustainable development conferences. By 2012, however, the mandate and functioning of the CSD had become the subject of increasing contention.[35] Many governments and NGOs began calling for major reform, and some even proposed that the CSD should be replaced or abolished because of its lackluster performance. By Rio+20, a clear consensus had emerged that the CSD had outlived its usefulness. To replace the CSD or, more accurately, to move beyond it, negotiations at Rio+20 focused on establishing a "high-level political forum" to "provide political leadership, guidance and recommendations for sustainable development."[36]

Later in 2012, the UNGA, in its follow-up to Rio+20, formally established the new High-Level Political Forum on Sustainable Development (HLPF), which operates under both the UN Economic and Social Council (ECOSOC) and the UNGA, giving it a much higher political profile than the CSD ever had. Every four years the forum is to be convened at the highest possible level of heads of state and government for two days at the beginning of the annual UNGA session in September. The HLPF will also meet annually for eight days—including a three-day ministerial meeting—under the auspices of ECOSOC to ensure regular high-level discussions. The HLPF is charged with providing political leadership, guidance, and recommendations for sustainable development; following up and reviewing progress in the implementation of sustainable development commitments; enhancing the integration of the three dimensions of sustainable development; and ensuring the appropriate consideration of new and emerging sustainable development challenges.[37]

The forum held its inaugural session in September 2013 at the level of heads of state and met in both 2014 and 2015 under the auspices of ECOSOC. Although the forum got off to an inspiring start, it did not accomplish much in its first few years and seemed to be waiting until the 2030 Agenda for Sustainable Development and the SDGs were formally launched in 2016. The forum will conduct regular reviews on the follow-up and implementation of the sustainable development commitments and objectives, including the SDGs, and will oversee follow-up and review of the 2030 Agenda for Sustainable Development at the global level.[38] By 2017, the 17 SDGs and 169 targets are to be joined by a set of global indicators developed under the auspices of the UN Statistical Commission. These indicators have the potential to demonstrate which goals are on track and where further effort should be expended and should facilitate the HLPF's work. Yet, until the mandate and working methods for the HLPF reviews are clarified,[39] it is still too soon to determine whether the UN's new institutional structure for this important follow-up and review effort will be effective.

Does Evolution Mean Change?

The ongoing evolution within the institutional architecture of global environmental governance does not guarantee that positive change will occur on the ground or that there will be reduced GHG emissions, an end to trade in endangered species, decreased levels of air and water pollution, restoration of the earth's protective ozone layer, and conservation of the world's biodiversity, fisheries, land, and forests. Perhaps the biggest obstacle to improving the architecture and impact of global environmental governance is political will.

Many internationally agreed-upon declarations and documents have called for new policies and practices, but actual progress has been limited. Some of the political and economic leaders that oppose action appear to believe they live in isolation from fairly well accepted ecological, economic, and technological trends. They dismiss the idea that climate change, biodiversity loss, persistent organic pollutants

(POPs), hazardous wastes, and ozone depletion undermine the future of their country or interests.[40] Others worry that strengthening environmental governance could challenge the fundamental concept of state sovereignty. Still others express concern that strong environmental policies will hinder economic growth, at least in the short term. There are those, however, who agree that more significant action is necessary and aspects of the system need to be changed, but they either don't have the political influence or the necessary resources to build effective domestic or international coalitions.

Given these constraints, it is perhaps not surprising that global environmental governance is not nearly as ambitious as many would like it to be. Whether the UNEA, HLPF, and new or expanded MEAs discussed in Chapters 3 and 4 will make global environmental governance more effective in practice remains to be seen. But as the international community continues to evolve and as the understanding of the interrelationship between environmental and development issues continues to gain traction, the political will to further strengthen the structures of global sustainable development governance may follow.

CONCLUSION: THE PROSPECTS FOR GLOBAL ENVIRONMENTAL POLITICS

The year 2015 will likely be remembered as a landmark year for environmental diplomacy. In September 2015, heads of state and government gathered at the UN Sustainable Development Summit in New York and adopted the 2030 Agenda for Sustainable Development and the 17 SDGs and 169 targets to shape domestic and international sustainable development policy making through 2030. Unlike the MDGs that preceded them, the SDGs are universal and address the environment, social development, economic development, and peace, equality, and human rights. In conjunction with this, in July 2015, governments adopted the Addis Ababa Action Agenda (AAAA) to provide the financial and technical means to implement the SDGs and the sustainable development agenda.

In December 2015, for the first time in more than twenty years of UN climate negotiations, delegates from almost two hundred nations adopted the Paris Agreement, an ambitious, binding, and universal agreement under the UNFCCC aimed at keeping the global temperature rise to well below 2°C.

But that wasn't all. In January 2015, governments agreed—after years of preliminary talks—to negotiate a new international instrument on the conservation and sustainable use of marine biodiversity in areas beyond national jurisdiction (the high seas) under the UN Convention on the Law of the Sea, as mandated by Rio+20. Negotiations began in 2016 and are expected to be completed by 2017.[41]

Parties to the Montreal Protocol took a major step forward in November 2015 toward regulating HFCs, a potent GHG. Meeting in Dubai, the parties agreed to begin talks in 2016 on an amendment to the protocol or other mechanisms that will address HFCs, replacements for ozone-depleting substances (ODS) that are often used in refrigeration, air conditioning, and insulation. Adopting a worldwide phasedown of HFCs could avoid global warming of 0.5°C, a big contribution to climate-change mitigation efforts (see Chapter 3).

In May 2015, parties to the Stockholm Convention added new chemicals to the control regime, overcoming significant opposition from entrenched economic interests to safeguard a much, much larger number of global citizens (see Chapter 3). The UN Forum on Forests (UNFF), also in May, adopted a historic resolution on the International Arrangement on Forests (IAF) beyond 2015, which strengthened the IAF, defined its strategic direction until 2030, and promoted coherence between the IAF and the 2030 Agenda for Sustainable Development (see Chapter 4). The UNCCD adopted decisions in October 2015 that placed it at the center of both implementing SDG target 15.3 on land-degradation neutrality and examining the relationship between land-degradation neutrality and climate-change mitigation (see Chapter 4).

The events of 2015 bode well for the future of multilateralism and global environmental governance, but the international community cannot afford to rest on its laurels. Disturbing environmental trends and unsustainable development continue unabated.

Can the international community develop effective cooperative efforts to address our major global environmental problems successfully? The case studies presented in this book show that, on some issues, states have taken collective actions that significantly reduced specific environmental threats, such as hunting endangered species of whales. In the case of the ozone layer, states have devised a regime that has been innovative in its rule making and largely effective and cost-efficient in phasing out most of the damaging chemicals.

But the successful regimes have had favorable circumstances. The ozone case involved a relatively small number of interested economic actors and substitute technologies that turned out to be cost-effective. The initial whaling ban passed because only a few countries wanted to continue to hunt whales and there was no large worldwide market for whale products. The ivory ban initially succeeded because a few major countries were able to shut down most of the market for elephant ivory. It is hoped that the September 2015 announcement by Chinese President Xi Jinping and US President Barack Obama to enact near-complete bans on ivory import and export and to take significant and timely steps to halt the domestic commercial ivory trade will make a difference.[42] However, none of these regimes have been completely successful. The black market for ivory still exists, and elephant poaching continues unabated; Iceland, Japan, and Norway still hunt whales; and the ozone layer has not fully recovered.

We have outlined the importance of continued efforts to improve the effectiveness of environmental regimes even after they are adopted. Parties can strengthen regimes by tightening the requirements for regulating activities that are causing the environmental disruption or resource depletion, by improving compliance with those requirements, or by broadening state participation in the regime. The biodiversity regime has focused work on seven thematic work programs addressing marine and coastal biodiversity, agricultural biodiversity, forest biodiversity, island biodiversity, inland waters biodiversity, dry and subhumid lands biodiversity, and mountain biodiversity. Yet, despite this, the international community failed to meet the 2010 target for significantly reducing biodiversity loss and may similarly struggle to meet the Aichi biodiversity targets, as noted in Chapter 4.

The desertification regime still faces considerable administrative and financial problems in fulfilling its mandate to reduce land degradation in the drylands. Although nearly universal ratification of the convention can be seen as recognition of the problem of drylands degradation, the issue is complicated by the fact that combating land degradation must work hand in hand with efforts to address poverty eradication, water resources management, agriculture, deforestation, biodiversity conservation, climate change, and population growth. The success or failure of this regime is a key indicator for the overall success or failure of sustainable development.

The regime for global fisheries management needs a stronger compliance system and increased participation. The Fish Stocks Agreement lacks a COP, relying entirely on regional fisheries management organizations to track compliance, and many of the major distant-water fishing states have refused to ratify it.

But environmental regimes are not the only forces that influence global environmental governance. Multilateral institutions affect environmental politics and the development of regimes, be it by helping to set the global agenda (e.g., UNEP), bringing states together to negotiate (UNEP, FAO), monitoring global environmental trends (UNEP), conducting comprehensive scientific assessments (Intergovernmental Panel on Climate Change [IPCC], Intergovernmental Science-Policy Platform on Biodiversity and Ecosystem Services [IPBES]), or providing financial support for environmental activities (GEF). But these institutions do not always have the resources or the mandate to promote strong regimes. The GEF has funding that can accomplish only a fraction of what is needed to support effective international cooperation in biodiversity, climate change, chemicals and waste, land degradation, international waters, and sustainable forest management. UNEP and other intergovernmental organizations have been subject to the weak political will of key states.

The world's global trade and financial institutions—the World Bank, the International Monetary Fund (IMF), and the WTO—also play important roles. Although the World Bank and the IMF have made some progress, critics argue that these institutions, which are controlled by developed countries, are unlikely to become truly effective tools for sustainable development without changing their power structures. Power in the World Bank is presently apportioned according to members' shares, just like that in a corporation. Major decisions require 85 percent of the vote, and the United States, which holds about 16 percent of the shares (and controls the presidency), wields de facto veto power. The same is true of the IMF, whose presidency is controlled by Europe, although reforms are in the works.[43] Although the establishment of the New Development Bank may provide an alternative to the World Bank or challenge its modus operandi (see Chapter 2), change is not guaranteed unless the finance ministries or legislatures of the world's major industrialized countries compel them to, something that will likely require domestic political pressure.

As for the WTO, its ministerial conference in Nairobi in December 2015 brought only one bit of good environmental news. The 164 member countries agreed to phase out export subsidies for some agricultural products. That's a small but worthy accomplishment that eluded the global trading system for five decades. Otherwise deep divides on trade issues persist between rich and poor countries and among competing economic powers; the Doha Round is on life support, with no new road map for action on other environmentally damaging subsidies, and doubts exist about whether the WTO will be able to agree on meaningful multilateral trade liberalization, including on environmental goods and services.[44]

The leadership of the industrialized countries, especially the United States, is a key to effective regimes. Since the 1970s, the United States has been the one state without whose leadership any environmental regime is certain to be much weaker. When the United States has actively engaged in trying to achieve consensus on stronger institutions or actions, it has often been able to overcome reluctance on the part of other industrialized countries, as in the negotiations on ozone depletion, African elephants, whaling, fish stocks, and the most recent round of climate negotiations. When the United States has been a veto state, as in the case of the hazardous waste trade, or has played a much lower-profile role, as in cases of desertification, POPs, and biodiversity, the resulting regime has been negatively affected. The US executive branch has wavered on some of these issues for years, through multiple administrations, and Congress has often been a force impeding US leadership.

China, India, and the EU have joined the United States as countries whose leadership is essential on global environmental issues. The size of their economies, resource consumption, and GHG emissions, as well as their central roles in international trade and financial relations, make their full participation in environmental regimes essential in the twenty-first century.

Although their resources and interests are increasingly diverse, developing countries as a group must also show leadership and move beyond the traditional interpretation of the principle of CBDR and participate fully in global environmental regimes. Developing countries need to take the initiative and accept new commitments in each of the major areas in return for financial or other forms of compensation, but the commitments and compensation need not be uniform for all developing countries. The Paris Agreement on climate change marks the first major breakthrough in the discussions of developing-country commitments. Governments finally agreed that if major developing countries do not take on GHG-reduction commitments, there is nothing that developed countries alone can do to prevent significant climate change.

There is increasing awareness among business groups regarding the implications of global environmental threats and global environmental regimes for their interests. As a result, more and more corporations and trade associations play active roles in global environmental politics. Because treaties could impose significant new costs or open up new opportunities, depending on their details, the business sector recognizes that early involvement in the negotiating process will often bring long-term benefits once a regime is in place.

Sometimes this involvement is negative. Some corporations and industry associations have worked against strong international or national environmental measures. Exxon/Mobil reportedly funneled more than $32 million to researchers and activist groups promoting disinformation about global warming over the years, as well as to members of Congress and corporate lobbying groups that deny climate science and block efforts to fight climate change.[45] The agro-industrial complex in the United States, along with the chemical companies producing methyl bromide, worked to create a large loophole in the phaseout provisions for methyl bromide under the Montreal Protocol.

At other times, corporate interests have assisted the creation of strong environmental regimes. During the Montreal Protocol negotiations, US chemical companies that manufactured chlorofluorocarbons (CFCs) realized significant regulations were on the way and finished developing alternatives. Their success enabled US negotiators to take a stronger position and emerge as a lead state in the negotiations. The Munich Climate Insurance Initiative, which brings together insurers, climate experts, economists, and independent organizations, is working on the innovative uses of risk-transfer tools to manage climate risks in conjunction with the UNFCCC. Companies that produce or use energy that does not emit GHGs employ ever greater numbers of people and have become more influential in promoting green energy and GHG-reduction policies at the local, state, national, and international levels.

Domestic political support for new political commitments on global environmental issues likely will not happen without environmental movements and civil society influencing national public opinion and pushing governments into action. At the international level, NGO networks on climate change, chemicals, biodiversity, and desertification map strategies for monitoring treaty implementation and facilitate public participation in national action programs and strategies. The Trade Records Analysis of Flora and Fauna in Commerce (TRAFFIC) monitors the international trade in endangered species. International NGOs such as Greenpeace and WWF contribute substantial ideas on climate change, marine pollution, marine biodiversity, whales, and fisheries. Nevertheless, the most important challenge for NGOs and civil society is to build political pressure on reluctant states to support participation in, or strengthening of, global environmental regimes.

Global environmental politics has grown significantly more complex since the first global environmental conference in Stockholm in 1972. Many more issues, treaties, institutions, and policy initiatives exist, and the environment is now integrated into a broad array of international economic, trade, and development issues. In some ways, this growth is a sign of the progress made in the last forty years by the international community in learning how to address global environmental issues.

Caution is necessary, however. Although recent MEAs have applied the precautionary principle and made genuine efforts to grapple with equity issues, many observers believe these steps are not enough to meet the significant challenges of the twenty-first century.[46] Aspects of the exclusionist paradigm based on neoclassical economics continue to influence important policy discussions. The shift to a sustainable development paradigm—something that seemed imminent in 1992—has not come to pass.

It is possible that the 2030 Agenda for Sustainable Development and the SDGs may facilitate such a shift. Yet, remaining definitional questions about universality, CBDR, and accountability may provide a few bumps in the road or possibly major detours. Supporters of the SDGs hope that individual national commitments will add up to worldwide results that help all people, especially those living in extreme poverty (living on less than $1.25 a day), live better lives while also ensuring a healthy environment. For the first time, a UN development agenda recognizes the interlinkages among sustainability of ecosystem services, poverty eradication, eco-

PHOTO 7.3 Echoing UN Secretary-General Ban Ki-moon, "There is no 'Plan B' for action to reduce climate change as there is no 'Planet B'." Courtesy Leila Mead, IISD/*Earth Negotiations Bulletin,* www.iisd.ca.

nomic development, and human well-being. However, it is comparatively easy to agree that the shift to sustainable development is necessary. Almost no one challenges that statement. The difficulty is to reach agreement on what that means, to develop appropriate policies, and, in particular, to muster the political will to implement them effectively.

This book has examined the principal paradigms, actors, issues, and challenges in global environmental politics. What the future will bring is unclear. There are reasons for both optimism and grave concern. What we do know is that today's environmental challenges are global in nature, unprecedented in scope, and closely linked to economic and social development. The need for innovative and creative global solutions is greater than ever.

Appendices

APPENDIX A: PERSISTENT ORGANIC POLLUTANTS CONTROLLED UNDER THE STOCKHOLM CONVENTION

The Dirty Dozen—Persistent Organic Pollutants Included in the Original Convention

- Pesticides: aldrin; chlordane; dichlorodiphenyltrichloroethane (DDT); dieldrin; endrin; heptachlor; mirex; toxaphene
- Industrial chemicals: polychlorinated biphenyls (PCBs), hexachlorobenzene (which is also a pesticide)
- By-products (unintentionally produced substances created when certain substances burn or through particular industrial activities): dioxins; furans

Persistent Organic Pollutants Added to the Stockholm Convention

(Note: Some are listed in more than category.)

- Pesticides: chlordecone; endosulfane; alpha hexachlorocyclohexane; beta hexachlorocyclohexane; lindane; pentachlorobenzene; and pentachlorophenol
- Industrial chemicals: hexabromobiphenyl; hexabromocyclododecane; hexabromodiphenyl ether and heptabromodiphenyl ether; hexachlorobutadiene; pentachlorobenzene; perfluorooctane sulfonate (PFOS), its salts, and perfluorooctane sulfonyl fluoride; polychlorinated naphthalenes; tetrabromodiphenyl ether/pentabromodiphenyl ether
- By-products: alpha hexachlorocyclohexane; beta hexachlorocyclohexane; pentachlorobenzene

Persistent Organic Pollutants Listed in Annexes A, B, and C

(Note: Some POPs are listed in more than one annex and thus subject to more than one type of control measure.)

Annex A: Elimination

- Included in the original convention: aldrin, chlordane, dieldrin, endrin, heptachlor, hexachlorobenzene, mirex, PCBs, toxaphene
- Added in 2009: chlordecone, hexabromobiphenyl, hexabromodiphenyl ether and heptabromodiphenyl ether, alpha hexachlorocyclohexane, beta hexachlorocyclohexane, lindane, pentachlorobenzene, tetrabromodiphenyl ether/pentabromodiphenyl ether

- Added in 2001: endosulfan
- Added in 2013: hexabromocyclododecane
- Added in 2015: hexachlorobutadiene, pentachlorophenol, polychlorinated naphthalenes

Annex B: Restricted

- Included in the original convention: DDT
- Added in 2009: PFOS

Annex C: Minimize and Where Feasible Eliminate

- Included in the original convention: dioxins, furans, hexachlorobenzene, PCBs
- Added in 2009: pentachlorobenzene
- Added in 2015: polychlorinated naphthalenes

APPENDIX B: THE AICHI BIODIVERSITY TARGETS

Strategic Goal A: Address the Underlying Causes of Biodiversity Loss by Mainstreaming Biodiversity Across Government and Society

Target 1: By 2020, at the latest, people are aware of the values of biodiversity and the steps they can take to conserve and use it sustainably.

Target 2: By 2020, at the latest, biodiversity values have been integrated into national and local development and poverty-reduction strategies and planning processes and are being incorporated into national accounting, as appropriate, and reporting systems.

Target 3: By 2020, at the latest, incentives, including subsidies, harmful to biodiversity are eliminated, phased out, or reformed in order to minimize or avoid negative impacts, and positive incentives for the conservation and sustainable use of biodiversity are developed and applied, consistent and in harmony with the convention and other relevant international obligations, taking into account national socioeconomic conditions.

Target 4: By 2020, at the latest, governments, businesses, and stakeholders at all levels have taken steps to achieve or have implemented plans for sustainable production and consumption and have kept the impacts of use of natural resources well within safe ecological limits.

Strategic Goal B: Reduce the Direct Pressures on Biodiversity and Promote Sustainable Use

Target 5: By 2020, the rate of loss of all natural habitats, including forests, is at least halved and, where feasible, brought close to zero, and degradation and fragmentation is significantly reduced.

Target 6: By 2020, all fish and invertebrate stocks and aquatic plants are managed and harvested sustainably, legally, and applying ecosystem-based approaches so that overfishing is avoided, recovery plans and measures are in place for all depleted species, fisheries have no significant adverse impacts on threatened species and vulnerable ecosystems, and the impacts of fisheries on stocks, species, and ecosystems are within safe ecological limits.

Target 7: By 2020, areas under agriculture, aquaculture, and forestry are managed sustainably, ensuring conservation of biodiversity.

Target 8: By 2020, pollution, including from excess nutrients, has been brought to levels that are not detrimental to ecosystem function and biodiversity.

Target 9: By 2020, invasive alien species and pathways are identified and prioritized, priority species are controlled or eradicated, and measures are in place to manage pathways to prevent their introduction and establishment.

Target 10: By 2015, the multiple anthropogenic pressures on coral reefs and other vulnerable ecosystems impacted by climate change or ocean acidification are minimized so as to maintain their integrity and functioning.

Strategic Goal C: To Improve the Status of Biodiversity by Safeguarding Ecosystems, Species, and Genetic Diversity

Target 11: By 2020, at least 17 percent of terrestrial and inland water, and 10 percent of coastal and marine areas, especially areas of particular importance for biodiversity and ecosystem services, are conserved through effectively and equitably managed, ecologically representative, and well-connected systems of protected areas and other effective area-based conservation measures and integrated into the wider landscapes and seascapes.

Target 12: By 2020, the extinction of known threatened species has been prevented and their conservation status, particularly of those most in decline, has been improved and sustained.

Target 13: By 2020, the genetic diversity of cultivated plants and farmed and domesticated animals and of wild relatives, including other socioeconomically as well as culturally valuable species, is maintained, and strategies have been developed and implemented for minimizing genetic erosion and safeguarding their genetic diversity.

Strategic Goal D: Enhance the Benefits to All from Biodiversity and Ecosystem Services

Target 14: By 2020, ecosystems that provide essential services, including services related to water, and contribute to health, livelihoods, and well-being are restored and safeguarded, taking into account the needs of women, indigenous and local communities, and the poor and vulnerable.

Target 15: By 2020, ecosystem resilience and the contribution of biodiversity to carbon stocks has been enhanced through conservation and restoration, including restoration of at least 15 percent of degraded ecosystems, thereby contributing to climate-change mitigation and adaptation and to combating desertification.

Target 16: By 2015, the Nagoya Protocol on Access to Genetic Resources and the Fair and Equitable Sharing of Benefits Arising from Their Utilization is in force and operational, consistent with national legislation.

Strategic Goal E: Enhance Implementation Through Participatory Planning, Knowledge Management, and Capacity Building

Target 17: By 2015, each party has developed, adopted as a policy instrument, and commenced implementing an effective, participatory, and updated national biodiversity strategy and action plan.

Target 18: By 2020, the traditional knowledge, innovations, and practices of indigenous and local communities relevant for the conservation and sustainable use of biodiversity and their customary use of biological resources are respected, subject to national legislation and relevant international obligations, and fully integrated and reflected in the implementation of the convention with the full and effective participation of indigenous and local communities at all relevant levels.

Target 19: By 2020, knowledge, the science base, and technologies relating to biodiversity, its values, functioning, status and trends, and the consequences of its loss are improved, widely shared and transferred, and applied.

Target 20: By 2020, at the latest, the mobilization of financial resources for effectively implementing the Strategic Plan for Biodiversity 2011–2020 from all sources, and in accordance with the consolidated and agreed-upon process in the Strategy for Resource Mobilization, should increase substantially from the current levels. This target will be subject to changes contingent to resource needs assessments to be developed and reported by parties.

Source: Convention on Biological Diversity, "Aichi Biodiversity Targets," 2010, www.cbd.int/sp/targets/.

Notes

Chapter 1: The Emergence of Global Environmental Politics

1. United Nations Environment Programme (UNEP), *GEO 5: Global Environmental Outlook—Environment for the Future We Want* (Nairobi: UNEP, 2012).

2. WWF, *Living Planet Report 2014* (Gland, Switzerland: WWF, 2014), 32.

3. Ibid.

4. "World Footprint," Global Footprint Network, www.footprintnetwork.org/en/index.php/GFN/page/world_footprint/.

5. United Nations (UN), *World Population Prospects: The 2015 Revision* (New York: UN, 2015), 2.

6. Ibid.

7. Ibid.

8. Ibid., 3

9. Ibid., 4.

10. Peter Dauvergne, *The Shadows of Consumption* (Cambridge, MA: MIT Press, 2008), 4.

11. UNEP, *GEO 5,* 4–30.

12. WWF, *Living Planet Report 2012* (Gland, Switzerland: WWF, 2012), 56.

13. UNEP, "UNEP-Hosted Global Partnership on Waste Management Answering Call as Municipal Waste to Grow to 2.2 Billion Tonnes per Year by 2025," UNEP Newsdesk release, November 6, 2012.

14. WWF, *Living Planet Report 2014*, 59.

15. "The State of Consumption Today," Worldwatch Institute, www.worldwatch.org/node/810#1.

16. Mark J. Perry, "Today's New Homes Are 1,000 Square Feet Larger Than in 1973, and the Living Space per Person Has Doubled over Last 40 Years," AEIdeas Blog, February 26, 2014, www.aei.org/publication/todays-new-homes-are-1000-square-feet-larger-than-in-1973-and-the-living-space-per-person-has-doubled-over-last-40-years/.

17. Jonathan Vespa, Jamie Lewis, and Rose Kreider, *America's Families and Living Arrangements: 2012* (Washington, DC: US Census Bureau, 2013), 7.

18. WWF, *Living Planet Report 2014*, 37.

19. UN, *Millennium Development Goals Report 2014* (New York: UN, 2014), 5, 8–9.

20. "Water Quality," UN Water, www.unwater.org/statistics/statistics-detail/en/c/260727/.

21. Roddy Scheer and Doug Moss, "Use It and Lose It: The Outsize Effect of U.S. Consumption on the Environment," *Scientific American*, September 14, 2012, www.scientificamerican.com/article/american-consumption-habits/.

22. International Energy Agency (IEA), *World Energy Outlook 2014 Factsheet* (Paris: IEA, 2014), 5, www.worldenergyoutlook.org/media/weowebsite/2014/141112_WEO_FactSheets.pdf.

23. "Energy Use (kg of oil equivalent per capita)," World Bank, http://data.worldbank.org/indicator/EG.USE.PCAP.KG.OE/countries/1W-US-CN-IN?display=graph.

24. John Banks, *Key Sub-Saharan Energy Trends and Their Importance for the US* (Washington, DC: Brookings Institute, 2013).

25. "Global Energy Statistical Yearbook 2015," Enerdata, http://yearbook.enerdata.net/.

26. Ibid.

27. A. Boden, G. Marland, and R. J. Andres, *Global, Regional, and National Fossil-Fuel CO_2 Emissions* (Oak Ridge, TN: Carbon Dioxide Information Analysis Center, Oak Ridge National Laboratory, US Department of Energy, 2013), doi:10.3334/CDIAC/00001_V2013.

28. Global Carbon Project, "Fossil Fuel Emissions," www.globalcarbonatlas.org/?q=en/emissions.

29. World Bank, "CO_2 Emissions (metric tons per capita)," http://data.worldbank.org/indicator/EN.ATM.CO2E.PC.

30. Ibid.

31. IEA, *World Energy Outlook Factsheet: Global Energy Trends to 2040* (Paris: IEA, 2015), www.worldenergyoutlook.org/media/weowebsite/2015/WEO2015_Factsheets.pdf.

32. World Meteorological Organization, "WMO: 2015 Likely to Be Warmest on Record, 2011–2015 Warmest Five Year Period," press release no. 13, November 25, 2015, www.wmo.int/media/content/wmo-2015-likely-be-warmest-record-2011-2015-warmest-five-year-period.

33. Intergovernmental Panel on Climate Change, *Climate Change 2013: The Physical Science Basis,* Contribution of Working Group I to the Fifth Assessment Report of the Intergovernmental Panel on Climate Change, eds. T. F. Stocker, D. Qin, G. K. Plattner, M. Tignor, S. K. Allen, J. Boschung, A. Nauels, Y. Xia, V. Bex, and P. M. Midgley (New York: Cambridge University Press, 2013).

34. UNEP, *GEO 5.*

35. Ibid.

36. UN-Water, *World Water Development Report 2014* (Paris: UN, 2014), 4, 23.

37. Ibid., 23.

38. Ibid., 2, 24.

39. A hectare is 10,000 square meters.

40. UNEP, *Annual Report 2014* (Nairobi: UNEP, 2015), 22.

41. Food and Agriculture Organization of the UN (FAO), *Global Forest Resources Assessment 2015: How Are the World's Forests Changing?* (Rome: FAO, 2015), 18.

42. UNEP, *Annual Report 2014*, 4.

43. UNEP, *Protected Planet Report 2014* (Nairobi: UNEP, 2014), 17.

44. World Resources Institute (WRI), *Ecosystems and Human Well-Being: Biodiversity Synthesis* (Washington, DC: WRI, 2005).

45. FAO, *State of the World Fisheries and Aquaculture* (Rome: FAO, 2014), 37.

46. FAO, "Ecosystems, Biodiversity and Genetics," in *The Post-2015 Development Agenda and the Millennium Development Goals* (Rome: FAO, 2014), 2.

47. FAO, *State of the World Fisheries and Aquaculture*, 37.

48. FAO, "Ecosystems, Biodiversity and Genetics."

49. J. Samuel Barkin and Elizabeth R. DeSombre, *Saving Global Fisheries: Reducing Fishing Capacity to Promote Sustainability* (Cambridge, MA: MIT Press, 2013).

50. FAO, *Review of the State of World Marine Fishery Resources*, 13–14.

51. Secretariat of the Convention on Biological Diversity and the Scientific and Technical Advisory Panel–Global Environment Facility, *Impacts of Marine Debris on Biodiversity: Current Status and Potential Solutions*, Technical Series No. 67 (Montreal: Secretariat of the CBD, 2012). See also UNEP, *Marine Litter: A Global Challenge* (Nairobi: UNEP, 2009).

52. World Economic Forum and Ellen MacArthur Foundation, *The New Plastics Economy: Rethinking the Future of Plastics* (Cologne and Geneva: World Economic Forum, 2016), www3.weforum.org/docs/WEF_The_New_Plastics_Economy.pdf.

53. Daniela Russi et al., *The Economics of Ecosystems and Biodiversity for Water and Wetlands: A Briefing Note* (Geneva: UNEP, 2012).

54. Ibid.

55. UNEP, *Protected Planet Report 2014* (Nairobi: UNEP, 2014), 9.

56. Russi et al., *The Economics of Ecosystems.*

57. Worldwatch Institute, *Vital Signs* (Washington, DC: Worldwatch, 2014).

58. UN-Water, *World Water Development Report 2014*, 54.

59. Asbjørn Eide, *The Right to Food and the Impact of Liquid Biofuels (Agrofuels)* (Rome: FAO, 2008), 14.

60. UN-Water, "Statistics," www.unwater.org/statistics/statistics-detail/en/c/211815/.

61. See Eide, *The Right to Food*, 44. Analyses of the links between climate change and weather include Vladimir Petoukhov et al., "Quasiresonant Amplification of Planetary Waves and Recent Northern Hemisphere Weather Extremes," *Proceedings of the National Academy of Sciences* (March 1, 2013), doi:10.1073/pnas.1222000110; C. B. Fields et al., eds., *Managing the Risks of Extreme Events and Disasters to Advance Climate Change Adaptation: Special Report of the Intergovernmental Panel on Climate Change* (Cambridge: Cambridge University Press for the IPCC, 2012); and Department of Climate Change and Energy Efficiency, Government of Australia, *The Angry Summer* (Canberra: Commonwealth of Australia, 2013).

62. "Drought Information," California Department of Water Resources, www.water.ca.gov/waterconditions/; Soumaya Belmecheri, "Multi-century Evaluation of Sierra Nevada Snow-pack," *Nature Climate Change* (2015), doi:10.1038/nclimate2809.

63. International Resource Panel, UNEP, *Towards Sustainable Production and Use of Resources: Assessing Biofuels* (Nairobi: UNEP, 2009); Mireille Faist Emmenegger et al., *Harmonisation and Extension of the Bioenergy Inventories and Assessment* (Bern, Switzerland: EMPA [Swiss Federal Laboratories for Material Science and Technology], 2012), www.empa.ch/plugin/template/empa/*/125527; Michael Hagman, "New Data on the Biofuel Ecobalance: Most Biofuels Are Not 'Green,'" EMPA, September 24, 2012, www.empa.ch/plugin/template/empa/3/125597/—-/l=2; Damian Carrington, "Leaked Data: Palm Biodiesel as Dirty as Fuel from Tar Sands," *Guardian*, January 27, 2012.

64. National Corn Growers Association (NCGA), *World of Corn: Unlimited Possibilities* (Washington, DC: NCGA, 2013), www.ncga.com/upload/files/documents/pdf/WOC%20 2013.pdf.

65. Timothy Wise, "The Cost to Developing Countries of U.S. Corn Ethanol Expansion," Global Development and Environment Institute Working Paper No. 12-02, Tufts University, October 2012, 2, www.ase.tufts.edu/gdae/Pubs/wp/12-02WiseGlobalBiofuels.pdf.

66. UNEP, *GEO 5*, 46–48.

67. UNEP, "UNEP-Hosted Global Partnership on Waste Management."

68. "Global Health Observatory Data: Urban Health," World Health Organization, www.who.int/gho/urban_health/en/.

69. UN Human Settlement Program (UNHSP), *World Habitat Day Voices from Slums: Background Paper* (Nairobi: UN Habitat, 2014), 1, http://unhabitat.org/wp-content/uploads/2014/07/WHD-2014-Background-Paper.pdf.

70. UN, *World Urbanization Prospects, 2014 Revision* (New York: UN, 2014), 93.

71. UNHSP, *World Habitat Day Voices from Slums: Background Paper*, 2.

72. For an early effort to categorize environmental problems, see Clifford Russell and Hans Landsberg, "International Environmental Problems: A Taxonomy," *Science* 172 (June 25, 1972): 1307–1314.

73. Garrett Hardin, "The Tragedy of the Commons," *Science* 162, no. 3859 (December 13, 1968): 1243–1248.

74. Oran Young, *International Governance: Protecting the Environment in a Stateless Society* (Ithaca, NY: Cornell University Press, 1994), 19–26.

75. Diane Bui, "The Instance of Environmental Regimes," in *Delegating State Powers: The Effect of Treaty Regimes on Democracy and Sovereignty*, ed. Thomas Franck (Ardsley, NY: Transnational Publishers, 2000), 33.

76. Lars-Göran Engfeldt, "The Road from Stockholm to Johannesburg," *UN Chronicle* 39, no. 3 (September–November 2002): 14–17.

77. UN Conference on Environment and Development, *Agenda 21, Rio Declaration, Forest Principles* (New York: UN, 1992).

78. This definition builds explicitly on the definition developed in Stephen Krasner, ed., *International Regimes* (Ithaca, NY: Cornell University Press, 1983). Compare the definition and use of the term *regime* in John Gerard Ruggie, "International Responses to Technology: Concepts and Trends," *International Organization* 29 (1975): 557–583; Ernst Haas, "On Systems and International Regimes," *World Politics* 27 (1975): 147–174; Robert Keohane and Joseph Nye Jr., *Power and Interdependence: World Politics in Transition* (Boston: Little, Brown, 1977); Oran Young, "International Regimes: Problems of Concept Formation," *International Organization* 32 (1980): 331–356; Robert Keohane, *After Hegemony: Cooperation and Discord in the World Political Economy* (Princeton, NJ: Princeton University Press, 1984); Jack Donnelly, "International Human Rights: A Regime Analysis," *International Organization* 40 (1986): 599–642; Stephan Haggard and Beth Simmons, "Theories of International Regimes," *International Organization* 41 (1987): 491–517; and David Downie, "Road Map or False Trail: Evaluating the Precedence of the Ozone Regime as Model and Strategy for Global Climate Change," *International Environmental Affairs* 7 (Fall 1995): 321–345.

79. For influential discussions of the study of international cooperation, see and compare Friedrich Kratochwil and John Gerard Ruggie, "International Organization: A State of the Art on an Art of the State," *International Organization* 40 (1986): 753–776; James Dougherty and Robert Pfaltzgraff Jr., *Contending Theories of International Relations: A Comprehensive Survey*, 5th ed. (New York: Pearson, 2001), ch. 10; and Joseph Grieco, "Anarchy and the Limits of Cooperation: A Realist Critique of the Newest Liberal Institutionalism," *International Organization* 42 (1988): 485–507.

80. Classic examples include Thucydides, Machiavelli, and Hobbes. Influential modern examples include Hans J. Morgenthau, *Politics Among Nations: The Struggle for Power and Peace*, 5th ed. (New York: Knopf, 1973); Robert Jervis, "Cooperation Under the Security Dilemma," *World Politics* 30 (1978): 167–186; and Kenneth Waltz, *Theory of International Politics* (Reading, MA: Addison-Wesley, 1979).

81. Constitutionalists believed "international governance is whatever international organizations do; and formal attributes of international organizations, such as their charters, voting procedures, committee structures and the like, account for what they do" (Kratochwil and Ruggie, "International Organization," 755). The institutional process approach examines influence, how information is produced and digested, who speaks to whom, how decisions are made, and so on. It argues that the outputs of international organizations do not always reflect their charters or official procedures. A classic example is Robert Cox and Harold Jacobson, eds., *The Anatomy of Influence: Decision Making in International Organization* (New Haven, CT: Yale University Press, 1973).

82. For example, Richard Falk, *A Study of Future Worlds* (Princeton, NJ: Princeton University Press, 1975).

83. Important examples and discussions of functionalism include David Mitrany, *A Working Peace System: An Argument for the Functional Development of International Organization* (1943; repr., Chicago: Quadrangle Books, 1966); David Mitrany, *The Functional Theory of Politics* (London: M. Robertson, 1975); and A. J. R. Groom and Paul Taylor, eds., *Functionalism: Theory and Practice in International Relations* (New York: Crane, Russak, 1975).

84. See and compare discussions in Kratochwil and Ruggie, "International Organization," 756–763; Dougherty and Pfaltzgraff, *Contending Theories of International Relations*, ch. 10; and Groom and Taylor, *Functionalism*, ch. 1.

85. Leading examples and discussion include Ernst Haas, *Beyond the Nation State: Functionalism and International Organization* (Stanford, CA: Stanford University Press, 1964);

Ernst Haas, "The Uniting of Europe and the Uniting of Latin America," *Journal of Common Market Studies* 5 (1967): 315–343; Philippe Schmitter, "Three Neo-Functional Hypotheses About International Integration," *International Organization* 23 (1969): 161–166; Ernst Haas, "The Study of Regional Integration: Reflections on the Joy and Anguish of Pretheorizing," *International Organization* 24 (1970): 607–646; Kratochwil and Ruggie, "International Organization," 757–759; and Groom and Taylor, *Functionalism*, chs. 11–12.

86. Examples are Ernst Haas, "On Systems and International Regimes," *World Politics* 27 (1975): 147–174; and Ernst Haas, *When Knowledge Is Power: Three Models of Change in International Organizations* (Berkeley: University of California Press, 1990).

87. Robert Keohane and Joseph Nye Jr., eds., *Transnational Relations and World Politics* (Cambridge, MA: Harvard University Press, 1972); Robert Keohane and Joseph Nye Jr., "Transnational Relations and International Organizations," *World Politics* 27 (October 1974): 39–62.

88. Keohane and Nye, *Power and Interdependence.* Complex interdependence and turbulent fields share important concerns and insights.

89. This paragraph is adapted from I. William Zartman, ed., *The 50% Solution: How to Bargain Successfully with Hijackers, Strikers, Bosses, Oil Magnates, Arabs, Russians, and Other Worthy Opponents* (1976; repr., New Haven, CT: Yale University Press, 1983), 9–10.

90. R. Michael M'Gonigle and Mark Zacher, *Pollution, Politics, and International Law: Tankers at Sea* (Berkeley: University of California Press, 1979), 58–59, 84–85, 93–96.

91. Keohane, *After Hegemony*, provides an influential discussion of why it is easier to change international regimes to make them more effective than it is to create new ones.

92. For more information on the Convention on Migratory Species initiative on migratory sharks, see "CMS Convention on Migratory Species: Meetings on Migratory Sharks," Convention on Migratory Species, 2010, www.cms.int/bodies/meetings/regional/sharks/sharks_meetings.htm.

93. For an early analytical overview of these approaches, see Haggard and Simmons, "Theories of International Regimes."

94. Keohane and Nye, *Power and Interdependence*, 50–51.

95. For the former approach, see Robert Gilpin, *The Political Economy of International Relations* (Princeton, NJ: Princeton University Press, 1987); Grieco, "Anarchy and the Limits of Cooperation"; and Susan Strange, "Cave! Hic Dragones: A Critique of Regime Analysis," *International Organization* 36 (Spring 1982): 479–496. Susan Strange, "The Persistent Myth of Lost Hegemony," *International Organization* 41 (Summer 1987): 570, argues that inconsistency in US policy rather than loss of US global hegemony caused erosion of international regimes.

96. Oran Young, "The Politics of International Regime Formation: Managing Natural Resources and the Environment," *International Organization* 43 (Summer 1989): 355.

97. Fen Osler Hampson, "Climate Change: Building International Coalitions of the Like-Minded," *International Journal* 45 (Winter 1989–1990): 36–74.

98. See Peter Haas, "Do Regimes Matter? Epistemic Communities and Mediterranean Pollution Control," *International Organization* 43 (Summer 1989): 378–403.

99. The issue of ocean dumping of radioactive wastes, in which scientific evidence was explicitly rejected as the primary basis for decision making by antidumping states, is analyzed in Judith Spiller and Cynthia Hayden, "Radwaste at Sea: A New Era of Polarization or a New Basis for Consensus?" *Ocean Development and International Law* 19 (1988): 345–366.

100. Robert Putnam, "Diplomacy and Domestic Politics: The Logic of Two-Level Games," *International Organization* 42, no. 3 (Summer 1988): 427–460.

101. For example, David Downie, "Understanding International Environmental Regimes: Lessons of the Ozone" (PhD diss., University of North Carolina, Chapel Hill, 1996).

102. For an influential and accessible discussion of paradigm shifts, see Thomas Kuhn, *The Structure of Scientific Revolutions* (Chicago: University of Chicago Press, 1962). Our discussion

of paradigm shifts is not offered as a new theory to compete with existing theories of international regimes but rather as a supplementary set of lenses through which to discuss environmental issues.

103. Harold and Margaret Sprout, *The Ecological Perspective on Human Affairs, with Special Reference to International Politics* (Princeton, NJ: Princeton University Press, 1965); Kenneth Boulding, "The Economics of the Coming Spaceship Earth," in *Environmental Quality in a Growing Economy: Essays from the Sixth RFF Forum*, ed. Henry Jarrett (Baltimore: Johns Hopkins University Press, 1966).

104. For an analysis of neoclassical economic assumptions as they bear on environmental management, see Daniel Underwood and Paul King, "On the Ideological Foundations of Environmental Policy," *Ecological Economics* 1 (1989): 317–322.

105. See Michael Colby, *Environmental Management in Development: The Evolution of Paradigms* (Washington, DC: World Bank, 1990).

106. John McCormick, *Reclaiming Paradise: The Global Environmental Movement* (Bloomington: Indiana University Press, 1989), 67.

107. See Clem Tisdell, "Sustainable Development: Differing Perspectives of Ecologists and Economists, and Relevance to LDCs," *World Development* 16 (1988): 377–378.

108. Donella Meadows et al., *The Limits to Growth: A Report for the Club of Rome's Project on the Predicament of Mankind* (New York: Universe Books, 1972); Council on Environmental Quality and Gerald Barney, *Global 2000: The Report to the President Entering the Twenty-First Century* (New York: Pergamon, 1980).

109. Julian Simon and Herman Kahn, eds., *The Resourceful Earth: A Response to Global 2000* (Oxford: Basil Blackwell, 1984).

110. For background on the sustainable development concept, see UN Center for Transnational Corporations, *Environmental Aspects of the Activities of Transnational Corporations: A Survey* (New York: UN, 1985).

111. World Commission on Environment and Development, *Our Common Future* (Oxford: Oxford University Press, 1987).

112. See Edith Brown Weiss, "In Fairness to Future Generations," *Environment* 32 (April 1990), 7–11, 30–31; and similar arguments made in the Latin American and Caribbean Commission on Development and Environment, *Our Own Agenda* (New York: Inter-American Development Bank, 1990).

113. See Alan Durning, "How Much Is Enough?" *Worldwatch* 3 (November–December 1990): 12–19.

114. See Yusuf Ahmad, Salah El Serafy, and Ernst Lutz, eds., *Environmental Accounting for Sustainable Development* (Washington, DC: World Bank, 1989). For an early example of natural resource accounting, see Robert Repetto et al., *Accounts Overdue: Natural Resources Depreciation in Costa Rica* (Washington, DC: WRI, 1991).

115. See Herman E. Daly, "Toward a Measure of Sustainable Social Net National Product," in Ahmad, Serafy, and Lutz, *Environmental Accounting for Sustainable Development*, 8–9; and Herman Daly and John Cobb Jr., *For the Common Good: Redirecting the Economy Toward Community, the Environment and a Sustainable Future* (Boston: Beacon, 1989), 368–373, 401–455. A similar effort to rate the distributive effects of national policies is embodied in the UN Development Programme's human development indicators in its annual *Human Development Report.*

116. Centre for Bhutan Studies, *A Short Guide to Gross National Happiness Index* (Thimphu, Bhutan: Centre for Bhutan Studies, 2012), www.grossnationalhappiness.com/wp-content/uploads/2012/04/Short-GNH-Index-final1.pdf.

117. See World Bank, "National Capital Accounting," May 20, 2015, www.worldbank.org/en/topic/environment/brief/environmental-economics-natural-capital-accounting.

118. See UN Statistics Division, "The System of Environmental-Economic Accounts (SEEA) Measurement Framework in Support of Sustainable Development and Green Economy Policy," Briefing Note, http://unstats.un.org/unsd/envaccounting/Brochure.pdf.

119. See "Measuring Well-Being and Progress," Organization for Economic Cooperation and Development, www.oecd.org/statistics/measuringwell-beingandprogress.htm.

120. For information on the Environmental Sustainability Index, see www.yale.edu/esi.

121. Commission of the European Communities, *GDP and Beyond: Measuring Progress in a Changing World*, http://eur-lex.europa.eu/LexUriServ/LexUriServ.do?uri=COM:2009:0433:FIN:EN:PDF. See also "Indicators," European Commission, http://epp.eurostat.ec.europa.eu/portal/page/portal/sdi/indicators.

122. See, for example, Partha Dasgupta and Karl Goran Maler, "The Environment and Emerging Development Issues," paper presented at the World Bank Conference on Development Economics, April 26–27, 1990, 22; and Sander Tideman, "Gross National Happiness: Towards a New Paradigm in Economics," in *Gross National Happiness and Development: Proceedings of the First International Seminar on Operationalization of Gross National Happiness*, ed. Karma Ura and Karma Galay (Thimphu, Bhutan: Centre for Bhutan Studies, 2004), 222–246.

123. See Robert Repetto, *Promoting Environmentally Sound Economic Progress: What the North Can Do* (Washington, DC: WRI, 1990); and Daly, "Toward a Measure of Sustainable Social Net National Product."

124. Pamela Chasek and Lynn Wagner, "An Insider's Guide to Multilateral Environmental Negotiations Since the Earth Summit," in *The Roads from Rio: Lessons Learned from Twenty Years of Multilateral Environmental Negotiations*, eds. Pamela Chasek and Lynn Wagner (New York: RFF, 2012), 1–2.

125. Tideman, "Gross National Happiness," 229.

126. UNEP, *GEO 5*.

127. Martin Khor, "Globalisation and Sustainable Development: Challenges for Johannesburg," *Third World Resurgence* 139/140 (March–April 2002).

128. For example, James Gustave Speth, "Two Perspectives on Globalization and the Environment," in *Worlds Apart: Globalization and the Environment*, ed. James Gustave Speth (Washington, DC: Island, 2003), 12.

129. UNEP, *Towards a Green Economy: Pathways to Sustainable Development and Poverty Eradication* (Nairobi: UNEP, 2011).

130. Ibid.

131. Ibid., 14.

132. UN, *Secretary-General's Report on Objectives and Themes of the United Nations Conference*, December 22, 2010, 5, www.uncsd2012.org/index.php?page=view&type=400&nr=10&menu=45.

133. UNEP, *Towards a Green Economy*, 14.

134. Ibid., 16–17.

135. "Summary of the United Nations Conference on Sustainable Development: 13–22 June 2012," *Earth Negotiations Bulletin* 27, no. 51 (June 25, 2012): 21.

136. Martin Khor, "Global Debate on 'Green Economy,'" *Star* (Malaysia), January 24, 2011.

137. UN, *The Future We Want*, July 24, 2012, 10, www.uncsd2012.org/thefuturewewant.html.

138. Neil Carter, *Politics of the Environment: Ideas, Activism, Policy*, 2nd ed. (Cambridge: Cambridge University Press, 2007), 272–273. For additional views on this argument, see Jagdish Bhagwati, *In Defense of Globalization* (Oxford: Oxford University Press, 2004); and Jennifer Clapp and Peter Dauvergne, *Paths to a Green World: The Political Economy of the Global Environment* (Cambridge, MA: MIT Press, 2005).

139. Carter, *Politics of the Environment*, 273; and Ronnie D. Lipschutz, *Global Environmental Politics: Power, Perspectives, and Practice* (Washington, DC: Congressional Quarterly Press, 2004), 121.

140. Carter, *Politics of the Environment*, 273; and Arthur Mol, *Globalization and Environmental Reform* (Cambridge, MA: MIT Press, 2003), 71–72, 126.

141. Paul Raskin et al., *Great Transition: The Promise and Lure of the Times Ahead* (Boston: Stockholm Environment Institute, 2002). Compare with Kuhn's analysis of paradigm shifts in science in *The Structure of Scientific Revolutions*.

142. For updated information on EU sustainable development policy, see the relevant official websites, including "Environment: Sustainable Development," European Commission, http://ec.europa.eu/environment/eussd.

143. See, for example, Thomas Homer-Dixon, "On the Threshold: Environmental Changes as Causes of Acute Conflict," *International Security* 16, no. 2 (1991): 76–116; Thomas F. Homer-Dixon, "Environmental Scarcities and Violent Conflict: Evidence from Cases," *International Security* 19, no. 1 (1994): 5–40; Thomas F. Homer-Dixon and Jessica Blitt, eds., *Ecoviolence: Links Among Environment, Population and Security* (Lanham, MD: Rowman & Littlefield, 1998); and Thomas Homer-Dixon, *Environment, Scarcity, and Violence* (Princeton, NJ: Princeton University Press, 1999). For current news and reports, see the Environmental Change and Security Program website: www.wilsoncenter.org/program/environmental-change-and-security-program.

144. UNEP, *Sudan: Post Conflict Environmental Assessment* (Nairobi: UN, 2007); Clionadh Raleigh, "Political Marginalization, Climate Change, and Conflict in African Sahel States," *International Studies Review* 12, no. 1 (2010): 69–86.

145. See Doug Hawley, "Drug Smugglers Curtail Scientists' Work," *USA Today*, December 27, 2007.

146. Christian Nelleman, UNEP, and INTERPOL, *Green Carbon, Black Trade: Illegal Logging, Tax Fraud and Laundering in the World's Tropical Forests* (Nairobi: UNEP, 2012).

147. Maura O'Connor, "Two Years Later, Haitian Earthquake Death Toll in Dispute," *Columbia Journalism Review*, January 12, 2012.

148. See, for example, Geoffrey Dabelko and P. J. Simmons, "Environment and Security: Core Ideas and U.S. Government Initiatives," *SAIS Review* (Winter/Spring 1997): 127–146; German Advisory Council on Global Change, *Climate Change as a Security Risk* (Oxford: Earthscan, 2007); The White House, *Findings from Select Federal Reports: The National Security Implications of a Changing Climate* (Washington: The White House, May 2015), www.whitehouse.gov/sites/default/files/docs/National_Security_Implications_of_Changing_Climate_Final_051915.pdf.

149. Oli Brown and Alec Crawford, *Climate Change and Security in Africa* (Winnipeg, Canada: International Institute for Sustainable Development, 2009), 2.

150. Oli Brown and Alec Crawford, *Rising Temperatures, Rising Tensions: Climate Change and the Risk of Violent Conflict in the Middle East* (Winnipeg, Canada: International Institute for Sustainable Development, 2009), 2.

151. For discussion, see J. Oglethorpe, J. Shambaugh, and R. Kormos, "Parks in the Crossfire: Strategies for Effective Conservation in Areas of Armed Conflict," *IUCN Protected Areas Programme: Parks* 14, no. 1 (2004): 2–8.

152. G. Debonnet and K. Hillman-Smith, "Supporting Protected Areas in a Time of Political Turmoil: The Case of World Heritage Sites in the Democratic Republic of Congo," *IUCN Protected Areas Programme: Parks* 14, no. 1 (2004): 11.

153. See, for example, Talli Nauman, "Illegal Drugs Root of Evil for Conservation Community," *Herald Mexico*, August 1, 2006; Hawley, "Drug Smugglers Curtail Scientists' Work."

154. "Rio Declaration on Environment and Development," in *Report of the United Nations Conference on the Human Environment*, Stockholm, June 5–16, 1972, ch. 1, www.un-documents.net/rio-dec.htm.

155. These concepts are adapted from David Kriebel et al., "The Precautionary Principle in Environmental Science," *Environmental Health Perspective* 109, no. 9 (September 2001): 871–876.

156. Carolyn Raffensperger and Katherine Barrett, "In Defense of the Precautionary Principle," *Environmental Health Perspective* 109, no. 9 (September 2001): 811–812.

157. For a collection of examples, see Joel Tickner, Carolyn Raffensperger, and Nancy Myers, *The Precautionary Principle in Action: A Handbook*, www.sehn.org/rtfdocs/handbook-rtf.rtf.

158. Ministerial Declaration, Second International Conference on the Protection of the North Sea, London, November 24–25, 1987, www.vliz.be/imisdocs/publications/140155.pdf.

159. Preamble, Montreal Protocol, 26 ILM 1541, September 16, 1987.

160. UN Framework Convention on Climate Change, UN, May 9, 1992, www.un-documents.net/unfccc.htm.

161. See Article 10 and Article 11 of the Biosafety Protocol, http://bch.cbd.int/protocol/text/.

162. Article 1 of the Stockholm Convention on Persistent Organic Pollutants, May 22, 2001, http://chm.pops.int/Portals/0/download.aspx?d=UNEP-POPS-COP-CONVTEXT-2009.En.pdf.

163. Communication from the Commission on the Precautionary Principle COM 1.1 Final, Commission of the European Communities, February 2, 2000.

164. See Tickner, Raffensperger, and Myers, *The Precautionary Principle in Action*, 16–17.

165. Ibid.

166. Ibid.

167. Personal observations by David Downie during negotiations related to the Montreal Protocol and the Rotterdam and Stockholm Conventions.

168. Jon Van Dyke, "The Evolution and International Acceptance of the Precautionary Principle," in *Bringing New Law to Ocean Waters*, eds. David Caron and Harry Scheiber (Leiden, Netherlands: Martinus Nijhoff, 2004), 357.

Chapter 2: Actors in the Environmental Arena

1. David Day, *The Whale War* (Vancouver: Douglas and MacIntyre, 1987), 103–107.

2. These data come from the Indonesian Ministry of Forest's *Production Forest Utilization Quarterly Report* in 2011. See "7 Conglomerates Control 9M ha of Land in Indonesia," mongabay.com, May 5, 2011, http://news.mongabay.com/2011/0504-indonesia_conglomerates.html. REDD is a program that seeks to create economic incentives for developing countries to protect and better manage their forest resources, thereby helping to combat climate change. REDD aims to make forests more valuable standing than cut down by creating a financial value for the carbon stored in trees. For information, see www.un-redd.org.

3. Richard Benedick, *Ozone Diplomacy: New Directions in Safeguarding the Planet*, 2nd ed. (Cambridge, MA: Harvard University Press, 1998), 59.

4. The German Green Party was routed in the first all-German elections since 1932 because it opposed reunification. It began to rebound in the mid-1990s and then won thirty-four seats in the German parliament in 1998 and made history by becoming part of a coalition government with the Social Democratic Party. In 2002, the Green Party won fifty-five seats and continued its role in the coalition government with the Social Democratic Party, which lasted until 2005.

5. *Earth Summit Update* 7 (March 1992): 3.

6. Detlev Sprinz and Tapani Vaahtoranta, "The Interest-Based Explanation of International Environmental Policy," *International Organization* 48, no. 1 (1994): 77–105.

7. Brian Gareau, *From Precaution to Profit: Contemporary Challenges to Environmental Protection in the Montreal Protocol* (New Haven, CT: Yale University Press, 2013), details the development of and strongly criticizes the methyl bromide exemptions.

8. On EU ambitions for global leadership on the environment, see Brian Wynne, "Implementation of Greenhouse Gas Reductions in the European Community: Institutional and

Cultural Factors," *Global Environmental Change Report* 3 (March 1993): 101–128; Yannis Paleokrassas is quoted in *Energy, Economics and Climate Change* 4, no. 7 (July 1994): 14.

9. Eugene Robinson and Michael Weisskopf, "Bonn Pushes Tough Stand on Warming; U.S. Puts Pressure on 3 Allies to Drop 2nd Stiff Initiative," *Washington Post*, June 9, 1992, A1.

10. Philippe Le Prestre and Evelyne Dufault, "Canada and the Kyoto Protocol on GHGs," *ISUMA* 2, no. 4 (Winter 2001): 40.

11. Bill Curry and Shawn McCarthy, "Canada Formally Abandons Kyoto Protocol on Climate Change," *Globe and Mail*, December 12, 2011.

12. United Nations Environment Programme (UNEP), *Climate Commitments of Subnational Actors and Business: A Quantitative Assessment of the Emission Reduction Impact* (Nairobi: UNEP, 2015), 11.

13. "Cities to the Rescue," *US News and World Report*, October 15, 2015, www.usnews.com/opinion/articles/2015/10/16/cities-are-leading-the-way-on-climate-action.

14. For information, see the US Conference of Mayors Climate Protection Center's website: www.usmayors.org/climateprotection/revised/.

15. Carbon Neutral Cities Alliance, http://usdn.org/public/Carbon-Neutral-Cities.html.

16. "Cities to the Rescue."

17. Ibid.

18. City of New York, "Mayor de Blasio Commits to 80 Percent Reduction of Greenhouse Gas Emissions by 2050, Starting with Sweeping Green Buildings Plan," press release, September 21, 2014, www1.nyc.gov/office-of-the-mayor/news/451-14/mayor-de-blasio-commits-80-percent-reduction-greenhouse-gas-emissions-2050-starting-with/#/0.

19. Matt Richtel, "San Diego Vows to Move Entirely to Renewable Energy in 20 Years," *New York Times*, December 15, 2015.

20. C40 Cities, *Working Together: Global Aggregation of City Climate Commitments*, http://c40-production-images.s3.amazonaws.com/researches/images/24_Working_Together_Global_Aggregation.original.pdf?1411483385.

21. See, for example, "Greenhouse Gas Emissions Targets," Center for Climate and Energy Solutions, www.c2es.org/us-states-regions/policy-maps/emissions-targets.

22. Sierra Club, "Oregon Governor Kate Brown Signs Historic Coal Transition Bill into Law," press release, March 11, 2016, http://content.sierraclub.org/press-releases/2016/03/oregon-governor-kate-brown-signs-historic-coal-transition-bill-law.

23. Robert Semple Jr., "California Leads the Way on Climate Change," *New York Times*, October 14, 2015, http://takingnote.blogs.nytimes.com/2015/10/14/california-leads-the-way-on-climate-change/?ref=topics&_r=0.

24. "Minnesota Climate and Energy Profile: Sources of Electricity Produced in Minnesota in 2013," Georgetown Climate Center, http://energy.georgetownclimate.org/clean-energy-and-climate-data?state=MN#.

25. "Washington Climate and Energy Profile: Sources of Electricity Produced in Washington in 2013," Georgetown Climate Center, http://energy.georgetownclimate.org/clean-energy-and-climate-data?state=WA.

26. Paul Hibbard, Andrea Okie, Susan Tierney, and Pavel Darling, *The Economic Impact of the Regional Greenhouse Gas Initiative on Nine Northeast and Mid-Atlantic States: Review of RGGI's Second Three Year Compliance Period (2012–2014)*, (Boston: Analysis Group, 2015), www.analysisgroup.com/uploadedfiles/content/insights/publishing/analysis_group_rggi_report_july_2015.pdf; Alex Nussbaum, "Carbon-Trading Program Generates $1.3 Billion in U.S. Northeast," *Bloomberg Business*, July 13, 2015, www.bloomberg.com/news/articles/2015-07-14/carbon-trading-program-generates-1-3-billion-in-u-s-northeast.

27. Ben Cubby, "Carbon Neutral NSW by 2020," *Sydney Morning Herald*, May 9, 2008.

28. Rowena Mason, "Most of Britain's Major Cities Pledge to Run on Green Energy by 2050," *Guardian*, November 23, 2015.

29. British Columbia Ministry of Environment, "B.C. Celebrates Five Consecutive Carbon Neutral Years," press release, June 30, 2015, http://news.gov.bc.ca/stories/bc-celebrates-five-consecutive-carbon-neutral-years.

30. Province of Quebec, "A Brief Look at the Quebec Cap and Trade System for Emission Allowances," 2014, www.mddelcc.gouv.qc.ca/changements/carbone/documents-spede/in-brief.pdf.

31. United Nations Environment Programme (UNEP), *GEO 5: Global Environmental Outlook—Environment for the Future We Want* (Nairobi: UNEP, 2012), 355.

32. United Nations Environment Assembly of the UNEP, *Proposed Biennial Programme of Work and Budget for 2016–2017,* UNEP/EA/1/7, April 12, 2014, 16, www.unep.org/unea/download.asp?ID=4833.

33. For a similar discussion that uses different terms, see David Downie, "UNEP and the Montreal Protocol: New Roles for International Organizations in Regime Creation and Change," in *International Organizations and Environmental Policy*, eds. Robert Bartlett, Priya Kurian, and Madhu Malik (Westport, CT: Greenwood, 1995).

34. Richard Benedick, "The Ozone Protocol: A New Global Diplomacy," *Conservation Foundation Letter* 4 (1989): 6–7; and Benedick, *Ozone Diplomacy*, 109–110.

35. David L. Downie and Marc Levy, "The United Nations Environment Programme at a Turning Point: Options for Change," in *The Global Environment in the Twenty-First Century: Prospects for International Cooperation*, ed. Pamela Chasek (Tokyo: United Nations University Press, 2000).

36. UNEP, *State of the Environment and Contribution of the United Nations Environment Programme to Addressing Substantive Environmental Challenges: Report of the Executive Director*, UNEP/GC.23/3, October 21, 2004, www.unep.org/gc/gc23/working_docs.asp.

37. See UNEP, *United Nations Environment Programme Medium-Term Strategy 2010–2013*, UNEP/GCSS.X/8, 2007, www.unep.org/PDF/FinalMTSGCSS-X-8.pdf; and UNEP, *United Nations Environment Programme Medium-Term Strategy 2014–2017*, www.unep.org/pdf/MTS_2014-2017_Final.pdf.

38. See United Nations (UN), *Report of the Governing Council of the United Nations Environment Programme on Its Twelfth Special Session and the Implementation of Section IV.C, Entitled "Environmental Pillar in the Context of Sustainable Development," of the Outcome Document of the United Nations Conference on Sustainable Development*, resolution 67/213 (March 15, 2013), www.un.org/en/ga/search/view_doc.asp?symbol=A/RES/67/213; and UN, *Change of the Designation of the Governing Council of the United Nations Environment Programme*, resolution 67/251 (July 25, 2013), www.un.org/en/ga/search/view_doc.asp?symbol=A/RES/67/251.

39. See "Summary of the First UN Environment Assembly of the UN Environment Programme: 23–27 June 2014," *Earth Negotiations Bulletin* 16, no.122 (June 30, 2014).

40. Stine Madland Kaasa, "The UN Commission on Sustainable Development: Which Mechanisms Explain Its Accomplishments?" *Global Environmental Politics* 7, no. 3 (August 2007): 114–115. For details on the consultative process, see "United Nations Open-Ended Informal Consultative Process on Oceans and the Law of the Sea," www.un.org/Depts/los/consultative_process/consultative_process.htm.

41. UN, *The Future We Want*, A/RES/66/288, September 2012, http://sustainabledevelopment.un.org/futurewewant.html.

42. Gunnar Sjöstedt and Bertram Spector, conclusion to *International Environmental Negotiation*, ed. Gunnar Sjöstedt (Newbury Park, CA: Sage, 1993), 306.

43. Pamela Chasek, "Scientific Uncertainty in Environmental Negotiations," in *Global Environmental Policies*, ed. Ho-Won Jeong (London: Palgrave, 2001).

44. For information on the Millennium Ecosystem Assessment, see www.millenniumassessment.org.

45. For information on the Intergovernmental Science-Policy Platform on Biodiversity and Ecosystem Services, see www.ipbes.net.

46. Andrew Hurrell and Benedict Kingsbury, eds., *The International Politics of the Environment: Actors, Interests, and Institutions* (Oxford: Clarendon, 1992), 2; Pamela Chasek, *Earth Negotiations: Analyzing Thirty Years of Environmental Diplomacy* (Tokyo: United Nations University Press, 2001).

47. United Nations Development Programme, *Changing with the World: UNDP Strategic Plan 2014–1017* (New York: UNDP, 2013).

48. "Our Work: Sustainable Development," UNDP, www.undp.org/content/undp/en/home/ourwork/sustainable-development/overview.html.

49. "Our Work: Climate and Disaster Resilience," UNDP, www.undp.org/content/undp/en/home/ourwork/climate-and-disaster-resilience/overview.html.

50. Analytical discussions of secretariats include Frank Biermann and Bernd Siebenhüner, eds., *Managers of Global Change: The Influence of Environmental Bureaucracies* (Cambridge, MA: MIT Press, 2009); and Sikina Jinnah, *Post-Treaty Politics: Secretariat Influence on Global Environmental Governance* (Cambridge, MA: MIT Press, 2014).

51. This list is adapted from Rosemary Sandford, "International Environmental Treaty Secretariats: Stage-Hands or Actors," in *Green Globe Yearbook of International Cooperation on Environment and Development 1994*, ed. Helge Ole Bergesen and Georg Parmann (Oxford: Oxford University Press, 1994), 21.

52. Discussion of these two topics has been based on the analysis presented in Steffen Bauer, Per-Olof Busch, and Bernd Siebenhüner, "Administering International Governance: What Role for Treaty Secretariats?" Global Governance working paper 29, October 2007, www.glogov.org/images/doc/WP29.pdf.

53. Personal observations of the authors during attendance at more than seventy global environmental negotiations since 1990. For discussion, see Richard Benedick, "Perspectives of a Negotiation Practitioner," in *International Environmental Negotiation*, ed. Gunnar Sjöstedt (Newbury Park, CA: Sage, 1993), 224.

54. Bauer, Busch, and Siebenhüner, "Administering International Governance," 5.

55. Ibid., 18–19.

56. Ibid., 10.

57. United Nations Framework Convention on Climate Change (UNFCCC) website statistics, 2013, http://unfccc.int/essential_background/about_the_website/items/3358.php.

58. Jinnah, *Post-Treaty Politics*, 52.

59. Ibid., 53.

60. Oran R. Young, *International Governance: Protecting the Environment in a Stateless Society* (Ithaca, NY: Cornell University Press, 1994), 170.

61. Jinnah, *Post-Treaty Politics*, 52.

62. Johan Kaufmann, *Conference Diplomacy: An Introductory Analysis*, 3rd ed. (London: Macmillan, 1996), 93–94.

63. Benedick, "Perspectives of a Negotiation Practitioner," 225. Downie also observed this while attending the 1990 ozone negotiations in London.

64. Farhana Yamin and Joanna Depledge, *The International Climate Change Regime: A Guide to Rules, Institutions and Procedures* (Cambridge: Cambridge University Press, 2005); Bauer, Busch, and Siebenhüner, "Administering International Governance."

65. Bauer, Busch, and Siebenhüner, "Administering International Governance," 13.

66. Personal observations of the authors and conversations with secretariat and government officials during attendance at global environmental negotiations since 1990.

67. See, for example, Steffen Bauer, "The United Nations and the Fight Against Desertification: What Role for the UNCCD Secretariat?" in *Governing Global Desertification: Linking Environmental Degradation, Poverty, and Participation*, eds. Pierre Marc Johnson, Karel Mayrand, and Marc Paquin (Aldershot, UK: Ashgate, 2006), 83.

68. GEF, "What is the GEF?" www.thegef.org/gef/whatisgef.

69. For a critical analysis of the environmental impacts of various multilateral development bank loans, see Bruce Rich, *Mortgaging the Earth: The World Bank, Environmental Impoverishment, and the Crisis of Development* (Boston: Beacon, 1994).

70. Navroz Dubash and Frances Seymour, "World Bank's Environmental Reform Agenda," *Foreign Policy in Focus*, March 1, 1999, www.fpif.org/reports/world_banks_environmental_reform_agenda.

71. Ibid.

72. Ibid.

73. World Bank, *Making Sustainable Commitments: An Environment Strategy for the World Bank* (Washington, DC: World Bank, 2001).

74. Independent Evaluation Group–World Bank, *Environmental Sustainability: An Evaluation of World Bank Group Support* (Washington, DC: World Bank, 2008), xvi.

75. Frances Seymour, "Mainstreaming and Infrastructure," *Environment Matters 2004* (Washington, DC: World Bank, 2004), http://siteresources.worldbank.org/INTRANET ENVIRONMENT/Resources/EM04Mainstreaming.pdf.

76. Ibid., 69.

77. World Bank, *Toward a Green, Clean, and Resilient World for All: A World Bank Group Environment Strategy 2012–2022* (Washington, DC: World Bank, 2012).

78. Ivy Mungcal, "New World Bank Environment Strategy Draws Mixed Reactions," *Devex*, June 8, 2012, www.devex.com/en/news/78385/print.

79. Ibid.

80. World Bank, "World Bank Board Committee Authorizes Release of Revised Draft Environmental and Social Framework," press release, August 4, 2015, www.worldbank.org/en/news/press-release/2015/08/04/world-bank-board-committee-authorizes-release-of-revised-draft-environmental-and-social-framework.

81. "World Bank: Dangerous Rollback in Environmental, Social Protections," Human Rights Watch, August 4, 2015, www.hrw.org/news/2015/08/04/world-bank-dangerous-rollback-environmental-social-protections.

82. "IMF Reviews Its Approach to Environmental Issues," *IMF Survey*, April 15, 1991, 124.

83. IMF, "IMF and the Environment," www.imf.org/external/np/fad/environ/.

84. Ved P. Gandhi, *The IMF and the Environment* (Washington, DC: IMF, 1998).

85. Information on the New Development Bank, including its creation and stated purpose, can be found on its website: http://ndb.int.

86. Raj Desai and James Raymond Vreeland, "What the New Bank of BRICS Is All About," *Washington Post*, July 17, 2014, www.washingtonpost.com/news/monkey-cage/wp/2014/07/17/what-the-new-bank-of-brics-is-all-about/.

87. Ibid.

88. "Our Purpose," New Development Bank, http://ndb.int/our-purpose.php.

89. Belgium, West Germany, Luxembourg, France, Italy, and the Netherlands formed three organizations: the European Economic Community, the European Coal and Steel Community, and the European Atomic Energy Community.

90. The European Community (EC) takes part in activities and negotiations within the context of many international institutions, especially the UN. It is a party to more than thirty international environmental conventions and agreements and takes an active part in negotiations.

91. EU, *EUROPE 2020: A Strategy for Smart, Sustainable and Inclusive Growth*, 3.3.2010 COM(2010) 2020 final, 2010, http://eur-lex.europa.eu/LexUriServ/LexUriServ.do?uri=COM:2010:2020:FIN:EN:PDF.

92. EC, *2030 Framework for Climate and Energy Policies*, http://ec.europa.eu/clima/policies/2030/index_en.htm.

93. Organization of American States, "Securing Our Citizens' Future by Promoting Human Prosperity, Energy Security and Environmental Sustainability," Declaration of Commitment

of Port of Spain, Fifth Summit of the Americas, Port of Spain, Trinidad and Tobago, April 19, 2009, www.summit-americas.org/V_Summit/decl_comm_pos_en.pdf.

94. VI Summit of the Americas, "From Cartagena Forward, Statement by the President of Colombia at the Close of the Sixth Summit of the Americas," 82, www.summit-americas.org/pubs/ctg_fwd_en.pdf.

95. VII Summit of the Americas, "Prosperity with Equity: The Challenge of Cooperation in the Americas—Mandates for Action," April 17, 2015, www.summit-americas.org/vii/docs/mandates_en.pdf.

96. African Union, *Agenda 2063: The Africa We Want* (Addis Ababa, Ethiopia: African Union Commission, 2015).

97. APEC, "Sydney APEC Leaders' Declaration," APEC Summit, Sydney, Australia, September 9, 2007, www.apec.org/Meeting-Papers/Leaders-Declarations/2007/2007_aelm.aspx.

98. APEC, *APEC at a Glance* (Singapore: APEC Secretariat, 2014), http://publications.apec.org/publication-detail.php?pub_id=1610.

99. Ibid.

100. Adil Najam, "The View from the South: Developing Countries in Global Environmental Politics," in *The Global Environment: Institutions, Law and Policy*, 2nd ed., eds. Regina S. Axelrod, David Leonard Downie, and Norman J. Vig (Washington, DC: Congressional Quarterly Press, 2005).

101. This description is based on "About the Group of 77," Group of 77, www.g77.org/doc; and Najam, "The View from the South."

102. The organization was originally called the South Pacific Regional Environment Program. For information on SPREP, see its official website at www.sprep.org.

103. See Michele Betsill and Elisabeth Corell, eds., *NGO Diplomacy: The Influence of Nongovernmental Organizations in International Environmental Negotiations* (Cambridge, MA: MIT Press, 2008); Thomas Weiss and Leon Gordenker, eds., *NGOs, the UN, and Global Governance* (Boulder, CO: Lynne Rienner, 1996); Paul Wapner, "Politics Beyond the State: Environmental Actions and World Civic Politics," *World Politics* 47, no. 3 (April 1995): 311–340; Thomas Princen and Matthias Finger, eds., *Environmental NGOs in World Politics: Linking the Local and the Global* (London: Routledge, 1994); and Barbara Bramble and Gareth Porter, "Non-Governmental Organizations and the Making of U.S. International Environmental Policy," in Hurrell and Kingsbury, *The International Politics of the Environment.*

104. Friends of the Earth International, "About FoEI," www.foei.org/about-foei.

105. Greenpeace, "About Greenpeace," www.greenpeace.org/international/en/about/.

106. WWF, "Our Work," www.worldwildlife.org/initiatives.

107. European Environmental Bureau, *EEB Work Programme and Budget 2015* (Brussels: EEB, 2015), 3–4.

108. Ramachandra Guha, "The Environmentalism of the Poor," in *Varieties of Environmentalism: Essays North and South*, eds. Ramachandra Guha and Juan Martinez-Alier (London: Earthscan, 1997), 15.

109. See Julie Fisher, *The Road from Rio: Sustainable Development and the Nongovernmental Movement in the Third World* (Westport, CT: Praeger, 1993), 123–128; and Monsiapile Kajimbwa, "NGOs and Their Role in the Global South," *International Journal of Not-for-Profit Law* 9, no. 1 (December 2006): 58–64.

110. Guha, "The Environmentalism of the Poor," 4.

111. See Third World Network, *The Battle for Sarawak's Forests* (Penang, Malaysia: World Rainforest Movement, 1989).

112. For representative press reports, see "Villagers Protest Against Alleged Illegal Logging," *Borneo Post*, May 21, 2011; Bettina Wassener, "Tracing the Money, and the Masterminds, of Illegal Logging, *New York Times*, April 6, 2013; "Nine Villages Join Protest Against Illegal Logging," *Sarawak Mirror*, June 27, 2012; and "Villagers Protest Illegal Logging,"

Malaymail Online, September 21, 2014, http://www.themalaymailonline.com/malaysia/article/villagers-protest-illegal-logging; Andrew Revkin, "Conservationists Decry Slaying of Cambodian Forest Guraeds, Pointing to China Timber Trade," *New York Times*, November 14, 2015; Rachel Nuwer, "Illegal Logging Has Become More Violent Than Ever," *National Geographic*, February 3, 2016, http://news.nationalgeographic.com/2016/02/160202-Illegal-loggers-murders-violence-defending-land/; and "Cambodia's Zeal for Rubber Drives Ethnic Group from Land," *New York Times*, March 26, 2016.

113. For information about the Green Belt Movement, see its website: www.greenbeltmovement.org.

114. "Introduction," Third World Network, www.twn.my/twnintro.htm.

115. "IPEN's Impacts," International POPs Elimination Network, www.ipen.org/site/ipens-impacts.

116. "About IUCN," International Union for the Conservation of Nature and Natural Resources, www.iucn.org/about/.

117. Working with Merck and Genentech, the World Resources Institute, the World Wildlife Fund, and the Environmental and Energy Study Institute drafted an interpretive statement and persuaded President Clinton in 1993 to sign the treaty with such a statement attached.

118. For references to the boycott as well as broader discussion, see "Iceland," in *The Europa World Yearbook, 2004* (London: Taylor and Francis, 2004), 2049; Guillermo Herrera and Porter Hoagland, "Commercial Whaling, Tourism and Boycotts: An Economic Perspective," *Marine Policy* 30, no. 3 (May 2006): 261–269; Steinar Andresen, "Science and Politics in the International Management of Whales," *Marine Policy* 13, no. 2 (April 1989), 88–117; and "Burger Chain Targeted," *Los Angeles Times*, June 19, 1988.

119. Scott Couder and Rob Harrison, "The Effectiveness of Ethical Consumer Behavior," in *The Ethical Consumer*, eds. Rob Harrison, Terry Newholm, and Deirdre Shaw (London: Sage, 2005), 89–104.

120. Robert Boardman, *International Organization and the Conservation of Nature* (Bloomington: Indiana University Press, 1981), 88–94.

121. Patricia Birnie, "The Role of International Law in Solving Certain Environmental Conflicts," in *International Environmental Diplomacy: The Management and Resolution of Transfrontier Environmental Problems*, ed. John Carroll (Cambridge: Cambridge University Press, 1988), 107–108.

122. Personal communication from a member of the US delegation to the biodiversity negotiations, February 1994.

123. Kal Raustiala, "States, NGOs and International Environmental Institutions," *International Studies Quarterly* 41 (1997): 728.

124. The *Earth Negotiations Bulletin* was initially published as the *Earth Summit Bulletin* and was created by Johannah Bernstein, Pamela S. Chasek, and Langston James Goree VI. For information, see www.iisd.ca.

125. Raustiala, "States, NGOs and International Environmental Institutions," 730. See also Pamela Chasek, "Environmental Organizations and Multilateral Diplomacy: A Case Study of the *Earth Negotiations Bulletin*," in *Multilateral Diplomacy and the United Nations Today*, 3rd ed., eds. James Muldoon Jr. et al. (Boulder, CO: Westview, 2005).

126. Laura Kosloff and Mark Trexler, "The Convention on International Trade in Endangered Species: No Carrot, But Where's the Stick?" *Environmental Law Reporter* 17 (July 1987): 10225–10226.

127. See Gareth Porter, *The United States and the Biodiversity Convention: The Case for Participation* (Washington, DC: Environmental and Energy Study Institute, 1992). The Industrial Biotechnology Association merged with the Association of Biotechnology Companies in 1993 to form the Biotechnology Industry Organization.

128. *International Environment Reporter*, June 2, 1993, 416.

129. For example, in 2012, Swiss Re announced that insured losses came in at $60 billion in 2011, up from $5 billion forty years ago. "Fostering Discussion on Climate Change Risks at Swiss Re Roundtable in New York," the Climate Group, www.theclimategroup.org/what-we-do/news-and-blogs/fostering-discussion-on-climate-change-risks-at-swiss-re-roundtable-in-nyc/.

130. M'Gonigle and Zacher, *Pollution, Politics and International Law*, 58–62.

131. S. Res. 98, "A Resolution Expressing the Sense of the Senate Regarding the Conditions for the United States Becoming a Signatory to Any International Agreement on Greenhouse Gas Emissions Under the United Nations Framework Convention on Climate Change," 105th Congress, 1st Session, http://thomas.loc.gov/cgi-bin/bdquery/z?d105:SE00098. It is widely known as the Byrd-Hagel Resolution.

132. Day, *The Whale War*, 103–107.

133. Laura Eggerton, "Giant Food Companies Control Standards," *Toronto Star,* April 28, 1999.

134. Alon Tal, *Pollution in the Promised Land: An Environmental History of Israel* (Berkeley, CA: University of California Press, 2002), 305.

135. Interview with William Nitze, Alliance to Save Energy, June 20, 1994.

136. Jennifer Clapp, "Transnational Corporate Interests and Global Environmental Governance: Negotiating Rules for Agricultural Biotechnology and Chemicals," *Environmental Politics* 12, no. 4 (2003): 1–23. Prominent industry groups at the negotiations included the Biotechnology Industry Organization (a US-based biotechnology lobby group), BioteCanada, Japan Bioindustry Association, the International Chamber of Commerce, and the International Association of Plant Breeders for the Protection of Plant Varieties.

137. Personal observations by the authors while attending such meetings since 1998.

138. Alan Miller and Durwood Zaelke, "The NGO Perspective," *Climate Alert* 7, no. 3 (May–June 1994): 3.

139. *Daily Environment Reporter*, August 27, 1992, B2.

140. Examples include the Ceres Company Network (www.ceres.org/company-network), the Business for Innovative Climate and Energy Policy (www.ceres.org/bicep), and the Business Environmental Leadership Council (www.c2es.org/business/belc/climate-energy-strategies/targets).

141. Robert Paarlberg, "Managing Pesticide Use in Developing Countries," in *Institutions for the Earth: Sources of Effective International Environmental Protection*, eds. Peter Haas, Robert Keohane, and Marc Levy (Cambridge, MA: MIT Press, 1993), 319.

142. See Stephen Schmidheiny, with the Business Council for Sustainable Development, *Changing Course: A Global Business Perspective on Development and the Environment* (Cambridge, MA: MIT Press, 1992).

143. See the World Business Council for Sustainable Development website: www.wbcsd.org.

Chapter 3: The Development of Environmental Regimes: Stratospheric Ozone, Hazardous Waste, Toxic Chemicals, and Climate Change

1. United Nations Environment Programme (UNEP), *Environmental Effects of Ozone Depletion and Its Interactions with Climate Change: 2010 Assessment* (Nairobi: UNEP, 2011), details the impacts of ozone depletion.

2. Mario Molina and F. Sherwood Rowland, "Stratospheric Sink for Chlorofluoromethanes: Chlorine Atom–Catalysed Destruction of Ozone," *Nature* 249 (June 28, 1974): 810–812.

3. World Meteorological Organization (WMO) et al., *Scientific Assessment of Stratospheric Ozone: 2010* (Geneva: WMO, 2011), provides a comprehensive discussion of the ozone layer and ozone-depleting substances.

4. The discussion of the ozone regime in this chapter explicitly follows and builds on previous writings by David Downie, including "Understanding International Environmental

Regimes: The Origin, Creation and Expansion of the Ozone Regime" (PhD diss., University of North Carolina, Chapel Hill, 1996); "The Vienna Convention, Montreal Protocol and Global Policy," in *Chemicals, Environment, Health: A Global Management Perspective*, eds. Philip Wexler et al. (Boca Raton, FL: CRC Press, 2012); "Stratospheric Ozone Depletion," in *The Routledge Handbook of Global Environmental Politics*, ed. Paul Harris (New York: Routledge, 2013); and "Still No Time for Complacency: Evaluating the Ongoing Success and Continued Challenge of Global Ozone Policy," *Journal of Environmental Studies and Sciences*, 5, no. 2 (2015): 187–194. Other detailed discussions include Sharon Roan, *Ozone Crisis: The 15-Year Evolution of a Sudden Global Emergency* (New York: John Wiley & Sons, 1989); Karen T. Litfin, *Ozone Discourses: Science and Politics in Global Environmental Cooperation* (New York: Columbia University Press, 1994); Richard Benedick, *Ozone Diplomacy: New Directions in Safeguarding the Planet*, 2nd ed. (Cambridge, MA: Harvard University Press, 1998); Stephen Anderson and K. Madhavea Sarma, *Protecting the Ozone Layer: The United Nations History* (London: Earthscan, 2002); Penelope Canan and Nancy Reichman, *Ozone Connections: Expert Networks in Global Environmental Governance* (Sheffield, UK: Greenleaf, 2002); Edward Parson, *Protecting the Ozone Layer: Science and Strategy* (Oxford: Oxford University Press, 2003); and Ozone Secretariat, *Montreal Protocol on Substances That Deplete the Ozone Layer, 2012: A Success in the Making* (Nairobi: UNEP, 2012).

5. See, in particular, Iwona Rummel-Bulska, "The Protection of the Ozone Layer Under the Global Framework Convention," in *Transboundary Air Pollution*, eds. Cees Flinterman et al. (Dordrecht, Netherlands: Martinus Nijhoff, 1986), 281–296; and Benedick, *Ozone Diplomacy*.

6. For discussion of the early stages of the negotiations, see Downie, "Understanding International Environmental Regimes"; Benedick, *Ozone Diplomacy*; and Parson, *Protecting the Ozone Layer*.

7. For analysis of this point, see David Downie, "The Power to Destroy: Understanding Stratospheric Ozone Politics as a Common Pool Resource Problem," in *Anarchy and the Environment: The International Relations of Common Pool Resources*, eds. J. Samuel Barkin and George Shambaugh (Albany: State University of New York Press, 1999).

8. Benedick, *Ozone Diplomacy*, stresses US leadership on this point. Benedick led the US delegation to these negotiations.

9. J. Farman et al., "Large Losses of Total Ozone in Antarctica Reveal Seasonal ClO_x/NO_x Interaction," *Nature* 315 (May 16, 1985): 207–210. Disagreements exist in various historical accounts regarding the awareness and use of data from US satellites. It is clear, however, that British scientists using ground-based measurements published the first peer-reviewed reports of the ozone hole.

10. For representative discussion, see Downie, "Understanding International Environmental Regimes," ch. 6; Litfin, *Ozone Discourses*, 96–102; Benedick, *Ozone Diplomacy*; and Roan, *Ozone Crisis*, 125–141, 158–188.

11. See, for example, Anderson and Sarma, *Protecting the Ozone Layer*, 93–94, and relevant discussions in Benedick, *Ozone Diplomacy*.

12. For discussion and citations of the information in this paragraph, see WMO et al., *Scientific Assessment of Stratospheric Ozone: 1989* (Geneva: WMO, 1989).

13. Hydrochlorofluorocarbons (HCFCs) have shorter atmospheric lifetimes, and one HCFC molecule destroys far fewer ozone molecules than one chlorofluorocarbon (CFC) molecule. But ozone destruction by HCFCs takes place sooner.

14. For example, at the first Meeting of the Parties (MOP), in 1989, European Community members joined eighty nations (including the United States but not Japan or the Soviet Union) to support a nonbinding declaration calling for a complete CFC phaseout by 2000.

15. For the text of the ozone treaties, amendments, and adjustments, as well as official reports from each MOP, visit the Ozone Secretariat's website: http://ozone.unep.org.

16. Countries with economies in transition (CEITs) include the countries in Eastern Europe formerly aligned with the Soviet Union, as well as Russia, Ukraine, and other countries created

when the Soviet Union collapsed, which were transitioning from communist to capitalist economies. The Global Environment Facility (GEF) later took over most of the responsibility for assisting CEITs on ozone issues.

17. The fund has been replenished nine times: $240 million (1991–1993), $455 million (1994–1996), $466 million (1997–1999), $440 million (2000–2002), $474 million (2003–2005), $400 million (2006–2008, 2009–2011, and 2012–2014), and $437.5 million (2015–2017). The extra $70 million in the 2015–2017 budget is leftover funds and interest. For these figures and details of the history and operation of the fund, see the Multilateral Fund homepage: www.multilateralfund.org.

18. David Downie's observations and conversations with national delegates during the ozone negotiations in 1995, 1997, 1999, and 2015.

19. A small "servicing tail" is permitted beyond the HCFC phaseout date to allow for the continued use of existing equipment.

20. The Implementation Committee under the Non-compliance Procedure for the Montreal Protocol and the MOP has considered many cases of potential noncompliance, most involving countries with economies in transition and developing countries. Although the regime allows for the application of specified trade sanctions in response to severe cases of intentional noncompliance, the committee and MOP decided that each instance fell below the threshold for sanctions, and opted for consultation and targeted technical and/or financial assistance to remove barriers to implementation and, on occasion, the equivalent of a public rebuke to try harder.

21. Brian Gareau, *From Precaution to Profit: Contemporary Challenges to Environmental Protection in the Montreal Protocol* (New Haven, CT: Yale University Press, 2012), provides detailed information on the methyl bromide debates. Information about the issue in this and the next paragraph is based on observations by David Downie and his conversations with Australian, EU, NGO, secretariat, US, and other officials during the ozone negotiations from 1992 to 1997. See also the official meetings of these MOPs (which Downie helped to write), available on the Ozone Secretariat website.

22. "Summary of the Nineteenth Meeting of the Parties to the Montreal Protocol: 17–21 September 2007," *Earth Negotiation Bulletin* 19, no. 60 (September 24, 2007). For other summaries of the HCFC debate and other developments at MOP19, see *Report of the Nineteenth Meeting of the Parties to the Montreal Protocol on Substances that Deplete the Ozone Layer*, UN Document UNEP/OzL.Pro.19/7, September 21, 2007; Keith Bradsher, "Push to Fix Ozone Layer and Slow Global Warming," *New York Times*, March 15, 2007; and David Ljunggren, "Ozone Deal Hailed as Blow Against Climate Change," Reuters Newswire, September 22, 2007.

23. "Summary of the Nineteenth Meeting."

24. For examples, see UNEP, *Report of the Twenty-Third Meeting of the Parties to the Montreal Protocol on Substances That Deplete the Ozone Layer*, UNEP Document UNEP/OzL.Pro.23/11, December 8, 2011, paragraphs 15–17 and 103–119; UNEP, *Report of the Thirty-Second Meeting of the Open-Ended Working Group of the Parties to the Montreal Protocol on Substances That Deplete the Ozone Layer*, UN Document UNEP/OzL.Pro/WG.1/32/7, August 8, 2012, paragraphs 69–77; UNEP, *Report of the Twenty-Fourth Meeting of the Parties to the Montreal Protocol on Substances That Deplete the Ozone Layer*, UNEP Document UNEP/OzL.Pro.24/10, November 25, 2012; and UNEP, *Report of the Twenty-Seventh Meeting of the Parties to the Montreal Protocol on Substances That Deplete the Ozone Layer*, UNEP Document UNEP/OzL.Pro.27/13, November 30, 2015.

25. UNEP, *Report of the Twenty-Seventh Meeting of the Parties to the Montreal Protocol on Substances That Deplete the Ozone Layer.*

26. UNEP, *Information Provided by Parties in Accordance with Article 7 of the Montreal Protocol on Substances that Deplete the Ozone Layer*, UNEP Document UNEP/OzL.Pro.23/7, September 16, 2011. However, evidence of unreported intentional or by-product carbon tetrachloride production exists. See UNEP, *Report of the Twenty-Seventh Meeting of the Parties to the Montreal Protocol on Substances That Deplete the Ozone Layer*, Decision 27/7.

27. Compare the information in COP decisions that approved exemptions from COPs in the late 1990s and 2000s to those from 2013–2015.

28. WMO et al., *Scientific Assessment of Stratospheric Ozone: 2010.*

29. Downie, "Stratospheric Ozone Depletion."

30. UNEP, "Backgrounder: Basic Facts and Data on the Science and Politics of Ozone Protection," press release, September 18, 2008. See similar discussions based on computer simulations in WMO et al., *Scientific Assessment of Stratospheric Ozone: 2010*; and Paul Newman, Paul McKenzie, and Richard McKenzie, "UV Impacts Avoided by the Montreal Protocol," *Photochemical and Photobiological Science* 10, no. 7 (2011): 1152–1160.

31. UNEP, *Environmental Effects of Ozone Depletion and Its Interactions with Climate Change: 2010 Assessment*, 2010; US Environmental Protection Agency (EPA), *Protecting the Ozone Layer Protects Eyesight: A Report on Cataract Incidence in the United States Using the Atmospheric and Health Effects Framework Model* (Washington, DC: EPA, 2010); Arjan van Dijk et al., "Skin Cancer Risks Avoided by the Montreal Protocol: Worldwide Modeling Integrating Coupled Climate-Chemistry Models with a Risk Model for UV," *Photochemistry and Photobiology* 89, no. 1 (January–February 2013): 234–246.

32. For a representative discussion, see Guus Velders et al., "The Importance of the Montreal Protocol in Protecting Climate," *Proceedings of the National Academy of Science* 104, no. 12 (March 20, 2007): 4814–4819.

33. Ozone Secretariat, "Montreal Protocol Parties Devise Way Forward to Protect Climate Ahead of Paris COP21," press release, November 6, 2015, http://unep.org/newscentre/Default.aspx?DocumentID=26854&ArticleID=35543&l=en.

34. National Oceanic and Atmospheric Administration (NOAA), "Annual Antarctic Ozone Hole Larger and Formed Later in 2015," press release, October 29, 2015, http://research.noaa.gov/News/NewsArchive/LatestNews/TabId/684/ArtMID/1768/ArticleID/11409/Annual-Antarctic-Ozone-Hole-Larger-and-Formed-Later-in-2015.aspx.

35. Downie, "Still No Time for Complacency."

36. Downie, "The Vienna Convention, Montreal Protocol and Global Policy," 255.

37. WMO et al., Executive Summary, *Scientific Assessment of Stratospheric Ozone: 2010.*

38. Downie, "The Vienna Convention, Montreal Protocol and Global Policy," 255.

39. Downie, "Understanding International Environmental Regimes"; Downie, "Stratospheric Ozone Depletion."

40. For detailed and sometimes differing analyses of the complex interrelationships between the development of scientific knowledge and policy developments, see, among others, Lydia Dotto and Harold Schiff, *The Ozone War* (Garden City, NY: Doubleday, 1978); Downie, "Understanding International Environmental Regimes"; Downie, "Stratospheric Ozone Depletion"; Peter Haas, "Banning Chlorofluorocarbons: Epistemic Community Efforts to Protect Stratospheric Ozone," *International Organization* 46, no. 1 (winter 1992): 187–224; Litfin, *Ozone Discourses*; Benedick, *Ozone Diplomacy*; Anderson and Sarma, *Protecting the Ozone Layer*; Canan and Reichman, *Ozone Connections*; Parson, *Protecting the Ozone Layer*; and Gareau, *From Precaution to Profit.*

41. Downie, "Stratospheric Ozone Depletion." For detailed and sometimes differing analysis of different aspects of the impact of changing economic interests on the development of ozone policy, see, among others, the works cited in the previous note and Kenneth Oye and James Maxwell, "Self-Interest and Environmental Management," *Journal of Theoretical Politics* 64 (1994): 599–630.

42. Ronald Mitchell, "Regime Design Matters: International Oil Pollution and Treaty Compliance," *International Organization* 48, no. 3 (summer 1994): 425–458.

43. For an extended discussion, see Downie, "Understanding International Environmental Regime." See also Downie, "The Vienna Convention, Montreal Protocols and Global Policy."

44. UNEP, *GEO 5: Global Environmental Outlook—Environment for the Future We Want* (Nairobi: UNEP, 2012), 223.

45. General analyses of the international hazardous waste issue and regime include David Hackett, "An Assessment of the Basel Convention on the Control of Transboundary Movements of Hazardous Wastes and Their Disposal," *American University Journal of International Law and Policy* 5 (Winter 1990): 313–322; Mark A. Montgomery, "Travelling Toxic Trash: An Analysis of the 1989 Basel Convention," *Fletcher Forum of World Affairs* 14 (Summer 1990): 313–326; Katharine Kummer, *International Management of Hazardous Wastes: The Basel Convention and Related Legal Rules* (New York: Oxford University Press, 2000); Kate O'Neill, *Waste Trading Among Rich Nations: Building a New Theory of Environmental Regulation* (Cambridge, MA: MIT Press, 2000); Henrik Selin, *Global Governance of Hazardous Chemicals: Challenges of Multilevel Management* (Cambridge, MA: MIT Press, 2010). The Basel Convention Secretariat (www.basel.int) and the Basel Action Network (www.ban.org), a prominent NGO, provide extensive information on the regime and the waste issue, including links to news articles and reports.

46. An organizational meeting took place in 1987, and five formal negotiation sessions occurred in 1988 and 1989.

47. Carol Annette Petsonk, "The Role of the United Nations Environment Programme (UNEP) in the Development of International Environmental Law," *American University Journal of International Law and Policy* 5 (Winter 1990): 374–377; *International Environment Reporter*, April 1989, 159–161.

48. For the text of the convention, reports from the COPs and other meetings, official documents, updated lists of ratifications, and information on other aspects of the regime, see the Basel Convention website (www.basel.int). For independent summaries and analyses of the COP meetings, see reports by the *Earth Negotiations Bulletin* at www.iisd.ca/vol20/.

49. See Hackett, "An Assessment of the Basel Convention"; and Montgomery, "Travelling Toxic Trash."

50. *International Environment Reporter*, 159–160.

51. *Greenpeace Waste Trade Update*, no. 3 (July 1989); and *Greenpeace Waste Trade Update*, no. 4 (December 1989).

52. During this period, only the republics of the former Soviet Union, desperate for foreign exchange and willing to disregard the health and environmental consequences, appeared openly willing to accept significant shipments of hazardous wastes. See Steven Coll, "Free Market Intensifies Waste Problem," *Washington Post*, March 23, 1994.

53. Greenpeace, *The International Trade in Wastes: A Greenpeace Inventory*, 5th ed. (Washington, DC: Greenpeace, 1990). See also "Chemicals: Shipment to South Africa Draws Enviro Protests," *Greenwire*, February 18, 1994; Michael Satchell, "Deadly Trade in Toxics," *US News and World Report*, March 7, 1994, 64–67.

54. John Cushman Jr., "Clinton Seeks Ban on Export of Most Hazardous Waste," *New York Times*, March 1, 1994; "Basel Convention Partners Consider Ban on Exports of Hazardous Wastes," *International Environment Reporter*, March 22, 1994, A9.

55. Charles Wallace, "Asia Tires of Being the Toxic Waste Dumping Ground for Rest of World," *Los Angeles Times*, March 23, 1994. For a detailed account of the Geneva meeting, see Jim Puckett and Cathy Fogel, "A Victory for Environment and Justice: The Basel Ban and How It Happened," Basel Action Network, September 1994, www.ban.org/about_basel_ban/a_victory.html.

56. Greenpeace, *The International Trade in Wastes: Database of Known Hazardous Waste Exports from OECD to Non-OECD Countries: 1989–March 1994* (Washington, DC: Greenpeace, 1994). See also Jim Puckett, "The Basel Ban: A Triumph over Business-as-Usual," Basel Action Network, October 1997, http://archive.ban.org/about_basel_ban/jims_article.html.

57. In 2011, after years of debate regarding interpretation of Article 17(5), parties agreed that the Ban Amendment requires ratification by three-quarters of the parties that were parties at the time of its adoption for the amendment to enter into force. Some countries had argued for an alternative "current time" approach in which the number of ratifications required for

the Ban Amendment to enter into force would be based on the current number of parties to the Basel Convention. For analysis, see "Summary of the Ninth Meeting of the Parties to the Basel Convention: 23–27 June 2008," *Earth Negotiations Bulletin* 20, no. 31 (June 30, 2008).

58. See comments by the Basel Action Network as reported in "Summary of the Meetings of the Parties to the Basel, Rotterdam and Stockholm Convention: 4–15 May 2015," *Earth Negotiations Bulletin* 15, no. 230 (May 19, 2015).

59. See "Summary of the Ninth Meeting."

60. In February 2007, the company that had leased the tanker, Trafigura, settled with the government for the equivalent of $198 million. As part of the agreement, the Côte d'Ivoire government released three jailed Trafigura executives, dropped criminal charges against the company and its executives, and sealed the investigation results. International Network for Environmental Compliance and Enforcement (INECE), "Côte d'Ivoire Toxic Waste Scandal Triggers Legal Action in 3 Countries," *INECE Newsletter* 14 (April 2007).

61. "Summary of the Tenth Meeting of the Parties to the Basel Convention: 17–21 October 2011," *Earth Negotiations Bulletin*, 20, no. 37 (October 24, 2011).

62. Ibid.

63. For details, see the ESM section of the Basel Secretariat website: www.basel.int/Implementation/CountryLedInitiative/EnvironmentallySoundManagement/Overview/tabid/3615/Default.aspx.

64. C. P. Balde et al., *The Global E-Waste Monitor - 2014* (Bonn: United Nations University, IAS-SCYCLE, 2015); UNEP, "Urgent Need to Prepare Developing Countries for Surge in E-Wastes," press release, February 22, 2010; UNEP, *Recycling: From E-Waste to Resources* (Nairobi: UNEP, 2009).

65. I. Rucevska et al., *Waste Crime—Waste Risks: Gaps in Meeting the Global Waste Challenge* (Nairobi and Arendal: UNEP and GRID-Arendal, 2015).

66. For information on COP8, see the official report and documents from the meeting, available on the Basel Convention website (www.basel.int). See also "Summary of the Eighth Meeting of the Parties to the Basel Convention: 27 November–1 December 2006," *Earth Negotiations Bulletin* 20, no. 25 (December 4, 2006).

67. For details, see the PACE section of the Basel Secretariat website: www.basel.int/Implementation/TechnicalAssistance/Partnerships/PACE/Overview/tabid/3243/Default.aspx.

68. For information on COP12, see the official report and documents from the meeting, available on the Basel Convention website (www.basel.int). See also "Summary of the Meetings of the Parties to the Basel, Rotterdam and Stockholm Conventions: 4–15 May 2015."

69. For official information, see the synergies website: http://synergies.pops.int.

70. David Downie and Jessica Templeton, "Pesticides and Persistent Organic Pollutants," in *Routledge Handbook of Global Environmental Politics*, ed. Paul Harris (New York: Routledge, 2013).

71. For information on the most recent joint COPs, see the official report and documents from the meeting, available on the Basel, Rotterdam, and Stockholm Convention websites and the synergies website (http://synergies.pops.int). See also "Summary of the Meetings of the Parties to the Basel, Rotterdam and Stockholm Conventions: 4–15 May 2015."

72. UNEP, "Urgent Need to Prepare Developing Countries"; UNEP, *Recycling.*

73. "Summary of the Meetings of the Parties to the Basel, Rotterdam and Stockholm Conventions: 4–15 May 2015."

74. David Downie, personal observation and discussion during Basel COP7 and the Basel and Stockholm COPs in 2013 and 2015.

75. Selin, *Global Governance of Hazardous Chemicals*, 40.

76. UNEP, *GEO 5*, 170.

77. Ibid., 174, citing *OECD Factbook: Economic, Environmental and Social Statistics* (Paris: Organization for Economic Cooperation and Development, 2010).

78. UNEP, *GEO 5*, 174.

79. Ibid., citing *OECD Factbook*.

80. Lowell Center for Sustainable Production, *Chemicals Policy in Europe Set New Worldwide Standards for Registration, Education and Authorization of Chemicals (REACH)*, 2003, cited in UNEP, *GEO 5*, 223.

81. EPA, *Guidelines for Carcinogen Risk Assessment*, Document EPA/630/P-03/001F (Washington, DC: EPA, 2005), cited in UNEP, *GEO 5*, 223.

82. Masanori Kuratsune et al., "Epidemiologic Study on Yusho, a Poisoning Caused by Ingestion of Rice Oil Contaminated with a Commercial Brand of Polychlorinated Biphenyls," *Environmental Health Perspectives* 1 (April 1972): 119–128.

83. Thomas R. Dunlap, *DDT: Scientists, Citizens, and Public Policy* (Princeton, NJ: Princeton University Press, 1981); Janna G. Koppe and Jane Keys, "PCBs and the Precautionary Principle," in *The Precautionary Principle in the 20th Century: Late Lessons from Early Warnings*, eds. Poul Harremoës et al. (London: Earthscan, 2002), 64–78.

84. The action plan the conference produced called for improved international efforts to develop and harmonize procedures for assessing and managing hazardous substances and to augment resources available to developing countries for building domestic capacity.

85. Global agreements include the 1972 International Convention on the Prevention of Marine Pollution by Dumping of Wastes and Other Matter (London Convention) and the MARPOL Convention, which includes the 1973 International Convention for the Prevention of Pollution from Ships and its 1978 protocol. Early regional and river agreements include the 1972 Convention for the Prevention of Marine Pollution by Dumping from Ships and Aircraft (Oslo Convention); 1974 Convention for the Prevention of Marine Pollution from Land-Based Sources (Paris Convention); 1974 Convention on the Protection of the Marine Environment of the Baltic Sea Area (Helsinki Convention); 1976 Convention on the Protection of the Rhine Against Chemical Pollution; 1976 Protocol for the Prevention of Pollution of the Mediterranean Sea by Dumping from Ships and Aircraft; and the 1978 Great Lakes Water Quality Agreement.

86. Jonathan Krueger and Henrik Selin, "Governance for Sound Chemicals Management: The Need for a More Comprehensive Global Strategy," *Global Governance* 8 (2002): 323–342.

87. David Victor, "Learning by Doing in the Nonbinding International Regime to Manage Trade in Hazardous Chemicals and Pesticides," in *The Implementation and Effectiveness of International Environmental Commitments: Theory and Practice*, eds. David Victor et al. (Cambridge, MA: MIT Press, 1998), 228.

88. The participating organizations in the Inter-Organization Programme for the Sound Management of Chemicals are the Food and Agriculture Organization, International Labour Organization, UN Development Programme, UNEP, United Nations Industrial Development Organization, United Nations Institute for Training and Research, World Health Organization, World Bank, and OECD.

89. For the text of the convention, reports, and official documents from the COPs and other meetings, lists of parties, national reports, country contacts, and other information, see the Rotterdam Convention website: www.pic.int. Analyses of the development and content of the convention include Victor, "Learning by Doing"; Richard Emory Jr., "Probing the Protections in the Rotterdam Convention on Prior Informed Consent," *Colorado Journal of International Environmental Law and Policy* 23 (2001): 47–91; and Selin, *Global Governance of Hazardous Chemicals*.

90. For broader discussions of the science of POPs, see Arnold Schecter, *Dioxins and Health Including Other Persistent Organic Pollutants and Endocrine Disruptors* (Hoboken, NJ: Wiley and Sons, 2012); David Leonard Downie and Terry Fenge, eds., *Northern Lights Against POPs: Combatting Threats in the Arctic* (Montreal: McGill-Queen's University Press, 2003); Joe Thornton, *Pandora's Poison: Chlorine, Health, and a New Environmental Strategy* (Cambridge, MA: MIT Press, 2000); and Theo Colborn, Dianne Dumanoski, and John Peterson Myers, *Our*

Stolen Future: Are We Threatening Our Fertility, Intelligence, and Survival?—A Scientific Detective Story (New York: Dutton, 1996).

91. For examples and discussion of these studies, see Downie and Fenge, *Northern Lights Against POPs*; and Arctic Monitoring and Assessment Programme (AMAP), *AMAP Assessment Report: Arctic Pollution Issues* (Oslo: AMAP, 1998).

92. See Downie and Fenge, *Northern Lights Against POPs.*

93. Personal observations and discussions by David Downie with UNEP chemicals and national government officials during this period and during the negotiating sessions from 1998 to 2001.

94. The World Health Organization (WHO) estimated that about 3.2 billion people are at risk of malaria and that 214 million new cases occurred in 2015, with an estimated 438,000 deaths. People living in the poorest countries are the most vulnerable, especially in Africa, where its effects lead to a significant percentage of childhood deaths ("10 Facts on Malaria," www.who.int/features/factfiles/malaria/en/index.html). For detailed information and links, see WHO, "Health Topics: Malaria," www.who.int/topics/malaria/en.

95. The decision by the UNEP Governing Council to initiate the talks included specific mandates to address both issues.

96. For the text of the convention, reports, and other official documents from the COPs and the POPs Review Committee (POPRC), lists of parties, national reports, country contacts, documents from the negotiations that produced the treaty, detailed information on the chemicals controlled under the convention, and other information, see the Stockholm Convention website: http://pops.int. For detailed secondary-source reports on the COP, see www.iisd.ca/process/chemical_management.htm.

97. Very small amounts of DDT can also be used as an intermediate in the production of the chemical dicofol if no DDT is released into the environment.

98. For information on exemptions, including which countries have requested and can use particular exemptions, see http://chm.pops.int/Procedures/Exemptionsandacceptablepurposes/tabid/4646/Default.aspx.

99. For a detailed discussion of this process, including the original version of Figure 3.2, see Downie and Fenge, *Northern Lights Against POPs*, 140–142.

100. See, in particular, paragraphs 7(a) and 9 of Article 8 of the Stockholm Convention.

101. Sources of information and analyses of POPRC include Jessica Templeton, "Framing Elite Policy Discourse: Scientists and the Stockholm Convention on Persistent Organic Pollutants" (PhD diss., London School of Economics and Political Science, 2011); Downie and Templeton, "Pesticides and Persistent Organic Pollutants"; and reports on POPRC meetings by the *Earth Negotiations Bulletin.*

102. Opt-in parties include Australia, Canada, China, India, Republic of Korea, and Russia. If it ratifies the convention, the United States would likely be an opt-in party

103. The opt-in and opt-out options could lead to some parties being bound by controls on new substances while others are not. This could deter listing more live substances if some countries believe that doing so will put them at a competitive disadvantage in comparison with opt-in states. Uneven patterns of ratification could also create legal uncertainties with regard to restricting trade in products made with or containing POPs. See Downie and Templeton, "Pesticides and Persistent Organic Pollutants."

104. Although special obligations are placed on developed countries, all countries with the resources and expertise to do so are called on to provide technical assistance (Article 12). This is one of several examples in the Stockholm Convention in which the principle of common but differentiated responsibilities is implemented slightly differently than it was in previous treaties.

105. Because the United States had already controlled the dirty dozen, its costs to implement the original treaty would be low. President Bush participated in a Rose Garden ceremony

heralding the convention and stating his intention to push for ratification. In the absence of 9/11, it is logical that he would have done so, if for no other reason than to provide his administration with an environmental victory before the 2004 election. It is possible that another president will submit the treaty for consideration.

106. Chemicals under review, as of December 2015, include decabromodiphenyl ether (commercial mixture, c-decaBDE), dicofol, short-chained chlorinated paraffins, and pentadecafluorooctanoic acid.

107. "Summary of the Fourth Meeting of the Persistent Organic Pollutants Review Committee of the Stockholm Convention: 13–17 October 2008," *Earth Negotiations Bulletin* 15, no. 161 (October 20, 2008).

108. Ibid. Personal observations by David Downie during these meetings and subsequent COPs.

109. For details of the debate and vote, see UNEP, "Report of the Conference of the Parties to the Stockholm Convention on Persistent Organic Pollutants on the Work of Its Seventh Meeting," UN Document UNEP/POPS/COP.7/36; and "Summary of the Meetings of the Parties to the Basel, Rotterdam and Stockholm Conventions: 4–15 May 2015."

110. Ibid. See, in particular, comments by the EU and Africa. Also, personal observations by David Downie and communications with delegates and observers during the 2015 COPs.

111. Downie and Templeton, "Pesticides and Persistent Organic Pollutants."

112. For details of the meeting, see background documents and the official meeting report on the Stockholm Convention's website (http://pops.int) and the daily and summary reports provided by the *Earth Negotiations Bulletin* at www.iisd.ca/chemical/pops/cop4. This section draws heavily on personal observations and notes made by David Downie while attending the meeting; the official report of the meeting; and "Summary of the Fourth Conference of Parties to Stockholm Convention on Persistent Organic Pollutants: 4–8 May 2009," *Earth Negotiations Bulletin* 15, no. 174 (May 11, 2009).

113. David Downie, personal observations during the COP.

114. GEF, *Report of the GEF to the Fifth Meeting*, 4.

115. Ibid.

116. "Executive Summary of the Report of the Council of the GEF to the Conference of the Parties to the Stockholm Convention on Persistent Organic Pollutants at Its Seventh Meeting," UN Document UNEP/POPS/COP.7/23, January 22, 2015. We extrapolated one figure. Updated figures can be found in GEF documents submitted to more recent COPs.

117. Downie and Templeton, "Pesticides and Persistent Organic Pollutants."

118. "Summary of the Third Meeting of the Stockholm Convention on Persistent Organic Pollutants: 30 April–4 May 2007," *Earth Negotiations Bulletin* 15, no. 154 (May 7, 2007).

119. Including for travel, interpretation, translation, facilities, and conference services.

120. Personal observations by David Downie and communications with delegates and observers during the 2013 and 2015 COPs.

121. Personal communication between David Downie and James Willis. Related to the synergies initiative in theme but springing from a different legal and operational basis is UNEP's Strategic Approach to International Chemicals Management (SAICM).

122. WHO and UNEP, *State of the Science of Endocrine Disrupting Chemicals* (Geneva: WHO and UNEP, 2013); UNEP, *GEO 5*, 223.

123. As of January 2016, Australia, Bangladesh, India, New Zealand, and Venezuela had ratified controls on none of the chemicals added to the treaty.

124. US policy on toxic chemicals is generally strong, and the United States supports the convention financially. However, it is possible that over time the regime could move beyond US chemical policy, potentially creating a market haven for certain substances.

125. Downie and Templeton, "Pesticides and Persistent Organic Pollutants."

126. For an overview of the science of climate change, see Intergovernmental Panel on Climate Change (IPCC), *Climate Change 2014: Synthesis Report*, Contribution of Working

Groups I, II and III to the Fifth Assessment Report of the Intergovernmental Panel on Climate Change (Geneva, Switzerland: IPCC, 2014), http://ar5-syr.ipcc.ch/ipcc/ipcc/resources/pdf/IPCC_SynthesisReport.pdf.

127. Ibid.

128. Svante Arrhenius, "On the Influence of Carbonic Acid in the Air upon the Temperature of the Ground," *Philosophical Magazine* 41 (1896): 237–276.

129. G. S. Callendar, "The Artificial Production of Carbon Dioxide and Its Influence on Climate," *Quarterly Journal of the Royal Meteorological Society* 64 (1938): 223–240.

130. Richard Houghton and George Woodwell, "Global Climatic Change," *Scientific American* 260 (April 1989): 42–43.

131. Daniel Bodansky, "The United Nations Framework Convention on Climate Change: A Commentary," *Yale Journal of International Law* 18, no. 2 (Summer 1993): 461.

132. For a more holistic look at the work of the UN Framework Convention on Climate Change (UNFCCC) subsidiary bodies, see the UNFCCC website, http://unfccc.int/bodies/items/6241.php.

133. See Matthew Paterson, *Global Warming and Global Politics* (London: Routledge, 1996), 77–82.

134. Japan subsequently backtracked by proposing a process of "pledge and review" in place of binding commitments. Individual countries would set for themselves appropriate targets that would be publicly reviewed. Most EC member states and NGOs opposed the idea. Bodansky, "The United Nations Framework Convention on Climate Change," 486.

135. For country greenhouse gas emissions, contributions to total emissions, and rankings at the time of the negotiations, see World Resources Institute, *World Resources, 1992–1993* (New York: Oxford University Press, 1992), 205–213, 345–355. For an early discussion of different methods of greenhouse gas accounting, see Peter M. Morrisette and Andrew Plantinga, "The Global Warming Issue: Viewpoints of Different Countries," *Resources* 103 (Spring 1991): 2–6.

136. *Earth Summit Update* 9 (May 1992): 1; *Wall Street Journal*, May 22, 1992, 1.

137. "Status of Ratification of the Convention," UN Framework Convention on Climate Change, http://unfccc.int/essential_background/convention/status_of_ratification/items/2631.php.

138. See the Climate Secretariat website (http://unfccc.int) for text of the Kyoto Protocol. Also see Herman Ott, "The Kyoto Protocol: Unfinished Business," *Environment* 40, no. 6 (1998), 16 ff.; Clare Breidenrich et al., "The Kyoto Protocol to the United Nations Framework Convention on Climate Change," *American Journal of International Law* 92, no. 2 (1998): 315.

139. International Centre for Trade and Sustainable Development, "EU Attacks Bush's U-Turn on Climate Change," *Bridges Weekly Trade News Digest* 5, no. 11 (March 27, 2001), http://ictsd.org/i/news/bridgesweekly/81784.

140. See, for example, Alex Rodriguez, "Russian Move on Global Warming Treaty Sets Stage for Enactment," *Chicago Tribune*, October 1, 2004.

141. The protocol, like most treaties, specifies a ninety-day delay between the final ratification required and the actual entry into force.

142. The Climate Group, *The Copenhagen Climate Conference: A Climate Group Assessment*, January 2010, www.theclimategroup.org/_assets/files/TCG-Copenhagen-Assessment-Report-Jan10.pdf.

143. Daniel Bodansky, "The International Climate Change Regime: The Road from Copenhagen," Viewpoints, Harvard Project on International Climate Agreements, October 2010, http://belfercenter.ksg.harvard.edu/publication/20437/international_climate_change_regime.html?breadcrumb=%2Fproject%2F56%2Fharvard_project_on_climate_agreements%3Fpage_id%3D234.

144. Ibid.

145. "Summary of the Copenhagen Climate Change Conference: 7–19 December 2009," *Earth Negotiations Bulletin* 12, no. 459 (December 22, 2009): 1.

146. "Summary of the Cancun Climate Change Conference: 29 November–11 December 2010," *Earth Negotiations Bulletin* 12, no. 498 (December 13, 2010): 28.

147. UNFCCC, *Report of the Conference of the Parties on Its Fifteenth Session, Held in Copenhagen from 7 to 19 December 2009*, FCCC/CP/2009/11/Add.1, March 30, 2010.

148. Bodansky, "The International Climate Change Regime," 3.

149. "Summary of the Cancun Climate Change Conference: 29 November–11 December 2010," *Earth Negotiations Bulletin* 12, no. 498 (December 13, 2010): 28.

150. Ibid.

151. Climate Focus, *CP16/CMP6: Cancun Agreements: Summary and Analysis*, January 10, 2011, http://theredddesk.org/sites/default/files/resources/pdf/2011/Cancun_Briefing_Jan_2011_v.1.0.pdf; UNFCCC, "The Cancun Agreements," http://cancun.unfccc.int.

152. Bolivian Ministry of Foreign Affairs, "Bolivia Decries Adoption of Copenhagen Accord II Without Consensus," press briefing, December 11, 2011, http://pwccc.files.wordpress.com/2010/12/press-release-history-will-be-the-judge.pdf.

153. "Summary of the Cancun Climate Change Conference: 29 November–11 December 2010," 1.

154. Ibid.

155. "Summary of the Durban Climate Change Conference: 28 November–11 December 2011," *Earth Negotiations Bulletin* 12, no. 534 (December 13, 2011): 1.

156. See UNFCCC, *Report of the Conference of the Parties on Its Seventeenth Session, Held in Durban from 28 November to 11 December 2011, Addendum, Part Two: Action Taken by the Conference of the Parties at Its Seventeenth Session*, FCCC/CP/2011/9/Add.1, March 15, 2012.

157. "Summary of the Doha Climate Change Conference: 26 November–8 December 2012," *Earth Negotiations Bulletin* 12, no. 567 (December 11, 2012): 26.

158. As of April 8, 2016, sixty-one countries have ratified the Doha Amendment. See UNFCCC, "Status of the Doha Amendment," http://unfccc.int/kyoto_protocol/doha_amendment/items/7362.php.

159. "Summary of the Warsaw Climate Change Conference: 11–23 November 2013," *Earth Negotiations Bulletin* 12, no. 594 (November 26, 2013): 29.

160. Members of the Like-Minded Developing Countries group include Algeria, Argentina, Bolivia, Cuba, China, Democratic Republic of the Congo, Dominica, Ecuador, Egypt, El Salvador, India, Iran, Iraq, Kuwait, Libya, Malaysia, Mali, Nicaragua, Pakistan, Philippines, Qatar, Saudi Arabia, Sri Lanka, Sudan, Syria, and Venezuela.

161. "Summary of the Warsaw Climate Change Conference: 11–23 November 2013," 29.

162. The White House, "U.S.-China Joint Presidential Statement on Climate Change," press release, September 25, 2015, www.whitehouse.gov/the-press-office/2015/09/25/us-china-joint-presidential-statement-climate-change.

163. William J. Antholis, "The U.S. and China's Great Leap Forward . . . For Climate Protection," Brookings Institution Planet Policy Blog, November 12, 2014, www.brookings.edu/blogs/planetpolicy/posts/2014/11/12-us-china-great-leap-forward-climate-protection-antholis.

164. UNFCCC, "Lima Call for Climate Action," Decision 1/CP.20, February 2, 2015. http://unfccc.int/resource/docs/2014/cop20/eng/10a01.pdf.

165. "Summary of the Lima Climate Change Conference: 1–14 December 2014," *Earth Negotiations Bulletin* 12, no. 619 (December 16, 2014): 43.

166. "Summary of the Bonn Climate Change Conference: 19–23 October 2015," *Earth Negotiations Bulletin* 12, no. 651 (October 25, 2015): 9.

167. Ibid., 10.

168. "Summary of the Paris Climate Change Conference: 29 November-13 December 2015," *Earth Negotiations Bulletin* 12, no. 663 (December 15, 2015): 43.

169. Ibid.

170. For more information on what the Paris Agreement needed to gain US approval, see Daniel Bodansky, *Legal Options for U.S. Acceptance of a New Climate Change Agreement* (Arlington, VA: Center for Climate and Energy Solutions, 2015).

171. Coral Davenport, "Nations Approve Landmark Climate Accord in Paris," *New York Times*, December 12, 2015.

172. Daniel Bodansky, "Reflections on the Paris Conference," *Opino Juris* blog, December 15, 2015, http://opiniojuris.org/2015/12/15/reflections-on-the-paris-conference/.

173. Ibid.

174. Davenport, "Nations Approve Landmark Climate Accord in Paris."

Chapter 4: The Development of Environmental Regimes: Natural Resources, Species, and Habitats

1. Oran Young, *International Environmental Governance: Protecting the Environment in a Stateless Society* (Ithaca, NY: Cornell University Press, 1994), 21.

2. Ibid., 21–22.

3. Ibid., 23.

4. "IUCN Red List," International Union for Conservation of Nature (IUCN), http://www.iucnredlist.org/.

5. S. L. Pimm et al., "The Biodiversity of Species and Their Rates of Extinction, Distribution, and Protection," *Science* 344, no. 6187 (2014), doi:10.1126/science.1246752.

6. National sovereignty over natural resources implies that a government has control over its resources, such as oil, minerals, and timber. Common heritage implies that no one can be excluded from using natural resources, except by lack of economic and technological capacity; conversely, everyone has a right to benefit from the exploitation of the resources. See G. Kristin Rosendal, "The Convention on Biological Diversity: A Viable Instrument for Conservation and Sustainable Use," in *Green Globe Yearbook of International Cooperation on Environment and Development 1995*, eds. Helge Ole Bergesen et al. (Oxford: Oxford University Press, 1995), 69–81.

7. United Nations Environment Programme (UNEP), *Report of the Ad Hoc Working Group on the Work of Its Second Session in Preparation for a Legal Instrument on Biological Diversity of the Planet*, UNEP/Bio.Div2/3, February 23, 1990, 7.

8. For text of the Convention on Biological Diversity (CBD) and subsequent agreements, official documents from its negotiation and subsequent meetings, and lists of ratifying states, see the official CBD website at www.cbd.int.

9. The Senate Foreign Relations Committee approved the ratification of the CBD by a vote of sixteen to three on June 29, 1994. However, in a dramatic move in September 1994, CBD ratification was removed from the Senate's agenda, and since then the ratification issue has never come up for a vote.

10. "Thematic Programmes and Cross Cutting Issues," CBD, www.cbd.int/programmes/.

11. Elisa Morgera and Elsa Tsioumani, "Yesterday, Today, and Tomorrow: Looking Afresh at the Convention on Biological Diversity," *Yearbook of International Environmental Law* 21, no. 1 (2011), doi:10.2139/ssrn.1914378.

12. Ibid., 8. As noted by Morgera and Tsioumani in footnote 42, "CBD parties have long complained of this . . . Note that the Subsidiary Body on Scientific, Technical, and Technological Advice's (SBSTTA) recommendations form the basis of the majority of the CBD COP decisions and that this problematic drafting practice is reflected across all of the other sub-processes that contribute to formulating the rest of the CBD COP decisions."

13. Ibid.

14. See CBD, "COP Decision VI/26 on Strategic Plan for the Convention on Biological Diversity," Doc. CBD UNEP/CBD/COP/6/20 (2002) at para. 11; World Summit on Sustainable

Development, "Johannesburg Plan of Implementation," UN Doc. A/CONF.199/20, September 4, 2002, Resolution 2, Annex, para. 44; and UN General Assembly, "2005 World Summit Outcome," Resolution 60/1, October 24, 2005, para. 56.

15. CBD and UNEP–World Conservation Monitoring Centre, *Global Biodiversity Outlook* (Montreal, Canada: Secretariat of the Convention on Biological Diversity, 2010), http://gbo3.cbd.int.

16. Ibid.; and Morgera and Tsioumani, "Yesterday, Today, and Tomorrow."

17. CBD, "COP Decision X/2 2010 on Strategic Plan for Biodiversity 2011–2020," www.cbd.int/decision/cop/?id=12268.

18. See CBD, *Global Biodiversity Outlook 4* (Montreal: CBD Secretariat, 2014), www.cbd.int/gbo4/.

19. CBD, "UN Report Calls for Bold and Accelerated Global Action to Meet Biodiversity Targets by 2020," press release, October 6, 2014, www.cbd.int/doc/press/2014/pr-2014-10-06-gbo4-en.pdf. The EU is a party to the treaty, in addition to member states being parties to the treaty. As part of normal burden sharing among EU member states, some EU countries might exceed the 15 percent commitment, some might equal it (like Belgium and the UK), and some might do less, but the overall action within all EU countries as a whole will equal 15 percent.

20. Ibid.

21. For analysis of the World Trade Organization ruling, see ITCSD, "A Preliminary Analysis of the WTO Biotech Ruling," *Bridges* 10, no. 7 (November 2006), http://ictsd.net/i/news/bridges/11680.

22. Nicholas Kalaitzandonakes, "Cartagena Protocol: A New Trade Barrier?" *Regulation* 29, no. 2 (Summer 2006): 18–25, www.cato.org/pubs/regulation/regv29n2/v29n1-4.pdf.

23. For a summary of the negotiations and the protocol, see "Report of the Resumed Session of the Extraordinary Meeting of the Conference of the Parties for the Adoption of the Protocol on Biodiversity to the Convention on Biological Diversity: 24–28 January 2000," *Earth Negotiations Bulletin* 9, no. 137 (January 31, 2000).

24. *Nagoya–Kuala Lumpur Supplementary Protocol on Liability and Redress to the Cartagena Protocol on Biosafety* (Montreal: Secretariat of the Convention on Biological Diversity, 2011), http://bch.cbd.int/protocol/NKL_text.shtml.

25. The protocol will enter into force on the ninetieth day after the date of deposit of the fortieth instrument of ratification, acceptance, approval, or accession (Article 18).

26. "Summary of the Third Meeting of the Parties to the Cartagena Protocol on Biosafety: 13–17 March 2006," *Earth Negotiations Bulletin* 9, no. 351 (March 20, 2006).

27. Ibid. Exporting parties' preexisting bilateral trade agreements with large nonparties, such as the United States, were widely acknowledged as one reason why some Latin American parties resisted consensus.

28. "Summary of the Seventh Meeting of the Parties to the Cartagena Protocol on Biosafety: 29 September–3 October 2014," *Earth Negotiations Bulletin* 9, no. 635 (October 6, 2014).

29. Ibid.

30. "Summary of the Fifth Meeting of the Parties to the Cartagena Protocol on Biosafety: 11–15 October 2010," *Earth Negotiations Bulletin* 9, no. 533 (October 18, 2010).

31. For more information, see Rhett Butler, "Anti-HIV Drug from Rainforest Almost Lost Before Its Discovery," mongabay.com, September 13, 2005, http://news.mongabay.com/2005/09/anti-hiv-drug-from-rainforest-almost-lost-before-its-discovery/.

32. See Kabir Bavikatte, Harry Jonas, and Johanna von Braun, "Shifting Sands of ABS Best Practice: Hoodia from the Community Perspective," United Nations University Institute of Advanced Studies, March 31, 2009, www.unutki.org/default.php?doc_id=137.

33. Article 1 of the CBD states, "The objectives of this Convention, to be pursued in accordance with its relevant provisions, are the conservation of biological diversity, the sustainable use of its components and the fair and equitable sharing of the benefits arising out of the utilization of genetic resources, including by appropriate access to genetic resources and by

appropriate transfer of relevant technologies, taking into account all rights over those resources and to technologies, and by appropriate funding."

34. CBD, "Access and Benefit-Sharing: Background," www.cbd.int/abs/background.

35. "Summary of the Tenth Conference of the Parties to the Convention on Biological Diversity: 18–29 October 2010," *Earth Negotiations Bulletin* 9, no. 544 (November 1, 2010).

36. Ibid., 27.

37. Sachiko Morita, "After 18 Years, a Protocol on Access to Genetic Resources Is Adopted at COP 10," World Bank, December 2010, http://go.worldbank.org/KWVLRFHC10.

38. Ibid.

39. CBD, *Nagoya Protocol Access to Genetic Resources and the Fair and Equitable Sharing of Benefits Arising from Their Utilization, Article 3* (Montreal, Canada: CBD, 2010), www.cbd.int/abs/doc/protocol/nagoya-protocol-en.pdf.

40. Ibid.

41. CBD, *Nagoya Protocol Access to Genetic Resources*, Article 3.

42. Morita, "After 18 Years, a Protocol on Access."

43. CBD, *Nagoya Protocol Access to Genetic Resources.*

44. "Summary of the Tenth Conference," 27.

45. Ibid.

46. CBD, "Strategic Plan for Biodiversity 2011–2020, Including Aichi Biodiversity Targets," Decision X/2 (October 29, 2010), www.cbd.int/decision/cop/?id=12268.

47. Morgera and Tsioumani, "Yesterday, Today, and Tomorrow."

48. For more information about the Intergovernmental Science-Policy Platform on Biodiversity and Ecosystem Services, which was established in 2012, see www.ipbes.net/.

49. CITES, "What is CITES?" www.cites.org/eng/disc/what.php.

50. Detailed and updated information on CITES, including its text, history, operation, species covered, current parties, and other issues, can be found on the regime's official website: www.cites.org. For history of the regime, see also *CITES World*, March 3, 2003, www.cites.org/sites/default/files/eng/news/world/30special.pdf.

51. Ed Stoddard, "CITES Does Not Follow Standard U.N. Divisions," *Environmental News Network*, October 14, 2004, www.enn.com/top_stories/article/169.

52. For updated lists and other information concerning the species listed in each appendix, see www.cites.org.

53. Suzanne Sharrock, *A Guide to the GSPC: All the Targets, Objectives and Facts* (Richmond, UK: Botanic Gardens Conservation International, 2012), 25, www.plants2020.net/files/Plants2020/popular_guide/englishguide.pdf.

54. Ibid., 27.

55. UNEP, *UNEP Yearbook: Emerging Issues in Our Global Environment* (Nairobi, Kenya: UNEP, 2014).

56. Liana Sun Wyler and Pervaze Sheikh, "International Illegal Trade in Wildlife: Threats and U.S. Policy" (Washington, DC: Congressional Research Service, July 23, 2013), 1, http://fas.org/sgp/crs/misc/RL34395.pdf.

57. See Sarah Fitzgerald, *International Wildlife Trade: Whose Business Is It?* (Washington, DC: WWF, 1989), 3–8, 13–14.

58. David Harland, "Jumping on the 'Ban' Wagon: Efforts to Save the African Elephant," *Fletcher Forum on World Affairs* 14 (Summer 1990): 284–300.

59. "CITES 1989: The African Elephant and More," *TRAFFIC Dispatches* 9 (December 1989): 1–3.

60. World Resources Institute, *World Resources 1990–1991* (New York: Oxford University Press, 1990), 135.

61. "U.S. Ivory Market Collapses After Import Ban," *New York Times*, June 5, 1990, C2; Raymond Bonner, *At the Hand of Man: Peril and Hope for Africa's Wildlife* (New York: Vintage Books, 1994), 157.

62. In each case the proposals were withdrawn prior to a formal vote. WWF, "The Challenge of African Elephant Conservation," *Conservation Issues*, April 1997.

63. "CITES and the African Elephants: The Decisions and the Next Steps Explained," *TRAFFIC Dispatches* (April 1998): 5–6.

64. CITES, "Verification of Compliance with the Precautionary Undertakings for the Sale and Shipment of Raw Ivory," Doc. SC.42.10.2.1, Forty-Second Meeting of the Standing Committee, Lisbon, Portugal, September 28–October 1, 1999.

65. "Summary of the Thirteenth Conference of the Parties to the Convention on International Trade in Endangered Species of Wild Fauna and Flora: 2–14 October 2004," *Earth Negotiations Bulletin*, 21, no. 45 (October 18, 2004): 16.

66. Julie Gray, *TRAFFIC Report of the 14th Meeting of the Conference of the Parties to CITES* (Cambridge: TRAFFIC, 2007), www.traffic.org/cop-papers.

67. "Summary of the Fourteenth Conference of the Parties to the Convention on International Trade in Endangered Species of Wild Fauna and Flora: 3–15 June 2007," *Earth Negotiations Bulletin* 21, no. 61 (June 18, 2007): 21.

68. CITES, "Ivory Sales Get the Go-Ahead," June 2, 2007, www.cites.org/eng/news/press/2007/070602_ivory.shtml.

69. CITES, *Report on the One-Off Ivory Sale in Southern African Countries*, SC58 Doc. 36.3, Fifty-Eighth Meeting of the Standing Committee, Geneva, Switzerland, July 6–10, 2009, www.cites.org/eng/com/SC/58/E58-36-3.pdf.

70. CITES, *Elephant Conservation, Illegal Killing and Ivory Trade*, SC62 Doc. 46.1 (Rev. 1), 2012, www.cites.org/eng/com/SC/62/E62-46-01.pdf.

71. "Summary of the Sixteenth Meeting of the Conference of the Parties to the Convention on International Trade in Endangered Species of Wild Fauna and Flora: 3–14 March 2013," *Earth Negotiations Bulletin* 21, no. 83 (March 18, 2013): 26; "CITES Conference Takes Decisive Action to Halt Decline of Tropical Timber, Sharks, Manta Rays and a Wide Range of Other Plants and Animals," press release, Bangkok, Thailand, March 14, 2013, www.cites.org/eng/news/pr/2013/20130314_cop16.php.

72. Brandon Keim and Emma Howard, "African 'Blood Ivory' Destroyed in New York to Signal Crackdown on Illegal Trade," *Guardian*, June 19, 2015.

73. Adam Vaughan, "Global Accord on Combatting Illegal Wildlife Trade Agreed by 46 Nations," *Guardian*, February 13, 2014.

74. Keim and Howard, "African 'Blood Ivory.'"

75. Food and Agriculture Organization of the UN (FAO), *Global Forest Resources Assessment 2015* (Rome: FAO, 2015), 14.

76. Ibid.

77. See Chapter 1 of Millennium Ecosystem Assessment, *Ecosystems and Human Well-Being* (Washington, DC: Island Press, 2005).

78. World Bank, "Trees: Not Just for Treehuggers," March 20, 2015, www.worldbank.org/en/news/feature/2015/03/20/trees-not-just-for-tree-huggers.

79. World Bank, "Trees: Not Just for Treehuggers."

80. Ibid.

81. FAO, *The Challenge of Sustainable Forest Management* (Rome: FAO, 1993), 9.

82. Even prior to the formation of the UN, forests had been discussed as an international issue between Canada and the United States as early as the late nineteenth century. See R. Peter Gillis and Thomas Roach, *Lost Initiatives: Canada's Forest Industries, Forest Policy, and Forest Conservation* (Westport, CT: Greenwood, 1986). There is also a long history of international conferences on forestry convened by the British under the banner of "empire forestry." See Gregory Barton, *Empire Forestry and the Origins of Environmentalism* (Cambridge: Cambridge University Press, 2002).

83. FAO, "History of the Committee on Forestry," COFO/2005/INF/8, 2005, www.fao.org/docrep/meeting/009/J4566e.htm.

84. Constance L. McDermott, "REDDuced: From Sustainability to Legality to Units of Carbon—The Search for Common Interests in International Forest Governance," *Environmental Science and Policy* 35 (2014): 13.

85. Ibid., 14.

86. This is a non–legally binding authoritative statement of principles for a global consensus on the management, conservation, and sustainable development of all types of forests (Rio de Janeiro, June 13, 1992).

87. Agenda 21, 1992 Report of the United Nations Conference on Environment and Development (UNCED), I (1992), UN Doc. A/CONF.151/26/Rev. 1, ch. 11.

88. David Humphreys, "The UNCED Process and International Responses to Deforestation," paper presented to the Inaugural Pan-European Conference on International Studies, Heidelberg, Germany, September 16–20, 1992, 34–35.

89. *Earth Summit Update* 8 (April 1992): 7.

90. These initiatives included the Conference on Global Partnerships on Forests organized by Indonesia, the India–United Kingdom initiative to establish reporting guidelines for forests to the Commission on Sustainable Development (CSD), and the Intergovernmental Working Group on Global Forests, convened jointly by Malaysia and Canada, which met twice in 1994.

91. For a summary of the international initiatives in support of the International Panel on Forests (IPF) process, see A. J. Grayson and W. B. Maynard, *The World's Forests: Rio+5—International Initiatives Towards Sustainable Management* (Oxford: Commonwealth Forestry Association, 1997), 29–46.

92. The IPF's report to the CSD (E/CN.17/1997/12) can be found at www.un.org/documents/ecosoc/cn17/ipf/1997/ecn17ipf1997-12.htm.

93. The former Canadian natural resources minister, Anne McLellan, said in a 1997 speech to the Canadian pulp and paper industry that Canada was leading a push for a forest convention to secure an internationally recognized ecolabel for wood-based products. She linked the project to the threat posed to pressures on the Canadian forest industry. See "Americans, Canadians at Odds over 'Sustainable Forestry' Plan," *Ottawa Citizen*, February 1, 1997.

94. NGO briefings on developments in IPF and the CBD at BIONET, January 26, 1996, and December 5, 1996.

95. David Humphreys, "The Elusive Quest for a Global Forests Convention," *Review of European Community and International Environmental Law* 14, no. 1 (April 2005): 1–10.

96. Ibid.

97. "Summary of the Nineteenth United Nations General Assembly Special Session to Review Implementation of Agenda 21: 23–27 June 1997," *Earth Negotiations Bulletin* 5, no. 88 (June 30, 1997): 5–6; David Humphreys, "The Report of the Intergovernmental Panel on Forests," *Environmental Politics* 7, no. 1 (Spring 1998): 219–220.

98. United Nations Economic and Social Council (ECOSOC) Resolution E/2000/3, Economic and Social Council Official Records (2000), Supplement No. 1, para. 11.

99. The Collaborative Partnership on Forests currently comprises fourteen international organization members: Centre for International Forestry Research, FAO, International Tropical Timber Organization, International Union of Forestry Research Organizations, Secretariat of the CBD, Secretariat of the Global Environment Facility (GEF), Secretariat of the UNCCD, Secretariat of the United Nations Forum on Forests (UNFF), Secretariat of the United Nations Framework Convention on Climate Change (UNFCCC), United Nations Development Programme, UNEP, World Agroforestry Centre, World Bank, and World Conservation Union (IUCN).

100. Deborah Davenport and Peter Wood, "Finding the Way Forward for the International Arrangement on Forests: UNFF5, 6 and 7," *Review of European Community and International Environmental Law* 15, no. 3 (2006): 317.

101. For more information on UNFF5, see "Summary of the Fifth Session of the United Nations Forum on Forests: 16–17 May 2005," *Earth Negotiations Bulletin*, 13, no. 133 (May 30, 2005).

102. ECOSOC Resolution E/2006/49, Economic and Social Council Official Records (2006), E/2006/INF/2/Add.1, www.un.org/esa/forests/pdf/2006_49_E.pdf.

103. See General Assembly Resolution 62/98, "Non–Legally Binding Instrument on All Types of Forests," January 31, 2008, www.un.org/esa/forests/about-resolutions.html.

104. ECOSOC, UNFF, *Report of the Seventh Session, 24 February 2006 and 16 to 27 April 2007*, E/2007/42 (New York: United Nations, 2007), 13.

105. Jan McAlpine, personal communication, June 9, 2015.

106. UNFF, *UNFF11 Factsheet* (New York: UNFF, 2015). See also UN, *United Nations Forum on Forests: Report of the Eleventh Session*, E/2015/42-E/CN.18/2015/14 (New York: United Nations, 2015), www.un.org/ga/search/view_doc.asp?symbol=E/CN.18/2015/14.

107. Gunilla Reischl, "The EU and the UN Forest Negotiations: A Case of Failed International Environmental Governance?" in *Global Environmental Agreements: Insights and Implications*, ed. Asha B. Joshi (Hyderabad, India: Icfai Press: 2008).

108. UNCCD, *Land Degradation Neutrality: Resilience at Local, National and Regional Levels* (Bonn: UNCCD Secretariat, 2014).

109. Ibid.

110. UNEP, *Desertification: The Problem That Won't Go Away* (Nairobi: UNEP, 1992); Ridley Nelson, "Dryland Management: The 'Desertification' Problem," working paper 8, World Bank Policy Planning and Research Staff, Environment Department, September 1988, 2.

111. For a news report on these findings, see William K. Stevens, "Threat of Encroaching Deserts May Be More Myth Than Fact," *New York Times*, January 18, 1994, C1, 10.

112. UN Governmental Liaison Service, "Second Session of Desertification Negotiations, Geneva, 13–24 September 1993," E and D File 2, no. 13 (October 1993).

113. "A Convention for Africans," *Impact* 6 (September 1992): 3.

114. UNEP, *Desertification Control Bulletin (Nairobi)* 20 (1991); Mostafa K. Tolba, "Desertification and the Economics of Survival," statement to the International Conference on the Economics of Dryland Degradation and Rehabilitation, Canberra, Australia, March 10–11, 1986.

115. *World Bank News*, May 27, 1993, 4; *Crosscurrents* 5 (March 16, 1992): 13.

116. E. U. Curtis Bohlen, deputy chief of the US delegation, recalls that he made the decision personally without consulting with higher US officials. Private communication from Bohlen, August 15, 1994. On the earlier suggestion by African countries of a possible bargain linking African support for a forest convention with US support for a desertification convention, see *Crosscurrents* 5 (March 16, 1992): 13.

117. "A Summary of the Proceedings of the United Nations Conference on Environment and Development: 3–14 June 1992," *Earth Summit Bulletin* 2, no. 13 (June 16, 1992): 3, www.iisd.ca/download/pdf/enb0213e.pdf.

118. "Summary of the First Session of the INC for the Elaboration of an International Convention to Combat Desertification, 24 May–3 June 1993," *Earth Negotiations Bulletin* 4, no. 11 (June 11, 1993): 2–6, www.iisd.ca/linkages/vol04/0411000e.html.

119. "Summary of the Fifth Session of the INC for the Elaboration of an International Convention to Combat Desertification, 6–17 June 1994," *Earth Negotiations Bulletin* 4, no. 55 (June 20, 1994), 7–8, www.iisd.ca/linkages/vol04/0455000e.html.

120. "Summary of the Second Session of the INC for the Elaboration of an International Convention to Combat Desertification, 13–24 September 1993," *Earth Negotiations Bulletin* 4, no. 22 (September 30, 1993): 11, www.iisd.ca/vol04/0422000e.html.

121. "Summary of the Fifth Session of the INC," 9–10.

122. Detailed and updated information on the convention, including its text, history, operation, current parties, and other issues, can be found on the regime's official website: www.unccd.int.

123. For more information on the challenges the convention faced, see "Summary of the Second Conference of the Parties to the Convention to Combat Desertification, 30 November–11

December 1998," *Earth Negotiations Bulletin* 4, no. 127 (December 14, 1998), www.iisd.ca/download/pdf/enb04127e.pdf.

124. "Summary of the Seventh Conference of the Parties to the Convention to Combat Desertification, 17–28 October 2005," *Earth Negotiations Bulletin* 4, no. 186 (October 31, 2005): 16, www.iisd.ca/download/pdf/enb04186e.pdf.

125. Ibid.

126. Even Fontaine Ortiz and Guangting Tang, *Review of the Management, Administration and Activities of the Secretariat of the United Nations Convention to Combat Desertification (UNCCD)* (Geneva: UN Joint Inspection Unit, 2005), 7, www.unjiu.org/dataen/reports/-notes/archive/JIU_REP_2005/en2005_5_English.pdf.

127. Ibid.

128. UNCCD, "Ten-Year Strategic Plan and Framework to Enhance the Implementation of the Convention (2008–2018)," document ICCD/COP(8)/16/Add.1, October 23, 2007, www.unccd.int/Lists/OfficialDocuments/cop8/16add1eng.pdf.

129. Steffen Bauer and Lindsay Stringer, "The Role of Science in the Global Governance of Desertification," *Journal of Environment & Development* 18, no. 3 (2009): 248–267.

130. Ibid.

131. For information about the science–policy interface, see www.unccd.int/en/programmes/Science/International-Scientific-Advice/Pages/SPI.aspx?HighlightID=282. For information about the Scientific Knowledge Brokering Portal, see www.unccd.int/en/programmes/Science/Knowledge-Management/Pages/Scientific-Knowledge-Brokering.aspx.

132. Charles Bassett and Joana Talafré, "Implementing the UNCCD: Towards a Recipe for Success," *Review of European Community and International Environmental Law* 12, no.3 (2003): 133–139.

133. Lindsay Stringer et al., "Implementing the UNCCD: Participatory Challenges," *Natural Resources Forum* 31 (2007): 198–211.

134. Pamela Chasek et al., "Operationalizing Zero Net Land Degradation: The Next Stage in International Efforts to Combat Desertification?" *Journal of Arid Environments* (2014), http://dx.doi.org/10.1016/j.jaridenv.2014.05.020.

135. UN, *The Future We Want,* A/RES/66/288* (New York: United Nations, 2012), para. 206, www.uncsd2012.org/thefuturewewant.html.

136. UN, *Transforming Our World: The 2030 Agenda for Sustainable Development,* A.69/L.85, August 15, 2015, www.un.org/ga/search/view_doc.asp?symbol=A/69/L.85&Lang=E.

137. UNCCD, "Integration of the Sustainable Development Goals and Targets into the Implementation of the United Nations Convention to Combat Desertification and the Intergovernmental Working Group Report on Land Degradation Neutrality," Decision 3/COP.12, October 23, 2015, www.unccd.int/Lists/OfficialDocuments/cop12/20add1eng.pdf.

138. UNCCD, "Land Matters for Climate: Reducing the Gap and Approaching the Target," November 2015, www.unccd.int/Lists/SiteDocumentLibrary/Publications/2015Nov_Land_matters_for_climate_FLYER_ENG.pdf.

139. Noel Oettlé, "Land Degradation Neutrality and a New Fund to Advance the Concept," *Africa Report,* October 2, 2015, www.theafricareport.com/East-Horn-Africa/land-degradation-neutrality-and-a-new-fund-to-advance-the-concept.html.

140. For more about operationalizing land-degradation neutrality, see Pamela Chasek et al., "Operationalizing Zero Net Land Degradation."

141. UNCCD, "World Governments Agree on How to Stop Land Degradation by 2030," press release, October 23, 2015, www.unccd.int/en/media-center/MediaNews/Pages/highlightdetail.aspx?HighlightID=418.

142. "Summary of the Twelfth Session of the Conference of the Parties to the Convention to Combat Desertification, 12–23 October 2015," *Earth Negotiations Bulletin* 4, no. 267 (October 27, 2015): 22.

143. FAO, *State of the World Fisheries and Aquaculture* (Rome: FAO, 2014), 37.

144. Ibid.

145. Ibid.

146. See Gareth Porter, *Estimating Overcapacity in the Global Fishing Fleet* (Washington, DC: WWF, 1998). WWF, *Living Blue Planet Report: Species, Habitats and Human Well-being* (Gland, Switzerland: WWF, 2015), 26.

147. FAO, *State of the World Fisheries and Aquaculture*, 6.

148. World Bank, *The Sunken Billions: The Economic Justification for Fisheries Reform* (Washington, DC: World Bank, 2009).

149. Its official title is the United Nations Agreement for the Implementation of the Provisions of the United Nations Convention on the Law of the Sea of 10 December 1982 Relating to the Conservation and Management of Straddling Fish Stocks and Highly Migratory Fish Stocks.

150. According to European law, the European Commission, on behalf of the EU, negotiates fisheries agreements with third countries.

151. See, for example, Commission of the European Communities, "Fishing on the High Seas: A Community Approach," Communication from the Commission to the Council and the European Parliament, SEC (92) 565, April 2, 1992, 5.

152. On Canadian mismanagement, see Raymond Rogers, *The Oceans Are Emptying: Fish Wars and Sustainability* (Montreal: Black Rose Books, 1995), 96–147; on EU allocations and Spanish and Portuguese catches, see Senate Standing Committee on Fisheries and Oceans, Report on Straddling Fish Stocks in the Northwest Atlantic, 37th Parliament of Canada, 2nd Session, June 2003, www.parl.gc.ca/Content/SEN/Committee/372/fish/rep/rep05jun03-e.pdf.

153. "Canada Hits EU's Atlantic Overfishing," *Washington Times*, February 19, 1995, A11.

154. Marvin Soroos, "The Turbot War: Resolution of an International Fishery Dispute," in *Conflict and the Environment*, ed. Nils Petter Gleditsch (Dordrecht, Netherlands: Kluwer Academic, 1997), 248.

155. "Summary of the Fifth Substantive Session of the UN Conference on Straddling Fish Stocks and Highly Migratory Fish Stocks: 24 July–4 August 1995," *Earth Negotiations Bulletin* 7, no. 54 (August 7, 1995), www.iisd.ca/vol07/0754000e.html.

156. To date there are thirteen technical guidelines relevant to data in fisheries management: (1) fisheries operations, 1996; (2) precautionary approach to capture fisheries and species introductions, 1996; (3) integration of fisheries into coastal-area management, 1996; (4) fisheries management, 1997; (5) aquaculture development, 1997; (6) inland fisheries, 1997; (7) responsible fish utilization, 1998; (8) indicators for sustainable development of marine capture fisheries, 1999; (9) implementation of the International Plan of Action to deter, prevent, and eliminate illegal, unreported, and unregulated fishing, 2002; (10) increasing the contribution of small-scale fisheries to poverty alleviation and food security, 2005; (11) responsible fish trade, 2009; (12) information and knowledge sharing, 2009; and (13) recreational fisheries, 2012. For more information and updates, see "Technical Guidelines for Responsible Fisheries," FAO, www.fao.org/fishery/publications/technical-guidelines/en.

157. The other international plans of action are the 1999 International Plan of Action for Reducing Incidental Catch of Seabirds in Longline Fisheries and the 1999 International Plan of Action for the Conservation and Management of Sharks. For more details, see FAO, "Activities—Introduction," www.fao.org/fishery/activities/en.

158. "Summary of the UN Fish Stocks Agreement Review Conference: 22–26 May 2006," *Earth Negotiations Bulletin* 7, no. 61 (May 29, 2006).

159. Ibid.; and "Summary of the Resumed Review Conference of the UN Fish Stocks Agreement: 24–28 May 2010," *Earth Negotiations Bulletin* 7, no. 65 (May 31, 2010), www.iisd.ca/download/pdf/enb0765e.pdf..

160. To learn more about the 2016 Resumed Review Conference, see www.iisd.ca/oceans/review-fish-stocks/2016.

161. A revised version of the 1973 Endangered Species Conservation Act banned whaling in US waters or by US citizens, outlawed the import of whale products, and required that the United States initiate bilateral and multilateral negotiations on an agreement to protect and conserve whales.

162. The effort to build an International Whaling Commission (IWC) majority to ban whaling was stymied in the latter half of the 1970s because states such as Canada and Mexico that were otherwise opposed to whaling were primarily concerned about protecting rights to regulate economic activities within their own two-hundred-mile exclusive economic zones and opposed the jurisdiction of an international body over whaling.

163. Teresa Watanabe, "Japan Is Set for a Whale of a Fight," *Los Angeles Times*, April 20, 1993.

164. Paul Brown, "Playing Football with the Whales," *Guardian*, May 1, 1993. The Caribbean states cooperating with Japan were Grenada, St. Lucia, St. Kitts and Nevis, Antigua and Barbuda, Dominica, and St. Vincent.

165. "During Clinton's Watch Global Whaling Triples," Greenpeace, May 20, 1997, http://archive.greenpeace.org/majordomo/index-press-releases/1997/msg00126.html.

166. "Catches Under Objection Since 1985," IWC, http://iwc.int/catches.

167. Ibid.

168. "Japan Ends Whale Hunt with Less than a Third of Its Target Catch," *Telegraph*, March 9, 2012.

169. For example, see Dennis Normile, "Japan's Whaling Program Carries Heavy Baggage," *Science* 289, no. 5488 (September 29, 2000): 2264–2265; and Nicholas J. Gales et al., "Japan's Whaling Ban Under Scrutiny," *Nature* 435 (June 16, 2005): 883–884.

170. Since 2008, EU member countries of the IWC have been bound by a "common position," requiring that they all vote and speak in the same manner at meetings of the IWC (Denmark has an exception related to Greenland). This means that EU countries that formerly expressed some support for sustainable whaling (Sweden, Finland, and Denmark) can no longer do so. See Dan Goodman, "The 'Future of the IWC': Why the Initiative to Save the International Whaling Commission Failed," *Journal of International Wildlife Law & Policy* 14, no. 1 (2011), 66.

171. Ibid.

172. Fisheries Agency head Masayuki Komatsu in an Australian Broadcasting Corporation radio interview. See "Japan 'Buys' Pro-Whaling Votes," CNN.com, July 18, 2001, http://edition.cnn.com/2001/TECH/science/07/18/japan.whale/index.html; and "Japan Denies Aid-for-Whaling Report," CNN.com, July 18, 2001, http://edition.cnn.com/2001/WORLD/asiapcf/east/07/19/japan.whaling. See also Andrew R. Miller and Nives Dolšak, "Issue Linkages in International Environmental Policy: The International Whaling Commission and Japanese Development Aid," *Global Environmental Politics* 7, no. 1 (February 2007): 69–96.

173. International Convention for the Regulation of Whaling, December 2, 1946, www.iwcoffice.org/cache/downloads/1r2jdhu5xtuswws0ocw04wgcw/convention.pdfarchive.iwc.int/?r=3607&k=2fae4a45c4.

174. Goodman, "The 'Future of the IWC,'" 65; IWC, "Resolution 2006-1: St. Kitts and Nevis Declaration," Fifty-Eighth Annual Meeting, St. Kitts and Nevis, June 16–20, 2006, http://archive.iwc.int/?r=2081. The following countries sponsored the declaration: St. Kitts and Nevis, Antigua and Barbuda, Benin, Cambodia, Cameroon, Côte d'Ivoire, Dominica, Gabon, Gambia, Grenada, Republic of Guinea, Iceland, Japan, Kiribati, Mali, Republic of the Marshall Islands, Mauritania, Mongolia, Morocco, Nauru, Nicaragua, Norway, Republic of Palau, Russian Federation, St. Lucia, St. Vincent and the Grenadines, Solomon Islands, Suriname, Togo, and Tuvalu.

175. Goodman, "The 'Future of the IWC,'" 64.

176. IWC, *Annual Report of the International Whaling Commission 2010* (Cambridge, UK: IWC, 2011), 6, https://archive.iwc.int/?r=65.

177. Richard Black, "Whaling 'Peace Deal' Falls Apart," *BBC News*, June 23, 2010.

178. IWC, *Annual Report 2010*, 7.

179. International Court of Justice, "Australia Institutes Proceedings Against Japan for Alleged Breach of International Obligations Concerning Whaling," press release no. 2010/16, June 1, 2010, www.icj-cij.org/docket/files/148/15953.pdf.

180. Ibid.

181. United Nations News Center, "UN Court Rules Against Japan's Whaling Activities in the Antarctic," press release, March 31, 2014, www.un.org/apps/news/story.asp?NewsID=47468#.VZW1aPlVhBc.

182. Yoko Wakatsuki and Sophie Brown, "Japanese Whaling Fleet Set to Sail Despite Recent Ruling," CNN.com, April 24, 2014, www.cnn.com/2014/04/24/world/asia/japan-whaling/.

183. IWC, "Resolution on Whaling Under Special Permit," Resolution 2014–5, Resolutions adopted at the 65th meeting, 2014, http://archive.iwc.int/?r=3723.

184. Chris Parsons, "Wailing About Whaling—The 2014 International Whaling Commission Meeting," Southern Fried Science blog, October 17, 2014, www.southernfriedscience.com/?p=17800.

185. Dennis Normile, "Scientists Renew Objections to Japan's Whaling Program," *Science* (June 19, 2015), http://news.sciencemag.org/plants-animals/2015/06/scientists-renew-objections-japan-s-whaling-program; Tim Hornyak, "Japan Defends Scientific Value of New Plan to Kill 333 Minke Whales," *Science*, December 7, 2015, http://news.sciencemag.org/asiapacific/2015/12/japan-defends-scientific-value-new-plan-kill-333-minke-whales.

186. Ronald B. Mitchell, "Discourse and Sovereignty: Interests, Science, and Morality in the Regulation of Whaling," *Global Governance* 4 (1998): 277.

187. Ibid.

188. Rebecca Goldman, "Notes from the IWC/60—Will Comity Save the Whales?" *Whales Alive* 17, no. 3 (July 2008): 3, http://csiwhalesalive.org/csi2008_07.pdf.

Chapter 5: Effective Environmental Regimes: Obstacles and Opportunities

1. United Nations Environment Programme (UNEP), *Auditing the Implementation of Multilateral Environmental Agreements (MEAs): A Primer for Auditors* (Nairobi: UNEP, 2010), 3, www.unep.org/environmentalgovernance/Portals/8/documents/Auditing_Implementation_of_MEAs.pdf.

2. The figures of 1,150 and 1,500 come from the International Environmental Agreements Database Project (http://iea.uoregon.edu) directed by Ronald Mitchell.

3. Broader and influential discussions of implementation and compliance include Edith Brown Weiss and Harold K. Jacobson, eds., *Engaging Countries: Strengthening Compliance with International Environmental Accords* (Cambridge, MA: MIT Press, 1998); James Caermon et al., eds., *Improving Compliance with International Environmental Law* (London: Earthscan, 1996); David Victor, Kal Raustiala, and Eugene Skolnikof, eds., *The Implementation and Effectiveness of International Environmental Commitments* (Cambridge, MA: MIT Press, 1998); Oran Young, ed., *The Effectiveness of International Environmental Regimes* (Cambridge, MA: MIT Press, 1999); Edward Miles et al., *Environmental Regime Effectiveness* (Cambridge, MA: MIT Press, 2001); Ronald Mitchell, "Problem Structure, Institutional Design, and the Relative Effectiveness of International Environmental Agreements," *Global Environmental Politics* 6, no. 3 (August 2006): 72–89; and Oran Young, "Effectiveness of International Environmental Regimes: Existing Knowledge, Cutting-Edge Themes, and Research Strategies," *PNAS* 108, no. 50 (2011): 19853–19860.

4. The discussion of the first five sets of factors draws extensively on publications by one of the coauthors. See particularly David Downie, "Understanding International Environmental Regimes: Lessons of the Ozone" (PhD diss., University of North Carolina, Chapel Hill, 1996); and David Downie, "Global Environmental Policy: Governance Through Regimes," in *Global*

Environmental Policy: Institutions, Law, and Policy, 2nd ed., eds. Regina Axelrod, David Downie, and Norman Vig (Washington, DC: Congressional Quarterly Press, 2005).

5. Classic examples include Thucydides, Niccolò Machiavelli, and Thomas Hobbes. Influential modern examples include Reinhold Niebuhr; Hans Morgenthau, *Politics Among Nations: The Struggle for Power and Peace*, 5th ed. (New York: Knopf, 1973); Robert Jervis, "Cooperation Under the Security Dilemma," *World Politics* 30 (1978): 167–186; and Kenneth Waltz, *Theory of International Politics* (Reading, MA: Addison-Wesley, 1979).

6. Waltz, *Theory of International Politics*.

7. Discussion of the impact of positional concerns on cooperation includes Joseph Grieco, "Anarchy and the Limits of Cooperation: A Realist Critique of the Newest Liberal Institutionalism," *International Organization* 42 (Summer 1988): 485–507.

8. Jervis, "Cooperation Under the Security Dilemma"; Kenneth Oye, ed., *Cooperation Under Anarchy* (Princeton, NJ: Princeton University Press, 1986), 1–22.

9. Mancur Olson, *The Logic of Collective Action* (Cambridge, MA: Harvard University Press, 1965).

10. Garrett Hardin, "The Tragedy of the Commons," *Science* 162, no. 3859 (December 13, 1968): 1243–1248; J. Samuel Barkin and George Shambaugh, eds., *Anarchy and the Environment: The International Relations of Common Pool Resources* (Albany: State University of New York Press, 1999).

11. Robert Keohane, *After Hegemony: Cooperation and Discord in the World Political Economy* (Princeton, NJ: Princeton University Press, 1984).

12. Robert Jervis, *Perception and Misperception in International Politics* (Princeton, NJ: Princeton University Press, 1976).

13. M. A. Giordano and A. T. Wolf, "Sharing Waters: Post-Rio International Water Management," *Natural Resources Forum* 27 (2003): 163–164.

14. Elli Louka, *International Environmental Law: Fairness, Effectiveness, and World Order* (New York: Cambridge University Press, 2006).

15. 1972 Stockholm Declaration and Action Plan, UN Document A/CONF.48/14, 118.

16. Gary Bryner, *From Promises to Performance: Achieving Global Environmental Goals* (New York: Norton, 1997), 59.

17. Peter Sand, *Lessons Learned in Global Environmental Governance* (Washington, DC: World Resources Institute, 1990), 21.

18. See, for example, Naomi Klein, *This Changes Everything: Capitalism vs. The Climate* (New York: Simon & Schuster, 2014).

19. Discussions of trade and environment include Chris Wold, Sanford Gaines, and Greg Block, *Trade and the Environment: Law and Policy* (Durham, NC: Carolina Academic, 2011); Erich Vranes, *Trade and the Environment: Fundamental Issues in International and WTO Law* (New York: Oxford University Press, 2009); Kevin Gallagher, *Handbook on Trade and the Environment* (Northampton: Edward Elgar, 2009).

20. For general discussion, see the Carbon Tax Center's website: www.carbontax.org.

21. Intergovernmental Panel on Climate Change (IPCC), *Climate Change 2014: Synthesis Report—Contribution of Working Groups I, II and III to the Fifth Assessment Report of the Intergovernmental Panel on Climate Change* (Geneva, Switzerland, IPCC, 2014).

22. Peter Haas, Robert Keohane, and Marc Levy, eds., *Institutions for the Earth: Sources of Effective International Environmental Protection* (Cambridge, MA: MIT Press, 1993). This discussion slightly expands their definition of the three conditions.

23. For discussion of aspects of this and the next category, see Lawrence Susskind, *Environmental Diplomacy: Negotiating More Effective Global Agreements* (New York: Oxford University Press, 1994); and Sand, *Lessons Learned in Global Environmental Governance*.

24. UNEP, *Report of the Conference of the Parties to the Rotterdam Convention on the Prior Informed Consent Procedure for Certain Hazardous Chemicals and Pesticides in International Trade on the Work of Its Seventh Meeting*, Geneva, 4–15 May 2015, UNEP/FAO/RC/COP.7/21;

"Summary of the Meetings of the Conferences of the Parties to the Basel, Rotterdam and Stockholm Conventions, 4–15 May 2015," *Earth Negotiations Bulletin*, 15, no. 230 (May 19, 2015). The stated reason was Sudan's concern that listing would lead to cost increases, something Sudan was reportedly told by a company that makes fenthion. Some at the meeting speculated privately to the author that inappropriate economic activity may also have been involved.

25. Ibid. Ecuador insisted that the official meeting report reflect that its delegation had been approached during the meeting by private-sector representatives in "unacceptable" ways seeking to persuade it to oppose listing paraquat.

26. See World Health Organization (WHO), "At Least One in Three Europeans Can Be Exposed to Asbestos at Work and in the Environment," press release, May 1, 2015, www.euro.who.int/en/media-centre/sections/press-releases/2015/04/at-least-one-in-three-europeans-can-be-exposed-to-asbestos-at-work-and-in-the-environment.

27. Sand, *Lessons Learned in Global Environmental Governance.*

28. Most spills occur in industrial facilities and laboratories and are relatively contained but can expose particular individuals to high doses. Large spills and area contaminations also occur as a result of industrial accidents; fires; accidents involving trains, ships, or trucks transporting chemicals; and inadequate pollution controls at production facilities. Famous examples include the explosions in 2008 at a large chemical plant in Guangxi Province, China, that released toxic gas into the air and contaminated the Longjiang River, forcing evacuation of nearby towns. In 1991, seven train cars carrying the pesticide metam sodium derailed, spilling chemicals into the Sacramento River and killing downriver plant and aquatic life for forty-three miles. In December 1984, a cloud of poisonous gas escaped from a Union Carbide chemical plant that produced the pesticide sevin in Bhopal, India, killing thousands of people and exposing hundreds of thousands. In 1983, the US government purchased the town of Times Beach, Missouri, and relocated more than twenty-two hundred residents because the land was so badly contaminated from nearby industries.

29. WHO and UNEP, *State of the Science of Endocrine Disrupting Chemicals* (Geneva: WHO and UNEP, 2013).

30. IPCC, *Climate Change 2014: Synthesis Report.*

31. Recent examples include deliberations on pentachlorophenol, short-chained chlorinated paraffins, and dicofol. Committee members from India stand out, but some other members (and some government and industry observers) have taken positions influenced by economic interests (personal observations by David Downie during these meetings). See also the official reports from the Persistent Organic Pollutants Review Committee meetings, available from the Stockholm Convention Secretariat, and reports by the *Earth Negotiations Bulletin* (www.iisd.ca/vol15).

32. "Summary of the Eleventh Meeting of the Rotterdam Convention's Chemical Review Committee: 26–28 October 2015," *Earth Negotiations Bulletin* 15, no. 238, (October 31, 2015).

33. Observations by David Downie during the POPs and mercury negotiations.

34. David Downie, personal observations during the mercury negotiations. See also the official reports of these negotiations (which Downie helped to draft), as well as the *Earth Negotiations Bulletin* (www.iisd.ca/vol28).

35. See Knut Midgaard and Arild Underdal, "Multiparty Conferences," in *Negotiations: Social-Psychological Perspectives*, ed. Daniel Druckman (Beverly Hills, CA: Sage, 1977), 339; and Pamela Chasek, *Earth Negotiations: Analyzing Thirty Years of Environmental Diplomacy* (Tokyo: United Nations University Press, 2001), ch. 3.

36. Barkin and Shambaugh, *Anarchy and the Environment.*

37. Research continues on developing biofuels from plants that can grow on marginal land without fertilizer or from algae that can be grown in greenhouses with recycled water, which could alleviate many of these negative impacts.

38. Ronald Mitchell, "Regime Design Matters: Intentional Oil Pollution and Treaty Compliance," *International Organization* 48, no. 3 (Summer 1994): 425–458. See also Ronald Mitchell,

"Problem Structure, Institutional Design, and the Relative Effectiveness of International Environmental Agreements," *Global Environmental Politics* 6, no. 3 (August 2006): 72–89.

39. Jacobson and Weiss, "A Framework for Analysis," in *Engaging Countries: Strengthening Compliance with International Environmental Accords*, eds. Edith Brown Weiss and Harold K. Jacobson (Cambridge, MA: MIT Press, 1998), 4.

40. J. Timmons Roberts, Bradley Parks, and Alexis Vásquez, "Who Ratifies Environmental Treaties and Why? Institutionalism, Structuralism and Participation by 192 Nations in 22 Treaties," *Global Environmental Politics* 4, no. 3 (August 2004): 22–64.

41. In addition to those cited above or below (in particular those by Jacobson and Weiss, Miles et al., Sand, Victor et al., and Young), prominent examples of this literature include Peter Sand, ed., *The Effectiveness of International Environmental Agreements* (Cambridge, MA: Grotius, 1992); Ronald Mitchell, *Intentional Oil Pollution at Sea* (Cambridge, MA: MIT Press, 1994); Michael Kelly, "Overcoming Obstacles to the Effective Implementation of International Environmental Agreements," *Georgetown International Environmental Law Review* 9, no. 2 (1997); Ronald Mitchell, "Compliance Theory: A Synthesis," *Review of European Community and International Environmental Law* 2, no. 4 (1993): 327–334; Patrick Bernhagen, "Business and International Environmental Agreements: Domestic Sources of Participation and Compliance by Advanced Industrialized Democracies," *Global Environmental Politics* 8, no. 1 (2008): 78–110; and David McEvoy and John Stranlund, "Self-Enforcing International Environmental Agreements with Costly Monitoring for Compliance," *Environmental and Resource Economics* 42, no. 4 (2009): 491–508.

42. Sand, *International Environmental Agreements*, 82.

43. Kelly, "Overcoming Obstacles," 462–463.

44. For example, in an experiment conducted by WWF, volunteers declared or displayed a cactus to customs officials in several countries, including the United Kingdom, Switzerland, Germany, Sweden, Denmark, and the United States. Although virtually all cacti are protected under CITES, officials asked no questions in any of these countries about the plant species or its origins. See Bill Padgett, "The African Elephant, Africa and CITES: The Next Step," *Indiana Journal of Global Legal Studies* 2 (1995): 529, 538–540, as cited in Kelly, "Overcoming Obstacles," 469–470.

45. See, for example, Duncan Brack, "Combating International Environmental Crime," *Global Environmental Change* 12, no. 2 (July 2002): 79–147; William Laurance et al., "Deforestation in Amazonia," *Science* 304, no. 5674 (May 21, 2004): 1109–1111; Christian Nelleman, UNEP, and INTERPOL, *Green Carbon, Black Trade: Illegal Logging, Tax Fraud and Laundering in the World's Tropical Forests* (Nairobi: UNEP, 2012).

46. Personal observations by David Downie during meetings of the Stockholm, Rotterdam, and Basel Conventions in 2013 and 2015 and personal communications from senior environmental officials from several African countries during the fourth Conference of the Parties to the Stockholm Convention on Persistent Organic Pollutants, Geneva, Switzerland, May 4–8, 2009.

47. Personal observations by David Downie during negotiation of the Minamata Convention.

48. David Vogel and Timothy Kessler, "How Compliance Happens and Doesn't Happen Domestically," in Weiss and Jacobson, *Engaging Countries*, 24.

49. Nelleman, UNEP, and INTERPOL, *Green Carbon, Black Trade.*

50. Andrew Heimert, "How the Elephant Lost His Tusks," *Yale Law Journal* 104 (1995): 1473, as cited in Kelly, "Overcoming Obstacles," 465.

51. Environmental Investigation Agency and Telepak, *The Final Cut: Illegal Logging in Indonesia's Orangutan Parks* (Washington, DC: Environmental Investigation Agency, 1999); David Brown, *Addicted to Rent: Corporate and Spatial Distribution of Forest Resources in Indonesia—Implications for Forest Sustainability and Government Policy* (Jakarta: Indonesia-UK Tropical Forest Management Programme, 1999).

52. Peter Tsai and Thomas Hatfield, "Global Benefits from the Phaseout of Leaded Fuel," *Journal of Environmental Health* 75, no. 5 (December 2011): 8–14.

53. UNEP and Kenya Forest Service, *The Role and Contribution of Montane Forests and Related Ecosystem Services to the Kenyan Economy* (Nairobi: UNEP, 2012).

54. Matthew Wald, "Fossil Fuels' Hidden Cost Is in Billions, Study Says," *New York Times*, October 19, 2009; Committee on Health, Environmental, and Other External Costs and Benefits of Energy Production and Consumption, National Research Council, *Hidden Costs of Energy: Unpriced Consequences of Energy Production and Use* (Washington, DC: National Academies Press, 2010).

55. UNEP, *UNEP Year Book 2014 Emerging Issues Update* (Nairobi: UNEP, 2014), 43.

56. Robert Costanza et al., "The Value of the World's Ecosystem Services and Natural Capital," *Nature* 387 (May 15, 1997): 253–260.

57. Robert Costanza et al., "Changes in the Global Value of Ecosystem Services," *Global Environmental Change* 26 (May 2014): 152–158.

58. For information, see the Economics of Ecosystems and Biodiversity (TEEB) website: www.teebweb.org.

59. See Patrick ten Brink et al., *The Economics of Ecosystems and Biodiversity for Water and Wetlands: A Briefing Note* (Geneva: UNEP TEEB, 2012); and Daniela Russi et al., *The Economics of Ecosystems and Biodiversity for Water and Wetlands: Final Consultation Draft*, UN Document UNEP/CBD/COP/11/INF/22, September 26, 2012.

60. UNEP FI and Global Footprint Network, *A New Angle on Sovereign Credit Risk: E-RISC—Environmental Risk Integration in Sovereign Credit Analysis* (Geneva: UNEP, 2012).

61. See Nicholas Stern, *The Economics of Climate Change: The Stern Review* (Cambridge: Cambridge University Press, 2007); McKinsey & Co., *U.S. Greenhouse Gas Emissions: How Much and at What Cost?* (New York: McKinsey, 2007); Frank Ackerman and Elizabeth Stanton, *The Cost of Climate Change: What We'll Pay If Global Warming Continues Unchecked* (Washington, DC: Natural Resources Defense Council, 2008); Ernst von Weizsäcker et al., *Factor Five: Transforming the Global Economy Through 80% Improvements in Resource Productivity* (London: Earthscan, 2009); Economics of Climate Adaptation (ECA) Working Group, *Shaping Climate Resilient Development: A Framework for Decision-Making* (Washington, DC: ECA, 2009); Council of Economic Advisers to the President of the United States, *The Cost of Delaying Action to Stop Climate Change* (Washington, DC: The White House, 2014); US Environmental Protection Agency (EPA), *Climate Change in the United States: Benefits of Global Action* (Washington, DC: EPA, 2015).

62. ECA Working Group, *Shaping Climate.*

63. "Too Hot to Work: Climate Change Puts South-east Asia Economies at Risk," *Guardian*, October 27, 2015; Jeremy Pal and Elfatih Eltahil, "Future Temperature in Southwest Asia Project to Exceed a Threshold for Human Adaptability," *Nature Climate Change* (2015), doi: 10.1038/nclimate2833.

64. See Tammy Thompson et al., "A Systems Approach to Evaluating the Air Quality Co-benefits of US Carbon Policies," *Nature Climate Change* 4 (October 2014): 917–923.

65. Coral Davenport, "Economies Can Still Rise as Carbon Emissions Fade," *New York Times*, April 7, 2016.

66. Ibid.

67. UNEP-GEF, "New Countries to Start Phase-Out of Inefficient Lighting, with Major Economic and Climate Benefits," press release, June 21, 2012. Information on the initiative is available at www.enlighten-initiative.org. National data on the benefits of a transition to energy-efficient lighting can be viewed at www.unep.org/PDF/PressReleases/Table_Energy_Efficient_Lighting_Transition.pdf.

68. See UNEP, "World-Wide Action on Black Carbon, Methane and Other Short-Lived Pollutants Grows as Seven More Countries Join New Coalition," press release, July 25, 2012. For information on the coalition, see www.unep.org/ccac.

69. Michael Renner et al., *Green Jobs: Towards Decent Work in a Sustainable, Low-Carbon World* (Nairobi: UNEP, 2008).

70. *UNEP Year Book 2009* (Nairobi: UNEP, March 2009); UNEP, *Global Green New Deal: Policy Brief* (Nairobi: UNEP, March 2009).

71. Andy Gouldson et al. *Accelerating Low-Carbon Development in the World's Cities* (London and Washington, DC: New Climate Economy, 2015).

72. For specific information, see the relevant reports of the ozone regime's Implementation Committee, available at the Ozone Secretariat's website: http://ozone.unep.org.

73. Personal observations by David Downie during these negotiations.

74. John Vidal, "Many Treaties to Save the Earth, but Where's the Will to Implement Them?" *Guardian*, http://www.theguardian.com/environment/blog/2012/jun/07/earth-treaties-environmental-agreements.

75. Personal observations.

76. David Downie and Jessica Templeton, "Pesticides and Persistent Organic Pollutants," in *Routledge Handbook of Global Environmental Politics*, ed. Paul Harris (New York: Routledge, 2013).

77. UNEP, *GEO 5: Global Environmental Outlook—Environment for the Future We Want* (Nairobi: UNEP, 2012).

78. See Stern, *The Economics of Climate Change*, xvii and chs. 14–17; Carbon Tax Center's website (www.carbontax.org); and Eric Marx, "More than 2,000 Companies Call for Lowering Emissions Using a Price on CO_2," *Environment and Energy Publishing*, May 22, 2015, www.eenews.net/stories/1060018992.

79. For discussion, see UNEP and WTO, *Trade and Climate Change: A Report by the United Nations Environment Programme and the World Trade Organization* (Geneva: WTO Publications, 2009).

80. Such provisions were even included as part of climate-change legislation that passed the US House of Representatives in 2009 (HR 2454: American Clean Energy and Security Act of 2009) but did not pass in the Senate.

81. David Cosby et al., *How Large Are Global Energy Subsidies*, International Monetary Fund (IMF) working paper, May 2015, www.imf.org/external/pubs/ft/wp/2015/wp15105.pdf.

82. International Energy Association (IEA), *2014 World Energy Outlook* (Paris: IEA, 2014).

83. See, for example, John Conti, *Direct Federal Financial Interventions and Subsidies in Energy in Fiscal Year 2013* (Washington, DC: US Energy Information Agency, 2015); Shakuntala Makhijani, *Fossil Fuel Exploration Subsidies: United States* (London: Overseas Development Institute, 2014); Oil Change International (OCI), *Cashing In on All of the Above: US Fossil Fuel Production Subsidies Under Obama* (Washington, DC: OCI, July 2014).

84. J. Samuel Barkin and Elizabeth DeSombre, *Saving Global Fisheries: Reducing Fishing Capacity to Promote Sustainability* (Cambridge, MA: MIT Press, 2013).

85. Edith Brown Weiss, "The Five International Treaties: A Living History," in Weiss and Jacobson, *Engaging Countries*, 115–116.

86. See Victor, Raustiala, and Skolnikoff, *International Environmental Commitments*.

87. Personal communications from regime officials.

88. Examples include the Alliance for Responsible Atmospheric Policy, an industry group, which tracked ozone-depleting substance production for many years, and the Environmental Investigation Agency's investigations of CFC smuggling.

89. For additional information, see the TRAFFIC website: www.traffic.org.

90. For additional information, see the International Fund for Animal Welfare website, particularly www.ifaw.org/international/our-work/wildlife-trade/ifaw-and-interpol-working-together-fight-wildlife-crime.

91. For discussion, see Mitchell, *Intentional Oil Pollution at Sea*, 47–48.

92. See Susskind, *Environmental Diplomacy*.

93. Personal communication.

94. See the website of the Environmental Performance Index: www.epi.yale.edu.

95. For example, see Pamela Chasek, "Confronting Environmental Treaty Implementation Challenges in the Pacific Islands," *Pacific Islands Policy* 6 (2010).

96. Personal observation by the authors during negotiations on the ozone, chemical, climate, and mercury regimes. For specific examples, see *Earth Negotiations Bulletin* reports from the negotiations at www.iisd.ca.

97. Organization for Economic Cooperation and Development (OECD), "Development: Aid to Developing Countries Falls Because of Global Recession," press release, April 4, 2012, www.oecd.org/newsroom/developmentaidtodevelopingcountriesfallsbecauseofglobal recession.htm.

98. See particularly Jeffrey Sachs, *The End of Poverty: Economic Possibilities for Our Time* (New York: Penguin, 2005); and Jeffrey Sachs, *Common Wealth: Economics for a Crowded Planet* (New York: Penguin, 2008).

99. For official information on the EU Emissions Trading System, see http://ec.europa.eu /clima/policies/ets/index_en.htm.

100. See the Regional Greenhouse Gas Initiative webpage: www.rggi.org; and the California trading system webpage: www.arb.ca.gov/cc/capandtrade/capandtrade.htm.

101. For information, see the Adaptation Fund website: www.adaptation-fund.org/.

102. For information, see the Green Climate Fund website: www.greenclimate.fund/.

103. Stephen Seidel and Daniel Blank, "Closing an Ozone Loophole," *Environmental Forum* 7 (1990): 18–20; "Effect of Ozone-Depleting Chemicals Tax Could Be Wide-Ranging, IRS Attorney Says," *Environment Reporter* 21 (November 2, 1990): 1257.

104. For information, see www.fin.gov.bc.ca/tbs/tp/climate/carbon_tax.htm.

105. For an early example, see International Institute for Sustainable Development, "Financing Climate Change: Global Environmental Tax?" *Developing Ideas* 15 (September–October 1998).

106. UN Commission on Sustainable Development, *Financial Resources and Mechanisms for Sustainable Development: Overview of Current Issues and Developments, Report of the Secretary-General,* E/CN.17/ISWG.II/1994/2, February 22, 1994, 24.

107. "Levy on International Air Travel Could Fund Climate Change Fight," *Guardian*, June 8, 2009, 13.

108. See, for example, John Vidal, "Oil Nations Asked to Consider Carbon Tax on Exports," *Guardian*, November 21, 2012.

109. The original proposal, by Nobel Prize–winning economist James Tobin, was for a 0.5 percent tax on speculative currency transactions that would raise $1.5 trillion annually and was aimed at deterring such transactions. The United Nations Development Programme (UNDP) proposed a much smaller tax. See UNDP, *Human Development Report 1994* (New York: Oxford University Press, 1994), 69–70; Martin Walker, "Global Taxation: Paying for Peace," *World Policy Journal* 10, no. 2 (summer 1993): 7–12.

110. See section 921 of the United Nations Reform Act of 1999, commonly referred to as "Helms-Biden."

111. Updated information on the HIPC initiative can be found on the World Bank and IMF websites: www.worldbank.org/debt; and www.imf.org/external/np/exr/facts/hipc.htm.

112. Jim VandeHei, "G-8 Leaders Agree on $50B in Africa Aid," *Washington Post*, July 9, 2005.

113. See the Jubilee USA Network website: www.jubileeusa.org.

114. María José Romero, *What Lies Beneath? A Critical Assessment of PPPs and Their Impact on Sustainable Development* (Brussels: Eurodad, 2015), 4, http://eurodad.org/files/pdf /559e6c832c087.pdf.

115. World Bank Public-Private Partnership in Infrastructure Research Center, "Potential Benefits of Public-Private Partnerships," http://ppp.worldbank.org/public-private-partnership /overview/ppp-objectives.

116. United Nations Foundation, *Understanding Public-Private Partnerships* (Washington, DC: UN Foundation, 2003).

117. See the UN Global Compact website, www.unglobalcompact.org/; also see UN, *The Future We Want,* A/66/L.56, July 24, 2012, 10, www.uncsd2012.org/thefuturewewant.html; and UN, *Report of the World Summit on Sustainable Development,* A/CONF.199/20, www.unmillenniumproject.org/documents/131302_wssd_report_reissued.pdf.

118. Romero, 6.

119. Karin Bäckstrand, "Multi-stakeholder Partnerships for Sustainable Development: Rethinking Legitimacy, Accountability and Effectiveness," *European Environment* 16 (2006), 290–306.

120. Kacper Szulecki, Philipp Pattberg, and Frank Biermann, "Explaining Variation in the Effectiveness of Transnational Energy Partnerships," *Governance* 24, no. 4 (2011): 713–736.

121. Ibid.; Jonathan Volt, "Opinion: Why Does United Nations Secretary-General Insist on Placing Public-Private Partnerships in the Heart of the Post 2015 Development Agenda?" Earth Systems Governance Project, March 23, 2015, http://sdg.earthsystemgovernance.org/sdg/news/2015-03-19/opinion-why-does-united-nations-secretary-general-insist-placing-public-private-part.

122. "What Is South–South Cooperation?" United Nations Office for South–South Cooperation, http://ssc.undp.org/content/ssc/about/what_is_ssc.html.

123. Ibid.; International Trade Union Confederation, "Briefing Note: What Are South–South and Triangular Cooperation?" August 3, 2012, www.ituc-csi.org/briefing-note-what-are-south-south?lang=en.

124. United Nations Office for South–South Cooperation.

125. UNEP, *South Trade in Renewable Energy: A Trade Flow Analysis of Selected Environmental Goods* (Nairobi: UNEP, 2014).

126. See UN, "The Future We Want"; UN, *Addis Ababa Action Agenda of the Third International Conference on Financing for Development* (New York: UN, 2015); and UN, *Transforming Our World: The 2030 Agenda for Sustainable Development,* A.69/L.85, August 15, 2015, www.un.org/ga/search/view_doc.asp?symbol=A/69/L.85&Lang=E.

127. International Trade Union Confederation.

128. Personal observations.

129. "Triangular Cooperation," OECD, www.oecd.org/dac/dac-global-relations/triangular-cooperation.htm.

130. Guido Ashoff, "Triangular Cooperation: Opportunities, Risks and Conditions for Effectiveness," *Development Outreach,* October 2010, 23, http://siteresources.worldbank.org/WBI/Resources/213798-1286217829056/ashoff.pdf.

131. See UN, "The Future We Want"; UN, *Addis Ababa Action Agenda;* and UN, "Transforming Our World."

132. Ashoff, 23–24.

133. Ibid., 24.

Chapter 6: Environmental Politics and Sustainable Development

1. United Nations Development Programme (UNDP), *Human Development Report 2011: Sustainability and Equity—A Better Future for All* (New York: Palgrave Macmillan, 2011), 27.

2. Ibid., 24.

3. *Development and Environment* (Paris: Mouton, 1971), report and working papers of experts convened by the secretary-general of the UN Conference on the Human Environment, Founex, Switzerland, June 4–12, 1971.

4. Adil Najam, "The View from the South: Developing Countries in Global Environmental Politics," in *The Global Environment: Institutions, Law and Policy*, 2nd ed., eds. Regina Axelrod,

David Downie, and Norman Vig (Washington, DC: Congressional Quarterly Press, 2005), 224–243.

5. *Development and Environment*, 5–6, as cited in Adil Najam, "Why Environmental Politics Looks Different from the South," in *Handbook of Global Environmental Politics*, ed. Peter Dauvergne (Cheltenham, UK: Edward Elgar, 2005), 111–126.

6. Lars-Göran Engfeldt, *From Stockholm to Johannesburg and Beyond* (Stockholm: Government Offices of Sweden, 2009), 81.

7. Ibid., 67; UN, *Report of the United Nations Conference on the Human Environment*, A/CONF.48/14/Rev 1 (1973), www.un-documents.net/unche.htm.

8. Pamela Chasek, "Sustainable Development," in *Introducing Global Issues*, 5th ed., eds. Michael Snarr and D. Neil Snarr (Boulder, CO: Lynne Rienner, 2012), 256–257.

9. World Commission on Environment and Development, *Our Common Future* (New York: Oxford University Press, 1987), 5.

10. World Commission on Environment and Development, *Our Common Future*, 43.

11. Engfeldt, *From Stockholm to Johannesburg*, 111.

12. Marian Miller, *The Third World in Global Environmental Politics* (Boulder, CO: Lynne Rienner, 1995), 9.

13. Najam, "The View from the South." See also Andrew Jordan, "Financing the UNCED Agenda: The Controversy over Additionality," *Environment* 36, no. 3 (1994): 16–34.

14. Pamela Chasek, "The Convention to Combat Desertification: Lessons Learned for Sustainable Development," *Journal of Environment and Development* 6, no. 2 (1997): 147–169.

15. Najam, "The View from the South."

16. See *Outreach* 1, no. 24 (April 22, 1997).

17. See the final communiqué from the Gleneagles Summit, 2005, www.g7.utoronto.ca/summit/2005gleneagles/communique.pdf.

18. See the outcome document from the 2005 UN summit, www.un.org/summit2005.

19. "Development Aid Stable in 2014 but Flows to Poorest Countries Still Falling," Organization for Economic Cooperation and Development (OECD), April 8, 2015, www.oecd.org/dac/stats/development-aid-stable-in-2014-but-flows-to-poorest-countries-still-falling.htm.

20. Ibid.

21. Data from OECD StatExtracts, 2010, http://stats.oecd.org/index.aspx?DataSetCode=CRS1. The figures represent total bilateral and multilateral official development assistance in 2013 for all sectors and total for environmental protection.

22. United Nations Environment Programme (UNEP), *GEO 5: Global Environmental Outlook—Environment for the Future We Want* (Nairobi: UNEP, 2012).

23. Najam, "The View from the South." See also Anil Agarwal and Sunita Narain, *Global Warming in an Unequal World: A Case of Environmental Colonialism* (New Delhi: Center for Science and Environment, 1991); Anil Agarwal, Sunita Narain, and Anju Sharma, eds., *Green Politics: Global Negotiations*, vol. 1 (New Delhi: Center for Science and Environment, 1999).

24. Najam, "The View from the South."

25. United Nations Department for Public Information, "Press Summary of the Secretary-General's Report on Implementing Agenda 21," press release, January 2002.

26. Chasek, "Sustainable Development," 252.

27. "Addressing Inequities of Globalization 'Overarching Challenge' of Times Says Secretary-General, Presenting Millennium Report to General Assembly," press release SG/SM/7343, UN, April 3, 2000, www.un.org/News/Press/docs/2000/20000403.sgsm7343.doc.html.

28. Pamela Chasek and Richard Sherman, *Ten Days in Johannesburg: A Negotiation of Hope* (Cape Town: Struik, 2004); and International Institute for Sustainable Development (IISD), *Millennium Review Meeting Bulletin* 104, no. 2 (March 16, 2005), www.iisd.ca/sd/ecosocprep1/sdvol104num2e.html.

29. Ibid.

30. UN, *The Millennium Development Goals Report 2015* (New York: UN, 2015), 4–7.

31. Liz Ford, "Sustainable Development Goals: All You Need to Know," *Guardian*, July 19, 2015.

32. UN, *The Millennium Development Goals Report 2015*, 8.

33. Jeffrey Sachs and Walter Reid, "Investments Toward Sustainable Development," *Science* 312 (May 19, 2006): 1002.

34. Raymond Ahearn, *Rising Economic Powers and the Global Economy: Trends and Issues for Congress*, Congressional Research Service Report 7–5700 (Washington, DC: Congressional Research Service, 2011).

35. See Karl Sauvant and Hajo Hasenpflug, eds., *The New International Economic Order: Confrontation or Cooperation Between North and South?* (Boulder, CO: Westview, 1977).

36. James Sebenius, "Negotiating a Regime to Control Global Warming," in *Greenhouse Warming: Negotiating a Global Regime*, ed. Jessica Tuchman Mathews (Washington, DC: World Resources Institute, 1991), 87.

37. South Commission, *The Challenge to the South: The Report of the South Commission* (Oxford: Oxford University Press, 1990); Mohammed Ayoob, "The New-Old Disorder in the Third World," *Global Governance* 1, no. 1 (1995): 59–77; Adil Najam, "An Environmental Negotiation Strategy for the South," *International Environmental Affairs* 7, no. 3 (1995): 249–287; Najam, "The View from the South," 224–243.

38. This was part of a longer-term decline in the real prices of primary products in the world market, caused by slow growth in demand, the development of cheaper substitutes, and overproduction. See UNDP, *Human Development Report 1992* (New York: UNDP, 1992), 59.

39. UNDP, "Financial Inflows and Outflows," *Human Development Report 1998* (New York: Oxford University Press, 1998). The term *least-developed countries* (LDCs), was originally used at the UN in 1971 to describe the "poorest and most economically weak of the developing countries, with formidable economic, institutional and human resources problems, which are often compounded by geographical handicaps and natural and man-made disasters." There are currently fifty LDCs.

40. "World Development Indicators and Global Development Finance," World Bank, 2015, http://databank.worldbank.org/data/home.aspx.

41. Ibid.

42. Ibid.

43. M. Ayhan Kose and Eswar Prasad, *Emerging Markets: Resilience and Growth Amid Global Turmoil* (Washington, DC: Brookings Institution Press, 2010), 1.

44. Credit Suisse Research Institute, *Credit Suisse Global Wealth Report, 2014* (Zurich: Credit Suisse Research Institute, 2014), 11, http://publications.credit-suisse.com/tasks/render/file/?fileID=60931FDE-A2D2-F568-B041B58C5EA591A4.

45. Winnie Byanyima, "Inequality and Climate Change: 2015's Challenges," World Economic Forum Blog, January 19, 2015, http://agenda.weforum.org/2015/01/inequality-and-climate-change-twin-challenges-of-2015/.

46. Chasek, "Sustainable Development," 262.

47. Mark Halle, "Sustainable Development Cools Off: Globalization Demands Summit Take New Approach to Meeting Ecological, Social Goals," *Winnipeg Free Press*, July 29, 2002.

48. World Bank, *Global Economic Prospects and the Developing Countries* (Washington, DC: World Bank, 1992), 13.

49. *Barriers to entry* are any obstacle that impedes a potential new entrant (a company or country) from entering a market to produce or sell goods or services. Barriers to entry shelter incumbent companies against new entrants. They can include government regulations, subsidies, intellectual property rules, restrictive practices, preexisting supplier or distributor agreements, control of resources, economies of scale, advantages independent of scale, consumer preferences, and other factors.

50. Kevin Gallagher, "The Economics of Globalization and Sustainable Development," in "Trade, Environment and Investment: Cancún and Beyond," special issue, *Policy Matters* 11 (September 2003).

51. Steve Charnovitz, "Environmentalism Confronts GATT Rules," *Journal of World Trade* 28 (January 1993): 37; Daniel Esty, "Economic Integration and the Environment," in *The Global Environment: Institutions, Law, and Policy*, eds. Norman Vig and Regina Axelrod (Washington, DC: Congressional Quarterly Press, 1999), 192.

52. General Agreement on Tariffs and Trade (GATT) and World Trade Organization (WTO), preamble to "Agreement Establishing the World Trade Organization," WTO, 1994, www.wto.org/english/docs_e/legal_e/04-wto.pdf.

53. Ibid.

54. For more information on the WTO Bali agreements, see Christophe Bellmann, "The Bali Agreement: Implications for Development and the WTO," *International Development Policy/ Revue internationale de politique de développement* 5.2 (2014), doi:10.4000/poldev.1744; and International Centre for Trade and Sustainable Development, "Success in Bali Sparks Questions over Doha, WTO Future," *Bridges* 17 (December 12, 2013): 41, www.ictsd.org/bridges-news/bridges/news/success-in-bali-sparks-questions-over-doha-wto-future.

55. Roberto Azevêdo, "Address to the MC10 Closing Ceremony," WTO, December 19, 2015, www.wto.org/english/news_e/spra_e/spra108_e.htm.

56. "World Trade Organization's 10th Ministerial Conference in Nairobi," World Bank, January 7, 2016, www.worldbank.org/en/news/feature/2016/01/07/world-trade-organizations-10th-ministerial-conference-in-nairobi. See also International Centre for Trade and Sustainable Development (ICTSD), "Bridges Daily Update #5: Overview of Outcomes of WTO's 10th Ministerial in Nairobi," *Bridges* (December 19, 2015), www.ictsd.org/bridges-news/bridges/news/bridges-daily-update-5-overview-of-outcomes-of-wto%E2%80%99s-10th-ministerial-in.

57. WTO, Nairobi Ministerial Declaration, WT/MIN(15)/DEC, December 19, 2015, paragraph 30, www.wto.org/english/thewto_e/minist_e/mc10_e/mindecision_e.htm.

58. New York Times Editorial Board, "Global Trade After the Failure of the Doha Round," *New York Times,* January 1, 2016, A22.

59. Ibid.; and Joseph Stiglitz, "In 2016, Let's Hope for Better Trade Agreements and the Death of TPP," *Guardian,* January 10, 2016, www.theguardian.com/business/2016/jan/10/in-2016-better-trade-agreements-trans-pacific-partnership?CMP=share_btn_tw.

60. Devinder Sharma, "Time to Admit Honestly that WTO Is Dead!" *ABP Live,* January 9, 2016, www.abplive.in/blog/time-to-admit-honestly-that-wto-is-dead.

61. For a matrix of selected MEAs and their trade provisions, see WTO, "Matrix on Trade Measures Pursuant to Selected Multilateral Environmental Agreements," WT/CTE/W/160/Rev.6., October 4, 2013, www.wto.org/english/tratop_e/envir_e/envir_matrix_e.htm.

62. UNEP and IISD, *Environment and Trade: A Handbook*, 2nd ed. (Winnipeg, Canada: IISD/UNEP, 2005), 66.

63. Ibid., 67.

64. "Doha Ministerial Declaration," WT/MIN(01)/DEC/1, WTO, November 20, 2001, www.wto.org/english/thewto_e/minist_e/min01_e/mindecl_e.htm; and "The Doha Mandate on Multilateral Environmental Agreements (MEAs)," WTO, www.wto.org/english/tratop_e/envir_e/envir_neg_mea_e.htm.

65. Richard Tarasofsky, *Trade, Environment, and the WTO Dispute Settlement Mechanism,* report commissioned by the European Commission, June 2005, 4, http://ecologic.eu/download/projekte/1800–1849/1800/4_1800_cate_wto_dispute_settlement.pdf.

66. The term *environmental trade measures* is used in Steve Charnovitz, "The Environment vs. Trade Rules: Defogging the Debate," *Environmental Law* 23 (1993): 490. Charnovitz lists all of these forms of environmental trade measures except mandatory ecolabeling.

67. Sang Don Lee, "The Effect of Environmental Regulations on Trade: Cases of Korea's New Environmental Laws," *Georgetown International Environmental Law Review* 5, no. 3 (Summer 1993): 659.

68. One exception was when Ecuador sought WTO approval for retaliatory sanctions against the European Union (EU) for the EU's failure to comply with the WTO ruling on its banana-import regime, which discriminated against some South and Central American banana-exporting countries. However, realizing that, as a small country, imposing punitive tariffs on EU imports would have little impact on the EU but a devastating effect on Ecuador's consumers, Ecuador said it would target intellectual property rights and services for retaliation. See International Centre for Trade and Sustainable Development (ICTSD), "Ecuador, U.S. Reject EU Banana Proposal; Ecuador to Cross-Retaliate," *Bridges Weekly Trade News Digest* 3, no. 45 (November 15, 1999).

69. Daniel Esty, *Greening the GATT: Trade, Environment and the Future* (Washington, DC: Institute for International Economics, 1994), 188. In an ironic twist, research undertaken by the Inter-American Tropical Tuna Commission found that dolphin-safe tuna fishing results in catching tuna at least thirty-five times more immature (because young tuna do not school beneath groups of dolphins as mature tuna do) and thus threatens to deplete tuna fisheries. See Richard Parker, "The Use and Abuse of Trade Leverage to Protect the Global Commons: What We Can Learn from the Tuna-Dolphin Conflict," *Georgetown International Environmental Law Review* 12, no. 1 (1999): 37–38.

70. For environmental critiques of the decision, see Steve Charnovitz, "GATT and the Environment: Examining the Issues," *International Environmental Affairs* 4, no. 3 (Summer 1992): 203–233; Robert Repetto, "Trade and Environment Policies: Achieving Complementarities and Avoiding Conflict," *WRI Issues and Ideas* (July 1993): 6–10. For an alternative view of the decision, see John Jackson, "World Trade Rules and Environmental Policies: Congruence or Conflict?" *Washington and Lee Law Review* 49 (Fall 1992): 1242–1243.

71. In April 2007 a California appeals court ruling agreed with the environmental groups. Moreover, due to the perceived threat to the integrity of the US government label, the largest tuna brands declared they would not buy purse seine tuna products even if government labeling requirements allowed it. See ICTSD, "GATTzilla vs. Flippa Revisited? The Tuna-Dolphin Dispute's Second Round," *BIORES* 5, no. 1 (April 6, 2011), www.ictsd.org/bridges-news/biores/news/gattzilla-vs-flippa-revisited-the-tuna-dolphin-dispute%E2%80%99s-second-round.

72. ICTSD, "GATTzilla vs. Flippa."

73. Marie Wilke, "Tuna Labelling and the WTO: How Safe is 'Dolphin-Safe'?" *BIORES* 6, no. 2 (June 18, 2012), www.ictsd.org/bridges-news/biores/news/tuna-labelling-and-the-wto-how-safe-is-dolphin-safe.

74. Janet Welsh Brown, "Trade and the Environment," in *Encyclopedia of Violence, Peace and Conflict*, vol. 3, ed. Lester Kurtz (San Diego, CA: Academic Press, 1999), T12–14.

75. The appellate body also noted that the United States had not signed the Convention on Migratory Species and the United Nations Convention on the Law of the Sea, ratified the Convention on Biological Diversity, or raised the issue of sea turtles during recent CITES conferences. These inconsistencies on protecting endangered species do not prove, of course, that the US intention in the shrimp/turtle case was not to protect endangered sea turtles.

76. See "Revised Guidelines for the Implementation of Section 609 of Public Law 101–162 Relating to the Protection of Sea Turtles in Shrimp Trawl Fishing Operations," Public Notice 3086, *Federal Register*, July 1999.

77. For additional information about the Forest Stewardship Council, see www.fsc.org.

78. For more information, see the Marine Stewardship Council's website: www.msc.org.

79. Food and Agriculture Organization of the United Nations (FAO), *State of World Fisheries and Aquaculture 2014* (Rome: FAO, 2014), 47.

80. Since 1994, labeling and related issues have been discussed in the WTO's Committee on Trade and Environment, the Committee on Technical Barriers to Trade (TBT), and the Committee on Sanitary and Phytosanitary Measures, as well as during two triennial reviews of the TBT agreement, at various informal WTO symposia, in external conferences attended by WTO Secretariat staff, and in dispute-settlement panels and appellate bodies. See also WTO, "Labelling."

81. Marie Wilke, "Tuna Labeling and the WTO: How Safe Is 'Dolphin-Safe'?"

82. See WTO, Committee on Trade and Environment, *Environmental Benefits of Removing Trade Restrictions and Distortions: Note by the Secretariat* (Geneva: WTO, 1997); Gareth Porter, *Fisheries Subsidies, Overfishing and Trade* (Geneva: UNEP, 1998); International Monetary Fund (IMF), *Energy Subsidy Reform: Lessons and Implications* (Washington, DC: IMF, 2013).

83. U. Rashid Sumaila et al., "Global Fisheries Subsidies," European Parliament, 2013, www.europarl.europa.eu/RegData/etudes/note/join/2013/513978/IPOL-PECH_NT(2013)513978_EN.pdf; U. Rashid Sumaila et al., "A Bottom-Up Re-estimation of Global Fisheries Subsidies," *Journal of Bioeconomics* 12 (2010): 201–225.

84. Ibid.; ICTSD, "Trade Leaders Call for Fisheries Subsidies Reform on World Oceans Day," *Bridges Weekly Trade News Digest* 13, no. 21 (June 10, 2009), http://ictsd.net/i/news/bridgesweekly/48339; J. Samuel Barkin and Elizabeth DeSombre, *Saving Global Fisheries: Reducing Fishing Capacity to Promote Sustainability* (Cambridge, MA: MIT Press, 2013).

85. ICTSD and IISD, "Trade and Environment."

86. WTO, "Ministerial Declaration," WT/MIN(05)/DEC, Annex D, December 22, 2005, www.wto.org/english/theWTO_e/minist_e/min05_e/final_text_e.pdf.

87. ICTSD, "Bridges Daily Update #5"; See the ministerial declaration at www.wto.org/english/thewto_e/minist_e/mc10_e/fishsubsippmc10_e.pdf.

88. "Eliminating Trade Barriers on Environmental Goods and Services," WTO, www.wto.org/english/tratop_e/envir_e/envir_neg_serv_e.htm.

89. OECD, "Opening Markets for Environmental Goods and Services," September 2005, www.ciaonet.org/attachments/11402/uploads.

90. ICTSD, "'Green Goods' Trade Talks Kick Off in Geneva," *Bridges* 18, no. 25 (2014), www.ictsd.org/bridges-news/bridges/news/green-goods-trade-talks-kick-off-in-geneva.

91. ICTSD, "Environmental Goods Agreement Trade Talks Look to Hone Product List," *BioRes*, June 24, 2015, www.ictsd.org/bridges-news/biores/news/environmental-goods-agreement-trade-talks-look-to-hone-product-list; Office of the US Trade Representative, "Fact Sheet: WTO Environmental Goods Agreement—Promoting Made-in-America Clean Technology Exports, Green Growth and Jobs," July 8, 2014, http://iipdigital.usembassy.gov/st/english/texttrans/2014/07/20140708303542.html#axzz3iiV9XGIX.

92. ICTSD, "Environmental Goods Agreement Trade Talks Stall Ahead of Nairobi Ministerial," *BioRes*, December 9, 2015, www.ictsd.org/bridges-news/biores/news/environmental-goods-agreement-trade-talks-stall-ahead-of-nairobi.

93. Ibid.

94. Ministry of Foreign Affairs, Republic of Colombia, "Rio+20: Sustainable Development Goals (SDGs)—A Proposal from the Governments of Colombia and Guatemala," 2012, www.uncsd2012.org/content/documents/colombiasdgs.pdf.

95. UN, *Report of the United Nations Conference on Sustainable Development*, A/CONF.216/16 (New York: UN, 2012), 46–47, www.uncsd2012.org/content/documents/814UNCSD%20REPORT%20final%20revs.pdf.

96. See UN, *Transforming Our World: The 2030 Agenda for Sustainable Development*, A.69/L.85, August 15, 2015, www.un.org/ga/search/view_doc.asp?symbol=A/69/L.85&Lang=E.

97. Liz Ford, "UN Begins Talks on SDGs, 'Carrying the Hopes of Millions and Millions'," *Guardian*, September 24, 2014, www.theguardian.com/global-development/2014/sep/24/un-begins-talks-sdgs-battle-looms-over-goals.

98. "Unsustainable Goals," *Economist*, March 25, 2015, www.economist.com/news/international/21647307-2015-will-be-big-year-global-governance-perhaps-too-big-unsustainable-goals.

99. Howard LaFranchi, "In New UN Goals, an Evolving Vision of How to Change the World," *Christian Science Monitor*, September 1, 2015, www.csmonitor.com/USA/Foreign-Policy/2015/0901/In-new-UN-goals-an-evolving-vision-of-how-to-change-the-world.

100. Ibid.

101. Bhumika Muchhala, "North–South Debate in the UN Within Context of Sustainable Development Goals," Third World Network Info Service on UN Sustainable Development, March 14, 2014, www.twn.my/title2/unsd/2014/unsd140303.htm.

102. UN, *Monterrey Consensus of the International Conference on Financing for Development* (New York: UN, 2003).

103. UN, *Doha Declaration on Financing for Development: Outcome Document of the Follow-up International Conference on Financing for Development to Review the Implementation of the Monterrey Consensus* (New York: UN, 2009).

104. See paragraph 43 of UN, "Follow-up to the International Conference on Financing for Development," A/RES/68/204, January 14, 2014.

105. UN, *Addis Ababa Action Agenda* (New York: UN, 2015).

106. UN, "Addis Ababa Conference Opens Path for Robust Implementation of New Sustainable Development Agenda," press release, July 17, 2015, www.un.org/esa/ffd/ffd3/press-release/addis-ababa-conference-opens-path-for-robust-implementation-of-new-sustainable-development-agenda.html.

107. United Nations Department of Economic and Social Development, "Financing Sustainable Development and Developing Sustainable Finance," briefing note, July 2015, www.un.org/esa/ffd/ffd3/wp-content/uploads/sites/2/2015/07/DESA-Briefing-Note-Addis-Action-Agenda.pdf.

108. "Civil Society Response to the Addis Ababa Action Agenda on Financing for Development," http://csoforffd.files.wordpress.com/2015/07/cso-response-to-ffd-addis-ababa-action-agenda-16-july-2015.pdf.

109. Olav Kjorven, Nalinee Nippita, Frank Borge Wietzke, "The Addis Ababa Action Agenda: Strengths, Weaknesses, and the Way Ahead," UNICEF blog, August 18, 2015, http://blogs.unicef.org/blog/the-addis-ababa-action-agenda-strengths-weaknesses-and-the-way-ahead/.

110. International Council for Science (ICSU), *Review of the Sustainable Development Goals: The Science Perspective* (Paris: ICSU, 2015), www.icsu.org/publications/reports-and-reviews/review-of-targets-for-the-sustainable-development-goals-the-science-perspective-2015/SDG-Report.pdf.

111. UN, *Transforming Our World.*

112. This paragraph has been adapted from Pamela Chasek, "Sustainable Development."

Chapter 7: The Future of Global Environmental Politics

1. United Nations Environment Programme (UNEP), *GEO 5: Global Environmental Outlook—Environment for the Future We Want* (Nairobi: UNEP, 2012), 482.

2. Lars-Göran Engfeldt, *From Stockholm to Johannesburg and Beyond* (Stockholm: Government Offices of Sweden, 2009).

3. Andrew Deutz, "Rio+20: What Does Success Look Like in the Post-Copenhagen Era?" *Guardian*, June 19, 2012.

4. World Bank, "GDP at Market Prices (Current US$), World Development Indicators," http://data.worldbank.org/indicator/NY.GDP.MKT.

5. United Nations (UN), "List of Least Developed Countries (as of 11 December 2015)," www.un.org/en/development/desa/policy/cdp/ldc/ldc_list.pdf.

6. World Bank, "GDP at Market Prices."

7. World Bank, "GNI Per Capita, Atlas Method (current US$)," December 22, 2015, http://data.worldbank.org/indicator/NY.GNP.PCAP.CD/countries.

8. Deutz, "Rio+20."

9. Ibid.

10. Philipp Pattberg and Oscar Widerberg, "Theorising Global Environmental Governance: Key Findings and Future Questions," *Millennium: Journal of International Studies* 43, no. 2 (2015): 687.

11. Robert Falkner, "The Crisis of Environmental Multilateralism: A Liberal Response," in *The Green Book: New Directions for Liberals in Government,* eds. Duncan Brack, Paul Burall, Neil Stockley, and Mike Tuffrey (London: Biteback Publishing, 2013), 347–358.

12. Pamela Chasek, Lynn Wagner, and Peter Doran, "Lessons Learned on the Roads from Rio," in *The Roads from Rio: Lessons Learned from Twenty Years of Multilateral Environmental Negotiations*, eds. Pamela Chasek and Lynn Wagner (New York: RFF, 2012), 256.

13. As discussed in Chapter 3, hydrofluorocarbons (HFCs) were developed as a substitute for ozone-depleting chlorofluorocarbons (CFCs). Widely used around the world, HFCs do not deplete stratospheric ozone but are powerful greenhouse gases.

14. Chasek, Wagner, and Doran, "Lessons Learned on the Roads from Rio," 259–260.

15. UNEP and Office of the High Commissioner for Human Rights, "Universality in the Post 2015 Sustainable Development Agenda," UNEP Post-2015 Note #9 (Nairobi: UNEP, 2014), www.unep.org/post2015/Portals/50240/note_9.pdf.

16. "Summary of the Doha Climate Change Conference: 26 November–8 December 2012," *Earth Negotiations Bulletin* 12, no. 567 (December 11, 2012): 26.

17. Richard Gardner, "The Role of the UN in Environmental Problems," in *World Eco-Crisis*, eds. David A. Kay and Eugene Skolnikoff (Madison: University of Wisconsin Press, 1972).

18. Fiona Harvey, "Paris Climate Change Agreement: The World's Greatest Diplomatic Success," *Guardian,* December 14, 2015, www.theguardian.com/environment/2015/dec/13/paris-climate-deal-cop-diplomacy-developing-united-nations.

19. Pamela Chasek, *Earth Negotiations: Analyzing Thirty Years of Environmental Diplomacy* (Tokyo: United Nations University Press, 2001), 1–2.

20. Francesco Francioni and Christine Bakker, "The Evolution of the Global Environmental System: Trends and Prospects," Transworld working paper 8, January 2013, 5, www.transworld-fp7.eu/wp-content/uploads/2013/01/TW_WP_08.pdf.

21. Ulrich Beyerlin and Thilo Marauhn, *International Environmental Law* (Oxford: Hart, 2011), 10–11.

22. Francioni and Bakker, 5.

23. Ibid., 20.

24. Ibid., 21.

25. Ibid.

26. *Synergies* is the name given to this process within the three treaty regimes.

27. UN Department of Economic and Social Affairs, Basel Convention, Rotterdam Convention, Stockholm Convention, UNEP, and Food and Agriculture Organization of the UN, *Synergies Success Stories: Enhancing Cooperation and Coordination Among the Basel, Rotterdam and Stockholm Conventions* (New York: UN, 2011), 4.

28. The six conventions are the Convention on the Conservation of Migratory Species of Wild Animals, the Convention on International Trade in Endangered Species of Wild Fauna and Flora (CITES), the Convention on Wetlands of International Importance (Ramsar Convention), the World Heritage Convention, the International Treaty on Plant Genetic Resources for Food and Agriculture, and the Convention on Biological Diversity (CBD). See also UNEP, *Sourcebook of Opportunities for Enhancing Cooperation Among the Biodiversity-Related Conventions at National and Regional Levels* (Nairobi: UNEP, 2015).

29. Adil Najam, David Runnalls, and Mark Halle, *Environment and Globalization: Five Propositions* (Winnipeg, Canada: IISD, 2007), 32. See also Adil Najam, Mihaela Papa, and Nadaa Taiyab, *Global Environmental Governance: A Reform Agenda* (Winnipeg, Canada: IISD, 2006).

30. James Gustave Speth, "Beyond Reform," *Our Planet* (February 2007): 16, www.unep.org/pdf/OurPlanet/OP_Feb07_GC24_en.pdf. For more on the World Environmental Organization proposal, see Daniel Esty, "The Case for a Global Environmental Organization," in *Managing the World Economy: Fifty Years After Bretton Woods*, ed. P. Kenen (Washington, DC: Institute for International Economics, 2004), 287–307; Frank Biermann, "The Rationale for a World Environment Organization," in *A World Environmental Organization: Solution or Threat for Effective Environmental Governance*, eds. Frank Biermann and Steffen Bauer (Aldershot, UK: Ashgate, 2005): 117–144.

31. A specialized agency is an autonomous organization linked to the UN through a special agreement, such as the Food and Agriculture Organization, the International Atomic Energy Agency, and the International Labor Organization, among others.

32. UN, *Report of the United Nations Conference on Sustainable Development*, A/CONF. 216/16 (New York: UN, 2012), 18.

33. Ibid., 17–18.

34. "Summary of the First UN Environment Assembly of the UN Environment Programme: 23–27 June 2014," *Earth Negotiations Bulletin* 16, 122 (June 30, 2014): 15.

35. "Summary of the United Nations Conference on Sustainable Development: 13–22 June 2012," *Earth Negotiations Bulletin* 27, no. 51 (June 25, 2012): 20, www.iisd.ca/download/pdf/enb2751e.pdf.

36. UN, *Report of the United Nations Conference on Sustainable Development*, 16.

37. UN General Assembly (UNGA), *Format and Organizational Aspects of the High-Level Political Forum on Sustainable Development*, Resolution 67/290, July 9, 2013, www.un.org/ga/search/view_doc.asp?symbol=A/RES/67/290&Lang=E.

38. Ibid.; UNGA, *Transforming Our World: The 2030 Agenda for Sustainable Development*, Resolution 70/1, October 21, 2015, www.un.org/ga/search/view_doc.asp?symbol=A/RES/70/1&Lang=E.

39. Issues that still require clarification include the High-Level Political Forum on Sustainable Development's organizational arrangements for state-led review, institutional responsibilities, and annual themes and the sequence of thematic reviews to be considered, among other aspects of the follow-up and review framework.

40. Massoumeh Ebtekar, "Market Messengers," *Our Planet* (February 2007): 15, www.unep.org/pdf/OurPlanet/OP_Feb07_GC24_en.pdf.

41. For more information, see "Summary of the Ninth Meeting of the Working Group on Marine Biodiversity Beyond Areas of National Jurisdiction: 20–23 January 2015," *Earth Negotiations Bulletin*, 5, no. 94 (January 26, 2015).

42. Rachael Bale, "U.S.-China Deal to Ban Ivory Trade Is Good News for Elephants," *National Geographic*, September 25, 2015, http://news.nationalgeographic.com/2015/09/150925-ivory-elephants-us-china-obama-xi-poaching/.

43. Andrew Mayeda, "Congress Approves IMF Change in Favor of Emerging Markets," *Bloomberg Business*, December 18, 2015, www.bloomberg.com/news/articles/2015-12-18/congress-approves-imf-changes-giving-emerging-markets-more-sway.

44. Greg Rushford, "The WTO Struggles in Nairobi," *Wall Street Journal*, December 21, 2015.

45. Suzanne Goldenberg, "ExxonMobil Gave Millions to Climate-Denying Lawmakers Despite Pledge," *Guardian*, July 15, 2015.

46. Neil Carter, *The Politics of the Environment: Ideas, Activism, Policy*, 2nd ed. (Cambridge: Cambridge University Press, 2007), 268.

Index

Lightning Source UK Ltd.
Milton Keynes UK
UKHW011256151019
351624UK00020BA/295/P